Torkildsen's Sport and Leisure Management

Sixth edition

For nearly thirty years George Torkildsen's classic textbook has been the most comprehensive and engaging introduction to sport and leisure management available to students at all levels. Now in a sixth edition – fully revised and updated by Peter Taylor and a team of specialist contributors – it is still the only textbook that covers all the key topics taught within contemporary sport and leisure management courses.

This new edition includes expanded coverage of the practical managerial skills that students must develop if aiming for a career in the sport and leisure industry, from managing people and planning to marketing and entrepreneurship. It includes five completely new chapters reflecting important developments in contemporary sport and leisure: leisure in the home, financial management, quality management, law and enterprise. The new edition retains the hallmark strengths of previous editions, including in-depth discussion of the social and cultural context of sport and leisure; full analysis of the public, private and voluntary sectors; and a review of key products and services, including sport, tourism, the arts, play and leisure in the natural environment.

Richly illustrated throughout with up-to-date evidence, data, case studies and international examples, each chapter also contains a range of useful pedagogical features, such as discussion questions, practical tasks and structured guides to further reading and resources. For the first time, a dedicated companion website offers additional teaching and learning resources for students and lecturers.

Peter Taylor is Professor of Sport Economics at the Sport Industry Research Centre, Sheffield Hallam University, UK. He has researched and written many publications on sport and leisure economics and management, including *Economics of Sport and Recreation* (with Chris Gratton).

Praise for *Torkildsen's Sport and Leisure Management*, sixth edition

This book should be compulsory reading for all students studying sport, leisure or related courses.

Leigh Robinson, University of Stirling, UK

I can see this becoming a key text for many types of undergraduate in sport, leisure or recreation management. It is written in true Torkildsen style, and is a tribute to his memory and contribution to this study area.

Ray Barker, University of Hull, UK

This new edition of a classic text not only retains the strengths of the original but the new material and the sharper focus on the management element have enhanced its reputation. I am sure it will become a key text across a number of courses in this area.

Peter Mann, University College Birmingham, UK

The sixth edition of *Torkildsen* has seen some huge and much needed changes from the fifth edition. It has been well and truly overhauled to bring it up to date with the modern sport leisure industry, and sets this against the challenging economic and political environment in which it now operates. Where the author team have made a real impact and added great value in the sixth edition is in the inclusion of up-to-date case studies and in particular the incorporation of recent statistical data about sport and leisure management. This gives the text the currency and hence the credibility that makes this the 'must-have' reference book for undergraduate students of sports and leisure related programmes who aspire to a career in this field. Further, the text contains enough cutting-edge information about the leisure industry as it is today, to make it a very useful companion to those managers who already have a career in this field.

Martin Steer, Education Development Manager,
The Institute of Sport and Recreation Management, UK

Torkildsen's Sport and Leisure Management combines current thinking about management with relevant theory about managing sport and leisure organisations. The contemporary practical, real-life examples articulated in the case studies interspersed throughout each chapter provide excellent vehicles to contextualise theoretical concepts and showcase good practice in sport and leisure organisations. The book is written in such a way as to provide the reader with great versatility, as it can be read as a stand-alone textbook or it can be used as a reference for particular aspects of sport and leisure management, enabling the reader to access relevant sections or chapters as required. This comprehensive book combines extensive coverage of contemporary topics critical to an understanding of effective sport and leisure management, with an accessible writing style and design.

Overall it provides a good balance of theory and hard data that allows the student to develop ideas and discussion, whilst enabling sport and leisure managers to reflect upon their own practices.

Tracy Taylor, University of Technology Sydney, Australia

Peter Taylor's revision of *Torkildsen's Sport and Leisure Management* is a nice addition to the literature. The author provides useful teaching tools for undergraduate students and has used industry examples to illustrate a broad array of topics including economics, planning, marketing and international tourism.

Glenna G. Bower, University of Southern Indiana, USA

Torkildsen's Sport and Leisure Management

Sixt

Edit

Routledge
Taylor & Francis Group

LONDON AND NEW YORK

First edition published 1983 as *Leisure and Recreation Management* by Spon Press
Second edition published 1986 by Spon Press
Third edition published 1992 by Spon Press
Fourth edition published 1999 by Spon Press
Fifth edition published 2005 by Routledge

This edition published 2011
by Routledge
2 Park Square, Milton Park, Abingdon, Oxon, OX14 4RN

Simultaneously published in the USA and Canada
by Routledge
270 Madison Avenue, New York, NY 10016

Routledge is an imprint of the Taylor & Francis Group, an informa business

Typeset in Sabon and Frutiger by Wearset Ltd, Boldon, Tyne and Wear
Printed and bound in Great Britain by MPG Books Group, UK

British Library Cataloguing in Publication Data
A catalogue record for this book is available from the British Library

Library of Congress Cataloging in Publication Data
Torkildsen's sport and leisure management/edited by Peter Taylor.
p. cm.
Rev. ed. of: Leisure and recreation management, 2005.
1. Leisure. 2. Leisure–Management. 3. Recreation. 4. Recreation–Management. I.
Taylor, Peter, 1949- II. Torkildsen, George, Leisure and recreation management.
GV181.5.T67 2005
790.069–dc22

2010016 413

ISBN13: 978-0-415-49792-3 (hbk)
ISBN13: 978-0-415-49793-0 (pbk)

Contents

Contents

Contents

Figures

Tables

Case studies

Preface

When George Torkildsen died in 2005, he left a massive hole in the leisure management profession. He was one of the founding fathers of this profession in the UK and his achievements stretched across facility management, consultancy, service for *World Leisure*, professional presentations and writing. It is for the last of these that he is perhaps most well known, to countless students wanting an authoritative overview of leisure, leisure industries and leisure management. The legacy George left is typified by the fifth edition of this book, his last edition, which has remained one of the best-known texts in leisure management.

So it is with some trepidation that this sixth edition has been written – George Torkildsen is a hard act to follow! Nevertheless, leisure is a dynamic field and it was necessary in planning this new edition to tread a careful line between preserving the 'essence of George' whilst developing the text to fit the changing leisure scene. The fundamental principles on which to plan and manage leisure are consolidated and expanded in this edition. Although leisure management is interdisciplinary, to structure this sixth edition clearly it retains the same constituent parts as before:

1 setting the scene with definitions and trends;
2 reviewing the three major sectors supplying and influencing leisure – commercial, government and the 'third sector';
3 examining the major leisure products and services provided;
4 analysing separately the important management disciplines that coalesce in leisure management in practice.

The title of the book has changed from *Leisure and Recreation Management* to *Sport and Leisure Management*. This is because although leisure is still the binding concept, it is clear that a major interest of many students and readers of the book in the past has been sport and physical activity. Therefore whilst leisure remains the primary focus, sport is an important secondary focus.

This edition sharpens the focus of the book on applied management by:

● removing much of the historical and philosophical material from the early parts of the previous edition;
● adding four new chapters on applied management considerations in Part 4: i.e. quality and performance management, finance, law and enterprise;
● making major revisions to most of the remaining chapters.

In one respect the concept of leisure has been extended for this book, with the addition of a new chapter on leisure in the home. This is not only a major competitor of what is conventionally seen as the province of the leisure manager, leisure away from home, but also the subject of some very large and dynamic parts of the leisure industry.

Two other, more embedded changes have been attempted in this edition. First, more international examples have been added. It is clear that whilst a UK focus is important for UK readers, and it provides a coherent core relating to one country, most of the principles in the book are not confined to the UK, but extend to other countries, particularly more developed countries. Second, more evidence has been included, because knowledge of what the sport and leisure industries consist of is important, and because evidence brings principles 'to life'.

The market for this book remains the same – anyone who wants a thorough introduction to the dimensions of sport and leisure markets and industries, and to key disciplines and principles of managing sport and leisure. In the main, this may well mean first year undergraduates in a range of subjects, including not just sport and leisure management but also sports and leisure studies, sports sciences, human movement, physical education, and more generic business and management studies. However, the book will also be useful to sub-degree students and postgraduates first acquainting themselves with the study of sport and leisure management; and also to those already in the sport and leisure industries who are looking to develop their knowledge and skills.

Several pedagogical features have been retained and developed in this new edition of the book:

- key questions and summaries at the beginning of each chapter;
- case studies of around 500 words in each chapter;
- discussion questions embedded at appropriate points throughout the text;
- practical tasks which will help readers to understand key points;
- structured guides to key readings;
- web references for most chapters;
- comprehensive list of documentary references for each chapter.

In addition, an accompanying website for this book contains:

- PowerPoint slides summarising each chapter;
- for some chapters, additional textual material;
- downloadable figures and tables;
- for some chapters, additional or extended case studies;
- elaboration of the discussion questions;
- web links for each chapter.

Acknowledgements

First and foremost, it is important to acknowledge and thank Margaret Torkildsen for her permission to keep George's name associated with this book.

The task of rewriting such a comprehensive text would not have been possible without several people with specialist knowledge agreeing to take charge of rewriting specific chapters. These contributing authors have done a tremendous job and have been very patient in dealing with suggestions to ensure that their contributions fit the style and purpose of the book. They are:

- Chris Cooper, Oxford Brookes University, for Chapter 7: International tourism;
- Lynn Crowe, Sheffield Hallam University, for Chapter 8: Leisure and the natural environment;
- Elizabeth Owen, independent consultant, for Chapter 9: Arts, museums and libraries;
- Perry Else, Sheffield Hallam University, for Chapter 11: Managing play services for children;
- Chris Wolsey and Jeff Abrams, Leeds Metropolitan University, for Chapter 13: Managing people in sport and leisure;
- Rob Wilson, Sheffield Hallam University, for Chapter 18: Financial management in sport and leisure;
- Peter Charlish, Sheffield Hallam University, for Chapter 19: Law and sport and leisure management;
- Guy Masterman, Sheffield Hallam University, for Chapter 20: The importance and management of events.

In addition the editor would like to thank the following people for essential information in the rewriting of this book:

- Helen Broadbent, Ponds Forge International Sports Centre, for an insight into programming at a major sports and events centre;
- Peter Jennings, University of Sheffield, for invaluable advice on enterprise and entrepreneurship;
- Themis Kokolakakis, Sheffield Hallam University, the principal architect of Leisure Forecasts and Sports Market Forecasts, for invaluable and unique data on the profiles of sport and leisure markets in the UK;
- Tony Veal, University of Technology, Sydney, Australia, for considerable help with planning and policy in sport and leisure.

The editor received extensive and detailed feedback on each draft chapter from Russell George, at the publishers Taylor & Francis, and from eight independent reviewers. This feedback was tremendously helpful in putting together the final version and a huge debt of gratitude is due to Russell and his reviewers.

Finally, I would like to thank Janice, who has had to be more patient than anyone else in coping with the demands of me trying to emulate George Torkildsen!

Peter Taylor
Sport Industry Research Centre
Sheffield Hallam University

Part 1

Introducing leisure management concepts and trends

Contents

1 Introduction

2 People's needs and leisure demand

3 Trends in the leisure industry

This part lays a foundation for the rest of the book by defining key concepts, describing overall dimensions of sport and leisure activity, and providing information on important trends over time. Chapter 1 discusses and defines sport, leisure and management, as well as some other important complementary concepts such as play, recreation and culture and a concept devised by George Torkildsen – 'pleisure'.

Chapter 2 defines need, an important root to people's choices in leisure; and demand, the end result of their choices. It also provides statistical evidence of the dimensions to sport and leisure demands and the demographic and socio-economic factors that most influence sport and leisure participation.

Chapter 3 identifies important trends over time in leisure time, sport and leisure participation, and leisure expenditure. It also explores trends in some important influences on sport and leisure trends, including population size and structure, incomes and inequality, and health.

Chapter 1

Introduction

In this chapter

- What is the purpose and structure of this book?
- How is management defined and what is the role of management in sport and leisure?
- How are sport and leisure defined?
- What is George Torkildsen's 'pleisure' principle?

Christophe Simon/Getty Images

Summary

This chapter sets the scene for the management of leisure by exploring some of the dimensions and meanings of key terms, particularly 'sport', 'leisure' and 'management'. Sport and leisure is big business, particularly in more developed countries. An agreed definition of the subject of this business is, however, elusive – sport and leisure mean different things to different people. Definitions of sport are sometimes confined to competitive sports but are more often wider and include a range of non-competitive physical activities. Definitions of leisure include leisure as time, as activities and as a state of being. Definitions of management have evolved in line with different theories of management. A clear understanding of these basic concepts provides leisure managers with a clearer focus on their customers, and their decision-making.

The chapter also explains how this book is structured and what its underpinning themes are. Part 1 reviews basic concepts and evidence about the sport and leisure business and how it is changing. Part 2 examines the main sport and leisure providers, arranged in three sectors: commercial, government and the third sector, which is non-profit. Part 3 explores major product and service types in leisure, including tourism, sport and leisure in the home (the object of some of the most dynamic leisure industries). Finally, the largest part of the book (Part 4) is devoted to different management disciplines, including human resource management, marketing, finance, quality management and enterprise.

Today we have more knowledge, more resources and more opportunity than before, with which to have a fullness of living undreamed of in times past. Leisure has an increasingly important role to play in modern lifestyles, but the question is: has leisure achieved its potential in a fulfilling way of life? The extent to which it hasn't is a fundamental reason for improving leisure management. At the heart of sport and leisure management is a concern to provide and manage opportunities for people to get the most out of their sport and leisure experiences, however these are defined.

1.1 Introduction

By taking an interest in leisure management, you are stepping away from your individual leisure consumer's focus on having a good time, and beginning to take other people's leisure as a professional interest. Although leisure is enjoyable, it is also a serious business which requires knowledge, analysis, skills and perceptive decision-making to make it work successfully. Just because it is leisure, doesn't mean we can take it for granted or relegate it to an unimportant part of society. As Roberts (2004) suggests:

Even today, tabloid newspapers, probably for want of better headlines, occasionally mock recreation management, sport, tourism and media studies as joke subjects, and evidence of dumbing-down in higher education. All such talk is grotesquely out of date.

It is not just journalists who get it wrong – no lesser figure than the Chief Inspector for Schools in England denigrated contemporary interdisciplinary subjects such as sport and leisure studies in the late 1990s. Such an attitude is as irrelevant as those which criticise service industries generally and bemoan the decline of manufacturing in more developed countries. The fact is that the economic prosperity of many more economically developed countries has for the last thirty years and more been increasingly based on service industries. In the UK, for example, service jobs represented 61.5 per cent of the total in 1978, and by 2009 they were 81.5 per cent of the total (ONS, 2010). And leisure is an important part of these service industries.

This book is part of a continuing process, which is now several decades old, of educating students in sport and leisure and its management. Before this process began, managers in sport and leisure were often selected for superficial reasons that were not closely related to their abilities as managers – for example sports managers because they used to be good at sport, museum managers because they were educated in history. However, the modern-day sport and leisure organisation needs managers with not just knowledge of their branch of leisure but also a multitude of applied management skills, including quality management, human resources management, finance, law and marketing. This book is an introduction to such knowledge and skills.

One reason the management of sport and leisure, and its education, is now taken seriously is because leisure is a large and growing set of industries, particularly in more developed economies. It involves professional management not only in the commercial sector, but also by government at the central and local level, and in many private, non-profit organisations. A symptom of leisure's importance is spending by consumers. In the UK in 2008, for example, leisure spending was over a quarter of consumer spending on all goods and services (Leisure Industries Research Centre, 2009). In 1999, for the first time, spending by consumers on leisure exceeded spending on each of food, housing and transport.

At the time of writing, as the world is emerging tentatively from economic recession, leisure spending has not disappeared, but as with other forms of spending it has suffered either reduced growth or even reduced levels of economic activity for a while. However, when 'normal service is resumed' in terms of economic growth – and in the long term the trend is for economic growth – leisure industries will continue to play a leading role. In more developed economies, any rise in income is typically spent disproportionately on leisure. This is because after people have attended to the basic needs for housing, food and transport, leisure provides an endless opportunity for increased enjoyment and fulfilment.

Leisure is not a trivial luxury but an essential part of people's lifestyles. Benjamin Disraeli, a nineteenth-century British Prime Minister, believed that increased means and increased leisure are the two civilisers of man. Bertrand Russell (1935), English pacifist, philosopher and mathematician, was of the opinion that to be able to fill leisure intelligently is the best product of civilisation. Today, people of all ages demand choice and have higher expectations for healthier lifestyles, quality services, more facilities and better customer service and management. This applies as much to leisure industries as to any other, because leisure is an expression of people's free time preferences. By taking an interest in how to manage leisure, you are taking an interest in an increasingly important set of activities and industries.

Another reason for taking leisure management seriously in education is that it is complex. It involves two interdisciplinary concepts – leisure and management. Management covers a range of disciplines and skills which are required to run organisations effectively and efficiently. Leisure is a subject that has been analysed by economists, sociologists, geographers, political scientists, philosophers and management scientists, to name just a few. The management of sport and leisure embraces:

- planning the products, services, facilities and other infrastructure that combine to give people leisure;
- managing the available resources to produce high quality services;
- monitoring and improving the resulting outcomes in the form of participation in and enjoyment of leisure activities;

and it stretches to:

- contributing to possible impacts of sport and leisure on people's health, quality of life and sense of community.

Therefore, to understand leisure management requires a substantial breadth of considerations.

Discussion question

If you were studying sport and leisure management and a fellow student, who is studying a more traditional subject (e.g. history, maths or engineering), accused you of studying a 'Mickey Mouse' subject, how would you reply?

Leisure can be perceived in many contexts: individual, community, regional, national and international. Its delivery is both local and global. Global conditions have a considerable influence on leisure. The world economic climate, for example, has an impact on individuals and nations alike – the 'credit crunch' of 2008–9 is a stark reminder of this. Environmental issues are arguably a more long-term danger and they impact on travel and tourism in particular. The terrorist tragedy inflicted on the United States of America on 11 September 2001 continues to have profound effects, not only in the military, political and economic arenas, but also on our ways of life, including leisure. The clashes of ideologies of the first half of the twentieth century have been replaced by clashes of cultures in the early twenty-first century which are expressed in both global and local decision-making. In addition to global considerations and contexts, however, it is important to identify the demands of local people in designing and delivering appropriate sport and leisure services. One size does not fit all!

1.2 Why manage leisure?

Is there a need to manage people's leisure? Nature provides us, in the natural environment, with abundant resources for leisure and recreation. One could argue that there is no need for expensive additional facilities, services, programmes and management. Nature has provided fields, woods, rivers, beaches and sunshine. We have the challenge of the mountains, winter snow, the seas and the sky. There is beauty to behold, solitude in the country and peace away from the crowds.

Yet even in natural environments, management of sport and leisure is very important. Access to natural amenities is necessary for a range of sport and leisure visitors – e.g. surfers, hang-gliders, horse riders, walkers, bird-watchers and sightseers – and this access needs to be provided and maintained in a way that facilitates visiting but without spoiling the attraction. The visitors will want ancillary services such as food and drink and accommodation. The sport and leisure activities of visitors may need to be controlled in the light of environmental issues in specific areas, or conflicts between different users. All such functions require planning and managing.

The demand for man-made resources for sport and leisure is greater now than it has ever been, because people often have more time and money for leisure, and there is a wider choice than ever of what to do in leisure. Leisure opportunities have to be provided and managed for all ages – from young children wanting to play in safe and exciting environments, to old people wanting enjoyable experiences away from their home environment. Planning provision is very important, as is managing facilities to achieve the best effects for individuals and communities.

When the energies of some young people are channelled into acts of violence or vandalism, we see evidence of unsatisfied needs. Leisure opportunities could surely provide the challenges, experiences, adventure, noise, speed and independence that young people seek and help meet some of those needs? Opportunities are also needed for adults, for families, for the lonely, the old, the disabled and the disadvantaged to experience the satisfactions that leisure provides. It is the leisure manager's job to ensure that such experience can happen and people can get the most out of their leisure.

1.2.1 Defining management

The meaning of the term 'management' has evolved through several phases of theories, all of which contribute to a contemporary understanding of what management is:

- The foundation of **management sciences,** in the early years of the twentieth century, is commonly credited to the work of Frederick Taylor, who emphasised the scientific systems necessary to improve productivity and the efficiency of organisations.
- **Classical management** theory followed, extending the concept of efficiency to the structure and operation of organisations. Leading proponents of classical management theory were Henri Fayol and Max Weber. The theory concentrates on five managerial processes: planning, organising, commanding, coordinating and controlling. It entails hierarchical chains of command which are now criticised for their formality and bureaucracy, but are nevertheless still an important feature of many organisations.
- In the 1950s and 1960s a **human relations movement** in management thinking concentrated more on the motivations and needs of the individuals in organisations, inspired by such writers as Abraham Maslow, Chester Barnard and Elton Mayo. This movement concentrated on managerial effectiveness, rather than the efficiency of organisations, with concern for interpersonal relationships and the effects of supervision on the morale as well as the productivity of workers.
- The human relations movement led to a more general **behaviourist** view of management, which concentrated on more informal and flexible organisational structures, and greater employee involvement. It emphasised the importance of motivators in generating staff

satisfaction, such as achievement, recognition and personal development; and also the importance of hygiene factors in creating dissatisfaction, such as working conditions, salary, status and job security.

● Finally, towards the end of the twentieth century emphasis in management theories switched firmly to **customer orientation**, which is at the heart of not only marketing theory but also quality management. The simple premise behind this approach is that customer needs are the starting point for the design and delivery of products and the structures and processes in organisations.

1.2.2 The sport and leisure services to be managed

Leisure and recreation are made possible by means of a range of services and facilities, both indoor and outdoor, in and around the home, in the urban environment, in rural areas and in the countryside – see Table 1.1 for an illustrative rather than exhaustive list. A range of services and programmes are provided by the commercial, public and third sectors to meet the diverse needs and demands of individuals, families, groups, clubs, societies and businesses.

Demands are met, however, not just by providing infrastructure and facilities, but also by attracting people to use and enjoy them through services, management policy and effective management action. Problems inevitably occur, e.g. a strike at airports or a political dispute can cause immense hardship for business and leisure passengers, sometimes stranded at locations around the world. A greater number of resources are available for leisure today than before. With them come greater opportunities and greater problems – opportunities which should be seized and problems which leisure managers must help to solve.

Discussion question

Is there such a thing as sport or leisure that does not need management to help it? Discuss examples such as a walk in the countryside, reading a book or chatting with friends.

1.3 The structure of the book

The purpose of this book is to describe and analyse issues relevant to sport and leisure managers and in doing so help these managers to make better decisions. Sport and leisure planners, providers and managers are in key positions for using resources and creating opportunities which can help to enhance the quality of life for many people. This book deals with important contextual information for sport and leisure managers and best practice principles for sport and leisure management. It is not, however, a technical textbook dealing with leisure 'hardware', such as facility design and construction, physical maintenance requirements, and catering and bar requirements. Instead, this book is concerned with what might be termed 'soft' skills – namely, knowledge of sport and leisure markets and the nature of demand, the quality of sport and leisure services, facilities and experiences, the principles and techniques for planning provision, and principles underpinning management decision-making.

Table 1.1 Sport and leisure facilities: examples

In the home	Resources and equipment in the home for exercise, relaxation, social recreation, entertainment, hobbies and pastimes
Out of home facilities	Gardens and open spaces, allotments, play areas and sports grounds. Facilities for entertainment, the arts, music, drama, literary activities, education, sport and physical activities: including halls and meeting rooms, libraries, theatres, museums, sports and leisure centres, swimming pools, community centres, entertainment centres, pubs, clubs, cinemas, concert halls, studios and art and craft workshops
Countryside infrastructure	Roads and rail networks, maps and signposting, stopping-off points, scenic viewing points, picnic sites, car parking, camping and caravan sites, clean beaches and lakes, water recreation areas, walkways, footpaths, nature reserves and many others
Tourism	Tourist Information Centres, travel agents, visitor attractions, roads, rail and air transport, accommodation and hospitality

The book is structured broadly in four parts:

- Part 1 considers the scope and development of sport and leisure by examining definitions of key terms; exploring the nature of people's needs and sport and leisure demands; and identifying trends in leisure time, participation and expenditure, as well as general demographic and socio-economic trends which impact on leisure.
- Part 2 is focused on the providers of sport and leisure services, facilities and activities in the commercial, public and third sectors; and the relationships between these sectors.
- Part 3 reviews the main areas of leisure activity, i.e. tourism, countryside, the arts, sport, play and leisure in the home.
- Part 4 examines core disciplines important to the management of leisure, i.e. human resource management, planning, marketing, programming, quality management, financial management, law, event management and enterprise.

1.3.1 Part 1: concepts and trends

Having set the scene and introduced key definitions in this first chapter, a key concept of George Torkildsen's is introduced – the 'pleisure principle'. This illustrates the essence of the leisure experience, a concept which helps leisure managers understand what is needed to satisfy people's needs through leisure.

Chapter 2 explores in detail the concepts of human needs and sport and leisure demands – fundamentals of any examination of sport and leisure management in an era when 'the customer is king'. The following questions are raised: what are the factors which influence leisure activity and, importantly, what circumstances constrain them?

Chapter 3 establishes a statistical overview of leisure by reviewing some major trends in leisure over time, including leisure time, participation and expenditure. Leisure is a changing, volatile industry and is affected by changes in legislation, demography, technology and the economy.

1.3.2 Part 2: providers

Chapters 4–6 focus on the major providers of leisure services and facilities in the commercial, public and third sectors. Chapter 4 deals with the commercial sector. This provides for many popular leisure activities in the home, such as audio-visual media, gardening, DIY and household pets. The products that these activities consume come from important leisure businesses, and at-home leisure is subject to considerable government regulation. Leisure outside the home is examined by looking into specific markets, including eating and drinking out, going to the cinema or sports events, playing tenpin bowling or bingo, and visiting leisure parks and theme parks. These include many activities with a recent history of considerable growth, as well as some with more volatile trends.

Chapter 5 explores central and local government and the influence that they have on sport and leisure, both through direct provision and through regulation and legislation. Government enables and also constrains what sport and leisure providers may and may not do. The influence of lead departments, such as the Department for Culture, Media and Sport in the UK, is explored, along with their national agencies. Local government plays a significant role in supplying sport and leisure opportunities.

The 'third sector' is covered in Chapter 6 and it includes voluntary organisations, non-profit social enterprises and sport and leisure provision by companies for their employees. The opportunities offered to people through thousands of voluntary clubs, associations and organisations represent collectively a massive contribution to sport and leisure. The increasing importance of social enterprises to the management of public sector sport and leisure services and facilities is assessed.

1.3.3 Part 3: products and services

Chapters 7–12 provide overviews of leisure products and services. Chapter 7 deals with tourism, in recent years arguably the largest and fastest expanding leisure sector globally. Covered in this chapter are tourist visit profiles, management issues for tourism and its destinations, and the rising importance of e-tourism.

Chapter 8 considers issues about leisure and the natural environment. It reviews participation and volunteering in the natural environment, and the range of services and facilities provided, including protected areas such as national parks, and recreation provision in forests, green spaces, water spaces, country parks and urban parks. The natural environment is a vital leisure resource but it needs well thought out policies and good management to deal with issues such as access, rights of way and damage to sensitive areas.

Chapter 9 is concerned with core aspects of cultural provision – the arts, museums and libraries. It reviews the main agencies responsible for promoting, supporting and supplying cultural opportunities, particularly in the UK. The government is very active in these fields, with national policies and subsidies to providers at national and local levels – a conspicuous example in the UK being the funding of free entry to museums of national status. In addition, the voluntary and commercial sectors play important roles, particularly in the arts and museums.

Chapter 10 deals with sport and physical activity – increasingly important areas in leisure provision and leisure management at a time when there are multi-national concerns about increasing obesity and related health problems. The leisure opportunities provided by sport are varied – from recreational participation for fun and fitness, through competitive participation for performance, to elite participation for medals and championships. All three main providing sectors have important roles to play in sport and physical activity – the commercial sector is very active in major sports and activities such as football and fitness, as well as in media coverage; governments support, promote and provide sporting opportunities, from local to national sports centres; whilst volunteers are the bedrock of a large majority of sports clubs.

Chapter 11 focuses on children's play, which is the foundation stone upon which many adult leisure activities are built. Children's play attracts national government policies and government support, and much of the provision is by local government. This raises a lot of management and policy issues for playwork – not only for the design and management of different types of play facilities, but also for the use of play workers to lead play activities.

Chapter 12 focuses on leisure in the home, particularly the increasing importance of technology in the form of computers and the internet, games consoles and audio-visual systems. The supply of such leisure opportunities is largely in the hands of the commercial sector and demonstrates the power of technological change and marketing in driving consumer demands and expenditure. Government policy is also concerned, particularly in such issues as competition, standards and censorship. Computing and the use of the internet connect strongly with other leisure pursuits, particularly tourism, to the extent that increasing numbers of people search for and book trips online.

1.3.4 Part 4: management skills and techniques

Chapters 13–21 introduce and explore a number of key management disciplines which a leisure manager needs to be aware of. Management involves a multi-disciplinary set of theories, principles and skills. Each problem encountered by managers is likely to involve a number of these disciplines. Whilst specialism by managers in any one of these disciplines is not unusual – e.g. finance, marketing, human resources – any manager should have a strong awareness of the other disciplines.

Chapter 13 is concerned with human resource management. Leisure is often termed a 'people business' not only because of the importance of customers but also because the main purpose of staff is to satisfy customers' demands. Managing staff, or human resources, involves key issues, including leadership and appropriate organisational structures to empower staff to perform to their potential.

Chapter 14 considers planning from two important perspectives. First, the formal planning process involves government processes, planning policy guidance, planning models and development plans. Second, planning from an organisational perspective involves such techniques as demand forecasting and public consultation.

The marketing of sport and leisure is covered in Chapter 15. It explains the marketing approach, the concept of social marketing and the influence that marketing has on potential customer behaviour. Core concepts of marketing are explained, including mission and vision, market research, marketing strategies, market positioning, segmentation and the use of the marketing mix to meet the objectives of marketing plans.

Chapter 16 examines one of the most important leisure management skills, that of programming for leisure services and facilities. Managers must have sufficient knowledge of programming because it is the principal means by which sport and leisure are delivered to customers and through which organisational objectives can be met. The chapter explains what programming consists of, different programming strategies, and programming methods for general and target markets.

Chapter 17 looks at vital aspects of contemporary management – quality management and performance management. Total quality management systems are commonplace in the sport and leisure industry, particularly Quest, a system devised specifically for sport and leisure organisations in the UK. There are numerous quality awards available, and the chapter reviews these and their relationship with organisational performance. Performance management is closely related to quality management and relies not only on accurate measurement of organisational performance, e.g. by benchmarking, but also on appropriate management processes to act on this information.

Chapter 18 examines core principles of financial management. On the one hand, an understanding of financial accounting is important as an essential context within which all managers operate. On the other hand, management accounting principles enable managers to act appropriately in order to improve financial performance.

Chapter 19 is an introduction to the role of law in managing sport and leisure. Whereas managers are rarely legal experts, the law is an essential context for their decision-making. Basic principles of legal liability and negligence, working with children, employment law and risk management will help managers to be aware of their legal responsibilities and how their decision-making is constrained by the law.

Chapter 20 deals with the planning and management of special events. Events are an important part of any comprehensive sport and leisure programme. Well organised, they can be a boon; badly organised, they can spell disaster and deter people from coming to such events in future. Leisure managers must be capable of controlling the planning and staging of events. This chapter demonstrates the importance of events at local, regional and international levels. It covers the event planning process and demonstrates how events can be managed, from beginning to end.

Chapter 21 examines entrepreneurship and enterprise in sport and leisure. It explores the characteristics of entrepreneurs – are they born or are they the products of their environments? Examining enterprise involves a set of principles and techniques, including feasibility assessment, business start-up financing, business planning, investment appraisal and managing risk. It has a close relationship with many other management disciplines, particularly finance, marketing and human resource management. Enterprise establishes best practice principles not just for new ventures, but also for innovation and change in businesses generally. As such it is a fitting conclusion to the book.

1.4 Key definitions

Before discussing the meanings of sport and leisure in depth, it is instructive to outline these and other definitions of key concepts involved in leisure. These concepts are not all mutually exclusive, and arguably the most all-embracing concept is leisure. Individual chapters, particularly in Part 3 of the book, provide further discussion of these and other concepts in leisure.

- **Leisure** is perceived in a variety of ways – as a type of time, as a set of activities or as a state of being. At its most ideal, leisure can be perceived as experiencing activities, unpaid and chosen in relative freedom, that are personally satisfying and have the potential to lead towards self-actualisation, i.e. personal growth and fulfilment.
- **Recreation** is usually thought of as leisure time activities which are more organised and institutional and sometimes it is used as another term for leisure. In its purest sense, recreation is re-creation – an inner-consuming experience that leads to revival of the senses

and the spirit. In this sense, recreation renews, restores and 'recharges the batteries'. Physical recreation refers to physical activities which have this restorative value.

- **Sport** is an informal or formally organised physical activity, typically but not always competitive and typically governed by a set of rules and officials. However, as elaborated below, there are many activities which are commonly labelled sports but which do not have one or more of the basic characteristics which typically define sport.

- **Play** can be described as activity freely chosen and indulged in for its own sake for the satisfaction it brings in the doing – see Chapter 11. Play exhibits childlike characteristics of joy, spontaneity, self-expression and a creation of its own special meaning in a play world.

- **Culture** has different meanings in different countries. In the UK, culture is typically used to describe activities such as the arts, heritage and libraries. In Europe, culture is used in the wider sense of a range of artistic and social pursuits which populations engage in, including sport. Chapter 9 discusses culture in more detail.

- **Creative industries** is a term that has come to be used in the UK to mean a set of creative and commercial activities, which include: some leisure industries such as music, radio, television and film production, and performing arts; some industries that are partly leisure such as publishing and crafts; and some industries that lie outside leisure, such as advertising and architecture.

The two concepts at the core of this book are sport and leisure and we explore their definitions further below (pp. 14–20). Sport is a major interest of many further education (16 plus) and higher education (18 plus) courses in leisure, and is therefore a specific focus throughout most of this book. Leisure covers a wide range of activities and organisations, the management of which is the main subject of this book.

1.5 Defining sport

Identifying sports is relatively easy from a commonsense point of view, e.g. by listing activities that are considered to be sports. Core sports activities such as football, baseball and athletics are clearly sports, but what about darts and snooker? The latter are reported in the media as sports, but many would dispute their identification as sports because they involve little physical effort. And what about climbing and long-distance walking? They both require physical effort but typically are not competitive. It is in defining the characteristics of sport that difficulties arise, because characteristics such as physical effort and competition are not shared by all the activities that we label 'sport'.

For an activity to be identified as a sport typically requires one or more of a number of characteristics, including physical activity, skill, competition and also regulations with officials to enforce them (e.g. referees, umpires). Rodgers (1977) suggests two other criteria – that the activity is practised for a recreational purpose (i.e. physical renewal) and that it has a framework of institutional organisation (e.g. leagues, competitive events, rankings, etc.).

Gratton and Taylor (2000) add a more pragmatic criterion – that there is general acceptance that an activity is a sport, e.g. by the media and government sports agencies. They suggest three categories of sport:

1 a core of sports which have all the required attributes, such as football and athletics;
2 physical, recreational but mainly non-competitive activities, which include fitness activities, most swimming, and possibly long-distance walking;

3 non-physical but competitive activities which have institutional organisation and are generally accepted as sports, such as darts and snooker.

However, both the media and government are biased and selective in their coverage of sports. The media is full of popular sports but even world champions in minority sports hardly get a mention. Government recognition of sports, e.g. for funding purposes, is often conditioned by major events such as the Olympic Games, but these Games are very selective in what sports they include – a major example being golf, which is not in the Olympics.

Another example of political selectivity in sport is a recent change in the UK. Sport is within the remit of the Department for Culture, Media and Sport (DCMS) and government funded national agencies such as Sport England. For a long time the interpretation of sport by government and national agencies was broad, embracing competitive sports and an array of sports/physical activities such as climbing, fishing and fitness activities. These sports and physical activities were collectively seen to contribute to important government objectives, such as health, community cohesion and reduction in crime and vandalism. In 2008 the government strategy changed (DCMS, 2008) and the definition of sport for DCMS and national sport agencies was narrowed to competitive sports. Physical activity was seen as more of a remit for other government departments, e.g. the Department of Health and the Department for Transport.

The change in the UK policy on sport is not consistent with one of the most often cited definitions of sport, by The Council of Europe as part of their 1992 European Sports Charter:

> Sport means all forms of physical activity which, through casual or organised participation, aim at expressing or improving physical fitness and mental well-being, forming social relationships or obtaining results in competition at all levels.

This is a very inclusive definition, embracing physical activities as well as competitive sports. It implicitly acknowledges a spectrum of sport and physical activity, with formal, competitive sports at one end and informal physical activities at the other. These activities share basic attributes, including health and well-being and social relationships.

However, whatever definition is used there will always be activities which will be disputed as 'proper sport'. For example, sport typically includes some activities that involve aesthetic movement, such as gymnastics and ice skating. Dance is consistent with the Council of Europe definition – it is physically active, skilful and at the elite end it is competitive – yet many would deny it is a sport. Another source of debate concerns competitive activities where the winner is decided by subjective judgement, e.g. gymnastics, ice skating, equestrian dressage, freestyle skiing and even boxing (in cases where a knockout is not achieved).

How important are these definitional considerations to the sport and leisure manager? On the one hand, many such managers are involved at the community level. They recognise the competitive structure of sport and the desire of many sports participants to improve. They also have to acknowledge and cater for the array of other reasons for sports provision, from the demand by individuals for relaxing, invigorating and social sport, to broader objectives such as improving community health. Management to these non-competitive objectives will necessarily emphasise attributes such as enjoyment, health benefits and social relationships. It will not make a distinction between sport and physical activity. On the other hand, fewer sport and leisure managers will be more narrowly focused on performance sport. Their efforts will be engaged in managing participants in order to improve their skills and competitive positions. Definitions of sport do matter, then, because they bring precision to the objectives of the manager.

> **Discussion question**
>
> Are the following activities sports: (1) long-distance walking; (2) darts; (3) dance; (4) skateboarding; (5) extreme ironing?

1.6 Defining leisure

What is leisure? This question has been discussed for a long time by philosophers, researchers, lecturers, sociologists and leisure directors, managers and students. The United Nations Universal Declaration of Human Rights states:

> Everyone has the right to rest and leisure, including reasonable limitation of working hours and periodic holidays with pay.
>
> (Article 24)

> Everyone has the right freely to participate in the cultural life of the community, to enjoy the arts and to share in scientific advancement and its benefits.
>
> (Article 27)

The word 'leisure' appears on the surface to be a self-explanatory concept and most people will have little difficulty, on a 'commonsense' basis, describing what it means to them. Yet scholars have been unable to agree with clarity descriptions of leisure, let alone define what the word means. Indeed, leisure has been debated for well over two thousand years. Edginton *et al.* (2003) provided over 200 definitions of leisure and recreation.

A starting point for understanding is the derivation of key words. The Greek word '*schole*' was synonymous with leisure, the implication being that leisure was non-work but also was associated with learning and culture. The English word 'leisure' is derived from the Latin '*licere*', 'to be permitted' or 'to be free'. So here, at least, there are common denominators which convey that in order for us to be 'at leisure' there must be an essential freedom to choose what we want to do and what we want to be.

The concept of leisure permits widely varying responses. Leisure is commonly thought of as the opposite of work, but one person's work can be another person's leisure, e.g. art and crafts. Freedom from obligation is often regarded as a key attraction of leisure, but many non-work activities involve considerable obligation, e.g. volunteering. Some regard leisure as being an opportunity for relaxation and pleasure, but often people spend their leisure time in dedicated service, study, personal development or hard training. Whatever leisure is, it is important to people's quality of life. And it is important for leisure professionals to understand what leisure is and what it does for people – in a customer-focused industry, this is essential.

1.6.1 Leisure as time

This approach treats leisure as a residual of time, after taking out of total time everything that is not regarded as leisure, i.e. paid work and 'obligated' time such as sleeping and personal hygiene. However, some uses of time are difficult to categorise in this way. Eating, for example, could be seen as obligated time but is definitely a leisure activity when it is a social occasion with family or friends. Do-it-yourself and gardening might be obligated chores to some but pleasurable choices for others.

In leisure time one has choice over how to spend it – the terms 'discretionary time' and 'free time' have been used to describe such choice. However, such time is not always seen as leisure. Those people who are made to retire early or are made redundant can find themselves feeling alienated, isolated and robbed of a purpose in life. Such situations make it a mistake to consider 'leisure' as simply time free from work or obligations. The American Association for Health, Physical Education and Recreation (AAHPER) qualify their understanding of leisure with how time is used:

> we view leisure as time – time that is free for man to choose among alternatives {…} [There exist] three basic functional aspects of leisure – relaxation, entertainment, and development {…} Leisure is the absence of pressure, the freedom from the obligation to work {…} Leisure is the restorative, creative use of free time.
>
> (AAHPER, quoted in Edginton *et al.*, 2003)

Discussion question

What is the difference between leisure and free time? Give examples of people with one but not the other.

1.6.2 Leisure as activity

Another classical understanding of leisure is that it is made up of an activity or a 'cluster of activities'. Dumazedier (1967), for example, suggests:

> Leisure is activity – apart from the obligations of work, family and society – to which the individual turns at will, for relaxation, diversion, or broadening his individual and his spontaneous social participation, the free exercise of his creative capacity.

Many look at leisure as activities freely chosen. However, in reality some leisure activities are not freely chosen. Dumazedier (1967) coined the term 'semi-leisure' to describe those activities which one was obliged to do but that brought about satisfactions in the doing, e.g. do-it-yourself, family obligations.

Case Study 1.1 illustrates the range of activities which are identified in national surveys of leisure. They demonstrate that such lists are context specific and also time specific. And typically the list of activities does not include what Rojek (2000) calls the 'dark side' of leisure, e.g. recreational drugs, joy-riding, hooliganism, graffiti.

Discussion question

What leisure activities could be leisure or work, depending on the circumstances? For example, what about volunteering?

CASE STUDY 1.1

Leisure in practice

Table 1.2 Leisure activities in Australia

Home-based leisure

watch TV	entertain at home
electronic and computer games	exercise, keep fit
swim in own/friend's pool	play musical instrument
arts, crafts	reading
listen to music	gardening
indoor games	outdoor play with children
talk on telephone (15 mins+)	relax, do nothing

Social/cultural leisure

visit friends/relatives	dining, eating out
dancing, disco	visit pub
visit licensed club	cinema/movies
pop concerts	theatre
musical recital/opera	other live performances
special interest courses	church activities
library activities	museums, galleries
exhibitions	arts, crafts
hobbies	picnic/barbeque away from home
parks	horse/dog races
sport spectating	drive for pleasure
bird-watching	play electronic games

Sport

archery/shooting	athletics
Australian rules football	badminton
baseball/softball	basketball
bowls	cricket
cycling	fishing
golf	gymnastics
hockey	horse riding
martial arts	motor sport
netball	orienteering
rink sports	rugby league
rugby union	soccer
squash	surfing/lifesaving
swimming	tennis
ten-pin bowling	touch football
water activities – non-powered	water activities – powered

Recreation

walk dog	walk for pleasure
aerobics	jogging/running
bushwalking/hiking	skateboarding
shooting/hunting	shopping for pleasure

Source: Veal, in Cushman *et al.* (2005).

Whilst it is important for a leisure manager to consider the concept of leisure in order to understand what it is that actual and potential customers want from leisure, in practical terms the clearest expression of leisure demand is what people do. National surveys demonstrate this by asking what leisure activities people undertake. Table 1.2 gives a list of leisure activities from one of the most comprehensive national surveys – the Australian National Recreation Participation Survey, 1991.

However, even this extensive list does not contain all leisure activity. Under home-based leisure, for example, it does not include do-it-yourself or listening to the radio. And, because the survey was in 1991, it does not include leisure use of the internet, particularly social networking. Also, typically for many national leisure surveys, the list does not include domestic or foreign tourism trips. Furthermore, the list specifies details of sports but not other activities, such as the arts or visits to heritage attractions.

Leisure has a strong cultural, traditional orientation, parts of which are common to many countries, such as many of the activities listed in Table 1.2. However, sometimes popular leisure activities are specific to particular countries or regions of the world, such as berry picking in Finland, which 60 per cent of the population do at least once a year; story telling in New Zealand, which 12 per cent of the population do at least once a month; and going to the tea house in Hong Kong, which 59 per cent of the population do at least once a month (Cushman *et al.*, 2005).

1.6.3 Leisure as a state of being

In the society of ancient Greece – at least at the educated, privileged strata – the 'treasures of the mind' were the fruits of leisure which contained the joy and delight of life. Hence, Aristotle thought of leisure as a state of being, free from the necessity of work, and characterised by activity for its own sake or as its own end. The 'ideal man' would strive for perfection in arts, music, sport, school and in military service. This ideal leisure made for an advanced society and for good governance. Neulinger (1974), in similar vein, suggests:

> Leisure is a state of mind; it is a way of being, of being at peace with oneself and what one is doing {…} Leisure has one and only one essential criterion, and that is the condition of perceived freedom. Any activity carried out freely without constraint or compulsion, may be considered to be leisure. To leisure implies being engaged in an activity as a free agent, and of one's own choice.

Pieper (1952) went further and stressed the idea from a spiritual perspective:

> Leisure it must be understood, is a mental and spiritual attitude – it is not simply the result of external factors, it is not the inevitable result of spare time, a holiday, a weekend or a vacation. It is, in the first place, an attitude of the mind, a condition of the soul.

Leisure, to Pieper, was not a means to an end, but rather an end in itself. Leisure, for Pieper, is a mental or spiritual attitude, a 'condition of the soul'. It produces an inward calm; it means not being busy, but letting things happen. Kraus (2001) also identifies a 'spiritual' dimension:

> Leisure implies freedom and choice and is customarily used in a variety of ways, but chiefly to meet one's personal needs for reflection, self-enrichment, relaxation, or pleasure. While it usually involves some form of participation in a voluntary chosen activity, it may be regarded as a holistic state of being or even a spiritual experience.

Is it possible to have leisure as a way of life? Discuss what types of people might be able to do this.

1.7 The 'pleisure' principle

This term was devised by George Torkildsen in an attempt to get to the heart of the leisure experience. It is reproduced in his words, as a testimony to his endeavour to go beyond the immediate concerns of leisure managers and explore the fundamental meaning of the products they manage. The term 'pleisure' was introduced by Torkildsen in 1992 and this section explains it and the implications for leisure managers.

Three concepts are the foundation stones for leisure management: 'play', 'recreation' and 'leisure'. In debating and dissecting each concept, a case can be made for treating each as a distinct concept, and in common language we can all distinguish children at play, young people and adults taking part in organised recreation, and being at leisure. However, the feelings we might experience could be the same whatever words we care to use. Why, then, the concern, one might well ask? It is tempting to dismiss this line of enquiry as mere semantics which simply adds to the jargon. However, there is more to it than just words because we often provide for these three aspects of life in different ways. We provide play space, community recreation facilities or multi-use and family leisure centres.

At the core of play, recreation and leisure, there exist a number of similarities and overlaps, so much so that we can use each word at times to mean much the same thing. Indeed, several words, ideas or themes are used frequently in describing something of their collective essence: freedom; absence of necessity; choice; self-initiation; self-expression; satisfaction in the doing; playfulness. There are, of course, differences. Playfulness and spontaneity are found more in children's play. Recreation carries a badge of respectability – doing things that are good for you. Leisure is a looser, more casual, less constrained term than recreation and encompasses a vast range of active and passive, casual and serious pursuits. Despite the differences and nuances, there are times, whether at play, recreation or leisure, that people experience a feeling of immense satisfaction in the doing; or of well-being or a quality of experience that can lead to revitalisation or an uplifting of the spirit. This can, of course, occur in many different life situations, including work, but it is when we are 'at leisure', free to make choices and be ourselves, that we are more likely to achieve a quality we might describe as 'wholeness' or an inner-consuming experience. The experience goes beyond the description afforded by words – but it needs to be called something!

As there is no word to describe this experience in the English language, Torkildsen invented the word 'pleisure'. Figure 1.1 illustrates better than words the concept of the pleisure experience at the heart of play, recreation and leisure.

What implications does this 'discovery' have for leisure professionals and managers? The 'pleisure principle' implies that in meeting the needs of individual people, clients and customers of leisure and recreation services, facilities and programmes, it is the quality of the experience that is more important for them than the activities, programmes, numbers attending or the income generated. The activity itself may be quite secondary to what it

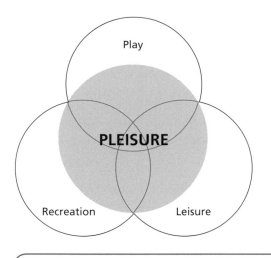

Figure 1.1 'Pleisure' at the heart of play, recreation and leisure experience.

does for a person, or what it means to him or her. Moreover, appreciating that leisure managers have business goals to fulfil, people are more likely to be attracted to and 'buy' activities that they perceive to be worthwhile or that bring satisfying experiences – pleisure.

1.7.1 From 'pleisure' principles to leisure management actions

Putting principles into practice is not easy. Expediency is often the option we take and, understandably, management practices tend toward efficiency. If, as leisure professionals, we want to provide a choice of activities and the opportunity for people to experience and develop their leisure participation, then we must provide favourable environments: the right conditions; satisfactions; and positive outcomes:

- **The right conditions** – leisure programmes need to be designed with sufficient options for different people. There needs to be freedom of choice and also the opportunity for some self-initiation and spontaneity.
- **Satisfactions** – for leisure to be satisfying, some of the following experiences need to be present: self-expression; challenge; novelty; stimulation; joy; playfulness; 'pleisure' experiences; re-creative moments.
- **Positive outcomes** – for leisure to be effective, there should be some positive outcomes; for example: accomplishment; physical, emotional, social and psychological well-being; heightening of self-esteem.

Favourable experiences give satisfactions. Satisfactions lead to consuming interests. Consuming interests can lead to life-enhancing experiences, a goal of leisure. Providing for client and customer satisfactions can also lead to successful business outcomes.

Regrettably, it is not so simple. There are a number of individual and institutional barriers to providing services and programmes based on maximising the 'pleisure' experiences of people. The reasons are complex. People, generally, are not agents free to do as they please and are limited in their response to leisure services and programmes; some people have physical, mental and social limitations or their environments limit choice (e.g. family, peer group, culture, resources). Leisure for others is eroded through obligations, lack of time or through enforced free time without the means or motivation to use it. Activities one might consider as leisure, such as sport, can be practised in such a manner that the spirit of play and fair play are submerged and dominated by the desire to win at all costs. And there are inequalities of opportunity – physical, social and economic.

Successful private sector organisations, although concerned with financial profits, realise that maximising 'pleisure' experiences can lead to greater profits. However, if as a society we want to provide 'pleisure', then government, in particular, must have appropriate aims and objectives:

- Services should be open to all and meet individual needs, so that a person can choose activities, in relative freedom.
- Priorities should be balanced to serve the greatest number and those in greatest need, recognising that those in greatest need may well be in the minority.

The question is: with the emphasis on freedom, can 'pleisure' actually be organised, planned and managed? The activity can be organised, but the experience cannot. What is the manager's role? Normally considered as managing resources, services, facilities and pro-grammes, sport and leisure managers have a wider remit. Their role is to:

- consult and involve people and then create environments and services to match the market profiles and their expectations;
- extend the range of activities to offer a wide and varied choice;
- help groups through supportive services – some can be enabled to create their own opportunities and manage themselves;
- assist employers in giving their employees recreation activities at workplaces and outside work;
- help provide leisure education for schools, colleges and organisations to develop leisure skills (physical, social, cultural and intellectual) which can help people, particularly young people, to make choices to realise their potential.

In these and other ways, leisure managers and other professionals can help to extend opportunities. These actions amount to an enhanced 'people approach' in public leisure services. This stems from the belief that each individual has worth, has a need to express himself or herself, and that society will benefit from citizens who have the ability and resourcefulness to be creative and find fulfilment in their lives, through leisure.

1.8 Conclusions

It is clear that leisure is a complex concept and certainly not as simple as 'free time'. It involves fundamental principles of free and informed choice and appropriate opportunities. It requires a relationship with paid work which is not in conflict but is again a choice for the individual. It has the potential to become central to both a way of life and a sense of identity. And given the considerable constraints that exist, which often prevent the realisation of leisure's potential, there is a clear role for managers. Leisure managers need to know what leisure is in order to hope to satisfy the aspirations of their customers and to realise the potential benefits that leisure can provide for individuals and society.

Many of the definitions above feature freedom of choice, to which some add intrinsic motivations. What, then, is the role of management? If leisure is so self-determined, is management a contrived and redundant skill in leisure? The ethos of this book and of the leisure management profession is that management has key roles to play in facilitating leisure, however defined. Management of facilities and services provides opportunities for people to express their leisure demands. Even natural resources are typically the outcomes of man's management of the land, e.g. in the provision of footpaths and canals, and in access to coastal and inland amenities. Policy also has an important role – in Japan, for example, legislation was passed to limit the number of working hours; and in Europe the European Working Time Directive has a similar objective.

Customers are the starting point for sport and leisure management and are at the heart of many management decisions. Quality management begins with consideration of what the customer wants. Marketing may be seen by some as a manipulation of people's free expressions of choice, but for marketers themselves the mission is to develop the offer of products to consumers, i.e. to extend the choice of activities. Even human resource management, with an explicit concern for staff, is designed to enable staff to satisfy customer preferences.

Practical tasks

1 Complete a diary recording your use of time and identify what percentage of it is leisure. Compare this with diaries recorded by other people in different situations, e.g. relatives, friends. Consider how important leisure is to each person.
2 Consider the list of leisure activities in Table 1.2 and add any activities which you think are leisure but are not included in the list.

Structured guide to further reading

For numerous definitions of concepts related to leisure and recreation:
Edginton, C., Coles, R. and McClelland, M. (2003) *Leisure Basic Concepts*, AALR, Reston, VA.

For a consideration of the way in which definitions of leisure have developed to create a more complex and fundamental concept:
Goodale, T. and Godbey, G. (1988) *The Evolution of Leisure*, Venture Publishing, State College, PA.

For practical lists of leisure activities for a variety of countries:
Cushman, G., Veal, A.J. and Zuzanek, J. (eds) (2005) *Free Time and Leisure Participation: international perspectives*, CABI Publishing, Wallingford.

Chapter 2

People's needs and leisure demand

In this chapter

- Do leisure needs exist?
- What is the difference between leisure needs, wants and demands?
- What factors influence leisure participation?
- What are the planning and management implications of leisure demands?

Summary

All humans have the same basic needs that have to be satisfied. In theories of motivation, need is seen as a force within the individual to gain satisfaction, enjoyment and completeness as well as survival and safety. There appear to be many levels and types of need, including important needs of self-actualisation and personal development that sport and leisure help to achieve. 'Leisure needs' as such may not exist; rather there are human needs which can find satisfaction through leisure. Need is not just an individual concept but should also be considered in the form of social need, which embraces a number of different types, including normative, felt, expressed, comparative, created, false and changing needs.

Many discrete and interrelated factors condition people's choices and participation in leisure activities, which is the most obvious expression of their demand. These include personal factors, social and circumstantial factors, and opportunities presented by leisure providers. People's use of facilities and services is affected, to a considerable degree, by management policy and management actions, which should be designed to both fulfil customers' expectations and counter barriers to participation. Facilities must both be accessible and provide attractive leisure opportunities.

2.1 Introduction

It could be argued that the understanding of leisure is only of academic interest and of limited value, unless this understanding helps towards meeting some of the needs of individuals and groups of people and thereby is of value to the wider community. Leisure services are claimed by their providers to be based on the needs of the people they are intended to serve. But is this the case or is it wishful thinking? After all, do policy-makers, planners, providers and managers of leisure services have sufficient insights into people's needs? Should they be concerned with needs, wants or demands, and what is the difference? Policy-makers, facility managers and club officers all seek to identify what their citizens, customers and members need and how their demands can be satisfied.

This chapter first attempts to throw light on the concept of need. It addresses such questions as: what are human needs; can leisure meet some of these needs; and do leisure needs exist? More pragmatically, leisure providers are faced with evidence of demand in the form of participation in sport and leisure activities, so after clarifying the distinction between needs, wants and demand, we review evidence on demand. In particular we attempt to clarify the major demographic and socio-economic influences on participation in sport and leisure, using evidence from the UK and beyond. Such evidence is important in informing policy-makers and service managers, who are interested in designing and managing appropriate opportunities for their citizens and customers. Participation evidence drives the market segmentation which managers, and particularly marketing managers, employ when planning, providing and promoting services for specific groups of people (see Chapter 15).

2.2 Needs, wants and demand

Leisure policy-makers, researchers, planners and managers often equate 'needs' with wants or demands. But there are differences between the three:

- **Needs** are deficiencies which relate to fundamental human requirements. Arguably sport and leisure are most relevant to health and self-development needs.
- Leisure **wants** are many and various and exist as responses to the desire to satisfy needs and preferences. They include the desire for new leisure experiences such as gym membership, holidays, computer games, theatre shows and football games.
- Leisure **demands** are similar to wants but are often interpreted as actual, revealed demands, i.e. leisure activities and expenditures that have been realised. Many wants may not be so realised, e.g. simply because of the lack of sufficient money.

Policy-makers and leisure planners have generally been concerned with identifying sport and leisure demands rather than understanding people's needs. Large scale government and commercial surveys, for example, have identified certain demands, but have not elaborated what motivates people to leisure and why people participate. 'Whereas a "need" appears to be conceptually "woolly" and operationally elusive, "demand" appears tangible, measurable, even predictable' (Kew and Rapoport, 1975). However, Torkildsen, among others, believed that if researchers are to provide information of real value to policy-makers and planners, they must explore people's needs and values, not just their demands. To reach a full understanding of demand, it is necessary to know not only what people do, as provided by social surveys, but also reasons for participation and non-participation, and the needs that underpin demand, which are better explored by qualitative research.

2.3 Needs, drives and motivation

One simple view is that human need is caused by something that is missing, a deficit. Of relevance to sport and leisure, for example, are the need for physical health when overweight, the need for relaxation when stressed and the need for excitement when bored. Needs here are the causes of motivation, rather than the motivation itself. Drives are goal directed; they release energy. They are generally considered to be the motivating factors within human personality.

Many psychologists who see the motivational aspects of human needs as drives do so in conjunction with the concept of 'homeostasis', which is a fundamental need to maintain a state of relative internal stability. Homeostasis is easiest to understand in terms of physiological needs, for example the relief of cold or hunger. Needs which are more social in nature, such as the needs for achievement, self-fulfilment and acceptance, are less easily accounted for in terms of homeostasis. However, the principle of 'psychological homeostasis' is used by Shivers (1967) as the basis of 're-creation', i.e. purposeful leisure.

'Need' is often used to denote some inner state that initiates a drive; for example, 'humans need to sleep'. This is the approach taken by Maslow, whose analysis of the 'hierarchy of needs' is the most well-known theory of needs. Maslow (1954, 1968) discerned five levels of need. If humans are chronically hungry or thirsty, the biological and physiological need to secure food and water will be most powerful. After hunger and thirst needs have been met other higher needs emerge. Next will be the needs for safety, orderliness and a predictable world. When these have been met, the need for belonging and love (family, personal and work relationships) is followed by the need for esteem (achievement, status, responsibility, reputation) and then finally the need for self-actualisation, i.e. for personal growth and intellectual fulfilment. It is at the highest levels of need – belonging, esteem and self-actualisation – that sport and leisure have a role to play.

Doyal and Gough (1991), however, do not accept Maslow's 'Needs Hierarchy': 'its strict temporal sequencing of motivations in question is simply false. Some people seem far more concerned with their self-actualisation than their safety – mountain climbers, for example'. Maslow's categories seem either to be combined or at times to conflict. Thompson (1987) takes a similar stance: 'one can have a drive to consume something, like lots of alcohol, which one does not need and at the same time have a need for something, like exercise or diet, which one is in no way driven to seek.'

Perceived need, therefore, may be a matter of individual preference. Subjective feeling, however, is not a reliable indicator of human need; it is more an expression of wants. We can strongly want things which are seriously harmful, such as recreational drugs or excess alcohol, and, in our ignorance, not desire things which we require to avoid harm, such as exercise. The message should not go unheeded by leisure managers. We can provide excellent, accessible services and programmes which are good for our health, and charge nothing for them, yet people will buy alternatives which they desire but which are not good for their health, such as sweets and snacks. You cannot even give away leisure products and services if people do not want them. In practice, this is why management decisions on what to supply are typically based on revealed demand, rather than more fundamental concepts of need.

Discussion question

Should a sport or leisure manager be more interested in what leisure activities people undertake or what leisure means to people?

Doyal and Gough (1991) reason that there are two main types of need: one concerned with survival, security and health; and the second concerned with what they term 'autonomy' and learning. By autonomy, Doyal and Gough mean they believe that a basic personal need is to recognise ourselves as distinct and separate individual people; and through learning and education we grow and develop. Human beings are not capable of growing up and developing alone; therefore basic needs are provided for in a social context. Society has therefore created 'institutions' to provide for the realisation of individual needs; among them, leisure facilities and organisations.

It appears to be a reasonable conclusion that there is a relationship between need and motivation: 'In theories of motivation need is seen as a state or force within the individual. This can be either a deficit state leading to a search for satisfaction, or else a stage of psychological incompleteness leading to a movement towards completeness' (IFER/DART, 1976). In either case, need is the trigger for a motivational process – conscious or unconscious – involved in goal-oriented behaviour.

Significant contributions to the understanding of motivations in leisure are provided by Csikszentmihalyi (1975) and Scitovsky (1976). Scitovsky analysed how people's preferences are formed, and suggested, in contrast to the state of homeostasis, that optimum arousal was a key criterion for success in consumption. Csikszentmihalyi uses the term 'flow' to describe a similar state of optimum consumption experience – 'a holistic sensation that people feel when they act with total involvement'. To take the example of playing a game of football, if the level of competition and standard of playing is too low, arousal is too low and it will be a boring experience. If, however, the standard of play is too high, arousal is too high and it will cause anxiety and dissatisfaction. When arousal is optimum, the game will be a pleasure to play.

According to Scitovsky, the key factors in determining optimum arousal are the degree of novelty of the consumption experience and the skill of the individual in coping with this novelty. For example, an experienced mountain climber has the skill to cope with very difficult and risky climbs and optimise arousal. A beginner, however, may get just as much of a 'buzz' from a relatively easy climb. Many sports organisations organise activities, and particularly the learning of appropriate skills, in a way that implicitly acknowledges these principles of motivation by 'optimum arousal', and many aspire to a condition from playing sport that is equivalent to Csikszentmihalyi's 'flow'.

Discussion questions

What needs and motivations does television viewing service? Do they justify television's importance in leisure participation?

2.4 Do leisure needs exist?

Both 'leisure' and 'needs', seemingly easily understandable in commonsense language, have been shown to be complex concepts. Linking leisure to needs and asking the question 'Do leisure needs exist?' is even more complex.

Despite the limitations of Maslow's theory, one benefit it has is that it emphasises the developmental needs of the individual. Need is not just seen as the reduction of a state of tension, or the return to homeostatic equilibrium. In addition, people are seen as striving towards self-actualisation and growth. If leisure has a place in this process, self-actualisation could be perceived as one of the goals of leisure or, indeed, the ultimate goal.

Tillman (1974) is one of many authors who have examined needs and identified those which are important to leisure. He listed needs for:

- new experiences like adventure;
- relaxation, escape and fantasy;
- recognition and identity;
- security – being free from thirst, hunger or pain;
- dominance – to direct others or control one's environment;
- response and social interaction, to relate and react to others;
- mental activity – to perceive and understand;
- creativity;
- service to others – the need to be needed;
- physical activity and fitness.

Discussion questions

What needs does sport and leisure fulfil for you? Are any of these needs not capable of being met by non-leisure activities such as paid work, household work or community work?

However, the concept of 'leisure needs' is misleading. People have needs which can be satisfied in a variety of ways, including not just leisure but also other means such as housing, work and family. One way of meeting needs may be through taking up leisure opportunities; but it is only one way. Leisure needs as such may not exist. The case study of empirical investigations of leisure consumers' benefits (Case study 2.1) relates three different leisure experiences to concepts very similar to some of the needs identified above.

CASE STUDY 2.1

Exploring benefits for leisure consumers: three examples

How are leisure needs analysed in practice? This case Study summarises three studies in *Managing Leisure: an international journal* which attempt to empirically identify the benefits for customers of different services and which give important indications of the needs that these services are satisfying. These examples are cricket spectators in the UK, visitors to a zoo in the USA and children at a summer camp in Greece.

All three studies used quantitative techniques to identify benefits to, motivators for and preferences of consumers. This involved questionnaire surveys, the responses for which were grouped, through factor analysis, to identify the main types of benefit. Whereas the questions did not use the term 'need', the results relate closely to some of the concepts of needs reviewed in this chapter.

In the cricket study (Kuenzel and Yassim, 2007) the purpose is to identify the relationship between the emotion of joy, customer satisfaction, the informal promotion by them of the experience by 'word of mouth', and the revisit intentions of customers. Sport spectating is described as hedonic consumption, in the pursuit of personal pleasure, and one of the principal drivers of customer satisfaction in such an activity is the feeling of joy it generates. Three variables are explored relating to joy:

1   **the quality of the game** – represented by the performance of the two teams, but particularly the team that the individual supports;
2   **social facilitation** – represented by the spectator's interaction with friends, family and other spectators, as well as sharing the experience of the game with others;
3   **auditory elements** – represented by the atmosphere created by the different noises of the crowd.

The results of the study show a significant relationship between the three variables and joy, which influences customer satisfaction positively, which in turn influences word-of-mouth and revisit intentions favourably. Social facilitation was found to be the most important dimension of joy.

In the study of Fort Worth zoo customers in the USA (Tomas *et al.*, 2002), four major benefits emerged as important for visitors:

1   **family togetherness** – bringing the family together in an enjoyable experience;
2   **companionship** – being with and doing things with friends;
3   **wildlife enjoyment** – enjoying rare sights and discovering new elements;
4   **wildlife appreciation and learning** – including learning more about wildlife, appreciating it more and thinking what to do to help wildlife.

In the study of children at a Greek summer camp (Alexandris and Kouthouris, 2005), six factors emerged as the main motivations for respondents to attend the camp:

1 **camp experience** – including memorable experiences, community life, and fun;
2 **socialisation among old friends**;
3 **socialisation with new friends**;
4 **independence** – including feeling free, and getting away from parents;
5 **participation in activities** – i.e. the experience of sporting, outdoor and water activities;
6 **parents' decisions** – not really a benefit, just reflecting the fact that some children are sent to camp against their preferences.

Socialisation with new friends was identified as the most important motivation, with camp experience the second most important.

In all three of these investigations the socialisation element emerges strongly and this relates closely to Maslow's 'belonging' need and to Tillman's 'response and social interaction' need. Other consumer benefits to emerge as important relate more to the specific experiences offered by the different services, i.e. the quality of the cricket match, wildlife attributes at the zoo and camp experience at the children's camp. These relate most closely to Tillman's need for 'new experiences' and possibly also to Maslow's 'self-actualisation' need.

Another aspect of these studies needs emphasising. All were undertaken to inform providers of what their customers valued most, in order for them to improve their services. They are very much in the spirit of finding out, not just what your customers do, but what they need from and value about the service provided.

2.5 Social needs

Needs, then, have important social dimensions. Bradshaw (1972) classified social needs into four categories: 'normative', 'felt', 'expressed' and 'comparative'. Godbey (1976) and others expanded the number of classifications by adding additional categories: 'created needs', 'false needs' and 'changing needs'. These seven needs are described below within the context of providing leisure services.

2.5.1 Normative needs and leisure

These represent value judgements made by professionals in the sport and leisure field, for example the standards that are set by policy-makers for the amount of open space needed in local communities. They are usually expressed in quantitative terms and have been commonly used in sport and leisure planning. However, the use of such normative needs as the major determinant of leisure provision can be challenged on a number of points – a full discussion of the problems and benefits of standards is presented in Chapter 14.

2.5.2 Felt needs and leisure

These can be defined as the desires that an individual has but has not yet actively expressed; they are the determinants of what a person thinks he or she wants to do. Felt needs are largely learned patterns, from personal experience and the experiences of others. They are limited by an individual's knowledge and perception of available leisure opportunities.

However, mass communication has expanded individuals' knowledge beyond the realm of their experience. Clearly sport and leisure managers have an opportunity to influence individuals' felt needs, by promotion.

2.5.3 Expressed needs and leisure

These are felt needs that have been able to be realised, i.e. activities in which individuals actually participate. They provide the leisure manager with knowledge about current leisure preferences, tastes and interests and are typically the most common frame of reference for sport and leisure planning, if only because they are relatively easy to identify. However, if leisure resources, programmes and services are based solely on expressed needs, there is less incentive to initiate new services and programmes. Expressed need itself does not give a total picture of felt need, or of why people do or do not participate.

2.5.4 Comparative needs and leisure

Often an individual or organisation will compare itself with another individual or organisation. This may be done purely out of interest, or it may provoke feelings of deficiency. Care must be exercised when utilising the comparative method in assessing needs – one cannot assume that what works well in one situation will automatically be effective in another.

2.5.5 Created needs and leisure

Godbey (1976) suggests that policy-makers and professionals can create leisure interests. Created needs refer to those activities which organisations have 'introduced to individuals and in which they will subsequently participate at the expense of some activity in which they previously participated'. In other words, created needs refer to those programmes, services and activities solely determined by the organisation and accepted by the participant without prior felt need or knowledge. Some analysts are critical of created needs, seeing them as stimulating demand simply to feed growth in commercial business. However, according to Edginton et al. (1980) the created needs approach can be useful to the participant and to the organisation:

> Many individuals are grateful to organizations for helping them identify an area of interest that previously they had not considered. In a sense, the approach is a form of leisure education that is an important component of the philosophy of recreation and leisure service organizations. The organization also benefits by serving as an agency that creates opportunities for stimulation and enrichment. As a result, individuals may look to the organization as a vehicle for providing innovative experience.

There are many examples within leisure of what might be seen as created needs which demonstrate innovation and enterprise, such as theme parks, 3D cinema, budget airlines and even fast food restaurants. The ultimate judges of the value of such products are consumers, who vote with their feet and their money. It is probably more appropriate to term such products created demands, rather than created needs.

2.5.6 False needs and leisure

Needs may be created which are inessential, which are in fact false needs, i.e. there is a distinction between what an individual is aware of needing (felt needs), what are usefully 'created needs' and what is created but not needed. Marcuse (1964) suggested that society encourages the individual to develop certain sorts of 'need', which serve the interests of society as a whole but may be false needs for the individual. Thus people acquire the 'need' for cars, washing machines, televisions, computers, etc., which it is in the general interests of the economy to promote. But they are false needs to the extent that they are not strictly essential. However, it is hard to prove the existence of false needs and it is ethically dubious to challenge the expressed demands of customers, who react positively to innovative products and services, by labelling them 'false needs'.

2.5.7 Changing needs in leisure

Rhona and Robert Rapoport (1975) claim that although every person has needs, these needs change as one progresses from one phase of life to another. The Rapoports' thesis is that all people have a quest for personal identity. Each person is seen as having a 'career' consisting of separate but interrelated strands. Three major strands relate to family, work and leisure. Each life strand produces changes in needs, interests and activities at critical points in life such as marriage and the birth of children. It is important for sport and leisure providers to consider the needs attributed to each stage in the life-cycle if they are to make the most appropriate provision for different age segments of the population.

Another dimension to social needs is **social control**. One of the assumptions made in this book is that what is fulfilling, meaningful and worthwhile for the individual is in the main likely to be worthwhile for the community also. Leisure needs, therefore, should be considered in a social and community context. Stokowski (1994) suggested that leisure is a consistent feature of life in 'human gatherings', but often for social control purposes:

> leisure is something that human beings need just as they need food, shelter, warmth, security and protection. At the same time {...} leisure is seen as quite low down on the scale of essential social values {...} leisure is regarded as something to be given as a reward to the individual and society or withheld as a punishment or as a way of controlling social behaviour.

This view of leisure sees it as part of a social system, including family, employment, education and government, which determines what an individual does, even to a large extent what he or she chooses to do. Leisure in this system is designed to provide opportunities for people which are controlled and conform to social norms. This is perhaps best demonstrated by an example of deviation from such social norms. UK government policy in response to riots in Brixton and Liverpool in 1981 included efforts to improve leisure opportunities, and one way of looking at this policy response is to see leisure as a tool to bring dissatisfied young people back within social control. Another more subtle example of social control is the way that unemployed people often reduce their formal leisure participation, not just because they have less income, but also because they feel unworthy of such leisure – they have not earned it.

Discussion question

Discuss the key differences between wanting to know how sport and leisure can satisfy people's needs and being able to research more easily what people choose to do in sport and leisure activities.

2.6 Sport and leisure participation

Revealed demand is documented in many countries by data on participation. The most common indicator used is participation rates, i.e. the percentage of a population or sub-group that participates in an activity over a given time period. Table 2.1 gives English participation rates for the year 2005–6 in a variety of sport and leisure activities. This evidence is produced by an annual *Taking Part* survey of adults (16 years and older) conducted in England since 2005 (DCMS, 2007a). Another large national survey in England, *Active People*, concentrates on sports participation, so results from this survey are reviewed in Chapter 10.

The *Taking Part* survey illustrates some of the problems when moving from conceptual discussions about needs and demand to more practical expressions of demand through evidence. *Taking Part* is comprehensive but it does not ask questions about needs, and it does not cover all leisure activities – it is confined to the seven categories in Table 2.1. And within each category it is selective about which activities are included – in arts events, for example, it does not ask about cinema visiting. Nevertheless, it is a relatively comprehensive overview of national participation in leisure.

According to the *Taking Part* results, the most popular activities for adults in England are:

- **at historic sites** – cities (participation rate, 52 per cent in the year), buildings (37 per cent) and parks/gardens (38 per cent);
- **arts events** – theatres for musicals/pantomimes (26 per cent) and plays/drama (23 per cent), live music events (24 per cent) and art exhibitions (22 per cent);
- **arts activities** – buying original crafts (16 per cent) – although it is arguable whether this is an arts 'activity' or not – painting/drawing/sculpture (13 per cent) and textile crafts (13 per cent);
- **active sports** – indoor swimming (16 per cent in the previous four weeks), health/fitness activities (14 per cent) and cycling (10 per cent);
- **gambling** – the National Lottery (57 per cent in the year), horse racing (12 per cent) and scratchcards (10 per cent).

Table 2.1 Annual participation rates for adults in various leisure activities in England, 2005–6

Leisure activity	Percentage of adults participating in the year
Attending a historic environment site	70
Attending a museum/gallery	42
Attending a library	48
Attending at least one type of arts event	67
Participating in at least one type of arts activity	53
Participating in at least one type of active sport	69
Participating in at least one type of gambling activity	65

Source: DCMS (2007a).

Table 2.2 Adult participation rates for a sample of leisure activities in different countries

	Great Britain	Australia	Canada	Israel	Japan	Netherlands	New Zealand	Russia
Date	2002	1991	2000	1998	2003	1999	1997/8	1999
Reference period in survey	4 weeks	1 week	3 months, 1 month* or 1 year**	1 year	1 year	1 year	1 month	'regular'
Percentage of population participating in reference period								
Watch television	99	94	n/a	94	n/a	n/a	95	74
Listen to music	83	65	69	n/a	41	n/a	75	21
Read books	65	70	41	77	n/a	n/a	71	28
Gardening	48	n/a	43	n/a	35	n/a	50	n/a
Walking	35	27	68	n/a	n/a	11	n/a	21
Swimming	14	16	20	n/a	20	32	n/a	n/a
Cinema	19	25	15*	41	37	46	32	n/a
Theatre	n/a	4	20**	41	12	23	13	n/a

Source: Cushman et al. (2005).

Table 2.2 provides some comparative evidence, for different countries, of participation in leisure activities. The table shows some similarities and differences in participation rates. However, the national surveys from which these data are drawn cover different dates and also different time periods, e.g. the last year or the last month. It is also likely that for some activities the definitions used in the surveys were slightly different. These differences in survey methods account for at least some of the apparent differences in participation between countries.

Table 2.2 shows the ubiquity of television as a leisure pursuit in more economically developed economies. This applies not just to the very high percentages of populations watching television but also to the time they spend watching television. For example, in Australia, out of an average of 313 minutes of leisure a day in 1997, 119 minutes were spent watching television. In Canada, out of an average of 299 minutes of free time a day in 1998, employed people spent 102 minutes watching television. And in Great Britain in 2000–1, out of an average of 313 minutes leisure time a day, 147 minutes were spent watching television. All this evidence is cited in Cushman *et al.* (2005).

One transnational study that attempted to make consistent comparisons across different countries was COMPASS (UK Sport, 1999), which examined sports participation in European countries – this study is featured in Case Study 2.2.

CASE STUDY 2.2

COMPASS: sports participation in Europe

This study investigates the availability of sports participation data across seven European countries and allows for differences in data collection methods (e.g. samples, phrasing of questions, prompting, etc.). The results enable an accurate comparison to be made of sports demand across different countries.

The COMPASS project (UK Sport, 1999) examined a structure of sports participation from no participation to high intensity, frequent participation at a competitive level. The main findings are summarised in Table 2.3. They show a quite significant difference in sports participation rates, which are systematically higher in Northern European countries and lower in Southern European countries.

Finland and Sweden have both the highest levels of participation in the high frequency, intensive categories and the lowest percentages in the non-participant categories. In contrast, Italy and Spain have the lowest participation rates in the high frequency, intensive categories, and the highest percentages in the non-participant categories. The UK, Ireland and the Netherlands have lower overall participation rates than Finland and Sweden, and more people in the irregular and occasional categories.

The evidence from COMPASS leads to some interesting questions, particularly about why the differences in sports participation exist. Is participation simply determined by the weather and average temperatures, i.e. does a generally colder climate encourage greater activity? Or are there different traditions and cultures of sport between Scandinavian, Latin and other European countries? The differences are not caused by age structures – all the countries have similar population structures and the differences in participation rates are maintained for different age groups.

37

How does such evidence help providers of sport services? In an increasingly international leisure business, commercial sector providers in particular need consistent information of this type in order to plan their development in new countries. On the one hand, Scandinavian countries might be seen as showing such strong demand that there is considerable commercial potential from new provision there. On the other hand, the large rates of non-participation in Southern European countries, together with increasing transnational concern for rising levels of obesity and associated health problems, might suggest that the greater potential market lies in countries like Italy and Spain. It depends what objectives the providers have in terms of target markets; and what types of supply are being planned.

Table 2.3 Adult sports participation in European countries, 1999

	Percentage of adult populations						
	Finland	Ireland	Italy	Netherlands	Spain	Sweden	UK
Competitive, organised, intensive	6	7	2	8	2	12	5
Intensive	33	11	3	8	7	24	13
Regular, competitive and/or organised	5	7	2	10	2	5	4
Regular, recreational	28	3	3	6	4	17	6
Irregular	6	15	8	25	10	11	19
Occasional	2	21	5	6	6	n/a	20
Non-participation but participation in other physical activities	16	10	37	38	43	8	15
Non-participation and no other physical activities	3	26	40		26	22	19

Source: COMPASS (UK Sport, 1999).

Table 2.4 provides some evidence of the leisure pursuits of young people aged 11–15 years in England (DCMS, 2007b). It demonstrates the differences between total participation and participation outside school, the latter being more voluntary. Those children who participate in each type of leisure do on average two activities, e.g. those who participate in sport do on average two sports. The most popular activities are football, swimming and basketball for sport; theatre and festivals for arts events; painting, playing musical instruments, computer art and dance for arts activities; and cities, monuments and buildings for historic sites.

The *Taking Part* evidence in Tables 2.1 and 2.4 typically records what percentages of adults and children in England undertook each type of leisure activity at least once in the year. *Taking Part* asks other relevant questions about participation, including frequency of participation, which varies considerably. At one extreme, half of adults participating in moderate intensity sports (i.e. excluding passive sports such as darts, bowls and fishing) do so at least three times a week. At the other extreme, over half of adults attending arts events or museums and galleries do so just once or twice a year.

The evidence on what people actually demand in leisure is vital as a set of signals to sport and leisure managers, expressing people's revealed preferences. Despite the huge variety of leisure activities engaged in, there are a few activities that are very popular and in that sense leisure demand is largely predictable. Participation evidence identifies which are the mainstream markets and which are minority markets, at least in terms of revealed demand.

2.7 What factors influence leisure participation?

Many factors influence people's leisure choices. The first group of factors relates to the individual: his or her stage in life, interests, attitudes, abilities, upbringing and personality. The second group relates to the circumstances and situations in which individuals find themselves, the social setting of which they are a part, the time at their disposal, their job and their income. The third group relates to the opportunities and support services available to the individual: resources, the quality of activities, facilities and programmes, and the management of them.

Table 2.5 summarises many of these different factors – it is an illustration of the complexity and variety of influences on an individual's leisure participation and expenditure decisions. In addition, even if people have identical circumstances and opportunities, one person may choose one activity and another something entirely different – personal preferences are important too.

In England, the *Taking Part* survey provided direct evidence of what individuals think prevents them from participating in various leisure activities. Table 2.6 summarises the top three responses for 2005–6. For arts and heritage activities, personal preferences are at the root of the most common constraint – a lack of interest. This is difficult for leisure managers to overcome because it indicates that these people may not even be potential attenders; although new interest might be generated by effective education and promotion. For sport the main constraint is perceived health status, which is more capable of being modified by managers. Physical activities can be designed to take into consideration all kinds of health problems, and indeed physical activity is typically promoted as a means of improving health status. For libraries the main reason for non-attendance is that there is no need to go – presumably because alternative sources of reading and reference materials are readily available, i.e. purchases and the internet.

By understanding the major relationships between leisure participation and the influences and constraints in Tables 2.5 and 2.6, leisure managers can foresee some of the difficulties encountered by potential participants, and management approaches can be modified accordingly. Care is needed in examining the evidence, however, because the influences often interact in their relationship with leisure participation. For example, income and education are highly correlated. Evidence shows that people with low education and low income participate least in leisure activities that are felt to be important to health needs, e.g. moderate intensity sport and physical activity (DCMS, 2007a). What is appropriate policy intervention? Reduce entrance charges to sports facilities for the poor? A targeted sports education programme in deprived areas? Would either of these have much of an impact when the culture people are born into and their upbringing might also be correlated with income and education? It is because of such problems that more 'joined up' policies are seen as the way to tackle social exclusion, which is itself the result of a number of interrelated factors.

Table 2.4 Annual participation rates in leisure for young people in England, 2005–6

Leisure activity	Percentage of 11–15-year-olds participating
In the year	*Outside school*
All	
Attending a historic environment site	72	n/a
Attending a museum/gallery	55	45
Attending a library	72	58
Attending at least one type of arts event	74	68
Participating in at least one type of arts activity	91	77
In the previous four weeks	
All	*Outside school*
Participating in at least one type of active sport	95	89

Source: DCMS (2007b).

Table 2.5 Influences on leisure participation

Personal	Social and circumstantial	Opportunity factors
Age	Occupation	Resources available
Stage in life-cycle	Education and attainment	Facilities – type and quality
Gender	Disposable income	Awareness
Ethnicity	Material wealth and goods	Perception of opportunities
Marital status	Car ownership and mobility	Recreation services
Dependants and ages	Time available	Distribution of facilities
Will and purpose of life	Duties and obligations	Access and location
Personal obligations	Home and social environment	Activities provided
Resourcefulness	Friends and peer groups	Transport
Leisure perception	Social roles and contacts	Costs: before, during, after
Attitudes and motivation	Environment factors	Management: policy and support
Interests and preoccupation	Mass leisure factors	Marketing
Skills and ability – physical, social and intellectual	Population factors Cultural factors	Programming Organisation and leadership
Personality and confidence	Upbringing and background	Social accessibility
Health	Culture born into	Political policies

Table 2.6 Major reasons for adults not participating in leisure activities

	Percentages of non-participants citing:			
	Not really interested	Difficult to find the time	Health not good enough	No need to go
Arts activity	37	30	14	
Arts event	31	29	16	
Historic environmental sites	30	30	14	
Museums and galleries	33	27	8	
Sport	18	18	48	
Libraries	19	19		30

Source: DCMS (2007a).

2.7.1 Personal and family influences

The personality of an individual, his or her interests, physical and social ability, a person's will and purpose in life, and a whole range of other personal factors will influence choice and participation in sport and leisure. Some important personal factors are now reviewed.

2.7.1.1 Age and stage in the family life-cycle

Age has an important influence on sport and leisure participation, but its effect will vary depending on the person, the opportunities and the type of activity. For children, there is a rapid change in the space of a few years. For adults, participation profiles by age groups are different for different leisure pursuits, as shown in Figure 2.1 for the seven types of leisure activities covered by the *Taking Part* evidence for England. For sport there is a steady decline by age; for arts activity there is a more gradual decline with age. However, for attending historic sites, arts events, museums and galleries, and for gambling, participation rates increase until middle age, then fall with older age. Such profiles are important for sport and leisure managers to understand who their main markets are and where the main problems of drop-out occur. In sport for example, given current understanding of the beneficial effects of physical activity for the physical and mental health of older people, the declining participation rates by age disclose a major challenge to policy-makers and sports managers alike.

Veal (in Cushman *et al.*, 2005) examines the relationship between age and the participation in the 40 leisure activities in Australia and finds that for 29 of the 40 listed activities the lowest participation rate is among the 60+ age group. For half the activities the highest participation rates are in the 14–19-year-old group. This pattern is not just for the more active pursuits such

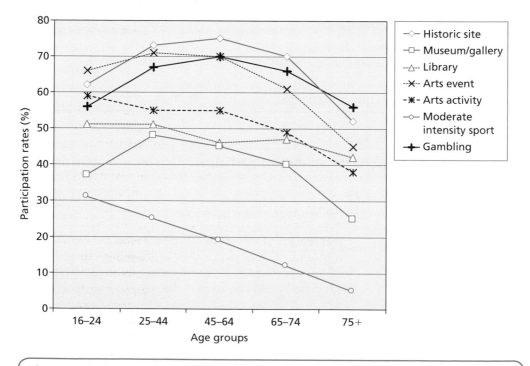

Figure 2.1 Age and leisure participation in England, 2005–6.
Source: DCMS (2007a).

as sport, but also for watching television, playing musical instruments, listening to music, telephoning friends, hobbies and the cinema. Similar results are to be found in Cushman *et al.* (2005) for Canada, Finland, France, Great Britain and Hong Kong. It is not surprising that, by common consent, age is one of the main influences on leisure participation. It therefore presents a major challenge to leisure managers, particularly as such countries are typically experiencing a long-term ageing of their populations.

> ## Discussion question
>
> Given the evidence of declining leisure participation by age, should leisure managers spend a lot of effort trying to get older people to attend their facilities, or simply concentrate on the ages where they know demand is strong?

The *Taking Part* survey in England also asks respondents to compare their participation in leisure now with their participation when they were children. This compares participation for the same respondents, rather than comparing participation by different generations, which is influenced by many factors other than age. The results for sport, arts and museums/galleries are given in Table 2.7. They demonstrate not only how much participation falls from childhood to adulthood, but also the influence of encouragement as a child, which leads to significantly higher participation rates for children and adults alike. Interestingly, the one exception to the patterns shown is that participation in arts activities by adults who were not encouraged as children is higher than when they were children. This suggests they have compensated for earlier missed opportunities.

Age should not be considered in isolation, however. Age may be less restrictive for certain leisure activities than life-cycle changes, such as getting married and having children. For some, participation may increase with age as a result of the children leaving home or a person retiring from work. Although age may influence the level of fitness and energy, a reduction in family and work responsibilities may more than compensate for this.

Table 2.7 Adult versus child participation in leisure

	Moderate intensity sport activities	Arts activities	Museums and galleries
	Percentages of adults		
Participation as a child			
encouraged as a child	72	86	56
not encouraged as a child	29	14	44
Participation in 2005–6			
encouraged as a child	24	58	53
not encouraged as a child	15	35	29

Source: DCMS (2007a).

2.7.1.2 Gender

The leisure patterns of males and females are typically different. Evidence for England is given in Figure 2.2. It demonstrates that for three of the leisure sectors covered, male participation rates are higher than female, but for three others female participation rates exceed those of men.

Men and women face different constraints on their leisure participation. A higher proportion of men work full time in the paid labour force in most countries, including the UK. However, women typically have higher time commitments to home and family obligations, particularly looking after children; and in England a high proportion have part-time paid work (Green *et al.*, 1987). The net effect of these different constraints, however, is that typically women have less leisure time than men.

Time constraints and whatever is behind them are probably a major influence on the different participation rates of men and women in many leisure activities. In the USA, for example, out of 31 outdoor recreation pursuits listed in Cushman *et al.* (2005), 24 have higher adult participation rates for men than women. In General Household Survey evidence for UK sports and physical activities in 2002 (Fox and Rickards, 2004), male participation rates exceed female for 22 out of 30 major sports listed, and female participation rates were higher for just five sports.

However, the picture changes depending on the leisure activities chosen and the country investigated, as demonstrated in Cushman *et al.*, 2005. In Finland in 1991, for example, out of 42 leisure activities listed, female participation rates were higher in 20, whilst male participation rates were higher in 19. In France in 1997, out of 30 sport and leisure activities

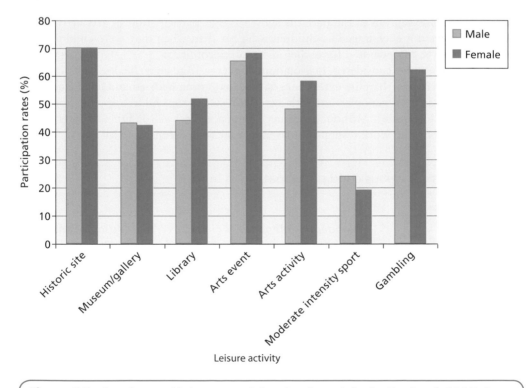

Figure 2.2 Gender and leisure participation by adults in England, 2005–6.
Source: DCMS (2007a).

listed, men had higher participation rates for 16 activities, women had higher participation for 13 activities, including watching television, reading books, going to a library, gardening, collecting and gymnastics. In Australia in 1991, out of 40 sport and leisure activities listed, men had higher participation rates in 14, women in 15. And in a list of popular sports and physical activities in Hong Kong in 2000, men had higher participation rates in eight but women had higher participation rates in the other seven, including badminton, jogging, walking and martial arts.

Women have had, and continue to have, greater constraints placed upon them than men, which shows unambiguously in leisure time evidence. However, one of the misleading factors in looking for similarities and differences stems from the fact that most surveys have studied traditional leisure activities. Once a wider view of leisure is taken, encompassing the range of activities in and around the home, holidays, socialising, entertainment, etc., a more complex picture starts to emerge.

2.7.1.3 Ethnicity

As the flow of peoples between countries increases, whether for economic, political or other reasons, so an increasingly important personal dimension to leisure participation is ethnic origin. Figure 2.3 shows some evidence of differences in leisure participation by different ethnic groups in England.

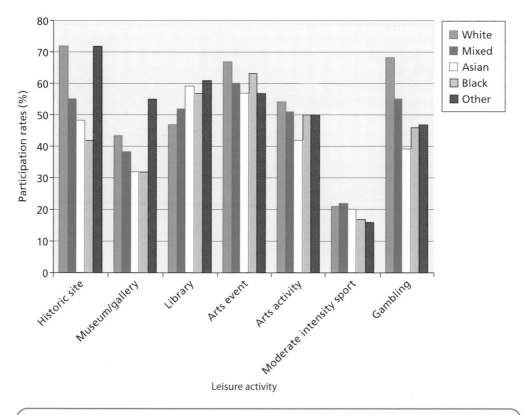

Figure 2.3 Ethnicity and leisure participation by adults in England, 2005–6.
Source: DCMS (2007a).

The highest participation rates are typically for white people. However, for libraries white people have the lowest participation rates, possibly reflecting a relationship between ethnicity and income. It is important to emphasise that within these broad ethnic groups there are considerable variations in participation rates, e.g. between different Asian groups.

In many other countries, evidence of leisure participation by ethnicity is not available. In the USA, however, evidence for outdoor recreation pursuits in Cushman *et al.* (2005) shows that people of Caucasian origin had higher participation rates than those of African American or Hispanic origins for all but two of 31 activities listed. This finding may be as much a reflection of cultural traditions and preferences as inequality of opportunity, although it is likely to be influenced by inequalities of income too. But it draws attention to the need for sport and leisure planners and managers, particularly in the public sector, to cater for diverse cultural needs and demands in contemporary communities.

Discussion question

Are the lower participation rates in many leisure activities by ethnic minorities a sign of discrimination, or differences in culture, or are they due to other reasons?

2.7.1.4 Education

The type of education, the length of education and the educational attainment of people are closely related to upbringing, class, occupation, income and other factors. In general, the higher the qualification, the greater the degree of participation in leisure activities. This is evidenced in many surveys over the past twenty years. *Taking Part* survey evidence for England endorses this finding, as shown in Figure 2.4. A particular challenge for policy-makers, however, is that female educational performance is increasingly stronger than male's, yet the gender differences in activities such as sport persist.

For six of the seven types of leisure, participation rates are higher for those with qualifications below A-levels than for those with no qualifications; and those with A-levels or above have the highest participation rates. The main exception to this pattern is gambling, where the most educated have the lowest participation rate.

The strong influence of education on leisure participation rates is endorsed by international evidence (Cushman *et al.*, 2005). In Canada, the participation rates of those with higher education qualifications are higher for a range of at-home and away from home sport and leisure activities, compared with those with just high school or elementary school qualifications. In France the picture is much the same, whilst in Spain the only activities listed with higher participation rates for lower educational qualifications are family activities, listening to the radio and watching television.

2.7.2 Social and circumstantial factors

The range of social and situational circumstances that affect leisure participation include the home, school, work environment, income, mobility, time, social class and social roles. Evidence for some of these in relation to leisure is reviewed here.

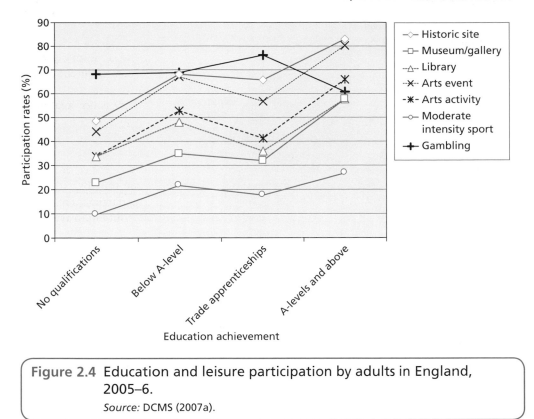

Figure 2.4 Education and leisure participation by adults in England, 2005–6.

Source: DCMS (2007a).

2.7.2.1 Time availability

According to Lader *et al.* (2006), reporting on a national survey of time use, the average breakdown in the use of time in the UK is as shown in Figure 2.5. It shows that on average 23 per cent of time was spent on leisure, the second largest use of time after the 36 per cent spent on sleep. However, Figure 2.5 is an average across all adults, and it is clear that leisure time availability is conditioned heavily by the employment status and domestic responsibilities of a person, e.g. those in full-time work tend to have less leisure time, as do those with children.

Table 2.8 details leisure time availability in the UK for a variety of circumstances. Unfortunately women have less leisure time than men of the same working or domestic status, mainly because of home obligations. Women still do the majority of household chores, on average, despite their increased participation in the labour market. Overall, women from all social classes spend more than three times longer than men on average on cooking and routine housework and more than twice as long on caring for children and adults, despite the apparent 'new man' sharing in the household duties.

The greatest amount of leisure time appears to be concentrated at the ends of the age continuum, with younger people and the retired having considerably more time at their disposal than the middle age groups, who live under a greater degree of time pressure from both paid work and family. Retired people and unemployed men have the most time for leisure, although much of it may be more accurately identified as free time rather than leisure time.

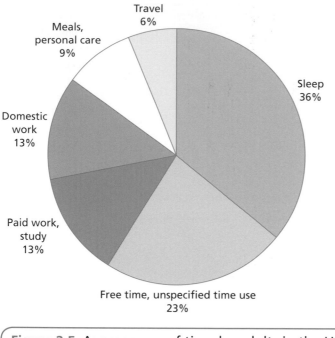

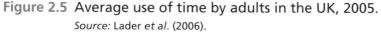

Figure 2.5 Average use of time by adults in the UK, 2005.
Source: Lader *et al.* (2006).

Table 2.9 provides some comparisons of leisure time availability in different countries. There are considerable variations here which may emanate from different working or domestic cultures, but which may also be explained more simply by differences in either the year the data was collected or the methods used to collect the data, e.g. the questions asked in time-use surveys.

Table 2.8 Adult leisure time in the UK, 2000

Age	Domestic situation	Average minutes of leisure time per day	
		Men	*Women*
8–24	Single, no children, living with parents	356	319
<45	Couple, no children	321	296
All ages	Single parent, youngest child <18	301	264
All ages	Parent, couple, youngest child 0–6	233	217
45–64	Mid-age couple, no children at home	319	291
65+	Older couple	427	383
All people		327	299

Source: ONS (2001).

Table 2.9 Adult leisure time in different countries

Date	Country	Average minutes per day of leisure time
2000	Netherlands	380
1995	USA	377
1998	Canada	362
1987	Finland	353
1990	Israel	335
1997	Australia	313
2000	UK	313
1998–9	New Zealand	278
1998–9	France	276
1996	Poland	271

Source: Cushman *et al.* (2005).

2.7.2.2 Income and leisure participation

Income levels are closely linked to participation rates, and for many leisure activities the proportion of the adult population participating increases with income. Figure 2.6 summarises the relationship for England. Two of the seven types of leisure in Figure 2.6 do not show increasing participation with higher income – libraries and gambling. These exceptions are probably for different reasons – in the case of libraries there are commercial alternatives that higher income people will probably prefer and be willing to pay for, i.e. bookshops, the internet. In the case of gambling, the influence of background, social class and cultural preferences may explain the greater participation of lower income groups.

It is perhaps not surprising that since income correlates with both education and social class, the higher income group has the higher participation rates for most leisure activities. If lower income groups are to be attracted in larger numbers to leisure activities a more social service approach will need to be applied. This is one of the principal roles of public sector leisure provision (see Chapter 5).

2.7.2.3 Socio-economic class and leisure participation

The nature and meaning of social class are generally regarded as being problematic, because class relates not simply to income or occupation but also to upbringing and parental background. Social class is often regarded as grouping on the basis of occupation, which is 'socio-economic class' rather than social class. Socio-economic class is more easily identified for most people because it is related to occupations. However, classification of those not in paid work is obviously more difficult – and is normally done by reference to the partner's occupation for those full time in the home, or previous occupation in the case of the unemployed or the retired.

Evidence of the effect of socio-economic class on leisure participation in England is shown in Figure 2.7. For most of the types of leisure covered, the relationship echoes that of income in Figure 2.6 – not surprisingly, because occupation and income are closely related. However, for libraries the relationship between participation and socio-economic class is different to the

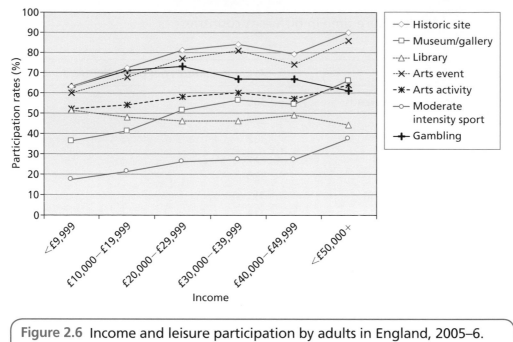

Figure 2.6 Income and leisure participation by adults in England, 2005–6.
Source: DCMS (2007a).

relationship with income, which demonstrates that whilst there is a close relationship between income and socio-economic class, it is not universal – sometimes they have different effects.

Evidence of the influence of socio-economic class on leisure participation in other countries is provided in Cushman *et al.* (2005). In France in 1997, for example, the highest occupational groups (managers/professional, skilled non-manual) had the highest participation rates for 20 out of 30 leisure activities listed. In Australia in 1991, managers/professionals had the highest participation rates for 23 out of 40 leisure activities listed.

IFER/DART (1976) explored the issue of socio-economic class and referred to the importance of 'social climate', a complex of factors in addition to those which relate to age, gender, income, occupation and education. The attitudes and values of people in their social setting are seen as enabling or inhibiting factors concerned with leisure choices. The review of evidence on pp. 42–50 relating to personal and social circumstances and leisure shows a powerful interrelationship between factors such as income, education and occupation, which leads to clear differences in leisure participation between those at one end of the scale and those at the other. People towards the top end of the income, education and occupation scales have much higher participation rates in most leisure activities, i.e. sport, the arts, heritage. And this conclusion extends to other leisure activities not covered in the evidence reviewed above, e.g. tourism.

At the other end of the spectrum, the evidence points unambiguously to what are termed 'the socially excluded' – i.e. people with lower education attainment, lower income, lower skill jobs, etc. – with a much lower probability of engaging in many leisure activities. It is this sector of society that public leisure policy has been directed to, in an attempt to improve opportunities. The very term 'socially excluded' suggests that the low participation rates are because of constraints, but the extent to which they result from constraints rather than

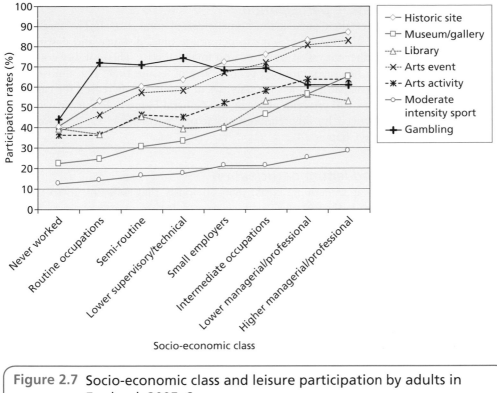

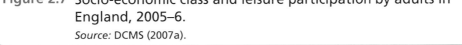

Figure 2.7 Socio-economic class and leisure participation by adults in England, 2005–6.
Source: DCMS (2007a).

preferences is not well researched. Table 2.6 contains an important reminder that one of the most common reasons given for lack of participation is 'not really interested'. However, the lack of interest may itself be partly determined by the socio-economic class a person belongs to.

2.7.3 Opportunity and leisure participation

The opportunities that sport and leisure managers provide through the facilities and pro-grammes they offer are a form of social filter. For example, some swimming pools in England have adapted their facilities and staffing in order to programme Asian women's swimming sessions, with great success. There are both formal and informal social filters – programming is an example of formal, whilst the appearance and culture of a facility are informal, an example being the way many old people are deterred from using sports facilities because they have the image of only being for young, fit people.

The way people perceive their neighbourhood can have as significant an effect on leisure participation as the way they perceive local leisure provision. For example, if residents per-ceive their neighbourhood as being violent, the elderly in particular will be fearful of ventur-ing out of the house at night. Sport and leisure management should include or interact with actions which might change people's perceptions for the better, not only of leisure facilities and their local neighbourhood but also of themselves.

2.7.3.1 Access and leisure participation

Leisure participation undertaken outside the home involves some travel. The method of travel can affect the level of satisfaction – it can determine time, distance and destination. Apart from walking, all other means of travel incur a financial cost. The mobility conferred by the ownership of a car has revolutionised people's use of leisure time. For almost every activity the chances of participating in leisure activities in Britain are increased for car users by between 50 per cent and 100 per cent, according to General Household Survey evidence. Accessibility is also influenced by other important factors, particularly the location of a sport or leisure facility (see Chapter 14).

2.7.3.2 Awareness and leisure participation

If people do not know that something exists, then obviously they will not go to visit it, unless they stumble upon it. One of the key functions of leisure marketing is to inform potential users of the leisure opportunities provided for them (see Chapter 15). Because leisure facilities are not sought in the same way as a shopping centre or place of work, knowledge about them derives from seeing them, hearing about them or reading about them. The influence of the media is critical in informing many leisure choices, as is the internet.

2.8 The influence of planning and management on leisure participation

People's take-up of leisure opportunities and use of leisure facilities are determined, as we have seen, by some discrete factors and a number of interrelated factors. Effective planning and management are no less important as an influence on demand. The way services and facilities are managed can have a profound effect on the extent to which they are used and who uses them.

Obviously the most direct way in which planning and management can affect leisure participation is through the quality of decisions by leisure providers. Planning the location and design of a facility, management policy, marketing, the attitudes of staff, sensitive customer service, skilled programming reflecting the 'needs' of the community – all such decisions go towards creating an accessible service, a welcoming atmosphere, an attractive image and a set of leisure opportunities that is known and valued by potential customers. Even the administrative and booking systems at a leisure facility can consciously or unconsciously act as a type of social filter, encouraging some people from attending but possibly deterring others.

Although many of the constraints on leisure demand are seemingly beyond the reach of leisure managers – e.g. they can't alter a person's income or education – there are actions they can take to target and attract specific groups. In the public sector particularly, explicit management decisions are often taken to attract hard-to-reach groups such as the socially excluded. Even people who think they are not interested in an activity may be targeted by management efforts to persuade them that they should be interested! This is not unusual, for example, in management of sports facilities and outreach services (i.e. mobile services taken into specific communities).

People use leisure facilities for a variety of reasons. Sport centres, for example, can be places to go and socialise. The activity itself may be of quite secondary importance compared with getting out of the house, having 'quality time' with the children, and meeting and talking with friends. Management needs to be aware of such motivating factors in deciding on management policy and delivery.

Leisure planning and management exist, in large measure, to provide opportunities for individual people to participate actively or passively, seriously or casually in their time for leisure. People's preferences can be met, in part, by effective leisure planning and management, but only if the needs and demands of different people are identified. Therefore, a broad base of research, consultation and (for the public sector) community involvement will help to plan appropriate provision. It is suggested that such an approach will provide:

- an increase in individual and community stakeholders' inputs and involvement in planning and decision-making;
- a better understanding of the community's needs;
- accurate and up-to-date information on the activities in which people are involved, the activities in which they would like to be involved and how these can be provided.

Chapter 14 includes an examination of demand forecasting techniques and public consultation alternatives.

Discussion question

What should be the more important influences on leisure provision, countering barriers to participation or concentrating on attractors in services?

2.9 Conclusions

There are many constraints on sport and leisure choices, and in practice few people are agents free to choose whatever they will. This means that there are clear differences between leisure needs (what we must have), wants (what we desire) and what we actually demand and consume (what we commit time and money resources to doing). Leisure can offer significant options for individual action and for personal decisions, should opportunities permit these decisions to be realised. As choice concerns the individual, two factors have to be stressed. First, there is a strong link between leisure and other elements of life; and, second, because it matters to the individual, the quality of the experience is of paramount importance.

People can still enjoy leisure, even though they might face severe difficulties and constraints in accessing leisure activities. It is clear that a great many people overcome the limitations of a poor education, family obligations and personal handicaps, and even overcome the obstacles of low income, insufficient facilities and resources, to find themselves satisfying interests, fulfilling experiences and 'mountains to climb'. Sport and leisure management, therefore, has much to offer in the way of enabling people to discover themselves and achieve fulfilment in their leisure choices.

> **Practical tasks**
>
> 1 Interview two people of very different ages. Identify what they need from their leisure activities and assess the similarities and differences between them.
> 2 Visit a sport or leisure facility and assess the extent to which its offer is limited in the types of people it attracts (by age, gender, ethnicity, etc.), both by formal filters such as its programme and by informal filters such as its image and dominant user types.

Structured guide to further reading

For a review of leisure and needs:

IFER/DART (Institute of Family and Environmental Research and Dartington Amenity Research Trust) (1976) *Leisure Provision and Human Need: Stage 1 Report (for DoE)*, IFER/DART, London.

For participation data on 15 countries:

Cushman, G., Veal, A.J. and Zuzanek, J. (eds) (2005) *Free Time and Leisure Participation: international perspectives*, CABI Publishing, Wallingford.

For a review of sports participation concepts and economic influences on demand decisions:

Gratton, C. and Taylor, P. (2000) *Economics of Sport and Recreation*, E & FN Spon, London.

Search appropriate leisure and sport journals for case studies of specific target groups, analysing their needs and drawing implications for policy and management.

Useful websites

For *Taking Part* survey reports and data:
www.culture.gov.uk/reference_library/research_and_statistics/4828.aspx

Chapter 3

Trends in the leisure industry

In this chapter

- What is happening to sport and leisure participation over time?
- How are leisure spending and leisure time changing over time?
- Is leisure at home, especially TVs and computers, taking over?
- Is sport and leisure away from home growing?
- What general demographic and socio-economic trends are affecting sport and leisure?

Summary

Trends enable sport and leisure managers to be aware of changes over time which are important to their industry. They help managers to plan for the right provision to suit people's changing circumstances and preferences. The most obvious trends of relevance are for key dimensions of leisure, such as participation in sport and leisure activities, the amount and use of leisure time and changes in leisure expenditure. This chapter identifies trends in leisure at home and leisure away from home. The former are only a quarter of leisure spending in the UK but they include important growth areas such as televisions, computers and use of the internet. These sectors demonstrate the importance of technological change to trends in leisure, particularly at home. Leisure away from home is the focus for the majority of leisure expenditure in the UK, with eating and drinking out and overseas holidays being the largest sub-sectors.

Although leisure as a whole is a growth industry, it contains some sectors which show strong growth over time, such as use of the internet, holidays and gambling, and other sectors which show slow growth or even decline, such as reading and alcohol consumption away from home. Some sectors are relatively stable over time, but others, such as visits from overseas tourists, are relatively volatile.

In addition to leisure trends, it is also wise for leisure managers to be aware of more general demographic, social and economic trends, because they impact on current and future leisure business. These more general trends include changes in population levels and structures, changes in incomes and inequality, and changes in health. Each has major implications for the nature of leisure demands; and also the way in which governments will attempt to change them by regulation or by promotional initiatives.

3.1 Introduction

In recent years, the pace of change not only in sport and leisure, but in our quality of life generally, has been rapid. We are now enjoying higher standards of living, filled with goods, services, activities and opportunities that in past years seemed unimaginable. This has been fed by rising incomes, technological advances and greater mobility of people, to name a few of the underlying factors. But many of the more developed economies also have increasing inequality between the 'haves' and the 'have nots' (see pp. 75–6), which has implications for leisure, particularly for public sector providers. And there are worrying trends in the proportions of populations who are overweight and obese – particularly in the USA and UK but also in other more developed countries.

This chapter explores major trends relevant to sport and leisure, i.e. changes over time, five years and more. The core evidence used relates to the UK because of the availability of consistent data, particularly from *Leisure Forecasts*, which is a trends and forecasting publication from the Leisure Industries Research Centre at Sheffield Hallam University (e.g.

Leisure Industries Research Centre, 2009). However, many of the issues covered relate to other countries, particularly the more developed.

Leisure commentators, forecasters, social scientists and researchers provide information on trends in areas such as leisure time, leisure participation, consumers' expenditure on leisure, travel, and economic, social and demographic changes, which all impinge on leisure provision and participation. Exploring the past and predicting the future in terms of leisure provision and participation are essential planning and management tools. They are used in numerous ways, including:

- to draw attention to specific areas of growth and decline;
- to predict the most likely future leisure activities of consumers;
- to plan leisure services and facilities strategically;
- to reduce the element of risk in decision-making on future provision and policy;
- to provide information for use in marketing of future facilities, services and programmes.

Trends are important indications of future needs and demands. However, they are normally indications of national movements. It is important for leisure planners and managers to remember that what is happening nationally may not be occurring locally. National trends need to be supplemented where possible by local information, on needs and demands, and on provision, to ensure accurate interpretation. Moreover, some 'trends', so called, are short lived, emphasising the volatility of the leisure industry. Also, forecasting future trends is fraught with uncertainty because the future does not always follow past trends. It was predicted in the 1960s, for example, that by now the UK would have moved to the 'three 30s'. i.e. 30 years of working life, 30 working weeks per year and a 30-hour working week. This has only been achieved in part, and for the very few. Indeed, many people in full-time employment are working longer hours now than two decades ago.

3.2 General leisure trends

3.2.1 Leisure participation

Many of the more developed countries have statistics on changes in leisure participation over time. Table 3.1 summarises some of the data in Cushman *et al.* (2005). It is not meant to provide exhaustive coverage of all leisure activities. The time periods for different activities and countries vary. But the table demonstrates the variation in leisure participation over different time periods and between countries.

The most reliable long-term evidence of leisure participation rates in Great Britain is from the *General Household Survey* (e.g. ONS, 2009a), which periodically asked questions about a range of leisure and sport activities. Figure 3.1 shows how stable the participation rates of the main domestic leisure pursuits are in the last quarter of the twentieth century. Most of the activities in the figure were stable or rising in this period. Only dressmaking/needlework/knitting declined.

> ### Discussion question
>
> Why do you think participation rates for dressmaking/needlework/knitting declined in Britain in the last quarter of the twentieth century?

Table 3.1 Examples of changes in leisure participation over time in different countries

Countries	Time periods	Increasing participation rates[1]	Decreasing participation rates
Australia	1991–2002	art galleries, cinema, classical music concerts, library, theatre	dance, museums, opera, pop concerts
Canada	1981–98	ballet	art gallery, cinema, classical/music/jazz/pop concerts, theatre, opera, museum, historical sites, park, zoo
	1988–2000	aerobics, gardening, golf, jogging	bowling, cycling, swimming, tennis, volleyball
Finland	1981–91	art exhibitions, dancing library, roulette, TV	chess, cinema, concerts, dance, listening to music, radio, reading books and magazines, summer sports, theatre
France	1973–97	concerts, dancing, listening to music, museums, reading books and magazines, theatre, TV	cinema, gardening, historical sites, radio
Israel	1970–90	domestic and foreign holidays, hobbies, listening to music, pubs/nightclubs, sports, TV	cinema, gambling, radio, reading books and magazines, spectator sports, theatre
Japan	1982–2003	art exhibition, bowling, cinema, concerts, foreign holidays, soccer	badminton, baseball, cycling, DIY, exhibitions/events, fishing, golf, jogging, knitting/sewing, skiing, spectator sport, table tennis, tennis, theatre
Netherlands	1979–99	cinema, concerts, jogging, museums, solo sports, theatre, theme parks	cycling, ice skating, team sports
USA	1960–2001	camping, cycling, fishing, riding, sailing, swimming	hunting

Note: 1: participation rate = % of population participating in a given time period (e.g. a year or a month)
Source: Cushman *et al.* (2005).

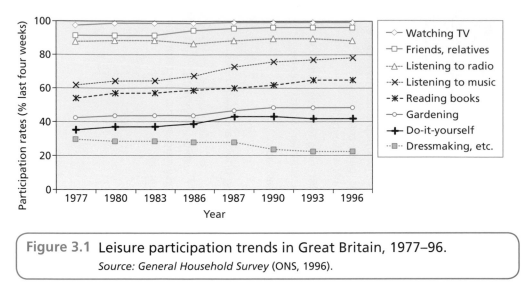

Figure 3.1 Leisure participation trends in Great Britain, 1977–96.
Source: General Household Survey (ONS, 1996).

Sports and physical activities participation evidence for Great Britain is presented in Figure 3.2. It shows steady or rising participation for all the main activities until 1996, except for snooker/pool/billiards, which fell through the 15 years covered by the figure. The reason for the significant fall in 2002 for walking is probably the 2001 outbreak of foot and mouth disease in the countryside, which led to the closure of many footpaths and general publicity deterring people from visiting the countryside. Although the problem cleared by 2002, it is likely to have had a negative effect on recreational walking that year.

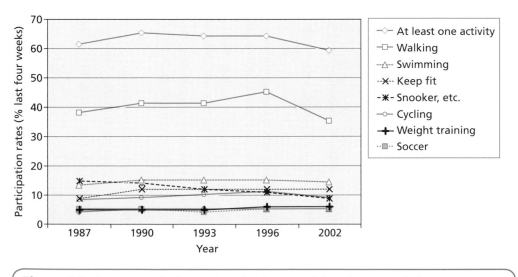

Figure 3.2 Sports and physical activities participation trends in Great Britain, 1987–2002.
Source: General Household Survey (ONS, 2002).

CASE STUDY 3.1

Leisure participation trends in Poland, 1980–99

In Poland the fall of communism in 1989 proved to have little effect on the supply of leisure opportunities but it seems to have had a dramatic effect on leisure participation trends (Jung, 2005). Table 3.2 shows trends in supply and demand for a few leisure activities and there are some dramatic changes, with changes in demand often very different from changes in supply.

Table 3.2 Supply of and demand for organised leisure in Poland

	1980	1985	1990	1995	1999	% change 1980–99
Newspaper titles	88	97	130	108	74	−16
Newspaper circulation	2,627	2,467	1,390	1,434	1,190	−55
Museums	427	528	563	589	623	+46
Museums visits	20,079	19,857	19,282	17,060	18,582*	−7
Theatres	134	139	143	181	190	+2
Theatres visits	17,803	17,032	12,873	10,198	10,667	−40
Cinemas	2,228	2,057	1,435	721	695	−69
Cinema visits	97,540	107,080	32,798	22,613	27,475	−72
Sports clubs	1,815	1,866	1,846	2,901	3,638	+100
Sports club memberships (000s)	1,394	951	641	443	372	−73

Note: * 1998 figure (1999 n/a).
Source: Jung (2005).

Jung refers to a mass withdrawal from institutionalised forms of leisure provision as one of the post-communism trends that emerged – all the attendances/memberships in Table 3.1 fell during this period. Yet supply typically did not fall as much as demand, or it actually increased, giving post-communist Polish leisure consumers much more choice.

Another trend which Jung identifies is a large rise in Polish tourism. Over the same twenty-year period from 1980 to 1999 the number of people visiting Poland rose tenfold, while the number of Poles travelling out of the country rose by a factor of eight. Again, it was the fall of communism which stimulated these increases in travel.

> **Discussion question**
>
> Why do you think participation rates in snooker/pool/billiards fell in Britain in the 15 years to 2002?

A contrast to the British participation trends is provided by Poland (see Case Study 3.1) demonstrating that in a very different political context another more developed economy has had very different leisure trends.

3.2.2 Leisure spending

Table 3.3 identifies the scale of leisure spending in the UK, both at home and away from home. It is clear from this evidence that leisure away from home dominates leisure spending, being about three quarters of the total in 2008. These are the markets of most direct interest to sport and leisure service managers.

Table 3.3 Leisure spending in the UK, 2008

Consumer spending on leisure	Market value, £ billion, 2008
Reading	7.58
Home entertainment	22.06
House and garden	16.16
Hobbies and pastimes	9.72
Leisure in the home	*55.52*
Eating out	43.42
Alcoholic drink	43.26
Eating and drinking	*86.68*
Local entertainment	6.37
Gambling	9.94
Active sport	11.81
Neighbourhood leisure	*28.12*
Sightseeing	1.26
UK holiday accommodation	10.52
Holidays overseas	36.76
Holidays and tourism	*53.46*
Leisure away from home	*168.26*
TOTAL LEISURE	*223.78*

Source: Leisure Industries Research Centre (2009).

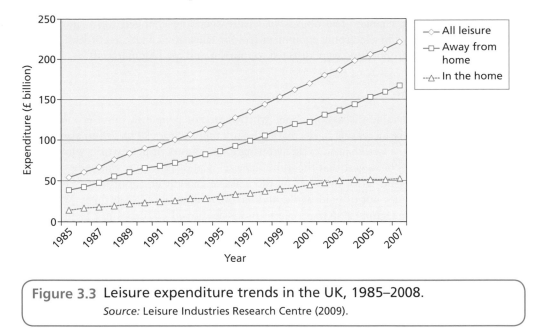

Figure 3.3 Leisure expenditure trends in the UK, 1985–2008.
Source: Leisure Industries Research Centre (2009).

Over the past two decades the spending on leisure goods and services in the UK has nearly quadrupled, as shown in Figure 3.3. This may be related to the increased availability of credit, which suffered an abrupt reverse in the current economic recession. It is leisure services which are the most dynamic element of leisure expenditure. In the last two decades average spending per household in the UK on leisure services just about doubled in real terms, i.e. after allowing for inflation (ONS, 2008c). *Leisure Forecasts* (Leisure Industries Research Centre, 2009) distinguishes four categories of consumer spending in terms of their trends over time: high growth services, which include leisure services; high growth goods, which include leisure goods; low growth sectors, such as non-alcoholic drinks; and declining sectors, such as alcoholic drinks. Leisure spending is typically around 27 per cent of total consumer spending in the UK. It reached a peak of 28 per cent in 1989 but has fallen slightly as a percentage of total consumer spending in recent years, probably because of large increases in housing costs.

Discussion questions

What are the main factors which determine how much you spend on leisure in a typical month? To what extent do you think the same factors are important in determining leisure spending at a national level?

A contrast to the UK trend in leisure spending is provided by Poland (Jung, 2005). Before the fall of communism in 1989, leisure spending in Poland was 10.5 per cent of total household expenditure. By 1993 it had fallen to about 5 per cent of household expenditure and it stayed at 5 or 6 per cent for the rest of the 1990s – the result of a greater concentration of expenditure on more basic goods and services at a time of national uncertainty and fundamental economic change. The objects of leisure spending changed too – in the late 1980s it was dominated by electronic equipment (colour televisions, video recorders), but by the late 1990s higher proportions were directed to tourism and reading materials.

3.2.3 Leisure time

There has been considerable discussion about whether or not people in more economically developed countries have increasing or decreasing leisure time. Schor (1992, 2006) argues that people are trapped into a work/spend cycle involving longer hours of paid work; whilst Robinson and Godbey (1999) suggest that the 'time squeeze' is perceptual, i.e. time pressures are created not by longer paid work time but by the massive growth in opportunities to spend time on different activities out of paid work, and having to choose between them. Whatever the facts, there is little argument that people in more developed countries are feeling more 'time pressured' over time, and this is a very important consideration in designing sport and leisure services – ideally they need to be time flexible.

Gratton and Taylor (2005) present UK evidence for the last 25 years of the twentieth century, from the New Earning Survey, which shows that since the early 1980s the actual working hours of manual and non-manual workers, male and female, have increased slightly over time. Gershuny (2000) suggests that people are working longer hours in order to afford the increasing opportunities for spending money on leisure. Time pressures will apply differently to people in different situations: Martin and Mason (1998) have characterised groups as time poor/money rich, time rich/money poor or possibly poor in both respects; and this will impact on their experience of leisure. Of course, many people are not in paid work, so time pressures can't be attributed just to working hours.

Gershuny (2000) presents some evidence that unpaid work time, i.e. mostly housework, increased in the period 1950–1970, just when domestic technology (e.g. the vacuum cleaner, the washing machine) was doing so much to increase the productivity of housework. The most likely explanation for this is that technology not only increased productivity but also increased the number and range of domestic tasks that people aspired to, e.g. changing clothes more often, cleaning more often. More recently the evidence suggests a fall in unpaid work time, although Gershuny (1997) presents evidence that time caring for children was twice as long in the 1990s as it was in the 1960s. Gershuny puts the rise in childcare time down to the increasing distance between families and services; to the collapse of children's 'license to roam'; and also to the greater commitment of many modern parents to 'quality time' with their children. Looking after children is not simply a chore but more probably a mix of unpaid work and leisure. And this characteristic is important for sport and leisure service managers, the implication being that family choices are often more important than individual choices.

What are the net effects on UK leisure time of leisure's increasing opportunities, and of changes in paid and unpaid work time? According to Gershuny and Fisher (1999) leisure time increased from an average of 285 minutes a day per person in 1961, to an average of 305 minutes a day in 1995. And according to Lader et al. (2006) leisure time reached an average of 326 minutes per person per day in 2005. This is a 14 per cent rise in 45 years – hardly a dawning of a 'leisure age', as was once predicted, but nevertheless a positive trend in leisure time. It should be noted, too, that this is caused not necessarily by people choosing more leisure time, but by other structural reasons, such as an ageing population. The increase in leisure time is an important relaxing of one of the major constraints to sport and leisure participation, although the perception of 'time pressures' remains.

Evidence for the USA (Aguiar and Hurst, 2007) shows that leisure time, defined as enjoyable activities, i.e. excluding housework and childcare, increased on average for non-retired adult men by 5.6 hours a week between 1965 and 2003, an 18 per cent increase which was largely the result of less time in paid work. For non-retired adult women in the USA, leisure time increased by 3.65 hours over the same period, a 12 per cent increase. For women the increase in leisure time was accompanied by an increase in their paid work, so it was household work which was reduced significantly to allow leisure time to expand.

By comparison, in Poland Jung (2005) suggests that leisure time has increased from an average of 246 minutes per person per day in 1976 to 292 minutes per day in 1996, which is less leisure time than in the UK and USA, but with a faster growth rate over a shorter period. Clearly, trends in leisure time availability will be conditioned heavily by demographic (especially age structure) and political and economic changes in a country.

Discussion question

If leisure time is increasing over time in many countries, why do people feel under such time pressures?

3.2.4 Attitudes to leisure

People's expectations of leisure are changing. Consumers are becoming more discerning and knowledgeable and want value for money. And what happens in commercial markets spills over to other sectors. In terms of community leisure, residents expect to be provided with good facilities and a quality of service that would be expected from the commercial sector. In the voluntary sector, members of clubs are less willing to give time to volunteering and more likely to view clubs as providers for their needs (see Chapter 6).

Leisure provision and choice of activity are increasingly affected by outside variables, e.g. health, food standards, fashion and concern about the environment. The catering industry, for example, is under greater scrutiny about not just the content of food provided, but also the methods by which it is produced. Some leisure activities have come under scrutiny simply for environmental reasons, e.g. overseas tourism (especially by air transport) and motor sports. Developers applying for planning permission, particularly in protected areas, will continue to face strong objections from local pressure groups and a less favourable attitude from local authorities. Leisure planners and managers will have to ensure that provision of facilities and services fits in with changing individual, community and political expectations.

Discussion question

Do you think that social attitudes to leisure have changed in the last twenty years? Think of specific examples such as (1) going out for a drink in a pub/bar, (2) going out to see an opera, (3) going to a fitness club and (4) going on a weekend trip to another country.

3.3 Leisure at home

Although leisure at home appears out of reach of leisure managers, in fact it is heavily conditioned by leisure industries, which provide the choices for leisure at home, and by governments, which regulate many of the at-home activities. Furthermore, at-home leisure provides some important leads for away from home leisure managers – particularly in the use of technology and innovation to feed market growth. Leisure at home is a major competitor for leisure away from home, in the use of leisure time and in leisure expenditure, so it is important for managers of leisure services away from home to take note of the strategies and decisions of industries servicing leisure at home.

As Table 3.3 shows, leisure in the home can be divided into four main sectors: home entertainment, house and garden, reading, and hobbies and pastimes. The first two are the largest at-home leisure sectors in the UK (Leisure Industries Research Centre, 2009). Home entertainment attracted 39 per cent of leisure spending at home by consumers (nearly one-tenth of total leisure spending) in 2008. House and garden is also a large sector, with 29 per cent of at-home leisure spending in 2008. Reading is 14 per cent, and hobbies and pastimes (which includes toys, games and pets) 18 per cent, of at-home leisure spending.

In this section we review some of the main trends in leisure at home. It is investigated in more detail in Chapter 12. In Figure 3.4 we identify the trends in leisure spending at home in the UK over more than two decades. It shows strong growth in the value of spending in the 1990s but a faltering of this growth from about 2004.

Figure 3.1 shows just how embedded certain leisure habits are in a more developed economy such as the UK. This is especially so of watching television, which not only is an activity which 99 per cent of the population does, but also takes up a major slice of people's leisure time – according to Lader *et al.* (2006), 48 per cent of the average person's leisure time is spent watching television in the UK – that's 157 minutes per person per day. This is one long-term trend that is unlikely to change. The latest technological developments are

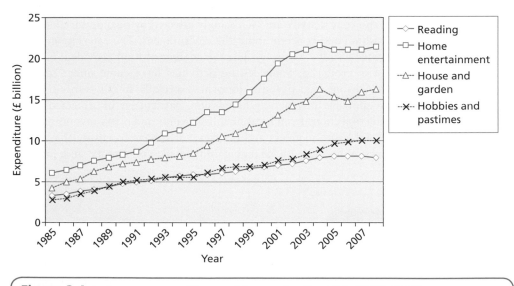

Figure 3.4 Leisure expenditure at home in the UK, 1985–2008.
Source: Leisure Industries Research Centre (2009).

'on-demand' services, whereby viewers can watch 'catch-up' or classic programmes at times of their choosing. This is a good example of producing a time-flexible product to fit a time-pressured market. Initial evidence suggests that the BBC's successful iPlayer service has expanded viewing hours, rather than substituting for the viewing of 'live' shows.

Technology is a key driver of trends in leisure at home. Audio-visual technology demonstrates this, with continued growth of expenditure on equipment stimulated by new developments, e.g. from DVDs to Blu-ray; from analogue to digital; from flat screen to HD television. And the take-up of new technology by households is increasingly rapid. Whereas video recorders took seven years to reach three million sales in the UK, DVD players took three years to reach similar sales. It is now estimated by the Leisure Industries Research Centre (2008) that 95 per cent of households in the UK have a video or DVD player. Such market penetration is achieved not only by technological advances but also the falling prices of new technology. Prices of video/DVD equipment, for example, fell 18 per cent between 2002 and 2007.

Other leisure at home markets are similarly affected by technology, including photography, which has seen substantial growth in recent years caused by the switch from traditional to digital cameras. Arguably the most significant growth trend has been in the purchase of home computers and use of the internet. Home computer ownership has increased in Great Britain from 13 per cent of households in 1985 to 71 per cent of households in 2007 (ONS, 2009a). It is not coincidental that prices of computing hardware fell over 20 per cent in the period 2002–7. The implications for leisure managers are clear – a combination of technological innovation and affordability is a powerful attraction to leisure consumers.

Playing music on home music systems is another popular activity influenced by technology changes – from records to cassettes, to compact discs, to DVDs which can play music, videos and games. However, technology changed again and now the biggest growth is in downloading music and films from the internet. Furthermore, traditional home music systems are being replaced by more mobile platforms such as MP3 players and mobile telephones. Mobile telephones not only now facilitate the ever proliferating calls and texts, but also have integrated music systems, photographic and video recording capabilities, satellite navigation systems and access to the internet.

According to the Office of National Statistics (2009b) 65 per cent of people in Britain utilised the internet in 2008, at home or work, compared with 45 per cent in 2002. Furthermore, 56 per cent of all households had broadband connections. This is more evidence of the strong take-up of new technology, possibly driven by cash-rich, time-poor consumers. The internet is increasingly being used as a source of information about, and direct booking for, leisure opportunities. The power of the internet is illustrated by top class sport and sports teams with websites carrying advertisements for online gambling, ticket sales, sponsorship and merchandising. In 2002, £100 million worth of bets were placed on the Grand National; 10 per cent of these were online betting. At the 2003 Wimbledon tennis championships, over four million 'unique users' logged on to the Wimbledon website, visiting the site over 27 million times, and staying for an average of over two hours.

Discussion question

What are the advantages and disadvantages of technological change for the leisure consumer?

Reading is an important part of many people's daily routine – over half of adults in Britain read books and magazines and 60 per cent read newspapers. Over half the population are members of their local library and in Great Britain over 400 million books are borrowed from public libraries each year. Many libraries have collections of CDs, records, audio and video-cassettes, and DVDs for loan to the public. The library sector is included in Chapter 9.

The books industry in Britain expanded sales by 26 per cent in real terms (i.e. after allowing for inflation) over the period 1998–2003 but traditional retailers have been squeezed by the expansion of the internet and by promotions in supermarkets. In recent years the economic cycle in book sales peaked with the publication of the Harry Potter books (see Case Study 12.1), so it will be interesting to see how the post-Potter period unfolds. Table 3.1 shows that trends in reading books and magazines differ by country, e.g. falling over time in Finland and Israel, rising over time in France.

Magazines, books and newspaper sales all declined in real terms in 2007 and forecasts suggest that the industry as a whole is in decline, with one of the principal reasons being the increased use of the internet – consumers in Britain doubled their average time online in the two years from 2005 to 2007, from two to four hours per week. Another threat to the traditional sector is the growth of free newspapers and magazines, although their future is uncertain as advertising revenues fall in the recession at the time of writing. The main exception to the downward trend in the commercial reading business is likely to be reading using electronic formats – online, e-books and electronic readers.

House and garden leisure consists principally of do-it-yourself (DIY) and gardening. Both sectors flourish in a buoyant housing market, because moving house stimulates house and garden improvement. DIY achieved strong growth in UK consumer spending in the early 2000s – increasing by 14 per cent in real terms in the period 1999–2004. Growth in expenditure on gardening is also stimulated by a trend for 'easier gardening', with ready-made plants and plug plants appealing to cash-rich, time-poor consumers. However, increasing personal debt and the competing attraction of expenditure on new technology in televisions and home computing are said to have contributed to a decline in DIY spending from 2005 and gardening from 2004 (see Figure 3.4). This is likely to be have been exacerbated by the slump in the housing market in 2008–9, and in the case of gardening other negative factors are the rapid growth of flats in city centres and the increasing use of land for parking in urban areas, particularly front gardens.

Another important at-home leisure sector is toys and games, which demonstrated consistent growth in UK consumer spending (in value and in real terms) throughout the 1990s and early 2000s. In the case of toys, this growth is despite falling numbers of children aged 0–4 throughout most of the 1990s and consequently falling numbers of children aged 5–9 and 10–14 in the early 2000s. This means that expenditure per child is rising faster than the fall in numbers of children. An important trend in toys is that the toy industry has become very dependent on Chinese production – 80 per cent of the world's toys are manufactured in China. This gives the advantage of cheaper toys for consumers – in the period 2002–7, the toys market grew in value by 16 per cent, whilst at the same time prices fell by 15 per cent. However, 2007 demonstrated one of the risks of such high dependency on imports when millions of toys were recalled because of safety concerns. This, however, was a temporary 'shock' to the longer term trend of importing cheap toys, which is likely to continue.

Electronic games has also achieved substantial growth in UK expenditure during the early 2000s. This sector is not so dependent on the numbers of young people, since many adults participate in such games. The market growth is again helped by falling prices, mainly driven by the intense competition between Nintendo (DS and Wii), Sony (Play-Station) and Microsoft (Xbox).

Expenditure on pets also shows consistent increases in real terms in the long term. Over half of UK households own pets, the most common choice being cats. It is no longer just young families with children that keep pets. As people have children later in life, pets are often seen as 'surrogates'. With more fragmented families (see p. 75), higher divorce rates and more single adult households, pets can fulfil an important need for company.

A significant trend in spending on pets is that a greater proportion of spending is being spent on non-food items, and a falling proportion on pet food – in 2006 for the first time the former overtook the latter to become the largest share of the pet market. This echoes household expenditure generally, where over time, as incomes grow, lower proportions of expenditure are spent on food and higher proportions on non-food items such as household assets, holidays, etc. In the case of pets, non-food expenditure includes insurance, health care and general pet pampering – increasing amounts are being spent on pet fashions and accessories. A clear implication for leisure managers in the commercial sector is to increase market spend by evolving and augmenting the product with additional features (see Section 15.7.1).

3.4 Leisure away from home

Table 3.1 shows a variety of trends for leisure activities away from home in different countries. There was growth in participation rates for art galleries, for example, in Australia, Finland and Japan, but decline in Canada. There has been decline in participation rates for cinema in Canada, Finland, France and Israel, but growth in Australia, Japan and the Netherlands. And some sports' participation rates have grown in the Netherlands and USA, but others have declined in Japan and Canada. The variations in trends by countries demonstrates that it is not just global trends that matter to sport and leisure managers, but also national trends. Furthermore, a manager in a specific sport or leisure service needs to gather intelligence on local trends too, since these can vary significantly in comparison with national trends.

It is not cultural and sporting activities which dominate leisure spending away from home, but more typically eating and drinking out and overseas holidays. The Leisure Industries Research Centre divides leisure away from home into three main sectors: eating and drinking; neighbourhood leisure (the entertainment element of which includes cinema, live arts and other entertainments); and holidays and tourism. Table 3.3 shows leisure away from home to be about three-quarters of total leisure spending in the UK (Leisure Industries Research Centre, 2009). Figure 3.5 shows the trends in expenditure on the main components of away from home leisure in the UK, over the last two decades and more. Holidays overseas has seen the most rapid growth in expenditure – six times larger in 2007 than 1985. The slowest growth has been in alcoholic drink, which has grown just threefold in the same period.

The most common leisure activity outside the home among adults in Great Britain is eating out, with 95 per cent of adults eating out in their free time. Over the five years 2002–7, the eating out market grew by 16 per cent in real terms (after allowing for inflation) and by 34 per cent in value. Figure 3.5 shows that, for the first time, in 2008 eating out overtook alcohol consumption as the largest away from home market, in expenditure terms. The frequency of eating out increased as a direct result of the ban on smoking in indoor public places in 2007. The restaurant sector is a very fragmented market and is therefore highly competitive. Coffee shops, by comparison, are dominated by three major chains, but there is still intense competition between them.

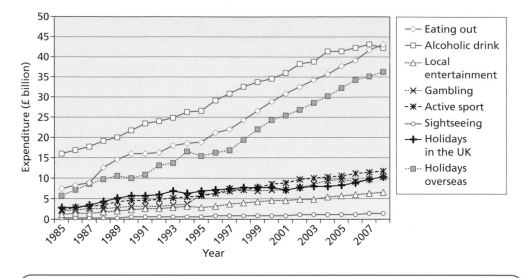

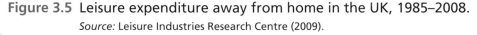

Figure 3.5 Leisure expenditure away from home in the UK, 1985–2008.
Source: Leisure Industries Research Centre (2009).

Unlike eating out, consumption of alcohol away from home shows a flat or declining trend over time in the UK. Sales of wines and spirits saw modest growth in the early 2000s but beer sales have been negatively affected by the ban on smoking in public houses and also by social concerns over binge drinking and tougher anti-drink-driving legislation. Pub closures were reported to be running at 27 a week in mid-2008 (British Beer and Pub Association, 2008), a closure rate which is 14 times faster than in 2005. There is a high business failure rate for the hospitality sector generally – three times more likely to fail than other businesses in the UK (UHY Hacker Young, 2007). Nevertheless the closure rate for pubs is particularly high and it is clearly a long-term trend that has not been reversed by the diversification of pubs into food, by the extension of opening hours or by a trend towards the production and sale of more real ales. Whilst the decline of the pub is bad for the industry, an interesting social concern is also being expressed – that it threatens an important hub of the UK's social fabric and community history.

Discussion questions

Is the decline of the British pub inevitable? Should politicians be concerned because of the significance of pubs to local communities?

Holidays are a major form of leisure spending in more developed countries. In Germany they comprised over one-quarter of the average household leisure budget in 1997 (Tokarski and Michels, 2005). Table 3.3 shows that in the UK holidays and tourism accounted for 24 per cent of total leisure spending in 2008. Over two-thirds of this expenditure is on foreign holidays. Tourism is rising steadily worldwide, as demonstrated in Chapter 7. In the Netherlands, for example, the total number of holiday trips rose by 20 per cent in the 1990s (Knulst and van der Poel, 2005). In the UK the total number of visits abroad for holidays and visiting friends and relatives rose from just over 25 million in 1990 to over 57 million in 2008, with consumer spending on holidays rising fourfold in the same period (Leisure Industries Research Centre, 2009). Such growth has been fed by rising disposable incomes, the emergence and growth of budget airlines, and a continuing demand for overseas holiday sunshine and experiences. The recent recession has seen a reversal of this growth and a surge in demand for holidays at home – so-called 'staycations'.

Compared with the largest away from home leisure sectors in the UK, gambling is relatively small. However, it has seen considerable changes over the last two decades because it is a part of the leisure sector which is arguably most affected by changes in government regulation. The biggest change came with the National Lottery, which started in 1995. Before the National Lottery, lotteries comprised about 1 per cent of the gambling market. In 1995 the National Lottery caused the UK gambling market to grow by 54 per cent and took a 41 per cent share of this market. By 2000 the National Lottery had a 47 per cent share of the UK gambling market, but since then its popularity has waned and in 2007 it was estimated to have a 25 per cent share (Leisure Industries Research Centre, 2008).

Betting, by comparison, has had relatively stable growth through the last twenty years and is now back to having the largest market share in gambling, at about 31 per cent. It will almost certainly continue to grow, but it is also changing in character – from being away from home leisure to being at-home leisure. This is because the fastest growing gambling activity in recent years is online – it grew over sixfold in the period 2002–7. Another activity with significant growth is gaming machines, which in 2007 were estimated to be 25 per cent of the UK gambling market. This growth was stimulated in part by relaxation of the government's regulation of gaming machines.

Local entertainment is in a relatively steady state in the UK, with modest growth in visits to the cinema, live arts, spectator sports and dances/clubs throughout the 1990s, but a slight decline, of 7.5 per cent, in these combined visits from 2002 to 2007 (Leisure Industries Research Centre, 2008). Nevertheless, because prices rose by 22 per cent in this period, the total expenditure on local entertainment increased in real terms. Live arts are the largest sub-sector in terms of consumer spending – taking 41 per cent of total sales in local entertainment in 2007. This is not because of more visits than other sub-sectors, though; it is because of the higher prices paid for live arts. Festivals are an increasingly important feature of local entertainment – there were over 400 registered in 2007. There will be important boosts to this market from time to time, e.g. in 2008 for Liverpool, European Capital of Culture, and, of course, in 2012 with the London Olympics.

In 2007 about 17 million adults in Great Britain participated in indoor sports and physical activities, and over 25 million participated in outdoor sports and physical activities (including walking). This generated expenditure of different types, of which spending on sports clothing and footwear takes the largest share (37 per cent throughout the early 2000s). Other major elements of active sports spending include fitness club memberships, sports equipment (especially boating), paying for public facilities and voluntary club memberships. Interestingly, the increases in consumer spending on sports equipment, clothing and footwear are not matched by increases in sports and physical activities participation, which have only grown a little in the last twenty years. In the case of sports clothing and footwear it may simply be the increase in purchases for fashion rather than sport. In the case of sports equipment, it seems that consumers are happy to spend money on sports hardware but less happy to use it on a regular basis.

Sport and leisure managers need to forecast future trends to plan their services appropriately. Case Study 3.2 examines a contemporary question for which analysis relies on past

CASE STUDY 3.2

The effects of recession on sport

The Sport Industry Research Centre at Sheffield Hallam University has analysed past trends in participation and spending to identify the likely effects of the 2008–9+ recession on sport in the UK. Past recessions, in 1980–1 and 1990–1, provide evidence of the effects of a national downturn on the sports market. These recessions both caused falls in national gross domestic product (GDP) and national consumer spending. The 1980–1 recession was characterised by very high energy prices at the beginning of the recession. The 1990–1 recession occurred alongside a crash in the housing market. What makes the 2008–9+ recession different and probably worse is that it started not only with these two adverse conditions – high energy prices and a housing market crash – but also a credit crunch and financial crisis caused by excessive high risk lending by financial institutions.

Data suggest that the recessions in 1980–1 and 1990–1 had little if any negative impact on sports participation as a whole. Although the sports participation data available is periodic rather than annual, it does show a steady increase from 1977 to 1980 and then to 1983; and then an increase from 1987 to 1990, followed by stable participation rates up to 1993 and 1996. Therefore, given this previous evidence, there is no reason to believe that a recession will cause sports participation to fall.

Spending on sport, however, does fall simultaneously with falling consumer spending in a recession, according to the UK evidence. In 1990–1, for example, total consumer spending grew in real terms by just 0.78 per cent in 1990 and then fell by 1.61 per cent in 1991. In the same two years spending on sport in real terms fell by 0.85 per cent, in 1990, and then again by 2.1 per cent, in 1991. However, when the economy began to recover, in 1992, spending on sport grew rapidly, by 4.13 per cent, compared with a modest recovery of 0.46 per cent in total consumer spending.

The 1990–1 recession provides evidence of differences in the impact of the recession within the sports sector which reconcile an apparent contradiction between stable or rising participation and falling expenditure. In 1990–1 relatively large falls in spending occurred for sports equipment, skiing goods and skiing holidays – relatively expensive and infrequent items. On the other hand, spending on sports admissions (subscriptions and fees) actually grew by 0.5 per cent in 1990 and 6.5 per cent in 1991. Such spending is on relatively continuous and cheaper items. It appears, therefore, that people under deteriorating economic circumstances changed their spending habits to defend their sports participation.

The remaining uncertainties about the 2008–9+ recession are how long and how deep it will be. Much more complex and severe circumstances have triggered this recession and it remains to be seen whether or not sports participation and spending will resist the recession in the way they did before. However, there are some promising early signs:

- In a survey of sports clubs, CCPR (2009) report that the average numbers of members and volunteers increased slightly at the time the UK was entering the recession in 2008; and the proportions of clubs making surpluses and losses remained fairly stable in this period.
- The Fitness Industry Association (2009) report that membership of health and fitness clubs in the UK grew slightly in the year ending 31 March 2009, and the market value of the sector (total number of members multiplied by the average membership fee) grew by 3 per cent.

trends – what effect will the recession in 2008–9 have on sport? It relies primarily on comparisons with past periods of recession, although there are already promising signs of sport's resilience to the effects of recession.

> ## Discussion question
>
> Why, when leisure time and incomes have been increasing over time, has sports participation grown so slowly or not at all in the UK?

Active sport is another leisure sector which the government would like to influence, although in this case its influence is through facilitation rather than regulation. Various government initiatives have been a regular feature of the sports market, attempting to increase participation. Chapter 5 reviews the reasons for such initiatives, the most important of which is improving health. At the time of writing, the UK government's objective is to increase active sports participation by an additional one million people participating by 2012–13, which is an ambitious target given that participation rates in overall active sport have been fairly static for the last two decades. The government intention is an important signal to sports managers, who have the opportunity not only to share the ambition for growth in their markets, but also possibly to benefit from some of the associated government spending. Ironically, the fastest growth in sport and physical activity in recent years has been in the commercial sector, at health and fitness clubs.

Holiday-taking in more developed economies typically demonstrates an upward trend, as shown in Figure 3.5 for the UK. For the UK, Table 3.2 and Figure 3.5 demonstrate that spending on sightseeing and UK holiday accommodation is exceeded by expenditure on overseas holidays – the latter being more than twice the size of the former. This has been a structural feature of the tourism market for more than three decades. Overseas holidays also exhibit the strongest growth over time – particularly recently, with the advent of budget airlines and the increased competition they have imposed on the travel industry. Chapter 7 examines the tourism industry in detail.

The market for trips to the UK by overseas tourists tends to be more volatile than that for holiday trips at home and abroad by British residents. The market expenditure in real terms by overseas tourists in the UK achieved double digit annual growth rates in 1995 and 2004. On the other hand this expenditure fell in real terms in 1997–9, 2001, 2003 and again in 2008. This volatility is caused by a number of factors, including fluctuations in exchange rates, which happen regularly, wars (e.g. Iraq) and the one-off (hopefully) negative effects of such events as the 9/11 terrorist attacks in New York in 2001, foot and mouth disease in Britain in 2001, the SARS virus outbreak in 2003 and the 7/7 terrorist attacks in London in 2005.

3.5 General demographic and socio-economic trends

Many general demographic, social and economic trends impact on leisure markets, as has already been noted in relation to specific leisure trends. In this section we review some of the more important general trends from a leisure perspective.

3.5.1 Population growth

The population in the UK has grown steadily over recent decades and in 2007 stood at 61 million. It is forecasted to rise to 63.2 million by 2012. Such growth is important for leisure because it feeds growth in many leisure markets. Population worldwide is expected to grow for the next fifty years and more (United Nations, 2004), but growth rates across the world are forecasted to decline. Population growth is expected to be fastest in Africa and slowest in Europe, with the Americas and Asia in between. If the participation rate for an activity – the percentage of the population who participate in it – stays constant but population size increases, so the market expands. If both the population and participation rates in sport and leisure increase, then the growth in sport and leisure markets will be that much greater. Alternatively, if participation rates fall, as they have in active sport in England recently, this may be 'compensated' by population increases such that the market for sport stays the same size, or even increases. It is important for a leisure manager to anticipate such considerations, alongside demographic changes such as those reviewed below, in order to forecast their future market size and plan provision accordingly.

3.5.2 Ageing population

In 2007, for the first time in the UK the number of people of pensionable age exceeded the number aged under 16 (Dunnell, 2008). Factors leading to an ageing population include the post-Second World War 'baby boomer' generation reaching retirement age and the fact that older people are living longer – the fastest growing age group in 2007 was 80+ years. Another factor over recent decades is the general tendency for women to delay having children. This tendency is linked to participation both in higher education and in the labour force. In addition, many women start a second family following the breakdown of a former marriage or partnership.

It is forecasted that the number of people of 'young pension' age (aged 60–74) will rise from 13.2 per cent of the population in 2002 to 14.8 per cent of the population by 2012 – this would be an increase of over 1.5 million people of this age, taking into account both the increased percentage and the forecasted increase in population size. Similarly the number of 'old pension' people (aged 75+) is forecasted to rise by over 600,000 in the same ten-year period.

An ageing population changes the nature of demand because different ages have different demands and these demands change over time. Many leisure market analysts have warned the industry to be aware of, and prepare for, the increasing power of the 'grey pound'. An example in sport is that many public facilities have devised programmes, prices and promotion to attract older customers and succeeded in not only attracting such customers but doing so in off-peak periods, e.g. weekday mornings and afternoons. By such means, initiatives to attract older customers need not substitute in a significant way for the traditional younger customers, who attend more in peak periods.

> ### Discussion question
>
> Is an ageing population a threat or an opportunity for leisure providers?

3.5.3 Fragmented population

Another striking change in social structure in the UK is the increase in one-person households. In 1971 they represented 17 per cent of households; by 2007 they were 31 per cent of households (ONS, 2009a). There are a number of reasons for this. First, there is a growing number of 'never married' men and, to a lesser extent, 'never married' women. Second, the number of separations and divorces has risen in the long term. In 2007 there was a 45 per cent chance of a marriage ending in divorce in the UK (Wilson and Smallwood, 2008), although the divorce rate had fallen in 2004–7 to its lowest level since 1981. Third, there is an increasing number of elderly widowed women. In 2007, over half of people aged 75+ lived by themselves. Another contributory factor is that the UK has the highest rate of births to teenage girls in the European Union. One-fifth of dependent children lived in lone parent families in 2003, almost twice the proportion in 1981.

> **Discussion question**
>
> **Which leisure activities will benefit from (1) an ageing population and (2) a more fragmented population?**

3.5.4 Growth of ethnic minority groups

Sport and leisure managers need to be aware of the shifts in the ethnic make-up of their markets, because different ethnic groups have different sport and leisure needs and demands. Many of the more developed countries are becoming more multi-racial. For example, a major trend in Europe since 2004 is immigration from the eight former Eastern Bloc countries which joined the European Union, facilitated by regulations on the freedom of movement of labour within the EU. Out of 1.42 million immigrants who arrived in the UK from May 2004 to November 2006, for example, 427,000 were people registering to work from these countries, with the vast majority coming from Poland. However, these are legal economic migrants, not all of whom will stay. Evidence in early 2009 suggested that, with the economic downturn in the UK, the number of immigrants from Eastern Europe fell by 40 per cent. In the UK immigration has exceeded emigration since 1993, with an annual net inflow of between 100,000 and 200,000. However, the percentage of the British population which is of 'white' ethnic origin is falling only slowly over time – it was 90 per cent in 2007 (ONS, 2009a).

3.5.5 Income and inequality

The leisure industry is a growth industry, employing around 2.5 million people. Income is an important measure of the standard of living of individuals and the country as a whole. It directly influences leisure behaviour. One of the most commonly used measures of living standards is disposable income, defined as the amount of money people have available to spend as they wish, after tax has been deducted and benefits added. Household disposable income in the UK more than doubled in real terms (after allowing for inflation) between 1987 and 2006 (ONS, 2008a), which was good news for spending on leisure – it rose consistently in the same period. However, now that a recession has started in 2008, the prospects are for a reversal in both income and leisure spending.

Income inequality also has an impact on leisure spending, with those on low incomes having little room for leisure spending once essentials have been bought, whilst those on high incomes having much more scope for leisure spending. Sport and leisure managers may not be able to do anything about inequalities in income but they can make decisions, particularly about the prices of their services, which respond to such inequalities. In the UK public sector, for example, price discounts are available in a wide number of local authorities for disadvantaged groups, including those on low incomes – typically through leisure card schemes. Even commercial sector companies are increasingly recognising that discounts at particular times for low income groups in the community, such as students, old people or the unemployed, might actually be good for business at off-peak times.

Statistics for the UK show a widening of the inequality between the top and bottom fifths of the population, particularly in the 1980s (ONS, 2008b). Since then the top 20 per cent have earned over 40 per cent of total income, whilst the bottom 20 per cent have earned about 7 per cent of total income. The impact of income inequality on leisure spending in the UK is clear from Family Expenditure Survey evidence (ONS, 2008c). This shows that in 2007 those in the bottom 10 per cent of incomes spent on average £28.10 per week on recreation, culture, restaurants and hotels, which was 16.3 per cent of their average total spending per week. By comparison, those in the top 10 per cent of incomes spent £210.20 per week on the same items, or 21.3 per cent of their average total weekly spending.

One of the most significant changes in income distribution in the UK over the last thirty years has been for retired households. In 1977, over half of retired households were in the bottom 20 per cent of incomes. By 1996–7, however, this proportion had fallen to 29 per cent, and it stayed at this percentage through to 2006–7. This is because a greater proportion of retired people had occupational pensions – it is those on just state pensions that are poor.

Couples with non-dependent children have the highest gross household income in the UK. Lone parents with dependent children receive nearly half their income in the form of non-contributory state benefits and they are among the poorest households. An increase in the number of one parent households has led to the proportion of children living in households in the bottom 20 per cent of incomes increasing from 19 to 29 per cent between 1977 and 1997. By 2007 the proportion of children living in households in the bottom 20 per cent of incomes had fallen slightly, to 25 per cent (ONS, 2008a).

3.5.6 Personal debt

A recent trend in the UK which has been causing concern is rising levels of personal debt. Between 1993 and 2005 total lending to individuals in the UK more than doubled in real terms, to a total of over £1 trillion (i.e. £1,000 billion). There is an important debate about whether or not debt is a bad thing – on the one hand debts have to be paid back, but on the other hand they are an important means of preserving and expanding expenditure for individuals, companies and governments alike. In the recent financial 'credit crunch' at the time of writing, most of the concern is ironically that lending has suddenly shrunk to too low levels and this is economically damaging.

> ### Discussion question
>
> Is increasing personal debt good or bad for the leisure industry?

3.5.7 Health

Despite progressive improvements in the health of the nation and advances in medicine, there remain significant health concerns and health inequalities in more developed countries. Obesity is increasingly a cause of concern in the USA, UK, Canada and other countries. In a Health Survey for England (NHS Information Centre, 2006), it was reported that 65 per cent of men were overweight or obese, with 22 per cent being obese. For women, over 55 per cent were overweight or obese, with 23 per cent being obese. The survey found that nearly 17 per cent of children aged 2–10 years were obese; and over 20 per cent of those aged 11–15 years were obese.

Overweight and obesity lead to a variety of serious health problems and this issue has been described as an 'epidemic'. Various government policies have been enacted to try to deal with the problem, including a number of initiatives to increase physical activity which are of direct relevance to sports managers. The health survey disclosed a strong and consistent inverse correlation between physical activity and overweight/obesity problems. This is probably reflective of a two-way relationship – increasing physical activity undoubtedly contributes to losing weight, but being overweight is likely to cause less physical activity. Whichever is true, sports managers have a potentially major role in helping to reduce levels of overweight and obesity. This opportunity represents an important and growing market segment, a potentially important source of funding from government (i.e. to set up or support targeted programmes for the overweight) and a potentially major contribution to one of the most important social objectives of the day.

Discussion questions

What is likely to be the strongest causal effect: physical activity producing weight loss or overweight causing less physical activity? How might a sports manager encourage more of the former?

3.6 Conclusions

Sport and leisure managers need to investigate both leisure and general trends carefully in order to plan for changes in their future products and services. Changes in sport and leisure participation and spending are conditioned by society-wide changes, e.g. in time use, in population, in income and in health. Knowledge of major, relevant, changing circumstances can provide positive leads for product and market development. An example is the ageing population, which provides considerable opportunities not only for developing sport and leisure markets with specific initiatives to attract older people, but also for developing products so that they are more enjoyable for older people.

The simplest forecasting assumption one can make is to assume that what has happened in the past will continue to happen in the future. However, whilst this may be reasonable for some general trends, such as an ageing population, it is not necessarily reasonable for more specific trends, such as leisure participation and spending. At the time of writing, a large uncertainty hangs over the continuation of fairly well-established trends, particularly in spending, because of economic recession. It is a reminder that, even with knowledge of how things have changed in the past, the future can still be uncertain.

> **Practical tasks**
>
> 1 For a particular country, use the internet or other appropriate sources to find the changes over the last twenty years in participation rates for two sport or leisure activities of your choice; and changes in population over the same period. Calculate for these two activities what has happened to the number of people participating, i.e. to the size of the market. What are the implications of your results for planning the two sport or leisure activities?
>
> 2 From a reliable source of data, such as your local authority, identify the extent to which the local population structure has got older or younger in the last twenty years. Select an appropriate sport or leisure provider in the area and investigate to what extent have they accommodated the change in the local population's age structure? Consider what likely changes will occur in the local population's age structure in the next twenty years and what measures local providers of sport and leisure might take in anticipation of such changes.

Structured guide to further reading

For a detailed trend analysis and forecasts of all at-home and away from home leisure sectors, and a commentary on the current situation in each sector:
Leisure Forecasts (annual from the Leisure Industries Research Centre).

For trends in participation and time use in a number of different countries:
Cushman, G., Veal, A.J. and Zuzanek, J. (eds) (2005) *Free Time and Leisure Participation: international perspectives*, CABI Publishing, Wallingford.

For trends in Great Britain for participation in a range of sport and leisure activities:
General Household Survey (1973, 1977, 1980, 1983, 1986, 1987, 1990, 1993, 1996, 2002).

For a compendium of national trends drawn from a range of sources; covering population, households and families, education and training, the labour market, income and wealth, expenditure, health, social protection, crime and justice, housing, environment, transport and lifestyles:
Social Trends (annual from Office for National Statistics).

For results for Great Britain since 1971 on such topics as households and families, smoking and drinking, consumer durables, marriage, pensions and health:
General Household Survey (annual from Office for National Statistics).

For detailed information on people's spending patterns and trends:
Family Spending (annual from Office for National Statistics).

Useful websites

For time-use evidence in the UK for 2000:
www.statistics.gov.uk/TimeUse/default.asp

For time-use evidence in the UK for 2005:
www.statistics.gov.uk/cci/article.asp?ID=1600

For the Office for National Statistics (ONS):
www.statistics.gov.uk/

For the *General Household Survey*:
www.statistics.gov.uk/ssd/surveys/general_household_survey.asp

For the Leisure Industries Research Centre:
www.shu.ac.uk/research/sirc/

Part 2

Sport and leisure providers

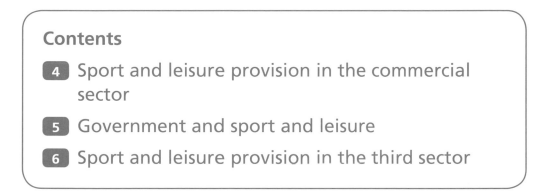

Contents

People's sport and leisure is made possible through a wide range of providers, including central government agencies; local authorities; schools, colleges and universities; commercial companies; not-for-profit companies; charitable trusts; and voluntary organisations. These are described and analysed in this part of the book under three major sector headings: commercial sector, public sector and third sector.

In the past, there was a clear distinction between what was provided by these three sectors, but today there are overlaps, with some of the same sorts of services, facilities and programmes provided from more than one sector. Furthermore, funding of a service can often involve a mix of the three sectors, and they often act in partnership in delivery of sport and leisure services. There are still distinct differences between different types of provider in philosophy and approach, though even these are gradually becoming blurred. There are sometimes signs of convergence of objectives: examples include when a commercial organisation has clear social objectives or runs a public service under contract; when a charitable trust finds it difficult to break even and acts in a very similar manner to commercial management; and when a public sector organisation is oriented towards efficiency gains and reducing subsidies.

Management issues can be different in each sector – for example managing full-time paid staff effectively can be different in the commercial and public sectors because the first is driven by efficiency and profit considerations whilst the second is arguably more driven by public service motives. Managing volunteers is very different again, simply because volunteers do not receive any monetary reward. But some aspects of management across the three sectors can also be very similar, e.g. seeking to satisfy customers, and achieving cost savings and best value for money in operations should be common goals.

Chapter 4

Sport and leisure provision in the commercial sector

In this chapter

- What does commercial sport and leisure consist of?
- What are the objectives of commercial sport and leisure providers?
- What is the typical structure of commercial sport and leisure industries?
- How does globalisation affect commercial leisure?
- What are the key drivers of commercial leisure?
- What are the major commercial leisure industries and how have they evolved?

Christie Goodwin/Getty Images

Summary

The commercial leisure sector is typically the largest, at least in terms of monetary dimensions. It involves more expenditure than either the public or the voluntary sector.

The structure of the commercial leisure sector can be identified in two main ways: first, by the activities supplied; and, second, by the size structure of companies in each industry, i.e. the proportion of market sales from the largest firms. The major commercial leisure industries by financial size typically include alcohol production and distribution, eating out, home entertainment (TV, games, music, etc.) and holidays. A typical size structure of commercial leisure in more developed countries is oligopoly, with a few firms dominating market supply.

Commercial leisure firms, like commercial firms generally, are motivated by profit. It is profit that enables them to satisfy shareholders, increase their value on stock markets, reinvest, grow, diversify and merge with or take over other firms – so profits are linked to many other objectives.

Key drivers for commercial leisure companies have historically included society-wide factors which influence all sectors, such as the amount of leisure time available, and to whom it is available; the income people have to spend; laws laid down by government; and technological changes.

A number of important commercial leisure industries are reviewed, i.e. eating and drinking out, betting and gambling, commercial sport, cinemas, leisure parks, theatres, nightclubs and theme parks.

4.1 Introduction

The leisure market in the UK was worth just under £224 billion in 2008 according to the Leisure Industries Research Centre (2009), accounting for one-quarter of total consumer spending. A large proportion of this spending is in the commercial sector, as is the case in other developed economies. Millions of people buy domestic and overseas leisure tourist trips, sports equipment and cinema tickets, eat out socially, drink alcohol, gamble, watch television and are entertained in their leisure time through services and products provided commercially.

Commercial leisure providers are often defined as those which make profit, but that simplification ignores some important complications. Many other types of provider often use 'commercial practices' to achieve their objectives, such as efficiency savings (i.e. cost cutting, for example in the public sector), target marketing (all sectors) and quality management (important in the public as well as the commercial sector). Furthermore, commercial providers have many more objectives than profits, as is discussed on pp. 86–7.

Entrepreneurial and risk-taking qualities are often the hallmarks of commercial sector leaders, such as Ryanair's Michael O'Leary and Virgin's Richard Branson. Chapter 21 looks in more detail at enterprise and leisure.

4.2 The commercial leisure sector: an overview

There are two main kinds of commercial leisure business:

1 commercial operators managing commercial activities for profit, e.g. public houses, ski holiday companies;
2 commercial operators managing not-for-profit or public sector facilities/activities, such as UK contract companies Leisure Connection, DC Leisure and Parkwood.

In addition, there are two other forms of business that have commercial characteristics:

1 not-for-profit operators managing some activities commercially to improve financial performance, for example to help repay capital costs, pay for minor investments or cross-subsidise non-profitable community activities, e.g. health suites and cafes in public sector leisure centres;
2 commercial companies providing resources for not-for-profit organisations in return for publicity, brand awareness, beneficial image and possible increases in sales; this, of course, is commercial sponsorship and it is discussed in Chapter 15 as an important marketing tool.

Table 4.1 identifies the major elements of commercial leisure, with examples. It shows the range of businesses involved. According to Leisure Industries Research Centre (2009) the largest elements are leisure travel and tourism (particularly holidays overseas), eating out, alcoholic drink and home entertainment – the most significant element of the home environment in Table 4.1, comprising TV, DVD, audio, games and home computers. Table 3.3 provides more detail of the size of some of these industries in the UK. Furthermore, these commercial sectors have achieved significant growth in the last thirty years, as shown in Figures 3.4 (p. 66) and 3.5 (p. 70).

For obvious reasons Table 4.1 does not include what some commentators would identify as significant commercial leisure industries but which are illegal – particularly drugs and prostitution. Of course this opens the debate about what is leisure, and this could be extended to such industries as tobacco. But for the purposes of definition, this debate is avoided here by excluding illegal activities, although the debate is an important one and if, for example, recreational drugs were legalised, they would become part of the formal commercial leisure sector.

> ### Discussion question
>
> Should recreational drugs be included in definitions of commercial leisure?

4.3 Commercial sector objectives

The major difference between a commercial organisation and a public or voluntary organisation is that a primary objective of the commercial operator is to achieve financial profit or an adequate return on investment. The other sectors may also make financial surpluses on occasion, but they are established primarily for other reasons. Yet, profit-making and not-for-profit organisations in leisure have similarities – they must both attract sufficient clients, customers or members, or they will fail. Public and not-for-profit managers increasingly use some of the skills and techniques of commercial operators, such as market research, targeted promotion, and product innovation and development.

Despite the fundamental objective of making profit to both survive and prosper, many private businesses do not make profits. Forty per cent of American commercial ventures apparently never make a profit, but break even or go under, and half the rest make only marginal profits, the major problem being the mounting capital repayment debts. In such a climate, many commercial leisure organisations find it hard to stay in business and, compared to public sector services, competition is fierce and many companies may fail. Leisure is a volatile market and changes in leisure spending add to this uncertainty.

Making profit is a simplification of the objectives of the commercial provider. There are many other short run and medium term commercial sector objectives which either need profit to accomplish them or are designed to increase profit. These include:

- increase stock market value, which is often but not always related to short-term profitability;
- growth, through organic, endogenous means of product and market developments, or through merger and acquisition;
- maximising sales, which can sometimes be risky in terms of profitability and is closely related to the growth objective;
- increasing market share, which is a means of gaining power in the market, as discussed in the later section on size structure (see below);
- controlling risk, e.g. through diversification – moving into other markets to develop a portfolio of activities is a strategy which can reduce the risks of confining supply to one market in a sector which can have quite volatile movements in demand.

4.4 The size structure of commercial leisure companies

The commercial leisure industry is made up of many thousands of businesses, from independent gyms and craft shops to giant multinationals producing sports clothing and footwear or alcoholic drinks. It is the large companies that tend to dominate in a number of commercial leisure industries. Irvine and Taylor (1998) investigated the size structure of 15 leisure markets in the UK in 1990 (the year with the most reliable data). They found a high level of market concentration in the 15 leisure markets examined, measured by the proportion of market sales supplied by the largest five firms – called the 'five firm concentration ratio' (see Figure 4.1).

The average market concentration across all 15 sectors (in the 'Average' column) is 53 per cent. However the range is quite wide, from airlines and airports, betting and gaming, and photography, where over 70 per cent of market sales are from the five largest firms in each market, to books, DIY and sports, where less than 40 per cent of sales are from the five largest firms. These data are the only ones available but they are rather dated. They are likely to have changed over time – for example, the market concentration in airlines is likely to have fallen with the recent successes of budget airlines.

This concentration of market power in a few large companies is termed an 'oligopoly' and it is characterised by both interdependence and uncertainty. The companies are interdependent because one large company's actions in supply have an effect on the other large companies, e.g. a price decrease by one company can cause a reduction in demand and sales for another company. This can cause stability in that no one company wants to 'rock the boat'. Sometimes oligopolistic companies collude illegally in cartels, for example to fix prices and prevent price competition. There are national and international laws (e.g. for the

Table 4.1 Commercial leisure

Area	Examples		Examples
Arts	Reading material		Cinema
	CDs/records/tapes		Television relay services
	Radio relay services		Photography/films/processing
	Musical instruments		Music, video tapes
	Galleries		Theatre and concerts
Sports	Participation (e.g. fitness clubs)		Spectating
	Equipment		Clothing
Attractions	Country houses		Amusement parks
	Historic attractions		Wildlife parks
	Zoos		Theme parks
Leisure travel & tourism	Travel agents		Tour operators
	Airlines		Rail and bus operators
	Ferry companies		Channel Tunnel
Transport	To and from leisure activities, or as a leisure activity in its own right, e.g. motoring for pleasure, rail, boat trips		
Accommodation	Hotels		Holiday camps
	Leisure villages		Caravanning
	Boats		Camping
	Second homes		Timeshares

Eating out	Restaurants	Banqueting halls
	Fast food	Snack bars
	Take away	Clubs
Alcohol	Off licence	Licensed premises
	Home brewing	
Gambling	Amusement arcades	Pools
	Bingo	Betting
	Gaming	Lotteries
	Casinos	
Dancing	Dance schools	Nightclubs
	Discos	Dance halls
Tobacco	All tobacco products	
Home environment	Home computers	Games
	TVs, DVDs, etc.	Audio equipment
	Gardening	Hobbies
	Toys	DIY
	Car maintenance	Pets and pet foods
	Art and antiques	
Sponsorship		

Source: adapted from Irvine and Taylor (1998).

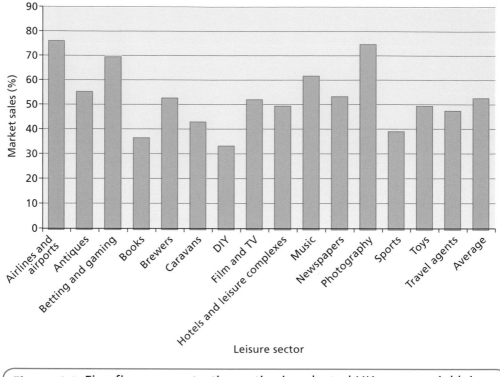

> **Figure 4.1** Five firm concentration ratios in selected UK commercial leisure sectors, 1990.
>
> *Source:* Irvine and Taylor (1998).

European Union) against such behaviour and large penalties are imposed if companies are proven guilty.

Other oligopolistic markets are characterised by extreme competition, which is the source of considerable uncertainty and instability, and which can threaten the financial viability of even large companies. This has happened, for example, in the package holiday market in the UK, where even the market leaders have gone out of business. It is also increasingly the case with airlines, with budget airlines competing fiercely on price and some large conventional airlines suffering as a consequence.

Discussion question

What are the main advantages and disadvantages of an oligopoly market structure in the production of beer?

4.5 Globalisation

Many commercial markets have in recent decades become more global, with multinational companies serving customers on a global basis. Leisure provides many of the most quoted examples, i.e.:

- McDonalds and KFC, which are globally recognised fast food restaurants, reaching as far as Russia and China;
- Disney, with not only theme parks in the USA, Paris, Tokyo and Hong Kong, but also films and merchandise which are universally recognised;
- large international hotel chains, such as Hilton and Best Western, which aim to ensure the same standard of facilities and service wherever they are in the world.
- sports clothing and footwear producers such as Adidas and Nike.

These brands are classic examples of what has been termed 'globalisation', a term which is used in a variety of disciplines to mean different things. In economics it signifies expanding international trade, international supply chains, and particularly the economic significance of large multinational companies producing and trading in a global market. In politics and international relations, it refers to the increasing importance of global relations and the diminishing importance of nation-states. In sociology and cultural studies, the term has been used to signify the emergence of a global society, with common values driven by international media; and standardisation of culture internationally, often denigrated with terms such as 'Cocacolanisation' or McDonaldisation'. Clearly it is an interdisciplinary concept, but one thing is at the heart of it – commercial activity. And from the examples given above it is obvious that commercial leisure provides some of the most conspicuous examples.

Many simplified claims have been made under the banner of globalisation and such is the international recognition of leading multinational brands that it is easy to use them to portray a global normality in terms of product and service offerings, and customer needs and values. This is reinforced by the market concentration referred to earlier, with many large multinational companies having significant proportions of market sales, not just nationally but also internationally. It is also reinforced by the exponential increases in communications, driven by technology – particularly through the media, the internet and mobile phones – which free many people from restricted national communications.

Nevertheless, it is easy to overstate the significance of globalisation. For example, the international presence of McDonalds etc. may be significant but a large majority of the eating out business is conducted in independent restaurants and food outlets with distinctive characteristics that attract customers. Irvine and Taylor (1996) explored the significance of commonly held principles of globalisation by interviewing six commercial leisure sector managers and found that whilst international activity is important regardless of the size of the organisation, simplified concepts of globalisation did not fit with commercial realities. Factors such as strong national (and local) cultures, language, religion and politics remain as important defining characteristics of nation-states, which are the main reference points for developing international business. Technology has facilitated international communications but has also enabled increased sensitivity to the needs of local markets. Brands often cross international boundaries but there are examples where they are hidden behind local brands which have more credibility in a particular country.

There is no disputing the rise in international business activity, the presence and power of some international brands, and the mobility of international capital to find the most cost-effective production locations. However, to assume that this is where the majority of commercial leisure business is positioned would be an overstatement. For the commercial production and distribution of leisure goods, globalisation is an economic reality. However, in leisure services much commercial activity is rooted in local communities, particularly those elements that rely on direct personal service. In such circumstances the scope for globalisation is limited.

> ### Discussion question
>
> **Discuss the advantages and disadvantages of globalisation to the production and distribution of a sports shoe, compared with a fitness centre.**

4.6 Key drivers for the commercial leisure business

This section reviews four key drivers for commercial leisure – time, money, government and technology. These factors determine the scale and nature of commercial leisure business, and constrain, liberate or actively facilitate commercial leisure development. They are derived from common considerations in the relevant literature.

4.6.1 Time

Chapter 2 identifies time as a key determinant and constraint of leisure demands. Free time in the UK comprises on average 23 per cent of the 24 hours a day available, according to Figure 2.5 (p. 62). Despite the fact that this has not changed a great deal (Gratton and Taylor, 2000; Gershuny, 2000), there is clear evidence that people feel more time pressured, i.e. they perceive that they have less time for the things they want to do, including work and leisure (Robinson and Godbey, 1999). Time availability is a key determinant of people's demand for leisure, whatever sector is supplying it. It is also the most commonly cited constraint on leisure demand, as identified for the UK in Table 2.6 (p. 41). The implications for leisure managers are clear – time convenience is an important attribute for leisure services.

Another crucial feature of time availability is its variation across different types of people, particularly by age and working status. Table 2.8 (p. 48) shows, for example, that older people have the longest amount of leisure time per day out of the categories compared. Combined with the ageing population which is common across many more developed economies, this results in an important, growing market for commercial leisure. Many holiday companies, for example, have identified the growing importance of older people, with specifically targeted promotions at off-peak times of the year.

Time constraints can be lessened by appropriate design of services and appropriate use of technology. Some commercial leisure businesses have been very astute at doing this – none more so than broadcasting, with services such as the Sky+ Box enabling viewers to watch programmes when they want, rather than when they are scheduled.

4.6.2 Money

For demand to be realised in the commercial sector it is necessary to have not only the time but also money. Figure 3.3 (p. 63) shows a rising trend in leisure expenditure, whether in the home or away from it. This trend is fed by rising disposable incomes across more developed economies. OECD statistics disclose a common feature over the last twenty years or more: rising disposable income for most of the period, even after allowing for inflation (see 'Useful websites', pp. 109–10). In real terms, gross national disposable income increased between 1988 and 2008 by 68 per cent in the UK, 73 per cent in the USA, 90 per cent in Japan and 98 per cent in Australia. Some of this increase will be accounted for by population growth and inflation, but generally inflation rates were fairly low during this period and much of the increase signifies real increases in spending power.

In the UK data on household expenditure (ONS, 2008d), recreation and culture accounted for over 13 per cent of weekly household spending in 2007, whilst between them restaurants and hotels, alcoholic drinks, tobacco and narcotics took another 10 per cent of household spending, on average. So it is clear that leisure spending takes a significant slice of disposable income. This is the spending that commercial leisure industries are interested in, and a large majority of leisure spending goes on their goods and services.

Discussion question

What is the most important constraint on buying more leisure goods and services, time or money? Consider this question for yourself and others in different employment circumstances to you.

4.6.3 Government regulation

Government both facilitates and constrains commercial leisure markets. There is no better example of this than the sale of alcoholic drinks in licensed establishments in the UK. In recent years there has been a general deregulation of licensing such that there are more opportunities to drink alcohol now and these opportunities last longer in the average day. However, as Case Study 4.1 shows, government regulation has also had a significant effect on the ownership of public houses, breaking up an oligopoly by the large brewing companies in the supply of beer to consumers.

Government also has significant effects in a number of other major commercial leisure industries, such as broadcasting and gambling (see Chapter 12). In broadcasting, governments not only allow public funding of public service broadcasters, such as the BBC in the UK, but also regulate the structure of broadcasting. In gambling, national and sometimes regional governments dictate through both law and planning regulations exactly what gambling is allowed in what premises. This leads, for example, to very different gambling regulations in different states in the USA.

4.6.4 Technology

Technology has had a longstanding historical effect on commercial leisure. Think of the impact of the railways on domestic holiday-taking and the development of traditional seaside resorts in the UK. Think also of various developments in air transport and the effects on leisure trips – the most recent being budget airlines. In Irvine and Taylor's examination of key factors influencing the commercial leisure sector (Irvine and Taylor, 1996), technological change emerged as one of the most important – even the humble fax machine was seen as a significant development for one travel company interviewed.

The internet is arguably having the most dramatic technological impact on commercial leisure today. In particular, e-commerce is growing rapidly and all commercial sectors are actively examining the opportunities and threats it brings. The internet is already changing the structure and delivery of leisure products and services. This is particularly the case with holidays and leisure trips (see Chapter 7), where increasing numbers of customers are planning and booking their own travel and accommodation online. It is also the case with home

Government regulation of public houses in the UK

By the end of the 1980s, the market for beer production was dominated by six national brewers – an oligopoly typical of many commercial industries. They accounted for three-quarters of UK beer production and controlled over half of all public houses (pubs) – 32,000 pubs out of a total of 60,000 – and also a substantial proportion of off-licence sales. The brewery-owned pubs were 'tied' to selling the brewer's beers only, and many other independent pubs (not owned by a big brewery) also entered into agreements with the big brewers to supply their beers in return for loans at favourable interest rates.

In 1986 the UK government's Director General of Fair Trading asked the Monopolies and Mergers Commission to investigate the beer market. It reported in 1989 that the beer market was controlled by a 'complex monopoly' which favoured the brewers, who controlled not only the production but also the distribution of beer. This prevented competition and restricted choice for consumers. The report recommended that the number of pubs which brewers were allowed to own should be capped.

The government then legislated in 1989 with 'Beer Orders'. These required brewers with more than 2,000 pubs either to dispose of their breweries or release from their 'ties' half of the pubs above the 2,000 threshold by November 1992, i.e. they had to pull out of production or radically cut their control over distribution. The Beer Orders also legislated that the remaining 'tied' pubs must sell one brand of cask beer and one brand of bottled beer from any supplier – so-called 'guest beers' – to give consumers more choice. Furthermore, they forbade any ties concerning non-alcoholic beers, low alcohol beers and non-beer drinks, many of which had higher profit margins and were also controlled by the major breweries.

The reaction to the legislation by the major brewers was to sell their pubs. From owning 32,000 pubs in 1989, by 2004 they owned none. Instead, through acquisition and merger activity, there emerged a new oligopoly of what are termed 'pubcos', i.e. pub-owning companies whose main business is running pubs. The House of Commons Select Committee report (House of Commons, 2004) identified seven pubcos with more than 1,000 pubs each, the largest two owning over 8,000 pubs each. The top six pubcos own about 40 per cent of all pubs. However, all the pubco pubs are leased to tenants, who run the pubs independently.

Therefore, the government regulation of the beer market has led to a radical restructuring of the industry, splitting what was previously a vertically integrated set of companies which controlled production and distribution into two separate industries – one for production, the other for distribution. Ironically, the market concentration of beer producers is as high as ever – the top six brewers supplied 84 per cent of sales in 2003. And a new oligopoly has emerged for distribution, the pubcos. But breaking the ownership link between the two has led to what the government has described as 'a reasonable amount of competition'. Furthermore, as the ties between production and distribution have been broken, the Beer Orders became irrelevant, and they were revoked in 2003. Job done!

Source: adapted from House of Commons, 2004

entertainment, with online games and downloading or streaming of music, films and television programmes (see Chapter 12).

> ### Discussion question
>
> Besides time, money, government and technology, what other key drivers of commercial leisure can you identify and why are they important? Take one of the key drivers and discuss the main implications of recent changes for managers in a sport or leisure industry of your choice.

4.7 Commercial leisure industries: a review

This section reviews some major commercial leisure industries, to illustrate contemporary developments. It concentrates on commercial leisure away from the home: Chapter 12 reviews the major at-home commercial leisure industries – reading, home entertainment, DIY, gardening, photography, toys and games, and pets. It also excludes consideration of major tourism-related industries – accommodation and transport – since these are reviewed in Chapter 7.

4.7.1 Eating and drinking out

The alcohol production industry is dominated by the few major breweries, as indicated in Case Study 4.1. However, as is typical of oligopolistic industries, consumer demand also sustains a large number of small, independent breweries. One institution which performs a unique and distinctive function in the UK is the public house and, as the case study also shows, the ownership of pubs has changed dramatically in the last twenty years. As a focal point for social activity, the selling of alcohol and food, and often the staging of live music events, the pub caters for a variety of demands. It remains one of the most popular free-time activities outside the home among adults, although, as noted in Chapter 3 (p. 70), it is in sharp decline.

In the long term, the decline in pubs is because of changing preferences, e.g. 40 per cent of all alcohol sold in the UK is now for home drinking and there is fierce competition on alcohol prices from supermarkets particularly. Other negative influences on pubs include drink-driving laws; health-conscious eating and drinking; and, for pubs in the south of England particularly, cheap purchases from France and Belgium. In the shorter term, many commentators have pointed to the ban on smoking in enclosed public spaces as the main reason for the decline in pubs in the UK. The ban was introduced in Scotland in 2006 and the rest of the UK in 2007. PricewaterhouseCoopers predicted that up to 5,000 pubs could close by 2011 as a result of the ban and in Scotland it was reported that one-third of pubs had to lay off staff as a result of falling business.

Another major influence on the industry is taxation – a favourite target of governments being alcohol. In 2008, for example, the UK government introduced higher than average tax increases for alcohol, which one study estimated will lead to a loss of 75,000 jobs in the industry in the following four years. However, the government's role is not always negative; in the UK, for example, the Licensing Act 2003 modernised the archaic licensing laws of England and Wales and provided for flexible, longer pub licensing hours.

Nevertheless, the public house market has shown that it can adapt to the changing nature of demand and to its changing circumstances. A growing diversification of products and segmentation of the market has been brought about by the growth in sales of pub food. And the smoking ban is an incentive for such a change: a poll conducted by the market research company BMRB International found that 'a non-smoking venue' was the second most important factor for parents after 'quality of food' when deciding where to take their children. Food expands the market to a wider public and profit margins on food are greater than on drinks. Family pubs are increasingly characterised by the provision of indoor and outdoor play areas and children's soft play facilities so that families can enjoy meals out. Although sales of beer are in long-term decline in pubs, the sales of food are increasing and 'gastro pubs' are expanding in number. According to Mintel (2009) pub meals showed the highest growth in sales of all eating out venues between 2001 and 2008.

In the UK, there are over 50,000 enterprises in the licensed restaurant industry, including fast food and takeaway outlets. Mintel (2009) reports that dining out is among consumers' top spending priorities after paying household bills. The market structure of the eating out industry varies according to the type of venue. The eating out sector as a whole is very competitive, particularly with many small independent restaurants in a very price competitive market. However, coffee bars and fast food chains have a different structure.

Coffee bars are in an oligopolistic market in many of the more developed economies. In the UK, three companies dominate the market and between them Starbucks and Costa have over half the market share. Branded fast food restaurants are also dominated by a few large companies. Demand for fast food outlets is strong, but they have been criticised for selling unhealthy foods and been the subject of protesters' actions as symbols of globalisation and capitalism. Nonetheless, the McDonalds' logo is said to be the most recognised worldwide.

Although a very varied and dynamic industry with plenty of new entrants, eating out is also a risky business. Hospitality businesses such as restaurants, hotels, pubs and bars are much more likely to fail than other businesses and Mintel (2009) report a 32 per cent rise in failures in restaurant businesses in 2008. The reasons for this include the time it takes to establish a customer base and the difficulty of raising working capital against the typically small assets of independent restaurant owners.

4.7.2 Betting and gambling

Gambling had a turnover in Britain of £84 billion in 2006–7 (Gambling Commission, 2009) and employs over 115,000 people. It is a service industry and therefore shares many of the service management requirements of the rest of the leisure industry. It has particular ethical and legal issues, however, which managers have to be aware of.

The *British Gambling Prevalence Survey 2007* found that 68 per cent of all adults gamble, 71 per cent of men and 65 per cent of women (Wardle *et al.*, 2007), so it is a mass participation leisure activity. Groups more likely to gamble include higher income households, those of white ethnicity, in paid employment and in lower supervisory and technical occupations, but different socio-demographic groups favour different gambling activities. In the UK gambling is dominated by betting, gaming machines and the National Lottery, which together account for about 80 per cent of the market. Other forms of gambling are relatively small scale, including bingo and online gambling, although the latter has grown the most rapidly recently (Leisure Industries Research Centre, 2009).

The government has a strong influence on the gambling industry, through a number of means. UK examples include introducing the National Lottery in 1994 and significant deregulation of gambling in the early 2000s. In the UK, there is a non-departmental public body set up by the 2005 Gambling Act to regulate commercial gambling – the Gambling Commission. Its regulatory objectives are to keep gambling crime free, to ensure players are not exploited and to protect children and vulnerable people from the dangers of gambling – these are the ethical considerations which good managers in the gambling industry will be watchful for. The 2007 survey identified that 0.6 per cent of gamblers are problem gamblers (gambling that compromises, disrupts or damages family, personal or recreational pursuits), which is about 284,000 people in the UK.

The rest of the gambling sector in the UK was hit hard in the mid- to late 1990s by the advent of the National Lottery; for example, it was held responsible for the closure of a substantial number of betting offices and bingo halls and a fall in business for the football pools companies. One consequence was the easing of regulations under the 2005 Gambling Act, designed in part to 'level the playing field' between the National Lottery and other forms of gambling (see 'Useful websites', pp. 109–10).

The UK gambling industry as a whole contains some elements which are in decline, e.g. bingo, and others which are growing, such as online betting. It has also seen quite radical shifts in ownership over the years. For example, Ladbroke sold all of its casinos to Gala in 2000. With so much depending on government regulation and a difficult public image, this is perhaps not surprising. However, it remains big business, not only in its own right but also in relationship with other leisure sectors, particularly sport. The review that follows does not include lotteries, because the National Lottery is really a government initiative and is reviewed in Chapter 5, whilst other lotteries are typically run by charities, sporting clubs and cultural bodies, so they are not commercial operations.

4.7.2.1 Betting and racing

Licensed betting offices account for around 90 per cent of off-course betting revenues in the UK. Growth areas are betting by telephone, internet and the television. The Gambling Commission (2009) reports that in 2009 three companies owned 67 per cent of the betting shops – Ladbroke, William Hill and Coral – i.e. another oligopoly. A number of regulatory changes have enabled betting shops to keep customers and attract new ones; for example, up to two amusement machines can be installed.

Fifty-nine per cent of betting shops' turnover is on horse racing, which is now second to football as the most televised sport. It is shown seven days a week on the internet and terrestrial television channels. There are 60 racecourses in Britain, with a combined total attendance of over 5.7 million in 2008. The horse racing industry generates direct expenditure of over £1 billion a year and employs 18,600 people (Deloitte, 2009). Another major betting subject is greyhound racing, which accounts for 15 per cent of betting shops' turnover. The Greyhound Board of Great Britain governs and regulates the industry, which has 28 racing tracks that attracted three million attendances in 2008. The sport employs around 20,000 people, including owners, trainers, stewards and operators.

4.7.2.2 Casinos

There were 144 casinos in Britain in 2009, operated by 24 companies in England, Scotland and Wales. Casinos are not permitted in Northern Ireland. Four companies own 79 per cent of the casinos in Britain – Gala, Genting Stanley, Grosvenor (Rank) and London Clubs International – another oligopoly. The location of casinos is strictly regulated in the UK. As well as putting forward the plan to build a 'supercasino' in Manchester, which was later withdrawn, the 2005 Gambling Act identifies eight areas for large casinos, and eight more for small casinos.

Changes in the law have benefited casinos through, for example, longer licensed drinking times; the abolition of the 'cooling-off' period, i.e. the time between joining a club and being allowed to gamble; and payment for chips with debit cards. However, the rise in the top rate of gaming duty from 33 per cent to 40 per cent in 1998, the smoking ban and the growth in competition have led to a downturn in business for some operators. The main growth in competition recently is from online casinos.

4.7.2.3 Bingo

Bingo was first developed in the sixteenth century in Italy as a game for the intelligentsia, but then it came to be regarded as an undemanding 'working class' pursuit. However, bingo does have surprising benefits socially. It is one of the few leisure activities which has good participation by lower socio-economic groups, lower income groups, divorced/separated people, the long-term unemployed, older people and women (Wardle *et al.*, 2007). There are lots of subsidised public sector leisure providers that would like that profile of users! Bingo also requires levels of concentration that may strengthen neural pathways in older people and can improve the accuracy and speed of short-term memory.

The Gambling Commission (2009) reports that Great Britain had 641 licensed bingo clubs operating in 2009, which is a fall of 60 clubs since 2004. Bingo has suffered from the advent of the National Lottery and more recently from the smoking ban in enclosed public spaces. However, it has also benefited from 'The National Bingo Game', run jointly by the largest bingo companies. It is the UK's second largest computer controlled game (after the National Lottery). Approximately 500 licensed bingo clubs link up every night of the year, except Christmas Day, to play, and over £1 million a week in prize money is distributed. Bingo is also altering its 'older generation' image, with new young players entering the game.

The industry is dominated by two operators, Gala Clubs and Mecca, which have over 40 per cent of the clubs, Gala with nearly one-quarter and Mecca with 16 per cent. As with other leisure industries dominated by a few large operators, however, there are a lot of small independent operators in bingo, which comprise nearly half the clubs.

4.7.2.4 Gaming machines

Amusement machines are a major source of income for many leisure providers. It is estimated that nearly 250,000 gaming machines were available for public use in Britain in 2009 (Gambling Commission, 2009), in public houses, arcades, bingo clubs, betting shops, restaurants, roadside service stations, leisure complexes and other venues. Prize machines earn substantial sums of money for their owners and operators. The British Amusement Catering Trade Association estimates that these machines can generate up to 30 per cent of public house income.

With the introduction of the National Lottery, followed soon after by the Scratchcard Lottery, amusement sector turnover reduced substantially. However, after deregulation the sector is recovering. Changes to the law have included: increases in cash payouts; amusement machines in betting shops; and increases in the number of machines allowed on one site for casinos, bingo clubs and members' clubs. New ways of winning back market share

are also being developed, e.g. high tech video games are being created which can compete with the home games market.

Discussion question

Deregulation is obviously good for commercial leisure business but is there still too much 'nanny state' interference in the gambling market?

4.7.3 Sport

In a study of the economic importance of sport, the Sport Industries Research Centre (Sport England, 2007a) estimated that the commercial sector was the most important sector in sport, with commercial sport accounting for 28 per cent of the value added (a measure of output). Together with commercial non-sport (i.e. commercial businesses that support or supply sport organisations, such as sponsors and travel companies) the commercial sector represents 74 per cent of sport output. Consumer spending on all commercial sport products was estimated to total over £2.5 billion in England in 2003 (Sport England, 2007a).

Commercial providers are concerned with sport in a number of key areas, i.e. spectator sports, sports clothing and footwear, sports equipment, sport gambling and sport media (in newspapers, magazines, on radio and television).

Furthermore, the commercial sector is involved in the provision of facilities for participants in a number of sports. In outdoor sports, this includes skiing, golf, tennis, water sports and five-a-side football. The last of these in particular has shown strong growth recently in the UK, with two companies running over eighty commercial centres. In indoor sports, health and fitness clubs, snooker, tenpin bowling, ice skating and indoor tennis are often provided by commercial organisations. Case Study 4.2 examines the best known and oldest form of sports tourism, which involves considerable commercial sector provision of various types – skiing. It demonstrates not only the multiple product nature of the ski holiday, but also important environmental considerations. Like much of sports provision, commercial or otherwise, the management role is largely to provide and operate a suitable infrastructure within which leisure experiences take place.

CASE STUDY 4.2

The skiing industry in the UK and Europe

Recreational skiing dates back to the nineteenth century in Europe. It now represents about 20 per cent of the European holiday market, dominated by the Alpine countries of Germany, France, Switzerland, Austria and Italy, which have 36 per cent of global resorts and cater for 47 per cent of global skiers (Mintel, 2008a). In the UK it is a niche market, just 3 per cent of all UK holidays, with the Alps being the most popular destination. It is an industry that not only combines two major leisure sectors, sport and tourism, but also combines a number of commercial industries, particularly travel, accommodation, specialist clothing, footwear and equipment, lifts and piste preparation, ski schools, restaurants, bars and car parking. Managers in the ski industry have to be acutely aware of the package of products which are important to the consumer, even if they are not supplying the whole package, because it is only as a package that it works as a leisure activity.

The term 'skiing industry' is a simplification because the industry now comprises two major activities – skiing and snowboarding – plus a host of more specialist activities such as cross-country skiing, telemark, snowmobiling, heli-skiing and tobogganing. The main market segments are inclusive tours, independently organised trips and school/college trips (Weed and Bull, 2004). In the UK market, inclusive tours have seen long-term increases in business, whilst school trips have seen long-term decreases. The independent trips were stable in the early 2000s but are likely to increase because of an increasing trend towards using the internet to make holiday arrangements.

The main drivers for the ski-related businesses have included rising disposable incomes in more developed countries, a rise in holiday entitlements and a complex mix of attractions to motivate consumers, including aesthetics, thrill/escape and opportunities for social engagement with friends, family and others. Also important has been the expansion of skiing opportunities by developers. There are now over 40,000 kilometres of ski runs in the Alps, serviced by 14,000 ski lifts which together are capable of moving 1.5 million skiers per hour (Weed and Bull, 2004).

The independent trip market is serviced by a vast array of independent operators, for travel and accommodation. The inclusive tours business is much more oligopolistic – in the UK, for example, six companies control 74 per cent of the market (Mintel, 2008a). As with the inclusive tour business generally, this market structure has led to extreme price competition in the past, which is good for most consumers but carries the continual risk of failure for some of the businesses concerned.

The skiing industry services customers which are in the main from higher income and younger age groups (under 45 years). The income bias is not surprising because skiing is an expensive form of tourism. Not only are there the usual expenses of travel and accommodation, but it is also necessary to buy or hire specialist clothing, footwear and equipment, a ski pass for the area being visited and, for beginners, ski school. Mintel (2006a) estimates that 37 per cent of consumer spending on skiing is on retail goods, with 22 per cent on lift passes, 21 per cent on accommodation, 9 per cent on transport and 11 per cent on spending at the resort. The ski clothing, footwear and equipment industry is oligopolistic, with a few major brands such as Rossignol and Salomon taking a significant proportion of sales.

Ski resort development falls into two broad types (Hudson, 2000). One is more organic development of existing settlements, with more community-based investment. The other is more holistic, integrated resort development. La Plagne in France is a major example of the latter, with a ten-village complex created by a development company from a natural, high altitude mountain wilderness.

The future of the skiing industry in Europe is uncertain in the medium to long term because of one factor – global warming. This threatens the depth and duration of snow cover, which threatens the commercial viability of the skiing season. Even if it does not occur, global warming has helped to provoke an environmental concern for activities such as skiing. Nevertheless, many winter resorts have already diversified to embrace summer mountain activities such as walking, mountain biking and white water activities.

4.7.3.1 Spectator sport

Commercial spectator sports are dominated worldwide by football, motor sports and horse racing, whilst different countries have their own favourites, e.g. American football, ice hockey, baseball and basketball in the USA. The most popular attract large numbers of spectators and huge television audiences. The spectator sports market is worth around £770 million in the UK, about the same size as the cinema market. It has grown only slowly in the early 2000s, however, possibly because of price rises to boost the income of clubs. Over the period 2002–7 spectator sports prices increased by 22 per cent, which was more than twice the general rate of price increases in the economy. For grounds with strong demand and limited capacity, such price increases may simply choke off excess demand, but for other clubs they pose a real threat to ticket sales revenue if demand is sensitive to price rises. In 2009, a Virgin Money survey indicated that nearly one-quarter of Premier and Football League season ticket holders were considering not renewing their season tickets, in order to purchase tickets on a game-by-game basis instead.

Live spectator numbers for football fell in the UK from the late 1940s to the mid-1980s. Then a number of factors contributed to a strong recovery in attendances (although not to the levels of the 1940s). These probably included stadia improvements following the Bradford and Hillsborough disasters; the formation of the Premier League in 1992; the flotation of some clubs on the Stock Market; the increasing revenue from and coverage on television; and more international stars attracted to the Premier League.

As businesses, professional sports often live up to the cliché 'it's a funny old game' and they provide the most tangible evidence that so-called commercial businesses are often not just in it for profit. Year after year the professional football industry in the UK, for example, demonstrates that, apart from a few notable exceptions, many clubs operate with financial losses and many are technically insolvent and only sustained by rescheduled debts. Emery and Weed (2006) report that in 2002–3, for example, although the Premier League in England made an overall operating profit of £124 million, the rest of the Football League made a combined loss of £110 million. The ownership of many clubs changes hands frequently and this is partly because they have such an uncertain (or downright poor) financial prospect.

Discussion question

Is professional football a commercial leisure industry? Consider the profitability of professional clubs – and not just Manchester United!

Nevertheless, there are outstanding examples of business success in professional sport. In football the most conspicuous example is Manchester United, a club which, despite its large debts at the time of writing, generates significant profits and enormous revenues from merchandise and media rights as well as from live spectators attending matches at Old Trafford. Furthermore, there are other examples of football clubs at every level of the professional game that are successful businesses in the conventional manner of making profits. The trouble with professional sport is that commercial success is never enough – sporting success is equally and often more important. One of the most conspicuous examples of the business 'knife edge' walked by some professional football clubs is Leeds United, which went from being one of the top Premier League sides in England to a League 1 side in a few seasons – principally because of financial problems, in particular escalating debts.

4.7.3.2 Sport media

Whereas professional football often presents a poor image of commercial business, sport media provide some of the most successful examples of commercial success. An example featured in Case Study 12.2 is football and television, in particular the success of Sky television. There is a powerful, symbiotic relationship between the commercial sport and television industries, which the case study illustrates. The business model of subscription television took an interesting twist in the autumn of 2009 with the broadcasting of an England World Cup qualifier exclusively on the internet.

The relationship between professional sport and the media is a very important business alliance. Professional sport gets valuable revenue for media coverage, which helps to overcome the gap between costs and the revenue from finite live spectator numbers. The media is able to reach many more people interested in professional sport and make successful businesses out of this communication. Gratton and Solberg suggest:

> The most significant change in the sports industry over the last 20 years has been the increasing importance of broadcast demand for sport which has led to massive escalation in the prices of broadcasting rights for professional team sports and major sports events.
>
> (Gratton and Solberg, 2007: 1)

The escalation in the prices of broadcasting rights, however, has shown the risks involved in sport media. Setanta, having paid part of a record fee for Premier League football broadcasting rights in England and Scotland, then did not realise sufficient subscription income and their business folded in 2009. This left more than a few football clubs in financial trouble, such has been their increasing dependency on television revenues. The Setanta failure demonstrates the difficulties of breaking into a sport broadcasting market which is dominated by a few large companies.

4.7.3.3 Sports clothing, footwear and equipment

Although the sports industry is dominated by expenditure on sports services, according to the Sport Industry Research Centre (2009) about 38 per cent of consumer spending is on sports goods, with sports clothing, footwear and equipment taking the lion's share of this (see Figure 10.1, p. 257). This involves the manufacture, distribution and retailing of a vast range of goods, from yachts, canoes, tents, bicycles and hang-gliders, to tracksuits, specialist footwear for a variety of different activities, rackets, balls, snooker tables, dartboards, trampolines and goalposts.

The Sport Industry Research Centre (2009) estimates that about 20 per cent of all footwear spending and 7 per cent of all clothing spending is attributable to sport in the UK. The trend over the last ten years and more has been for falling prices but increasing sales volumes in sports clothing and footwear. The forecast at the time of writing is for sports clothing and footwear to be hit hard by not only the recession, but also the influence of changing fashion. Two of the four leading sports clothing and footwear retail companies in the UK faced financial difficulties in 2008–9.

Manufacture of sports clothing and footwear is very often 'outsourced' to countries with low labour costs, such as Taiwan, China and the Philippines. This raises ethical issues about 'exploitation' in less developed countries, but the commercial logic is that it keeps production costs low and allows high wholesale and retail margins in more developed countries. Gratton and Taylor (2000) reproduce an example of a Nike sports shoe which in 1995 cost $20 dollars to produce; with Nike costs and profits raising the wholesale price to $35.50; and retail costs and profits raising the final retail price to the customer to $70.

Discussion question

Is it 'exploitation' when a multinational sports goods company organises production in a less developed country?

The largest element of the sports equipment industry in terms of consumer spending in the UK is boats. It is a minority participation activity but the value of the market is boosted by the high prices of many sailing boats. Boats represent about half the value of the UK sports equipment market and include not just sailing boats but also canoes, kayaks and, in some countries, canal boats. Apart from boats, bicycles, outdoor equipment and indoor fitness equipment are major markets, with the last of these benefiting from increased health awareness and concern.

4.7.3.4 Health and fitness clubs

The fitness sector is comprised mainly of commercial providers, although fitness facilities are common in public sector leisure centres too. It is a sector that has seen substantial growth in the past two decades. In the UK, the number of members of clubs has risen from just over 1.5 million in 1995 to more than 4.7 million in 2009, with about 95 per cent of these in the commercial sector. Public sector fitness participants are more likely to be pay-and-play than members. Commercial sector growth has been driven by a significant increase in the number of commercial fitness clubs, with development by a number of chains, including Bannatyne's, Cannons, David Lloyd, Esporta, Fitness First, LA Fitness, and Virgin. Most of the clubs are standalone but some are located in hotels and run by the hotel or by outside contractors.

Health and fitness clubs have evolved over the past forty years into a widespread, sophisticated market leader. With a move towards individual health and fitness, supported by government policy, a burgeoning market has grown in the private sector with new kinds of equipment – resistance, cardio-vascular, treadmills – and these have led to highly sophisticated machinery, computerised and incorporating club members' personal workout information. Personal trainers are an important development from this industry.

The nature of some clubs has been moving from physical fitness to health and wellbeing, a shift which forward-thinking leisure managers should take seriously. An interesting development in fitness clubs is that private health insurance companies in the USA and UK have recently offered reduced health insurance premiums for club members who have attended regularly. The links between commercial fitness and health took another step in the UK in 2007 when a private health care company, Nuffield, acquired Cannons Health and Fitness clubs.

It is not uncommon today to find private health companies with a range of services which have a synergy with health and fitness clubs, i.e. treatments and therapies including acupuncture, the Alexander technique, aromatherapy, chiropracty, homeopathy, hypnotherapy, massage, meditation, osteopathy, reiki, reflexology, relaxation training, sports injury clinics, t'ai chi and yoga. While it provides a few of such services, the trend in the private fitness sector is more towards the concept of 'wellness' and health spas, which have been extremely popular in parts of Europe for the last hundred years. The American 'wellness' market sector has also moved towards provision of health spas and holistic approaches.

It is not only in the commercial sector that health and fitness centres are moving to a more holistic approach. The whole idea behind government and National Lottery backing for the concept of Healthy Living Centres in the UK is to provide a range of opportunities that deal with the needs of 'the whole person' (see more on Healthy Living Centres in Chapter 10).

4.7.4 Cinema

The hundredth anniversary of the cinema was celebrated in 1997. The peak audiences for cinema-going were in the years immediately after the Second World War. However, with the invention of television came a decrease in cinema ticket sales – in the UK from a peak of 1,635 million in 1946 to an all-time low of 54 million in 1984. Yet cinemas experienced an upturn in their fortunes, so that by 2008 cinema-going reached 164 million visits (Cinema Exhibitors' Association – see 'Useful websites', pp. 109–10). The Office for National Statistics (2009) reports that 42 per cent of adults attend the cinema at least once a year in the UK.

Global cinema attendances are dominated by two countries – India, with 2.9 billion visits in 2002, and the USA, with 1.4 billion visits in 2002 (Cinema Exhibitors' Association – see 'Useful websites', pp. 109–10). Of course these figures are influenced by much higher population numbers than the UK, but even so, per capita cinema visiting is much higher in these countries than in the UK – for example 4.6 visits per head in the USA, compared with 2.7 in the UK. This may be related to supply. Despite the growth of multiplexes, the UK is still under-screened compared to many other countries, with 59 screens per million people in 2007, compared to nearly 129 per million in the USA.

Young adults are the most likely age group to go to the cinema. In 2008, over 80 per cent of 15–24-year-olds in the UK reported that they went to the cinema once a year and over 40 per cent went once a month or more (ONS, 2008). Equivalent figures for 45–54-year-olds were that 59 per cent visited once a year and 10 per cent once a month or more. A particular growth market is attendance by 7–14-year-olds, with 87 per cent going at least once a year, comprising nearly one-fifth of total visits.

The recovery in cinema attendances in the last two decades has been stimulated in part by reinvestment, particularly the multiplex – an attractive cinema environment providing a choice of films. Although there has been a decline in the number of cinema sites in the UK, there has been an increase in the number of screens, brought about by the division of many of the existing cinemas into multi-screen units. The structure of the industry is once again oligopolistic, with leading brands including Odeon, UCI and UGC.

Although cinema audiences have increased in the UK in recent times, only around 10 per cent of cinema capacity is reached from Monday to Thursday, which accounts for 39 per cent of total visits, compared with 61 per cent of visits from Friday to Sunday. Technological change provides an opportunity to increase usage and revenue in off-peak times. Digital technology and projection, for example, enable cinemas to screen sporting events and pop concerts and to hold business conferences linking up with other cities and countries. It has been forecasted that film reels will disappear in time and film data will be stored digitally and sent to cinemas by satellite, DVD or cable. This should lead to substantially reduced costs. Another technological change which is already spreading rapidly is 3D cinema, with an estimated doubling of the number of 3D cinemas in 2009 (Palicki, 2009) and plans in North America to invest in 3D technology in up to 20,000 cinemas. 3D is now proven technology, having been adopted by increasing numbers of theme parks, museums and other visitor attractions.

> **Discussion question**
>
> Why do you think that cinema, football spectating and bingo have all recovered in popularity since low points in admissions in the mid-1980s?

4.7.5 Leisure parks

Leisure parks are clusters of leisure and other developments in one location, such as cinema, tenpin bowling, restaurants and clubs. Leisure experiences in attractive, safe environments attract families and the older age groups and provide an alternative to home entertainment. However, different groups in the community have different demands; these are largely age related and lead to a fragmented market. To cater for each separate market would be costly and less attractive to the family market. Multi-facility leisure schemes are increasingly being developed to attract a wide range of users within one complex. There are over 100 large scale leisure parks in the UK, but the more common mix, at over 900 sites, is retail parks with leisure elements (Mintel, 2008d).

In the 1990s interest from developers in the leisure park market was stimulated by evidence of increasing numbers of cinema-goers, greater interest in tenpin bowling and bingo and the popularity of nightclubs. As a result, nearly all leisure parks designed during this time are anchored by multiplex cinemas and restaurants, which then become a catalyst for other elements, particularly tenpin bowling and health and fitness clubs, but also bars/pubs, bingo and nightclubs (Mintel, 2008d). In retail parks with leisure, cinemas and restaurants are also the main anchors, with tenpin bowling the next most common leisure element.

4.7.6 Theatres

Commercial leisure provision for entertainment and the arts outside the home covers a number of areas, although these can be divided into two basic categories: those which encourage active participation (e.g. ballrooms; discos; drama, music and dance schools) and those in which provision is generally geared towards spectators. This section deals primarily with the latter.

In the UK, commercial theatres are in large measure centred on London. The London Theatre Guide shows 42 theatres in London's West End, whilst the Society of London Theatre (2009) identifies 45 theatres, of which only half a dozen have substantial government subsidies (e.g. Royal Opera House, London Coliseum, National Theatre, Sadler's Wells). The London commercial theatres are another oligopoly, with five companies owning 29 London theatres between them: Ambassadors, Delfont Mackintosh, Live Nation, Nimax and Really Useful Group.

London theatres put on 241 productions and attracted nearly 13.9 million visits in 2008 – this compares with the lowest figure, in 1986, of just over 10 million (Society of London Theatre, 2009). A survey of London's West End theatres in 2003 identified that 37 per cent of visitors came from London, 36 per cent from the rest of the UK, 17 per cent from North America and 11 per cent from other countries. West End theatres have much the same socio-demographic biases as theatres nationally – 65 per cent of audiences were female in 2003, 92 per cent were of white ethnic origin and 41 per cent had annual incomes exceeding £30,000 (Society of London Theatre, 2009).

The Wyndham Report (Travers, 1998), commissioned by the Society of London Theatre, reported that 41,000 jobs depend on London's West End theatres, with £250 million spent on tickets and £433 million spent by theatregoers on restaurants, hotels, travel and merchandise. The global earnings of the most successful UK theatre productions are greater than Hollywood blockbusters such as *Titanic*, and London theatres' contribution to the UK's balance of payments is greater than the UK film and television industry.

Further analysis of the implications of *The Wyndham Report* has subsequently focused on a number of key issues. First, creative new theatre works are largely confined to the public sector, which highlights the importance of partnership between the subsidised and commercial sectors to fully realise the commercial potential of such works. Second, an active partnership is necessary between theatres and education authorities, to sustain and broaden interest in theatre in the long term. Third, London theatres in particular are old (most were built in the nineteenth century) and many are in urgent need of renovation. Fourth, theatre is a high risk business and its biggest hurdle is raising investment to back new shows. Finally, a focus on London is inappropriate because of the interrelationships between regional and London theatres, and between subsidised and commercial theatres, in terms of productions and personnel.

Although London is the theatre capital of the world, commercial theatre is also present in the rest of the UK. About half of the professional theatres in Britain are owned or rented by commercial companies. Live Nation and Ambassadors, for example, own 14 theatres each outside London.

4.7.7 Nightclubs

The value to commercial operators of the nightclub/discotheque sector has continued to increase because of sustained high levels of admission. 'Clubbing' is a sector with around £1.9 billion turnover a year in the UK. Total admissions have been more or less static since 2003 in the UK, whilst the percentage of adults visiting clubs declined from nearly 30 per cent in 2003 to less than 27 per cent in 2008 (Mintel, 2008c), which suggests that average frequency of attendance per person has risen. For 15–17-year-olds, the percentage visiting fell from nearly 50 per cent in 2003 to less than 19 per cent in 2008. The main reason for this is likely to include the tighter checking of younger customers' age, related to the enforcement of a number of legislative changes, including a Security Industry Act and a Licensing Act.

The nightclub industry is very fragmented in ownership, with the largest operator running just 6 per cent of the 1,700 clubs. Getting the mix of activities right for specific market segments has seen leisure companies updating old concepts, finding new combinations and being innovative – a recent example in the UK being student events organised by Carnage UK. The major clubs need large regular throughputs and run a number of special events and promotions to increase business on quiet nights, i.e. early in the week.

One of the problems of this lucrative market is a clash of cultures. On the one hand there is the promotion of sales of alcohol and exciting entertainment, as these make for profitable business for the industry (and through taxes, also for the government) as well as satisfying the demands of consumers. Yet on the other hand there is public and policy concern about health, anti-social behaviour and crime, which gives rise to calls for further regulation. Leisure managers and other professionals need to identify ways in which appropriate compromises are reached, ensuring customers' demands are still satisfied, whilst protecting them and others from the excesses that can arise. Leisure education, in its widest sense, is one of the means of helping young people to make their own choices to meet their needs for excitement and fun without causing social concern.

4.7.8 Theme parks

Theme parks have become popular since the creation of Disneyland, which resurrected the amusement park industry in 1955 in the United States. Their philosophy has been one of providing excellence, cleanliness, courtesy and safety. They create an atmosphere of fantasy, glamour, escapism, prestige and excitement. Disney theme parks are successful in Tokyo, Hong Kong and Paris, as well as Florida and California, and are world leaders. Disneyland Paris, for example, is the most popular visitor attraction in Europe, with 15.3 million visits in 2008 (Harrison and Bland, 2009).

Britain's first theme park was Thorpe Water Park at Chertsey, with a theme of maritime history. Its development encouraged the provision of other 'theme' facilities elsewhere in the UK. Britain's largest, Alton Towers in Staffordshire, is the tenth largest theme park in Europe, with over 2.5 million visits in 2008. Apart from Disney, four other companies dominate the operation of theme parks in Europe: Merlin Entertainments, Parques Reunidos, Grevin et Cie and Aspro Ocio. Merlin Entertainments operates some of the largest UK theme parks – Alton Towers, Thorpe Park, Legoland, Madame Tussauds, Sea Life centres and Chessington World of Adventures – as well as the London Eye and theme parks in Italy and Germany.

Theme parks are a magnet for children and young people and are therefore attractive for day trips and family outings. They take up large amounts of land so need to be located at distances from urban settings, requiring longer travel times than to local facilities. But they are marketed as a 'day out' and have benefited during the recent recession from the trend towards 'staycations' – holidays at home.

The biggest commercial challenge is to generate sufficient visitors and revenue to cover not only the high running costs but the high capital costs of new, eye-catching major rides, which have become a necessity to encourage repeat visits. Generating visits is only partly controlled by management actions – particularly investment, advertising and pricing. Other major influences are the state of the general economy and, of course, the weather. Bad weather in the summer of 2007 in the UK, for example, contributed to a 5 per cent decline in the number of overall visits at UK theme parks (Mintel, 2008b).

As well as sustaining and growing attendances, theme parks have been successful at generating higher revenue from their assets through what is termed 'yield management' (Harrison and Bland, 2009). The initiatives which achieve this include advance ticket purchases, priority queuing tickets for popular rides (at premium prices), merchandising, photographic souvenirs and on-site accommodation. Market research reported by Mintel (2008b) identifies that the three developments most wanted by customers at theme parks were reasonably priced food and drink, being able to buy priority queuing tickets, and paying for rides on a pay-as-you-go basis rather than paying for expensive all-inclusive entry tickets.

Discussion questions

As an attraction manager, how would you prefer to ration excess demand: by a straightforward queue where everyone was equal; by higher prices generally to choke off the excess demand; or by selling priority queuing tickets at premium prices? Why?

4.8 Conclusions

Commercial providers of facilities, services and products for leisure consumption have by far the greatest influence on people's use of leisure time, compared to other providers. This chapter has reviewed some general considerations and some of the commercial markets for leisure away from home. However, there are other major commercial leisure interests covered in other chapters, particularly leisure in the home (Chapter 12), the holiday and tourist industry (Chapter 7) and sponsorship (Chapter 15).

Commercial businesses have to make profits or in the end they go out of business. In order to reap the best profits and returns on investment, management policies, approaches and techniques are important. A number of factors determine commercial leisure success, including:

- accessibility and location, either in town centres or in out-of-town sites;
- the range of facilities and activities;
- the catchment area and the market competition (not just from similar facilities but also other opportunities for children and families);
- the quality of products and services;
- investment in new products;
- pricing;
- promotion;
- catering and social opportunities;
- facilities and services for different market segments;
- car parking.

The commercial sector, whilst having to maintain profitability, does not operate in isolation from other sectors. Government is a key influence on commercial business, both facilitating and constraining. The commercial sector does generate important positive and negative social outcomes, which it is showing increasing regard for – it has to, otherwise it loses the support of communities and ultimately consumers.

Practical tasks

1 Visit a commercial leisure organisation. Identify how many different ways it tries to get you to spend money. Identify other possible ways in which it could tempt you to spend money.

2 Visit the venues of two major operators in any *one* of the following industries: cinema, bingo, fast food, coffee bars. Consider the similarities and differences between the sites and decide whether oligopoly is good or bad for customer choice and quality of service.

Structured guide to further reading

For an overview of leisure and sport industries:
Leisure Forecasts and *Sports Market Forecasts*, annual publications from the Sport Industry
Research Centre, Sheffield Hallam University, Sheffield.

For commercial leisure in the USA:
Vogel, H.L. (2007) *Entertainment Industry Economics: a guide for financial analysis*, 7th
edition, Cambridge University Press, New York.

For market reviews of different commercial leisure markets, international and UK:
Mintel reports.

For an overview of gambling in the UK:
Gambling Commission (2009) *Industry Statistics, 2008/2009*, Gambling Commission,
London.

For a review of the ownership of public houses in the UK:
House of Commons (2004) *Trade and Industry Second Report*, available at www.publica-
tions.parliament.uk/pa/cm200405/cmselect/cmtrdind/128/12802.htm.

For sports broadcasting:
Gratton, C. and Solberg, H.A. (2007) *The Economics of Sports Broadcasting*, Routledge,
London.

Useful websites

For international disposable income statistics, from the OECD:
www.oecd.org/LongAbstract/0,3425,en_2649_33715_36864949_1_1_1_1,00.html

For household expenditure statistics in the UK, from the Office for National Statistics:
www.statistics.gov.uk/downloads/theme_social/family_spending_2007/familyspend-
ing2008_web.pdf

For information on greyhound racing in Great Britain:
www.thedogs.co.uk

For information on horse racing in Great Britain:
www.britishhorseracing.com/inside_horseracing

For information on the 2005 Gambling Act:
www.culture.gov.uk/what_we_do/gambling_and_racing/3305.aspx

Providers

For information on gambling in the UK:
www.gamblingcommission.gov.uk/research__consultations/research/bgps/bgps_2007.aspx

For information on the attractions market:
Attractions Management online, http://attractionsmanagement.com/

For information on cinema in the UK:
Cinema Exhibitors' Association, www.cinemauk.org.uk/

Chapter 5

Government and sport and leisure

In this chapter

- How does government get involved in sport and leisure?
- What are the roles of central and local government and non-department public bodies (NDPBs) in sport and leisure?
- What is the rationale for government involvement?
- What are the key elements of legislation affecting sport and leisure?
- How does the National Lottery affect sport and leisure in the UK?
- How is the European Union involved in sport and leisure?

Summary

There are very few areas of leisure which are unaffected by government. The different ways in which government influences leisure include direct provision, financial support, and both enabling and controlling legislation. Different levels and agents of government are active in leisure, from the EU at the international level, through central government and many non-department public bodies (NDPBs) at the national level, to regional governments and local authorities. Central government typically has the most pervasive influence but most of this is indirect – it is NDPBs and local authorities which have the most direct effects on leisure markets.

The rationale for government intervention in leisure has evolved for almost two centuries, since mid-nineteenth-century legislation which facilitated leisure provision in order to achieve health, citizenship and social control benefits. Other rationales have developed, including a recognition that government funding is needed for excellence in various spheres of leisure, especially sport, the arts, heritage and museums and galleries.

The forms of government support for leisure have also changed over time, the most conspicuous new form in recent times being lotteries, licensed by government and with proceeds going to good causes which include sport and leisure.

The medium term future is one of uncertainty for government support for leisure, however, as governments which have engaged in fiscal stimulus to help recovery from the recession will have to significantly cut their expenditures.

5.1 Introduction

In earlier chapters, the concept of leisure has been debated in terms of what it is, what it does and what it can do for individual people and for the community at large. Leisure service and facility managers are encouraged to provide programmes and activities which enable people to find satisfying leisure experiences. Providing satisfaction can achieve two main objectives: first, it can help to meet some of the needs of people; and, second, it can help in meeting the business goals of leisure organisations by attracting more satisfied clients and customers. We now consider how providing for leisure satisfies government objectives too and what leisure provision takes place in the public sector. Many of the examples used are from the UK, to give a consistent and holistic picture, but similar provision and legislation are evident in other countries.

People's leisure and recreation are enhanced by powers and duties invested in, or assumed by, government. There are many different elements of government involved in the provision of leisure facilities, including central government, non-department public bodies, regional or state government and local authorities of different types (e.g. in different parts of the UK there are unitary authorities, county councils, district councils and parish councils at the local level).

Since Torkildsen's *Leisure and Recreation Management* was first published in 1983, there have been huge changes in central government and local government. In the UK, for example, there has been devolution of many central powers to the Scottish Parliament and the Welsh and Northern Ireland Assemblies. Legislation over much of the last thirty years has had the effect, on the one hand, of tightening councils' budgets and, on the other hand, bringing flexibility and accountability into the ways in which services could be delivered and facilities managed.

There is one issue of terminology that it is important to get straight. Throughout this book the term 'leisure' is used to encompass a wide range of activities such as sports, recreation, arts, play, heritage sites, etc. In government circles, and particularly in countries other than the UK, a more common term is 'culture'. Ironically, however, culture is the term used in the title of the main UK government department responsible for leisure – the Department of Culture, Media and Sport (DCMS) – although it is slightly confusing to identify sport separately because sport is part of culture. Another confusing matter is that culture in the UK is often seen more narrowly as a term covering the arts. In the USA a more commonly used term for leisure in policy is 'recreation'.

5.2 The scope of public leisure services and facilities

In the UK (as in many other countries, including France and Japan), central government has a powerful role but local authorities actually provide more leisure opportunities. USA, Germany and Australia are examples of a different model – a federal system – in which regional or state governments play a significant role. The regional role in the UK is at its most significant in the responsibilities devolved to the Scottish Parliament and the Welsh and Northern Ireland Assemblies.

The variation in the different sources of government support between countries is shown for the arts in the mid-1990s in a report by the Arts Council for England (1998):

- In the UK, 58 per cent of government funding for the arts came from central government, 42 per cent from local government (more recently, after devolution, there is now some regional government funding in Scotland, Wales and Northern Ireland).
- In Australia, 40 per cent was from central government, 49 per cent from state governments and 11 per cent from local government.
- In the USA, 41 per cent came from central government, 17 per cent from state governments and 42 per cent from local government.

5.2.1 Central government

Central government does not typically provide leisure services directly, but has a coordinating policy function. In more federated systems such as Australia and the USA, central government is only concerned with matters of national interest, such as national sports teams, national parks and world heritage sites. The lead department in the UK, DCMS, is responsible for government policy on the arts, sport, the National Lottery, tourism, libraries, museums and galleries, broadcasting, creative industries, press freedom and regulation, licensing, gambling and the historic environment (see 'Useful websites', p. 136). It is also the lead department for the 2012 Olympic Games and Paralympic Games. Similar leisure responsibilities exist in departments in the Scottish Parliament and Welsh and Northern Ireland Assemblies. Other central UK government departments also have links and influence in respect of leisure policy. They include departments responsible for schools, higher education, local government, health and environment.

Central government makes decisions on national policy and sets out the legal framework for its regional and local networks, its agencies and institutions. It regulates the way local government can act and deliver services at the local level. The legal framework laid down by central government controls how the country is run; its laws apply to most aspects of life, including social lives and leisure, whether inside or outside the home. For example, the law sets down the rules governing radio, television and press coverage, what age you have to reach before watching certain films at the cinema or drinking alcohol in a public house, what standards of hygiene are enforced in restaurants, and a whole range of safety standards for funfairs, rides and slides, sporting events, concerts and festivals.

Central government has a direct funding influence on national excellence in several types of leisure provision, for example in the UK:

- **sport** – financing several national sports centres and, through the UK Sports Council, elite sportspeople, as well as funding for the 2012 London Olympic Games;
- **arts** – financing internationally famous venues such as the Royal Opera House and the Royal Shakespeare Company at Stratford;
- **heritage** – financing major national heritage sites such as Stonehenge and Hadrian's Wall;
- **museums and art galleries** – financing national museums such as the National Gallery and the Natural History Museum (and free entrance to them – see Case Study 9.2).

Discussion question

Consider possible arguments for and against government funding of (1) a national sports stadium, such as Stade de France or Wembley Stadium; and (2) a national performing arts centre, such as the Royal Opera House or Sydney Opera House. How would you expect their operations to be different because of the public funding?

5.2.2 NDPBs

For actual delivery of leisure policies and services, many national governments rely on NDPBs to steer policy. NDPBs are separately constituted and typically run by an independent board of directors, but they receive funding mainly from central government, so they are often heavily influenced by central government policy. NDPBs used to be known as 'quangos' – quasi-autonomous national government organisations.

The DCMS is responsible for over 50 NDPBs in the UK. They are often the target for criticism when commentators are looking for cuts in public spending. However, in leisure they provide vital coordinating and focusing functions for government policy in their sectors. In the UK they include five sports councils (for England, Scotland, Wales, Northern Ireland and the UK); four arts councils (one for each country); English Heritage; the Museums, Libraries and Archives Council; 16 national museums directly funded by DCMS; VisitBritain, which is the national tourism agency responsible for marketing Britain worldwide; and no fewer than ten environmental agencies (see Chapter 8 for details).

There are a lot of NDPBs in the UK because leisure is a very diffuse area of responsibility, and because policy responsibility in the UK is typically devolved to the four countries. In Australia, Lynch and Veal (2006) report over 30 NDPBs at the national level:

CASE STUDY 5.1

VicHealth: building health promotion into sport and recreation organisations

One of the key contemporary rationales for government intervention and support for sport and physical activity rests on health improvement objectives. VicHealth is a health promotion foundation funded by the Victoria state government in Australia. Among its programmes, one which started in 2000 set out to change Regional Sports Assemblies in Victoria from being narrowly focused on sports competitions to being concerned with facilitating community sport and recreation programmes as part of the state-wide health promotion strategy. Casey *et al.* (2009) examined nine Regional Sports Assemblies which were funded by VicHealth to promote physical activity to specific target groups including: linguistically and culturally diverse; indigenous; women; older adults; and young people.

The first stage in the development of health promotion capacity in the Regional Sports Assemblies consisted of awareness raising. VicHealth engaged in direct discussions with executive officers of the sports assemblies; it funded community consultations to plan the implementation of health promotion by the sports assemblies and it conducted a health promotion education programme with the assemblies' staff and board members.

The second stage involved formal adoption by the Regional Sports Assemblies of a programme to promote participation in community sport and recreation. This process was facilitated by further funding by VicHealth to implement the programme. The implementation of the programme involved an initial three years of VicHealth funding and workforce development which helped to reorient the assemblies to health promotion activity via sport and recreation.

The final stage in the process of transforming Regional Sports Assemblies into health promotion agencies using sport and recreation was arguably the biggest test – could the transformation continue without continued VicHealth funding? Casey *et al.* suggest that this is not possible – the assemblies need continued funding to maintain their health promotion role. Nevertheless, this case study is a very clear and explicit example of government health funding used to facilitate sport and physical activity for health reasons.

Source: derived from Casey *et al.* (2009)

- five responsible to the Department of Environment and Heritage, including the Commonwealth National Parks, Reserves and Botanic Gardens and the Natural Heritage Trust;
- over 25 responsible to the Department of Communications, Information Technology and the Arts, including the National Library/Gallery/Portrait Gallery and National Museum, the Australian Broadcasting Corporation, the Australian Film Commission, the Australian Film Finance Corporation, Music Australia, Australian Sports Commission and the Australian Institute for Sport;
- one responsible to the Department of Tourism – Tourism Australia.

There are also NDPBs at the state level of government in a federal system such as Australia. Case Study 5.1 demonstrates how a health NDPB in the state of Victoria, Australia, has influenced sport organisations to take on more of a health remit. It also demonstrates an important government policy link, between sport and health.

NDPBs often provide more of the land-extensive facilities, such as major water resources (e.g. British Waterways, responsible for over 2,000 miles of canals and rivers) and national parks. Non-leisure NDPBs such as new town corporations also have major roles in leisure provision, with powers or duties to assist or initiate provision.

Discussion question

What advantages are there to organising public policy for leisure through a lot of NDPBs, rather than organising policy and strategy in a government department and funding providing organisations directly?

5.2.3 Local authorities

Arguably it is local authorities that have the largest scope of leisure services in many countries. They have a number of identifiable elements and spheres of influence, which are summarised in Figure 5.1. Different local authorities will have some or all of these elements, depending on the location and the size of the authority, its policies and its responsibilities. Many of the elements are combined or overlap; no two authorities are exactly alike in their leisure responsibilities – there are general similarities but specific differences.

Local authorities provide their services in a variety of ways. The public has access to a large number of free facilities, such as urban parks, playgrounds, libraries, museums, picnic areas, nature trails, beaches and country parks. While the public does not pay directly for these amenities, it does so indirectly through local and national taxes. Local authorities also provide facilities where there is a direct payment by the user, albeit often at highly subsidised charges, such as swimming pools, playing fields, golf courses, marinas, arts centres, theatres and sports centres. Leisure managers are essential to all such facilities, to ensure effective use by the public and efficient use of public money.

The importance of local authorities to provision of heritage, libraries, parks and sports facilities is similar in the central system of government in the UK and the federal systems in Australia (Lynch and Veal, 2006) and the USA (Heilbrun and Gray, 2001; Loomis and Walsh, 1997). In Australia, however, state governments are also major providers of parks, sport and recreation, museums, art galleries, performing arts venues and cultural heritage.

While local authorities often look to voluntary and commercial sectors to provide for social activity and entertainment, they nevertheless do provide for entertainment, both directly and indirectly. They provide directly, for example, through village halls, community centres and civic halls, which are often used for entertainment; and urban parks, which are used for events. Many sport and leisure centres contain the largest public halls in their district and are therefore prime venues for public entertainment, such as antique and craft fairs, concerts, exhibitions and large social events.

Local authorities are not simply providers of facilities, they support organisations of all kinds – private institutions, voluntary organisations and even commercial companies – when it is shown that greater service will be given to the public by so doing. The support given is

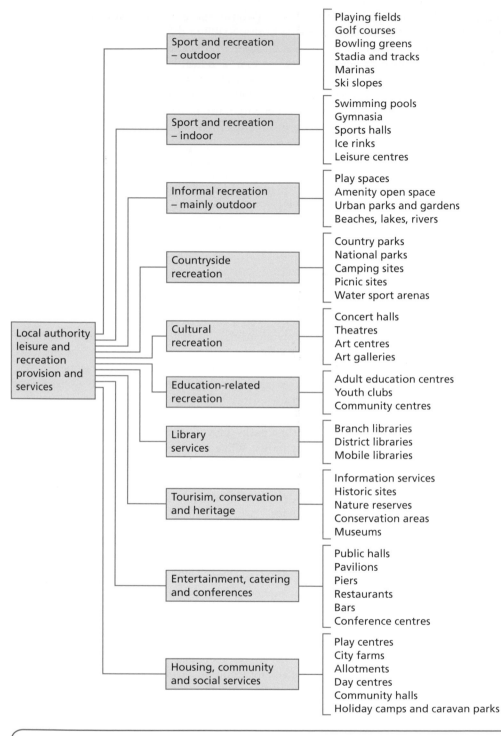

	Sport and recreation – outdoor	Playing fields
		Golf courses
		Bowling greens
		Stadia and tracks
		Marinas
		Ski slopes
	Sport and recreation – indoor	Swimming pools
		Gymnasia
		Sports halls
		Ice rinks
		Leisure centres
	Informal recreation – mainly outdoor	Play spaces
		Amenity open space
		Urban parks and gardens
		Beaches, lakes, rivers
	Countryside recreation	Country parks
		National parks
		Camping sites
		Picnic sites
		Water sport arenas
Local authority leisure and recreation provision and services	Cultural recreation	Concert halls
		Theatres
		Art centres
		Art galleries
	Education-related recreation	Adult education centres
		Youth clubs
		Community centres
	Library services	Branch libraries
		District libraries
		Mobile libraries
	Tourisim, conservation and heritage	Information services
		Historic sites
		Nature reserves
		Conservation areas
		Museums
	Entertainment, catering and conferences	Public halls
		Pavilions
		Piers
		Restaurants
		Bars
		Conference centres
	Housing, community and social services	Play centres
		City farms
		Allotments
		Day centres
		Community halls
		Holiday camps and caravan parks

Figure 5.1 Examples of local authority leisure facilities and services.

basically of two kinds. The first is to make their own resources (not just buildings but also labour and skills) available for use, with or without charge. The second is to make financial grants. Local authorities also enable leisure provision indirectly through planning decisions and generally by acting in an 'enabling' capacity.

Local education authorities are usually involved in support for youth and community services and organisations, for example by making schools available for youth and adult classes, and by making capital and annual grants to community associations and other social groups. They sometimes pay the salaries of wardens, leaders and managers of community centres.

The local authority planning function is crucial to recreation. As planning authorities, they can assist with the availability of land and resources. As housing authorities, they can assist with leisure in and around the home, in streets and walkways, in neighbourhood play areas and open spaces. Local authorities give (and withhold) planning consent. They make decisions on development proposals and give consent for recreational facilities provided by other agencies. Planning authorities have to consider proposals in the context of broad overall and long-term policy. In the UK, local authorities are guided by government Planning Policy Guidance Notes (PPGs) issued by central government. Planning for sport and leisure is covered in Chapter 14.

A political curiosity underlies local authority provision of leisure in the UK. Local authorities have a legal duty to provide leisure opportunities through education, museums and libraries. However, they only have discretionary powers in England and Wales to assist the arts, sports, informal recreation, countryside recreation, entertainment, tourism and youth and community services. Yet many of these services are legal obligations in Scotland and Northern Ireland. This may be an historical anomaly, but it matters when cuts in public expenditure are sought, because it is discretionary services which are likely to bear a heavier share of the cuts. With the inevitable fiscal measures necessary to reduce public debt after the recession, local authority leisure managers are in a difficult position to defend their services against cuts.

> ## Discussion question
>
> Why do you think local authorities in England and Wales finance the provision of sport and recreation when they are not obliged to do so?

5.3 The development of and rationale for public sector leisure services

In the UK the development of public leisure services can be perceived in historical stages, i.e. a long gestation period from the mid-nineteenth century to the mid-twentieth century; post-Second World War initiatives; an enlightened period of new ideas in the 1960s; local government reorganisation of the 1970s, with a surge of new facilities; and government-inspired changes from the 1980s to the early 2000s in the shape of new legislation, including Compulsory Competitive Tendering, Best Value, Education Reform, Children Acts and Disability Discrimination legislation.

The evolution of UK leisure policy is revealing of not only increasing government intervention, but also the reasons for this. Before concentrating on this evolution of leisure policy, however, Case Study 5.2 identifies a contrasting more recent development of leisure policy in a relatively new country, Israel.

CASE STUDY 5.2

Leisure policy in Israel

The first major study of leisure and culture in Israel, in 1970, was sponsored by the Ministry of Education. It led to two government committees considering the results and developing policies for a shorter working week, and culture and the arts. Ruskin and Sivan (2005) identify a remarkably logical and fundamental set of issues driving the policy-makers at this time:

- whether there is need for an explicit cultural policy in a democratic society;
- how Israel can blend disparate ethnic cultures into a national culture;
- how to blend religious tradition with secular modernisation;
- whether the mass media can avoid the international free flow of information, which is dominated by politically and culturally strong nations;
- whether Israel should take on European culture, arts and values, or a blend of this and other cultures;
- what the population should do with more leisure time;
- what cultural opportunities are created by more leisure time and the role of leisure education;
- how cultural policy-makers might help the less well-educated generation to overcome the constraints of age;
- how equal opportunities might be guaranteed in the provision and consumption of leisure.

Consideration of these and other issues led to the formation of leisure policies in a series of workshops with government practitioners. Two significant developments in the 1990s helped to consolidate the leisure policies. First, a national curriculum was developed for leisure education – 'intended to develop in pupils the skills, knowledge, attitudes and values to be wise consumers of leisure time, and have carry-over value for their future as adults' (Ruskin and Sivan, 2005: 148). Second, a leisure management administration was established in the key government-backed organisation, the Israel Association of Community Centres, which coordinates these key local providers of community services, including leisure.

It is the first of these initiatives that is groundbreaking for government policy. According to Sellick (2002), Israel is the first and only country to place leisure education directly into the education curriculum. To do so required the appointment of a National Commissioner of Leisure Education, the training of over 200 teachers in specific leisure education details, and the recruitment and training of a variety of health professionals to develop leisure education courses suited to their areas of expertise.

Source: derived from Ruskin and Sivan (2005)

Public sector leisure is made possible and is guided and constrained by a whole variety of Acts, laws, statutes, government circulars and reports and regulations. Acts of Parliament impose duties or confer authority or powers to provide for leisure. Acts cover such diverse areas as allotments, swimming pools, parks, waterways, catering, clubs and associations, betting and gaming, public entertainment, libraries, licensing, countryside recreation and preservation, employment, institutions, charities and companies. In the UK these have built up over a long period.

5.3.1 The first 100 years: mid-nineteenth century to mid-twentieth century

The origins of public sector leisure in the UK go back to the nineteenth century. Poverty and the unhealthy and debilitating social conditions led to concern in government for the moral and physical welfare of the urban working classes. It also led to a concern for social control, to modify the freely chosen activities of the populace into acceptable forms necessary for political and social progress. Such a rationale is not outdated – there are formal alcohol strategies in a number of countries today with a similar purpose.

The Baths and Wash-Houses Act 1846, from which many present-day local authority leisure departments originated in the UK, was concerned primarily with personal cleansing and hygiene. Swimming pools were built, mainly for instructional purposes but also for leisure. The Town Improvements Act 1847, which allowed local authorities to provide places for leisure, the Museums Act 1845 and the Libraries Act 1850 were all born of a paternalism – a perceived need for public buildings and amenities for recreational purposes – rather than public demand. They are examples of what has been termed the 'rational rec- reation movement' (Coalter *et al.*, 1986). The beginnings of public sector leisure, however, were only permissive, i.e. allowing local authorities to make provision if they wanted.

The Public Health Act 1875 was the first major statutory provision enabling urban authorities to purchase and maintain land for use as public walks or pleasure grounds. Later statutes had to be passed to empower local authorities to set aside parts of such lands for the playing of games. The parks movement was partly philanthropic and partly provided by the local authorities. Parks departments expanded their sphere of authority and took over areas for organised outdoor sports and facilities for tennis, athletics, golf, boating, bowls and a range of outdoor entertainments and festivals.

According to Coalter *et al.* (1986), by the end of the nineteenth century the principles of public leisure policy were clear, i.e.:

- improvement of the quality of life of the urban working classes;
- improvement of physical health, for health, productivity and fitness for war reasons;
- improvement in moral welfare, by providing 'better' alternatives to those available in private markets;
- social integration and control;
- promotion of self-improvement;
- government facilitating rather than directly providing leisure opportunities.

Discussion question

How relevant do you think the nineteenth-century reasons for govern- ment intervention in leisure are today?

Economists identify such a rationale as a 'merit good' (Gratton and Taylor, 2000), i.e. legislating for the provision of services which are thought to be good for people generally and which, left to their own devices, they would not consume in sufficient amounts to benefit society.

The beginning of the twentieth century saw a continuation of government concern for many of these principles. In the Public Health Act 1936 authority was given to provide public baths and wash-houses, swimming pools and bathing places. The Physical Training and Recreation Act 1937 was introduced as a result of unrest in Europe – there was a need for a strong, fit nation. It was the first major Act to use the word 'recreation'; however, support from government had come not because recreation was fun and enjoyable, but on the grounds of social and physical health and welfare, character training and improvement.

5.3.2 Post-Second World War initiatives

The period after the Second World War saw a significant change in UK government policy on leisure. Instead of simply facilitating provision, the government gave considerable funding to the Central Council for Physical Recreation to help implement its policies. It established the Arts Council in 1946, again with government funding. It established several other important NDPBs. Through these agencies it invested directly in national assets in leisure, particularly in sport, the arts, heritage, museums and galleries. National excellence had become another important rationale for government intervention.

Other legislation continued to facilitate leisure provision. The Town and Country Planning Act 1947 made it possible for the development plans of local planning authorities to define the sites of proposed public buildings, parks, pleasure grounds, nature reserves and other open spaces or to allocate areas of land for such use. The National Parks and Access to the Countryside Act 1949 gave local planning authorities whose areas included a national park the opportunity to provide accommodation and camping sites and to provide for leisure.

Education Acts of 1918 and 1944 gave education authorities permissive powers, first (in 1918) to create facilities for social and physical training and then (in 1944) to make it mandatory on all education authorities to provide adequate facilities for 'recreation and social and physical training' for primary, secondary and further education. This resulted in the growth not only of the Youth Service, adult education and physical education (and hence sport), but also of facilities such as sports grounds, swimming pools, larger gymnasia and halls.

5.3.3 The 1960s: an age of leisure enlightenment

Up to the 1950s, governments consistently viewed recreation as a beneficial means towards some other ends, such as health, fitness and moral welfare, rather than as beneficial in its own right. The report of the Wolfenden Committee led to the eventual recognition by Parliament of recreation's intrinsic merits. The Committee (Lord Wolfenden, 1960) examined the factors affecting the development of games, sports and outdoor activities in the UK. The report was a watershed in the eventual acceptance of recreation by Parliament.

The Wolfenden Report and the Albermarle Report on the Youth and Community Service (Ministry of Education, 1960) stressed the need for more and better facilities for indoor sport and recreation. There followed one of the most significant developments in the history of leisure provision – the growth of multi-use, indoor leisure centres, which was then given greater impetus with the reorganisation of local government in the 1970s.

In addition to this growth in indoor sport and recreation centres, youth and community services were developed by education authorities; country parks were promoted by the Countryside Commission, established in 1968; and library services and the arts were also part of this leisure renaissance. The Public Libraries and Museums Act 1964 placed a duty on every library authority to provide a comprehensive and efficient library service, and to promote and improve the services. The arts were the subject of numerous reports, for example a 1965 White Paper (Department of Education and Science, 1965) and the Maud Report (Lord Redcliffe-Maud, 1977).

The 1960s also witnessed a growing realisation that thousands of schools and education facilities were potential community leisure and recreation centres. The Department of Education and Science and the Ministry of Housing and Local Government (1964) advanced a new policy guideline which encouraged dual use of such facilities by schools and the public.

An organisational constraint on the development of public leisure was a proliferation of departments, with different policies, budgets and attitudes. Another inquiry (Lord Redcliffe-Maud, 1969), into local government structures, recommended the streamlining of committees and departments. As a result, a number of local authorities rationalised leisure services into departments covering previously separate services, including the arts, libraries, museums and art galleries, entertainments, parks, sport and physical recreation.

Discussion question

Were the 1960s an age of enlightenment in leisure policy or the signal of a 'nanny state' developing?

5.3.4 The 1970s and local government reorganisation

The Maud Commission into the structure of local government in England (Lord Redcliffe-Maud, 1969) also led to a radical reduction in the number of local authorities. As far as recreation services were concerned, the greatest impact was felt in the 296 non-metropolitan district councils. These councils were now larger and more powerful and had, in many cases, inherited a range of facilities. Reorganisation also encouraged the creation of new facilities, particularly indoor leisure centres – many as community legacies for the old councils.

Local government reorganisation coincided with an important government document which signalled further recognition of the value of leisure in its own right. The 1975 White Paper *Sport and Recreation* (Department of the Environment, 1975) stated that provision of recreational facilities is 'part of the general fabric of the social services'. Some analysts feel that this period was one of restructuring of government-funded social infrastructure for a new post-industrial age. However, another significant change in the late 1970s was that it marked the start of a long-term squeeze on local government spending.

5.3.5 Recent government measures

From the 1980s the rationale for public sector involvement in leisure in the UK changed according to the political party in charge of central government. In the Conservative administrations up to 1997, economic justifications were important, i.e. economic impacts, creating and sustaining employment. This has been termed a period of 'marketisation' of public leisure services (Henry, 2001), not only because of the emphasis on an economic rationale but also because of the main legislation to affect local government leisure provision – Compulsory

Competitive Tendering (see below). From 1997 onwards, the Labour administrations have had a more even handed rationale, continuing to promote the economic benefits arising from public investments in leisure, but also promoting social inclusion.

A major characteristic of public sector leisure management in recent decades has been what is termed 'new managerialism' (Robinson, 2004). This essentially concerns the adoption of commercial business practices such as strategic planning, customer orientation, performance measurement and quality programmes. The public sector leisure manager is no longer just administering a public asset but is actively managing it to facilitate change, improve effectiveness and increase efficiency.

A common feature of the last twenty years or so is a strengthening of the national excellence rationale for government financing in leisure, particularly in the funding of elite sportspeople and facilities but also in supporting arts and heritage venues of national significance. This has not been through specific legislation but rather through policy statements and funding support. It is nowhere more evident than in sport, where considerable funding of elite sportspeople led to significant improvements in UK performance at the Olympic Games, particularly in Beijing in 2008. There has also been substantial UK government investment in new national facilities, including Wembley Stadium, the National Velodrome in Manchester, English Institute of Sport facilities in Bath, Birmingham, Loughborough, Manchester, Sheffield and elsewhere, and, of course, the new sports facilities for the 2012 London Olympics.

Central government has the most powerful effect on public leisure services, even though most provision is by local authorities. A review follows of some of the key pieces of legislation in the UK in the last two decades or so. This is all general legislation – it is not specific to leisure – but it demonstrates the top-down influence of government legislation on leisure provision.

5.3.5.1 Compulsory Competitive Tendering

Two Acts in 1988 and 1989 introduced Compulsory Competitive Tendering (CCT) and extended it to the management of local authority sports and leisure facilities. CCT was compulsory but it was not out-and-out privatisation; local authorities still owned the facilities and had control over aspects such as pricing, programming and opening hours through the contract specifications; and the legislation simply required that these contracts must be open to competition should organisations other than the local authorities choose to bid for them. However, it opened the door to management of some of these public assets by commercial contract companies, charitable leisure trusts, management buy-outs and other management hybrids (Chapter 6 examines non-profit organisations).

CCT was designed to improve financial performance, by local authority teams (direct service organisations) as well as the other management organisations. The early results of CCT in sport and leisure management were identified via a survey of local authorities by the Centre for Leisure Research (1993). They concluded that CCT led to a focusing of performance evaluation on economic efficiency, i.e. finances. By comparison, measures of non-financial performance, such as service effectiveness, were largely absent. In another, later survey of local authorities, the Centre for Leisure and Tourism Studies (1996) identified the main effect of CCT in leisure management as being cost reductions, brought about by a number of measures, including reduced services, staff cuts, facility closures and maintenance cuts. The cost reductions were accompanied by price increases above inflation and increased income generation. This is consistent with many observers' fears of CCT – that it would lead to over-concentration on 'the bottom line' and insufficient attention to social objectives, such as satisfying the needs of disadvantaged customers.

Furthermore, the intention of CCT to introduce competition was only partially successful – initially 60 per cent of sport and leisure management contracts were uncontested and a further

22 per cent attracted only one external bid (Centre for Leisure Research, 1993). The commercial interest in leisure management contracts initially consisted mainly of ex-local authority managers bidding for single sites. However, after some commercial failures and some consolidation, by 1997 commercial contract companies had won just over one-quarter of the leisure management contracts and six of the largest companies managed over twenty centres each – although still over half the contracts were uncontested (Henry, 2001).

Many processes and procedures of CCT are still relevant. European procurement rules require all prospective contractors to be treated equally and are implemented in British law by secondary legislation which sets down transparent criteria for selecting tenderers and awarding contracts. These regulations and guidance include the Transfer of Undertakings (Protection of Employment) Regulations 1981 (TUPE) and the European Union Acquired Rights Directive. In a sense, a contractor is 'taking over' a business and TUPE regulations were designed to protect the employment rights of the existing employees. The 1988 Act also attempted to ensure that no anti-competitive practice entered into the tendering process. Later guidance specified five key principles of good tendering practice:

1 **Transparency** – authorities should require the same standards of performance from a successful in-house team as from an external contractor.
2 **Removing obstacles to a good market response** – authorities needed to demonstrate that a reasonable range of prospective tenderers had been considered.
3 **Focusing on outputs** – authorities should specify the outputs to be achieved, rather than the way the service was to be performed.
4 **Evaluating quality and price** – authorities should adopt clear procedures for evaluating tenders to ensure that the desired service quality could be achieved.
5 **Fairness between in-house and external bids** – authorities must act fairly to ensure that tendering did not put any provider at a disadvantage.

Discussion question

What are the respective advantages and disadvantages of a local leisure centre being managed by a local authority team or by a commercial contract company?

5.3.5.2 Best Value

The statutory duty of Best Value was introduced following the Local Government Act 1999 and came into effect on 1 April 2000. Local authorities, police, fire and national parks authorities were all required to make arrangements to secure continuous improvement in the services they manage. Part of the government's modernising agenda, Best Value championed an entirely new culture in public service administration, which sought to retain the benefits of the previous government's emphasis on efficiency and add an emphasis on service effectiveness. This compromise between what might be seen as right-wing and left-wing concerns has been called the 'Third Way'.

Best Value was structured around six key components:

1 **Performance indicators** – national indicators were developed and each authority was expected to set targets in respect of these indicators and publish both the targets and their performance in annual local performance plans.

2 **Performance standards** – government identified benchmarks for minimum acceptable standards of performance.
3 **Performance targets** – set locally for strategic objectives, including efficiency, cost, effectiveness, quality and fair access.
4 **Performance reviews** – to ensure that continuous improvements to all services are made. Quality schemes such as Investors in People, Quest and Customer Service Excellence also have important roles in achieving Best Value (see Chapter 17).
5 **Competition** – as an essential management tool. Ways to test competitiveness included: benchmarking against a range of alternative providers; contracting out services after competition between external bidders; partnership or joint ventures; asset disposal or sell-off. CCT is replaced under Best Value by Voluntary Competitive Tendering and a more flexible choice of management options.
6 **Audit and inspection** – new arrangements with rigorous external checks on the information provided in local performance plans.

The Local Government Act 1999 identified four 'Cs' as key aspects of the Best Value process:

1 **Challenge** whether the authority should be 'exercising the function now and in the foreseeable future', at what level, and the way in which it should be carrying out the service.
2 **Compare** the authority's performance by reference to the performance of other organisations using a range of relevant indicators and particularly the national indicators specified by the Audit Commission.
3 **Consult** with stakeholders, including providers, users and non-users of the services, employees and elected members at all stages of the review.
4 **Compete** to determine the 'optimal way of delivering services against agreed targets and objectives'.

In summary, the duty of Best Value requires local authorities to deliver services by the most economic, efficient and effective means available to meet the requirements of local communities and to provide ways and means to secure continuous improvements. Case Study 5.3 looks at performance evidence for public sports and leisure centres during the period of Best Value, comparing 2001 with 2006.

5.3.5.3 Education Reform Act

The sport and leisure resources in educational institutions in the UK make up a large volume of the built facilities available to the public. Indeed, half of the newly built leisure complexes of the past four decades are linked in some way with education. Moreover, schools are often the birthplace of our feelings about music, history, travel, art, crafts and sport.

Major Education Acts have each had substantial effects, not only on schools but also on leisure. The Education Acts of 1986 and 1988 aimed to make the education service 'more responsive to consumer needs', devolve responsibility to local levels and reduce bureaucracy. The 1986 Act encouraged greater community use of premises. The 1988 Act included the National Curriculum and local management and devolved budgets of schools.

Most people will agree that children and young people need a balanced education – mental, spiritual, physical and social – in order to become balanced, positive citizens. However, as teachers are required to reach curriculum and attainment targets, less time is

The performance of English sport and leisure centres under Best Value

Best Value policy in the UK, as the main text suggests, is an attempt to find a 'Third Way' – achieving both efficiency and service effectiveness in public services. Because it has been collecting performance data for sports and leisure centres since 2001, the National Benchmarking Service (NBS) provides evidence to demonstrate whether or not these public leisure facilities have achieved improvements in both efficiency and effectiveness since Best Value policy began, in 2000.

Three indicators are employed to represent efficiency:

1 **operating cost recovery** – the percentage of operating costs which are recovered by earned income (from entrance fees, catering sales, etc.);
2 **subsidy per visit** – a measure of the cost to taxpayers;
3 **annual visits per square metre of indoor floor space** – a measure of the extent to which the public assets are utilised.

For service effectiveness, six indicators represent usage by different customer groups, i.e. 11–19 years old; 60+ years old; black and other minority ethnic groups; females; customers using a discount card for which their eligibility was some kind of disadvantage (e.g. in receipt of government benefit); and the unemployed. The first three of these effectiveness indicators are measured by a ratio of percentage of visits divided by percentage of population in the catchment area of each facility. The last three are measured by the simpler 'percentage of visits'.

Table 5.1 shows the 50 per cent benchmarks from NBS for 2001 and 2006, i.e. the mid-points in the distributions of performance scores for each indicator. Whilst efficiency has improved consistently over this period, service effectiveness presents a more mixed picture. The implication is that for these public leisure facilities Best Value has promoted improved efficiency more consistently than improved service effectiveness.

Table 5.1 The performance of public sport and leisure centres in the UK during the era of Best Value

	2001	2006	Change
Efficiency			
Cost recovery (%)	75	80	positive
Subsidy per visit (£)	0.73	0.67	positive
Annual visits per square metre of indoor floor space	74	87	positive
Effectiveness			
11–19 years[1]	0.8	0.9	positive
60 + years[1]	0.5	0.5	constant
Black and other minority ethnic groups[1]	1.2	1.1	negative
Females[2]	59	55	negative
Disadvantaged discount card users[2]	10	12	positive
Unemployed[2]	1.4	1.8	positive

Notes: 1 measured by ratio of % of visits divided by % in catchment population. 2 measured by % of visits.

However, it is important to point out that Best Value is not the only change to have occurred in the provision of public services since 2001. Whilst it has an important influence, so do other factors such as the changing levels of financing of local government services, the changing priorities of local authorities, the obligations imposed by other legislation, competition from other facilities and the changing demands of customers. Therefore the results in Table 5.1 are not just the results of Best Value policy, but of a complex array of influencing factors.

available for extra-curricular activities. In sport the UK government's response has been an objective to achieve a 'five hour offer', i.e. at least five hours a week of sport for all children aged 5–16 years, comprising two hours of curriculum PE plus three hours of extra-curricular opportunities. It has funded School Sport Coordinators to this effect, to promote school sport and school–club links.

The local management of schools poses problems which can restrict a coordinated policy, resulting in different arrangements and standards from district to district, and from school to school. A policy, agreed and understood, between district schools and district leisure departments can do much to assist local organisations and clubs. One-off 'wheeling and dealing' may make for an individual school winning out in the marketplace, but is unlikely to be more than a short-term measure, lacking continuity and making it difficult to develop an integrated, comprehensive approach to the management of community sport and leisure.

It makes sound educational, social and economic sense to provide for the community within existing community structures such as schools. There can be benefits for all parties, but only given appropriate policies, facilities and management. Providing for sport and leisure in these ways needs careful investigation and planning. One of the basic issues with these school–community collaborations is the extent to which the facilities are 'school' facilities or 'community' facilities. Three types of ownership and management arrangements are common:

1 **Dual use** – where leisure facilities have been provided solely under local education authority powers and are managed entirely by the school, but they are open to community use at certain times, this arrangement is termed 'dual use'. The educational budget can only be used for school purposes and curricular activities, so the community use must not be subsidised; it has to be self-financed.
2 **Joint provision** – here the facility, whilst forming part of (or being adjacent to) the school and used by the students, has been financed at least partly by other agencies, such as the local authority. These other agencies are typically involved in the day-to-day running of the facilities, especially in public use time.
3 **The Community School** – a school which engages in non-school activities and in which the governing body has control over as well as the responsibility for those members of staff who are wholly or partly engaged in non-school activities.

Leisure services departments and leisure managers can play an important role in achieving the best from community use arrangements with schools. For example they can:

● provide an advisory service to school governing bodies and/or informally provide help and advice on community sport and leisure, sharing with schools ideas and systems relating to marketing, programming, pricing and operational management;
● achieve levels of parity, for example, in pricing, between different agencies;
● provide joint programmes and/or collaborative programming;

- offer to manage the non-educational use on a contract basis;
- organise courses for leaders and coaches, and courses for those teachers responsible for facility operation;
- in collaboration with the local education authority, Sports Council, Arts Council and the local authority, appoint Development Officers to work with schools;
- promote links between schools and local clubs;
- provide collaborative promotion, awareness and publicity of the facilities and activities offered at the school;
- advise on applications to the National Lottery, grant-making bodies and sponsors;
- include the school resources in district cultural strategies and local leisure plans.

Discussion questions

Should schools be obliged to open their sports facilities to public use, rather than leave the decision to the head teacher and the school governors? Should the national curriculum include components on how to make the most of your leisure time?

5.3.5.4 Children Acts

The Children Act 1991 was a significant legislative change on behalf of children in the UK, replacing in part or whole 55 other Acts of Parliament, one going back a hundred years. This Act affected the management of leisure, play and sport by providers of services for children; providers of facilities; employers of paid staff and volunteers; and providers of information.

Leisure managers in the public sector have to work with other departments, particularly Social Services, and take a coordinated approach. The 1991 Act contains regulations, duties and powers that affect everyone who is responsible for planning, managing and delivering services to children, particularly those to children under the age of eight. The clear direction and commitment behind the legislation is to put children at the heart of, and give priority to their needs in, all those processes which affect their lives.

For the first time in the sphere of play and recreation, the local authority has a statutory duty to provide services. One of the practical outcomes of the Act is the requirement for registration – any person or organisation providing services for children under eight years old, whether in public, voluntary or commercial sectors, must be registered. The facilities affected by the Children Act include:

- crèches; play groups; child minding services;
- before and after school clubs;
- playschemes, outdoors and indoors;
- activities in leisure centres, e.g. mini-gymnastics, ballet, trampolining, football and swimming classes;
- activities in museums and art galleries;
- adventure playgrounds;
- commercial play centres;
- city farms;
- theme parks;
- play spaces in shopping centres and supermarkets;
- holiday schemes in libraries, theatres and sport centres.

Another Children Act in 2004 gave legislative backing to a government programme to improve the welfare of children and young people from birth to the age of 19. This programme is called Every Child Matters and aims to support every child in the UK, whatever their background or circumstances, to:

- be healthy;
- stay safe;
- enjoy and achieve;
- make a positive contribution;
- achieve economic well-being.

The Children Act 2004 created Children's Trusts in each area, through which the legal 'duty to cooperate' is enforced. The Act also requires each area to have a Children and Young People's Plan, to cover all relevant government services, including relevant leisure services.

One major concern of recent times in the wake of the Children Acts is that of child protection. This has implications for all leisure and recreation services, whether in the public, private or voluntary sectors. Whilst there is almost universal acknowledgement of the need for child protection, there is also concern about the level of bureaucracy that all voluntary leaders and helpers are having to be put through, particularly being checked for a relevant criminal record. Getting the balance right, between child protection and burdening willing volunteers with requirements, is difficult. Recent research for **sport**scotland suggests that most volunteers do not mind the process of being checked and accept that child protection is necessary (Taylor *et al.*, 2008).

> ### Discussion question
>
> Should parents who regularly take their and other children to a voluntary club's events have to undertake a formal check of their criminal record in the interests of child protection?

5.3.5.5 Disability Discrimination Acts

Two Acts, in 1995 and 2005, have aimed at protecting disabled people from discrimination by giving them rights enforceable by law in the UK. These rights include rights of access to facilities and services, and rights regarding the functions of public bodies. Service providers, including leisure managers, are now obliged to make 'reasonable adjustments' to premises or to the way they provide their services. The government advice specifically identifies everyday services, including hotels, pubs, theatres and voluntary groups such as play groups.

Under this legislation, it is now against the law for service providers to treat disabled people less favourably than other people for a reason related to their disability. The 'reasonable adjustments' which leisure managers are expected to make include:

- installing an induction loop for people with a hearing impairment;
- providing an option to book tickets by email as well as by phone;
- providing disability awareness training for staff who have contact with the public;
- providing larger, well-defined signage for people with impaired vision;
- putting a ramp at the entrance to a building as well as steps.

Clearly, these measures have resource implications for services that have not previously undertaken them. What is considered a 'reasonable adjustment' is a matter of judgement, depending on, for example, the size of an organisation and the resources it has.

5.4 The links between central government and local government

The examples of important government legislation above demonstrate how much national policies affect local delivery of services. However, as well as legislation, UK central government also partly funds local authorities – which get the rest of their funding from local taxes and from direct charges. As an example, the DCMS/Cabinet Office (2002) estimated that nearly 90 per cent of central government spending on sport and recreation goes to local government, and this accounts for over half the spending by local authorities on sport and recreation.

In return for their major contribution to the funding of local authority services, it is not surprising that central government requires local authorities to conform to national policies and to be accountable for the efficiency and effectiveness of their services. Until recently in the UK, Comprehensive Performance Assessment (CPA) was a system of performance indicators which local authorities were obliged to report. This has recently been replaced by Comprehensive Area Agreements, with a slimmed down set of national performance indicators, from which local authorities choose those which reflect their local priorities. In addition, central government has set a number of Public Service Agreements (PSA) which specify objectives and targets for NDPBs and local authorities.

To achieve greater partnership between central and local government, the government and the Local Government Association (LGA) agreed a set of seven shared priorities for local government, fulfilling a commitment made in a White Paper on *Strong Local Leadership, Quality Public Services* (Secretary of State TLGR, 2001), to define a single list of main aims for local government. The key priorities are:

- raising standards across schools;
- improving the quality of life of children, young people, families at risk and older people;
- promoting healthier communities by targeting key local services, such as health and housing;
- creating safer and stronger communities;
- transforming the local environment;
- meeting transport needs more effectively;
- promoting the economic vitality of localities.

The sport and leisure services provided directly or indirectly by local authorities have a potentially significant role to play in terms of quality of life and healthy communities, and also contributions to make to raising standards in schools and creating safer and stronger communities.

Discussion question

Should all local authorities be obliged to offer sport, arts, museums and other leisure services to their local residents, or should they have the option of not doing so?

5.5 The National Lottery

The National Lottery was launched on 14 November 1994 to raise money for a variety of good causes which are beneficial to the public and enhance the quality of life of people living in the UK. The National Lottery etc. Act 1993 established five areas to benefit from the Lottery: sport; the arts; heritage; charities; and to promote the year 2000 (this is now closed). In addition, the National Lottery Act 1998 created a sixth good cause, NESTA (National Endowment for Science, Technology and the Arts), a national trust endowed from the Lottery but operating independently of government. NESTA's aim is to help talented individuals (or groups of such individuals) to achieve their potential; help people turn inventions or ideas into products and services; and contribute to public appreciation of science, technology and the arts.

The Lottery is included in this chapter on government because it is essentially a government controlled operation. The Lottery is regulated by the National Lottery Commission, which is an NDPB funded by the DCMS. DCMS has responsibility for the policy framework for the National Lottery, but remains at arms length from the regulation and operation of the Lottery. The responsibility for distributing proceeds from the Lottery at the time of writing rests with 16 distributing bodies, many of them NDPBs:

- four national Arts Councils:
  - Arts Council England
  - Scottish Arts
  - Arts Council of Wales
  - Arts Council of Northern Ireland
- four national Sports Councils:
  - Sport England
  - **sport**scotland
  - Sports Council for Wales
  - Sports Council for Northern Ireland
- UK Sport
- Olympic Lottery Distributor
- Heritage Lottery Fund
- the Big Lottery Fund – for improving communities and the lives of people most in need
- Awards for All – for local communities
- UK Film Council
- Scottish Screen
- NESTA.

The Big Lottery Fund is responsible for awarding over half the money raised by the National Lottery for good causes. Since 1994 the National Lottery has raised over £23 billion for good causes, which it has awarded in over 317,000 grants. In 2007–8 it raised £1.36 billion in ticket sales. Out of the total money raised:

- 50 per cent goes to the winners in prizes;
- 28 per cent is awarded to good causes;
- 12 per cent is taken by the government in Lottery duty;
- 5 per cent goes to National Lottery ticket retailers;
- 5 per cent is retained by the operator, Camelot, to meet costs and shareholder returns.

The early years of the Lottery resulted in substantial sums being raised, exceeding expectations. Then there was a substantial drop in ticket sales, followed by a stabilisation of revenues in recent years. At least three clear messages for change have been identified. First, too many grants were being awarded to large prestigious projects. Second, certain geographical areas in the UK were benefiting more than others. Third, certain types of activities and organisations, particularly those that were well organised in terms of being able to handle the whole application process, were being successful and other well-deserving causes were not coming forward or were not getting through the process. To ensure a greater spread of awards, the Lottery distributors have recently been committed to focusing funding into areas not previously funded. Small projects, for example, have benefited from the introduction of the Awards for All awards.

The criticism of awards for large national projects being made at the expense of many more smaller awards for community projects is one that endures, particularly because of the 2012 London Olympics. In total the National Lottery is committed to raising £750 million towards the Games and many leading figures in other good causes have claimed that this means less money for their areas. The Olympic Games Lottery funding also reopens another criticism which was made at the start of the National Lottery – that Lottery funding substitutes for government funding and therefore does not represent a net addition to total funding. However, this is difficult to verify because it raises the impossible question of what would have happened if the National Lottery had not happened. In respect of the 2012 Olympic Games, the UK government is funding considerably more than the National Lottery funds, but without the latter would it have had to pay more?

> ### Discussion question
>
> Is it fair that £750 million of National Lottery funds has been designated for the 2012 London Olympics?

Lottery funding to local authorities can be significant, though it is increasingly very difficult to obtain, as competition for funding mounts and available funds have decreased. Local authorities can apply for direct financial assistance for projects at council-owned facilities and also enable organisations within the district to obtain funding for projects which complement existing provision and fit into local strategies. To harness these opportunities effectively requires a coordinated and focused approach by local authorities and leisure managers. The creation of a leisure strategy (or wider cultural strategy) is an important step towards effective use of total resources (see Chapter 14, Section 14.3.4), and bids for lottery funding would be expected to fit in with such strategies.

5.6 The European Union

Clearly, in the UK, government is complex. It is made even more complicated with, on the one hand, national and regional devolved government 'pulling away' from central government and, on the other hand, elected representation in the European Parliament, being 'pulled towards' Europe. What is the relevance of EU membership to leisure management?

Earlier (p. 125), the implications of European legislation on the TUPE regulations were noted. There is a great deal more. The EU is a source of funding from bodies such as the

Regional Fund, the Social Fund and the European Coal and Steel Community; grants and loans are primarily for areas of deprivation, with high unemployment and in need of regeneration. These funds have been granted to a number of leisure projects in the UK. Another example concerns the Common Agricultural Policy, with the halting of subsidies where overproduction exists. Instead, farmers have been encouraged to convert land to non-agricultural uses, and leisure and tourism provision is a common alternative.

Being part of the EU means having to comply with a range of European standards pertaining to areas as diverse as children's playgrounds and tourism destination facilities. In terms of tourism, Britain has an extensive, often stunning coastline and some wonderful beaches, the envy of many inland European countries. However, many of the beaches in the past had high levels of pollution and did not conform to EU standards. In 1994, only 80 per cent of Britain's 457 designated beaches passed the minimum EU standards. Of interest, failures in 1994 included some of the most famous resorts, including Blackpool, the most-visited seaside resort in Europe. The EU also has other standards for high quality beaches, including visitor facilities. On achieving the standards, the resorts are awarded the EU's Blue Flag. This is an important award to help in the promotion of Britain's seaside resorts, many in great need of renewal.

Travel and tourism is of substantial interest to the EU. Most of the attention of the Committee on Transport and Tourism has been given to modes of travel, improving the effectiveness of trans-European transport infrastructure and the safety of travellers. Recent tourism initiatives recommended by the EU Parliament have included a 'tourism package' to protect consumers' rights, a 'European Destination of Excellence' award (similar to the European Capital of Culture), coordinated information on accessible tourism for tourists with reduced mobility, and certification of websites which provide information and other electronic services to tourists.

In Chapter 10 there is a case study of the emerging interest of the EU in sport (Case Study 10.3), with a White Paper and a Preparatory Action programme. The EU's interest in culture is more longstanding and more significant. Recent EU measures for culture include a 2007 Agenda for Culture, and a Culture Programme which has a budget of €400 million between 2007 and 2013 (see Case Study 9.1).

5.7 Conclusions

Government has a very strong influence on sport and leisure provision, at both the local and national levels. Its main agents for influence at the national level are a range of NDPBs and other partners. It influences sport and leisure not only by direct provision but also by laws and regulations, funding support, and policies which are implemented through NDPBs and local authorities. Leisure managers cannot escape responsibilities and constraints imposed by government. And, of course, many leisure managers are working directly for government.

The rationale for government intervention in leisure began by concentrating on the beneficial individual and social effects of leisure, including health, moral behaviour and social control. It then developed into a recognition that leisure in its own right was good for society – one UK government paper suggested that it was part of social services. More recently the rationale has been more focused on the social benefits (and costs) of leisure, including health, economic importance, excellence, social inclusion and social control. However, the power of this rationale is arguably about to face its sternest test.

As more developed economies emerge from the recent recession, one of the inevitable consequences of the fiscal stimulation employed by many governments to help recovery is that in the next decade or so there will have to be severe cuts in government spending to reduce levels of public sector borrowing. A key question for the medium term, therefore, is how much will government support for leisure be reduced? This is particularly pertinent in the UK when one of the main agents of government support, local authorities, have few mandatory obligations to provide for leisure – most of their support is discretionary.

Some sectors of leisure might be more sheltered from the government expenditure cuts to come. For example, excellence in sport has received substantial government funding in the UK and is likely to continue to do so, with the 2012 London Olympics beckoning. However, the extent to which the 2012 Games will substitute for government spending elsewhere, not just in sport but in other areas of leisure, is a real and as yet unknown threat.

One of the ways in which government spending on, and support for, sport and leisure can be defended is by evidence that it produces a social return. In the past public sector leisure has been criticised for not providing sufficient evidence of what is gained by government support. It will be increasingly important that in the coming years such evidence is collected and used effectively, to defend the rationale for a hands-on government role in leisure.

Practical tasks

1   Visit a leisure amenity or facility which is paid for largely by government. Study the uses to which it is put, the types of visitors and, if possible, the management strategy. With the manager's permission, interview a few users to identify, first, whether they know the extent to which it is publicly funded and, second, whether they think this public funding is justified. Then interview one or two people in the nearby community and ask them the same questions. Draw conclusions about the rationale for and benefits from public funding of this amenity/facility.

2   Find and read some of the media coverage of the 2012 London Olympics and Paralympics (e.g. use libraries and the internet). Do the media show any recognition of the rationale for public funding of these Games?

Structured guide to further reading

For the development of UK leisure policy:
Coalter, F., Long, J. and Duffield, B. (1986) *Rationale for Public Sector Investment in Leisure*, Sports Council and Economic and Social Research Council, London.

For contemporary development of leisure policy:
Henry, I. (2001) *The Politics of Leisure Policy*, 2nd edition, Palgrave, Basingstoke.

For public sector sport and leisure management:
Robinson, L. (2004) *Managing Public Sport and Leisure Services*, Routledge, London.

Useful websites

For information on DCMS policy:
www.culture.gov.uk/

For information on National Lottery distribution bodies:
www.lotteryfunding.org.uk/uk/lottery-funders-listing.htm
www.natlotcomm.gov.uk

For information on the EU and culture:
http://europa.eu/pol/cult/index_en.htm

Chapter 6

Sport and leisure provision in the third sector

In this chapter

- What is the scale and scope of volunteering in sport and leisure?
- Who volunteers in sport and leisure and what motivates them?
- What benefits and problems are there for volunteers in sport and leisure?
- What are the major barriers and incentives for volunteering in sport and leisure?
- How does government interact with the voluntary sector in sport and leisure?
- What are the advantages and disadvantages of charitable status for sport and leisure organisations?

Orlando Kissner/Getty Images

Summary

The 'third sector' contains a very diverse set of sport and leisure providers, including voluntary and charitable organisations and provision for staff in commercial companies. Many employ paid managers, although voluntary organisations are typically managed by volunteers, particularly at the local level. Voluntary organisations are very important for sport and leisure provision, with hundreds of thousands across a range of leisure interests, including sport, the arts, heritage, the environment and young people's activities. They range from small local clubs with a handful of members to large national organisations with millions of members. They bring huge benefits to members but they also have problems, the most important of which appears to be a shortage of volunteers.

Many voluntary organisations are charitable and many charitable organisations rely on volunteers. At the local level in the UK an increasing number of public sector leisure assets, such as museums and sports centres, are managed by charitable trusts, which do not utilise many volunteers. Charitable status brings both advantages and disadvantages.

The relationship between the third sector and the public sector is one which is important but which needs careful management at national and local levels. At the national level the government is interested in promoting the social outcomes of the third sector, because they are important to government objectives. It is also interested in promoting what is termed 'capacity building' in the third sector, i.e. making it more effective. However, there is a sensitive balance to be achieved between supporting the third sector with public funding and attempting to steer it towards a greater conformance with government policies.

The provision of sport and leisure for staff in commercial companies has declined since its high point in the 1950s. This is arguably inconsistent with an increasing concern for corporate wellness – the health, fitness and welfare of the workforce.

6.1 Introduction

Many commentators in sport and leisure refer to volunteers as the lifeblood of their activities. But volunteers, as with any other types of input to the provision of sport and leisure opportunities, need to be managed. And volunteers are not the only concern of this chapter – the private non-profit sector is large and complex. It is increasingly labelled the 'third sector' rather than 'voluntary sector' because it contains some types of organisation which are run by paid staff, not volunteers. Private non-profit organisations are also called non-government organisations (NGOs) by international bodies – one of the best-known examples in sport being the International Olympic Committee.

The third sector embraces any organisations which are not profit-making but also not government organisations. These can include:

- **voluntary organisations** – primarily run by volunteers, although quite a few have paid employees for key functions – for example, managers of larger clubs and governing bodies, some bar staff at clubs, increasing numbers of coaches in sports clubs;
- **charitable trusts** – often run by paid employees, e.g. many trusts have been set up to operate public sector leisure assets (e.g. leisure centres, parks) at the local level in the UK;
- **social enterprises** – businesses operating for a social purpose, often with charitable status (covered in more detail, with a case study, in Chapter 21 – see Case Study 21.2);
- **commercial companies that provide non-profit sport and leisure opportunities for their employees** – financed by profit-making organisations but run for the welfare of employees and often organised by paid employees.

The third sector is important for sport and leisure management because many paid leisure managers are employed in it, particularly in relevant charitable organisations; and many volunteers themselves have to manage the operations of voluntary organisations.

The voluntary part of the third sector is the largest, and the chapter starts with an exploration of volunteers and voluntary organisations in sport and leisure. Volunteers are people doing unpaid work in their own leisure time, using their energy, skills and often their own money, because it gives them satisfaction and because they want to do it. In this sense, volunteering – giving service to others – can be seen as a leisure activity in itself and the concept of **volunteerism** embraces this. Volunteering is often categorised as either **formal**, volunteering for clubs or other organisations, or **informal**, volunteering for friends and family.

Voluntary sport and leisure groups have existed for centuries but not in the number and variety of recent times. In the eighteenth century the coffee-house was, for 'gentlemen of leisure', a social group – a club in embryo. Before industrialisation in more developed countries, recreations were often communal affairs based on seasons, festivals and commemorative events. The sports, dances, processions and ceremonies were within the context of the whole community, as they are in less developed countries today and as is sometimes the case with festivals in more developed countries.

It was the rationalisation of work that led to a separate and identifiable sphere of social life (Thompson, 1967, quoted in Tomlinson, 1979). Unions, factories and schools established their own football clubs; YMCAs and the Sunday School movement created clubs for recreation. Most national governing bodies for sport were also formed from the creation of interest groups of like-minded people. A European Union study of volunteering (GHK, 2010) suggests that in most EU countries volunteering in sport emanated from either a variety of society-led group traditions, such as farmers in Denmark and the military in Sweden and the UK, or government-led movements, for example in France and Germany. One recent exception is the development of sports volunteering in Greece, which only came about as a result of the Athens Olympic Games in 2004 – before that it was not a tradition in Greece.

Historically then, third sector organisations in many countries have had a long and significant influence on the foundations of today's sport and leisure. Today, third sector organisations are important internationally, nationally and locally. Before examining voluntary and other third sector organisations, however, we begin with an analysis of volunteers.

6.2 The scale and scope of volunteering

GHK (2010), reporting for the European Union (EU), suggest that for Austria, the Netherlands, Sweden and the UK the scale of volunteering is very large, with over 40 per cent of adults volunteering. Numbers are also high in Denmark, Finland, Germany and Luxembourg, with between 30 and 39 per cent of adults volunteering. However, at the other end of the scale, less than 10 per cent of adults volunteer in Bulgaria, Greece and Italy. In the UK the Home Office (2003) suggests that more people do informal (i.e. for friends or family) than formal volunteering, although in sport the opposite is true.

Sport is a major reason for volunteering in many countries. Cuskelly *et al.* (2006) suggest that the percentage of the adult population volunteering in sport is 5 per cent in Canada and between 8.2 and 10 per cent in Australia. The EU study (GHK, 2010) suggests that over 10 per cent of adults volunteer for sport in Finland, Ireland, the Netherlands, Denmark and Germany. At the other extreme, less than 1 per cent of adults volunteer in sport in Estonia, Greece, Lithuania, Latvia and Romania. GHK (2010) cite one estimate that the 'labour force' for sports clubs in Europe is 86 per cent volunteers and just 14 per cent paid staff.

Estimates of the percentage of adults who volunteer for sport in England vary considerably, depending on the sources. For example the *Active People* survey reports a sports volunteering rate for England of 7.5 per cent of adults in the previous month. This is considerably below previous national estimates of volunteering in sport, including 15 per cent of adults in the previous year (Sport England, 2003a); 34 per cent of adults in the previous year (Attwood *et al.*, 2003); and 13 per cent of adults in the previous year (Low *et al.*, 2007). The differences are probably explained by differences in the survey methods, the questions and prompts used, and the reference time period for the responses.

In over half of EU countries, according to GHK (2010), sport and exercise is the most popular interest for volunteers. Other important fields of interest for volunteering across the EU are social welfare and health, religion, culture, leisure and education. Table 6.1 shows the scope and extent of volunteering in different fields of interest in 2007 in England (Low *et al.*, 2007). To an extent all of this voluntary activity, because it takes place in people's leisure time, is leisure time activity. However, certain voluntary activity leads to the production of leisure outputs as well as involving leisure time inputs. In Table 6.1 the more leisure oriented fields of interest include sport/exercise, hobbies/recreation/social clubs and arts/museums. However, some of the more generic interests will also include leisure activities, e.g. education, children/ young people and conservation/environment/heritage.

One estimate for sport in England is that there are over 5.8 million adult volunteers, contributing 1.2 billion hours of volunteering a year (Sport England, 2003a). Nearly half of these volunteers are in clubs organised by members, one-fifth are in more informal groups of friends or family, whilst nearly one-third are either at clubs organised at school or in youth organisations. Relatively minor proportions are volunteering at university (7 per cent), for specific sports events (5 per cent) or for disabled sports organisations (3 per cent).

6.3 Who are the volunteers?

In describing the characteristics of volunteers, all volunteers are profiled because volunteering is conducted in leisure time and is therefore a leisure time activity. However, leisure management interest is largely confined to management of volunteers in organisations which produce leisure outputs, so reference is made to specific characteristics of volunteers in sport and leisure.

Table 6.1 Volunteering and fields of interest in England, 2007

Field of interest for volunteering	Percentage of all adults (16+)	Percentage of adult formal volunteers[1]
Education: schools, colleges, universities	18	31
Religion	14	24
Sports/exercise	13	22
Health/disability	13	22
Children/young people	11	18
Local community/neighbourhood/ citizens' groups	10	17
Hobbies/recreation/social clubs	8	13
Overseas aid/disaster relief	6	11
Animal welfare	6	10
Elderly people	5	8
Arts/museums	5	8
Conservation/environment/heritage	4	8
Social welfare	4	7
Politics	2	4
Safety/first aid	2	4
Justice/human rights	2	4
Trade unions	2	3
Other	2	3
None	41	n/a

Note: 1 Volunteers who volunteered at least once in the previous year.
Source: Low *et al.* (2007).

6.3.1 Gender

According to the 2001 Citizenship Survey (Home Office, 2003), in certain leisure fields of interest men are more likely to be engaged than women, i.e. in sports and exercise, and hobbies/recreation/arts/social clubs. The male bias in sports volunteering is common across all EU countries (GHK, 2010) and also in Australia and Canada (Cuskelly *et al.*, 2006). This may simply reflect the fact that male sports participants outnumber female participants. However, Low *et al.* (2007) found that women were more likely to volunteer than men overall, across all fields of interest. And in youth/children's activities (outside school) and environment/animals, women are more likely to volunteer than men.

There are also gender differences in the functions that formal volunteers fulfil. Women are more likely to volunteer to raise or handle money and give other practical help. Men are more likely to volunteer to lead a group or be a member of a committee, to give advice/information/counselling and to provide transport/driving (Home Office, 2003).

6.3.2 Age

Low *et al.* (2007) found differences in the extent of formal volunteering between different age groups in the UK, with 35–44-year-olds and 55–64-year-olds having the highest rate of volunteering and 65+-year-olds having the lowest. However, in terms of regular volunteering (at least once in the previous four weeks) it is the 16–24 years, 55–64 years and 65+ years groups that had the highest rates, and 25–34-year-olds that had the lowest rate. This may be caused by differences in time availability and family responsibilities.

In sport, GHK (2010) suggests that for most EU countries volunteering is mainly undertaken by people aged between 30 and 50; but in a minority of countries, including the UK, it is the 16–30 age group that provides most of the volunteers. In Australia the largest proportion of sports volunteers comes from people aged 45+, whilst in Canada it comes from people aged 35–44. There are no clear reasons for the differences but they may include different age structures in the national populations, different work patterns and working hours, and different family structures and responsibilities.

6.3.3 Socially excluded

Low *et al.* (2007) demonstrate that certain groups at particular risk of social exclusion have significantly lower rates of formal volunteering. These 'at risk' groups comprise certain black and ethnic minority groups, people with no qualifications and people with a disability or limiting, long-term illness. The Home Office (2003) shows that people living in the most deprived areas, measured by an Index of Multiple Deprivation, have a significantly lower rate of formal volunteering compared with those from less deprived areas.

6.3.4 Education and income

The 2001 Home Office Citizenship Survey (Home Office, 2003) shows that people at the highest end of the social spectrum, i.e. with the highest levels of education, from the higher socio-economic groups or with the highest levels of household incomes, were most likely to be involved in formal or informal voluntary activity. GHK (2010) report that, in EU countries generally, people with higher education degrees or vocational training are more likely to volunteer in sport. This bias in sports volunteering may again reflect a similar bias in participation, or it might be indicative of the skills requirements of many of the voluntary tasks involved, e.g. administration, finance, coaching.

The Home Office (2003) suggests the vast majority of citizens recognise that they have rights and responsibilities towards the community. Yet formal volunteering is concentrated within more affluent social groups. The survey suggests that 'more encouragement is needed toward the contribution of poorer, deprived communities, and people lacking qualifications'. However, this raises a key issue of the degree of responsibility which voluntary organisations have to wider social objectives and particularly the social inclusion agenda of government – something examined in more detail later in this chapter (see pp. 159–61). This issue is very relevant to managers in voluntary organisations: in particular when seeking new volunteers, should managers select the easiest option, the more affluent base from which existing volunteers come? Or should they make the extra effort required to recruit from the lower volunteering sections in the community?

6.4 The nature of volunteering

People go to extraordinary lengths and exhibit wide variations of behaviour in expressing their individual and collective needs in their leisure. There are religious, community and welfare groups, men's, women's, old people's and young people's groups, advisory and counselling groups, paramedical and military groups. Some people join clubs and associations that are culturally 'uplifting' or educational. Some join acting, ballroom, jazz, line dancing, slimming, singing, operatic or pop groups; large numbers play sport in groups, sail the seas with yachting clubs and climb with mountaineering groups. Many leisure groups identify themselves by wearing badges or special clothing such as uniforms to create an alternative identity: a leisure identity. Some uniforms identify a way of living, for example members of the Salvation Army, who in their own leisure time give help to the needy.

Cnaan *et al.* (1996) identify four key dimensions in defining the volunteer (see Table 6.2). The alternatives within these four dimensions illustrate the variability of volunteering, with one or two of them challenging the very concept of volunteering, i.e. having an obligation to volunteer, which can occur, for example, on becoming a member of some clubs; and receiving a stipend (a fixed or regular payment, although typically a low figure).

Is volunteering all about good neighbourliness, giving of ourselves for the good of the community? Although they like to think it is, volunteers often gain something for themselves. Consider volunteers on committees of governing bodies or local government councillors wielding power, or coaches (particularly parents) looking for glory from the achievement of their children in a team, and think of the status conferred upon presidents and chairpersons in clubs and societies. Volunteering is undertaken with different motives and in pursuit of different purposes. Stanley Parker (1997) identifies four types of volunteering, each sharing certain elements with one or more of the others:

Table 6.2 Key dimensions and categories in definitions of the volunteer

Dimensions	Categories
Free choice	1 free will (to choose voluntarily)
	2 relatively uncoerced
	3 obligation to volunteer
Remuneration	1 none at all
	2 none expected
	3 expenses reimbursed
	4 stipend/low pay
Structure	1 formal
	2 informal
Intended beneficiaries	1 benefit/help others/strangers
	2 benefit/help friends or relatives
	3 benefit oneself (as well)

Source: Cnaan *et al.* (1996).

1 altruistic volunteering as giving of time and effort unselfishly to help others;
2 market volunteering as giving something 'freely', but expecting (later) something in return;
3 cause-serving volunteering as promoting a cause in which one believes;
4 leisure volunteering as 'primarily' seeking a leisure experience.

> I say 'primarily' because motives are often mixed. Who is to say a particular act of apparently altruistic volunteering does not also provide a leisure experience for the volunteer? Some leisure activities enable people to feel they are doing something worthwhile and serving a cause, while at the same time enjoying themselves.
>
> (Parker, 1997)

Low *et al.* (2007) support the mixed motives of volunteers, with evidence presented in Figure 6.1 of the reasons why people started to volunteer. These responses vary from the purely altruistic (e.g. there was a need in the community) to the purely selfish (I wanted to meet people, make friends), with a number of mixed motives in between. And typically people gave more than one response, showing a mixture of personal motives. In volunteering, people want to retain their own individuality, yet many want to belong to groups. A good deal of volunteering encompasses elements of 'leisure', doing something we like to do, but also accomplishing something.

Motivations to volunteer in sport are reported on an EU-wide basis by GHK (2010). They identify the following important motivators, which they suggest are different from other fields of interest due to the leisurely and relaxing context that the sports sector provides for its volunteers:

- personal interest in a particular club, e.g. parents volunteering in a club where their children play and ex-participants giving something back to their club;
- personal interest in the sport, such that volunteers can enjoy themselves and interact with people sharing the same interests;
- social benefits, including building new relationships;
- social responsibility, e.g. helping to keep a club going and strengthening the community's social fabric;
- acquisition of new skills and experiences, which can be useful in looking for paid work;
- opportunities to participate in big sports events and possibly meet famous sportspeople.

Having started volunteering, many people continue for a considerable time, particularly in formal volunteering. Stebbins (2004) identifies ongoing involvement with a voluntary organisation as one of three principal types of 'serious leisure' (the other two being amateurs and hobbyists). Others label it as 'formal volunteering' and 'constructive leisure'. Stebbins' term 'serious leisure' acknowledges the presence of a serious orientation to leisure. He uses the following definition:

> the systematic pursuit of an amateur, hobbyist, or volunteer activity that participants find so substantial and interesting that, in the typical case, they launch themselves on a career centred on acquiring and expressing its special skills, knowledge and experience.
>
> (Stebbins, 2004: 49)

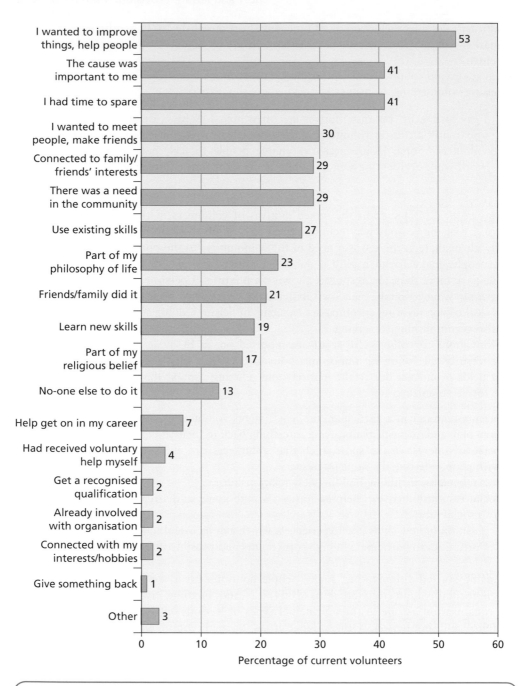

Figure 6.1 Reasons for starting to volunteer.

Note: All current formal volunteers (*n* = 1,351–1,352). Percentages sum to more than 100 as respondents could choose more than one reason. Don't know/refusal responses excluded.

Source: Low *et al.* (2007).

The use of the term 'career' in this respect signifies that many volunteers commit to a continuous engagement with their roles, which distinguishes them from the episodic, occasional volunteering contributions of other more casual volunteers. Many sports and leisure clubs depend on core volunteers of this type to fulfil key management positions. The committed, career volunteers in sport have been labelled 'stalwarts' (Cuskelly, 2004; Nichols, 2005). Case Study 6.1 looks at Nichols' study (2005) of stalwarts in sport. It has a relevance to other parts of voluntary leisure provision, where core volunteers are equally important.

> ## Discussion question
>
> What does the nature of volunteering tell us about the distinctions between work and leisure?

6.5 Benefits of volunteering and problems for volunteers

Volunteering in sport and leisure brings about benefits for both society in general and individual volunteers. One of the main social benefits is the way it contributes to 'social capital'. The term 'social capital' refers to:

> social networks based on social and group norms which enable people to trust and cooperate with each other and via which individuals or groups can obtain certain types of advantage.
>
> (Coalter, 2007)

According to Coalter, it is Putnam's (2000) view of social capital that has most influenced social policy, including policy efforts to engage with and facilitate third sector activities. Putnam suggests that civic engagement and third sector activity improve the efficiency of communities in realising collective interests. Two main types of social capital are:

1 **bonding capital,** among homogeneous types of people who are highly likely to associate with each other;
2 **bridging capital,** between more heterogeneous types of people, who are less likely to associate with each other.

Social capital is associated with community spirit and cohesion, citizenship, neighbourliness, trust and shared values. As such, community involvement and volunteering in leisure play significant roles in maintaining social capital. However, it is most likely to be of the bonding type, rather than bridging, because many clubs are exclusive in nature, bringing 'like people' together through common interests. In an EU-wide survey (GHK, 2010), when asked about benefits of sports volunteering to wider society 71 per cent of respondents identified 'increased social cohesion and inclusion', and 61 per cent acknowledged 'benefits to the local community'. Other benefits identified are low cost access to sport; health benefits from sport; and interaction between different age groups.

Evidence suggests that volunteers are generally very positive about their volunteering experiences, which is not surprising because they are volunteering out of free choice and in principle they can stop volunteering when they want to. The EU study by GHK (2010)

Stalwarts in English sport

In many clubs there are a few volunteers who seem to do a lot of the work. These are 'stalwarts', without whom clubs' effectiveness would suffer. Nichols (2005: 32–3) identifies four main reasons why stalwarts are important:

1 'in maintaining the club structure of sport in the UK and elsewhere – which is essential for participation in team sports and those where there is a competitive structure within a national framework';
2 'an overall decline in sports volunteers, or at least increased difficulty in the recruitment of volunteers. Thus more reliance is placed on those who remain';
3 'the increasing complexity of volunteers' roles and tasks' (an issue also found in Norway, Belgium, Greece and Australia, as well as England);
4 'they are the people who will determine how, and if, the voluntary sector in sport adapts and survives'.

Nichols (2005) estimates from the survey data used in Sport England (2003a) that stalwarts make up just 18.4 per cent of the volunteers who help in sports clubs, yet they gave 62 per cent of the total hours in 2002. Stalwarts are identified as those who volunteered for more than 300 hours a year, not for family or friends but in sports membership clubs. Nearly two-thirds of these stalwarts were in administrative positions – the voluntary sector equivalent of managers. Nearly half of the stalwarts were involved in coaching; over one-third were involved in refereeing or officiating; and 61 per cent were involved in fundraising. Clearly, the sum of these proportions is a total well in excess of 200 per cent – stalwarts are multi-taskers, like many volunteers.

Interestingly, Nichols found no distinctive personal characteristics for the stalwarts in his sport sample. There were no significant relationships with age, gender, having dependent children at home, education or employment status. The main significant difference between stalwarts and other volunteers was how they first became involved in volunteering. Stalwarts were more likely to have started because:

● their children participated in sport;
● they wanted to improve things and help people;
● they were helping with sport at school;
● they had a desire to continue involvement in sport after playing;
● they thought it would give them a chance to learn new skills.

It is easy to take volunteer stalwarts for granted but the Sport England evidence provides a warning against doing this. It points to

a dangerous downward spiral in that certain key volunteers expand the role they take, because of their own enthusiasm and expertise, or because they take over other roles because it is easier to do this than recruit new volunteers or because they perceive it impossible to recruit new volunteers. The role to be replaced is then defined by what the existing or last post-holder did, rather than with reference to what the club actually needs. Thus it becomes even harder to find a replacement for individuals.

(Sport England, 2003a)

Whilst stalwarts are essential for club sport, they also bring management problems, especially when they want to, or have to, stop volunteering. It becomes even more important than normal to plan for succession in such positions, and job splitting is almost certainly likely to be necessary.

identifies a range of individual benefits for volunteers, including satisfaction from making an active contribution to their community, enhanced employability and the contribution parents make to their children's sporting opportunities.

The work of volunteers in society and citizen participation is undergoing change. Arai (1997) believes that empowerment theory can help in understanding this change. She explores the relationship between empowerment, volunteering and Stebbins' concept of 'serious leisure'. She concludes that while volunteering is often in the form of serious leisure, it can have both desirable benefits and undesirable elements such as tensions and power relationships at a personal level and at a community level. Among the benefits community volunteers described are:

- opportunities for shared learning;
- opportunities to contribute to community;
- development of camaraderie, feeling connected to community;
- enhancement of individual knowledge about the community.

Thus volunteering is connected not only to psychological empowerment (self-conception, self-efficacy, locus of control), but also to social empowerment (increased access to information, knowledge, skills and resources; increased social connections) and political empowerment (access to decision-making processes, power of voice and collective action).

Low *et al.* (2007) report large majorities of the more regular, formal volunteers in England agreeing that they could cope with the tasks they were given by their organisation; they felt appreciated; and they were taking part in activities they liked to do. Low *et al.*'s (2007) evidence also testifies to a large measure of agreement about the personal benefits of volunteering. In this national survey evidence, 97 per cent of regular, formal volunteers testified to the importance of getting satisfaction from seeing the results of volunteering, and the same percentage agree that it is important that they 'really enjoy it'.

However, as well as a general level of satisfaction, there are specific issues which significant minorities of volunteers are concerned about. According to Low *et al.* (2007), 31 per cent of regular, formal volunteers agreed that 'things could be better organised', and 28 per cent felt there was 'too much bureaucracy'. Furthermore, the principle of choosing to stop volunteering was contested by 24 per cent of regular volunteers, who agreed that they 'would be unable to leave my role as there is no one else to take my place'.

Sport England (2003a) reports problems for volunteers within sport. Nearly three-quarters of core volunteers surveyed in sports clubs agreed that 'there are not enough other people willing to volunteer in the club', which of course places additional responsibilities on the club stalwarts (see Case Study 6.1). Sixty-five per cent of the same sample agreed that 'increasingly the work is left to fewer people', and there was qualitative evidence to support the difficulty of leaving important voluntary roles when there was no obvious replacement. One of the problems is that sports clubs sometimes have quite a demanding list of voluntary roles – including management, facility maintenance, coaching, supervision, match officials, welfare, fundraising, club development and communications. Another problem is that they are not very active in planning succession for key roles.

Discussion question

Why is there often a shortage of volunteers in sport in more developed countries?

Nichols and King (1998) investigated volunteer leaders in the Guides Association (now Girlguiding UK) and found very similar concerns to Sport England (2003a). The most common difficulty faced by Guides' leaders, identified by 71 per cent in a survey, was 'there are not enough other people to volunteer', and it was identified by 25 per cent of respondents as the most important difficulty faced over the previous two years. The second most common problem was 'increasingly, the work is left to fewer people', identified by 59 per cent of respondents. However, a major characteristic of the Guide leaders was loyalty: nearly half those surveyed had been leaders for ten years or more.

There seems to be a common problem of a lack of volunteers in at least the two areas identified above, sport and girlguiding. This problem is probably connected to the fact that a substantial minority of regular volunteers find it difficult to leave their roles (Low *et al.*, 2007). This changes the nature of volunteering from choice to obligation. 'Obliged' volunteers can be found in almost all branches of leisure activity and organisations. However, too much obligation can at times undermine the positive motives which cause people to volunteer.

Coalter (2007) cites Putnam (2000) in pointing to society-wide changes which have impacted negatively on volunteering, including suburban sprawl, increasing time pressures, greater use of television and other home entertainment, and the privatisation of public services. In sport, such factors impact not only directly on volunteering but also indirectly through changes in sports participation. A decline in traditional team sports and an increase in individualised sports activities such as fitness are apparent in a number of countries (Coalter, 2007), and the latter requires far less volunteering than the former.

Sport England (2003a) identifies a number of societal and institutional pressures on volunteering which have led to increasing problems of volunteer shortage. These pressures include:

- increased choice and competition for people's leisure time and expenditure;
- a 'time squeeze' caused by more time devoted to paid work and childcare;
- greater expectations of higher quality service delivery by members in sports clubs;
- more government requirements of and initiatives for voluntary sports organisations;
- increasingly demanding requirements by national governing bodies of sport, e.g. coach training, accreditation.

What causes people to stop volunteering? There is agreement across a number of surveys that 'not enough time' is by far the most common reason. Forty-one per cent of ex-volunteers gave this as a reason in Low *et al.* (2007); 23 per cent of ex-volunteers in sport blamed the lack of spare time (Sport England, 2003a); and 62 per cent of Guide leaders thought that one of the main reasons people stopped volunteering was 'there is little time left after your paid work'. Clearly, if there is a shortage of volunteers, there is a major recruitment challenge in at least some parts of the voluntary sector.

Sport and guiding share one characteristic which may have made the recruitment challenge more acute – they both tend to recruit primarily from within, i.e. from ex-participants/guides and from parents of young participants/guides. Nichols and King (1998) and Sport England (2003a) suggest that spreading the net wider to recruit volunteers may be necessary, for example using generic volunteer agencies in local communities.

6.6 Barriers to and incentives for volunteering

Low *et al.* (2007) identify the principal barriers to formal volunteering for those who do not volunteer at all (see Table 6.3). Time again is by far the most common response. In the 2001 Home Office Citizenship Survey, 34 per cent of people who did not volunteer or would like to spend more time in formal volunteering cited 'time commitments' as a reason and the next most common responses were also likely to be related to time constraints – 25 per cent cited 'personal circumstances' and 25 per cent cited 'working or educational commitments'. Whereas people's time availability is beyond the reach of leisure managers, the importance of this barrier suggests the need to design more volunteer tasks which are time constrained and not over-burdensome. This might include breaking down roles into more specific tasks and projects, or involving more volunteers, but each with more specific and time-limited contributions.

Other barriers in Table 6.3 are more specific to voluntary organisations and are more suited to actions by leisure managers wanting to recruit more volunteers. The most obvious barrier for such managers to attack is 'don't know how to find out about getting involved', which is a relevant barrier for 39 per cent of potential volunteers, according to Table 6.3. It would be remedied by effective promotion and information on volunteering opportunities. Worry about risk and liability might likewise be countered by reassurances about the low risks involved in practice. And self-doubt about skills and experience is also a target for effective promotion and information, with appropriate reassurance that any volunteer can usually find a useful role; and also careful induction processes for new volunteers.

A potential barrier to volunteering in the UK which has received a lot of media attention is child protection legislation, particularly the requirement for volunteers working with children and vulnerable groups to undertake criminal records checks. However, recent research undertaken with Scottish sports club volunteers (**sport**scotland, 2008) suggests that a large majority see the need for such legislation and checks, and only a relatively small minority of volunteers are sufficiently put off by these procedures that they might stop volunteering. The Scottish research suggests few potential volunteers are deterred by criminal records checks; they are much more likely to be deterred by a general lack of time or the demands of their paid work.

The Home Office (2003) research showed that large proportions of those who did not volunteer or only volunteered infrequently were interested in volunteering or volunteering more. Over one-quarter of those who had never been involved in formal volunteering and 44 per cent of those who were infrequent volunteers expressed this desire. Apart from attacking the barriers to their involvement, what can managers do by way of incentives to attract more volunteers? The most common responses by potential volunteers themselves are as follows:

- If someone asked me directly to get involved (44 per cent).
- If my friends or family got involved with me (40 per cent).
- If someone who was already involved was there to help get me started (32 per cent).

(Home Office, 2003)

These responses are clear signals to managers in voluntary organisations to proactively seek volunteers, use their members as agents in this recruitment process and induct any new volunteers with careful assistance.

Another incentive for volunteers is that there is a growing number of employer-supported volunteering schemes. Low *et al.* (2007) report that 36 per cent of employees identify that their employers support volunteering. For one-third of employees covered by such schemes the volunteering is done in their own time, but for another 20 per cent of such employees volunteering is done in paid work time, up to a specified maximum, and for another 17 per cent volunteering is covered by flexitime. This is clearly a good opportunity for managers of voluntary organisations – forming partnerships with local or national companies in order to promote recruitment of volunteers.

Table 6.3 Reasons for not volunteering

	Applies a lot (%)	Applies a little (%)	Does not apply at all (%)	Base (unweighted)
Not enough spare time	60	23	18	638
Put off by bureaucracy	17	32	51	632
Worried about risk/liability	16	31	53	635
Don't know how to find out about getting involved	12	27	61	636
Not got the right skills experience	6	33	61	635
Wouldn't be able to stop once got involved	7	29	64	632
Worried about the threat to safety	8	19	73	636
Worried I might end up out of pocket	6	19	75	637
Worried I wouldn't fit in with other people involved	4	20	77	638
Illness or a disability	13	9	78	638
Feel I am too old	8	11	80	638
Family/partner wouldn't want me to	5	15	80	638
Woried about losing benefits	3	4	93	638

Source: Low et al. (2007).

Finally, government can also offer incentives for volunteering, for example by special initiatives designed to stimulate it. One example in the UK is Millennium Volunteers, which had over £40 million of government funding between 1998 and 2002 and continues to operate in different guises in different UK countries, e.g. in England it has been superseded by a national youth volunteering programme, 'vinvolved'. Millennium Volunteers was designed to encourage young people aged 16–24 years old into volunteering. Its aims were to increase the number and range of volunteering opportunities for young people; to enable them to get national recognition for their volunteering through an awards scheme; and to bring added value to the community and to young people. By February 2002, there were over 52,000 participants (Institute for Volunteering Research, 2002) and over 10,000 awards had been given for reaching 100 or 200 hours of volunteering in a year.

6.7 Third sector organisations

The number of volunteer-involving organisations is subject to considerable estimation. It needs a clear definition of what constitutes a third sector organisation. The National Council for Voluntary Organisations in the UK (NCVO) estimates there were 870,000 'civil society organisations' in 2006–7 (NCVO, 2009). The NCVO is the largest umbrella body for voluntary organisations in the UK.

Third sector bodies vary greatly from neighbourhood groups to national and international organisations. Several different types of grouping can be identified; some of which are listed in Table 6.4, but the overlaps are many. For example, many uniform groups are youth groups; many women's groups are welfare groups, many young persons' groups do a lot of sport, and so on. Table 6.4 is by no means an attempt at classification; it is simply a means of showing the range and diversity of third sector leisure organisations.

The third sector has a number of national bodies representing almost every main field of social organisation. Leisure has a wide range of national organisations, including those for children's play, sports, arts, heritage, tourism and the environment. Most of these areas and their national bodies are mentioned in their respective chapters in this book. Some types of organisations, such as environmental organisations, have experienced very high levels of growth in membership. The National Trust, for example, had a membership of over 3.5 million in 2009, more than ten times the 1971 figure of 278,000.

Some more traditional third sector movements, for example young people's church groups, have witnessed a decline in numbers. Scouting and Guiding have been struggling with declining numbers of members in recent years, but they are still major young persons' organisations. There are 400,000 members of the Scouts in the UK and more than 28 million Scouts worldwide, in 216 countries and territories; compared with 12 million in 1970 (Scouting Association, 2009). Girlguiding UK is the country's largest third sector organisation for girls and young women, with 575,000 members and 65,000 trained volunteers in 2009 (Girlguiding UK, 2009). It is part of a World Association of Girl Guides and Girl Scouts, which has a combined membership of ten million in 145 countries. Girlguiding UK reports that the association members and adult helpers give ten million voluntary hours a year, equivalent to 5,500 full-time jobs.

Sport was identified in both the National Survey of Volunteering (Davis Smith, 1998) and the 2001 Citizenship Survey (Home Office, 2003) as the largest field of interest for volunteering, although the *Helping Out* survey evidence in Table 6.1 puts it at third largest. This volunteering, however, takes place in a very fragmented structure of organisations, as identified in Chapter 10. At the 'sharp end' of third sector sport provision in the UK are about 150,000 members' clubs.

Table 6.4 Range of third sector organisations

Community organisations	National Council for Voluntary Organisations, community associations, community councils
Children's groups	Pre-School Playgroups Association, Toy Library Association
Youth organisations	Scout Association, Girlguiding UK, National Council for YMCAs, National Association of Youth Clubs, DJ clubs
Women's organisations	National Federation of Women's Institutes, National Union of Townswomen's Guilds, Mother's Union, Women's Voluntary Service
Men's groups	Working men's clubs, servicemen's clubs
Old people's groups	Darby and Joan Clubs, Age Concern
Disabled groups	Gardens for the Disabled, Disabled Drivers' Motor Club, Gateway clubs
Adventure organisations	Outward Bound Trust, Duke of Edinburgh's Award, National Caving Association
Outdoor activity organisations and touring groups	Camping Club of Great Britain and Ireland, Youth Hostels Association, Central Council of British Naturism, Ramblers' Association, British Caravanners' Club
Sport and physical recreation organisations	Football Association, National Skating Association of Great Britain, Cycle Speedway Council, GB Wheelchair Basketball Association
'Cultural' and entertainment organisations	British Theatre Association, Museums Association, English Folk Dance and Song Society, British Federation of Music Festivals
Educational organisations	National Institute of Adult Education, Workers Educational Association, National Listening Library
Hobbies and interest groups	National Association of Flower Arranging Societies, Citizens Band Association, Antique Collectors Club, Handicrafts Advisory Association for the Disabled, British Beer Mat Collectors' Society
Animals and pet groups	Pony Club, Cats Protection League
Environmental, conservation and heritage groups	National Trust, Friends of the Earth, Royal Society for the Protection of Birds, Keep Britain Tidy Group, Save the Village Pond Campaign, Rare Breeds Survival Trust, Greenpeace groups
Consumer groups	Consumers' Association, Campaign for Real Ale

CCPR (2009) provides a comprehensive picture of the state of sports clubs in the UK (see 'Useful websites', p. 164). Typically these clubs are small, with an average of 117 adult members and 107 junior members in 2009, but with considerable variation by individual sports, e.g. golf clubs had an average of 527 adult members, while volleyball clubs had an average of 37 adult members. Sports clubs are not surprisingly very dependent on volunteers, with an average of 21 per club. So the average ratio of members to volunteers is just over 5.5:1. An encouraging finding was that entering the recession both the average number of members and the average number of volunteers increased slightly. However, the average financial surplus per club fell by one-third in 2008, to just under £2,000. Although such clubs are typically not in existence to make large surpluses, they have to remain viable. When asked what their biggest challenges were, they most commonly cited the following:

- recruitment and retention of members;
- finances, i.e. increasing costs and raising enough income;
- recruitment and retention of volunteers;
- facilities, i.e. getting access to the right quantity and quality, or owning facilities which need improvement.

For comparison with the UK position, Case Study 6.2 provides details for sports clubs in Germany. It demonstrates that the importance of sports clubs and sports volunteers in Germany mirrors their importance in the UK. It also shows that different countries share similar problems, particularly in acquiring sufficient sports volunteers in clubs.

In a review of the role of voluntary sports clubs, the Institute of Sport and Leisure Policy (ISLP, 2005) suggested that three themes emerged from appropriate literature:

1　There is an uncertain future for voluntary organisations, because of reductions in volunteering activity; the marginalisation of volunteers by an increase in the number of paid staff employed in voluntary organisations, such as coaches; and less need for voluntary clubs as sport and leisure demands become more individualised (see Chapter 10).
2　It is inappropriate to generalise about all voluntary organisations – they differ according to the type of organisation and the context (e.g. activity, country) in which the organisation operates.
3　If policy for voluntary sports clubs is to be more evidence based, more research is needed on them.

The ISLP review identifies similar issues in a variety of countries, including Belgium, Germany, Norway, the Netherlands, Canada and Australia. There seems to be a consensus on problems facing traditional sports clubs, particularly the shortage of volunteers.

6.7.1 Implications for managers

Study of the nature of voluntary clubs and associations reveals important factors for the leisure manager to consider, particularly managers in other sectors which may work in partnership with third sector organisations. These considerations are also important for managers in third sector organisations to acknowledge.

- All the clubs tend to be, at least partially, exclusive. Many clubs, theoretically open to all in principle, have been able to 'guarantee' their exclusiveness with high enrolment fees or membership systems. If a voluntary organisation seeks funding from or partnership with the public sector, a more inclusive outlook is necessary.

CASE STUDY 6.2

Sports clubs in Germany

In 2007 a national survey of over 13,000 sports clubs was conducted which led to estimates that Germany has over two million volunteers in sports clubs, giving a total of 36.6 million hours. This volunteering, as in the UK, is 'the most important part of civic involvement' (Breuer and Wicker, 2008: 1).

Sports clubs provide a substantial part of the sport infrastructure in Germany – 42 per cent of clubs own their own sports facilities. These include many gyms/fitness centres, sports halls, sports fields, swimming pools, shooting ranges and horse riding facilities. In addition they provide important social amenities, with over 30,000 club houses and over 11,000 youth centres. Thirty per cent of clubs have programmes with explicit health promotion/rehabilitation objectives, in addition to the obvious health benefits from their normal sports activities. Nearly 70 per cent of clubs cooperate with schools in some way.

Sports clubs in Germany are seen to provide an important function for specific age groups: 63 per cent of clubs have opportunities for children under six years and 93 per cent have opportunities for people over 60 years old. Participation in voluntary sports clubs in Germany is typically not expensive. Membership fees are very reasonable – with medians of €3.50 a month for children, €7.50 a month for adults and €14 for family memberships. And over half of the clubs do not charge admission fees (rising to 64 per cent of clubs in the case of children).

As well as volunteers, one-third of German sports clubs employ paid staff, largely in the functions of coaching/supervision, technology/maintenance and management/administration. Not surprisingly, the largest cost item for sports clubs was for coaches/trainers. Other large cost items included the maintenance of the clubs' facilities and the costs of sports equipment and clothing. In revenue terms the largest contribution by far was membership fees, followed by donations.

When asked about problems at their clubs, the one with the highest score was 'adherence/acquisition of voluntary workers', echoing the problems in UK sports clubs discussed earlier in this chapter (see pp. 149–50). For over 4 per cent of German sports clubs it is a problem which they suggest threatens their existence. Second and third most important problems in German sports clubs were 'adherence/acquisition of adolescent competitive athletes' and 'adherence/acquisition of trainers'. So human resources in various guises are the main focuses of managerial concern.

The German study is a good example of how evidence helps to show the importance of the voluntary sector, in this case to German sport. It led Breuer and Wicker to state: 'The contribution of sports clubs to the sports supply of the population is irreplaceable in Germany' (2008: 3).

Source: distilled from Breuer and Wicker (2008)

- Clubs are not static, but changing, organisations. The Wolfenden Committee Report on UK voluntary associations (Lord Wolfenden, 1978) found that 'New organisations are formed to meet newly discerned needs, others die. Yet others change their emphasis or venture into fresh fields {…} There is nothing static about the scene'. The leisure manager hoping to work with or in the voluntary sector should bear in mind therefore that new clubs, in particular, are likely to change in membership structure, and leadership priorities and styles, in the first few years.

- Clubs display similarities in behaviour – they are social groupings. It is important for leisure managers working with voluntary organisations to accommodate the imperative within clubs to keep members happy.

- Clubs are often dependent on support services, particularly the use of hired premises. Local authorities in particular can help by providing support services and premises. The local authority's enabling role plays an important part in this respect.

6.8 Charitable status

Within the third sector there are organisations of different legal status and a common type is a charity. Many but by no means all sport and leisure organisations in the UK are charities. The Charities Act 2006 provides a clear description of 'charitable purposes', which mainly concern public benefit. The activities which are listed as providing public benefit include a number relating to relief of poverty, education, religion, health, human rights, disability and animal welfare. They also include some which are more leisure relevant:

- the advancement of citizenship or community development (including the promotion of volunteering and the voluntary sector);

- the advancement of the arts, culture, heritage or science;

- the advancement of amateur sport – identified as sports or games which promote health by involving physical or mental skill or exertion;

- the advancement of environmental protection or improvement

The Charities Commission is the agency responsible for the registration, regulation and support of organisations that are charitable under the law of England and Wales (charity laws are different in Scotland and Northern Ireland). It has a statutory responsibility to ensure that charities make effective use of their resources. There were approximately 168,500 charities in England and Wales at the end of March 2009 according to the Charities Commission, with total annual income of just under £50 billion.

Health charities take the largest share of charitable income in the UK, whilst the arts, sport and the environment attract relatively minor proportions of donors – between 1 and 3 per cent (CAF/NCVO, 2008). Nevertheless, sports participation events present major opportunities for charity fundraising generally, e.g. in the UK the London Marathon and Sport Relief. The National Trust is the largest leisure-related charity, with a turnover of over £388 million in 2007–8, but the largest single element of its income is membership fees, at £111 million. Members may partly pay as a charitable donation but they also pay for discounted entry to National Trust properties; so they are not entirely, or even mainly, charitable donations.

6.8.1 Advantages and disadvantages of charitable status

There is continuing change in the management of public leisure assets in the UK, particularly an increase in the number being managed by charitable trusts. Organisations such as Greenwich Leisure, Edinburgh Leisure and Sheffield International Venues now have experience of running a wide range of facilities. It is therefore relevant to explore the advantages and disadvantages of being a charitable trust.

Advantages include the following:

- The governing body (e.g. the trustees for a charitable trust) can be built up on a widely representative basis, with external experts from commerce and professions, acting as 'critical friends'.
- Management autonomy, empowerment, independence and control, rather than having decisions imposed by key stakeholders. This compares favourably with the influence of politicians in the public sector and shareholders in the commercial sector.
- The opportunities for partnership are easier to establish.
- Fiscal benefits: charities can take advantage of financial benefits such as tax relief. For example, in the UK they benefit from 80 per cent mandatory reduction of national non-domestic rates (a business tax) and the tax authorities have discretion to allow relief on part or all of the remaining 20 per cent.
- Financial and forward planning: monies can be borrowed and invested with greater flexibility, provided the governing instrument permits it.
- Fundraising: charities can fundraise to support both capital and operational budgets. With further tax relief on charitable donations, they are better able to attract grants and sponsorship than either commercial or public sector organisations.
- Voluntary endeavour and community commitment: as a voluntary enterprise, a charity can encourage a strong spirit of belonging and community endeavour. Even paid staff can feel a greater sense of personal commitment.
- Low levels of bureaucracy, particularly compared with the public sector. Management has executive control, streamlining decision-making.

The **disadvantages** of charitable status include:

- Non-charitable activities are not allowed. Charities cannot undertake certain political, campaigning and pressure group activities. They cannot trade 'permanently', although charities often need to trade in order to provide the funds for the charity to do its work. Some charities set up separate trading companies, which covenant their profits to the charities.
- Raising capital resources is difficult. Often, there is a need to raise substantial sums of money, particularly in starting up a charity.
- Meeting operational expenditure can be difficult. A charitable body, whether run by paid staff or volunteers, can be at the mercy of local councils, needing to approach them 'cap in hand' for assistance every year. A charity can charge reasonable prices, but they should not be so high that the charity endangers its charitable status by ceasing to benefit a sufficient cross-section of the public.
- Constant fundraising is often required. Charities constantly need to raise money and some are having to sell/lease land to help fund projects.
- Some charities make surpluses but care has to be taken in case doubt is cast upon the 'public benefit' of what the charity is doing.
- Staff over-commitment is likely. There can either be too few staff or low paid staff, many giving service beyond the 'call of duty', similar to the stalwarts examined in Case Study 6.1.
- Charity trustees' commitment can be excessive. The key people on the management committees carry a heavy burden of responsibility and are usually busy people, often in paid employment elsewhere and sometimes engaged in many causes in the community.
- Public misconception is a risk. The public now have high expectations of leisure facilities

and services. People may not know, or even care, that a theatre or sports centre is being run by a charitable trust. To the public, it is a 'public' facility.

> **Discussion question**
>
> Is the growth of local leisure charitable trusts mainly due to the fact that they are a way of saving public expenditure?

6.9 Government and the third sector

GHK (2010) report that in nearly all EU countries a variety of public bodies share responsibility for volunteering, including volunteering in sport. However, the relationship between government and the voluntary sport is at its closest in a few countries, such as Germany and the Netherlands, where typically the government is responsible for the provision of infrastructure and facilities, which voluntary sports clubs then use. By contrast, in the UK, according to CCPR (2009), nearly one-quarter of sports clubs own their playing facility, whilst 68 per cent hire their facility – half of these from local authorities, one-quarter from education establishments, the rest from a variety of other facility owners.

Chapter 5 shows how important the partnership between local government and third sector organisations is to local sport and leisure. In many cases, third sector organisations are inextricably linked to public providers and public money. Charitable trusts are often partly sponsored by local authorities and, in some cases, largely subsidised. Local councils support and initiate many thousands of voluntary groups and projects and, in many cases, fund and staff them. The interdependence between many third sector organisations and public authorities is part and parcel of the wide framework of public community services, including sport and leisure.

An example is the financial influence over the voluntary sports sector by the UK government; the principal means being exchequer grants (i.e. direct from central government) to national governing bodies of sport (NGBs), and Lottery funding to NGBs and voluntary clubs. According to the DCMS/Cabinet Office (2002), 22 per cent of exchequer and Lottery grants for sport in 2001–2 were awarded to NGBs, and a further 12 per cent to voluntary clubs, so one-third of £307 million went to the voluntary sector.

Another example in UK sport is that Sport England, a government agency, has promoted 'Clubmark' since 2002. Clubmark is an accreditation system which is awarded to sports clubs which meet minimum operating standards in four areas: playing programme; duty of care and safeguarding and protecting children and young people; sport equity and ethics; and club management. By promoting such a scheme, Sport England can be seen to support and promote good practice in sports clubs, but on its terms – young people and sport equity will not be the concerns of many sports clubs. And the effects of Clubmark extend beyond good management practice – two of the benefits from Clubmark accreditation claimed by Sport England are that many funding bodies require applicants to be Clubmark accredited or working towards Clubmark; and more local authorities and other leisure operators give priority booking to Clubmark-accredited clubs and some also offer discounts for facility hire (see 'Useful websites', p. 164).

The national government in the UK is keen to encourage links between the public sector and the third sector. Government, increasingly, recognises the massive role played by the third sector, particularly in community and 'caring' organisations. Also, an increasing number of public and community services are delivered by third sector organisations on behalf of the government at national level and on behalf of local authorities at local levels – an example being trust management of an increasing number of sport and leisure centres in the UK. More specifically, formal volunteering, encouraged by government and its agencies, has both economic and social benefits – because of the volunteering alone, it provides cost-effective services, and it is a key factor in active citizenship.

A twin track approach to the relationship between government and the third sector is evident in the UK:

1   relying on the third sector to be an 'agent' of government policy in service delivery (and using government funding to 'leverage' the sector's compliance in this respect);
2   seeking to improve the effectiveness of the sector.

In 1998 a 'Compact' between the UK government and the third sector was drawn up after consultation with the voluntary sector (Home Office, 1998). This Compact was initially applicable to central government departments and offices, but with a stated intention to extend it to NDPBs and local government. The Compact provides undertakings by the voluntary and community sector, which include to:

- 'maintain high standards of governance and conduct and meet reporting and accountability obligations to funders and users';
- 'develop quality standards appropriate to the organisation';
- 'promote effective working relationships with Government';
- 'put in place policies for promoting best practice and equality of opportunity in activities, employment, involvement of volunteers and service provision'.

(Home Office, 1998: 7)

A later government review emphasises building the capacity of the voluntary sector to fulfil public service delivery. Building capacity 'is about ensuring that voluntary and community organisations have the skills, knowledge, structures and resources to realise their full potential' (HM Treasury, 2002: 19).

There are concerns, however, about the balance between supporting volunteering and seeking to control it (Davis Smith, 2003). Blackmore (2004) identifies a danger of 'mission drift', with resources in voluntary organisations diverted to delivering funders' priorities. She also warns against the growing audit and performance measurement culture in government, which may spill over into its expectations of the voluntary sector and undermine its distinctive character.

There are also concerns about the capacity or motivation of the voluntary sector to fulfil government objectives. Collins and Kay (2003), for example, express reservations about the capabilities of the voluntary sport sector in delivering the government's social inclusion objective. The ISLP review suggests:

> while there may be a temptation to see voluntary sports clubs as a policy tool for delivering participation and performance goals, to treat them as such may lead to a lack of volunteer commitment and problems in recruiting and retaining volunteers {…} That is not to say that voluntary sports clubs may not be able to contribute to these policy aims, just that considerable care needs to be taken when developing policy that encourages them to do so.
>
> (ISLP, 2005: 40)

Nevertheless, despite such concerns, the relationship between the third sector and the public sector is strong and getting stronger. Any leisure manager in either of these sectors needs to be aware of this relationship, and for positive reasons. There are synergies which lie behind the partnership in terms of strengthening communities and in terms of providing effective and efficient services for communities.

> ### Discussion question
>
> Is the voluntary sector capable of delivering government objectives?

6.10 The provision for sport and leisure for staff in commercial companies

This provision, often termed 'industrial recreation', is the provision of private facilities for the workforce as private individuals. In terms of management, such sport and leisure provision by companies is more akin to the private members' club than to commercial enterprise because its *raison d'être* is employee recreation, not financial profit. A happy and healthy workforce may achieve greater efficiency and output and thereby greater profits, so any financial benefit to the company is indirect and not from the leisure provision directly.

A number of factors have been put forward as being influential in or motivating the decision by employers to contribute capital and recurrent expenditure to sport and leisure provision. These include:

- philanthropy;
- fitness for work;
- reduction in staff turnover;
- company image;
- employee pressure.

The provision of company services and facilities is likely to have been influenced by a combination of these and other specific factors, such as land availability.

Whatever the motivation, the beginnings of industrial recreation provision in the UK started in the latter part of the nineteenth and the early part of the twentieth centuries, with pioneers such as Pilkington, Cadbury and Rowntree. Following the First World War, many industrial clubs sprang up, often associated with religious and welfare organisations. There was a boom in industrial recreation provision in the 1950s, when profits were high and a spirit of altruism led to a spate of companies 'investing' in sports and social clubs.

In the 1960s responsibility for the organisation and management of many of these clubs moved from employer to employee, under the guidance of a sports and social secretary and/or committee structures. Finance remained a joint effort, with the employers often providing for capital expenditure and an annual block grant. The employees contributed by membership subscriptions, lotteries, and bar and vending machine profits.

Company sports and social club secretaries, like managers in the public and voluntary sectors, have managerial responsibilities. As well as knowledge of management techniques, licensing laws and financial control, a company's sport and social manager should also be providing a programme relevant to the needs of the company's workforce.

Over the years, with some notable exceptions, there has been a general decline in the industrial recreation movement. Changes in the UK economy with a decline in the country's manufacturing base, allied to changes in employees' lifestyles and the increased choices in sport and leisure opportunities generally, have led to the closure of many company sports and social clubs. A decline in the number of participating staff members coincided with the increased cost of maintaining the grounds and the indoor facilities.

However, there remain exceptions to this general decline and industrial recreation has evolved into a more contemporary concept – corporate wellness. A number of large corporations in the UK offer employees extensive and often luxurious wellness facilities in recognition of the mutual benefits of corporate wellness to the employer and the employee. Good examples are the Royal Bank of Scotland's health and leisure centre in Edinburgh, and the Adidas Wellness International centre in Manchester. The latter has helped Adidas (UK) to reduce staff absenteeism to 2.63 days per employee per year and win European best practice awards for corporate wellness.

Another recent change in the management of some companies' facilities is to open access to the public, at a price of course. This helps to turn a loss-making staff facility into a more profitable enterprise and moves them out of the third sector and into the commercial sector. For example, Shell's facility in London, Lensbury, began in 1920 and has opened to the public since 1999; it is now a wholly owned subsidiary company of Shell. Another option for corporate wellness is for companies to include corporate health club memberships within their remuneration packages. Exclusive London sports, health and leisure clubs, for example, have a very high proportion of corporate memberships.

The concept of 'corporate wellness' has been gaining momentum – though slowly – in the UK as statistics become more widely publicised regarding the poor health of British workers and executives. The World Health Organization shows British workers at the top of the table when it comes to heart disease and lung cancer. British industry loses millions of working days per annum due to heart-related problems and back-related problems.

People's tastes are changing; more sophisticated leisure experiences are now in demand, boosted by television advertising, the fashion industry, and the concepts of fitness and 'wellness'. Clearly, sports and social club committees within commercial companies and the companies themselves need to be addressing these trends and defining the future role and nature of sport and leisure facilities for their employees. Forward-thinking company executives take corporate fitness seriously and there are enough large companies with comprehensive sport and leisure facilities to make this sub-sector of relevance to aspiring leisure managers.

Discussion question

Is provision of sport and leisure facilities for staff in commercial companies a relic of a bygone age?

6.11 Conclusions

Third sector organisations give people both the chance to participate and the opportunity to become involved in all levels of organisation and management. They also provide the opportunity to serve. In terms of community sport and leisure, managers must be aware that the third sector, more than other sectors, holds many of the keys to individual self-fulfilment, one of the main goals of effective leisure management. It is important, therefore, for leisure managers to understand something of what it means to be a volunteer.

Because third sector organisations are so critical to the provision of sport and leisure opportunities, it is important to consider management issues in them, but a problem is that they are often composed of unpaid volunteers, who in the main shun the concept of 'management'. Nevertheless, any organisation should be interested in providing its members with effective services and not wasting their membership income, so good management is still valid in this sector. And many third sector managers have some significant issues to contend with, particularly a shortage of volunteers in a number of areas of voluntary leisure provision, e.g. sport and young persons' organisations.

The third sector is extremely large and diversified and is linked particularly with the public sector. It is dominated by clubs, societies and associations. As a result of the sheer volume of organisations and numbers of people, there are more people involved in the management of leisure and recreation in the third sector than in the other sectors. Voluntary clubs offer individuals a group identity. Inter-club competition and rivalries reinforce the identity and sense of belonging. Membership can confer status and offer purposeful activity and a sense of importance. Voluntary organisations hold one of the keys to personal self-fulfilment. Leisure professionals need to harness their assets and public authorities should facilitate and encourage their development.

The relationship between the voluntary and public sectors is a very 'live' issue at national and local levels. At the national level, government is clearly interested in the role of voluntary organisations in promoting national policy objectives. At the local level, partnerships between local authorities and charitable trust organisations are growing in number. However, it is important at both national and local levels that the independence of the third sector is both recognised and valued – and not undermined by undue political pressure.

Practical tasks

1 Volunteer for one day with a sport or leisure organisation of your choice. Write a diary of your experience, including:

- the way you were treated as a new volunteer;
- the 'management' of volunteers;
- the attitude of your fellow volunteers to their tasks.

Compare your impressions with those of paid work situations with which you are familiar.

2 Interview a couple of volunteers in a sport or leisure organisation of your choice. Find out why they volunteer, what benefits they get out of it, and how important it is for them. Are your findings consistent with the literature?

Structured guide to further reading

For statistics on the number of volunteers:

Attwood, C., Singh, G., Prime, D. and Creasey, R. (2003) *2001 Home Office Citizenship Survey: people, families and communities*, Home Office, London, available at www.homeoffice.gov.uk/rds/pdfs2/hors270.pdf.

Low, N., Butt, S., Ellis Paine, A. and Davis-Smith, J. (2007) *Helping Out: a national survey of volunteering and charitable giving*, Office of the Third Sector/Cabinet Office, London, available at www.cabinetoffice.gov.uk/media/cabinetoffice/third_sector/assets/helping_out_national_survey_2007.pdf.

For volunteering in sport:

Sport England (2003a) *Sports Volunteering in England, 2002*, Sport England, London, available at www.sportengland.org/volunteering-in-england.pdf.

For volunteering in the European Union:

GHK (2010) *Volunteering in the European Union*, Educational, Audiovisual and Culture Executive Agency, Directorate General Education and Culture, Brussels, available at http://ec.europa.eu/citizenship/news/news1015_en.htm.

Useful websites

For 2001 Home Office Citizenship Survey:
www.homeoffice.gov.uk/rds/pdfs2/hors270.pdf

For 2007 Helping Out national survey of volunteering and charitable giving:
www.cabinetoffice.gov.uk/media/cabinetoffice/third_sector/assets/helping_out_national_survey_2007.pdf

For volunteering in the European Union:
http://ec.europa.eu/citizenship/news/news1015_en.htm

For Sport England's Clubmark accreditation scheme for sports clubs:
www.clubmark.org.uk/

For CCPR survey of sports clubs 2009:
www.ccpr.org.uk/ourcampaigning/uk/Research/Sports+Club+Survey+2009.htm

Part 3

Sport and leisure products and services

Contents

This part of the book has two major functions. First, it introduces and reviews major elements of the leisure industries, providing a comprehensive picture of leisure markets and organisations. Second, it flags up key management issues in each of the markets reviewed. All the different markets have specific issues of importance but many also share common issues.

Two of the chapters (Chapters 7 and 12) cover provision that is more the province of commercial supply and management than the other sectors. Three chapters (Chapters 8, 9 and 11) are largely concerned with voluntary sector and public sector management. The area covered by the other chapter in this part, Chapter 10, is managed by more of a mix of commercial, voluntary and public sector organisations.

The range of markets and industries covered is deliberately wide, because it is considered important for the study of leisure management that students interested in one element should be aware of other elements; and of their shared management problems as well as their different management issues. They are, after all, all competing for the same broad market – satisfying leisure demands. More critically, it is important for managers in a specific industry, such as any of the six represented in these chapters, not to become trapped by their own industry's history; and not to become so short-sighted that they think their specific industry is the only one to offer relevant examples and lessons.

Chapter 7

International tourism

Chris Cooper

In this chapter

- What are the key elements of international tourism?
- What are the basic characteristics of tourism demand?
- What are the essential features of a tourism destination?
- How does tourism impact on destinations?
- Why does government get involved in tourism?
- Why is tourism and destination marketing particularly important?
- How is technology changing tourism?

Summary

This chapter introduces you to the main elements of international tourism. The chapter begins by outlining a simple system of tourism that will inform the way that you consider all other aspects. Definitions of tourism are then considered, stressing the difference between supply and demand side definitions. The chapter then considers the tourist and demand for tourism. Here it is important to understand the motivations and determinants of demand and to see how these influence the global pattern of tourism flows, as well as the market for leisure products.

The destination is the element of the tourism system that energises the whole system and where many leisure businesses are located. Destinations have particular features and are impacted upon by visits from tourists. The chapter considers economic, environmental and social/cultural impacts. The nature of the tourism sector includes an important role for the public sector, though the tourism industry is dominated by small businesses.

Finally, the chapter examines the role of tourism marketing and the new 'services dominant' logic before examining destination marketing.

7.1 Introduction

Tourism is a significant economic sector in the world and one where much of the activity can be classified as leisure travel. Tourism generates significant flows of both travellers and money worldwide and is therefore an activity worthy of academic study. However, in a world that is changing rapidly it is important to provide a disciplined and stable framework to study tourism, as this chapter does. One interesting feature of tourism is its sustained growth and resilience since 1950, despite the recent 'shocks', which include 9/11, the 2004 Boxing Day Tsunami and the 2010 earthquake in Haiti.

Tourism is also a key source of business and opportunity for both leisure and sport operators. Leisure facilities, sporting events and cultural festivals all attract tourists, as well as local residents and day visitors, and the particular audience mix will depend upon the nature of that facility or event – the 2012 Olympics, for example, will attract significant numbers of both domestic and international tourists to the UK. In addition, the synergies between tourism and leisure and sport can be seen in the development of new products such as sport tourism. It is therefore important for the leisure manager to understand the operation of tourism and the opportunities it presents internationally, in order to better manage their businesses and to gain a competitive edge.

7.2 Leisure, recreation and tourism

Not only are the elements of tourism all interlinked, but we can also see that tourism has close relationships with other activities and concepts such as leisure, recreation and sport. For example, most tourism (though not all) throughout the world is a leisure activity and it is important to locate tourism on the spectrum of leisure activities as an activity that

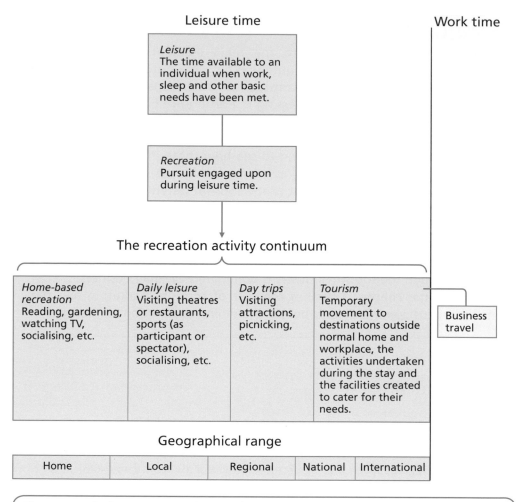

Figure 7.1 Leisure, recreation and tourism.
Source: Boniface and Cooper (2009).

requires an overnight stay (Figure 7.1). Although same-day visits or excursions are a common recreational activity, for tourism to occur leisure time has to be blocked together to allow a stay away from home. In other words, the relationship between leisure activities and tourism is a close one, as we show in Case Study 7.1, on sport tourism.

Discussion question

Should recreational pursuits such as fishing or cycling be considered sport tourism?

CASE STUDY 7.1

Sport tourism

One area where tourism and leisure are closely linked is sport tourism. Attention to sport tourism as both a research area and a product has grown since 2000. We know that tourists were travelling to sports events long before the term 'sport tourism' was coined, but in recent years satellite TV, the use of sport to signify prestige and status, and concerns with health and fitness have conspired to boost sport tourism. As a result, sport tourism is significant, estimated to account for between 4 per cent and 6 per cent of international tourism globally (WTO, 2001). Standeven and De Knop define sport tourism as:

> All forms of active and passive involvement in sporting activity, participated in casually or in an organized way for non commercial or business/commercial reasons that necessitate travel away from home and work locality.
>
> (Standeven and De Knop, 1999: 12)

Later in this chapter we identify three key components of tourism and it is useful to see how sport tourism fits into these:

1 The traveller-generating region includes both the passive tourist who travels to spectate and the active sport tourist travelling to compete or take part in, say, skiing, cycling, golf or fishing.
2 The tourist destination contains the sporting events, venues, accommodation and the powerful notion of sport as a tourism attraction.
3 The transit route region represents not only travel to sport events but also such products as sport tourism cruises.

There is a significant tourism industry that has grown around the concept of sport tourism, with specialist companies offering tailored tours to sporting events, visits 'backstage' to both current or heritage venues and for the travel needs of sporting clubs.

Event sport tourism is probably the best-known product, particularly tourism to hallmark or mega events such as an F1 Grand Prix or the soccer World Cup. These events are an increasing focus for research, especially in terms of their economic impact, as many are subsidised by national and regional governments in an attempt to leverage from their publicity and to boost local economies. In Australia, for example, the Melbourne F1 Grand Prix is heavily subsidised by the public sector.

Ritchie and Adair (2004) state that, as a new type of tourism, sport tourism raises a number of challenges. For example, it clearly overlaps with recreational pursuits such as fishing, as well as adventure tourism such as white water rafting. In fact the dimensions of sport tourism are the same as those that are familiar to students of leisure – work/play; freedom/constraint (Hinch and Higham, 2004). A further challenge is the lack of sophisticated planning and management of sport tourism. In part this is due to the lack of integration between sport and leisure policy and tourism policy.

7.2.1 Definitions of tourism

Tourism is a multidimensional, multifaceted activity which touches many lives and many different economic activities, including leisure and sport, and as a result it has proved difficult to define – the word 'tourist' first appeared in the English language in the early 1800s, yet more than two centuries later we still cannot agree on a definition. It is difficult to find an underpinning coherence of approach in defining tourism, aside from the need to characterise the 'otherness' of tourism from similar activities such as migration. Yet even this approach is under criticism as both geographers and sociologists increasingly believe that tourism is but one form of 'mobility' and should not be separated out. Yet it is important to attempt definitions of tourism, not only to provide a sense of credibility and ownership for those involved, but also for the practical considerations of both measurement and legislation. Definitions of tourism can be thought of as either:

- demand-side definitions; or
- supply-side definitions.

7.2.1.1 Demand-side definitions of tourism

For an economic sector, tourism definitions are unusual in that, until the 1990s, they were being driven more by demand-side than supply-side considerations simply because the industry is a difficult one to define. Demand-side definitions have been developed by the United Nations for use in measurement and for legal purposes. These definitions have been led by the need to isolate tourism trips from other forms of travel for statistical purposes; in other words, an activity has to pass certain 'tests' before it counts as tourism. Such tests include the following:

- minimum length of stay of one night (visitors who do not stay overnight are termed same-day visitors or excursionists);
- maximum length of stay of one year;
- strict purpose of visit categories, including leisure travel;
- a distance consideration, sometimes included on the grounds of delineating the term 'usual environment' – the UN World Tourism Organisation (UNWTO) recommendation is 160 kilometres.

> **Discussion question**
>
> Thinking of a leisure centre manager, how should they go about defining a tourist for the purpose of a user survey?

7.2.1.2 Supply-side definitions of tourism

The very nature of tourism as a fragmented, diverse product, spread over many industries (travel, accommodation, hospitality, retail, entertainment, etc.) and comprising both intangible and tangible elements, means that it is a difficult sector to define. The tourism satellite account (TSA) method is the agreed approach to defining the tourism sector. It measures the goods and services purchased by visitors to estimate the size of the tourism economic sector. The TSA:

- provides information on the economic contribution of tourism;
- provides information on tourism employment;
- allows tourism to be compared with other economic sectors.

For example, the most recent TSA (2007–8) for Australia paints a clear picture of the changing economic contribution of tourism to the country and provides a useful diagnostic tool (Australian Bureau of Statistics, 2010):

- in 2007–8, the overall contribution of tourism to the Australian economy increased – but not by as much as other key economic sectors;
- in 2007–8 the tourism share of gross domestic product was 3.6 per cent, representing a continuing decrease since 2000–1;
- the tourism industry employed 497,800 persons in 2007–8, representing almost 5 per cent of total employment in Australia;
- the major economic contributions from tourism come from long-distance passenger transport, takeaway and restaurant meals, shopping and accommodation.

The TSA shows a gradual decline in the economic contribution of tourism to the Australian economy since 2000–1 and allows us to diagnose the reasons for this. First, over the period Australian domestic travel declined at the expense of Australians travelling overseas. Second, the economic contribution of tourism was inflated in 2000–1 due to the successful Sydney Olympic Games.

The benefits of the TSA are clear – it delivers important data for planning and policy, as well as providing an important conceptual framework for studying and researching tourism.

7.2.2 A tourism system

For such a complex activity, it is important to provide an organising framework for the study of tourism. In this chapter we have adopted the model suggested by Neil Leiper in 1979 and updated in 1990 (Figure 7.2). This model works well as, whilst there are many more complex models available, when each of those is stripped down, at the core are the three elements of Leiper's system. The system considers the activity of tourists, allows industry sectors to be located and provides the geographical element inherent in all travel. It also places tourism in the context of a range of external environments such as society, politics and economies. The major advantages of Leiper's system are its general applicability and simplicity, which provide a useful 'way of thinking' about tourism. There are three basic parts to Leiper's model:

1   **Tourists** – the tourist is the actor in this system. Tourism, after all, is a very human experience, enjoyed, anticipated and remembered by many as some of the most important times of their lives. Defining the tourist is discussed later in this chapter (pp. 174–9).
2   **Geographical elements** – Leiper outlines three geographical elements in his model:
    - **The traveller-generating region** represents the generating market for tourism and, in a sense, provides the 'push' to stimulate and motivate travel.
    - **The tourist destination** represents the 'sharp end' of tourism, where the full impact of tourism is felt and planning and management strategies are implemented. The destination too is the *raison d'être* for tourism, with a range of special places distinguished from the everyday by their cultural, historic or natural significance. It is also where many leisure and sporting businesses are found.

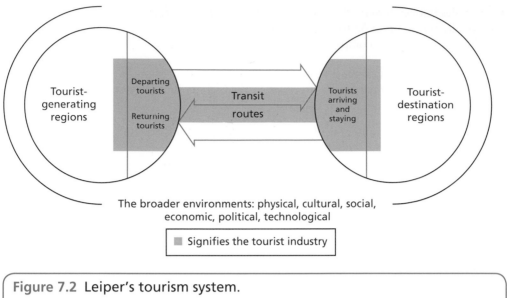

The broader environments: physical, cultural, social, economic, political, technological

■ Signifies the tourist industry

Figure 7.2 Leiper's tourism system.
Source: Leiper (1990).

- **The transit route region** does not simply represent the short period of travel to reach the destination, but also includes the intermediate places that may be visited en route.
3 **The tourism sector** – the third part of Leiper's model is the tourism sector – the range of tourism and leisure businesses and organisations involved in delivering the tourism experience.

All of the elements of Leiper's tourism system interact, not only to deliver the tourism product and experience, but also in terms of transactions and impacts and, of course, the differing contexts within which tourism occurs, as we saw in Case Study 7.1.

7.2.3 The tourist

Tourists have different personalities, demographics and experiences and this has led to various attempts to classify tourists. This has been done in two basic ways, both of which relate to the nature of their trip:

1 A basic distinction can be made between domestic and international tourists, although this distinction is blurring in many parts of the world, such as the European Union. Domestic tourism refers to travel by residents within their country of residence. International tourism involves travel outside the country of residence.
2 Tourists can also be classified by 'purpose of visit category'. Conventionally, three categories are used:
   - **leisure and recreation** – including holiday, sports and cultural tourism and visiting friends and relatives (VFR);
   - **other tourism purposes** – including study and health tourism;
   - **business and professional** – including meetings, conferences, missions, incentive and business tourism.

There are many other ways to classify tourists. These range from simple demographic and trip classifications through their lifestyles and personalities, to their perception of risk and familiarity and postmodern interpretations of consumers and commodities.

7.3 Tourist behaviour and tourism demand

Returning to Leiper's model, demand for tourism is the result of activities and decisions made in the generating region in response to opportunities in the destination region. Leisure managers will find that often a percentage of their market is made up of tourists. Uysal (1998) provides three reasons for analysing tourism demand which are relevant to leisure managers:

1   It is an essential underpinning for policy and forecasting.
2   It provides critical information to allow the balancing of provision/supply and demand at destinations.
3   It allows the tourism and leisure industry to better understand consumer behaviour and the tourism marketplace.

A useful definition of tourist demand is:

> The total number of persons who travel, or wish to travel, to use tourist facilities and services at places away from their places of work and residence.
>
> (Mathieson and Wall, 1982)

The notion that some individuals may harbour a demand for tourism but are unable to realise that demand suggests that demand for tourism consists of a number of components. We can identify three basic components that make up the total demand for tourism:

1   **Effective or actual demand** is the actual number of participants in tourism or those who are travelling.
2   **Suppressed or latent demand** is made up of that section of the population who do not travel for some reason, even though they want to. This may include problems with the supply environment, such as the 2004 Boxing Day Tsunami, which prevented travel to a region, or an issue with the person themselves, such as a disability.
3   Finally, there will always be those who simply do not wish to travel, constituting a category of **no demand**.

Economists view tourist demand in terms of demand schedules – the quantities of tourism that an individual wishes to purchase at different prices at a given point in time (Figure 7.3). Generally, the form of this relationship between price and quantity purchased is an inverse one, i.e. the higher the price of the product, the lower is the demand; the lower the price, the greater is the demand. The demand curve DD in Figure 7.3 can be characterised by a measure known as 'elasticity' – the responsiveness of quantity demanded to changes in price (see p. 413).

7.3.1 Motivations and determinants of tourist demand

There is a considerable literature on tourism consumer decision-making. No two individuals are alike and differences in attitudes, perceptions, images and motivation have an important influence on travel decisions.

Products and services

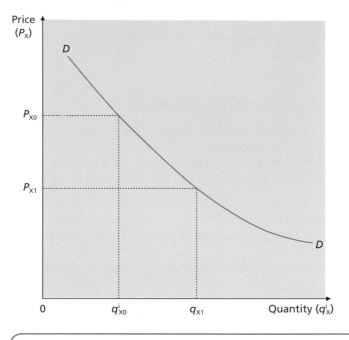

Figure 7.3 Tourism demand schedule.
Source: Cooper *et al.* (2008).

7.3.1.1 Motivations for tourism demand

An understanding of motivation is the key for leisure managers to understand tourist behaviour, answering the question of why people travel. McIntosh *et al.* (1995) utilise four categories of motivation:

1 **Physical motivators** are the most relevant to sport managers and relate to refreshment of body and mind, health purposes, sport and pleasure.
2 **Cultural motivators** relate to curiosity and the desire to see and know more about other cultures.
3 **Interpersonal motivators** include the desire to meet new people, visit friends or relatives, and to seek new and different experiences.
4 **Status and prestige motivators** include a desire for continuation of education, personal development, ego enhancement and sensual indulgence, such as, for example, a visit to a spa.

Case Study 7.2 illustrates a contemporary vision of the tourism experience, which is closely related to the tourist's motivation.

7.3.1.2 Determinants of tourism demand

Although an individual may be motivated to travel, their ability to do so will depend on a number of factors related to both the individual and the supply environment. These factors can be termed determinants of demand and represent the 'parameters of possibility' for the individual. Determinants can be divided into two groups:

1 **lifestyle** – including income, employment, holiday entitlement, educational attainment and mobility;

CASE STUDY 7.2

Tourism and the experience economy

Tourism is increasingly viewed as an experience, differing from manufactured goods when we come to assess its value or approach the marketing of tourism. As technology has constantly improved the quality of our leisure time through entertainment, visual images and sound in our own homes, so we have come to expect a similar level of quality from our tourism experience.

Engineering tourism experiences is the way of the future and it also matches perfectly the expectation of the marketplace. Pine and Gilmore's (1999) book *The Experience Economy* neatly captures the concept. They say that work is theatre and every business is a stage, a critical consideration for human resources in tourism, where front-line workers at the sport event or in the restaurant, hotel reception or lobby shop are always 'on stage'. The experience-based product is different to commodities, goods or services, as the nature of the offering is memorable. The Disney parade, for example, is memorable for young children; it is personalised – the children can relate to their favourite characters; and it delivers sensations to the audience.

Pine and Gilmore argue that there are four types of experience that can be engineered by 'experience providers':

1 **Entertainment** – here entertainment can be added to existing products, such as the old-fashioned aquarium that now has dolphin and seal shows. This 'engages' the visitor, but does not normally 'involve' all but one or two visitors in the entertainment.
2 **Education** – the visitor is a passive recipient of the experience but is more actively engaged than with a simple entertaining experience, because the very nature of an educational experience will change their levels of knowledge or awareness about a topic. Here the concepts of info-attainment or edu-tainment have been used to describe the process. Examples include the role of live interpreters in bringing to life heritage sites such as Sovereign Hill in Australia.
3 **Escapist** – this type of experience is much more about involving the visitor actively by immersing them in the experience. An example here is volunteer tourism cleaning up Everest.
4 **Aesthetic** – with this experience, the visitor is again immersed but does not impact upon the environment of the experience – gazing at the Taj Mahal or the Grand Canyon are examples.

As we go down this list the visitor is increasingly immersed in the experience and participates. Pine and Gilmore argue that the nature of the experience should be engineered to 'transform' the visitor. It is here that the ideas of the experience economy can be of great benefit for tourism. By transforming the nature of visits to, say, sensitive natural sites, managers can change behaviour such that the visitor understands the nature of the site, and therefore is more inclined to protect it and behave in an appropriate way. Here marketing and visitor management come together to deliver the experiences that the tourist desires, while also beginning to change the way the visitors behave in order to protect fragile destinations.

There is no doubt that the experience economy has many important insights for tourism and the leisure sector in general, not only in how products are formulated and engineered into experiences, but also for the workforce who have to deliver these experiences. The next stage of the process – transformation – may begin to change the behaviour of the tourists themselves to help protect the very resource that they have come to see.

2   **life-cycle** – where the age and domestic circumstances of an individual affect both the amount and type of tourism demanded.

Naturally, these factors are interrelated and complementary.

7.3.2 Lifestyle determinants of demand for tourism

There are five key lifestyle determinants:

1   **Income and employment** – income and employment are closely linked and exert important influences upon both the level and the nature of tourism demanded by an individual. Tourism tends to be an expensive activity that demands a certain threshold of income before participation is possible.
2   **Paid holiday entitlement** – the increase in leisure time experienced by most individuals in the developed world since 1950 is well documented. However, the relationship between an individual's total time budget, leisure time and paid holiday entitlement is complex. To enable tourism, leisure time has to be blocked into two or more days to allow a stay away from home.
3   **Education** – level of educational attainment is an important determinant of demand as education broadens horizons and stimulates the desire to travel. Also, the better educated the individual, the higher the awareness of travel opportunities, and exposure to information, media, advertising and sales promotion.
4   **Mobility** – personal mobility is an important influence on demand, especially with regard to domestic holidays. The car is the dominant recreational tool for both international and domestic tourism. It provides door-to-door freedom, can carry leisure equipment (such as tents or boats) and has all-round vision for viewing.
5   **Race and gender** – race and gender are two critical determinants of tourism demand, but the relationships are not clearly understood. Surveys of tourism participation in North America suggest that it is whites and males who have the highest levels of effective demand for tourism.

7.3.3 Life-cycle determinants of demand for tourism

Demand for tourism and leisure is closely related to an individual's chronological age and position on the family life-cycle. In fact the family life-cycle (FLC) discriminates well between types of tourist demand, referring to the stage in the FLC reached by an individual, with different stages characterised by distinctive tourism demand. The stages are:

1   childhood;
2   adolescence/young adult;
3   marriage;
4   empty nest stage;
5   old age.

The explanatory framework provided by the FLC approach is a powerful one. It has implications for the supply of tourism and leisure facilities, for the analysis of market needs of particular population groups (for example the growing numbers of elderly people in some Western countries) and has clearly been used as a basis for market segmentation by tour operators. However, the FLC as outlined above is only appropriate for developed Western economies and even here it is a generalisation as it does not consider, for example, one-parent families, divorcees or minority ethnic groups living within Western economies.

Clearly, for the purposes of analysing life-cycle and lifestyle determinants we have to separate them, but it must be remembered that they all are complementary and interrelated. As a result, some writers have attempted to analyse tourism or leisure behaviours by performing multivariate analysis on the determinants of tourism demand and then trying to group individuals into particular categories.

7.3.4 Macro determinants of tourism demand

Individual determinants identified above can be aggregated to see how they influence global patterns of demand. This can be done using 'STEP Analysis' (Cooper *et al.*, 2008), which analyses the impact of:

- Social factors;
- Technological factors;
- Economic factors;
- Political factors.

7.3.4.1 Social factors

Population density, distribution and degree of urbanisation of a country are important influences on tourism demand. Social changes since the Second World War in the developed world have changed travel demand patterns. Most Western countries are experiencing a slowing of the birth rate, with some having projections of population decline. This, combined with extensions in life expectancy, has created an ageing population. The consequent impact on demand is for greater tourism participation, but in particular forms of tourism such as domestic travel and short breaks.

7.3.4.2 Technological factors

Technology has been a major enabling factor in terms of converting suppressed demand into effective demand. This is particularly the case for transport technology, where the development of the jet engine in the late 1950s gave aircraft both speed and range and stimulated the development of a variety of tourism products to meet pent-up demand for international travel. Developments in aircraft technology have continued but so has the level of refinement of, and access to, the motor car. Similarly, the development of information technology, and, in particular, the internet and mobile technology, is a critical enabling factor in terms of tourism demand.

7.3.4.3 Economic factors

A society's level of economic development is a major determinant of the magnitude of tourist demand because the economy influences so many critical, and interrelated, factors. One approach is to consider a simple division of world economies into the affluent 'north', where the countries are major generators and recipients of both international and domestic tourism, and the poorer 'south'. In the latter, some countries are becoming generators of international tourism but mostly tourism is domestic, often supplemented by an inbound flow of international tourists.

7.3.4.4 Political factors

Politics affects travel propensities in a variety of ways. For example, the degree of government involvement in promoting and providing facilities for tourism depends upon the political complexion of the government. Governments that support the free market try to create an environment in which the tourism industries can flourish, rather than the administration being directly involved in tourism itself. Socialist administrations, on the other hand, encourage the involvement of the government in tourism and, through 'social tourism', often provide opportunities for the 'disadvantaged' to participate in tourism. This was common in the former socialist regimes in the Eastern European countries of Romania and Bulgaria, for example.

7.3.5 The scope of international tourism

The determinants of tourist demand identified above, allied to the characteristics of the mosaic of tourism destinations around the world, combine to produce the global rhythms and patterns of tourism. Understanding these global patterns of international tourism demand is essential to the successful marketing and development of tourism destinations and leisure businesses. The UN World Tourism Organisation has an impressive collection of statistics on international tourism, allowing us to trace the development of international demand (see 'Useful websites', p. 196).

The end of the Second World War represented the beginning of a remarkable period of growth for international tourism, with an annual average growth rate approaching 7 per cent for the second half of the twentieth century (Table 7.1). Until the early years of the twenty-first century, international tourism was remarkably resilient to factors that might have been expected to depress growth – recession, oil crises, wars and terrorism. Until 9/11, tourist demand globally demonstrated predictable growth and stable regional patterns. Although the aggregate effect of 9/11 was to only depress international arrivals by 4 million between 2000 and 2001, it heralded a new era of uncertainty in tourism markets. In 2008, stability was further disrupted as the world entered an unprecedented period of economic turbulence.

In addition to the historical trend, we can also identify a shift in the spatial pattern of international tourism demand, away from the dominance of Europe as a destination and towards the Asia/Pacific region – fuelled by a desire for long-haul travel, a maturing tourism product in the region and regional economic growth in Asia. For the future, the UN World

Table 7.1 International tourism arrivals: the historical trend

Year	International tourism arrivals (millions)
1950	25.3
1960	69.3
1970	159.7
1980	284.8
1985	321.2
1990	454.8
1995	567.0
2000	696.8
2001	692.6
2008	921.0

Source: UNWTO, at www.unwto.org

Tourism Organisation forecasts suggest that international tourism will reach 1.5 billion international arrivals in 2020 and that countries such as China will be dominant generators of international travel both within the Asia-Pacific region and beyond.

> ### Discussion question
>
> What are the main reasons why European countries such as Germany and Spain generate large numbers of international tourists compared to African countries such as Nigeria or Kenya?

7.4 The tourist destination

The destination energises Leiper's tourism system by providing the 'hook' that generates demand. It brings together all aspects of tourism – demand, transportation, supply and marketing in a common framework. While destinations are very varied, from beaches to cities or mountains to deserts, we can identify four common features of most destinations:

1 **Destinations are amalgams** – all the elements of a destination (attractions, transportation and support functions) have to be present for the destination to function. If, say, there is an attraction but no accommodation, then tourism will not occur.
2 **Destinations are cultural appraisals** – visitors have to perceive the destination as a worthwhile place to visit and these perceptions change over history. In Victorian times, for example, the Parisian sewers were a major attraction.
3 **Destinations are inseparable** – tourism is produced where it is consumed. In other words, tourists have to be physically present at the destination for tourism to occur. Hence there is an impact of those tourists upon the destination.
4 **Destinations are used not just by tourists** but also by many other groups, such as, say agriculture, and so multiple use has to be managed.

The components of a destination are:

- attractions, which can be manmade, natural or events;
- amenities such as retail;
- food and beverage;
- accommodation;
- transportation both to the destination and within it;
- destination organisations such as tourist boards.

Here, we must make the important distinction between attractions and support services. Attractions generate the visit to a destination, while support services and facilities are also essential for tourism to function at the destination; but support services would not exist without attractions. A particular focus of these components is the resort, such as Mexico's Acapulco. A resort is a destination that receives large numbers of tourists and one that has developed particular characteristics, such as a recreational business district where many of the tourism facilities are located. All resorts are dependent upon the revenue generated by tourism.

Another way of viewing the components of destinations is by looking at the fact that they comprise a mosaic of different actors that we can term stakeholders. A truly sustainable destination will recognise that it must satisfy all of its stakeholders in the long term.

This can be achieved by a strategic planning approach that balances a marketing orientation focused on tourists with a planning orientation focused on the needs of local people. In every destination there are several stakeholders, who have a wide range of both compatible and conflicting interests:

● The host community is the most important stakeholder as they live and work at the destination and provide the local resources to visitors.
● Tourists are looking for a satisfying experience, through properly segmented and developed products.
● The tourism and leisure businesses and other organisations are to a large extent responsible for the existing development of tourism and the delivery of the tourism product.
● The public sector sees tourism as a means to increase incomes, stimulate regional development and generate employment.
● Other stakeholders include pressure groups and chambers of commerce.

As markets and suppliers develop and change, destinations have had to respond to this in terms of their tourist facilities and services, for example through adaptation to climate change. A more formalised representation of this idea of destination evolution is expressed by Butler's (1980) tourist area life-cycle (TALC) (Figure 7.4). This states that destinations go through a cycle of evolution similar to the life-cycle of a product, where sales change as the product evolves through the various stages. Simply, numbers of visitors replace sales of a product. The broad stages are:

1 launch/discovery, e.g. Antarctica;
2 development, e.g. resorts in the Middle East;
3 maturity, e.g. Spanish coastal resorts;
4 decline, e.g. seaside resorts of northern Europe.

7.4.1 Consequences of tourism at the destination

The fact that tourism is produced where it is consumed means that visitors impact upon destinations and may change them. Here, the issue of carrying capacity is obviously key and

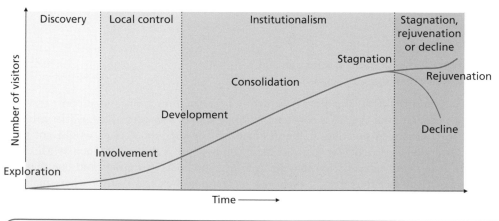

Figure 7.4 The tourism area life-cycle.
Source: Butler (1980).

we discuss this below (see pp. 184–6). Tourism is often a scapegoat for negative changes at the destination, such as the environmental degradation of the Spanish coast or the social change experienced in Cypriot villages. As a result, assessing the consequences of tourism at the destination is complex. This is also because we often do not have an accurate measure of the destination before tourism arrived and other variables are often at play as well as tourism. Measurement of the consequences of tourism is important but traditionally the economic consequences of tourism have proved easier to measure than, say, social or environmental consequences. We can think of the consequences of tourism at the destination in three main areas, although contemporary practice now views the destination as a total system and explores the linkages between these three areas.

7.4.1.1 Economic consequences

Traditionally the economic consequences of tourism have been dominant, not only because they are easier to quantify, but also because they tend to paint tourism in a positive light. The main technique used is known as 'the tourism multiplier', which represents the concept of a dynamic economy such that tourist spending, on, say, a mega sporting event, circulates and 'multiplies' through the economy to generate a greater benefit for the economy than the initial spend. The positive consequences of tourism for a destination economy include generation of income, generation of employment and economic development. As a result, governments often support tourism as a means to stimulate economies and support initiatives such as poverty reduction. However, there are also negative economic consequences of tourism at the destination, which include the danger of overdependence on tourism as a sector, opportunity costs of developing tourism as opposed to say health or education, and the risk of price inflation.

7.4.1.2 Environmental consequences

Since the post-war environmental movement, tourism has been seen as in conflict with the environment. This led to strategies to develop low impact forms of tourism such as ecotourism. Despite tourism being seen as a problem for the environment, in fact it can bring many positive aspects. These include financial support for environmental initiatives such as national parks and conservation, the use of tourism as a powerful medium of environmental education, and tourism leaving a valuable legacy of resort landscapes and re-use of otherwise redundant buildings, as, for example, on the redeveloped harbour side in Cape Town. Nonetheless, tourism does bring problems to the environment in terms of impacts on:

- **climate change** – tourism is estimated to account for 5 per cent of the world's carbon emissions, mainly from air travel and accommodation operations;
- **flora** – through trampling and other impacts;
- fauna – through wildlife viewing, hunting and poaching;
- **water supply and energy** – tourists are major users of water and energy at the destination, tending to use more resources when they are away from home;
- **land use** – through loss of biodiversity;
- **the built environment** – through poor quality development.

Environmental impact assessment is a technique which provides evidence with which to plan to lessen the potential impact of a development. Environmental auditing helps to manage impacts once the development is operating, to try to ensure that tourism development has a minimal impact on the destination (see, for example, Goodall, 2003).

7.4.1.3 Social and cultural consequences

Realisation that tourism has consequences for both the host community and their culture at the destination came rather late in relation to the development of tourism. The main mechanism for these consequences is through the meeting of the host and the guest – known as 'the encounter'. Even in developed countries such as, say, Spain, the encounter is inherently unequal, with the host often serving the tourist, who in turn is seen as affluent and at leisure. Encounters where host and guest meet casually to discuss issues of the day are seen as beneficial but are rare. A particular feature of the encounter is known as the 'demonstration effect', where the host copies aspects of the tourists' behaviour and culture, as seen, for example, in Caribbean islands, where the local population has been exposed to American tourists, leading to what has been called 'Coca-Cola-isation'.

There is a view that the intermingling of people and culture through tourism can be beneficial in terms of learning about others and can promote peace. However, an alternative view is that this intermingling brings about changes in the host culture through an asymmetric borrowing process, as we can see in the Pacific islands resorts. Here weaker cultures borrow from stronger ones and as a consequence change through a process of acculturation. Culture can also become commodified as festivals or objects are sold to visitors, or local languages are displaced. The host society can also be irreversibly altered by tourism through changing power structures, shifts in the balance of family structures and the introduction of undesirable activities such as gambling, crime or sex tourism.

Many of these impacts are particularly relevant to less developed countries. Case Study 7.3 examines the role tourism can play in tackling poverty in such countries.

7.4.2 The sustainable destination

A tourist destination can be effective only if careful planning and management deliver a sustainable tourism product. In so doing it is important to ensure that one or more of the components does not surge ahead of the others, as occurred, for example, in Byron Bay, Australia, where accommodation provision outstripped the resort's ability to supply clean water or sanitation. The concept of sustainability demands a long-term view of tourism, to ensure that consumption of tourism does not exceed the ability of a host destination to provide for future tourists. In other words, it represents a trade-off between present and future needs. For tourism in the past, sustainability has been a low priority compared with the short-term drive for profitability and growth. However, with pressure growing for a more responsible tourism industry, there are serious initiatives to ensure sustainability. These include development of sustainability indicators and eco-labelling of tourism products such as accommodation. Increasingly for destinations, quadruple bottom-line sustainability is needed – environmental, social/cultural, economic and low carbon. To understand how to deliver such a sustainable tourism destination, three key concepts need to be considered:

1 **Carrying capacity** – this is a pivotal concept, intervening in the relationship between the visitor and the destination. Mathieson and Wall define it as:

> The maximum number [of visitors] who can use a site without an unacceptable deterioration in the physical environment and without an unacceptable decline in the quality of experience gained by visitors.

> (Mathieson and Wall, 1982: 21)

CASE STUDY 7.3

Pro-poor tourism

One of the key issues in the twenty-first century will be the development of strategies to tackle poverty. Tourism has the potential to help in alleviating poverty by providing 'sustainable livelihoods' for the poor in the developing world.

Poverty reduction tends to focus on income-based measures of poverty, with the UN viewing poverty as anyone living on less than US$1 per day. However, development agencies have increasingly realised that poverty is multidimensional and can be thought of as depriving individuals of capability – in other words a person is poor if they lack both income and basic capabilities. The majority of the world's poor live in Asia, although the most extreme poverty rates are in sub-Saharan Africa.

The use of tourism to reduce poverty is sometimes termed 'pro-poor tourism' (PPT). PPT is an approach to tourism development aimed at poverty reduction rather than being a specific product. It aims to 'tilt' tourism towards benefiting the poor and can be defined as 'tourism that results in increased net benefits for poor people'. Tourism brings a number of benefits as a sector for pro-poor development:

- Tourism is produced where it is consumed – the tourist has to visit the destination, allowing opportunities for economic gain.
- Tourism is labour intensive and employs a high percentage of women.
- In poorer parts of the world, tourism is naturally attracted to remote, peripheral areas where other economic options are limited.
- Tourism is a significant and leading source of income and employment in the developing and least-developed countries.

It is essential that PPT strategies are implemented at the local level. Ashley *et al.* (2000) identify three types of pro-poor tourism strategies:

1 **Strategies focused on economic benefits** – these include:
   – local job creation to deliver a measure of security in household income;
   – gap filling between other forms of income, for example in non-harvest times, as found in India;
   – small business opportunities in the tourism market, directly and indirectly supplying tourists with goods such as handicrafts and food, as found, for example, in Jordan;
   – local cooperative developments, for example in Malaysia;
   – increasing the economic benefits for the whole community – by renting communal land for camping, for example as found in Zimbabwe.
2 **Strategies focused on improving living conditions and capacity building** – strategies here include training and education, reducing the environmental impacts of tourism, reducing competition for natural resources, and improving access to services such as schooling, healthcare, communications and infrastructure improvements. Examples include ecotourism developments in Brazil and tourism-based projects in the shantytowns of South Africa.
3 **Strategies focused on participation, partnerships and involvement** – here strategies are designed to change the policy and planning frameworks to allow participation by local communities in tourism, decision-making and partnerships with the private sector. Examples include projects based around community home-stay in Malaysia and wildlife guides in India.

The success of tourism as a tool of poverty reduction will then depend upon implementing the most appropriate of these strategies for particular destinations, situations and communities.

Here of course the key word is 'unacceptable' and this becomes a value judgement on the part of both managers and the visitor. Chapter 8 contains a critique of the practicality of the concept of carrying capacity.

2   **Destination management and planning** – successful destinations are those that have instigated comprehensive planning and management to provide a framework to anticipate and manage change; the British national parks are a good example here. Destination planning and management is about delivering a high quality experience to the visitor whilst managing the impacts of visitation. It should take a holistic and integrative approach to the destination and involve the host community in key decisions. It tends to be implemented by a destination management organisation through the medium of policy, planning legislation and partnership building with relevant destination stakeholders, including the leisure industry. It also reflects contemporary thinking that the destination is the appropriate level for implementation of planning, as opposed to the national or the regional level.

3   **Competitiveness** – an imperative for all destinations is to be competitive in order to deliver benefits to all stakeholders. In the bigger picture, it is in fact destinations that compete with each other rather than the individual businesses within the destination. To be competitive demands that destinations thoroughly understand their positioning against their competitors' offering; and constantly innovate in terms of their products and their marketing.

Discussion question

The most important element of sustainable tourism destinations will be to reduce carbon emissions. Thinking of traditional sun, sand and sea destinations, how could they address this issue?

7.5 The tourism sector

Contrary to received wisdom, the tourism sector comprises not only the private sector, but also the public sector. We deal with the role of the public sector in tourism first in this section, before moving on to consider the private sector.

7.5.1 The public sector

It can be argued that tourism is a private sector activity and that government has no legitimate reason for being involved. In fact, exactly the opposite is true: government plays a central role in organising, managing and governing the tourism sector. In addition, government owns and manages many iconic tourism attractions, including national parks, coastlines and heritage attractions such as museums, art galleries and historic monuments.

Government is involved in tourism for a variety of reasons. Tourism plays a leading economic development role in many countries, and for the developed world, in countries such as Spain, tourism represents a significant proportion of the economy. As a result government cannot afford to leave such an important economic sector to the whim of the market and the private sector. Remember, too, that tourism is produced where it is consumed, creating many consequences for the environment and host communities, as we noted above. It is government's role to alleviate the negative consequences of tourism and to ensure that the sector is regulated and planned effectively. As a result, all levels of government play an active role in tourism. Government has to be involved in tourism for a range of reasons:

- **Authority** – government is the only body that has the authority to legislate and determine policy for tourism and is therefore able to coordinate the sector at national, regional and local levels.
- **Economics** – as noted above, tourism plays an important role in many national economies.
- **Education and training** – government has overall control of national education and training systems, including, for tourism, supplying trained manpower to the tourism sector, often through hotel schools, as, for example, with the government-funded Utalli hotel school in Kenya.
- **Statistics and information** – as the private sector is reluctant to pay for large scale tourism surveys, government provides this service, for example the International Passenger Survey in the UK.
- **Planning and control** – to ensure that tourism delivers benefits which outweigh the costs.
- **Market regulation and promotion** – government has the authority to regulate and intervene in markets, particularly in a fragmented sector such as tourism where quality control and quality management may need to be imposed. Increasingly this is done in cooperation with the sector through 'public–private partnerships'.
- **The nature of destinations** – we can view destinations as loosely articulated amalgams of organisations and communities. However, this creates a leadership vacuum and so it commonly falls to government to provide the coordination and leadership needed for destinations to function effectively.

Traditionally the role of government in tourism has been policy setting, regulation and planning. However, as the importance of tourism has grown and government's role has matured, the public sector is expected to provide a wider range of functions, including marketing and promotion, destination management, strategy and sector coordination. Government agencies have struggled to deliver all of these roles alone and so they have sought out partnerships with 'non-state actors', such as the industry and communities, to deliver these functions. This approach recognises the importance of market forces and reflects a more fundamental trend in government to more collaborative ways of working. As a result, government agencies now act to coordinate the activities of tourism through 'integrated tourism governance' – as we see in Scotland – rather than 'regulation', exemplified by the tourism policy approach of Bulgaria. Case Study 7.4 outlines the UK government's approach to leading the tourism strategy for the 2012 London Olympics.

7.5.2 The private sector

The contemporary tourism industry comprises a range of businesses each with different objectives. Bull (1995) summarises these objectives as:

- **profit maximisation** – requiring a long-term view of revenue and cost, a perspective often absent in tourism;
- **sales maximisation** – which is often the default option for service businesses and tourism due to capacity constraints;
- **empire building** – here as businesses grow there may be a separation of ownership and control and non-monetary objectives emerge;

Tourism strategy for the London 2012 Olympics

Hosting the 2012 Olympic and Paralympic Games represents a huge opportunity for the UK tourism sector. The government's tourism strategy for the Olympics was published in 2007 and is an excellent example of 'joined-up thinking', where both sport and tourism policy come together (DCMS, 2007c). The strategy rightly focuses upon preparing and coordinating the UK's tourism sector for 2012, as well as ensuring that the British economy and society receive maximum benefits from the Olympics, not simply in 2012, but also beyond in the so-called 'legacy' effects. These effects will include:

- the regeneration of East London;
- the creation of new green spaces;
- an overhaul of the country's tourism infrastructure through improving quality and providing new facilities such as a convention centre in London;
- improved airport gateways; and, of course,
- the legacy of the newly built stadia themselves.

The tourism strategy for 2012 is wide ranging, dealing with issues as diverse as 'skills training' and the need to 'facilitate' overseas visits through making visas easier to obtain. The strategy also deals with the lucrative domestic, day visit and business markets, as well as the more obvious overseas tourism dimension. For example, the strategy aims to boost domestic tourism by encouraging British residents to travel and to take longer breaks.

The aims of the strategy are as follows:

- engage all tourism businesses;
- improve international perceptions of Britain;
- deliver a first class welcome to all visitors;
- improve the skills of the workforce;
- drive up quality in accommodation and boost access for disabled visitors;
- maximise the opportunities for increasing business visits and events;
- spread the benefits beyond London, for example through the sailing events at Weymouth on the south coast of Britain;
- improve sustainability, particularly in terms of sustainable transport options.

The economic impact of the 2012 Olympics is in constant dispute. The government estimates that the Games will generate £2.1 billion over the period 2007–17 and generate over 8,000 job-years. The legacy effect alone will account for two-thirds of this amount, although, of course, there will be a significant impact from construction jobs before the Games. In contrast to these estimates, the European Tour Operators Association is one of the more cautious voices, even suggesting that many tourists may stay away from the UK whilst the Games are being staged.

Whatever the outcome, international visitors will make a significant contribution and the UK's tourism marketing agency, VisitBritain, will be promoting both the Games and the 'Cultural Olympiad' as 'must-see' destinations. Emerging markets such as China and Russia will be key targets here. And, of course, it will not simply be the spectators who visit, but also the media, sports officials and competitors themselves.

In addition to the sporting events, the Cultural Olympiad is a major cultural event running alongside the Games (see Chapter 9), promoting Britain's multiculturalism, contemporary outlook and rich heritage, involving museums, stately homes, libraries and digital technology (see 'Useful websites', p. 196).

- **output maximisation** – relevant for product-oriented businesses, where volume is more important;
- **satisficing** – where the goal is to achieve a satisfactory level of revenue or profit;
- **a quiet life** – where the business is small, often family owned and may be run for lifestyle reasons.

The tourism private sector provides the machinery of tourism production which manipulates and permits the tourist experience to happen. In recent years the industry has been restructured in response to technology, changing consumer demand, increasing concentration in the industry (see Chapter 4), and the demands of flexible specialisation creating networks of supply and destinations with vertical, horizontal and diagonal integration (Debbage and Ioannides, 1998). A key characteristic of the tourism industry is the low level of concentration of ownership, as these enterprises are often operated by small and medium-sized enterprises (SMEs). On the one hand, this is an advantage because it means that tourist expenditure flows quickly into the local economy. On the other hand, however, SMEs are both fragmented and lack a coherent lobby. Often, too, they lack both the investment capability to upgrade and the management/marketing expertise which is demanded by an increasingly discerning tourism marketplace.

The main industries comprising the private tourism sector are attractions, hospitality, intermediaries and transportation.

7.5.2.1 Attractions

The attractions of a destination, whether they are artificial features, natural features or events, provide the initial motivation to visit. Traditionally, attractions have been neglected by industry bodies and associations owing to their variety and fragmented ownership pattern. However, the sector is now demonstrating maturity, with increased professionalism in the management of attractions. This includes a closer match between the market and supply of attractions through:

- adoption of a marketing philosophy;
- better training for attractions' personnel;
- greater involvement of technology in the development of a wide range of exciting new types of attraction;
- renewed focus upon, and professional management of, sporting mega events, which have emerged as an important sector in their own right.

Alongside this more enlightened management approach, the attractions' industry is forming professional bodies and seeking representation in wider tourist industry circles. Attractions range from major international scale businesses such as the British Museum, with almost 6 million visits a year, to small local arts festivals which may attract more local people than visitors.

7.5.2.2 Hospitality

The hospitality industry includes accommodation for tourism, and food and beverages. Accommodation is essential to tourism, as by definition tourism requires an overnight stay. Accommodation demonstrates the multi-sectoral nature of tourism supply and the interdependence of the various contributing industries. For example, the supply of many facilities and services at a resort depends on the number of bed spaces available; that is, the number of tourists who will visit. For example, provision of around 1,000 beds will support up to six basic retail outlets, while 4,000 beds will support specialist outlets such as hairdressers.

The hospitality sector of the destination not only provides physical shelter and sustenance, but also creates the general feeling of welcome and a lasting impression of the local cuisine and produce – think, for example, of the gastronomic traditions of France. Traditionally dominated by SMEs, the hospitality sector usually offers a mix of types of establishment, and it is important for destinations to adapt and change this mix to meet market aspirations. In some resorts, for example, there is a movement towards flexible forms of accommodation, such as apartments and timeshare, and away from more traditional serviced establishments (such as hotels or guesthouses). It is also important to remember the private informal sector (such as second homes and caravans), which is a large, though neglected, part of the accommodation industry.

7.5.2.3 Intermediaries

Tourism is unusual in that the product is geographically separate from the purchaser. As a result intermediaries exist to broker the sale. Intermediaries are tour operators and travel agents. Tour operators package up the various elements of the product – usually transportation, accommodation and transfers – whilst travel agents showcase the tour operators' products, making them available to the public for sale.

Intermediaries have been severely affected by the internet. Effectively, consumers can purchase elements of the travel product online, often direct from the hotel or airline, and so cut out the tour operator and travel agent. This has been termed 'disintermediation' and both agents and operators are devising strategies to reinvent themselves in the face of this development. A key strategy has been the development of 'dynamic packaging', where the operators deconstruct their product and sell the various elements separately online to the consumer, in other words allowing the consumer to self-assemble their own product.

7.5.2.4 Transport

Clearly the development and maintenance of efficient transport links and transport gateways to the generating markets are essential for the success of destinations. Indeed, there are examples of destinations where transport has made, or broken, the tourist industry. Small islands such as those in the Caribbean, for example, are dependent upon their carriers to provide market access, while destinations such as Spain and Mexico are ideally situated to take advantage of international tourism from Europe and North America respectively. In international terms, developing countries such as the Gambia have particular problems attracting a share of the market because they are generally distant from the generating markets.

Transport for tourism can be classified as surface transport (sea, rail and road) or air transport. Surprisingly, it is road transport that provides the majority of trips worldwide, simply because the majority of these trips are domestic and short in duration. Air transport is coming under increased criticism for its role in climate change. The air transport sector has also been characterised in recent years by the rise of low cost, or no frills, carriers, which have allowed access to air travel and international tourism to a market that hitherto was unable to afford it. In 2008 there were almost 5 billion air passenger movements worldwide, testifying to the scale of the industry.

With climate change, surface transport is seeing a renaissance, particularly though high-speed rail links and fast ferries, such as catamarans. In terms of surface transport, cruising is a good example of a leisure industry that has reinvented itself, with glamorous ships, new destinations and on-board leisure activities. Since 1990 it has experienced annual passenger growth of more than 7 per cent, reaching 12.8 million passengers in 2008.

> ### Discussion question
>
> Discuss the assertion that tourism is a set of disparate businesses in search of an industry.

7.6 Tourism marketing

The contemporary approach of the 'service-dominant logic' of marketing recognises that tourism is a product comprising a bundle of both tangible and intangible elements, as well as focusing on consumer needs and their involvement in the 'co-creation' of the tourism experience (Vargo and Lusch, 2004). As such, it is vital for the leisure manager to understand the principles of tourism and service marketing in order to gain a competitive advantage. Whilst there are many definitions of marketing, they all focus around the need to identify and supply customer needs, and the contemporary approach is to go beyond *satisfying* those needs to really *delighting* the customer. Contemporary definitions of marketing reflect this thinking, with a focus upon the many actors in the marketplace.

There are two considerations to take into account in order to understand how best to approach tourism marketing:

1   It is vital to understand the nature of the tourism product itself, and the nature of the purchasing process.
2   Technology, and in particular the internet, has transformed the way that tourism marketing is done.

7.6.1 The nature of tourism

Tourism is simply a particular type of offering to the marketplace that demands a differentiated approach from other products. This approach includes the following characteristics:

- Wherever possible the product should be made tangible, for example through the use of staff uniforms and the careful design of the environment – or servicescape – where the product is delivered. Many theme parks do this particularly well, for example the Disney or Universal Studios parks.
- Employees become an additional part of the marketing mix and therefore need to be well trained. The tourism product is produced where it is consumed, and this means that employees can influence not only the successful delivery of the product but also the tourists' evaluation of the service during the short time that they are exposed to it.
- Perceived risk should be managed through strong quality assurance, to ensure consistent and standardised service delivery. This consistency should be communicated to the customer through strong branding of the product, which itself acts to reassure the customer about the service.
- Other elements of the marketing mix should be carefully aligned with tourism, with promotion stressing emotive aspects and relationship building with intermediaries.
- The nature of services as 'perishable' means that it is essential to manage both capacity and demand through yield management, which adjusts pricing to demand and so smoothes out the demand curve.

These bullet points can be summarised into two key approaches that characterise tourism marketing and are designed to help retain customers, avoid price competition, retain employees and reduce costs:

1   Relationship marketing is designed to secure a loyal customer base, creating, maintaining and enhancing strong relationships with consumers.
2   Service quality management is designed to 'industrialise' service delivery by guaranteeing standardised and consistent services.

7.6.2 The role of technology

The internet influences every aspect of tourism and has changed the culture and behaviour of how people purchase, search and communicate. It connects companies, customers and governments at low cost and without constraints of time or space, and as such is a transformative marketing tool. This is because it has significant advantages over traditional communication media: advantages such as reach, cost, richness, speed and interactivity. Indeed, technology facilitates many of the processes that are needed in the new marketing paradigm of relationship building and co-creation.

Technology has created a whole new marketing industry – e-marketing, which in tourism can be defined as the promotion of a tourism product, company service or website online and can include a variety of activities from online advertising to ensuring that products are easily found on search engines such as Google. It also provides a medium and delivery mechanism for consumers to gather information and to make purchasing decisions.

E-marketing is ideally suited to the nature of tourism and leisure as an experience. It allows the development of online brochures that can deliver rich multimedia content, blending text, images, sound and video into multimedia documents to overcome the intangible nature of the product. Through video and interactivity it delivers the ability to 'test drive' the product. It also gives tourism organisations the ability to instantly change dates, prices and availability online, so saving expensive brochure reprints. Technology also allows organisations to individually target customers through 'narrow casting' to customise messages, utilise email and web links to engage in 'viral marketing' and, of course, the internet gives small businesses and destinations a degree of global market reach previously unheard of.

7.6.3 Market planning in tourism

It is essential for tourism organisations to plan their marketing strategically in the long term as well as tactically in the short term (see Chapter 15). Tourism market planning provides a common point of reference for the organisation, acting as a coordination mechanism for the many stakeholders involved in delivering tourism at a destination. It encourages a disciplined approach to marketing by ensuring that objectives are set for markets and products; and that each market has activities and resources allocated. The planning process also sets out key performance indicators against which the success or otherwise of the plan can be monitored. Increasingly these plans are flexible and subject to constant revision.

For most organisations, the tactical level of tourism marketing is focused upon marketing campaigns. Here, the starting point is to identify the target market and then to use elements of the marketing mix to approach that market (see Chapter 15). We can think of the marketing mix as the set of marketing tools that the firm uses to pursue its marketing objectives in the target market, where each element of the mix supports the others and none stands alone. For example, the pricing of an inclusive tour is done with the target market in mind, which in turn determines the type of promotion and distribution channel used. Also, with the move to a service-dominant logic, the marketing mix can be expanded from the traditional four Ps of product, place, price and promotion to include other influencing variables such as the people involved in delivering the tourism service, the physical setting – or servicescape – where the service is delivered and the actual process of delivering the service (see Chapter 15).

7.6.4 Destination marketing

The **process** of destination marketing involves dealing with the complexities of destinations and their many stakeholders, whilst the **outcome** is a brand or the image of the destination. In other words, a good destination marketer will focus upon two key operations:

1 managing the destination's many stakeholders and networks;
2 formulating and managing the destination brand.

The idea of destination management continues to evolve and a view is emerging that it is 'branding' that is the glue that holds the marketing of the destination together. The two key components of destination branding are image and brand.

7.6.4.1 Destination image
Understanding the formation and characteristics of the destination image is critical for destination marketing. A destination's image is a simplified version of reality, a way of making sense of the many destination stimuli received and processed by the visitor or potential visitor. The image of a destination is critical to marketing as it affects an individual's perception and choice of a destination. The generation of the image is different for destinations compared with many other products, because it is the tourists themselves who generate a destination image by selecting different sources of information from media, personal contacts and experience. As a result, destination marketers have much less influence on images, despite their critical importance to destination choice. Whilst image formation is not the same as branding, it is closely related. This is because the choice of branding and brand attributes of a destination reinforces the destination image.

7.6.4.2 Destination branding
To quote Kotler, 'branding is the art and cornerstone of marketing' (2003: 418) and can be defined as:

> A name, term, sign, symbol or design or combination of them, intended to identify the goods or services of one seller or group of sellers and to differentiate them from those of competitors.
>
> (Kotler, 2000: 404)

Branding tends to be undertaken by public sector led destination management organisations, in consultation with destination stakeholders. Branding is a complex and controversial issue for destinations and is surrounded by a range of issues focused upon how appropriate it is to market destinations as products. Three key issues can be identified with regard to destination marketing:

1 **The nature of the tourist destination** – the development of destination brands may conflict with a community's perception and feelings for the place where they live. This

can be exacerbated by the delivery of the brand on the ground through the use of signage, street furniture and landscaping. Destinations are contested spaces and the various users of this space each hold their own images, identities and interests.

2 **The role of the public sector** – the public sector tends to take the lead in destination marketing, coordinating other inputs and stakeholders. However, it is possible to question whether government is the most appropriate agency to deliver destination marketing as the public sector is not renowned for being entrepreneurial or trained in marketing.

3 **The role of destination stakeholders** – a key issue for destination marketing is to ensure involvement and commitment by all stakeholders in the destination marketing process.

Discussion question

Select a range of advertisements from magazines of your choice. Using these as a resource, do you think that tourism marketing lags behind other economic sectors such as retail or motor manufacturing?

7.7 Conclusions

This chapter has demonstrated the scale and scope of tourism at an international level. For the leisure manager it is important to understand all aspects of tourism, including sports tourism, as it will represent a segment of demand for leisure facilities alongside local residents and day visitors. To help you to do this, the chapter has analysed tourism demand. Here, we must remember that with considerations of climate change and concern for destinations the nature of tourism demand will change. Already there is evidence of an ethical tourism consumer emerging.

The chapter has also stressed that tourism is produced where it is consumed and that this has implications for the planning and management of destinations. It is the destination that is at the sharp end of tourism, and the location of many leisure businesses. It is therefore important to plan for the consequences of visits to the destination and to ensure that the destination itself is well managed. The tourism sector is dominated by small businesses, with many in the leisure industry. Here there are implications for both expertise and the ability to invest and to deliver a quality experience to the visitor.

To manage leisure or tourism successfully, it is important to adopt the contemporary view of the 'services dominant logic'. Destination marketing remains a controversial activity; after all, destinations are also places where people live, work and play, and some question whether standard marketing approaches should be applied to them. There is no doubt that tourism plays a major role in the leisure industry – indeed they are so closely linked that the contemporary leisure manager must understand tourism in order to fully capitalise upon its opportunities.

Practical tasks

1 Visit the statistics section of the UNWTO's website at www.unwto.org and construct a list of the world's top ten generating countries for tourism and the top ten destinations. How do you explain the fact that many countries on these two lists are European?
2 Taking a destination with which you are familiar, draw up a balance sheet of the positive and negative consequences of tourism.
3 Draft a marketing brief to extol the 'green' virtues of an attraction or large event with which you are familiar.

Structured guide to further reading

For a comprehensive and definitive tourism text:
Cooper, C., Fletcher J., Fyall, A., Gilbert, D. and Wanhill, S. (2008) *Tourism Principles and Practice*, Prentice Hall, Harlow.

For a classic text on tourism and public policy:
Hall, C.M. and Jenkins, J.M. (1995) *Tourism and Public Policy*, 4th edition, Routledge, London.

For a thorough and accessible text on the relationship between tourism and the environment:
Holden, A. (2008) *Environment and Tourism*, Routledge, London.

For an excellent and comprehensive edited volume on the supply side of tourism:
Ioannides, D. and Debbage, K.G. (eds) (1998) *The Economic Geography of the Tourist Industry: a supply side analysis*, Routledge, London.

For a classic marketing text reoriented with a tourism flavour:
Kotler, P., Bowen, J. and Makens, J. (2005) *Marketing for Hospitality and Tourism*, 4th edition, Prentice Hall, Upper Saddle River, NJ.

For a thorough and well-researched compendium of tourism:
Lew, A., Hall, C.M. and Williams, A.M. (eds) (2004) *A Companion to Tourism*, Blackwell, Oxford.

For a comprehensive and contemporary approach to sustainable tourism:
Miller, G and Twinning Ward, L. (2005) *Monitoring for a Sustainable Tourism Transition: the challenge of developing and using indicators*, CABI Publishing, Wallingford.

Useful websites

For the world's leading UN agency for tourism:
www.unwto.org

For the world's main lobby group for tourism businesses:
www.wttc.org

For the most established organisation that espouses ethical travel:
www.tourismconcern.org.uk

For the Association of Leading Visitor Attractions:
www.alva.org.uk

For an inspiring website with excellent simulation scenarios of the future of tourism in Scotland:
www.visitscotland.com

For the London 2012 Olympics:
www.london2012.com

Chapter 8

Leisure and the natural environment

Lynn Crowe

In this chapter

- What are the main leisure uses of the natural environment?
- How important is volunteering in the natural environment?
- What are the international and national policies that affect leisure in the natural environment?
- What are the main organisations providing for leisure in the natural environment?
- What are the key management principles for leisure in the natural environment?

Summary

This chapter summarises the available evidence concerning our use of the natural environment for leisure purposes. It notes that although walking remains one of our most popular leisure activities, there are increasing concerns about the lack of participation in outdoor leisure among certain groups and a decrease in engagement with the natural environment particularly among young people. The range of environmental policies relevant to leisure managers at an international, European and local level are discussed, alongside an overview of the main agencies and organisations involved in this sector in the UK. Existing provision and facilities in the natural environment for leisure – particularly designated sites and protected areas – are examined. The chapter concludes with an overview of the tools and techniques which the leisure manager can employ to effectively promote and manage leisure in the natural environment, whilst also conserving the resource.

8.1 Introduction

The natural environment typically comprises the landscapes, habitats, wildlife and cultural heritage features of both rural and urban places. Although some authors would define 'natural environment' strictly in terms of the absence of any human interference or impact, in this chapter it is taken in its more general meaning – that is, the environment separate from (but sometimes found within) the built environment, more natural in character and appearance. A nation's natural heritage is unique – its mountains and valleys, coastal and marine sites, lakes, forests and woodlands, national parks, inland waterways, urban parks and open spaces. To walk in the countryside and along coastal paths, and to enjoy the hospitality of local towns, rural villages, pubs, restaurants, hotels, inns and bed and breakfast establishments – getting 'off the beaten track' – is to be at leisure; as is enjoyment of parks and green spaces in and around towns and cities.

This chapter considers this natural environment – whole landscapes and local green spaces – the use made of them for leisure and the management challenges that they present.

8.2 Enjoyment of the natural environment

In the early years of the outdoor recreation profession, facilities and services were often developed and managed without much information about the people they were aimed at or users' needs and demands. For example, so-called tourist 'honeypots' have developed often in an ad hoc manner over many years, occasionally leading to problems of overuse and erosion. Leisure facilities have been created where land has become available, such as in the creation of parks on restored derelict land. This rather opportunistic approach has led to the development of a range of facilities and services which some have argued is somewhat fragmented and unplanned (see, for example, Curry, 1994).

These days there is a plethora of surveys and research projects which seek to identify how people engage with the natural environment, their motivations for doing so and barriers to further engagement. In fact, most agencies and authorities now adopt what might be described as a 'marketing approach' to leisure provision, with a focus on people as 'customers' of their particular service. The essential point of the marketing process is developing services which meet people's real needs. Marketing as it is related to outdoor leisure has been defined as

> not merely a question of selling {...} but of the need to think through each stage of development before that point is reached. If countryside facilities are to be managed effectively, the recreation manager needs to know clearly what his objectives are, what sections of the community he is aiming to serve, which research and analysis can help in decision making and how to assess financial risk.
>
> (CRRAG, 1977)

So at all stages of leisure provision – through the development of services and products, pricing and promotion strategies – the manager should consult with potential users and consider their needs.

Important market research can be undertaken on site, but managers also need to know the views and experiences of those not yet using their services or facilities. These can be obtained through household surveys, citizens' panels and other local stakeholder involvement techniques (see Chapter 14). But there is also considerable evidence available at the national level which can inform management decisions.

Natural England (2008) explored how and where people enjoy the natural environment. Rather than focusing on the more traditional 'countryside pursuits' or outdoor activities, Natural England suggested that people can engage with the natural environment in a variety of ways:

- They enjoy it physically – through activities such as walking, climbing, bird watching, gardening, or through conservation volunteering – close to home or further afield.
- They enjoy it visually – from home and when on the move.
- They enjoy it vicariously – through literature, art, photography, television, and more recently, the internet.

(Natural England, 2008: 165)

This gives a much wider interpretation to the meaning of the word 'engagement' and to the meaning of enjoyment of the natural environment.

But one measure of leisure use of the natural environment remains the number and types of visits to it. The *England Leisure Visits Survey 2005* (Natural England, 2006) estimates that there were 763.4 million rural leisure visits in England in 2005, including trips to the countryside, the coast, woods and forests, and to water. However, comparison with an earlier survey in 2002–3 (Countryside Agency, 2004) suggests that there has been a fall in the number of similar visits, and agencies continue to discuss why this might be happening (although there also continues to be debate as to the validity of these figures, and whether changes are due to differences in survey methodology).

In all surveys of this type, walking appears to be overwhelmingly the main activity in which people wish to participate. The Sport England *Active People Survey 1* (2010) confirms that walking is the most popular recreational activity for people in England. It estimated that over 8 million adults aged 16 and over had gone on a recreational walk for at least thirty minutes in the four weeks up to the survey. Similarly in Scotland, 28 per cent of the population participate in walking – the highest sports participation figure (**sports**cotland,

1999). Other activities are also significant, particularly cycling and horse riding – but participation trends in all these pursuits are notoriously difficult to establish. Many researchers claim that so-called 'adventure sports', such as climbing, white water canoeing and air sports, are on the increase – but again data is extremely difficult to obtain, and there is now significant evidence that participation in all outdoor sports is declining in the UK (for example Sport England, 2002). This raises extremely worrying implications, both for engagement with the natural environment and for physical and mental well-being.

Regardless of specific trends in different countries, it is essential that leisure managers understand their target markets, and the needs and demands of their potential customers. Reflecting on national surveys undertaken by the relevant government agencies or departments is often an easy way to access such information.

8.3 Volunteering in the natural environment

Volunteering provides another measure of how people enjoy and value the natural environment. Opportunities available include land and species management, education, walk leadership, practical conservation tasks and public relations. A study by the Institute for Volunteering Research (Countryside Recreation Network, 2007) suggests that levels of volunteering in the outdoors are increasing in the UK. This study also confirmed the wide range of organisations and tasks in this area. The British Trust for Conservation Volunteers (BTCV) is one of the UK's largest practical conservation charities, founded in 1959; it now supports the work of over 130,000 volunteers each year. Wildlife Trusts claim involvement from over 32,000 volunteers, and English Nature (now Natural England) nearly 2,000. A great many volunteers also appear to be involved in smaller, community-based organisations. In 2003, a study of volunteering with urban parks and green spaces across the UK identified 4,000 independent volunteer-led groups, with an estimated membership of 500,000 volunteers (Ockenden and Moore, 2003).

Volunteers can gain much from their involvement in protecting and conserving the environment, and leisure managers can benefit from the additional support and activity. But volunteers must also be properly managed and supported in their turn, and do not come entirely cost free. A full discussion of the voluntary sector in leisure can be found in Chapter 6.

8.4 Issues and challenges for outdoor recreation management

Leisure managers must not fall into the trap of only responding to immediate demands for their facilities and services. The providers of leisure services need to understand their potential customers' needs and demands, and how these might change in the future. Predicting leisure demand is a difficult business, but researchers do now have access to some reliable data about existing forms and levels of participation, and these can be correlated with other socio-economic factors. Forecasting means making intelligent assumptions and extrapolations about how the future world of leisure will change (Elson, 1982).

A recent study of the emerging trends that are likely to have significant implications for the way that people engage with and take their recreation in the natural environment in the future (Henley Centre, 2005) showed that:

- People are spending more time on indoor-based and sedentary activities at home, and visits to the countryside are in decline.
- Society has become more risk averse and good reliable information is often sought before new experiences are tried. Parents are less likely to allow children to explore the natural environment close to home, alone.
- Health and well-being problems are costing society in terms of health budgets and quality of life.
- There is a trend for people to be more concerned about their health and to be interested in preventative means to keep them healthier.
- A 'convenience culture' means that people are drawn to activities that seem to use their time well; the more convenient the activity, the more likely they are to do it.
- The planning system is the key to creating more opportunities for outdoor recreation near to where people live, and agri-environment schemes have the potential to increase and diversify access opportunities in other areas.
- Information on the internet is increasingly used for leisure-based decisions.
- An ageing society means that there are more active and experience-seeking people over 65.
- The social justice agenda is leading to more expectation for equal opportunities to engage with and enjoy the natural environment.

These trends present leisure managers with a variety of challenges. For example, the social justice agenda requires leisure managers (particularly those responsible for public funds) to address the issue of diversity within outdoor recreation. There is a consistent body of evidence that certain groups – in particular young adults, low income groups, minority ethnic groups, people with disabilities, older people and women – are less likely to participate in activities related to the natural environment. Various initiatives have been promoted and guidance produced to attempt to address these issues. An example is the Mosaic Partnership, featured in Case Study 8.1.

Discussion question

What are the barriers which prevent access to leisure opportunities in the natural environment for particular disadvantaged groups in society?

Of increasing significance is the growing alarm concerning the lack of engagement with the natural environment by children and young people. For a variety of reasons – including parental fears about 'stranger danger', anxieties about traffic and competition from electronic games – it would appear that children rarely experience unsupervised play outdoors, and that as they get older there are also fewer opportunities to experience the adventure and excitement that might have traditionally come from high adrenalin sports and other activities (Natural England, 2009). There are implications here for the physical health of our society, as well as concerns about personal development and risk assessment, which may get significantly worse. A seminal book by Louv (2006) referred to this worrying trend as 'Nature-deficit disorder'.

The Mosaic Partnership

Mosaic is a national project in the UK, a partnership between the Campaign for National Parks, the Youth Hostel Association (YHA) and the nine National Park Authorities in England. It aims to build sustainable links between black and minority ethnic communities and National Parks and the YHA.

Mosaic was developed in response to evidence that although about 10 per cent of the UK population is of an ethnic minority background only about 1 per cent of visitors to National Parks are from ethnic minorities. UK National Parks were created for the benefit of the public, as well as protection of their landscapes. So Mosaic works to make sure that all people have an equal opportunity to enjoy the many benefits that National Parks offer. The Mosaic project works by training influential leaders from ethnic minority communities to become 'Community Champions' promoting the National Parks and the YHA in their communities, so that they have the skills and confidence to promote the National Parks independently and beyond the end of the project in 2012.

Mosaic also helps the National Park Authorities and the YHA make changes to their organisations that will help them reach ethnic minority audiences. For example, Mosaic staff and Community Champions help to identify new ways of making decisions, consulting, providing information, and increasing the range of people who care about and can influence the future management of these areas.

Mosaic is supported by Natural England through its Access to Nature project. There have already been considerable successes, with links developed between many local community groups and their nearest National Park. Examples include: an Asian elders group from Bolton visiting the Lake District National Park to take part in silk painting, walking and a cruise on Lake Windermere; asylum seekers and young male refugees from Birmingham visiting the Peak District National Park for a range of exciting activities, including mountain biking, kayaking, sailing and walking; a Bradford father and child group visiting the North York Moors National Park to take part in archery, abseiling, football and a historical hunt at Robin Hood's Bay; and a mental health support group from Swansea and Cardiff visiting the Brecon Beacons National Park to participate in badge making, a wildlife trail and a trip on a barge.

Often, an important element of each visit is a residential stay in youth hostels – sometimes the first time these groups will have stayed in such rural locations. The final success, however, will be measured by how many of these groups return independently to the National Parks for their own enjoyment. The Mosaic Project is carefully monitoring this element of the project.

For more information, visit www.mosaicpartnership.org.

Discussion questions

Why are children and young people increasingly 'disengaged' from their surrounding natural environment? What might leisure managers do to address this issue?

Removing barriers to leisure in the natural environment has become increasingly import-ant as different public agencies have begun to appreciate the wide range of benefits such activity can bring to individuals and communities. There is now a growing evidence base which links health and well-being with access to nature (Royal Society for the Protection of Birds, 2004). A large study of over 250,000 people in the Netherlands has shown that the perception of health was related to the percentage of green space within a 3 km radius of people's homes. Those with more green space felt the most healthy, with the strongest results amongst the poorest people (Maas *et al.*, 2006). In Chicago, those living in poverty yet with greenery around were found to be better able to cope with stress and major life events than those with barren surroundings (Kuo, 2001). There is an increasing understand-ing that physical activity undertaken in a natural environment, so-called 'green exercise', creates an immediate increase in self-esteem and a more positive state (Kuo, 2001).

It is clear that there are many reasons why government departments and agencies at all levels, along with a plethora of different organisations and charities, become involved in the provision of leisure services in the natural environment.

8.5 The international policy context

Protecting the natural environment, and enabling people to enjoy it more, has become a major issue at all levels of government – local, national, European and international. There are several international initiatives relating to conservation and protection (for more details of this, see the accompanying website):

- The United Nations Convention on the *Protection of the World Cultural and Natural Heritage* has been ratified by 186 state parties; it allows for the designation of World Heritage Sites.
- The International Union for Conservation of Nature (IUCN) is the world's oldest and largest global environmental network, with a membership of more than 1,000 govern-mental and non-governmental organisations.
- European Union legislation includes the Birds Directive and Habitats Directive, con-cerned with the conservation of European wildlife and natural habitats.
- The European Environment Agency provides decision-makers with the information needed to make policies to protect the environment and support sustainable develop-ment.
- The European Environment Information and Observation Network includes over 300 environment bodies in the public and private sectors across Europe.
- The European Landscape Convention sets out measures for the recognition, protection, management and planning of landscapes everywhere, through domestic policy and prac-tice and European cooperation.

Since 2001, scientists under the auspices of the United Nations have been working to cat-egorise all the public benefits which a healthy natural environment can deliver to society. The Millennium Ecosystem Assessment has defined these public benefits as 'ecosystem serv-ices' (see Figure 8.1), which include cultural services such as leisure and recreation. This is particularly helpful for leisure managers, who may have to prioritise resources or defend policies and projects.

Perhaps the most pressing environmental issue of our time is that of climate change and global warming. It is now clear that future climate trends will have a wide-ranging impact on all human activities, and that we must plan our use of environmental resources in order

Provisioning services	Regulating services	Cultural services
E.g. food, fresh water, fuel wood, genetic resources	E.g. climate regulation, disease regulation, flood regulation	E.g. spiritual, recreation and tourism, aesthetic, inspirational, educational
Supporting services		
Those needed for the provision of the other services, e.g. soil formation, nutrient cycling, primary production		

Figure 8.1 The Millennium Ecosystem Assessment typology.
Source: adapted from Defra Research Project, www.ecosystemservices.org.uk.

to mitigate the effects of climate change, but also to adapt to climate change. After seven years of debate between leaders, politicians and scientists, on 16 February 2005 the Kyoto Protocol to control climate change finally became international law. The Protocol was drawn up in Kyoto, Japan, in 1997 to implement the United Nations Framework Convention for Climate Change. Industrialised nations which sign up to the treaty are legally bound to reduce their worldwide emissions of six greenhouse gases by an average of 5.2 per cent below their 1990 levels by the period 2008–12. It is clear that leisure and tourism activities will have a role to play in meeting these targets. Leisure managers will have to not only monitor and reduce their own carbon emissions, but also consider their wider role in areas such as sustainable transport and the development of green networks to facilitate climate change adaptation.

Discussion question

What roles and initiatives might leisure managers develop in promoting climate change mitigation and adaptation?

8.6 The national policy context

The UK has incorporated much of the international and European legislation and thinking into its own statutes and organisational structures. But it also has its own unique legacy in terms of the development of laws and policy frameworks. Perhaps the most significant legislation which retains an impact on leisure managers working in the natural environment today is the 1949 National Parks and Access to the Countryside Act. This Act created new protected areas in England and Wales – National Parks and Areas of Outstanding Natural Beauty. It also enshrined in statute the previously informal rights of access along footpaths and bridleways, and required highways authorities to create Definitive Maps showing the public where legal rights of way existed.

The 1949 Act also formalised a split in approach towards, on the one hand, the conservation of wildlife and, on the other hand, landscape protection and recreation. Further laws reinforced this division. The 1968 Countryside Act created the Countryside Commission – a government agency whose responsibilities included landscape protection and recreation – alongside the existing Nature Conservancy Council, whose responsibilities were largely focused on wildlife and habitat protection. The 1968 Act also included provisions for the creation of Country Parks and picnic sites – largely seen at the time as initiatives to prevent the degradation of our more 'precious' landscapes by the seemingly ever-increasing numbers of visitors and tourists.

During the 1990s, people began to realise that this assumed conflict between conservation and recreation was not the problem traditionally supposed. The 1995 House of Commons Select Committee on the Environment inquiry into the impact of leisure on the environment (House of Commons, 1995) found that recreation in the natural environment was not, in itself, a problem. Indeed, many research studies demonstrate the importance of visitor spend to rural economies, and the wider social and health benefits which outdoor recreation could deliver to both individuals and communities. What is needed is effective management to secure the aims of recreation and conservation together. Robinson (2008) concludes that there was 'no starker evidence of this than the devastation to the local economies of many rural areas when visitors stayed away during the wholesale "closure" of the countryside during the Foot and Mouth epidemic in England and Wales in 2001'.

The UK government produced two important White Papers in 2000 – a Rural White Paper and an Urban White Paper – which proclaimed a set of policies under the banner of a 'Countryside For All'. They emphasised that access to a high quality environment within and around towns, as well as to the countryside, was essential for everyone's well-being. Work that has followed these policies, particularly the Sustainable Communities Plan and the Urban Green Spaces Task Force of 2002, has extended this thinking into a richer understanding of the role of parks and open spaces in and around where people live.

Policies now espouse 'green infrastructure' as an essential component of our towns and cities, just as important as other infrastructure such as roads, water and drains. Green infrastructure – networks and corridors of well-managed green space – can provide important leisure services and facilities, as well as wider benefits such as flood mitigation, sustainable transport routes and wildlife benefits, and it contributes to healthy living initiatives and social cohesion.

Thus the management of our natural environment should now be considered in a much more integrated and holistic manner – incorporating leisure and recreation opportunities alongside other benefits for our health, wealth and well-being. Recent legislation in the UK – for example the 2006 Natural Environment and Rural Communities Act in England and the 2003 Land Reform Act in Scotland – have reinforced these policy aims. There are now single government agencies in the four UK countries with a responsibility to both protect and enhance the natural environment and to make it increasingly available for the public to enjoy. These are summarised in the following section.

8.7 Relevant UK agencies and organisations

To laymen and women, including many leisure managers, there appears to be a range of overlapping bodies with an interest in environmental issues, including leisure in the natural environment (see Table 8.1). For example, there are government departments, non-departmental public bodies (NDPBs), local authorities, and independent, private and voluntary organisations (see 'Useful websites', pp. 223–4). A large proportion of statutorily protected areas are owned or managed by non-governmental organisations. The leisure manager will find these agencies to be essential sources of up-to-date research and evidence, potential funding, and partners on specific projects and new initiatives. A summary of their roles and responsibilities can be found on their websites.

Table 8.1 Examples of relevant UK agencies and organisations

UK government departments	Department for Environment, Food and Rural Affairs Department for Communities and Local Government Department for Culture, Media and Sport
Non-departmental public bodies	Natural England Environment Agency English Heritage Countryside Council for Wales Environment Agency Wales Cadw – Welsh Historic Monuments Executive Agency Scottish Natural Heritage Scottish Environment Protection Agency Historic Scotland Northern Ireland Environment Agency British Waterways Forestry Commission Commission for Architecture and the Built Environment
'Umbrella' organisations	Central Council for Physical Recreation Countryside Recreation Network The Environment Council
Independent non-governmental organisations	Angling Trust Association for the Protection of Rural Scotland British Association for Shooting and Conservation British Canoe Union British Horse Society British Mountaineering Council British Trust for Conservation Volunteers Campaign for the Protection of Rural England Campaign for National Parks Country Landowners and Business Association (CLA) Cyclists' Touring Club Game and Wildlife Conservation Trust International Mountain Biking Association Land Access and Recreation Association National Trust National Trust for Scotland Open Spaces Society Ramblers Association Royal Society for Nature Conservation Royal Society for the Protection of Birds Royal Yachting Association Scottish Conservation Projects Sustrans Wildfowl and Wetlands Trust Wildlife Trusts Woodland Trust World Wide Fund for Nature UK

The range of NDPBs might be said to be confusing for the public and could lead to duplication of effort. The new UK Prime Minister in 2010, David Cameron, has suggested that all NDPBs will be reviewed in order to increase their effectiveness and reduce their costs. So the future remains uncertain for many of these organisations. However, their various roles and statutory duties will clearly remain important and will undoubtedly continue in some form, whatever the organisational structure created by any new government.

In the UK, one of the most important independent organisations involved in environmental protection is the National Trust (see 'Useful websites', pp. 223–4). A registered charity, independent of government, the National Trust was founded in 1895 by three Victorian philanthropists concerned about the impact of uncontrolled development and industrialisation. They set up the Trust to acquire and protect threatened coastline, countryside and buildings.

The Trust now cares for around 250,000 hectares of land in England, Wales and Northern Ireland, including forests, fens, moorland, downs, farmland, nature reserves and stretches of coastline. In total, it is responsible for 300 historic houses and gardens and 49 industrial monuments and mills. Some 15 million people visit National Trust 'pay for entry' properties each year and an estimated 50 million visits are made annually to its coasts and countryside properties. The Trust also has over 3.5 million subscribing members and other supporters. A separate National Trust for Scotland (see 'Useful websites', pp. 223–4) owns 128 properties. Established in 1931, it has a membership of around 297,000 and 1.7 million visitors each year.

Many of the non-governmental organisations campaign for greater access for their particular target audiences. There can be an inherent weakness in such a range of narrowly focused user groups, in that they may provide a fragmented, even conflicting, voice for leisure users. However, they often work in partnership with local government to promote and manage leisure services and facilities, and they are represented by such umbrella groups as the Environment Council and the Central Council for Physical Recreation.

In 1968, it was recognised that this multitude of different agencies and groups, working across different national boundaries but often sharing the same issues and challenges, could collectively work together to share best practice and focus research. Thus the Countryside Recreation Research and Advisory Group was formed. It subsequently changed its name to the Countryside Recreation Network and it continues to act as a network dedicated to the outdoor recreation profession in the UK and the Republic of Ireland. It undertakes shared research and disseminates best practice through workshops, conferences, a managed website and a professional journal (see 'Useful websites', pp. 223–4).

8.8 Existing provision, services and facilities

The different places and facilities available to enjoy leisure in the natural environment are many and diverse and it is important for leisure managers to be aware of them. Some areas are specially protected – for their landscape or wildlife importance. Others are important because they provide a resource for a particular type of activity. Some are just as important because they lie close to where people live and work.

As is true of all countries, the UK has a range of different protected areas and relevant designations of significance to leisure managers working in the natural environment which are peculiar to the UK. These categories have often developed as a result of the history of land ownership patterns in each country, and the socio-economic and demographic characteristics of each area, and are thus unique to each jurisdiction.

8.8.1 Designated areas

The first laws pertaining to natural resource protection in the UK were the Forest Laws of King Canute in *c.*1014. Today independent Wildlife Trusts have over 2,500 nature reserves covering 82,000 hectares; and over 413,000 members in total. National Nature Reserves are designated by the relevant government agency in each country in the UK for their wild-life and geological importance. Natural England recognises more than 400 country parks visited by over 70 million visitors a year. There are 35 in Wales recognised by the Country-side Council for Wales, 36 recognised by Scottish Natural Heritage, and Northern Ireland has 11 country parks.

The most valued habitats and landscapes in the UK are protected by a number of national designations. However, their designation does not exclude their use for leisure and recreation. Protected areas in 2008 included the following:

- Sites of Special Scientific Interest (SSSIs) in Great Britain – 6,586 sites;
- Areas of Special Scientific Interest (ASSIs) in Northern Ireland – 196 sites;
- National Nature Reserves (NNRs) – 407 sites;
- Local Nature Reserves – over 1,500 sites;
- Marine Nature Reserves – three sites;
- Special Protection Areas (SPAS) – 256 sites;
- Areas of Outstanding Natural Beauty (AONBs) – 49 sites;
- National Scenic Areas (NSAs) (Scotland) – 40 sites.

8.8.2 National Parks

National Park status recognises the national importance of the area concerned in terms of landscape, biodiversity and recreation. There are 13 national parks in England and Wales; Scotland has two. Sound planning and sensitive management are essential to ensure that both the main purposes of their designation – to protect and enhance their environment and to provide opportunities for enjoyment – are achieved. The National Parks of England and Wales receive over 100 million visitor days a year (Campaign for National Parks, 2009). The key policy and managing bodies with responsibility for the National Parks are the National Park Authorities. These are similar to local authorities in their powers, including local planning policy and controlling development. They are completely funded by central government.

8.8.3 Access and the rights of way network

Public rights of way and common land have been part of the British countryside for centuries. These rights have developed over time, and are a result of the unique land ownership and management arrangements to be found in different jurisdictions in the UK. England has about 190,000 km of public rights of way, including public footpaths, bridleways (for horse riding), restricted byways (open to non-motorised vehicles) and byways open to all traffic – footpaths constitute around 78 per cent of the total (Natural England, 2008). There are 15 long-distance walking routes in England and Wales designated as National Trails, and five Long-Distance Routes in Scotland. The National Cycle Network (see 'Useful websites', pp. 223–4) currently provides more than 12,000 miles of cycling and walking routes throughout the UK. Over 354 million walking and cycling trips were made on the network in 2007.

In addition to these linear routes, the 2000 Countryside and Rights of Way Act also opened up 'access land' in England and Wales. Essentially, people are allowed to roam across uncultivated land and common land, now mapped as 'open country' by Natural England and the Countryside Council for Wales. The Land Reform (Scotland) Act 2003 established a much more extensive right of access to land and inland water for outdoor recreation and passage in Scotland. These rights cover many different forms of outdoor recreation, including informal activities such as picnicking, photography and sightseeing; and active pursuits, including walking, cycling, riding, canoeing and wild camping; as well as taking part in recreational and educational events. The Scottish Outdoor Access Code provides more guidance about these rights and their management (Scottish Natural Heritage, 2004).

8.8.4 Forests and woodlands

In total, forests cover about 2.81 million hectares or 11.6 per cent of the total area of the UK. The Forestry Commission has 17 Forest Parks in Great Britain (see 'Useful websites', pp. 223–4). Forests provide opportunities for walking, cycling, horse riding, orienteering, camping, caravanning, fishing, bird-watching and a whole host of other activities enjoyed by people of all ages. There are various other initiatives concerned with new woodlands and forests in the UK, including a new National Forest and 17 Community Forests. Each forest contains hundreds of green spaces, including parks, woodlands, wetlands and recreation areas – all places for local people to visit and enjoy in their leisure time, providing an appreciation of the countryside, their heritage and surroundings and improving their quality of life.

8.8.5 Green space in urban areas

Eighty per cent of the population of England live in towns and cities. According to Natural England (2008), over half of all visits to the countryside are within only five miles of home. CABE Space is a government funded agency with a remit covering all outside spaces, including parks and streets, with an initial focus on parks and green spaces. It was established for the following reasons:

- Parks and green spaces are as essential to our cities as roads and sewers, breathing communities, bringing charm, beauty, character, nature and wildlife.
- 30 per cent of the public say they will not use parks, usually because they do not feel safe.
- Even fewer people who are elderly or from minority ethnic groups used parks.
- If you live in a deprived area, your parks are likely to be in a worse condition than if you live in a wealthier area.
- Children's play areas are often unsafe, empty and have broken equipment.
- One-third of all people never walk alone in their area after dark; even fewer women or older people go out after dark.

Increasingly, local authorities and others are being encouraged to plan and manage all their green spaces in a more holistic and integrated manner. Green infrastructure includes parks, open spaces, playing fields, woodlands, allotments and private gardens. It should be designed and managed as a multifunctional resource capable of delivering a wide range of environmental and quality of life benefits for local communities, including:

- places for outdoor relaxation and play;
- space and habitat for wildlife with access to nature for people;

- climate change adaptation – for example flood alleviation and cooling urban heat islands;
- environmental education;
- local food production – in allotments, gardens and through agriculture;
- improved health and well-being – lowering stress levels and providing opportunities for exercise.

Discussion question

Is leisure in the natural environment still mainly a rural issue, or is it more important for the quality of life for urban communities?

8.8.6 Access to water

Britons have an affinity with water, with strong historical links to the sea, lakes, rivers and inland waterways. The Royal Yachting Association has undertaken an annual Watersports and Leisure Participation Survey since 2002 and now estimates that overall watersports participation stands at approximately 4 million adults, compared to 3.7 million in 2006, 3.5 million in 2005 and 4 million in 2004 (Royal Yachting Association, 2007).

The UK coast is extremely popular for leisure and recreation. Natural England estimates that its sandy beaches and cliff-top routes generate 72 million trips a year to the undeveloped coast, and 174 million to seaside towns. There are 46 Heritage Coast designations protecting 1,555 km, about 35 per cent of the total length of coastline. The National Trust, through its Neptune Coastline Campaign, raises funds to acquire and protect stretches of coastline of natural beauty and recreation value. The National Trust for Scotland cares for more than 400 km of the Scottish coastline; whilst in Wales, non-statutory protection has been given to heritage coasts which cover a large area of undeveloped coastline. At the time of writing, a new Marine and Coastal Access Bill is being considered by Parliament which will lay the basis for a long-distance walking trail around the English coast for the purposes of open-air recreation, together with appropriate spreading room en route where people will be able to explore, rest or picnic.

Access to inland waterways, lakes and rivers is also variable throughout the UK. The Scottish Land Reform Act 2003 has established a statutory right of access to inland waterways for outdoor recreation. But this situation is not replicated in England and Wales, where there exists a mixture of statutory and permissive rights, traditional uses and ongoing restrictions. There are many campaigning groups who continue to press for more universal rights of access to inland waterways in England and Wales. Leisure managers can be faced with the often difficult task of balancing conservation, angling and other recreation interests.

British Waterways is the custodian of a network of canals and inland waterways which were built to service the transport needs of the world's first industrial revolution. The waterways network includes 3,200 km of canals, 4,763 bridges, 397 aqueducts, 60 tunnels, 1,549 locks, 89 reservoirs, nearly 3,000 listed structures and ancient monuments and 66 SSSIs. The network is an attraction to domestic and international tourists, for leisure and heritage purposes. British Waterways report that the network is visited each year by 10 million people, of whom only a small proportion own boats or take holidays on the canals. In addition to activities on the water, the waterways are used for walking, angling, cycling, wildlife pursuits and visiting heritage buildings.

8.9 The management of leisure in the natural environment

In spite of the evidence concerning the public benefits of leisure in the natural environment and increasing concerns about barriers to participation, there are still sections of the profession which remain overly focused on the potential impacts of visitors on the resource and regard recreation as a major problem to be managed. This perception is contrary to much of the available evidence (see House of Commons, 1995). It appears that concern about damage to the natural environment from leisure use is more of a philosophical standpoint, rather than a conclusion based on any hard data. Other pressures – agricultural intensification, urban development, extensive pollution – are far more significant in terms of impacts on our environment (English Nature, 2003).

Many researchers now believe that the focus on achieving a balance between recreation and conservation of the natural environment is no longer as relevant to current leisure management practices as had previously been thought. Indeed, in most cases it is possible to meet the demand for leisure and to promote further opportunities through sensitive planning and management based on a series of principles contained within established frameworks. Rather than discussing a 'balance' or compromise between these two objectives, it is far better to aim to achieve the 'best of both worlds'.

Discussion questions

Are there any environments in which recreation should be banned? And are there any environments where conservation is irrelevant?

Elson *et al.* (1995) concluded that six major factors were pivotal in producing good management practice:

1 **state of the environment** – establishing baseline environmental conditions on site, and an agreed view of the nature of any impacts;
2 **clarity of purpose** – setting unequivocal objectives forming a realistic framework for future action;
3 **participatory management** – regarding management as a process, guided by regular engagement with and negotiations between relevant interests;
4 **importance of voluntary agreements** – the operation of restraint and self-policing by clubs and governing bodies;
5 **local involvement** – regular liaison and negotiation with local populations and sports organisations;
6 **monitoring and review** – a conscious, systematic process which informs future management decisions, and any changes in direction to site management.

8.9.1 Carrying capacity

Leisure managers are faced with an environmental resource used by a multitude of individuals and organisations, with many different interests and concerns. An early approach to the issue of potential conflict was the concept of carrying capacities – 'the level of recreation use an area can sustain without an unacceptable degree of deterioration of the character and quality of the resource or the recreation experience' (Countryside Commission, 1970). Four types of recreational carrying capacity were identified: physical, economic, ecological and social. The chief problem here lies in what different individuals and groups construe as 'acceptable change'. Not only is this an issue when related to social and perceptual factors, but it is also true of ecological change. Indeed, it has been notoriously difficult to provide any empirical evidence which can confidently demonstrate causal links between recreation use and environmental change.

Hall and Page (2002) have suggested that there are five main reasons which explain why the carrying capacity concept has failed to generate practical visitor use limits:

1 Different leisure activities have different impacts on a site – and thus influence the total carrying capacity of that site – yet they could potentially occur at different times or at varying levels.
2 Impacts on biological and physical resources do not necessarily help establish carrying capacities; other factors could also be significant.
3 A strong cause and effect relationship between amount of use and impacts does not exist. Where relationships do exist, they are generally anything but simple and linear, and a wide range of other variables will have an influence.
4 Carrying capacity is a product of value-judgements and is not purely a product of the natural resource base; therefore it cannot be determined through careful observation and research.
5 Carrying capacity does not help determine the balance between protecting the pristine qualities of a natural area and allowing visitor use.

8.9.2 Visitor Planning Frameworks

Despite the concept of carrying capacity being over thirty years old, it remains in currency, although successful implementation is highly elusive. In academic circles, the concept has largely been dismissed, but many practitioners continue to refer to carrying capacity as a useful technique. There are other techniques which may be more useful in the field – a range of 'Visitor Planning Frameworks' which seek to achieve the best of all worlds. A useful summary of these is provided by Crowe (2005). One of these alternatives is a framework known as Limits of Acceptable Change (LAC). Instead of asking 'How much is too much?', the LAC approach rephrases the question by asking 'How much change is acceptable?' (Newsome *et al.*, 2002).

The LAC approach has been used extensively in North America, Australia and New Zealand (see Case Study 8.2). In the UK, Sidaway (1991) has simplified the process into four steps:

1 detailed objectives to be agreed for each site by interested agencies and individuals;
2 thresholds for deterioration (i.e. the limits of acceptable change) to be agreed in advance;
3 regular, systematic measurements to be taken so that management can monitor change;
4 management responses triggered when these values are exceeded – also agreed in advance.

One of the most critical aspects of developing a LAC approach has been establishing stakeholder endorsement and support. Stakeholders from the local tourism sector and communities can provide valuable input in determining desired outcomes, and are usually essential in providing the economic and political support necessary to ensure programmes can be effectively delivered and monitored.

Further elaborations of the LAC approach have developed models such as the Recreation Opportunity Spectrum and the Quality of Life Capital (Crowe, 2005). These different

The Bob Marshall Wilderness Complex, Montana, USA

The Bob Marshall Wilderness Complex, in north central Montana, is managed by the US Forest Service (USFS). It comprises 600,000 hectares of un-roaded temperate forest and attracts 25,000 visitors a year, primarily from June through November. June to September is dominated by backpacking and horse-supported backcountry trips. In the autumn, most use is for big game hunting.

In 1982, the USFS embarked on a planning effort based on the Limits of Acceptable Change (LAC) process, largely because of the perceived need to involve the public more closely in the management process. It involved continuous public participation through a taskforce consisting of a range of stakeholders: the public, scientists and managers. The process took five years. The LAC framework focused effort on addressing how much change in wilderness, biophysical and social conditions was acceptable. By designing a public participation process that incorporated the full range of values involved in the Wilderness area, participants developed a set of management actions that were effective in reducing and controlling human-induced impacts, and achieved the social and political acceptability necessary for implementation.

The plan has three broad characteristics:

1 It establishes four zones designed to protect the pristine character of the wilderness, yet realistically permits some trade-offs between recreation use and human-induced impacts.
2 It identifies indicator variables – things to monitor to ensure conditions remain acceptable and to use to establish the effectiveness of actions implemented to control or mitigate impacts. For each indicator, quantifiable standards exist, indicating what limit of change from the natural baseline is acceptable in each zone.
3 It indicates for each zone the management actions in order of their social acceptability. This gives the manager a choice of tools and determines what management action will be most acceptable in controlling impacts. This procedure encourages the least intrusive management action first.

Some of the management actions implemented have been successful at reducing impacts on the ground, while other actions have caused unexpected results that have actually led to a degradation in overall resource condition in some locations. Lessons learnt include:

● **Education/enforcement** – direct visitor contacts by experienced wilderness rangers are important to educate the public about the value of wilderness and the best ways to protect this fragile resource.
● **Prepare for potential shifts in visitor use** – e.g. due to fire activity, managers need to prepare for increased pressure from the public in popular locations not impacted by fire.
● **Encourage the proper Leave-No-Trace principles for camping** – encouraging future users to camp at already popular sites, because research shows that approximately 90 per cent of the resource impact to a previously unused location is caused in the first four nights of use.
● **Closing campsites can lead to a net increase in resource impact** – temporary closure of campsites to public use for Wilderness 'rehabilitation' purposes has not

led to an improvement in their condition. Therefore, campsite rehabilitation needs to minimise the future expansion of the square footage of a site.

- **Coordination among commercial services** – active work with guides to minimise overlap of itineraries reduces the likelihood of organised groups being at the same place at the same time.
- **Stock holding facilities** – temporary hitch rails or high-lines encourage stock holding in more durable areas and reduce the spread of resource damage.

Overall, the implementation of the LAC process at the Bob Marshall Wilderness Complex has been regarded as a success, and the planning and management activities continue today, as does the involvement of the taskforce.

Source: www.fs.fed.us/r1/flathead/wilderness/bmwcomplex.shtml

models are all useful in different circumstances and leisure managers should adapt what works in their own circumstances. The following fundamental elements must be in place for these approaches to be successful (Masters *et al.*, 2002):

- **The need for a systematic approach must be accepted** – senior staff have to be convinced that there are benefits from spending more time and resources on site planning and management, and that any system for monitoring or decision-making is helpful rather than constraining.
- **Setting clear objectives is central to the process** – whatever method is adopted, clear objective setting at the strategic, site and individual zone level is vital. Setting objectives will involve achieving agreement between stakeholders, and will be enhanced through having trend data to inform the decisions. Where objectives are in potential conflict, zoning and prioritisation of objectives will be required.
- **Staff time and resources should follow any systematic planning and management approach** – a more systematic approach may mean spending more time and resources on meetings, site visits and monitoring. It is also important to recognise that one approach is unlikely to fit all circumstances, and that cheaper and quicker methods will be necessary for simple sites.

8.9.3 Participatory management

Effective leisure managers will base their decision-making on sound evidence about their customers' needs and demands, and on the special characteristics of their resource. In order to develop clear objectives, owned and shared by all stakeholders, it is essential that information and data are gathered from all those with an interest in a site. The different aspects of a site to be monitored must be agreed and performance measures decided in advance. All of these issues require resources in terms of staff time and finance. Both internal and external stakeholders should be involved in all stages of the process. External 'facilitators' may be required to ensure the process is a full and open engagement with all stakeholders. Case Study 8.3 is one example of this.

Because of the nature of land ownership and land use in the natural environment, the range of stakeholders with an interest in any leisure development is likely to be large. Equally, resources are often limited and this can lead to managers focusing on those stakeholders with the 'loudest voice', or where traditional relationships are already well established (such as with significant non-governmental organisations and known user groups).

CASE STUDY 8.3

Stanage Forum stakeholder engagement

The Stanage/North Lees Estate is owned and managed by the Peak District National Park Authority (NPA) in the UK. Its landscape value is exceptional, with internationally rare heather moorland and blanket bog, and its recreational value is equally outstanding. The estate receives over half a million visitors per year, with a wide range of activities including walking, cycling, hang-gliding and paragliding, and bird-watching. Stanage Edge is perhaps best known as an internationally important grit-stone climbing edge, arguably one of the birthplaces of the sport.

In 2000, the NPA wished to review the Management Plan for the estate. It was perceived that there were real conflicts between the various activities on the estate and its management for conservation and farming interests. Rather than embark on a traditional process involving the production of a draft plan followed by various consultation exercises, the NPA began with a blank sheet of paper and commissioned an independent facilitator to guide the subsequent process:

1 A website was established with an on-line discussion board to enable as wide a debate as possible.
2 An open public meeting was held, attended by over seventy people, in August 2000. This wider Forum agreed a set of consensus building principles in order to develop a shared vision for the Plan.
3 A Steering Group of 17 people was nominated through an open, democratic procedure.

The Steering Group framed a number of specific problems, which were then discussed in technical groups. The emphasis was on consensus building and improving understanding in order to reach agreed solutions. Over the next two years, large amounts of time were voluntarily given by individuals and groups contributing to the shared development of the Stanage/North Lees Estate Management Plan. In addition, 285 people receive the Forum newsletter, and in total 135 different people attended public events. From the first Forum event in August 2000 up to the production of the draft plan at the end of June 2002, there were 21,300 hits on the Forum website. The final ten year Management Plan was agreed in October 2002.

Since then there have been other notable successes. The rare 'mountain blackbird', the ring ouzel, is now successfully breeding on the Edge following close cooperation with local climbers to avoid their nesting sites. Difficult negotiations between different groups over the legal use of a byway by motorised vehicles has led to the agreement of voluntary codes of conduct by the motoring groups, including speed limits and other restrictions. An annual public forum reviews progress and continues to seek to encourage anyone with an interest in the area to become involved in its future management.

For further information visit www.peakdistrict.org/index/looking-after/stanage.htm.

Particular difficulties are faced in trying to work with 'hard to reach' groups, such as the elderly or young people, spatially or socially isolated groups, and other minorities who may not be formally represented or organised.

Considerable support may be needed to enable some participants to engage meaningfully. Leisure managers need to be creative and imaginative in reaching a wider audience and enabling them to engage as fully as possible. This could mean developing partnerships with groups not normally associated specifically with leisure activities such as community groups or youth services.

8.10 Strategies and actions

Sidaway (1991), in his guide on good practice for sport and recreation, mentions a range of specific site management strategies and actions. Several of these are discussed below.

8.10.1 Zoning at a local site scale

One of the key strategies for managing protected areas is through zoning. This involves recognising smaller zones or units within areas, each with prescribed levels of environmental protection and certain levels and types of use. Most planning frameworks include identifying and managing zones over large areas. But this process can also work effectively at a detailed, site level.

Zoning helps to provide choice for visitors, as well as clarifying future intentions. Zoning can also be used to separate incompatible uses in space and time (spatial and temporal zoning). Spatial zoning might segregate different recreational uses, such as motorised and non-motorised users, or horse riders and cyclists. An example of temporal zoning might include limiting access to particular areas of a site, such as a nature reserve, during bird nesting seasons.

8.10.2 Regulating access

The provision, location, style and quality of site infrastructure are key components of the management of visitors in the countryside. They also provide an indication of the quality of management and can be an interface between organisations and visitors. But the first question must be: do we need any infrastructure at all? Particularly in the natural environment, there may be special qualities such as a sense of 'wilderness' which should not be sacrificed. Often, people services – such as a ranger service or educational service – can be more effective in resolving management issues than new infrastructure.

However, infrastructure may be needed. Table 8.2 (adapted from Keirle, 2002) illustrates some of the infrastructure tools available. The general issues which relate to the use of such tools include:

- the design of the item, as reflected in its function and anticipated users;
- the nature of the site and location of the item;
- creation of local distinctiveness – through selection of appropriate materials, scale and design;
- costs – both of the initial installation and long-term maintenance requirements;
- robustness (for example against vandalism);
- needs of visitors with disabilities;
- health and safety issues.

Table 8.2 Function, type and design issues associated with different infrastructure tools

Function	Possible infrastructure tools	Design issues
Control of cars – providing places to park and preventing parking where it is undesirable	Car parks, bollards, ditches, banks, fencing, yellow lines	Design, materials and location, charging issues, enforcement and liaison with local police
Directing visitors effectively around a site	Signposts, waymarkers, orientation panels, information, desire lines, attractions, sight lines	Design, materials and location, communication, maintenance, ranger assistance
Control of visitor movement around a site	Fences, hedges, barriers, landscaping, information, paths	Design, materials and location, monitoring and maintenance
Allowing people to pass through barriers such as fences, walls and streams	Stiles, kissing gates, bridges	Design, materials and location, access for all issues, maintenance
Control of litter	Bins, skips, dog bins	Design, materials and location, enforcement
Increasing visitor comfort	Toilets, seats, picnic tables, refreshments	Design, materials and location, maintenance
Increasing visitor confidence and safety	Lighting, signs, quality of infrastructure and information	Design, materials and location, information and maintenance

Source: adapted from Keirle (2002).

8.10.3 Self-regulation, voluntary codes and voluntary agreements

The acceptance of responsibility for conserving landscapes and wildlife by participants themselves is one of the most effective conservation measures, but it works best as one of a series of measures. Self-regulation is most effective when there is an affinity of interests between the participants, who want access, and conservation organisations and landowners, who wish to see the resource safeguarded and wildlife protected. Usually this is more easily achieved when most participants belong to the same organisation or club, which can then negotiate access with a landowner. It can, however, lead to difficulties of exclusive agreements between a limited group of users and landowners. For example, many of the issues surrounding access to water by both anglers and canoeists can be related to the development of access arrangements between either or both of these groups and the waterway owners. But even where voluntary agreements between these groups can be negotiated, often the needs of the informal participant, with no access to special arrangements or information, can remain unclear and ambiguous.

The limitations of self-regulation are all too evident when there are large numbers of casual participants who are not members of any club. Self-regulation works best when the rationale is clear and well justified, and when individual participants are informed and aware and accept responsibility. Codes of practice and voluntary agreements help here. Case Study 8.4 illustrates such an approach.

8.11 Health and safety

Health and safety issues have become an increasing matter of concern for many leisure managers. Clearly, the well-being of their users is paramount, but managers are often faced with both professional and financial consequences if their actions apparently lead to unfortunate accidents or unwarranted risks (see Chapter 19). This is particularly challenging when working in a location where the resource's special qualities may include a sense of adventure and an 'untamed' environment. Different countries have different legal interpretations of issues such as public and private occupiers' liability, and these will take precedence. But leisure managers can also adopt good practice to demonstrate that they are taking reasonable and proportionate action to manage risk and enhance the visitor experience.

An excellent guide to principles and practice has been developed by the Visitor Safety in the Countryside Group (see 'Useful websites', pp. 223–4). This guide advocates that managers take account of cultural and landscape objectives and do not take away people's sense of freedom and adventure. But visitors should be informed and educated about the nature and extent of hazards, the risk control measures in place and the precautions they need to take themselves. It also recommends the development of reasonable risk assessment processes and safety plans for individual sites, with the emphasis always on what is a proportionate response for the particular site, and careful monitoring to demonstrate that the manager is aware of his or her site (Visitor Safety in the Countryside Group, 2005).

8.12 Information and interpretation

High quality information, both on and off site, is needed to enable visitors to make informed decisions; whereas interpretation helps visitors to understand and enjoy a site. Keirle (2002) outlines a range of information that can be provided at recreation sites and

CASE STUDY 8.4

Broads Authority Water Ski Working Group

Water skiing has long been an issue in the Norfolk Broads in the UK. The Broads are a nationally designated landscape, with equivalent status to a national park in the UK. Concerns have been expressed in the past over the impact of the sport on the flora and fauna of these important wetland sites, and the peace and tranquillity of the area for other leisure users.

After consulting on its proposed policy to remove the sport from the Broads, outlined in the Draft Broads Plan 1993, the Broads Authority set up a Water Ski Working Group to examine all aspects of the sport and implications for its continuance and future management. The group's membership included representation of national water skiing interests as well as local clubs, the boat hire industry, private yachtsmen, the Navigation Section of the Broads Authority and conservation interests.

The Working Group assessed the impact of the sport in the Broads, including environmental impacts, safety issues and impacts on other people's enjoyment of the Broads. The group was also invited to look closely at current management of the sport and to put forward suggestions for additional or alternative control measures. Representatives made site visits, commissioned technical reports and a series of public opinion surveys. The report of the Water Ski Working Group on the impact of this sport on the Broads was published in 1997. This included 11 possible options, ranging from no change through various possible amendments to existing byelaws to new byelaws.

In 1998, after much debate, the Broads Authority decided again to take measures to seek a cessation of water skiing on the grounds that it is an inappropriate activity within this nationally designated landscape. The Authority then worked with water skiers over a period of several years to try to identify a suitable alternative location for the sport, but without success.

The Authority reviewed the issue in 2003 and, having taken into account its earlier decision but also the views of its newly constituted Broads Forum (representing a wide range of stakeholders), decided to defer implementing its 1998 decision and instead allowing a new management regime to be introduced and evaluated. It was recognised that a wide range of management controls could be instituted in cooperation with water skiers and imposed through a voluntary code of practice, particularly if water skiing interests were represented by a single and clearly constituted body, rather than the existing unstructured local club arrangements.

Measures are now in place whereby water skiing may only take place subject to: a permit being issued by the Broads Authority; compliance with the conditions set out in the Speed Limit Byelaws; and adherence to a set of conditions agreed between the Broads Authority and Eastern Rivers Ski Club. A further review of the issue took place in 2007, when a review panel consisting of nine different interest groups and an independent chair examined the suitability of the sport on the Broads over an eight-week period and concluded it was safe enough to continue.

For further information visit www.broads-authority.gov.uk/boating/navigating/waterskiing.html.

the variety of methods for providing that information. He also suggests how information provision can be used to influence visitors:

- **where people go** – by providing information we can influence the sites that people go to, or the locations within sites that people go to;
- **when people go** – by letting people know about opening times, or the timing of events;
- **how people get to a site** – provision of clear information on how to get to a site by car, public transport or bike;
- **what they do when they get to the site** – what the attractions of the site are and how they get to them;
- **who goes to a site** – information can be targeted at particular market segments.

There is also an element of information provision which is largely concerned with promotion and publicity.

Interpretation goes beyond just information provision. An early definition of interpretation states that it is '[a]n educational activity which aims to reveal meanings and relationships through the use of original objects, by first-hand experience, and by illustrative media, rather than simply communicate factual information' (Tilden, 1977). Good interpretation enhances enjoyment and understanding. But as well as adding to the visitors' experience, interpretation can also develop visitors' understanding and support for the managers' role and their objectives and policies.

Increasingly, leisure managers are using new technology as a means to interpret the natural environment for visitors – and this can sometimes avoid the need for permanent new infrastructure on remote sites. A good example of this is the Moors for the Future project in the South Pennines, UK, where audio trails can be downloaded directly onto a mobile phone or MP3 player from the website (see 'Useful websites', pp. 223–4). These audio trails, often using the voices of local people working and living in the area, add a layer of meaning and understanding for visitors to enhance their leisure experience.

> ### Discussion question
> Can electronic communication be used to enhance the visitor experience in the natural environment, or is it a place to escape from such communication?

8.13 Monitoring and review

Monitoring and review are now an accepted stage in any programme or project management cycle, although all too often this stage is still under-resourced and ineffectively used. Managers need to accurately evaluate the success of the outcomes of their decisions in terms of managing visitors, and reflect on the results of such monitoring to then increase the effectiveness of their work.

As part of this process, managers should ask themselves, 'What will success look like?', and consider how their objectives are to be measured. At a local level, managers need to collect input, output and outcome data – each of these will assist in evaluating the success of any project. However, all too often only elements of these factors are recorded. For example, it is very easy for a local access manager to measure the overall resources spent on a project, the length of trails which are adequately surfaced or promotional leaflets produced, all of which are inputs. But it is much more meaningful to monitor the number of people who are actively using these services and facilities (outputs) and their enjoyment (outcomes).

Often by demonstrating a contribution to wider public benefits, the leisure manager can also enhance the justification of their work. This may be particularly important in the public sector, where competing priorities for scarce resources increase the pressure on leisure budgets. So monitoring the wider public benefits which leisure in the natural environment provides becomes an important tool for the leisure manager.

8.14 Conclusions

The natural environment is a hugely important leisure resource, in all its many and varied forms. It is not only important for individuals and communities, but also for governments. There is increasing recognition that use of the natural environment for leisure can bring a range of important public benefits, not just to individuals but also to wider society. Hence a variety of organisations have an interest in leisure in the natural environment; and there is a variety of designations of special status for important areas. This complicates the management of such areas, because there are considerations of national and long-term interest, as well as the preferences of local stakeholders, to take into account.

In management of leisure in the natural environment, it is no longer appropriate to envisage a conflict between conservation and leisure, or even to see a 'balance' between the two as the aim of good management. Instead, good management of leisure in the natural environment concentrates on ensuring the long-term sustainability of the resource and access for leisure by more people, alongside the wider benefits to society as a whole. The leisure manager has a vital role in helping to achieve these multiple goals.

Practical tasks

1 Conduct a survey of local green spaces in your own community. Assess the accessibility of these spaces to different socio-economic groups (for example children, young people, families, people without private transport, people with disabilities) and identify any possible barriers to leisure use (for example safety fears, physical barriers, lack of information). Suggest a range of practical measures which could be implemented to remove these barriers.

2 Select a specific leisure activity in the natural environment with which you are unfamiliar and investigate how easy (or difficult) it is to find out how to pursue that activity within your area. Establish what information is available on the internet or through other sources such as Visitor Information Centres or your relevant local authority.

Structured guide to further reading

For leisure participation in the natural environment:
Countryside Recreation Network (2007) *Volunteering in the Natural Outdoors*, CRN, Sheffield.
Henley Centre (2005) *Online Research supporting the Outdoor Recreation Strategy*, available at www.naturalengland.org.uk/ourwork/enjoying/research/futuretrends.
Natural England (2008) *State of the Natural Environment*, NE85, Natural England, Sheffield.
Royal Yachting Association (2007) *Watersports and Leisure Participation Report*, available at www.bcu.org.uk/files/RYA%20Watersports%20Participation%20Survey%202007.pdf.

For environmental policies and administration:
Countryside Recreation Network, www.countrysiderecreation.org.uk.
Defra (2004) *Delivering the Essentials of Life*, available at www.defra.gov.uk/corporate/5year-strategy/5year-strategy.pdf.
European Environment Agency (2009) www.eea.europa.eu.
Scottish Natural Heritage (2004) *Scottish Outdoor Access Code*, available at www.snh.org.uk/strategy/access/sr-afor01.asp (accessed May 2009).

(and all relevant government agency websites – see below)

For management of leisure in the natural environment:
Crowe, L. (2005) *Promoting Outdoor Recreation in the English National Parks: guide to good practice*, Countryside Agency CA214, Cheltenham.
Elson, M., Heaney, D. and Reynolds, G. (1995) *Good Practice in the Planning and Management of Sport and Active Recreation in the Countryside*, Sports Council and Countryside Commission, London and Cheltenham.
Keirle, I. (2002) *Countryside Recreation Site Management: a marketing approach*, Routledge, London.
Sidaway, R. (1991) *Good Conservation Practice for Sport and Recreation*, Sports Council and Countryside Commission, London and Cheltenham.
Visitor Safety in the Countryside Group (2005) *Managing Visitor Safety in the Countryside: principles and practice*, RSPB, Nottingham.

Useful websites

For an international overview of policies and protected areas:
International Union of Conservation of Nature, www.iucn.org

For relevant UK government agencies:
Natural England, www.naturalengland.org.uk
Environment Agency, www.environment-agency.gov.uk/aboutus/organisation/35675/aspx
English Heritage, www.english-heritage.org.uk
Countryside Council for Wales, www.ccw.gov.uk
Environment Agency Wales, www.environment-agency.gov.uk/regions/wales
Cadw Welsh Historic Monuments Executive Agency, www.cadw.wales.gov.uk
Scottish Natural Heritage, www.snh.org.uk

Products and services

Scottish Environment Protection Agency, www.sepa.org.uk
Historic Scotland, www.historic-scotland.gov.uk
Northern Ireland Environment Agency, www.ni-environment.gov.uk
Forestry Commission, www.forestry.gov.uk

For general information about research, new policy initiatives and good practice:
Countryside Recreation Network, www.countrysiderecreation.org.uk

For other national organisations:
The National Trust, www.nationaltrust.org.uk
National Trust for Scotland, www.nts.org.uk
National Cycle Network in the UK, www.sustrans.org.uk
Forestry Commission in Britain, www.forestry.gov.uk
Visitor Safety in the Countryside Group, www.vscg.co.uk
Moors for the Future, www.moorsforthefuture.org.uk/audio-trails
Mosaic Partnership, www.mosaicpartnership.org

Chapter 9

Arts, museums and libraries

Elizabeth Owen

In this chapter

- Who participates in the arts, museums and libraries?
- How are the arts identified and organised?
- How are the arts valued?
- How is management of the arts structured?
- What are the origins and functions of museums and libraries?
- How important are public sector museums and libraries?
- How are museums and libraries developing in a digital age?

Summary

The arts, museums and galleries, and libraries are three important sections of cultural activity. They contain activities which attract significant proportions of the population. They involve all three major supplying sectors – the public sector, the commercial sector and the third sector. Governments have a longstanding interest in cultural activities, with public funding of the arts, heritage and libraries in the UK, for example, having been established for over 300 years. Now there is an array of public and private organisations promoting the interests of cultural activities.

Over time, public policy priorities for culture have changed. Among them are instrumental values (i.e. tangible outcomes such as numbers of visitors, employment in cultural organisations and their monetary value) and intrinsic values (i.e. culture important for its own sake). Modern governments are interested not just in preserving culture but also in access to culture by as many people as possible, as well as the contribution that culture makes to the creative industries. Culture is not simply a national matter – the innovation and excellence of creative industries are promoted to the global creative economy.

9.1 Introduction

Culture is a complicated word, Yeoman *et al.* (2004) note that '[m]eanings of culture have grown and developed but universally accepted definitions are still lacking'. This chapter will deal with the three distinct cultural areas: the arts, museums and libraries. Each section will begin with clarification of the activity in each area. An important consideration of cultural activity is the policies of and allocation of resources by governments. The chapter focuses on the structure and organisation of these activities in the UK, to give a coherent and detailed picture, although there is some reference to the international context and examples in other countries.

Whilst the identity of museums and libraries is fairly clear, this is not the case with the arts. McMaster (2008) notes that '[t]he arts encompasses a variety of forms'. The way these forms have been identified and described has changed over time. Pick (1986) identified that until the middle of the nineteenth century '"the arts" referred to gardening, needlework, conversation {...} as readily as to making music, writing poems or acting a play' because at that time a skill was the primary meaning of the word 'art'. The Arts Council of Great Britain (1993) suggested that '[i]t is notoriously difficult to say what art is or what it is for. One possible definition runs: art is a symbolic communication by which an artist represents and arranges objects, signs and sounds or events in a manner likely to imply meanings or arouse emotions. But that definition does not conjure up a sense of what art does'.

Discussion questions

Is graffiti art? What about a friend's poem that they showed you? Or breakdancing?

Another definition relevant to, but broader in concept than the arts is 'the creative industries'. These are defined by the UK's Department of Culture, Media and Sport (see 'Useful websites', pp. 251–2) as 'those activities which have their origin in individual creativity, skill and talent and which have a potential for wealth and job creation through the generation and exploitation of intellectual property'. The creative industries include:

- advertising;
- architecture;
- crafts and designer furniture;
- fashion clothing;
- film, video and other audiovisual production;
- graphic design;
- educational and leisure software;
- live and recorded music;
- performing arts and entertainments;
- television, radio and internet broadcasting;
- visual arts and antiques;
- writing and publishing.

The Work Foundation (Work Foundation & NESTA, 2007) suggests that there is a subset of 'cultural industries' which includes film, TV, publishing, music, the performing arts and video games.

9.2 Participation

Participation in the arts, museums and libraries is part of the evidence provided in Chapter 2 and is an important consideration for managers in this field – for segmentation, marketing and policy purposes. In summary this evidence, from the *Taking Part* survey, suggests the following for England:

- Two-thirds or more of adults had attended a historic site or an arts event at least once in the previous year. Over half of adults had participated in an arts activity at least once in the previous year. Less than half of adults had attended a library or a museum or gallery in the previous year (Table 2.1).
- The most common reasons for adults not participating in arts and heritage, cited by around one-third of non-participants, are lack of interest and difficulty in finding the time to participate. The main reason for not using libraries is the perception that there is no need to go (Table 2.6).
- Between five and nine out of every ten young people aged 11–15 had visited a museum, arts event, library, historic site or participated in an arts activity at least once in the previous year. Significantly lower numbers participate in these activities outside school.
- More women than men participate in arts events, arts activities and use of libraries. Equal numbers of men and women visit historic sites and museums and galleries (Figure 2.2).
- Higher percentages of white people visit arts and heritage attractions than other ethnic groups; but higher percentages of other ethnic groups use libraries than white people (Figure 2.3).
- Educational achievements have a generally positive effect on participation in arts, heritage and libraries (Figure 2.4).

- Higher income has a generally positive effect on participation in arts and heritage, but has little effect on use of libraries (Figure 2.6).
- Higher socio-economic class has a positive effect on participation in arts, heritage and libraries (Figure 2.7).

9.3 The arts

The arts can be divided into three main categories, which contribute to the creative and cultural industries:

1 **performing arts** – including drama, music and dance;
2 **visual arts** – including painting, sculpture, crafts and images which are produced using the lens, e.g. photography;
3 **literary arts** – including texts and oral reproduction of prose and poetry.

These three arts categories are not mutually exclusive as they overlap, merge and combine. For example, a work of art in the view of the public, such as the lyrics of a song mounted on the side of a building, brings together the visual and literary arts. Within the three arts categories there are also genres, i.e. recognised types within an art form which are important identifiers, just as there are different disciplines within a sport such as gymnastics. The following illustrations give a genre (in italics) in an art form: *farce* in drama; *house* in music; *jazz* in dance; *impressionism* in painting; *romance* in novel; *horror* in film. Genres are used to further describe the content of the art. People can respond to this specialist vocabulary in two ways – for some it may act as a deterrent to interest and participation, for others it offers more information about the work of art. It is helpful for leisure managers to investigate and understand genres such as classical, traditional, popular, folk, high, modern and contemporary when applied to art forms, in order to appreciate their different audiences.

Discussion questions

Which genres of any art form do you not like? Is this dislike related to your actual consumption experience of them, or is it caused by something other than experience?

Colbert (2000) considers the way works of art are produced and 'clearly distinguishes between unique products not designed to be reproduced (a prototype industry) and products manufactured in runs or batches using a prototype so that many copies appear at the same time'. In the twenty-first century, the arts contribute greatly to people's leisure through the consumption of cultural goods and commodities, produced, often for multiple reproduction, and increasingly distributed by technological means. The use, consumption and exhibition of these commodities in the home are considered in Chapter 12.

9.4 How do people learn about the arts?

Adults and children learn about the arts in a wide variety of ways and places, informal and formal. They may learn at home, with friends, in their community, in an amateur group or have private lessons and study qualifications such as those of the Royal Academy of Dance and the Associated Board of the Royal Schools of Music (ABRSM), the world's leading music examining body. Music exam fees contribute to the UK in the form of direct earnings from overseas (Myerscough, 1988). Also arts professional associations offer links to training and teaching organisations on their websites – examples include South Asian Dance in the UK (SADA) and the British Dance Council. Some artists are self-taught, like Jack Vettriano, Scotland's most commercially successful artist.

In the programme notes to *The Pitmen Painters*, a play about miners studying art in a Workers Educational Association (WEA) evening class in the north of England in the 1930s, Hall writes:

> Quite clearly the Working Classes of the early part of last century were aspirational about High Art. They not only felt entitled, but felt a duty to take part in the best that life has to offer in terms of art and culture. That fifty years later I could write Billy Elliot, a story about the incomprehension of a mining community towards a similar aspirant to High Culture, seems to me some sort of index of political and cultural failure. Despite the advances in education and the blossoming of the welfare state, somehow we have failed to 'democratise' the riches of culture. That the Group (The Pitman Painters) managed to achieve so much unaided and unabetted should remind us that dumbing down is not a prerequisite of culture being more accessible.
>
> (Hall, 2009)

Discussion questions

Do people need to understand or have prior knowledge of art in order to enjoy and appreciate it? What are the implications of your discussion for provision and management of the arts?

The arts are often taught in schools. In England, the arts subjects in the National Curriculum are Music, and Art and Design, while Drama and Literary Arts are studied in English, and Dance can be studied in Physical Education. Pupils learn about their own and other's responses to the arts and consider how judgements are made about concepts such as beauty, taste and quality. Artists undertake work in schools and education settings. From 2002–3, Creative Partnerships (CP) has sought to foster innovative long-term partnerships between schools and creative professionals. CP is managed by Arts Council England (ACE) and funded by DCMS and the Department for Education. Artsmark, a national award scheme open to all schools in England, recognises a high level of provision in the arts and a commitment to raising the profile of the arts in the school and local community. The Learning and Skills Council, which seeks to improve the skills of England's young people and adults, also funds non-qualification, creative courses.

In Venezuela for more than thirty years an extraordinary music project, the Sistema, has been using classical music through a network of after-school centres all over the country to improve the lives of the nation's poorest children. This investment by governments and projects enabling people to learn about and acquire skills in the arts raises the following question: what is the value of the arts?

9.5 What is the value of the arts?

The assessment of value can be controversial and complex, but it is vital for managers to understand arts consumption and arts policy. Pearson suggests:

> The power and force of 'art' as a respected, valued and elevated social phenomenon flows from and is intimately bound up with the very 'general', 'vague' human and non-utilitarian values ascribed to it. It is its very lack of an obvious (and utilitarian) function that is held to demonstrate its importance.
>
> (Pearson, 1982)

Yet twenty years later in the UK, the Social Exclusion Unit (2001) asserted that art can 'make a valuable contribution to delivering key outcomes of lower long-term unemployment, less crime, better health and better qualifications'. These different perspectives illustrate that the arts can be a form of individual expression (intrinsic value) and also a force for social good (instrumental value).

McGuigan (1996) suggests that 'value has a range of connotations' and suggests that '[i]n addition to economic value, we may speak of aesthetic, ethical, political and religious values'. Matarasso (1997) considered the value of participation in the arts and identified the following themes under which its social impact could be reviewed:

- personal development;
- social cohesion;
- community empowerment and self-determination;
- local image and identity;
- imagination and vision;
- health and well-being.

Holden advises:

> It is essential to examine the concept of value in order to understand why the benefits of cultural investment are so difficult to measure and express. Some values can be monetised, some cannot, but in both cases we need to tease out what values we are talking about and to understand the relative ease and difficulty in articulating each of them.
>
> (Holden, 2005)

The instrumental value of the arts can be measured through the collection of data about the economy or the well-being of a community, e.g. the economic impact of the arts (Myerscough, 1988). Such evidence helps to defend public spending on the arts. Nevertheless, good evidence is required and Holden (2005) cites Selwood's concern: 'Until the collection and analysis of data is carried out more accurately and objectively, and until the evidence gathered is used more constructively, it could be argued that much data gathered in the cultural sector has been a spurious exercise.'

The intrinsic value of the arts is more difficult to determine. The expression of the English nineteenth-century Aesthetic Movement, 'art for art's sake', suggests that art is solely concerned with art and not with any other purpose, economic, moral or social. Holden (2005) identifies that 'cultural experiences are subjective'. This means that an individual can respond to the essential nature of art in a different way from another individual in terms of thoughts or emotions. Smiers (2003) agrees: 'What represents beauty and joy for one person may be objectionable to another. Seldom do people agree about what is valuable in theatre, film, dance, music, the visual arts, design, photography or literature.' It is hard to measure what the intrinsic value of art is, because it is different for different people. This makes management of the arts more speculative, particularly given the importance of producing new films, plays, music, etc.

> ### Discussion question
>
> What method would you use to evaluate an art experience you have had?

Hill *et al.* (2003) suggest that learnt values influence the decisions of individuals to attend and participate in the arts, which are influenced by social, personal and psychological factors. In 2006 ACE launched the arts debate, an inquiry into how people value the arts. Between 2008 and 2011, ACE is attempting to put public value at the heart of everything it does.

The appraisal of the value of arts projects raises problems and questions which need to be considered by leisure managers. ACE offers a self-evaluation information sheet (see 'Useful websites', pp. 251–2). This explains that evaluation 'involves gathering evidence before, during and after a project and using it to make judgements about what happened'. There are some examples of evaluations in the ACE Projects and Publications archive on the ACE website.

Woolf (2004) suggests five stages to evaluation:

1 planning;
2 collecting evidence;
3 assembling and interpreting;
4 reflecting and moving forward;
5 reporting and sharing.

Williams and Bowdin (2007) showed that evaluation could 'be driven by internal management requirements (for example, to evaluate against the objectives, evaluate finance and use of resources, audience satisfaction and aspects of programme) or external stakeholders (for example, economic, social/cultural and environmental impacts, achievement of audience development objectives)'. Regarding the evaluation of seven arts festivals, they found it difficult to determine the effectiveness of evaluation methods because of the range of methods used and the subjectivity of arts appreciation. It was suggested that interested stakeholders such as ACE, British Arts Festivals Association (BAFA) and local authorities could share best practice to develop robust evaluation of economic, social and environmental impacts.

As arts and cultural activities of all sizes have increased in visibility, so interest has developed in approaches to their evaluation. There is evidence of a wide variety of approaches taken. However, the subjectivity of responses to the arts can raise concerns regarding the effectiveness of the evaluation of arts activities. Opportunities continue for the development of robust methods and tools for this purpose.

More formally, the Audit Commission recently introduced a national indicator to measure engagement in the arts, for use by English local authorities. The indicator measures the percentage of adults in a local authority who have either attended an arts event or participated in an arts activity at least three times in the last twelve months for leisure purposes.

9.6 Organisations and management in the arts

The arts are essentially a competitive area whether for financial gain or critical acclaim. The management of the arts takes place in four major domains. Here, unlike in Part 2 of this book, the third sector is divided into two, because of the importance of non-profit social enterprises in the arts:

1   commercial;
2   government;
3   not-for-profit;
4   voluntary and amateur.

Discussion questions

Which management domains dominate the arts venues local to you – commercial, government, not-for-profit, or voluntary and amateur? As a consumer, how can you tell which is which?

Prior to consideration of these four domains, the terms used to describe managers in the arts are considered, as there are three key groups:

1   producers;
2   directors;
3   promoters.

Producers and production companies are the people and businesses which raise finance, select, commission and organise an arts activity through development to final exhibition for consumption. Cameron Mackintosh has been described as the most successful producer of our time. Producers appoint and work with directors and promoters. The director has overall responsibility for the creative or artistic content of a production. The promoter negotiates the financial return when arranging for the exhibition of the arts product in a venue of the right ambiance, size and with the right equipment. The promoter is also responsible for advertising to attract attendance by the public. The financial return to the artists may be a fee or a percentage of the receipts from box office sales. Live Nation has been described as the world's biggest concert promoter.

In large organisations these management functions are specialist positions. However, a smaller organisation or a single person, such as a professional visual artist, may have to undertake all these management functions themselves.

Two further terms need explanation, as artists in all art forms may employ the services of the following:

1   managers;
2   agents.

An artist's manager is someone who, for a fee or negotiated financial return, represents all the artist's interests, financial, legal, logistical, etc. An artist's agent finds and books work for an artist, again for a negotiated financial return. The word 'agent' can be applied to a lot of different areas of responsibility.

9.6.1 Commercial enterprise

A commercial arts organisation seeks to achieve profit. Colbert (2000) categorises cultural enterprises according to specific criteria, the first of which 'concerns the orientation of the enterprise's mission, which can be positioned on a continuum that has product focus and market focus as its extremes'. A commercial arts enterprise's focus is on its market.

An example of an internationally successful, commercial arts company illustrates the business success it is possible to achieve in the arts. The international entertainment company the Really Useful Group (RUG) owns and manage several theatres in London's West End. From head offices in London and Sydney they produce and coordinate Andrew Lloyd Webber's works throughout the world and are involved in theatre and concert production, recording, merchandising, music publishing, television, film and video. As a wholly owned subsidiary of RUG, the Really Useful Theatre Company produce and co-produce many popular shows.

Smiers raises questions about the power of commercial interests:

> In the contemporary world where cultural conglomerates are able to spread their ideas of what culture should be, the crucial questions are: Whose stories are told? By whom? How are they manufactured, disseminated and received? Who controls production, distribution and exhibition?
>
> (Smiers, 2003)

A recent illustration of interest by governments around the world in the power of commercial enterprise is a proposed merger between Ticketmaster, the world's largest seller of tickets to live events, and Live Nation, the world's biggest concert promoter. This has been probed by the Department of Justice in the USA, and referred to the Competition Commission by the Office of Fair Trading in the UK. Beyond the USA and UK, regulators became involved in Turkey and Norway. The proposed merger would affect operations in 13 markets worldwide (Wearden and Allen, 2009).

9.6.2 Government

Governments can engage with the arts in a variety of ways, which can include:

- the creation of legislation;
- the support of regulation;
- the allocation of resources and money;
- the creation of policy.

Governments use different structures in their engagement with the arts. Some have government departments; for example, the Ministry of Culture of the Government of India states that the mission of the department is to preserve, promote and disseminate all forms of art and culture. Other governments also support and work with independent bodies; for example, in the USA the National Endowment for the Arts was established by Congress in 1965 as an independent agency of the federal government and is the nation's largest annual funder of the arts. The Australian Government's arts funding and advisory body is the Australia Council for the Arts.

Discussion question

Should government subsidise opera?

Around the world there are different structures of government. In European nation-states the three tiers – central, regional and local government – may engage actively with the arts. Brown (in Selwood, 2001) notes that the majority of the funding to the arts from European Union funds 'came about as a result of successful bidding by cultural organisations and local and regional authorities for monies available under Structural Fund initiatives, primarily concerned with addressing economic imbalances in disadvantaged areas of the EU'. This suggests that artists benefit from government money intended for programmes other than the arts.

9.6.2.1 The European Union and the arts

The Directorate General for Education and Culture manages the annual Culture programme of the EU (see 'Useful websites', pp. 251–2):

> The general objective of the programme is to enhance the cultural area shared by Europeans, which is based on a common cultural heritage through the development of cultural cooperation between creators, cultural players and cultural institutions of countries taking part in the programme, with a view to encouraging the emergence of European citizenship.

Case Study 9.1 demonstrates the nature of EU transnational government intervention.

Another EU initiative was launched by Melina Mercouri in 1985 – the European City of Culture, renamed European Capital of Culture from 1999. From 2001 and in response to EU enlargement, two capitals have been selected as European Capitals of Culture each year.

9.6.2.2 UK regulation

The UK Parliament passes laws within which the arts operate, which leisure managers have to be familiar with. These include matters such as business competition, copyright, health and safety, and licensing. The Competition Act 1998 created the Competition Commission and the Enterprise Act 2002 introduced a new regime for the assessment of mergers and markets in the UK. Reference was made on the previous page to concerns in the USA and the UK about the proposed merger in 2009 of Live Nation and Ticketmaster.

The Copyright, Designs and Patents Act 1988 is the principal legislation covering intellectual property rights in the UK. The laws of copyright are complex and specialist legal advice should be sought. In simple terms, an original work of any art form is protected by copyright. When a work is recorded in a permanent form, copyright is owned by the author. Works of art may consist of many parts; each part is protected by copyright. For example, a poem could be the inspiration for a piece of choreographed dance, in which case the poem and the dance would each be protected by separate copyright. Members of creative teams such as costume designers and make-up artists may also have their work protected by copyright. In 1996, the period of copyright in the UK was extended to seventy years to bring it in line with other European countries.

The Health and Safety at Work Act 1974 underpins guidance on managing health and safety at exhibitions and events. The Health and Safety Executive's job is to protect people against risks to health or safety arising out of work activities. It is a manager's duty to ensure that all reasonable precautions have been taken to protect works of art, performing artists and audiences (see Chapter 19).

The Licensing Act 2003 established a single integrated scheme for licensing premises used for the supply of alcohol and to provide regulated entertainment. The descriptions of regulated entertainment in the Licensing Act are:

Products and services

- the performance of a play;
- an exhibition of a film;
- an indoor sporting event;
- boxing or wrestling entertainment;
- a performance of live music;
- any playing of recorded music;
- a performance of dance;
- entertainment of a similar description to live music, recorded music or dance.

CASE STUDY 9.1

The European Union's Culture programme

The EU's Culture programme 2007–13 supports projects and initiatives which celebrate Europe's cultural diversity and shared cultural heritage. It promotes the development of cross-border cooperation between cultural operators and institutions. The main objectives of the programme are to:

- promote cross-border mobility of those working in the cultural sector;
- encourage the transnational circulation of cultural and artistic output;
- foster intercultural dialogue.

The full details of good practice in over twenty projects to date are available at the EU Culture website (see 'Useful websites', pp. 251–2). This shows projects using cultural activity from both traditional – choirs, theatre and dance – and more contemporary uses of communication – such as blogs, comics and rock music – in the creation of art and the dissemination of information. Work can take place in a wide range of settings, including traditional cultural venues such as theatres; community settings such as schools and hospitals; and public outside spaces. A wide variety of themes have been the focus of different projects, including the creation of new works of art; the training of young artists; artists engaging with issues such as the stabilisation of the climate; and the lifestyle choices of young people. Projects have demonstrated ways to overcome barriers which inhibit peoples' physical and cultural access to cultural activities and sites.

There has been recognition in the programme of the traditions and cultural heritage of different groups, from European Entrepreneurs to Roma minorities. Research has been undertaken on diverse topics from shared European carnival and folk rituals to the pan-European cultural phenomenon of Art Nouveau. Intercultural co-creation and examination of signs and symbols have been explored by young people using photography. Artists have created an exhibition of work about regional identity in the landscapes of former industrial regions. Products from selected European cooperatives are displayed and sold in an exhibition and temporary shop. Three European publishers overcame the limits of small national markets by jointly publishing a new book to attract children who are less enthusiastic about reading.

Networks have been created and visits and exchanges have taken place, both within and beyond the borders of the thirty European countries participating in the good practice projects. International collaboration has been supported between visual artists from the EU and China and the translation of children's books from the EU and India.

The Licensing Act had four main objectives: protecting the public from crime and disorder; protecting children from harm; public safety; and the prevention of public nuisance. The DCMS is responsible for setting the framework of licensing law, which licensing authorities then administer. Licensing authorities, which are usually local authorities, are responsible for licensing the sale and supply of alcohol, the provision of regulated entertainment and the provision of late night refreshment in England and Wales. It is to these authorities that managers must apply for permission to provide regulated entertainment.

9.6.2.3 UK government support for the arts
9.6.2.3.1 CENTRAL GOVERNMENT DEPARTMENTS

The Department for Culture, Media and Sport (DCMS) is the government department responsible for supporting the arts with funding, policy and specific initiatives. Spending for the cultural sector is broken down into five main headings: Arts; Heritage; Libraries; Media; Museums and Galleries. As a central government department, the DCMS is responsible for maximising the contribution the arts sector makes to the strategic priorities set by the political administration in government. The DCMS's work in the arts includes:

- funding the Arts Council for England and other key organisations;
- advocating the role of the arts for social and education policies, to increase people's access to the arts;
- supporting the contribution the arts makes to the economy and promoting the arts internationally.

The Foreign and Commonwealth Office is the sponsoring department of the British Council, which was established in 1934 and incorporated by Royal Charter in 1940. The British Council operates at arm's length from the UK government and aims to strengthen understanding and trust between and within different cultures. The British Council Arts Group aims to link UK arts to the rest of the world, for example by helping to arrange touring exhibitions or collaborative work between UK and foreign artists.

9.6.2.3.2 THE NATIONAL LOTTERY

Although Lottery funding is not strictly government funding, the National Lottery Act 1993 was designed by the government to benefit five areas, the arts being one of them. The National Lottery Distribution Fund is administered by the DCMS, which passes the money to the Lottery distributors for the arts – the UK's four national Arts Councils.

9.6.2.3.3 THE NATIONAL ARTS COUNCILS

The four national arts councils in the UK are for Northern Ireland, England, Scotland and Wales. Prior to 1994 an Arts Council of Great Britain (ACGB) existed, established by Royal Charter in 1946. Sinclair (1995) cites the aspirations of the first chairman of the ACGB, John Maynard Keynes: 'We look forward to a time when the theatre and the concert-hall and the gallery will be a living element in everyone's upbringing, and regular attendance at the theatre and at concerts a part of organized education.' This is not dissimilar to the current mission of ACE – 'great art for everyone'.

Discussion question

Over sixty years on, do you think Keynes' aspirations for the performing arts have been achieved?

Arts organisations can apply for a financial grant in aid from the national arts councils. Some examples of grants schemes are: three-year funds to regularly funded organisations; grants to individuals; the purchase of contemporary art; and cultural leadership. Internationally recognised arts companies, such as the Royal Shakespeare Company or the Royal Opera House, receive a significant element of their revenue from government via ACE.

Information on how to apply, timescales and eligibility for each of the grant schemes is available on the national arts councils' websites. Recipients of grants are accountable for the expenditure of grants awarded and participation in evaluation of the activity supported. Arts Councils also offer advice and information, and their websites contain downloadable publications and information sheets.

9.6.2.3.4 THE UK FILM COUNCIL

The UK Film Council (which the new UK government is going to abolish) is the government-backed lead agency for film in the UK, ensuring that economic, cultural and educational aspects of film are effectively represented at home and abroad. It works with and funds partners such as the national and regional Screen Agencies, the British Film Institute, First Light Movies and Skillset.

9.6.2.3.5 THE CULTURAL OLYMPIAD

The London Cultural Olympiad was developed by ACE in partnership with London 2012, the Arts Council of Northern Ireland, the Scottish Arts Council and the Arts Council of Wales. The four-year Cultural Olympiad started in September 2008, with the launch of three sections – Ceremonies, Major Projects and Inspire Mark Projects, which celebrate cultures, people and languages (see 'Useful websites', pp. 251–2). The themes of the Cultural Olympiad are to use the Olympics and Paralympics to:

- bring culture and sport together;
- encourage audience participation;
- make public spaces exciting through street theatre, public art, circus skills and live big screen sites;
- raise environmental sustainability, health and well-being issues through culture and sport;
- honour and share the values of the Olympic and Paralympic Games;
- create unique collaborations and innovations between communities and cultural sectors;
- support the learning, skills and personal development of young people through links.

9.6.2.4 UK local government and the arts

Local authorities in the UK work with the arts in several ways.

9.6.2.4.1 LICENSING AUTHORITIES

Local authorities play an important role in the delivery of the arts to local communities through their role as licensing authorities. They keep a register of premises' licenses and personal licences issued and temporary event notices.

9.6.2.4.2 DISCRETIONARY FINANCIAL SUPPORT

Local authorities can also give financial support to arts venues and organisations. But this is discretionary – they are not required by law to support arts activities. This has influenced how local authority arts policies have developed. Gray (2002) explains that 'the absence of any clear set of priorities for the sector as a whole, or a specific value commitment to the arts {…} served to generate clear differences between local authorities in terms of what support was provided and reasons behind such provision'. He offers the concept of 'policy attachment' and suggests development of arts policy took place through the attachment to other policy objectives, for example economic development or social cohesion. He identifies that a lack of coherence in provision has resulted, with urban authorities having more arts officers in post and spending more on the arts than rural authorities.

9.6.3 The not-for-profit sector

Managers of not-for-profit arts organisations may seek to make a financial surplus which they will redistribute internally as financial support for the work of the organisation. The surplus could be made by, for example, the trading arm of the organisation, which might be a cafe in a subsidised gallery or a bar in a subsidised theatre. This surplus may be redistributed to pay for the education activities in the gallery or commission a play by a local playwright for the theatre. 'Social enterprise' is also a term used to describe organisations working in this sector (see also Chapter 21).

Some organisations in the not-for-profit sector may receive subsidies as financial grants from government and other bodies identified in earlier sections above. There are several business structures for organisations working in this sector, from private limited companies to charitable trusts (see Chapter 6). People appointed to the boards of management of these organisations are not paid but bring their expertise because of their interest in supporting the work of the organisation. Arts organisations benefit from board members with professional expertise in areas such as law, finance, computing, education and marketing. In the UK the organisation Arts and Business, which receives funding via central government, has encouraged private sector support of the arts through innovative partnerships, networks and consultancy.

9.6.4 Voluntary and amateur groups

This domain can be defined simply as self-motivated people who volunteer in arts activity, including management of voluntary organisations, for which they receive no payment. In many countries there is a large sector of amateur arts which is regarded as important social and cultural activity.

The Voluntary Arts Network (VAN) is the development agency for the voluntary arts in the UK and the Republic of Ireland. It aims to promote participation in the arts and crafts which contributes to health, social and economic development. VAN explains:

> The voluntary arts are those arts and crafts that people undertake for self-improvement, social networking and leisure, but not primarily for payment. The range of art forms is wide and includes folk, dance, drama, literature, media, music, visual arts, crafts and applied arts, and festivals. Over half the UK adult population is involved in the voluntary arts and crafts. They play a vital role in promoting community cohesion and through their activities pump an estimated £50 million into the economy each year.

(www.voluntaryarts.org)

Dodd *et al.* (2008) found that this sector of arts activity in the UK has an income of £545 million a year and that '[g]roups are entrepreneurial about generating income, including ticket income, subscriptions, selling programmes, local sponsorship and other fundraising. Groups take pride in this remarkable ability to be self sustaining and deliver quality artistic products.'

9.7 Museums

The first great museums were founded on collections of rare or beautiful objects: artefacts, paintings, sculptures and specimens. In the late twentieth century many new museums opened to attract people as the heritage industry and tourism flourished. Now contemporary museums tackle controversial topics such as drugs, mass extermination, slavery and warfare, as well as popular topics such as fashion, music, space and sport.

The diverse goals of museums include the interpretation and conservation of the world's cultural and natural heritage and through this they also reflect people's identities. A key management change over the years has been to develop their traditional 'treasure house' role of undertaking conservation, research and education, moving towards their promotion as leisure attractions for visitors. The traditions of conservation and scholarship established by museums have had to respond to policies which seek to build relationships with diverse audiences and increase visitor numbers to museums. Recently this has extended to making information for exhibitions available in many ways, including electronic and media technologies. Museums now seek to fulfil a range of purposes for visitors, including to:

- attract;
- educate;
- entertain;
- provoke.

Throughout the world the availability of limited resources can raise concerns for museum managers about what should be their priority. Managers have to decide what aspect money should be spent on, e.g. increasing acquisitions of exhibits, attracting visitors or academic study. Witcomb (2003) cites two authors' comments on recent developments. On the one hand, Flannery notes the investment in museums to increase their appeal as visitor attractions: 'Australia has spent $500 million in the past year on state-of-the-art, multimedia museums in Canberra and Melbourne that try to compete with amusement parks at the expense of research and artefacts.' On the other hand, Casey supports the re-presentation of collections using modern techniques: 'we find contemporary audiences are fairly sophisticated media consumers and less likely to value a museum that clings to a historic role as a repository of curious objects amassed by nineteenth-century specimen collectors.'

Discussion question

To what extent do museums offer a leisure experience?

Throughout the world there are famous museums, from Kabul Museum in Afghanistan to the museums in the Vatican City, and some support research centres, e.g. the Smithsonian Institution. There is a diverse range of types of organisations which own and run museums, including national, regional, local, university, military, company, charities, trusts and private foundations. Professional museum practice undertakes the stewardship of the world's material heritage in a sophisticated and regulated world. The management of museums is undertaken in two main domains:

1 public;
2 independent/private.

A public museum is an institution where the policy-making body or a board of trustees is controlled by or responsible to a form of government – national, regional or local. The management of an independent or private museum is not controlled by or responsible to any part of government.

9.8 The international cooperation of museums

There is a long established tradition of international cooperation and exchanges among museums. The International Council of Museums (ICOM) is an organisation of museums and museum professionals committed to the conservation, continuation and communication to society of the world's natural and cultural heritage, present and future, tangible and intangible. It was created in 1946 as a non-governmental organisation and it is financed by membership fees and supported by governmental and other bodies. It carries out part of UNESCO's programme for museums. It has 26,000 members in 139 countries who take part in national, regional and international activities including International Museum Day (18 May, annually). The cornerstone of ICOM is its Code of Ethics for Museums (see 'Useful websites', pp. 251–2). It sets minimum standards of professional practice and performance for museums and their staff. On joining the organisation, ICOM members undertake to abide by this code.

In the European Union, several museums' projects receive funding:

- The European Museums' Information Institute (EMII) is a collaborative, virtual network to strengthen the work of museums within the European Union. EMII receives financial support from its members and finance from grant aiding bodies, such as the European Commission. It offers national overviews of museum provision in the partner states or countries.
- NEMO is the Network of European Museum Organisations and has an informal structure. It has developed an online toolkit that will enable all European museums – lenders and borrowers – to create their own loan document online.
- Europeana, according to Davies (2008), is 'the European digital library, museum and archive {…} a two-year project that began in July 2007. It will produce a service giving users direct access initially to some two million digital objects, including film material, photos, paintings, sounds, maps, manuscripts, books, newspapers and archival papers, rising to a target of 10 million by 2010'.

9.9 The public sector and museums in the UK

The Museums, Libraries and Archives Council (MLA) is a non-departmental public body sponsored by DCMS as the strategic body working with and for the museums, archives and libraries sector. The MLA promotes best practice in museums, libraries and archives, to inspire innovative, integrated and sustainable services for all. The MLA's Museum Accreditation Scheme sets nationally agreed standards for UK museums. Regional MLA staff work closely with local government on the development of museums, libraries and archives in their areas. There are three English regions, North, East and West. MLA London continued as in independent charity during 2009–10, working in partnership with the MLA Council. The online information service Culture24 was launched in May 2009. Individual venues directly access the Culture24 server to update their collection and event information.

9.9.1 Public museums in the UK

One of the first national public museums was the British Museum. It was founded in 1753 when a collection of books, manuscripts and natural history specimens were purchased with funds from Parliament. Minihan (1977) notes that, with this, 'Parliament entered the field of museum administration'. The newly established British Museum grew through private generosity and bequests and occasionally funds from government. In 1772 Parliament granted money to enable the purchase of *objets d'art*: 'From its beginnings the British Museum was a new type of institution. Governed by a body of Trustees responsible to Parliament, its collections belonged to the nation, with free admission for all' (British Museum, see 'Useful websites', pp. 251–2).

The National Museum Directors' Conference (NMDC) represents the leaders of the UK's national collections and major regional museums. A key finding by Travers and Glaister (2004) is that '[t]he overall impact of the NMDC "sector", including indirect and induced effects, is in the range of £1.83 billion to £2.07 billion'.

The Association of Leading Visitor Attractions' data identify the top five most visited museums in the UK in 2008 (see Table 9.1). The proportion of visits to these public museums by overseas visitors has remained relatively static. A notable development for UK national museums towards the end of the twentieth century was the introduction of entrance charges and the subsequent removal of them in 2001, a policy and management issue explored in Case Study 9.2.

9.9.2 UK Local authority museums

In the UK local authorities are responsible for over 600 museums. Some of these originated in the nineteenth century from the gift, by individuals and societies, of collections to local communities. In1845 Parliament gave local authorities the power to provide cultural facilities. Local authority museums are not and never have been a statutory service.

There is no standard museum provision. Nevertheless, they are important local heritage assets. Funding of £300 million from the Museums Libraries and Archives Council's Renaissance Programme was made available to encourage regional museums to raise the standards of their services and contribute to education, learning, community development and economic regeneration, and make museums great centres of life and learning which people want to visit.

Performance measurement for local museums was a recommendation of the Audit Commission (1991b). Selwood (2001) notes that local authorities manage 'the largest group of

---

Table 9.1 Five most popular museums in the UK, 2008

Museum	Visitor numbers
British Museum	5,932,897
Tate Modern	4,862,581
National Gallery	4,382,614
Natural History Museum	3,698,500
Science Museum	2,705,677

Source: Association of Leading Visitor Attractions, www.alva.org.uk/visitor_statistics/.

Free admission to national museums in Britain

In December 2001, British museums subsidised by the national government abandoned admission charges for entrance to their permanent exhibitions. This was heralded as one of the main cultural policy achievements of the government of the time. Before free admission, nine national museums had introduced admission charges during the 1980s and 1990s, largely as a result of pressure on their finances from rising costs and static government funding. The free admission initiative by the government was accompanied by inducements of additional public subsidies (estimated to be about £40 million a year) and more favourable value-added tax (VAT) arrangements, such that no national museum retained admission charges after 2001.

The government's rationale for free admission is that national museums and galleries play a unique part in British cultural life and consequently everyone should have the right to free access to them. The initiative fitted particularly well with an important aspect of the government's policy, social inclusion, ensuring that a potentially important barrier to entry at national museums for disadvantaged people is removed.

What have been the effects of the free admission? Cowell (2007) reports substantial achievements, including a 30 per cent increase in total visits to national government-sponsored museums, from 26.9 million visits in the year before free admission started to 35.1 million visits in the fifth year of the policy, 2005–6. The increase in visits in this period was much more for those museums which had previously charged for admission – 87 per cent – compared with those museums which were already free in 2001 (8 per cent). Furthermore, the percentage of visits which were by people from black and minority ethnic groups increased from 3.2 per cent in 2000–1 to 4.9 per cent in 2005–6. The percentage of visits which were by people from the bottom three socio-economic groups was only measured from 2002–3, but even so, it increased from 15 per cent in that year to 16.7 per cent in 2005–6.

Regarding audience reach, around 50 per cent of visits are 'new' (typically 'new' means the visitor not having visited the particular museum before in the previous year). This percentage remained relatively constant from the year before free admission, 2000–1, to the year 2005–6. Another proportion that has remained relatively static is the percentage of visits to government-funded national museums by overseas visitors – around one-third of total visits.

It is not appropriate to credit free admissions alone for improvements in visiting to national museums. Cowell (2007) points out that, as well as free admission, many national museums had substantially improved their facilities, particularly with the help of National Lottery awards, and some had opened new branches in different parts of the country (e.g. Tate Modern, Imperial War Museum). Selwood and Davies (2005) suggest that it is the combination of free admission and new capital investment that has given the most consistent increases in visits, whilst those museums which were already free in 2000, or which did not have new investment, had stable or even declining visits in the period 1999–2003.

Furthermore, a Mori survey in 2003 found that only 15 per cent of those surveyed were aware of the free admission policy and had consequently made more visits after it was introduced. Forty-one per cent of those surveyed said that free admission had not altered their visiting. Another 40 per cent of respondents were unaware of the change to free admission. This supports earlier evidence (Glasgow Caledonian University, 1998) which suggests that admission price is not the most important barrier to potential visitors. This evidence came from a survey of adults which found that admission charges are an important constraint to just 4 per cent of people who had not visited a museum in the previous year. The most important barrier is time – cited by over half the adults surveyed. Lack of interest was cited by another 38 per cent of non-visitors.

Therefore, free admission clearly works in terms of increasing visits, even by some disadvantaged groups, but it is more likely to do so in conjunction with improved services. Furthermore, admission charges are not the most important barrier to admission in museums; and museums still have a lot of work to do in addressing the socio-economic bias in their visits towards the better-off. A final question, for both politicians and taxpayers, is whether free admission provides value for money, i.e. is a 30 per cent rise in visits worth £40 million a year in extra subsidies plus VAT revenue reductions?

museums in the country {...} As a result of the Local Government Act 1999, their efficiency, cost and quality will come under quinquennial review carried out on the basis of national performance indicators'. Quantitative measures were introduced for the 1999–2000 financial year to show how well museum services perform and how they meet local and national priorities. The current national indicator measures the percentage of adults in a local authority who have visited a museum or gallery in the previous twelve months for leisure, informal learning, studying or research.

9.10 Social benefits of museums

Measuring the social benefits of a cultural service, not least a museum, is a difficult thing to achieve. The Local Government Association and the Museums Association (2008) offer information and case studies. When discussing the long-term benefits to the community that museums provide, Scott suggests:

> Through objects, museums can provide unique experiences associated with the collective meaning, sharing, discussion and debate that are the foundation of good citizenry. Through objects, museums can reinforce personal identity and belonging. Objects convey a sense of place and can, therefore, introduce outsiders to the significance of culture through its material heritage.
>
> (Scott, 2007)

As museum managers are increasingly asked to demonstrate that they provide social value, Scott offers a range of qualitative research which has sought to collect information as evidence for performance evaluation. Scott suggests how museums facilitate collective and personal development:

> From even a cursory glance at the literature, there is evidence to support five areas:
>
> ● providing a forum for the discussion and debate of emergent social issues;
> ● affirming personal identity;

- fostering tolerance and understanding;
- providing reverential and commemorative experiences; and
- creating a collective identity through a shared history and sense of place.

(Scott, 2007)

9.11 Independent and private museums in the UK

The Association of Independent Museums (AIM) represents the interests of independent museums and contributes to national policy-making and improving standards. AIM is a registered charity which has a membership of over 1,000 independent museums, heritage centres and historical interpretation projects, which is about half the museum provision in the British Isles. Independent museums can range from small local organisations to large organisations such as Chatham Historic Dockyard; London's Transport Museum; Ironbridge Gorge Museum and the Scottish Mining Museum. A report on *Local Authorities and Independent Museums* by Babbidge (2007) showed that independent museums have a total income of £300 million per year but financial support to them from local authorities is small. He estimates that one-quarter of the total museum economy in the UK is due to the work of independent museums.

9.11.1 Volunteering in UK museums

Volunteers play many roles in independent museums, as trustees, experts and willing members of the workforce. Holmes (2007) states that '[m]useums and heritage attractions world-wide involve a large number of volunteers {…} Volunteering in museums and heritage visitor attractions has a long history within the UK, with many museums founded entirely by volunteers'.

Volunteers can be considered within two models, the economic model and the leisure model. The economic model notes that while volunteers are unpaid workers not bound by contracts of employment, their work can be measured in its contribution to the economy. A professional approach to the management of volunteers features induction, training and clear line-management responsibility for volunteers. The leisure model identifies volunteering as a leisure experience and considers people's motivations, which range from doing something enjoyable to personal achievement and helping others to learn. Managers working with volunteers should be aware that people's motivations are mixed and range from social opportunities and pursuit of an interest to gaining work experience.

9.12 Change and museums

Electronic media and new technologies have enabled developments in two ways which museum managers need to be aware of: (1) the presentation of museums' collections and interactive displays; and (2) the creation of virtual museums where images of items in collections are available for people to view. An example of the latter is the Public Catalogue Foundation (PCF), a registered charity set up in 2003 to photograph and record all paintings in UK public collections. PCF is working with the BBC to provide access through a website called Your Paintings, to give the public online access by 2012.

Museums have continued to change and develop since the initial preservation of rare collections, through the subsequent curatorial recognition of the importance of the visitor's comfort, to, now, the consideration of the effect of the use of technology. Current initiatives using new technology may challenge curatorial cultures, authenticity and quality. This has to be weighed against the added value these developments offer through the benefits of good digital records and the increased electronic access offered to people who do not or cannot go to museums.

9.13 Libraries

A library is a place where information is:

- collected;
- processed;
- stored;
- made available to users.

Users may make reference to materials in the library and a lending library allows borrowers to take materials from the library for a specified period. Currently there is a growth in the use of new technology to enable electronic access to library materials.

> **Discussion question**
>
> To what extent are libraries leisure facilities?

Information is stored in a variety of media, for example texts such as books in a range of formats from print to Braille; images such as photographs, maps, illustrations; audio sound recordings such as CDs; and films and moving images such as DVDs. Since the 1930s libraries in the UK have been developing materials such as Talking Books to make materials available to the widest range of users.

There is evidence of ancient libraries in Persia, Greece and China, which collected information which was then stored on clay tablets and silk scrolls. Early libraries were collections of manuscripts and archives by a private person, an organisation or a religious body. Many libraries were started when materials were bequeathed to an organisation such as a church, a school or a town. People also paid a membership subscription to some libraries to access learned and popular reading materials of fiction and non-fiction. A trust set up by an American, Andrew Carnegie, paid for many libraries in the USA and UK to be built. Now libraries around the world house collections of materials on the widest range of all topics, from art to science and sports. Some libraries are still private and many are open to the public to use.

9.14 Private and special libraries

The Special Libraries Association (SLA) is for librarians and information professionals working in special libraries. Special libraries are also sometimes known as 'information centres'. These can include law libraries, news libraries, corporate libraries, museum libraries and medical libraries. SLA is an international organisation with over 11,000 members in over 80 countries. This cooperative association serves its membership in three main areas: learning, networking and advocacy.

In the UK the Private Libraries Association is a registered charity and an international society of book collectors which works in liaison with the Chartered Institute of Library and Information Professionals (CILIP). Countries throughout the world have library associations.

9.15 National libraries

National libraries are supported by governments as repositories of information. On every continent, countries from Albania to Zimbabwe have a national library. The International Federation of Library Associations and Institutions (IFLA) is the global voice representing the interests of library and information services and their users. It has 1,600 members in approximately 150 countries and its headquarters are in the Royal Library, the national library of the Netherlands.

In 2004 the European Library Project funded by the European Commission was completed. The European Library Service is a portal which offers integrated access to the combined resources, both digital and bibliographical (books, posters, maps, sound recordings, videos, etc.), of the national libraries of Europe. Thus information on where materials are held in European libraries is now more easily available.

9.15.1 National libraries in the UK

In the UK there are three national libraries, which are registered charities and governed by boards of trustees. The British Library Act 1972 established the British Library, which is now funded by the DCMS. The maintenance of a national printed archive has been a principle supported for over three hundred years in the UK. The British Library works with public libraries and collaborates with higher and further education institutions in the UK. Publishers in the UK and the Republic of Ireland have a legal obligation to send one copy of each of their publications to the Legal Deposit Office of the British Library within one month of publication. In 2003 this legal deposit was extended to include electronic or e-publications and other non-print materials.

The National Library of Scotland is now answerable to the Scottish Parliament and funded by the Scottish government. The National Library of Wales receives grant in aid from the National Assembly for Wales.

Between 2001 and 2005 these three national libraries undertook strategic reviews and public consultations. They particularly sought to address the social inclusion agenda by simplifying admission rules and staging roadshows and touring exhibitions. Money from the New Opportunities Lottery Fund paid for the transfer of learning materials, maps, prints, drawings, sheet music, text and sound recordings into electronic digital format. These materials can now be accessed through virtual visits to libraries.

9.16 Public libraries

The role of public libraries as local gateways to information, knowledge and culture was identified by the UNESCO Public Library Manifesto, first published in 1948 and revised in 1994. A public library is a place of leisure and recreation and can offer a local base connected to global knowledge networks. Maddern (2002) suggests that '[o]ften it is easier to find the telephone number of the nearest foreign embassy than it is to find out the number and name of the current president of the local tapestry club'. Access to information in public libraries is not the same throughout the world, and Miao (2002) notes that, '[e]specially in developing countries, public libraries seem to be less advanced in terms of computing capabilities than academic and company libraries'.

9.16.1 Public libraries in the UK

Legislation in the mid-nineteenth century enabled local authorities in the UK to fund public libraries. The 1964 Public Libraries and Museums Act stated that local authorities had a statutory duty to provide access to a 'comprehensive and efficient' public library service for all persons who desire to make use of it; and to lend materials to those who live, work or study in the area. Fifty-eight per cent of people in the UK have a library card. Libraries can be located within different local authority service departments, for example cultural services or the education departments.

The MLA suggests public libraries in England provide safe, neutral and shared environments for everyone. Key figures from CIPFA for 2006–7 show:

- 81 million books in 3,500 public libraries;
- 288 million visits to public libraries;
- 269 million book loans;
- 27 million loans of audio/visual material (e.g. Talking Books, CDs, DVDs);
- 48 million visits to library websites;
- 33,000 People's Network computer terminals;
- 44 million enquiries answered by library staff.

Nevertheless, Grindlay and Morris (2004) point to a decline in annual adult book issues from UK public libraries and suggest a range of possible causes, which include an increase in magazine reading and other leisure time activities such as the increased use of home computers and the internet. For some people an increase in book buying may have replaced borrowing from libraries. Users may have found libraries less convenient to use due to closures, reduced opening hours and cuts in book purchase funds.

MLA seeks to offer strategic direction, priorities and objectives to the diverse services run by separate library authorities. DCMS (2003) asserted that the following three areas of activity should be at the heart of libraries' modern mission:

1 the promotion of reading and informal learning;
2 access to digital skills and services, including e-government;
3 measures to tackle social exclusion, build community identity and develop citizenship.

Along with other public services, public libraries in the UK have had to demonstrate their performance in recent decades. By 2004, library standards covered the following areas:

- the distance people lived from a service point;
- opening hours;
- numbers of libraries with internet access;
- number of electronic workstations;
- average request supply time;
- numbers of visits;
- user satisfaction;
- numbers of books purchased;
- the time taken to replace the lending stock.

More recently a national indicator for libraries has been devised which measures the percentage of adults in a local authority who have used a public library service in the previous twelve months for leisure purposes, including informal learning and studying or research for personal interests. This indicator is very similar to those devised for arts and museums identified earlier in this chapter (p. 232 and p. 244).

In 2005 the DCMS launched the Public Library Impact Measures as a tangible means of demonstrating the impact that public library services have on wider community issues. In 2009 the MLA relaunched the Inspiring Learning for All Toolkit website. This introduced the generic social outcomes identified by the MLA, which demonstrate the wider community contribution of museums, libraries and archives. They identify the impact of services on social cohesion, health and well-being. Such initiatives further demonstrate the importance of local cultural managers measuring the performance of their services.

9.17 Digital services

Library staff roles have developed from gatekeepers to facilitators for information technology, and information managers. Librarians have knowledge of a wide variety of sources, both off and on the internet. They are also able to offer independent analysis of the results of searches and help users develop their search skills.

December 2002 saw the completion of the People's Network Programme, which had placed 30,000 computer terminals in over 4,000 libraries in the UK, providing library users with free access to the internet and use of software packages. This development supports the UK government's aspiration for universal internet access. It cost £120 million, which came from the New Opportunities Lottery Fund. Big Lottery Fund Research Issue 7 (2004) claimed that the People's Network had 'changed the common perceptions that many people have of the library service, helping the library to reposition itself at the heart of the local community'. Bradley notes:

> It got an average of 27% of each library's users on to the internet, hundreds of people were able to harness the power of the internet to get new jobs, enrich their local communities, thousands made new friends, kept in touch with family via email, or started a new hobby.
>
> (Bradley, 2007)

New technology makes virtual visits to libraries possible for material which was previously only available for reference, through electronic access using a user reference number from home. Libraries are also responding to an increase in the previously non-traditional methods of accessing the internet, such as mobile phones and televisions.

However, the role of public libraries as places to find information about local leisure activities has not been altered by the development of online search engines. Small clubs' websites are not ranked high in major search engine returns – as normally only a small number of people access them they can be difficult to find electronically. Prior to the publication of the Integrated Public Service Vocabulary (IPSV) in 2005 there was no widely used standard for the provision of community information.

9.18 Future plans for libraries in the UK

Modernisation of libraries has been undertaken by some authorities, e.g. the development of Idea Stores in Tower Hamlets and Discovery Centres in Kent and Hampshire. Ward explains:

> Discovery Centres were similar in concept to Idea Stores. The first modernised library to be re-badged as a Discovery Centre was that in Dover {...} bringing together a modernised library service, adult education, and the District Council-run museum. Within the building were found a nursery, a café, a theatre, adult education and arts and crafts activities.
>
> (Ward, 2007)

It was found that the increase in the range of activities appealed to a wider user group. Library managers have to consider how to continue to widen their appeal to younger people whilst still meeting the needs of their current core users.

Successful applications were announced in 2007 for the £80 million Community Libraries Big Lottery Fund. This initiative was set up to invigorate libraries as centres of wider community learning and development; create, improve and develop library spaces; and be innovative and promote good practice. One award, to Leicestershire County Council, enabled the opening in April 2009 of the Newbold Verdon Library, the first of the new community libraries. The rebuilt library offers to the local community a computer suite, advice services and a reading garden.

In 2008 a Modernisation Review of Libraries was announced by the Secretary of State for Culture, Media and Sport. This review is still being conducted at the time of writing. Issues being considered include:

- libraries' ability to deliver what the public wants in the future;
- understanding of what encourages people to use libraries;
- the skills of library staff;
- resources to support the growth of the e-book;
- review of shared learning provided by libraries, from book groups to family history research;
- investment in libraries and new ways of delivering services, for example on shared sites;
- the use of buildings, from silent places for informal learning and reading to social places for people to meet and discuss, such as an internet cafe.

9.19 Conclusions

These three contemporary cultural areas have grown from ancient traditions. Current practice in them reflects the maintenance of values actively shared by people, both private initiative and government intervention; and also dynamic changes in their roles and management. Management is undertaken by the talent of the individual enthusiast, the organisation of public services and the cooperation of international organisations.

Globally, electronic and digital technologies are leading to evolutionary developments in the arts, museums and libraries. The implementation of the use of electronic and digital technologies is challenging intellectual property rights, the authenticity of materials and the experience of people in these cultural sectors. Accessibility to these cultural areas may be increased for those with the access and competence to use this technology and those whose personal values motivate them to participate in the arts, museums and libraries.

Currently international projects are developing the use of new technologies to support the identification of the location of materials in libraries and their transfer into electronic digital formats. Despite the growth of public libraries throughout the world, access to information for leisure and learning is not universal. Literacy, be it the ability to read and write or competent use of computers, is an important key to these gateways to information.

Practical tasks

1 From publicity material such as advertisements in newspapers, posters, leaflets and websites, find examples of promoters, directors and agents. Identify how, as a leisure manager, you would contact them to negotiate booking a performance or exhibition at your venue.

2 Conduct research amongst students who are non-users of museums to find out what constrains their use of them. Construct a strategy to change museums to attract such current non-users.

Structured guide to further reading

For the arts:

Dodd, F., Graves, A. and Taws, K. (2008) *Our Creative Talent: the voluntary and amateur arts in England*, DCMS, London.

Gray, C. (2002) 'Local government and the arts', *Local Government Studies*, 28, 1 (Spring), Frank Cass.

For museums:

Local Government Association and the Museums Association (2008) *Unlocking Local Treasure: collections management and the local authority museum*, LGA & MA, London.

For libraries:

Big Lottery Fund Research Issue 7 (2004) *The People's Network: evaluation summary*, November.

DCMS (2003) *Framework for the Future: libraries, learning and information in the next decade*, DCMS, London.

Useful websites

For EU arts policy:

http://ec.europa.eu/dgs/education_culture/calls/docs/C_2008_8656.pdf

For EU cultural projects:

http://ec.europa.eu/culture/our-programmes-and-actions/doc/good_practice_projects2009per_country.pdf

For the UK government department DCMS:

www.culture.gov.uk/what_we_do/creative_industries/default.aspx

For the Arts Council England, the national development agency for the arts in England:

www.artscouncil.org.uk/

For an arts evaluation information sheet:

www.artscouncil.org.uk/information-sheet/self-evaluation/

Products and services

For the Voluntary Arts Network, an agency for the development of voluntary arts and crafts:
www.voluntaryarts.org/

For the Cultural Olympiad:
www.london2012.com/get-involved/cultural-olympiad/index.php

For the Museums, Libraries and Archives Council, the NDPB promoting best practice:
www.mla.gov.uk/

For ICOM code of ethics:
http://icom.museum/ethics.html

For the British Museum:
www.britishmuseum.org/the_museum/history_and_the_building/general_history.aspx

For the People's Network, operated through public libraries:
www.peoplesnetwork.gov.uk/
See also: http://raceonline2012.org/manifesto

Chapter 10

Sport and physical activity

In this chapter

- How important is sport?
- Who provides sport?
- Who participates in sport?
- Why does government have an important role in sport?
- How is sport organised and funded in the UK?
- How do sport and physical activity impact on health?

Summary

Sport is big business both in the UK and internationally. It took over £21 billion of consumer spending in the UK in 2008, the majority on sports services. Sport is ever present in news in the media and sport at the top level gives us some of the most enduring cultural images. Sport events such as the Olympics and the World Cup in football attract global audiences, as do national sports such as the English Premier League. The bulk of sports activity, though, is concerned with mass participation – sport and physical activity by the population at large.

Sport is an activity that is supplied by all three major sectors – commercial, public and voluntary. They are faced with management problems which are sometimes common and sometimes different, depending on the sector. The structure of administration in sport is characterised by a multitude of different organisations, with many different sports governing bodies at the national and international levels, and numerous government agencies and departments, all with a significant influence.

The role of government in sport has come under particular scrutiny. Local and national governments, combined with National Lottery funding, total around £2.2 billion a year for sport in the UK. The reasons for such government intervention are an array of social benefits from sport, including health improvement, crime reduction, educational improvement and the feel-good factor when the country achieves international success. Government intervention in sport has a long history and is characterised by two principal objectives: getting more people playing sport and physical activities; and producing success at the international level.

Arguably the single biggest reason for government involvement in sport is public health. The UK faces potentially huge health problems from overweight and obesity and one of the keys to counteracting such problems is to get people more physically active. Sport and exercise are the most obvious way of achieving this and a lot of the strategic planning by government in sport has been for this purpose. This involves a number of government departments – not just the one responsible for sport, but also departments for health, transport, children and environment, to name a few.

10.1 Introduction

Sport affects most people's lives at some time, through playing sport, as parents of children playing sport, by getting or keeping fit, following a favourite team, or watching a mega event such as the Olympic Games. Sport consists of large numbers of participants, spectators, employees, volunteers, activities, facilities, events and organisations. All these elements need managers to operate effectively and efficiently.

Chapter 1 reproduced the Council of Europe's definition of sport:

> all forms of physical activity which, through casual or organised participation, aim at expressing or improving physical fitness and well-being, forming social relationships, or obtaining results in competition at all levels.

It is clear from this definition that sport extends well beyond a narrow concept of competitive, organised activity. It embraces a lot of activities which are not competitive and not comprehensively organised by representative governing bodies, e.g. recreational walking, recreational swimming, skateboarding. This is important when considering local and national strategies for sport.

This chapter concentrates mainly on sport in the UK, in order to portray the extent, variety and complications of the sports market with a clear and coherent focus. It reviews key elements of supply and demand for sport. Some conspicuous elements of sport are left to other chapters, including sponsorship (Chapter 15) and major events (Chapter 20). First, though, the importance of sport is reviewed – culturally, globally and socio-economically.

10.2 The importance of sport

10.2.1 National identity

Nelson Mandela, at the Rugby Union World Cup in South Africa in 1995, announced, 'Sport has the power to change the world.' It was certainly important to the identity of South Africa at this time, as the film *Invictus* testifies. Sometimes the nationhood of countries is viewed as indivisible from the fortunes of national teams in major spectator sports. Sports became 'patriot games' in the late nineteenth century and their significance has grown ever since, often involving governments at the highest levels. For example, several governments boycotted the 1980 Olympic Games in Moscow and then others the 1984 Los Angeles Games. And sport is also drawn into the 'theatre' of war, the most serious example being a World Cup qualifying match between El Salvador and Honduras in 1969, which sparked riots leading to a war – the so-called 'Football War'.

10.2.2 Globalisation

Sport today is beamed across the world, engaging the interest of billions of people worldwide. The mass media and professional sport are now inextricably merged and economically dependent. Only a few sports attract 'big money': the trinity of sports in the USA – American Football, baseball and basketball; whilst in much of the rest of the world it is football which rules the roost. The introduction of cable and satellite delivery systems gives 24-hour access to sports channels and pay-per-view audiences. The media has accelerated the globalisation of sport. A conspicuous example of this is the Olympic Games. Gratton and Solberg (2007) report that in 1956 just one nation broadcast the Summer Olympics in Melbourne. By 1976, 124 nations broadcast the Montreal Summer Olympics and by 2004 the number had risen to 220 nations for the Athens Games. In parallel, the fees paid for broadcasting rights rose at a tremendous rate, from $100 million for the 1984 Summer Olympics in Los Angeles to $898.2 million for the 1996 Games in Atlanta and $1.7 billion for the Beijing Games in 2008 (Gratton and Solberg, 2007).

It is the media which are perhaps most responsible for the international status of the world's leading sports stars. Whilst many people resent the ridiculously high earnings that they command, they are also a marketing manager's dream as an attractor for sport. Whenever a major sports programme is launched, it is likely to be fronted by a major sports star – this is the simple 'hook' that gets a lot of potential participants interested.

10.2.3 Economic and social importance

Arguably the clearest evidence of the national benefits of sport relate to economic benefits. In England, for example, the total value of consumer spending on sport in 2008 was over £21 billion, which was 2.5 per cent of consumer spending in the economy as a whole and more than double the equivalent figure in 1985 (Sport Industry Research Centre, 2009). Growth in consumer sport spending in this period occurred at nearly twice the rate for all commodities in the economy. This demonstrates not only the increasing relative economic importance of sport, but also the need for competent managers to help sustain this growth.

Figure 10.1 shows the main components of sport spending in the UK. Less than 40 per cent of consumer spending is on sports goods (clothing and footwear, equipment, publications and boats), whilst over 60 per cent of spending is on sport services (including sport gambling, sport TV, participant sports, sport-related travel, and health and fitness). Many of these sub-sectors are dependent on sports participation to sustain their growth, including not only membership subscriptions and admission fees, but also sports clothing and footwear, sports equipment and sport-related travel. A majority of sports managers will be

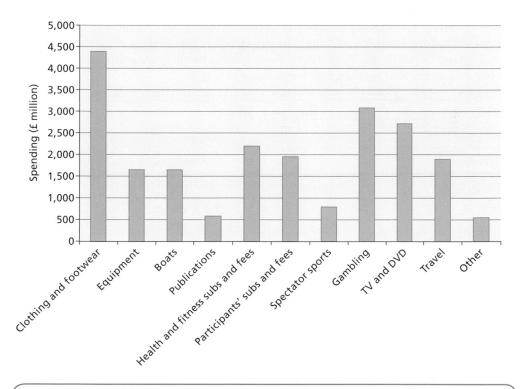

Figure 10.1 Components of consumer spending on sport in the UK, 2008.
Source: Sport Industry Research Centre (2009).

managing sports services with a direct interest in developing mass participation in sport, because this is what the majority of the sports market is about.

Sport and physical activity is also important to a range of social outcomes, including community health, citizenship and cohesion, education, crime and vandalism, and quality of life. These outcomes are not confined to individual participants – many impact on a much broader range of people. Sports managers, particularly in the public sector, should be aware not only of the relevant outcomes from sports participation, but also of how their management can best impact on such outcomes.

10.3 Provision for sport and physical activities

Provision of sporting opportunities is shared by all three of the major supply sectors – commercial, voluntary and government. Sport-related employment in England was estimated to be over 421,000 jobs in 2003, or just under 2 per cent of total employment (Sport England, 2007a). Three-quarters of paid employment in sport in England is in the commercial sector, 12 per cent in the public sector and 11 per cent in the voluntary sector. The voluntary sports sector also has an army of volunteers estimated to be worth 720,000 full-time equivalent paid workers (Sport England, 2003a).

10.3.1 Facilities

Sports participation depends to a large extent on sports facilities. The Audit Commission (2006) identified 3,489 sports centres and swimming pools open to the public in the UK. The Sport England Active Places Power website identifies the numbers of each type of facility in England for 2009 (see Table 10.1). These include not only government-funded facilities but also commercial facilities and membership facilities.

Table 10.1 Sports facilities in England, 2009

Facility type	Total count
Athletics track	379
Golf	3,019
Grass pitch	56,097
Health and fitness suite	6,737
Ice rink	44
Indoor bowls	366
Indoor tennis centre	325
Ski slope	159
Sports hall	9,311
Swimming pool	5,005
Synthetic turf pitch	1,651
Total	*83,093*

Source: Active Places Power, www.activeplacespower.com.

These facilities are not without problems. For example, the number of playing pitches in the UK fell in the latter part of the twentieth century as owners, often local authorities or schools, sold the land for development in order to relieve their budgets. The Labour government instituted a policy to protect playing fields, with strict guidelines controlling applications to develop such land (see Chapter 14, Sections 14.2 and 14.3).

Another problem is that the stock of facilities is ageing, particularly the indoor facilities such as sports centres and swimming pools, and considerable sums are needed to bring them up to modern standards (Carter, 2005). According to the Audit Commission (2006) 65 per cent of local authority sports centres and swimming pools are over twenty years old and in 2003 the assessed investment level needed to keep this stock in working order was £550 million (Sport England, 2003b), whilst total capital spending on sport was typically around £300 million a year, including new-build centres. However, in this period of ageing public facilities the private commercial sector invested heavily in health and fitness facilities – £10 billion in the fifteen years up to 2003 according to Sport England (2003b).

10.3.2 Voluntary clubs

It is estimated by the Central Council for Physical Recreation that around 150,000 voluntary clubs organise sport for eight million people in the UK. Most of these clubs are affiliated to national governing bodies of sport. The clubs are predominantly run by administrators, coaches and helpers who freely give of their time. Whilst this is big business, the management of voluntary organisations and volunteers is a very delicate balancing act between serving members' interests and balancing budgets, and between welcoming and nurturing volunteers and producing good quality sport at reasonable cost. Chapter 6 considers issues in the third sector, including voluntary clubs.

> ### Discussion question
>
> Voluntary clubs are very important providers of sport but they often struggle with insufficient numbers of volunteers. Does this mean that such clubs are not the future for sports provision?

10.4 Participation in sport and physical activities

The 'throughput' of people in sports facilities is large scale. Around 1.5 billion visits are made to UK public parks each year and 7.5 million adults and 2.1 million children are said to use parks for formal or informal sport. An estimated 80 million visits are made to UK local authority swimming pools and sports halls each year. One-quarter of adults are members of voluntary sports clubs. Football is the UK's main sport when spectator figures are added to those who play the game. There are around 42,000 football clubs. Premier League attendances have been fairly stable since the turn of the century despite price rises which were conspicuously higher than the rate of inflation. The total professional football league attendances for 2008 were nearly 30 million, with 13.7 million of these being in the Premier League.

Figure 3.2 introduced trends in sports and physical activities participation in Great Britain since the late 1980s, showing fairly stable participation rates from 1987 to 2002. Table 2.3 shows comparisons of sports participation in several European countries. A feature of such comparisons is that the UK lags behind Scandinavian countries in terms of intensive and regular recreational activity. This has raised concerns (e.g. DCMS/Cabinet Office, 2002) that sport is not contributing sufficiently to the health of the nation compared with the position in other countries. Health is a major reason for government intervention to promote sport, which is discussed later in this chapter (pp. 277–80). Given the emphasis by government on the importance of physical activity for improving health, any manager of a sports facility has a ready-made promotional line for their activities. Health and fitness are very contemporary concerns for today's society.

A major source of data on adults' (16 years and over) sports participation in England is *Active People* (Sport England, 2009a, 2009b), a national survey with a sample size of 363,000 in 2005/6 and over 190,000 in 2007–8 and 2008–9 – making it the largest survey of sports participation in Europe. The headline results for 2007–8 are shown in Table 10.2. These are more comprehensive than the published data for 2008–9, which are restricted to sports funded by Sport England.

It is important to note that the way *Active People* records participation is much stricter than the way the *General Household Survey* recorded sports participation, so the overall level recorded in Table 10.2 (21.3 per cent) is far lower than that recorded in Figure 3.2 (typically over 60 per cent). The latter was at least once in the last four weeks, whilst *Active People* and Table 10.2 record at least three times a week and the activity has to be of moderate intensity and of a continuous duration of at least thirty minutes on each occasion. The reason for this stricter measurement is that one of the primary drivers for Sport England measuring sports activities is for health improvement purposes, and 3 × 30 minutes a week of moderate intensity is considered by scientists to be the minimum necessary to have a health benefit.

Table 10.2 shows evidence of inequalities in sports participation, with higher participation rates for males, young people, those with no disability, white people and those with higher incomes. The Department for Culture, Media and Sport and Cabinet Office (2002) suggest that such levels of inequality, especially by age, need not be the case, when comparing the UK with more equal participation in Sweden and Finland. Managers of all types of provider should be interested in sports participation statistics such as those in Table 10.2. For commercial managers the statistics identify those with more potential to participate, which is important for marketing purposes. For public sector managers, the statistics identify those who are most deserving of special attention – e.g. through specific programmes, targeted promotion, price discounts – because they have relatively low participation rates.

Table 10.3 identifies the most popular activities in England but by the measure of participation at least once in the last four weeks. It demonstrates clearly how important non-competitive activities are. They comprise the top four places and include swimming and cycling because fewer than 2 per cent of swimmers and fewer than 20 per cent of cyclists had taken part in competitions in the previous year – most swimmers and cyclists are recreational participants. Non-competitive activities fill 11 of the remaining 21 places, including athletics because the largest number of athletics participants are joggers (just 5 per cent belong to clubs and only 20 per cent had taken part in a competition in the previous year).

Furthermore, many of these non-competitive activities are characterised by individual participation, rather than in teams or with playing partners. And many are also time flexible – with the participant being able to participate whenever he or she chooses. These non-competitive, individual, time-flexible activities are the ones to have shown most growth in the last two decades and many of them are available in gyms – it is not difficult to see what has fuelled the development of so many commercial fitness centres. It has been argued that such activities are more consistent with time-pressured lives (see Chapter 3).

Table 10.2 Sports participation in England, 2007–8

	Percentage of adults participating[1] at least 3 times a week for 30 minutes duration
All adults (16 years+)	21.3
Gender	
Male	24.2
Female	18.6
Age	
16–24 years	32.3
25–34 years	27.4
35–44 years	24.5
45–54 years	21.5
55–64 years	16.4
65–74 years	12.7
75–84 years	5.7
85 years+	2.3
Disability	
No disability	23.6
Limiting disability	9.1
Ethnicity	
White	21.7
Non-white	17.6
Children	
Children in household	24.0
No children in household	20.2
Income (£)	
52,000+	35.0
36,400–51,999	27.2
31,200–36,399	25.0
26,000–31,199	21.9
20,800–25,999	18.1
15,600–20,799	17.0
0–15,599	12.1
Socio-economic class[2]	
NS-SEC 1–4	23.3
NS-SEC 5–8	16.4

Notes:
1 Activities are of moderate intensity and include recreational walking and cycling, except for travel.
2 Socio-economic classes: 1 = higher managerial and professional occupations; 2 = lower managerial and professional; 3 = intermediate; 4 = small employers and own account workers; 5 = lower supervisory and technical; 6 = semi-routine occupations; 7 = routine occupations; 8 = never worked or long-term unemployed.

Source: Sport England (2009a).

Table 10.3 The 25 most popular sports and physical activities in England, 2007–8

		Percentage of adults participating[1] at least once in the last four weeks
1	Walking	22.0
2	Swimming	13.4
3	Gym	10.7
4	Cycling	8.5
5	Football	7.6
6	Athletics (including jogging)	6.0
7	Golf	3.7
8	Tennis	2.3
9	Badminton	2.3
10	Aerobics	1.6
11	Yoga	1.4
12	Exercise machines/bikes	1.4
13	Squash	1.2
14	Keep fit	1.2
15	Weight training	1.1
16	Bowls	1.1
17	Horse riding	1.0
18	Cricket	1.0
19	Pilates	0.9
20	Basketball	0.8
21	Rugby union	0.8
22	Conditioning/circuits	0.6
23	Fishing	0.5
24	Dance exercise	0.5
25	Health and fitness	0.5

Note: 1 Activities are of moderate intensity and include recreational walking and cycling, except for travel.
Source: Sport England (2009b).

Walking has always been the most popular of activities in Britain since the first national surveys were conducted in the 1970s. Improvements in rights of access will only have increased the incentive to walk in the countryside (see Chapter 8). Furthermore, an ageing population will lead to a growth in recreational walking activity because walking does not suffer as other activities do from the sharp decline with age demonstrated in Table 10.2.

Why are the top five sports in England popular, i.e. walking, swimming, going to the gym, cycling and football? To what extent do they appeal to different motivations?

Swimming has remained one of the most popular sports. Factors that contribute to this include a very strong attraction to water, its health benefits (being non-load-bearing) and its individual or family orientation. It is also relatively inexpensive, no equipment is required and it is readily available to the majority of the population. However, swimming opportunities are more constrained than those for walking and cycling because for most swimmers a swimming pool is required. Case Study 10.1 shows the relationship between the supply of pools and the demand for swimming. The investment implication is very obvious – if you want more swimmers, build more pools!

In comparison with walking and swimming, football is a low participation sport, with less than 8 per cent of adults participating once in the previous four weeks. National interest in football is more from spectating and media interest than from participation. Nevertheless, football participation is showing signs of growth, particularly the five-a-side market. In the commercial market two companies, Powerleague and Goals, operate multiple centres across the UK and claim that there is still untapped potential for greater participation numbers. This and the market for fitness centres, both commercial and public sector, show

CASE STUDY 10.1

Swimming pools and swimming participation

It seems almost simplistic to suggest that sports participation depends on available opportunities and facilities, but it is important for managers to remember this simple relationship. Recent analysis by Shibli (2009) has put together the swimming participation evidence from *Active People* and the availability of swimming pools from Active Places to examine the relationship in England.

The measure of supply used in the analysis is the surface area of swimming pool space (square metres) per 1,000 population. The measure of participation used is the percentage of the population who swam at least once in the previous four weeks. Comparisons were made on a regional basis. The results show significant differences in adult swimming participation rates between nine English regions, from the lowest (12.5 per cent in the North East) to the highest (14.9 per cent in the South East). They also show significant differences in available pool space, from 14.85 square metres per 1,000 people in the West Midlands to 21.27 square metres per 1,000 people in the South East.

The relationship between provision and participation is summarised in Figure 10.2. A line of best fit has been estimated through the data points for each of nine English regions. This line suggests a strong positive relationship, the logic of which is that with more pool space participation is higher.

The implications for planning and management are clear if it is desirable to get more people swimming. And there is a very strong case for wanting more people to swim, both on health grounds and on latent demand grounds (see below and pp. 277–80). The most obvious implication is to build more swimming pools. Sport England has a Facilities Planning Model through which planners can identify the areas most in need of more pools and the specific locations best suited to local populations (see Chapter 14, Section 14.4.8).

Another way of stimulating more participation would be to make more effective use of existing pool provision. The analysis by Shibli assumes that all the square meterage of pool space is available for public use but this is not necessarily the case. For example, many schools with swimming pools do not open them for public use on weekday evenings or at weekends.

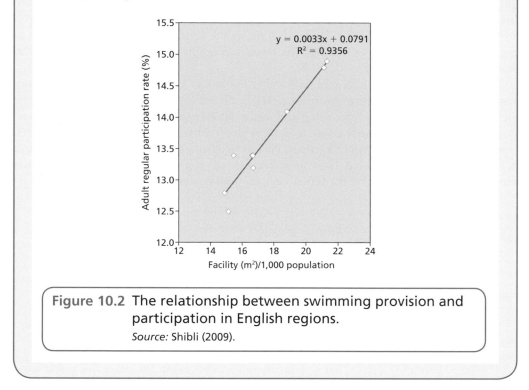

Figure 10.2 The relationship between swimming provision and participation in English regions.

Source: Shibli (2009).

the importance of managers accurately tracking trends in consumer preferences and capitalising on these preferences by either programming or investment.

Active People identifies other important dimensions to sports participation in England. It identifies latent demand – the sports which people would like to do, or do more of than they do at the moment. The most popular sports are also the ones with the largest latent demand, particularly swimming, which over five million people would like to do or do more of. Nearly two million would like to do (more) cycling and nearly 1.5 million would like to do (more) football. Such information is vital to sports centre managers, since it gives the clearest possible signals for service development in the case of swimming and football. It also points to the need for improvements in cycling environments to attract the latent demand for cycling, e.g. the provision of cycle lanes and signposted routes avoiding busy roads.

Active People discloses that nearly 5 per cent of adults volunteer to support sport for at least one hour a week (although this is a lower estimate than in many other surveys). Sport volunteering issues are explored further in Chapter 6. Eighteen per cent of adults had tuition from an instructor or coach to improve their performance in the previous year – another emerging trend for managers to react to. Just under 15 per cent had taken part in an organised competition for their sport in the previous year. And two-thirds of those surveyed were either very or fairly satisfied with sports provision in their local area.

Most of the evidence available on sports participation in England is for adults, because young people are more difficult to engage in surveys and their sports participation is a mix of school PE, extracurricular sport and out of school sport. However, there is some evidence of young people's participation in sport, particularly Sport England's surveys of young people and sport in 1994, 1999 and 2002 (MORI, 2003). The headline statistics for 2002 are shown in Table 10.4.

The overall sports participation rate out of school (excluding walking) for 11–16-year-olds (Y7–Y11) is given as 81 per cent in Table 10.4. Yet the equivalent participation rate for 16–19-year-olds in the 2002 *General Household Survey* is 73 per cent and for 20–24-year-olds it is 62 per cent. This demonstrates one of the most enduring problems in sport: the post-school drop-out, a substantial fall in participation of young people on leaving school. For football the decline is from 32 per cent of Y7–Y11 young people participating, to 23 per cent of 16–19-year-olds and to 12 per cent of 20–24-year-olds. Table 10.4 shows that for some kinds of activities the decline begins much earlier, during secondary school years – see the figures for swimming and athletics/gymnastics.

Discussion question

What are the likely reasons for young people dropping out of sport after leaving full-time education?

Table 10.4 Young people's participation in sport in England, 2002

	Percentage of young people who did sport out of lessons at least ten times in the previous year	
	Y2–Y6[1]	Y7–Y11[1]
Any sport (excluding walking)	88	81
Team games	53	52
Racquet games	26	36
Swimming, diving	63	37
Athletics and gymnastics	53	37
Outdoor, adventure activities	66	50

Note: 1 Y2–Y6 are primary school ages, approximately 7–11 years old; Y7–Y11 are secondary school ages, approximately 12–16 years old.

Source: MORI (2003).

The fall in participation rates among young people represents significant lost potential for sport and physical activity and the UK government has spent considerable policy effort and funding trying to reduce the post-school drop-out. The policy centres on achieving a consistent 'five hour offer' nationally, i.e. two hours a week of high quality physical education plus three hours a week of high quality extra-curricular opportunities. This policy effort includes the appointment of school sport coordinators to encourage more inter-school competition and promote school–club links; and a £28 million Sport Unlimited programme, designed to increase the activity of 'semi-sporty' young people.

10.5 The administration of sport in the UK

The structures for administering and delivering sport in the UK are complex, but it is important for sports managers to know what organisational networks can help them with information or funding. They can be structured according to four levels:

1 national (government);
2 national (non-government);
3 regional;
4 local.

Even at the national level there are a multitude of relevant organisations, both government and non-government, as shown in Table 10.5.

10.5.1 National organisations

Although the principal UK government department responsible for sport is the Department of Culture, Media and Sport (DCMS), a number of other central government departments are relevant to sport, including those responsible for health, children, schools, further education, higher education, local government, criminal justice and government finance. This reflects the fact that sport contributes to a number of cross-cutting agendas, such as social inclusion, crime reduction, citizenship, health, education and enterprise. Any leisure manager wanting government funding or help should be aware of the importance of these cross-cutting agendas.

There are also a number of non-departmental public bodies (NDPBs), funded by government and with sport in their remit, as shown in Table 10.5. Sports councils are accountable to Parliament but used to have a reputation for being 'quasi-autonomous' agents in the cause of sport. In the last two decades, however, it has been claimed that they are now much more agents of government policy. However, sports councils are considerable sources of funding for leisure managers for specific programmes. At the time of writing these include the Sport Unlimited programme for semi-sporty young people; and £10 million to encourage more sports participation at universities.

National sports institutes help the country's top sportsmen and women to win medals in major tournaments like the Olympics, the Commonwealth Games and World Championships in different sports. They provide world class facilities and a high standard of coordinated support services in areas such as coaching, sports science and physiotherapy. National Sports Centres also exist to promote excellence in sport. Sport England, for example, finances two multi-sport national centres at Lilleshall and Bisham Abbey, plus a National Centre for Mountain Activities at Plas y Brenin. A National Water Sports Centre

Table 10.5 Examples of national sports organisations in the UK

UK government department	Department for Culture, Media and Sport
National government departments	Department for Heritage, Wales
	Department of Arts, Culture and Sport, Scotland
	Department of Culture, Arts and Leisure, Northern Ireland
Non-departmental public bodies	UK Sports Council
	Sport England
	sportscotland
	Sports Council for Wales
	Sports Northern Ireland
	English Institute for Sport
	sportscotland Institute of Sport
	Welsh Institute of Sport
	Sports Institute Northern Ireland
	UK Anti Doping
	Football Licensing Authority
Independent non-government organisations	British Olympic Association
	British Paralympic Association
	Football Foundation
	Sportscoach UK
	Women's Sports Foundation
	Youth Sport Trust
	National Governing Bodies of Sport
'Umbrella' organisations	Central Council for Physical Recreation
	Scottish Sports Association
	Welsh Sports Association
	Northern Ireland Sports Forum
Professional associations	Institute of Sport, Parks and Leisure
	Institute of Sport and Recreation Management
	Chief Cultural and Leisure Officers Association
	Fitness Industry Association
	Business in Sport and Leisure

at Holme Pierrepont used to be run by Sport England but is now run by Nottinghamshire County Council. Sport England also grant-aided the development of other national facilities, including the National Indoor Arena, Birmingham; the National Cycling Centre, Manchester; the English Institute of Sport site at Sheffield; and the National Hockey Stadium, Milton Keynes. All these national facilities provide high quality opportunities for elite and improving sportspeople and many also have access for community groups, so they represent high profile opportunities for leisure managers in nearby locations.

National sports organisations are constitutionally independent of government. They are not-for-profit organisations; most are charitable and rely on funding from member clubs. However, some national sports organisations receive a substantial proportion of their funds from government, including the Central Council for Physical Recreation (CCPR), the Football Foundation and Sportscoach UK.

Individual sports are run by independent governing bodies, the majority of which are 'recognised' national governing bodies (NGBs). In the UK there are over 250 NGBs for just over 100 sports – many sports have more than one NGB. Some NGBs have a UK structure, some a GB structure and most are constituted separately in England, Wales, Scotland and Northern Ireland. Many of the major NGBs receive substantial funds from the government via the national sports councils. Any leisure manager organising sport development in specific sports should develop a close relationship with the appropriate NGBs.

In addition to the national structures for sport, most sports have international federations, which are responsible primarily for the rules of the sport and for international competitions. A number of international federations have their headquarters in the UK, including the Commonwealth Games Federation.

10.5.2 Regional organisations

These include:

- government offices;
- Sport England regional offices;
- Regional Sports Boards;
- County Sports Partnerships;
- NGBs at regional and county levels.

In England there are nine Regional Sports Boards (RSBs), grant-aided by Sport England. They work in partnership with Regional Development Agencies and Regional Assemblies. County Sport Partnerships (49 in England), also grant-aided by Sport England and overseen by RSBs, were set up to provide strategic coordination in their geographical areas. Their remit is to help deliver Sport England programmes in partnership with local authorities, healthcare providers, county level NGBs and others, to facilitate a 'joined-up' approach to increasing sports participation and building 'talent pathways' for promising sportspeople. The County Sports Partnerships are important networks for local leisure managers, with up-to-date information on funding opportunities for specific programmes in sport.

10.5.3 Local organisations

These include:

- local authorities;
- Community Sports Networks;
- schools;

- further and higher education institutions;
- local trusts and not-for-profit organisations;
- private sector owners and operators, e.g. health and fitness clubs;
- local sports councils, sports clubs and associations.

Local organisations are at the heart of sports provision in the UK and sports clubs and local authorities are the most significant. According to the Audit Commission (2006) there are 3,489 sport and recreation facilities with public access in England, three-quarters of these being local authority owned.

10.6 Funding for sport

Funding for sports comes from a variety of sources, including:

- central government;
- local government;
- the National Lottery;
- sponsorship;
- SportsAid (formerly Sports Aid Foundation), a private charity set up to provide funding to promising sportspeople;
- the Foundation for Sport and the Arts, set up in 1991 to channel funding from the New Football Pools to sporting and artistic causes;
- private sector companies;
- the voluntary sector, benefactors, donors and the public.

According to DCMS/Cabinet Office (2002), in 2000 nearly 90 per cent of central government funding for sport was distributed by local authorities, and this central government funding represented just over a half of local authorities' expenditure on sport. The rest was financed by fees and charges to users (23 per cent) and local taxes (25 per cent).

The National Lottery awards began in 1995 and sport has been one of the good causes throughout their existence. The DCMS website reveals a total of 47,703 grants awarded by the sports councils in the UK, totalling £37.4 billion in value since awards began. Table 10.6

Table 10.6 National Lottery funding for sport in the UK, 1995–2009

	No. of grants	£ million	Population (million)	£ per head of population
Sport England	18,716	2,777	51.092	54.35
sportscotland	8,378	248	5.144	48.21
Sports Council of Northern Ireland	3,319	129	1.759	73.33
Sports Council for Wales	6,161	141	2.980	47.32
Subtotal	*36,394*	*3,295*	*60.975*	*54.04*
UK Sport	11,309	443	60.975	7.27
TOTAL	*47,703*	*3,738*	*60.975*	*61.30*

Sources: www.lottery.culture.gov.uk/results.asp; www.statistics.gov.uk/statbase/Product.asp?vlnk=15106.

gives the national details of the funding distributed by the sports councils, with awards per head of population varying from over £73 per head in Northern Ireland to less than £48 in Wales. One of the contentious issues with Lottery awards is that increasing amounts have been going to major projects, such as the 2012 Olympics facilities, leaving less money for community level sport. Another concern is that Lottery funding has not all represented a net addition to investment in sport because it has been used as an excuse to reduce normal capital funding of sport by central government and local authorities.

Commercial sponsorship is a conspicuous form of funding, because it is evident on hoardings at all major sports events. Chapter 15 (Section 15.8) considers sports sponsorship as part of the marketing mix.

SportsAid raises funds and supports talented young people usually aged between 12 and 18 and disabled people of any age. Since it was founded in 1976, it has distributed more than £20 million, and now gives grants to around 1,500 sportspeople a year. The Scottish Sports Aid Foundation, SportsAid Cymru and the Ulster Sports and Recreation Trust play similar roles to SportsAid in the other UK countries.

The Foundation for Sports and the Arts, set up by the football pools promoters in 1991, has made awards of more than £350 million to over 100 sports, typically for projects on a relatively small scale compared to some of the large Lottery projects. It is due to close in 2012.

10.7 The rationale for a government role in sport

The DCMS and the Cabinet Office (2002) identified a total government and National Lottery investment in sport of £2.2 billion a year, and asked and answered the key question as follows:

> Why should government invest in sport and physical activity? Because they have a major part to play in promoting health, and as part of a basket of measures can contribute to improved educational outcomes, reduced crime and greater social inclusion.
>
> (DCMS/Cabinet Office, 2002: 14)

A series of reports by Sport England (2008b) identifies a comprehensive list of individual and community benefits which sport contributes to:

- increased social interaction and new relationships and role models;
- increased social and communication skills;
- increased sense of personal achievement, confidence and self-esteem;
- increased 'self-awareness' from experiences of winning and losing;
- improved skills and confidence to contribute to local decisions and take on new challenges;
- increased educational attainment and workforce skills;
- higher levels of knowledge, skills and qualifications;
- increased employment opportunities;
- increased use of community facilities and space;
- stronger local sporting infrastructure, image and identity;
- increased attractiveness of neighbourhoods as places to live and work;
- increased knowledge of local services and engagement with community issues;
- stronger identification with local community and sense of place;
- reduction in anti-social behaviour;
- adoption of more active and productive lifestyles;

and consequent key outcomes:

- participation in sport is increased and sustained, and sporting talent nurtured;
- better quality sporting experiences and the pride in communities that successful local participants and teams can generate;
- improved health and reduced health inequalities;
- strong, sustainable and cohesive communities;
- improved life chances for children and young people;
- increased skills, employment and economic prosperity;
- reduced anti-social behaviour and fear of crime.

(Sport England, 2008b: 4, Executive summary)

However, DCMS/Cabinet Office (2002) also makes clear that:

> The existence of benefits to society does not mean government should necessarily intervene in sport and physical activity. Intervention is justified when:
>
> - it corrects 'inefficiencies' in provision by the private or voluntary sectors (such as the health costs of inactivity); and
> - it addresses inequality of access or opportunity (e.g. differences in participation between social groups).
>
> (DCMS/Cabinet Office, 2002: 15)

Such inefficiencies and inequalities are termed 'market failure' because if the private commercial and voluntary sectors are left to their own devices, social benefits relating to health, education and crime will not be realised sufficiently, and inequalities will not be addressed. In addition, and important to sport, there are 'public goods', i.e. social benefits from which people cannot be excluded, and the enjoyment of which can be shared without affecting other people's enjoyment. Government intervention can take a number of forms – from direct supply subsidised from tax revenues, as in the case of local authority sports facilities and Sport England's national sports centres, to regulation of private activities through planning, monitoring/inspection and tax regimes.

A good example of public goods is excellence in sport, such as the tremendous performance of the UK Olympic and Paralympic stars at the Beijing Olympics in 2008, which gave the whole country a 'feel-good factor'. To try to resource the development of Olympic stars privately and get people to pay would be very difficult and would probably lead to fewer gold medals, through under-resourcing. So excellence in Olympic sports is largely funded by government money (e.g. the World Class Performance programme), which is drawn from tax revenues from those who benefit – the general public.

A persistent problem with designing government intervention, identified by both DCMS/Cabinet Office (2002) and Carter (2005), as well as other independent studies (e.g. Coalter, 2007) and the EU (2007), is that, apart from the health benefits, evidence of other social benefits from sport is patchy. As DCMS/Cabinet Office (2002) makes clear, '[t]his does not invalidate the case for action; but weakens the ability to make decisions fully based on evidence' (2002: 14). However, the main problem with improving the evidence is that the relationship between sport and social outcomes is typically multivariate, e.g. a whole host of factors determine whether or not someone does better or not in education, or is more or less inclined to commit crime. Therefore, to isolate the independent effect of higher sports participation on such outcomes is very difficult. Case Study 10.2 examines this issue in more detail.

Although assembling evidence of sport's effects on social outcomes is difficult, it is nevertheless important, and not just at the national policy-making level. At the local level, too,

CASE STUDY 10.2

Sport and crime

When young people participate in sports or have access to physical education, they can build up their health and self-esteem, use their talents to the fullest, learn the ideals of teamwork and tolerance, and be drawn away from the dangers of drugs and crime.

(Annan, 2005)

It is not hard to find endorsements of the beneficial effects of sport and physical activity on reducing crime and vandalism, especially among young people. According to Sport England (2008b) sport can make a contribution to creating safer communities through the following outcomes:

- reduction in youth offending and anti-social behaviour;
- increase in the culture of respect and tolerance among young people;
- reduction in crime and in alcohol and drug misuse;
- reduction in the fear of crime.

The Audit Commission (2009) agrees that sport and leisure have an important role in preventing anti-social behaviour. However, one of their six key messages for local and national governments concerns evidence, i.e. 'a general lack of data on costs and performance constrains effective commissioning'. Nearly half of the projects looked at by the Audit Commission did not have evidence of their outcomes. Nichols (2007) reviews eight case studies of projects and points to the variety of evaluation methods and evidence produced for them. Evaluations, when they do take place, vary because of the demands of the project funders and because of the preferences of the researchers.

A major programme in England designed to use sport to engage with disadvantaged and socially marginalised young adults is Positive Futures (Home Office, 2007). In 2007 this consisted of 124 projects which collectively engaged over 27,000 young people in around 490,000 contact hours. The programme demonstrates how sport can be used to tackle a range of social issues:

Positive Futures is not about a young person turning up once a week to a sports training session for six weeks. It's about a skilled team working with that young person to help them build their self-confidence, find out what they are good at and support them into education, training and employment by building their skills repertoire.

(Home Office, 2007: 5)

Positive Futures' evaluation measures five levels of engagement: disengagement, curiosity, involvement, achievement and autonomy. In 2007 they reported that 65 per cent of participants were involved or better, 25 per cent were curious and only 10 per cent disengaged – which is low for this type of programme working with hard-to-reach groups. Key lessons from the Positive Futures evaluation include the following:

- Whilst sport does have social value, this can only be fully realised if a personal developmental approach is taken, i.e. not just delivering sport.
- A developmental approach needs management and staff with considerable front-line skills in grassroots youth work.
- Research needs to be integral to project work, so that it informs progress.
- A mixture of sport and other activities is needed to generate wide and flexible appeal.

Positive Futures demonstrates the complexity of evaluating sport and crime. For one thing, it is not just sport in isolation that makes a difference, so any impacts are the result of sport as part of a package. For another, research is not just used to report on results – it is a dynamic process which has as much value in informing project delivery on the ground as in informing politicians and academics about the effects of a project.

Nichols (2007) endorses the importance of the personal developmental approach and the quality of staff needed to facilitate this. Sport is an appropriate hook for such personal development for some but not all young people, which is why Positive Futures uses other activities too. Nichols also stresses the importance of project managers and evaluators having an understanding of the theories which explain the processes by which sport has an influence on crime reduction. Through such knowledge the delivery will be appropriately designed and the evaluation will be aimed at appropriate processes and outcomes.

it is important for individual public facility managers and publicly subsidised sports programmes to help to identify the value for taxpayers' money that their services provide. Chapter 17 looks in more detail at issues of performance management but the main management implication for the moment is that the monitoring of performance is a vital management function.

10.8 The recent history of sport policy in the UK and Europe

Sport, historically, was promoted by individuals, clubs and associations and the governing bodies that they founded. Today, governments typically play a crucial role in terms of policy, sponsored agencies and funding. Because sport is organised in different ways in different countries, the UK is used as an example of the complexity and variability of sports policy. However, Case Study 10.3, on the European Union, demonstrates that international organisations acknowledge the importance of sport too.

For leisure and recreation management in the UK, a watershed document was published fifty years ago. The Wolfenden Report (Lord Wolfenden, 1960), commissioned by the CCPR, identified the need for a sports development council. The Sports Council was established in 1965 and granted independent status by Royal Charter in 1972. Three other national councils followed, for Scotland, Wales and Northern Ireland.

In parallel with the setting up of the Sports Council, the second report from the Select Committee of the House of Lords on Sport and Leisure (House of Lords, 1973) called for action to remedy deficiencies in sporting opportunities. This period was a turning point in sport and leisure policy:

> The state should not opt out of caring for people's leisure when it accepts the responsibility of caring for most of their other needs. The provision of opportunities for the enjoyment of leisure is part of the general fabric of the social services.
>
> (House of Lords, 1973)

Central government at the time had a belief that the provision of sports and leisure opportunities could help to alleviate anti-social behaviour and many ills of the world. This belief was documented in *Policy for the Inner Cities* (Department of the Environment, 1977) and the report of the Scarman Inquiry into riots in Brixton, London (Scarman, 1981). In 1974 the government produced a White Paper on sport and recreation, which proposed substantial changes (Department of the Environment, 1975). It was local authorities which took up the challenge and changed the face of public sports provision. In 1970, there were just 12 sports centres and 440 swimming pools in the UK. By 1980, this had risen to 461 sports centres and 964 swimming pools (Gratton and Taylor, 1991), and Table 10.1 shows that in 2009 there were 9,311 sports halls and 5,005 swimming pools in England alone.

In November 1994 came the launch of the National Lottery, one of the most influential decisions ever made for the sustained development of sport and physical recreation in the UK. Facilities funded by the National Lottery must be available for use by the whole community and Table 10.6 shows the significant scale of lottery funding for sport in the UK.

The next major development, in 1995, was a government policy document, *Sport: Raising the Game* (Department of National Heritage, 1995). Sports participation in schools had declined and the policy aimed at reversing the trend, promoting closer links between schools and sports clubs and establishing a new British Academy of Sport that would serve as a pinnacle of a national network of centres of excellence. This was later renamed as the English Institute of Sport. This development, together with Lottery funding for elite sportspeople, was significant because it marked a radical shift from earlier policies concerning excellence in sport; for example:

> Some countries invest vast public funds in special facilities, training programmes and financial and status rewards for elite athletes, in order to win prestige and trade internationally. It is neither tradition nor policy to treat top level sport in this way in Britain.
>
> (Sports Council, 1982)

Another pivotal government strategy for sport was produced by the government's Cabinet Office (DCMS/Cabinet Office, 2002). *Game Plan* was described by the prime minister in the foreword as 'a thorough analysis of where we are now and an essential route map to get us to where we want to be in the future'. It confirmed two major objectives for the government role in sport:

1 to increase participation, 'primarily because of the significant health benefits';
2 to improve Britain's success in international competition 'particularly in the sports which matter most to the public'.

Recommendations addressed not only these objectives but also the following:

● the need for 'a more cautious approach' to hosting major events, especially in relation to the government's role and the assessment of benefits;
● organisational reform to encourage closer working between public, voluntary and commercial sectors;
● identifying 'what works' before committing further government investment in sport.

A later independent review, the Carter Report (Carter, 2005) concentrated on the financing and organisation of sport. It echoed both the need for a better evidence base on which to build further public investment in sport and the need for organisational reform to eliminate wasteful duplication of effort. The most recent Sport England strategy for 2008–11 (Sport England, 2008a) attempts to address the organisational reform agenda. First, it creates a clear differentiation between responsibility for school sport, with the Youth Sport

Trust; responsibility for community sport when school is finished, with Sport England; and responsibility for elite sport, with UK Sport. Second, it restricts Sport England's remit to sport, narrowly defined, with physical activity being driven by a number of other government departments but particularly the Department of Health.

Furthermore, Sport England will work primarily through national governing bodies of sport to deliver their key outcomes, which are:

- 1 million people doing more sport by 2012–13;
- lower post-school drop-out in at least five sports;
- an increase in participants' satisfaction with the quality of their sport experience;
- improved talent development systems in at least 25 sports;
- a major contribution to the delivery of five hours a week high quality sports opportunities to young people aged 5–19 years.

The latest UK government plan for sport at the time of writing is Playing to Win, from the Department of Culture, Media and Sport (2008), which sets out 'a vision for sport to 2012 and beyond'. This plan reinforces the direction of change made clear in the Sport England strategy, the vision being 'to give more people of all ages the opportunity to participate in high quality competitive sport'. The means to deliver it is a 'system which will nurture and develop sporting talent, underpinned by a high quality club and competition structure'. This narrows the concept of sport to 'competitive', which is much more restricted than, for example, the commonly accepted definition of sport given earlier in this chapter (p. 256).

Discussion question

Discuss whether a policy of concentrating sports strategy on traditional sports and national governing bodies is too restricted. What are the risks of such a strategy?

Recreational, non-competitive sport is by inference no longer the remit of the DCMS, but instead is part of physical activity and therefore the remit of the Department of Health. The DCMS and Sport England plans are much more focused on a competitive sports system which delivers sporting success at the international level, particularly the 2012 Olympics; and also more focused on the voluntary sector – NGBs and clubs – to deliver this outcome. This is only partly consistent with one of the principal government aims for sport – to engage a million more people in regular sport participation by 2012–13. The major increases in UK sport participation in recent years have been both non-competitive (individual, fitness oriented activity – see participation evidence on pp. 259–66) and not in the voluntary sector but in the public (local authorities) and commercial (fitness) sectors. Furthermore, these trends are likely to continue.

However, the focusing of DCMS and Sport England strategies does not mean they are turning their backs on non-competitive sport and physical activity. DCMS (2008) does acknowledge its role in working with other government departments to promote physical activity and sports development. Furthermore, there is significant funding of initiatives to generate increases in physical activity, such as the £140 million free swimming programme for young and old people. The difference is that such initiatives are jointly funded by a number of government organisations, e.g. free swimming is a cross-government initiative

The European Union and sport

In 2007 the EU published a White Paper on sport and a consequent Action Plan. The White Paper is summarised in this case study. It begins with statements such as:

> Sport is a growing social and economic phenomenon which makes an important contribution to the European Union's strategic objectives of solidarity and prosperity.

and:

> It generates important values such as team spirit, solidarity, tolerance and fair play, contributing to personal development and fulfilment. It promotes the active contribution of EU citizens to society and thereby helps to foster active citizenship.

As well as promoting sport for its own sake, the EU Sport Unit also attempts to ensure that sport is taken into consideration in the development and implementation of relevant EU policies. The list of policies for which sport is deemed relevant is extensive: competition; the internal market; employment and social affairs; justice, freedom and security; regional policy; health and consumer protection; education and youth; environment; and external relations. The White Paper identifies the important societal roles for sport as follows:

- enhancing public health;
- combating doping;
- improving education and training;
- promoting volunteering and active citizenship;
- facilitating social inclusion, integration and equal opportunities;
- assisting the fight against racism and violence;
- sharing values with other parts of the world;
- supporting sustainable development.

The White Paper also acknowledges that sport 'can serve as a tool for local and regional development, urban regeneration or rural development'. It aspires to developing an agreed framework for good governance in sport – covering such principles as transparency, democracy, accountability and representation of stakeholders. It acknowledges the 'specificity of sport' in respect of EU law. This specificity comprises:

- sporting activities and rules, e.g. separate competitions for men and women, limitations on the number of competitors in events, and the need to ensure uncertainty of outcome to preserve a competitive balance in competitions;
- sport structures, particularly the autonomy and diversity of sport organisations.

Other issues covered by the White Paper include:

- the free movement of labour and how that interacts with national selection for competiton;
- transfer rules and the role of players' agents in professional sports;
- protection of minors, particularly in international competitions;
- licensing systems for professional clubs;
- the relationships between sport and the media (e.g. television rights).

The EU White Paper on Sport contains 58 action points, paralleling its discussion of the issues above, which form the Pierre de Coubertin Action Plan, named after the founder of the modern Olympics. Around one-third of these concern more effective communications with and between EU member states on issues such as health, doping, racism, eco-measures and licensing. There is a proposal to hold an annual Sports Forum involving all the key EU stakeholders in sport. Nine action points recommend research into issues including sports volunteers, challenges for non-profit sports organisations and the funding of grassroots sport. Another nine action points concern closer partnership working, particularly on issues such as doping, corruption, violence and racism in sport.

A relatively small proportion of action points suggest direct financing to support sports initiatives, or possible changes in EU law. Nevertheless, the White Paper is the strongest sign yet that the EU takes sport seriously. In December 2008 the European Parliament approved a €6 million budget for EU 'Preparatory Action in the field of sport' in 2009, which included: €4 million for sports projects focusing on health, education, disability sports and gender equality; €1 million for studies, surveys, conferences and seminars to support policy in sport; and €1 million for the 2009 Mediterranean Games. Clearly, EU policy and funding for sport are an emerging force to be reckoned with.

with funding from five government departments as well as investment from the Amateur Swimming Association and Sport England.

One puzzle remains, despite all this attention on government policy. Although over 90 per cent of government funding for sport and physical activity is distributed by local authorities, sports services have always been a discretionary service for local authorities in England and Wales. Other services such as education and refuse collection and disposal are mandatory. If sport is so important to government, why give local authorities the option to not do anything for sport?

European Union attention to sport as a policy interest is relatively recent, but it is another expression of the role of government, as Case Study 10.3 shows.

10.9 Sport, physical activity and health

Arguably it is the links between sport and health that most justify government intervention to promote mass participation in sport. As *Game Plan* suggests:

> The benefits of physical activity on health are clear, well evidenced and widely accepted. 30 minutes of moderate activity five times a week can help to reduce the risk of cardiovascular diseases, some cancers, strokes and obesity. Estimates put the total cost to England of physical inactivity in the order of at least £2bn a year. Conservatively, this represents about 54,000 lives lost prematurely. A 10 per cent increase in adult activity would benefit England by at least £500m a year (saving about 6,000 lives). These estimates exclude the costs of injuries. The burden of physical inactivity is an increasing problem, as the continuing rise in obesity and other inactivity-related health challenges demonstrates. As these escalate, so will the costs of physical inactivity.
>
> (DCMS/Cabinet Office, 2002: 15)

Products and services

Successive governments have warned of the dangers to health brought about by lack of physical activity. The White Paper *The Health of the Nation* (Department of Health, 1992), provided a strategic approach with the aims of 'adding years to life' and 'adding life to years':

> Health services are only one part of the strategy {...} Physical activity is a factor which may reduce early mortality and ill-health and contribute to healthy living. A lack of physical activity is accepted as a main risk factor for heart disease and stroke. With the decline in physical activity in everyday life and work, sport and physical recreation now account for most vigorous activity that a person engages in and they are central to the future health of the nation, as well as providing pleasure to millions of people of all ages and abilities.
>
> (Department of Health, 1992)

A more recent report has suggested:

> By 2050, 60 per cent of males and 50 per cent of females could be obese, adding between £5.5 and £6.5 billion to the annual cost of the NHS by 2050, with wider costs to society and business reaching £45.5 billion.
>
> (Government Office for Science/Foresight, 2007)

The Chief Medical Officer has reinforced the case for physical activity to combat this problem:

> The scientific evidence is compelling. Physical activity not only contributes to well-being, but is also essential for good health. People who are physically active reduce their risk of developing major chronic diseases by up to 50%, and the risk of premature death by about 20–30%.
>
> (Department of Health, 2004)

The European Union adds:

> As a tool for health-enhancing physical activity, the sport movement has a greater influence than any other social movement.
>
> (European Union, 2007)

According to Sport England (2008b), using sport and physical activity to improve health will generate the following key outcomes:

- reduce the specific risk factors that contribute to poor health, e.g. obesity, diabetes, cardiovascular disease and some types of cancer;
- increase life expectancy and reduce health inequalities;
- improve quality of life and increase independence, including among older people and people with health conditions;
- create a healthier workforce, with less absenteeism.

The message for sports managers is clear – if public funding is to be secured for development of sport in the community, then health benefits are the most influential underlying objective.

> ### Discussion question
>
> If the evidence relating sport and physical activity to better health is so strong, why don't more people choose to do more sport and physical activity?

10.9.1 Fitness facilities

The recent increase in positive awareness of health and fitness has meant a boom in the market and considerable interest from all sectors of supply. According to Sport England's Active Places website there are 6,693 health and fitness centres in England, in both the public and private sectors. This has grown from an estimated 2,900 centres in 1995. The most significant growth has been in the commercial fitness industry, as shown earlier (p. 259). In the public sector, nearly all large leisure centres now provide fitness centres, aerobics studios and health suites.

What has brought about this level of interest? Personal vanity and health and wanting to look good are prime reasons for individuals; public health and revenue are major motives for public sector providers; and market preferences and profit are major driving forces for commercial business. The drive for fitness, however, has not been founded in sport but rather in health and lifestyle.

Despite a developing and changing market, there are critical success factors for a fitness facility. They include:

- a fitness gym with cardio-vascular and resistance machines – the size of the gym has a direct bearing on the number of members that a club can accommodate;
- dance/aerobics studios – most clubs have at least one or two studios for aerobics, step classes, yoga, spinning, etc.;
- a swimming pool – providing for the most popular indoor activity;
- a health spa – with steam, sauna and water therapy pool suggests a holistic approach to health;
- a health and beauty salon – including facials, aromatherapy, hairdressing, massage and physiotherapy;
- support facilities – such as catering, bar, health drinks and food, and a crèche to attract the family market;
- personal trainers – to help customers get the most out of their participation.

10.9.2 Healthy Living Centres

As well as the conventional facilities promoting sport, physical activity and health, another type of facility has been developed in the UK – Healthy Living Centres. These were funded by the government, with an estimated £300 million allocated from the New Opportunities Fund. Lottery cash was targeted to areas of urban deprivation and social exclusion. Healthy Living Centres were aimed at helping to reduce the variations in health that arise as a result of differences in people's income, housing, education, employment, age and ethnic background.

Examples developed with Lottery funding include Peckham Pulse in London and the LIFE project on the Wirral. Peckham Pulse Healthy Living Centre comprises a main swimming pool, hydrotherapy pool with adjustable floor, gym, spa, crèche and a health suite with a National Health Service clinic. The Wirral national award-winning LIFE project was a collaborative scheme aimed at combating coronary heart disease. Following its success, the council and health authority provided joint funding to Wirral's Health Links programme: the Health Promotion School Scheme; Health Promotion Training Programme; Healthy Living Courses; and a Health Information and Research Centre.

These examples demonstrate the strong potential links between physical activity and healthy lifestyles and also demonstrate why central government and local authorities are anxious to provide these facilities. However, it should not be forgotten that most people taking part in sport and recreation do so for fun, comradeship and the enjoyment of taking part. Physical activity, like play, can be enjoyed for its own sake.

10.10 Conclusions

Sport has a complex organisational structure. Traditionally the province of the voluntary sector, which gave sport its rules, its governing bodies, its voluntary clubs and its major events, it now includes heavy involvement of both commercial and government interests. The commercial sector has clear areas of dominance, particularly in the manufacture and retailing of sports clothing and footwear, sports equipment and sport publications. But it also has substantial interests in significant sports services, such as TV, health and fitness clubs, sports sponsorship, sports gambling and professional spectator sports. The profit motive is a key driver of innovation and efficiency and it has a clear role in increasing the economic importance of sport to developed countries.

Governments have a complex array of objectives for sport, including health improvement, crime reduction and excellence in international competitions. To this end, government finances a considerable network of sports facilities, from local leisure centres to national training centres. A large majority of this funding is distributed at the local level. In local authorities there is a mix of management options, with in-house, commercial contractors and third sector trusts all operating different public sector sporting facilities, as discussed in Chapter 5.

The bedrock of sports provision, however, remains in the voluntary sector. National governing bodies of sport and their international federations dictate the structures of competition on which much sport thrives. Voluntary clubs supply an army of volunteers and it is in this sector that the UK government has recently put its trust, with a strategy firmly located in traditional sport, with NGBs as key partners.

However, looking at market trends, which managers must do, reveals a different story. It is not the traditional, competitive sports organised by NGBs that are growing in popularity the most. Rather, market growth favours individual, non-competitive, time-flexible activities such as walking, cycling or going to the gym and doing any number of exercise options. In this domain it is the commercial and public sector managers who are in the spotlight, and there is considerable competition for ever-more discerning customers looking for a high quality experience.

Practical tasks

1 Conduct a couple of interviews with people you know, assessing how important sport and physical activity are in their lives. Try and relate the discussions to their health, their social life and their self-confidence.

2 You want to form a new club for a specific sport or physical activity that you are interested in. By searching the internet and identifying what different organisations do, map out the network of local, regional and national organisations which might help you to develop your club.

Structured guide to further reading

For sports participation in England:

Sport England (2009a) *Active People Survey 2*, Sport England, London, available at www.sportengland.org/index/get_resources/research/active_people.htm.

MORI (2003) *Young People and Sport in England: trends in participation 1994–2002*, Sport England, London, available at www.sportengland.org/young-people-and-sport-2002-report.pdf.

For UK policy, including sport and health and sport and crime:

DCMS/Cabinet Office (2002) *Game Plan: a strategy for delivering government's Sport and Physical Activity Objectives Report*, DCMS, London, available at www.sportengland.org/gameplan2002.pdf.

DCMS (2008) *Playing to Win: a new era for sport*, DCMS, London, available at www.culture.gov.uk/images/publications/DCMS_PlayingtoWin_singles.pdf.

Sport England (2008b) *Shaping Places through Sport*, Sport England, London, available at www.sportengland.org/shapingplaces.

For UK sports markets:

Sport Industry Research Centre (2009) *Sport Market Forecasts 2009–2013*, SIRC/Sport England, Sheffield and London.

Useful websites

For *Taking Part* results:
www.culture.gov.uk/reference_library/publications/5396.aspx

For *Active People* results:
www.sportengland.org/research/active_people_survey.aspx
www.sportengland.org.uk/research/sport_facts/

For Active Places Power:
www.activeplacespower.com

Products and services

For sports councils in the UK:
UK Sports Council, operating as UK Sport, www.uksport.gov.uk
English Sports Council, operating as Sport England, www.sportengland.org
Scottish Sports Council, operating as **sport**scotland, www.sportscotland.org.uk
Sports Council for Wales, www.sports-council-wales.org.uk
Sports Council for Northern Ireland, www.sportni.net

For the British Olympic Association (BOA):
www.olympics.org.uk

Managing play services for children

Perry Else

In this chapter

- What is play and what are its benefits?
- Why does play provision have to be managed?
- What types of play are necessary to fulfil the requirements of children?
- What types of play provision are there and who provides them?
- What training is appropriate for people working in play?
- What does a play policy look like?
- What is good design for a play space?
- How can play provision be evaluated?

Summary

This chapter gives the reader an overview of play and playwork services for children and young people. Current definitions of play are examined, with some historical context. Play is an elusive and complex phenomenon and yet it is important for adults to understand what play offers children in order to make appropriate provision. Too often play decisions are made by adults, when the essence of play is that children should be making their own decisions.

There is a strong rationale for play provision, rooted in the benefits of good play opportunities for children. In particular, health and behaviour problems may be related to restricted play opportunities. This rationale is supported by government policies on children, including those of the United Nations and national movements. The chapter features examples from Sweden and the Netherlands, and focuses on key policy initiatives in the UK since 2000.

Policy and national support systems for playwork are briefly explained – the UK having one of the most connected national infrastructures for coordinating play policy and guiding playworkers. However public resources devoted to play services are typically relatively small. Detailed descriptions are given for frontline services for children and young people, involving many partnerships. The key issues involved in managing play services for children – staff training, policy, site design and evaluation – are outlined using relevant case studies from a variety of perspectives.

11.1 Introduction

> You don't stop playing as you grow old; you grow old because you stop playing.
>> (Attributed to both George Bernard Shaw and Benjamin Franklin)

> Play is a developmentally important human process.
>> (The National Institute for Play, http://nifplay.org/)

> Play is a process that is freely chosen, personally directed and intrinsically motivated. That is, children and young people determine and control the content and intent of their play, by following their own instincts, ideas and interests, in their own way for their own reasons.
>> (Playwork Principles Scrutiny Group, 2005)

As Shaw states, we are all capable of playing throughout our lives. Play is considered to be vital to human development in many ways, and children need opportunities to play that they can choose for themselves. There are many definitions of play; however, the professionally developed statement by the Playwork Principles Scrutiny Group is the one used by UK playworkers (adults working with children in their play).

What most modern descriptions recognise is that play is playing when defined by the player; when they are in control of the process, it can go where they want it to and it is felt to be playful. When children and young people are being told what to do it is not play; for example when it's being done for other reasons such as 'coaching' or 'education'. Interestingly, as part of the development of a city's sport strategy, adults were asked to say what had helped them become good – or bad – at sports. In both cases the dominant answer was the same – the adult involved. When as children they were forced to do something by an adult, they stuck in their heels and rebelled against it; when the activity was differently presented and they could choose how to engage, they saw it as playful, enjoyed it and stuck with it. Many adults still play when given the chance, but would they choose to do so if told to do it by someone else? When managing provision for play, managers should understand the key elements of play.

Play emerges spontaneously from children's natural activities (some describe this as an innate, biological drive). Children do not need equipment or special places to play; they can play everywhere and with everything. Think about children playing in the kitchen with cooking tools or food, or children out in the street playing tag or chase games in whatever space is available, or young people name-calling and chatting in parks or on street corners where they feel safe. Play has many dimensions; children can play alone or in groups; they can be very physically active or almost comatose, with their concentration on aspects of a game; play can be creative, destructive, loud, quiet, involving or isolating, depending on the players and the play themes. For many, childhood play leads to a lifetime interest in art, for others it is drama and stories, or sport and other leisure pastimes; adults too can play by using their minds, by interacting with others or by pushing their bodies to extremes. Because of these varied aspects, a lot has been claimed for the purpose of play over the years.

Play was discussed by the ancient Greeks and Romans, who stated that play was children's preparation for adulthood. In the modern era, this view was supported by Groos (1861–1946), who felt that play was how children made sense of adult roles; he also felt that play was evolutionary as more complex forms of play were practised by the more advanced species; all animals play, but big mammals, apes, monkeys and humans play in more intricate ways. Freud and Jung, writing in the 1920s, argued that the drive to play was more of a cognitive and emotional experience, and that the child's ideas and feelings would impact on their play, be it physical or imaginary. Piaget (1896–1980) was very influential in education and child development circles by stating that play served a developmental purpose, in that children played with the elements of the surrounding world to create mental models by which they could then make sense of that world. This led to his categorising of development into 'ages and stages' (where children were considered against developmental norms) that was very dominant in the later twentieth century.

Catherine Garvey (1977) broke away from Piaget's ideas of cognitive development by showing how play had separate lines of development in other areas, e.g. communication, motion, rules and rituals. Garvey felt that play was possible with different resources at different age levels for different benefits. She set out an inventory of the characteristics of play:

- Play is pleasurable, enjoyable.
- Play is spontaneous and voluntary.
- Play has no extrinsic goals.
- Play involves some active engagement on the part of the player.
- Play has certain systematic relations to what is not play, i.e. play has links to creativity, problem solving, socialisation and the development of language.

Garvey summed up her position by saying that it was 'difficult, if not impossible, to propose any single or uniform function for play'. Play is better described as a process, in that it has no defined goal or outcomes, and the play may start and finish in very different areas or topics. Thinking of play as a process also helps adults think about what is happening as children play, rather than thinking about the products of their play.

This process of play has been described as the play cycle (Sturrock and Else, 1998; see Figure 11.1). The parts of the play cycle are (i) the drive to play, which may be a conscious thought or a spontaneous impulse, that results in (ii) the play cue, the signal to others that the child wishes to play. The environment that contains the play is called (iii) the play frame, made up of the child's thought to play and the space it occupies. The play cycle is completed by (iv) the play return, which may be environmental or from another player. This cycle describes the first explorations of the environment by toddlers, for example in exploring textures or shapes, as it does teenagers teasing each other or challenging each other in risky play, for example by going higher on a climbing wall or faster on their bikes or boards. In all cases the play stops when the child or young person has got what they needed from the play opportunity.

One model that draws together the differing views on the purpose of play is the Integral Play Framework (Else, 2009; see Figure 11.2). This framework shows that all humans experience both the internal world of feelings as well as the world of objects shared with others. They interchange, so that what we think affects how we behave and what we experience affects our thoughts and feelings. For example, a group of children are playing tag chase, a physical game involving running around on the ground and over obstacles to evade capture. Ethan is 'it'; he tries hard to pass the role to another and races round energetically. Initially frustrated that he cannot catch the others, he becomes elated when he tags his friend Sohail and manages to escape onto a high platform. Later he and Sohail talk about the game and what it felt like to be 'on' and what it was like when they were running away. Similarly in a team game, adults will be using physical skills, thought-out strategies,

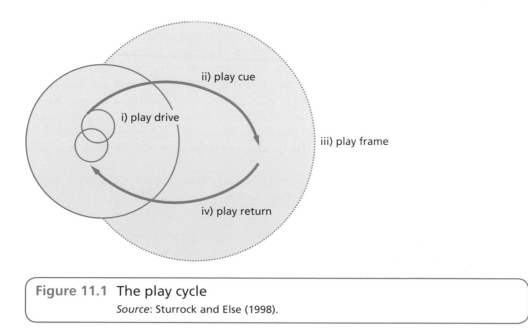

Figure 11.1 The play cycle
Source: Sturrock and Else (1998).

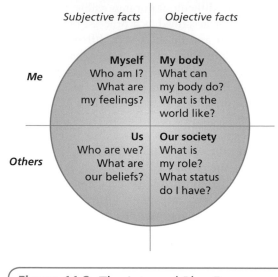

Figure 11.2 The Integral Play Framework.
Source: Else (2009).

communication and interaction skills and experiencing personal highs and lows as the game develops. Afterwards much reflection will take place in the locker room or local bar, where a different form of play may evolve.

This framework shows how play is important for feeling alive 'in the moment', how it supports physical and emotional interactions and how it helps us find out about the nature of things – all features that the writers quoted on p. 286 explain. In reality, many managers of play services will not have an appreciation of playwork concepts; this is doing a disservice to the children who they provide the service for. Children need access to environments and opportunities that encourage physical play – running and climbing – as well as play with others; imaginative and fantasy play as well as chances to perform and make (and destroy) things. In many settings, opportunities are designed to only engage with one or two dimensions. For example, the typical park playground has little opportunity for dressing up or creativity, and typically does not cater for team games. School playgrounds may be flat and unengaging tarmac spaces with few natural elements. Even natural environments, while offering many opportunities, may not feel socially or physically safe for many children. Providing varied and challenging environments for children helps us more fully meet their play needs.

Many of these thoughts have been influential in what is described in the UK as playwork, the practice of working with children to support their play.

Discussion questions

What philosophy of play do you share with the theorists? In what ways do you believe that play is beneficial for children?

11.2 Playwork

The play leadership movement started in Europe soon after the Second World War with the development of 'junk' or adventure playgrounds; 'creative playgrounds with tools and waste material'. An early champion of children's freely chosen play was Lady Allen of Hurtwood (1897–1976), who introduced adventure playgrounds to the UK after seeing them in Scandinavia in the late 1940s. Originally described as 'play leaders', practitioners soon realised that the role of the adult was better defined not as 'leading' children but as working alongside them. This was recognised by the Playwork Principles Scrutiny Group (2005), where the adult's role was defined as 'to support all children and young people in the creation of a space in which they can play', so playworkers help to create opportunities for play rather than leading play activities. This approach sets playwork apart from other work with children in that it is accepted that the impetus of the play comes from the children rather than being directed by adults.

11.2.1 Playwork concepts

In the early 1980s, the playwork movement in the UK started preparing papers to describe their emerging profession. Bob Hughes has contributed many papers and books (Hughes, 1996a, 1996b, 2001a, 2001b, 2003, 2006) that explore the practice and phenomenon of play. Perhaps the most widely quoted of his works is his list of play types (1996b), compiled from extensive reading of literature about children's play and development.

Play types describe different play behaviours that children may exhibit during their play, examples being locomotor play (playing through space and movement), social play (playing with others) and exploratory play (finding out about the nature of things) (Hughes, 1996b). The play types help adults see the different ways in which children play, not to direct the play but to recognise its variety and their need for resources. Hughes (1996a) also defined the characteristics of a rich play environment as a space that gives children and young people the opportunity to experience the following:

- interaction with the natural elements of earth, air, fire and water;
- sensory stimulation, smells, sights, sounds, textures, tastes;
- freely chosen social interaction;
- playing with identity, their own and that of others;
- emotional changes – happy/sad, angry/calm;
- challenge in relation to the physical environment and those in it;
- movement in all dimensions;
- change – construction and destruction;
- fabricated and natural materials;
- overall, an interesting and varied physical environment.

And, we could add, with 'sufficient space' to enable all of this to happen for the number of children in the setting. This checklist covers the fundamental elements of what should be offered to children through play spaces and playgrounds, and is as relevant for small community settings as it is for parks, schools and natural environments. All environments that provide for play will have some of these characteristics, and providers of services should help add greater variety. Case Study 11.1 illustrates a good example.

In 2000, three well-respected play organisations in the UK (National Playing Fields Association (NPFA), Children's Play Council (CPC) and PLAYLINK) wrote *Best Play: what play provision should do for children.* This explained the purpose of play, the values and principles underpinning play, its role in child development and the effects of play deprivation or lack of play. It then made the case for public investment in play, explained the adult roles in play provision and gave objectives for play provision.

Best Play also summarised the benefits of play in two ways: first, the benefits experienced by children at the time that they are playing:

> Play –
>
> - provides children with opportunities to enjoy freedom, and exercise choice and control over their actions;
> - offers children opportunities for testing boundaries and exploring risk;
> - offers a very wide range of physical, social and intellectual experiences for children.
>
> (NPFA *et al.*, 2000)

and, second, the benefits that develop over time:

> Play –
>
> - fosters children's independence and self-esteem;
> - develops children's respect for others and offers opportunities for social interaction;
> - supports the child's well-being, healthy growth and development;
> - increases children's knowledge and understanding;
> - promotes children's creativity and capacity to learn.
>
> (NPFA *et al.*, 2000)

In 2008, Play England (the English national organisation for play) commissioned 'a comprehensive review of the evidence underpinning current thinking on play'. The final review (Lester and Russell, 2008) argued for the importance of play and how it relates to social policy and practice. The review challenged the dominant view that play is a process for learning. Lester and Russell argued that as valid as the chance is that play gives children to find out about the world, equally valid is the experience of playing itself; in play children often do 'silly things' that have no apparent purpose other than for the fun of it. They also quoted the growing body of evidence that showed that brain development and plasticity are affected by the play opportunities that children experience; in effect, the more children play, the more connections the brain makes and the better it works. Similar views are promoted by the Association for Early Childhood Australia and by the National Institute for Play in the USA.

The works reviewed above provide lots of material to explain and justify the importance of play. With the benefits of play so well explained and understood, it may be surprising that opportunities for play are changing for the worse in many industrialised countries.

Discussion question

Why do you think that 'playwork' emerged as a profession towards the end of the twentieth century?

'Sportpunt' Centre, Netherlands

The 'Sportpunt' Centre in Goes, Zeeland, is an exceptional sports and leisure centre that serves the local population of 27,000. It is near the heart of town, directly accessible to people across town by a ten-minute cycle ride. The accommodation includes three sports halls, four squash courts, a climbing wall, two meeting rooms and a sports bar. At the heart of the centre is a subtropical swimming pool covering more than 1,000 square metres of water. In addition there are five other pools ranging through a toddlers splash pool, a bubble pool, training pools and a 25 metre lane pool, kept cool for serious swimmers. In the corner of the swimming area is a cafe selling cooked snacks, drinks and ice cream. The cafe and relaxed atmosphere help children and their families stay in the pool for in excess of three hours.

The supervision is quite relaxed, with children and other users expected to manage their own use of the facilities, even down to no supervision on the two water slides. The manager of the facility explained that such extensive provision was made possible by the fact that much of the water space was rented out to local schools for swimming lessons. In the 1980s, the Netherlands' government (in common with many European countries) decided that, to minimise drowning deaths, all children in the country should be competent swimmers by the age of seven years old, capable of swimming 200 or even 400 metres. So by the time they are old enough to roam through the environment, Dutch children are helped to be safer in a country much of which is close to water.

In addition to the indoor facilities there are 65 sports pitches and a nature area immediately adjacent to the sports centre. This environmental area was created with a variety of landscaped features that combine to create an excellent playful space with many opportunities for interaction for children. As well as the 'official' play area, there are a mini-golf area, petting zoo, local craft centre and environmental education centre. But the best area for free play is the waterway where children are encouraged to play unsupervised.

Planted directly in the dyke is a large pole with a chain and rope attached. On each side of the water is a landing platform and a little further along are a series of stepping-stones. Children take it in turns to swing across the dyke, and then run across the stones to have another go. No one supervises them, no one tells them to share the rope or be careful near the water (all the children can swim!). It is a wonderful example of the playful opportunities that the Dutch make freely available to their children. This whole area is bounded by woods and small hills and appears to be in the deepest countryside, though it is close to an industrial area and only 800 metres from the heart of town.

The Dutch were also a major developer of 'woonerf' – 'streets for living' – especially designed to encourage play and discourage high speeds by motor vehicles. In the Netherlands (as in other parts of Europe, notably Germany and Sweden), cars must give way to cycles and pedestrians in inner-city traffic environments. In a road accident between a bike and a car, it is taken for granted that the car driver is responsible. This attitude creates a positive approach to cycling that contributes, for example, to over 85 per cent of the population in Amsterdam having a cycle.

These two policy decisions, helping all children to swim and giving priority to pedestrians, create a country in which children are free to roam, play with friends, ride bikes and swim in a dyke, which perhaps helps explain why Dutch children are considered to be the happiest in the western world (UNICEF, 2007).

11.3 Why we need play provision

In the modern world, there are restrictions for children to play outside and many perceived threats. Work by Bird (2007) has shown how over an 80-year period children's opportunity to roam changed. Bird stated that in the 1920s children could roam up to 10 km from home, by the 1950s that had reduced to 1.5 km, and then to 275 metres for the generation growing up around the year 2000. The main restriction that has emerged in many western-ised countries since the 1970s is the large increase in traffic that has limited children's freedom to play outdoors. Combined with a change in the home circumstances of many children (more parents in employment, more single parent families and fewer contacts with an extended family), this has resulted in children who spend more time indoors, playing alone or in small groups. These changes in childhood have also been linked to increases in behaviour problems and childhood obesity. The years leading up to 2000 saw rises in the numbers of overweight or obese children in the UK (von Hinke Kessler Scholder, 2007) and USA and a tenfold increase in Scottish children diagnosed with attention deficit disorder (ADD) (NHS Quality Improvement Scotland, 2004). In the USA over 4 million children are prescribed drugs to treat ADD or attention-deficit hyperactivity disorder (ADHD) (O'Sullivan, 2005).

The importance of play and play provision to children's mental and physical health is being given greater importance. In 2004, the Chief Medical Officer in England recommended that '[c]hildren and young people should achieve a total of at least 60 minutes of {…} moderate intensity physical activity each day' (NCB, 2006). Mackett (2004) showed that in order to increase their energy expenditure, children need to spend more of their free time outdoors and playing freely. Mackett also found that children got more exercise from outdoor play than they did from clubs and formal sports activities. Play has been seen as contributing to chil-dren's mental health by increasing opportunities to make decisions, interact with others and learn their own strategies for coping with changes or developing resilience (NCB, 2006). Many adults recognise these benefits in their own lives, citing the need for active recreation to help keep them fit and healthy.

So while the need for children's play is clear, adults have a role in supporting play oppor-tunities for children, to help them play outdoors in spaces in which they feel comfortable and able to make choices.

11.4 Policy impacting on children's play

There has been a considerable shift away from the Victorian maxim that children should be seen and not heard. In 1989 the United Nations adopted the Convention on the Rights of the Child (UNCRC, 1989). This international treaty gave children and young people a com-prehensive set of rights that included the right to play (Article 31) and the right to be heard (Article 12). Since 1989, the Convention has been adopted by most countries, with the exception of the USA and Somalia. The Convention was adopted by the UK government in 1991 and influenced national policy in the UK in subsequent years. The Every Child Matters Framework, supported by the Children Act 2004, required all local authorities in the UK to provide services for children to 'be healthy, stay safe, enjoy and achieve, make a positive contribution and achieve economic well-being'.

Worldwide, play and playwork are promoted by the International Play Association (IPA). This non-governmental organisation was founded in 1961 and was partly responsible for the adoption of Article 31, children's right to play and leisure, in the UN Convention on the Rights of the Child. The IPA today operates in over 40 countries and holds a worldwide conference every three years, as well as continuing to speak for children's play at the United Nations.

Each member country has its own national IPA groups made up of representatives from other interested bodies. For example, there are the National Institute for Play and the Association for the Study of Play in the USA; the Korean Association for Safe Communities; the European Network of Child Friendly Cities; and, in Australia, the Playgrounds & Recreation Association of Victoria. Support for play varies from country to country, with some recognising the need for play only recently, whilst others have well-established national support systems.

In 2008 the first national Play Strategy in England set out the government's plans to improve and develop play facilities for children throughout the country (DCSF, 2009). This strategy was supported by £235 million of funding with the aim of creating 'safe, welcoming, interesting and free places to play in every residential community' (DCSF, 2009). The UK 'four nations' work closely together in these matters and similar initiatives have taken place in Scotland, Northern Ireland and, most notably, Wales, where the national agency Play Wales worked closely with the Welsh Assembly to produce a Play Strategy in 2002. The UK infrastructure for play is summarised in Case Study 11.2.

In support of the national Play Strategy, Play England has commissioned many papers (accessible from the organisation's website) that are useful in supporting play services. In addition to Lester and Russell (2008) these include the following:

- *The Charter for Children's Play* (2007) outlines eight statements that describe a vision of play for providers.
- *Design for Play: a guide to creating successful play spaces* (2008) describes how to design good play spaces that give children and young people the freedom to play creatively and still allow them to experience risk, challenge and excitement.
- *Managing Risk in Play Provision: implementation guide* (2008) shows how play providers can use an approach to risk management that takes into account the benefits to children and young people of challenging play experiences.
- *Developing an Adventure Playground: the essential elements* (2009) explains the key features of adventure playgrounds in the twenty-first century.

Discussion questions

How aware do you think the general public are of the rights and needs of children and young people? Are these rights and needs important in public debate?

In providing services for children's play, providers need to be aware of the conflicting philosophies and advice that may arise from working with different agencies. The clearest way through this maze is to have a service play policy that clearly states the vision, aims and expected outcomes of the provision being delivered. An example of this at the local level is given in Case Study 11.3.

CASE STUDY 11.2

The national infrastructure for children's play in the UK

The UK has one of the most developed infrastructures for children's play, with four national play agencies – Play England, Play Scotland, Play Wales and Playboard Northern Ireland – and also has a sector skills council which includes playwork, SkillsActive. The Play Unit in SkillsActive works towards the development of playwork education and training for all those working with children and young people. SkillsActive led on the accreditation and recognition of playwork qualifications, and worked with government and agencies such as the Children's Workforce Development Council (CWDC) to increase mobility within the children's and playwork workforce. Other agencies working mainly in the voluntary sector also offered considerable support for children's play.

The Free Play Network is a non-government agency which promotes greater understanding of the need for better play opportunities for children. It does this through discussion, exchanging information and offering guidance on best practice for children's play opportunities. While it has commented on policy, the Network's focus has often been on play spaces and play in the wider environment.

The KIDS Charity works to help disabled children live in an inclusive community which supports them and their families. KIDS also run the Play Inclusion Project, which offers strategic development, information and guidance to authorities and settings on inclusive play and childcare.

4Children is another charity which started with a focus on childcare for working parents and extended its remit to include all matters about children and families, including children's participation, work with schools, implementation of quality and policy development.

Ofsted (the Office for Standards in Education, Children's Services and Skills) is the public face of Her Majesty's Chief Inspector of Schools in England. Principally set up to inspect the standards of schools, local education authorities, child day care and childminding in England, Ofsted's remit was increased by government to include play care provision for children under 14, and in 2008 provision for under 5s became subject to the Early Years Foundation Stage, which set specific standards for the care and education of young children. The developmental, educational approach, criticised in Lester and Russell (2008), began to have an impact on the way that some providers supported play for young children.

11.5 Types of play provision

As will now be clear, children's play may be supported in a variety of ways: by encouraging play in the wider environment, by providing play spaces for them to freely use or by providing services that support play opportunities, whether free of charge or at a cost.

Each play space will be subject to a variety of management regimes, some provision will be unstaffed, some will have staff present, with assorted levels of support and different inspection systems, as well as issues such as health and safety, negligence, liability and legislative constraints having to be considered. The complexity and variety of these systems is

CASE STUDY 11.3

Play services in the inner-city UK

This inner-city borough (in Greater London) served a population of over 175,000, of whom around 38,000 were under 18 years of age (2001 Census). The borough delivered a variety of play services to its community. This was supported by an annual revenue budget of around £2 million, supplemented with various funds, including local charities and additional government resources for targeted work.

As well as developing the local service, the manager responsible for play had contributed over many years to the national development of play services by sitting on playwork training committees and relevant national voluntary committees. This contribution resulted in both a 'grassroots' informed national policy and local borough policy that was developed to national standards. For example, the borough's Play Statement was written considering the arguments in *Best Play* (NPFA *et al.*, 2000) and *Making the Case for Play* (Cole-Hamilton and Gill, 2002). The borough's playwork was developed in partnership with an active community and voluntary sector, and in conjunction with an independent play association. This partnership helped the play and youth service make links with newer communities in the borough and avoid 'separatist' provision.

A key part of the borough's success in developing play services over an extended period was its in-house playwork training service. This service had been reshaped several times over the years to include education, youth work and early years staff as well as play staff. Staff were supported to achieve relevant vocational qualifications and progressed in some cases to degree level qualifications with a local university. The training service also helped with service mobility as the divisions apparent between professional roles were blurred by all working together – a technique now being adopted nationally in the wider children's workforce. The strength of the manager's and staff's links to the national agenda was recognised when the borough was lead body in a consortium awarded a contract to be the regional playwork education and training agency. This further cemented the borough's reputation as a quality provider and helped draw in more playwork theorists and practitioners to help train its staff, through an active seminar programme.

The borough used two national playwork evaluation tools, Quality in Play and First Claim, to assess management processes and playworker skills, respectively. The borough also had an active programme of regular site visits to monitor work and direct staff. The senior manager took part in this programme, regularly joining staff teams as a team worker to keep up to date with practice and see what day-to-day employment was like for playwork staff.

In summary, this service has been successful in meeting the play needs of the community due to a combination of personal commitment from managers and staff, links to local development and national policy, and a clear and consistent vision for play that informed service development through varied political administrations and funding regimes.

extensive not only between countries but also between authorities, so it cannot be described in detail in this chapter (guidance is available in many formats both from lead agencies and on the internet). However, it is important to differentiate between 'care-based' and 'open access' provision. When staff are present, provision may be care based – with a register of users, who attend for fixed hours – or open access, where children are free to come and go as they wish; different philosophies and rules will apply according to which approach is

Table 11.1 Types of play provision

Type of provision	Description	Comments
Natural play spaces	Beaches, woodlands, fields, forests.	Open spaces of many descriptions provide spaces for children to run around and explore freely. Often adults are not present when children play in these spaces.
Parks and playgrounds	The spaces available for free recreation in towns and cities. Parks are the natural spaces set aside for all types of recreation; some of them have designed playgrounds that aim to meet children's play needs.	Parks often provide similar experiences to natural play spaces. Children may often be brought into conflict with adults over what is permissible behaviour in these public spaces.
Street play	In areas where traffic flow is slow or nonexistent, children play in the street or in the 'slack spaces' – those bits of land left over from all other formal uses.	Traditional games, cycling, den building, chase games can all take place in the streets close to where children live.
Play rangers	Some local authorities provide detached or mobile services that work with children in their communities.	Play rangers may work in an area for a limited time (say a school holiday) or for longer periods, often helping communities realise the chances for play available on their doorstep.
Adventure play	'An adventure playground can be described as a space dedicated solely to children's play, where skilled playworkers enable and facilitate the ownership, development and design of that space – physically, socially and culturally – by the children playing there' (Conway, 2009).	Adventure playgrounds are usually open access provision. The idea of dedicated space for children to play, supported by sensitive adults, caught on and spread UK-wide to reach a peak in the 1980s. In 2008, Play England was supporting the development of thirty new adventure playgrounds.

Holiday playschemes	A holiday playscheme is a service provided for children during school holidays. Typically based in a community hall, leisure centre or school, the playscheme offers a variety of experiences to children, including indoor and outdoor play and trips or camping holidays.	Holiday playschemes may be open access or care based. Some authorities run playschemes year round, others just in the summer months. Provision may be peripatetic or static. Sometimes the aim is to help the community operate the service for themselves.
After school provision	After school (or out of school) clubs offer a variety of play, care or occasionally homework sessions for children after school and sometimes in school holidays. Provision is very varied, with some sharing rooms in school, others in dedicated provision on school premises, and some on a remote site.	The growth in care provision for children under 14 years after 1990 led to the development of after school provision in many areas of the UK. The provision is usually care-based provision so subject to inspection by Ofsted.
School-based activity	Though the focus of school is education, play may occur there – in the playgrounds before and after school and during breaks (where they are permitted), and increasingly in 'free play' sessions for younger children in provision for early years.	In addition to the natural play times in school, some schools have play policies to set the standard for the play opportunities they offer. Playground supervisors may be employed to support free play rather than organised games.

taken and where the management team is based. The management of the service could be in the statutory or voluntary sector, in an educational service, a leisure service or a parks service – each will offer a different perspective that may be focused on the staff skills, equipment or landscape available.

Table 11.1 describes some of the most commonly available play provision, starting with the most 'natural' spaces, with no supervision, through to the most organised services, with dedicated staff.

11.5.1 Participation and consultation services

While not strictly play provision, these services are emerging worldwide, use playwork approaches to engage children and may be managed by agencies running play services. In support of Article 12 (UNCRC, 1989) and the Children Act 2004, in the UK Children's Voices programmes aim to listen to children and involve them in the development of services that meet their needs. Activities may vary from day-to-day involvement to one-off consultations. The ethos of Children's Voices projects is close to that of the Playwork Principles in that they aim to put children's agendas before those of adults.

> ### Discussion question
>
> In aiming to meet their needs, should children and young people be consulted on how resources are allocated?

11.6 Managing complex services

The complexity of delivering successful play services offers managers both challenges and opportunities.

The main challenge is to understand the nature of the service, how it may be delivered and to what standard. With no overarching professional approach that covers the many forms of provision, delivery is very prone to influence from the people implementing it and those funding it. It is very difficult to manage play services using a typical 'command and control' management structure; too many of the key influences and stakeholders will not be in the managers' control and so not subject to direct influence. It is significant that many play providers are active in partnership networks and rely on many forms of funding and support to deliver their services – this is as true of small voluntary providers as it is of large local government services. Partnership working requires agencies to be clear about their own aims and purposes, to communicate these clearly to others and then negotiate and reach consensus with others on the best way of meeting children's aims.

The opportunity that managing play services offers is to engage playfully, creatively and flexibly with the systems with which staff come into contact, in order to truly meet children's play needs. For many play services this flexible approach developed as a practical necessity in order to build consensus about the need for services and to attract the funds available for helping meet children's needs. Yet many management writers now comment on the creativity and playfulness needed in the modern world.

Kane argues that by approaching management playfully we 'maintain our adaptability, vigour and optimism in the face of an uncertain, risky and demanding world' (2004: 63). Battram (1999) has written about the states of order and chaos present in all living systems (including organisations) and how managers must be aware of behaviour that is predictable and stereotypical just as they should be aware of chaos and disorder – and the conditions that distinguish them. Battram has also commented (see Brown and Taylor, 2008) on these patterns of behaviour in services for children, arguing that static and ordered provision is not healthy for children who play at 'the edge of chaos', seeking out new experiences and new ways of interacting with the world. Senge *et al.* recognise the need to see organisations and systems as 'a set of overlapping communities formed around shared meaning' (1994: 300); in such cultures it is recognised that each member forges their own sense of meaning and unique contribution to the whole – very akin to the playwork principle that acknowledges that play is intrinsically motivated and emerges within the child; the behaviour cannot be predicted but becomes definable once it emerges.

11.7 Training for play provision

Just as a different form of management may be best for playwork provision, it has been argued that playwork training should reflect play in its delivery; it should be 'a more learner and work-base centred approach, experiential and reflective, issue-based, innovative, challenging, exciting and fun. The processes of learning should be akin to those of playing {…} becoming a playworker through doing the work' (Taylor, 2008). However, the reality of most training is much more prosaic, being driven by targets and financial constraints.

From 2005, the UK government worked towards the establishment of a 'world-class workforce for children and young people', as spelled out in the Children's Workforce Strategy (DFES, 2008). This strategy stated that more 'professional play workers' would be developed by enabling '4,000 playworkers to achieve an NVQ (National Vocational Qualification) Level 3 qualification by 2011' and by the development of a new playwork management qualification. The benchmark for practice in the UK was therefore set at NVQ Level 3, a qualification gained in the workplace for skills demonstrated. Some in the field have commented that 'world class' has a different meaning elsewhere. For example, in Denmark practitioners working with children are required to study for around three years to earn the equivalent of a UK degree level qualification (i.e. Level 6) before going into practice (Petrie *et al.*, 2005).

SkillsActive, the relevant sector skills council in the UK, has been working since 2003 to lead 'the skills and productivity drive' for the playwork industry. The dedicated Playwork Unit has supported the development of a national playwork training strategy (Quality Training, Quality Play 2006–2011) to improve the status of the playwork profession. In supporting playwork training, different routes to qualification in playwork are recognised: 'on the job' vocational qualifications, part-time or full-time attendance at further or higher education centres, and accreditation for prior education and learning, with flexible delivery and use of e-learning.

In 2009, the work of SkillsActive was joined to that of another agency in the creation of an Integrated Qualifications Framework for all practitioners in the children's workforce. When completed, this Framework was expected to provide 'a comprehensive set of qualifications that are agreed to be appropriate for people who work with children and young people' (Children's Workforce Network, 2009). A key part of this work was to create a shared understanding of the qualifications the children's workforce needed to help staff with career choices, progression and mobility.

Also in 2009, Play England supported the delivery of the Play Shaper training programme as part of the implementation of the National Play Strategy. This was designed to help professionals who plan, design, build and manage services to the public understand the importance of play and their role in creating child-friendly public spaces. The training was intended to help planners and developers, landscape architects, highways services, housing officers, schools and children's services, the police, parks and leisure officers understand how play provision and inter-agency cooperation help to improve the well-being of children, young people and their families (Play England, 2009b).

Case Study 11.4 shows how provision for play and education can be supported in a holistic way by professionals trained to a high level.

CASE STUDY 11.4

Play in Sweden

In Sweden, good links are present between formal education and play provision. Driven by the Swedish Education Act (1984), there is a continuous approach promoted between pre-school classes, formal school and 'leisure-time centres' (after school and holiday sessions). These services are provided free to all children and often include teaching materials, school meals, and health services and transport if needed.

Play is central to the Swedish childcare model. It is recognised that playing games helps children to understand the world around them, work with others and develop their imagination and creativity. This is a social model of education and play that recognises the importance of integrating their formal care with parenting and practice in the home.

Children may attend the pre-school classes until well into their sixth year, when they start formal school. The leisure-time centres are open year-round and support children whose parents are at work or in training. The focus on the whole curriculum helps ensure that services are provided to meet the children's need for 'meaningful recreation' as well as providing a care service for adults. The leisure-time centre staff are called pedagogues ('child leaders'):

> The pedagogue sets out to address the whole child, the child with body, mind, emotions, creativity, history and social identity. This is not the child only of emotions, the psychotherapeutical approach, nor only of the body, the medical approach, nor only of the mind, the traditional teaching approach.
>
> (Moss and Petrie, 2002)

Pedagogues have education and training comparable to the pre-school teachers and often work closely both with them and formal school teachers as part of an integrated team. A high proportion of staff have degree level qualifications and often studied together at university.

This integrated approach helps ensure that there is better understanding between education and childcare practice, with children supported in different environments, learning and playing together and from each other. In a recent survey, Swedish children were considered to be amongst the happiest in the western world (UNICEF, 2007).

11.8 The benefits of a play policy

Having a play policy is useful, not just for organising the work of the play team but also for demonstrating the value of play to all partners and stakeholders. Additionally, in the UK Play England stated in 2008 that authorities would not receive national funding without a relevant play policy or strategy.

A policy will set standards to which service providers should aspire and will clarify key priorities for the area under consideration, be that a service, a district, a town or a county. It is normal for play policies to include many of the following elements:

- a definition of play, to enable all to be clear about the purpose of the policy;
- a statement about the values underpinning the work, commonly the Playwork Principles;
- the social, political and environmental factors in the area for the policy;
- a declaration about children's right to play (UNCRC, 1989: Article 31);
- an argument for why provision for play should be supported;
- definitions of quality provision addressing questions of safety, risk and resilience;
- evidence of consultation with children and young people;
- the key policy statements in detail, which may cover spaces for play, elements to be included in play environments, non-staffed, fixed equipment playgrounds, children's rights for equality in play, resources and partnerships, networking and communication, training for people working in play, evaluation tools and processes;
- endorsements by and support from key stakeholders;
- a plan or strategy for change – how the policy will be implemented, by whom and over what timescale.

While some policies by necessity may be written by one or two people in a matter of weeks, it is considered best practice for policies to be written over a six- to twelve-month period and 'bottom up', i.e. based on the experiences of children and the adults closest to them. The processes used to involve children, young people and community members should be appropriate to their needs and expectations. Many authorities still use traditional meetings to call people together, although participation projects are increasingly going into communities to ask questions of people where they use the environment. Equally, it is important for lead officers to take draft policies to key agencies to secure their commitment; it is increasingly recognised in UK government policy that a number of agencies working together produces the best outcome for all children. Such agencies could include: early years and education staff; youth services to link in provision for teenagers; the police, as they are often involved in 'anti social' behaviour and offer diversionary activities to children and young people; and health agencies, who are interested because of concerns about the incidence of childhood obesity.

These processes will take time but if the policy is to gain the commitment of many stakeholders, time is essential. Once the process had been started, it is relatively easy to hold annual reviews of the document to ensure that it is meeting its aims and stated objectives.

Discussion questions

How does play fit into your thinking about the wider community's sport and recreational needs? How similar or different are the arguments for children's play to those for adult recreation?

11.9 Designing spaces for play

In many parts of the world, play provision for children is limited to unstaffed spaces set aside for children's use. In more industrialised countries, these spaces have been described as 'KFC' playgrounds (CABE, 2009); where the provision is based on Kit purchased from a manufacturer, in a Fenced space to keep it separate from other users and with a Carpet of 'safety surfacing' that removes the children from the natural environment. Helle Nebelong, a Danish landscape architect, has been in the vanguard of a movement in Europe that has created a resurgence in naturalised playgrounds. In contrast to many of her colleagues, who may prepare a design then offer it to the client for comment, Nebelong chooses to work with the community and potential users of the play space from the beginning. She often spends between twelve and eighteen months working in an area to design a space that emerges from the community and environment. Nebelong argues that KFC playgrounds do not meet the child's real need for play, being over-focused on safety standards. She states:

> Standardised playgrounds are dangerous {...} When the distance between all the rungs in a climbing net or a ladder is exactly the same, the child has no need to concentrate on where he puts his feet. Standardisation is dangerous because play becomes simplified and the child does not have to worry about his movements.
>
> (Nebelong, 2002)

Consistent with Nebelong's philosophy, in 2008 the UK agency Play England and the government's Department for Children, Schools and Families published ten principles for creating successful play spaces:

1 Designed to fit their surroundings and enhance the local environment
2 Located in the best possible place, 'to be where children would play naturally'
3 Close to nature, with grassy mounds, planting, logs and boulders to help attract birds and other wildlife
4 Designed so that children can play in different ways
5 Encouraging disabled and able-bodied children to play together
6 Loved by the community as a space that meets their needs
7 Where children of all ages play together instead of segregating children based on age or ability
8 Designed to enable children to stretch and challenge themselves in every way
9 Maintained for play value and environmental sustainability
10 Flexible and able to evolve as children grow

(Play England, 2008)

In North America, the design of spaces for play has more of a focus on provision for play than staffed resources. The Project for Public Spaces (PPS) is a non-profit organisation that aims to help people create and sustain places that build communities. PPS uses an approach that is similar to that of Nebelong and other designers who put children first: instead of adding public input after a plan has been drawn up, 'PPS gathers ideas from local stakeholders at the outset, helping the community create a vision for improvement'.

In the USA and Europe the trend has been to use natural material such as grassed surfaces, sand or loose fill materials (gravel or bark chippings) for playground surfacing. In the UK, many playgrounds were fitted with 'safety surfacing' in a mistaken bid to reduce injuries on playgrounds. Playgrounds have always been one of the safest places for children to play (statistically the home and local roads are the most harmful places for children), yet after a public campaign in the 1980s millions of pounds was spent on rubberised surfaces. Since 2002, after a report (No. 426) from the Health and Safety Executive, the UK has slowly been catching up with the rest of the world and is returning to 'natural' surfacing. It is now widely recognised that improving the quality of the play space experiences is the best way to spend resources for children's play. This approach is being supported by progressive play equipment manufacturers such as Richter Spielgeräte/Timberplay and Sutcliffe Play, both of which have strong play-based approaches to their work, and have been influential in developing play safety policy in their own countries and wider afield.

In the UK, the Health and Safety Executive has also led a campaign (2006) to reduce the myths surrounding safety and children's play, in a bid to reduce the number of children prevented from playing traditional games, playing outdoors or with the elements, due to exaggerated concerns about safety. Writer Tim Gill has described the situation in the UK as one where adults aim to create a 'zero-risk childhood'; one that may be physically safe, but where children are less able to develop resilience, personal responsibility and so autonomy. Those who would challenge this perspective should examine the play circumstances of the vast majority of the world's children, which take place in natural environments with no planned provision and usually with no adults present.

Elsewhere the cultural expectations are very different. In Scandinavian countries, it is quite common to see children playing outdoors in temperatures that would send many adults indoors. Commentators such as Asbørn Flemmen (Norway) and Gever Tulley (USA) have also emphasised the need for children to take risks in childhood, by playing with fire, sharp tools and weapons – and by breaking rules. In many countries around the world, children play where they live; they learn to navigate risk and opportunities in the world around them. These views have contributed to a reassessment of risk in play, from one that must be decided by adults to one where children are encouraged to make assessments of their own.

Discussion questions

Do you think 'KFC' playgrounds offer children 'safer' play experiences? What are the strengths and weaknesses of such playgrounds?

11.10 Funding for play

While play is recognised as a child's right under the United Nations Convention on the Rights of the Child, there are few countries where provision for play is a statutory responsibility. Where provision is made for play, it is often as an adjunct to education or care services. In many countries, including the UK and USA, provision is made available through funding programmes, local government or charitable trust money. Often funding is subject to competitive bids and so a case needs to be made to the fund managers to explain why the resources should be spent as requested. This ad hoc approach to provision has led to wide variety in the play services offered to children. In the UK the national agencies have tried to improve the planning and provision for play.

While the status of play and playwork has changed in recent years, and agencies like Play England and Play Wales promote services for children, there are still issues to be resolved in the delivery of services that support play for children. For some commentators the issues

Play services in a medium-sized metropolitan district in the UK

This metropolitan district served a population of nearly 470,000, with around 110,000 under 18 (2001 Census). The district delivered a variety of play services to its community, either directly or in partnership with others. The annual revenue budget for play provision within the district was the responsibility of the Leisure Services directorate and the Children's Services directorate; budgets for play were made up of a whole host of external grants in addition to base budgets in the two directorates. For example, additional funding had been awarded to the district through the Big Lottery Children's Play Programme and National Play Builder programme (£1 million) and had been secured in recent years from a variety of sources, including the Sure Start Fund, Children's Fund, local Neighbourhood Renewal Fund, Section 106 Funds (a fund created by housing developers to compensate for loss of open space) and through Friends Groups and local trusts.

The lead officer for the Play Strategy in this district was employed as an Early Years Childcare and Play Manager, with a remit to support play services across the district that comply with recommendations in the Strategy. This role had evolved in response to the recent establishment of the Children and Young People's Service, though the officer had worked in the area for many years, so had many 'on-the-ground' connections.

Being part of a developing Children and Young People's Service, the work was informed by a variety of policy initiatives, such as education, childcare, health, play, open space and recreation. Representatives from around 12 relevant agencies sat on the Play Partnership, the active voluntary sector being represented through a local play network. The figurehead role of 'play champion' had been filled by local councillors. The lead officer role was in Children's Services, yet the officer had good links with Parks staff, with whom the local strategy had been developed for the period 2008–11. The Play Strategy for the district was developed 'bottom up', with the involvement of staff and children – the latter through regular surveys designed to hear and respond to the voices of young people. The district also had good links to the regional and national structures, with representatives on the Play England Strategic Advisory Board and the Regional Play Board.

In addition to the Annual Performance Indicator, the TellUs annual service consultation – which gathers the views of young people at age 11, 13 and 15 on their life, school and local area – the service was evaluated in a number of ways. A Quality Improvement Support Programme was used for childcare and early years elements of the service, the Children's Integrated Service Improvement Framework was used to capture progress; and different tools were used to assess playworker settings and training provision.

In summary, this service had successfully 'played the game' as far as support and funding regimes were concerned. The play growth in recent years had been in childcare, education, leisure and health programmes. By engaging with these programmes, resources and services had been created that otherwise would not have emerged. However, by remaining true to the Playwork Principles, officers had been able to influence key strategies by advocating children's play needs. While not a primary aim of many strategies, the 'free play agenda' had been achieved by working with the dominant services rather than by arguing against them; this had been good groundwork on which to build the targeted resources latterly available through a range of national strategies.

may be summarised in two key concepts: the matter of statutory provision and the approach taken within that provision.

In most local authorities in the UK, play services have been provided by Education and Social Services (now Children and Young People's Services) or by Leisure (Parks or Sports) Services. For Children and Young People's Services, the statutory provision which must be provided by law, i.e. the education and care of children and young people, play services and the concept of 'extended schools' (where schools work more closely with partner agencies and the wider community), remains an ideal to strive for rather than the norm. Similarly, in Leisure Services the statutory requirement is to provide parks and green spaces for the community; services for children are often added extras after the considerations for adults. For example, in one large UK metropolitan area in 2006, the annual revenue budget spent on Children and Young People's Services was around £330 million; in the same year expenditure on Parks Services was £5 million, Sports Services £4 million, with around £500,000 allocated for direct play services to children. While it is difficult to get figures for detailed comparisons between authorities, it is reasonable to assume that the proportions of expenditure were similar across the country; for every £1 spent directly on children's play provision, £18 would be spent on adult leisure services and £600 on education and safeguarding services. It is not easy to argue for a disinvestment in the care and education of children; however, the growing evidence – supported by research showing that US and UK children were the unhappiest in a comparison of 21 industrialised countries (UNICEF, 2007) – strongly suggests that changes are necessary if children's play needs are to be met.

Case Study 11.5 demonstrates how pragmatic funding acquisition can enable a local authority to develop a range of play opportunities.

11.11 Evaluating play provision

Like many services provided for children and people in their leisure time, the evaluation of play experiences is fraught with difficulty. Frequently all that providers of services do is count the number of times that users of services attend sessions or use equipment. Such a blunt tool does not assess the quality of those experiences – it does not differentiate between the life-changing epiphany an individual may get from doing something well, or the boring repetition of an act done many times before. Those monitoring and evaluating services may form judgements on the experiences they observe in children using play spaces, and increasingly many providers of services ask children what they think of the experience themselves.

The UK is the leader in formal ways of assessing play provision. Spaces may be assessed for play value, for compliance with management policies and procedures, for safe operation and for user satisfaction.

A set of national indictors has been agreed by the UK government (Play England, 2009a). These provide the means of measuring national priorities; originally totalling 198, an extra one was added in 2009 – NI 199, which is the national indicator on children's satisfaction with parks and play areas. The indicator is assessed through the TellUs Survey, which asks children and young people across England their views about their local area, in this case about formal provision for play; results are available from the Ofsted website.

In looking at the quality of children's play provision in the UK, the Royal Society for the Prevention of Accidents (ROSPA) provides information on playground management and the safety of indoor and outdoor play areas. ROSPA may be commissioned to carry out an independent inspection of play spaces, including playing fields, play areas, 'safety' surfacing and skateboarding areas. ROSPA also offers advice and consultancy on playground management and has been used as an expert witness in legal matters.

When assessing play opportunities for children, Quality in Play is a quality assurance scheme offered by Play England for out of school play and childcare provision. The scheme was developed by playwork practitioners and is based on playwork values. The scheme operates through the production of a portfolio by staff. The content of the portfolio is dictated by the Quality in Play manual, which is made up of several sections covering the play environment, the organisational framework and the context in which the play setting is based. The scheme involves a mentor to guide staff through the process and to prepare them for assessment. There are costs attached to the scheme, including purchase of the manual, arranging for mentor and assessor time and for staff time in completing the portfolio.

Play Wales has produced two quality assessment tools, First Claim and Desirable Processes. First Claim aims to enable adults with an interest in children's play to analyse, by observation and reflection, the play environments they operate. It gives both Basic and Intermediate Frameworks to assess the quality of what is being provided and experienced by children and young people. Desirable Processes extends the method and contains an Advanced Framework that looks at the play process in more depth.

The formalisation of playwork evaluation tools started with the IMEE tool (Hughes, 1996a). The elements of the tool are:

- Intuitive judgements of what the playworker believes a good play environment should be;
- Memories from the worker's childhood of good play environments;
- Experience of good play environments from playworkers' own professional practice;
- Evidence of good play environments from the relevant literature.

While subjective and relatively informal, the IMEE protocol allows adults working with children to engage with the experience at a personal level, which may be enhanced by sharing evaluations with others in the team, to arrive at a joint assessment based on a variety of experiences and knowledge.

In addition to these nationally recognised tools, local authorities may create their local variations for local assessment. For example, Sheffield City Council (UK), as part of the preparation of its Play Strategy (2006), identified the Elements of Good Play Provision. For Sheffield, good provision offers a range of balanced activities:

- activities to promote the child's opportunity to experience;
- emotional/symbolic/problem solving;
- imagination/creativity/cultural understanding;
- elemental play/working with materials/physical skills;
- encouraging responsibility/cooperative play/social development;
- choice of activities;
- opportunities for challenge and risk-taking;
- equipment that is clean and accessible;
- sufficient space for all desired activities;
- involvement of children in planning and evaluation;
- celebration of personal, family and community events.

Wherever play provision is supported, those in charge of the service should have an understanding of how to measure the value of the provision for its primary users (usually children) as well as lead stakeholders such as parents, politicians and funders.

11.12 Conclusions

Provision for children's play varies according to many factors: the providers' understanding of play's benefits to children and the local community, the sources and allocation of funding for provision and the value given to provision by adults in control of the environment. A variety of approaches are used in different countries, with distinct policy approaches and legislation that reflects the value given to play in those countries.

Play services may be managed by a variety of agencies, including education, leisure and independent bodies, yet consistent patterns emerge of a need to identify a common aim and work in partnership with other providers in order to offer and coordinate services to best effect. The essentials of a successful play experience have been identified by theorists and lead agencies, with many common elements identified. Play and play provision make vital contributions to children's lives and are seen by many adults as the foundation on which to build healthy and lifelong leisure and sporting interests.

Practical tasks

1 Observe children playing. What do you see them doing and how would you describe the value of that to others?

2 Identify what support for play exists in your local area, town or city. How is the support made available to the community: through advice, funding, staff, equipment, local provision, district provision, a combination of all these or none of them?

3 Assess a local playground using the 'ten principles for creating successful play spaces' from Play England and the government's Department for Children, Schools and Families (see p. 302). Can you reach a sensible and unambiguous evaluation?

Structured guide to further reading

For more background to play theory and a detailed explanation of how play is valuable throughout our lives:

Else, P. (2009) *The Value of Play*, Continuum International Publishing Ltd, London and New York.

For more on play and playwork services:

Brown, F. and Taylor, C. (2008) *Foundations of Playwork*, Open University Press, Maidenhead.

For what to include and the process for creating a play space:

Play England (2008) *Design for Play: a guide to creating successful play spaces*, available at www.playengland.org.uk.

For an extensive summary of research into the importance of play and how it relates to social policy and practice:

Lester, S. and Russell, W. (2008) *Play for a Change*, Play England/National Children's Bureau, London.

Useful websites

For Children's Workforce Development Council (UK):
www.cwdcouncil.org.uk/playwork

For Free Play Network (UK):
www.freeplaynetwork.org.uk/

For Play England (UK):
www.playengland.org.uk/

For Playlink (UK):
www.playlink.org/

For International Play Association (Worldwide):
www.ipaworld.org/

For National Institute for Play (USA):
http://nifplay.org/

For Richter Spielgeräte:
www.richterplaygrounds.com/

For Sutcliffe Play:
www.sutcliffeplay.co.uk/

For Timberplay:
www.timberplay.com/

Chapter 12

Leisure in the home

In this chapter

- How is leisure in the home relevant to leisure management?
- How significant is spending on leisure in the home?
- Is reading a declining industry?
- What drives the growth and change in home entertainment?
- How important are DIY and gardening?
- How are hobbies and pastimes changing?
- Is gambling at home a problem or an opportunity?

Summary

Leisure in the home is big business. It includes some of the most vibrant parts of the leisure market, none more so than home entertainment. And leisure in the home is often characterised by technological change – major examples being in television, listening to music, electronic games, online gambling and photography. The devices used in entertainment – from mobile phones to computers and the internet, to televisions and games consoles – are increasingly designed as vehicles for a variety of leisure purposes. This convergence of use is an important feature of contemporary leisure and it means that much of it is no longer confined to the home, but is portable out of the home.

Other leisure in the home markets are less directly influenced by technological changes. These include reading, gardening and do-it-yourself (DIY). Reading books has been heavily influenced by the phenomenal *Harry Potter* success, which is said to have positively influenced children to read other books. Reading newspapers and magazines, however, is in long-term decline, possibly because of competition from the internet. Both gardening and DIY markets have moved away from purely functional spending and towards a greater variety of spending in tune with lifestyle aspirations.

The home is an important base for leisure. Although this is often simplified as 'watching television', because of the amount of time we spend doing this, there is a lot more to leisure in the home and significant elements of it are now available away from home. The developments it contains offer important lessons to the whole of the leisure industry – including the speed of adoption of technological change, the use of contemporary media, the importance of the pricing decision, the transformation of consumers' spending behaviour and the simplification of consumer choices. Governments have a potentially important regulatory role in leisure in the home, particularly in organising broadcasting and media infrastructures.

12.1 Introduction

What is leisure in the home doing in a book about leisure management? How is management relevant to leisure in the home? Well, leisure in the home may not be managed directly, but indirectly it is supported by, and the target of, considerable business interests. Table 2.2 shows us that some of the activities with the highest participation rates across a range of countries are those based largely at home, i.e. watching television, listening to music, reading books and gardening. Each of these activities is fed by large industries which produce the materials and equipment that make them possible. Leisure in the home represents major competition for leisure activities away from home.

Changes in leisure in the home vary according to the country and the time period examined (Cushman *et al.*, 2005). For example, in France between 1973 and 1997 participation rates for TV, music, and reading books and magazines increased, but for radio and gardening they decreased; and in Israel between 1970 and 1990 participation rates for TV, hobbies and listening to music increased, but those for listening to the radio and reading books and magazines decreased (see Table 3.1). In the period 1988–2000 in Canada, participation rates in home exercise decreased; whilst in Japan between 1982 and 2003 participation rates for DIY, knitting and sewing, and cooking all fell. Figure 3.1 shows that the participation rates for many of the major leisure activities in the home are growing in Britain; and Figure 3.3 shows that expenditure on leisure in the home is also growing, albeit at a slower rate than leisure out of the home. In the main this chapter will refer to UK evidence, to provide a consistent focus, but most of the major issues are common to developed countries and many are also relevant to developing countries.

Although leisure in the home might appear at first sight to be beyond the remit of management, in fact very similar management principles apply to the industries which service leisure in the home as to industries providing leisure out of the home. The only major difference is that the customer is remote from the industry, so direct personal service is less of a feature (but it is still often an element, e.g. home deliveries and visits). Leisure in the home is increasingly important because some traditionally out of home activities have become more prevalent in the home. Eating and drinking for pleasure certainly fall into this category, whilst more recently the internet has facilitated an increase in gambling at home. However, it is also the case that many of the home entertainments are now very portable away from home, including TV, radio, films, video games and the internet – via laptops, mobile phones, etc.

> ### Discussion question
>
> Does leisure in the home need 'managing'?

12.2 Spending on leisure in the home

Table 12.1 provides details from *Leisure Forecasts* (Leisure Industries Research Centre, 2008) concerning the scale of the different markets comprising leisure in the home in the UK. In this table, scale is measured by consumer spending on different sub-sectors. In a £57 billion sector in 2008, home entertainment takes the lion's share, with 38 per cent of leisure in the home consumer spending. The biggest individual sub-sector in Table 12.1, however, is not part of home entertainment – it is DIY, attracting nearly 20 per cent of leisure in the home consumer spending.

The markets in Table 12.1 support a considerable number of jobs in the production, distribution and retailing of goods and services for leisure in the home. The management of these processes can be seen as part of leisure management, because the consumers of these products are interested in fulfilling their leisure demands and needs. Accurate figures on the employment in these industries are difficult to identify, because they are often part of larger manufacturing sectors.

Consumer spending in leisure in the home markets shows very different changes over time, depending on the sub-sector examined. Table 12.2 shows these changes from 2002 to 2008 for the UK. Changes are measured in two ways: in value terms, i.e. at the current

Table 12.1 Principal markets for leisure in the home in the UK, 2008

Leisure in the home	Consumer spending, £ million in 2008	
Reading, comprising:	8,480	
books		3,956
newspapers		2,986
magazines		1,538
Home entertainment, comprising:	21,908	
television		9,816
DVDs, etc.		4,095
audio equipment		1,655
CDs, etc.		1,279
PCs		5,063
House and garden, comprising:	16,526	
do-it-yourself		11,243
gardening		5,283
Hobbies and pastimes, comprising:	10,084	
photography		2,299
toys and games		2,522
pets		5,263
TOTAL LEISURE IN THE HOME	56,998	

Source: Leisure Industries Research Centre (2008).

prices for each year; and in volume terms, i.e. at constant prices (in this case 2003 prices). The value measure includes price changes, whilst the volume measure excludes price changes, so the latter is a clearer indicator of changing sales volumes (i.e. how many products are sold). But changing sales volumes are also dependent on what has happened to prices – rising prices typically deter higher sales volumes and falling prices typically encourage higher sales volumes.

In value terms, the strongest growth over this period is demonstrated by books (37 per cent) and PCs (38 per cent). However, in the case of books this is largely because of rising prices – taking this factor away reduces the growth rate significantly, to 9 per cent. In the case of PCs prices actually fell, so the 38 per cent growth in the value of consumer spending was achieved by a considerable increase (77 per cent) in the number of PCs sold.

The weakest trends in the value of UK leisure in the home consumer spending in 2002–8 are shown by CDs/records/tapes and DVDs/videos, both of which fell in value terms. In both cases prices fell over this period but for CDs etc. so did the number sold. In the case of DVDs the volume of sales rose, but this did not compensate for the fall in prices, so that the value of sales actually fell.

In volume terms the most significant growth in the period covered by Table 12.2 was by photography and PCs, in both cases driven largely by falling prices. This can be contrasted with newspapers and magazines, where the volume of sales actually fell but the

Table 12.2 Changes in leisure in the home markets, 2002–8

Leisure in the home	% changes in consumer spending, 2002–8	
	Value = at current prices	Volume = at constant (2003) prices
Reading, comprising:	+20	−6
books	+37	+9
newspapers	+13	−12
magazines	+2	−21
Home entertainment, comprising:	+7	+24
television	+12	+15
DVD, etc.	−13	+14
audio equipment	+27	+36
CDs, etc.	−37	−11
PCs	+38	+77
House and garden, comprising:	+18	+14
do-it-yourself	+22	+16
gardening	+9	+10
Hobbies and pastimes, comprising:	+28	+46
photography	+27	+123
toys and games	+20	+46
pets	+34	+13
TOTAL LEISURE IN THE HOME	+15	+20

Source: Leisure Industries Research Centre (2008).

value of consumer spending rose because of increases in prices. Clearly the price decisions of managers have a significant bearing on both the value and volume of sales. These price decisions will be influenced by the strength of demand, the strength of competition in the markets and also by costs, particularly the effects of technological change on production costs.

Discussion question

To what extent is the management of the production and selling of a TV similar to the production and selling of a fitness class? Consider the importance of understanding customers, producing a high quality output, promotion and pricing.

12.3 Reading

Newspapers and magazines are in general decline in the UK, although there is a mixed picture in other countries, as noted above. National daily newspapers' circulation in the UK fell from 13 million in 2003 to 11.2 million in 2008 and is forecasted to keep on falling. Table 12.2 shows a 12 per cent fall in the volume of newspaper sales from 2002 to 2008 and a 21 per cent fall in the volume of magazine sales in the same period. The reasons for such decline are probably a mixture of, first, increasing competition from television (e.g. 24-hour news channels), radio and particularly the internet; second, rising prices of newspapers and magazines (largely because of the costs of raw materials); and, third, people generally feeling more time pressured (see Chapter 3). The Leisure Industries Research Centre (2007) reported that the average time consumers spent online has doubled from two to four hours per week, which exceeds the average of three hours per week spent reading newspapers and magazines. The teenage magazine market has suffered particularly, because this is the age group most likely to use the internet for a range of reasons but especially for social networking.

In addition to fierce competition, advertising has become more diversified away from traditional media such as newspapers and magazines, and again particularly towards the internet, where advertising can be more easily targeted to specific market segments associated with particular websites. The result is falling revenues in the newspaper and magazine industries. The Leisure Industries Research Centre (2007) reported a 9 per cent decline in national newspaper advertising and a 39 per cent increase in internet advertising. The recent recession and collapse in housing market sales has further hit the newspaper market because the revenue from classified adverts has fallen sharply.

Both newspapers and magazines markets serve as a reminder to leisure managers of how important the pricing decision is. In an extreme pricing decision, both markets have seen producers attempting to reverse the downward trends through free publications. The rationale for this is to attract higher advertising revenues through large circulation figures – *Metro*, for example, was distributed to one million readers in London in 2004. The Leisure Industries Research Centre (2005) reported over 130 free newspapers worldwide, with a total of 16 million copies given out every day. The largest operator is a Swedish group, Metro International, with 45 daily editions published in 67 cities around the world. However, it remains to be seen whether free titles have a long-term future, in particular in competition with the internet.

The market for books, like other markets, including CDs and DVDs, has become a sales battleground between the traditional retail outlets, supermarkets and the internet, once again illustrating the importance of the pricing decision. Supermarkets typically discount bestselling books to a greater extent than traditional bookshops can afford, sometimes as 'loss leaders' to attract customers; whilst the internet offers the convenience of shopping from home, often at discounted prices. Case Study 12.1 illustrates this intense competition very well.

An interesting development in the reading market is electronic reading devices. Sony and Amazon have launched digital readers which are about the size of a slim paperback. The latest model of Amazon's Kindle, for example, can hold around 1,500 books, includes a dictionary, can convert text to speech and has wireless connectivity to download new books, newspapers and magazines. There are considerable issues to resolve regarding format compatibility (ensuring books are available in a consistent electronic format) and digital rights management (ensuring payment to publishers and authors, similar to the issues faced by the music industry). Also the price of digital readers is considerable; for example, at the time of writing the Kindle2 is $259 and the Sony reader £150 in the UK. Nevertheless, the e-book market has considerable potential.

CASE STUDY 12.1

Harry Potter books

The *Harry Potter* series of books has been a publishing phenomenon. Each issue in the series coincided with growth in overall book sales in the UK and the economic cycle in books there became dependent on the *Harry Potter* publication dates. The final book of the series surpassed all previous book launches, with simultaneous releases in ninety countries in July 2007, and joint UK and US sales topping 11 million in the first 24 hours. This exceeded the achievements of the sixth book in the series, which sold nine million copies in the first 24 hours in the UK and USA. Prior to the final book, cumulative sales worldwide exceeded 325 million, in 63 different languages.

The *Harry Potter* books have transformed their publisher, Bloomsbury, from a small company to a significant player in the industry, demonstrating the power of a successful product. The books also illustrate the struggle taking place in book retailing internationally between traditional booksellers, supermarkets and the internet. Asda heavily discounted the final *Harry Potter* book (£5 each) in the UK, selling nearly all of its 500,000 copies in the first 24 hours. Amazon, meanwhile, had 2.2 million orders worldwide. Traditional bookshops became resigned to losing the bulk of sales to their competitive rivals, hoping instead to benefit from a general increase in reading by children.

It is claimed that the *Harry Potter* books not only were a reason for the success of the book industry in the last decade, but also introduced a whole generation of new children to reading books for pleasure, particularly boys, who are characterised more by their IT literacy than reading. A survey in Australia found a significant proportion of children were more interested in reading after reading the *Harry Potter* books and had since read a number of other titles. The books they read after *Harry Potter* encompassed a wide range of genres and titles and included fantasy, fairy tales, science fiction, historical fiction, realistic fiction and reference books. Whether or not this beneficial impact on 'Generation Y' (teenagers in the last decade of the twentieth century and first decade of the twenty-first century) will be sustained is yet to be seen now that the *Harry Potter* series has been completed.

In the UK, a survey by the book retailer Waterstone's suggested that children and teachers alike believe that *Harry Potter* has had a significant impact on children's literacy levels. Almost six out of ten children surveyed said that *Harry Potter* books had helped them improve their reading skills, and nearly half said that *Harry Potter* books made them want to read more books. Over eight out of ten teachers said that *Harry Potter* had a positive impact on children's reading abilities and nearly seven out of ten teachers said that *Harry Potter* had helped turn non-readers into readers.

Another electronic challenge to traditional books comes from Google's plans to put millions of copyrighted books online. This digitised service is likely to benefit authors as the new service will give users access to millions of out of print, but still copyright-protected, books. Nevertheless it is estimated that currently electronic books represent only just over 1 per cent of the market, and this is forecasted to rise to just over 5 per cent by 2012. So the switch to electronic books is much slower than the switch to electronic music downloads. This is partly because of the price difference but may also be because many people prefer to read hard copies rather than reading on a screen; plus electronic books need to be charged and may need repair.

12.4 Home entertainment

Home entertainment is defined in *Leisure Forecasts* (Leisure Industries Research Centre, 2008) by the electronic hardware which is increasingly prevalent in leisure in the home, i.e. watching television, listening to music and the use of personal computers for leisure purposes. It is not only the largest sub-sector of leisure in the home (see Table 12.1), but also has seen significant changes over time (see Table 12.2), largely because of changes in technology. And it is the sub-sector with which the public sector is most involved, largely through public broadcasting and regulation.

12.4.1 Television

The two largest elements in the UK television market are TV licenses and satellite TV, which comprise two-thirds of consumer spending on television in the UK. The other third consists mainly of set purchase and rentals, and repairs. The importance of TV licenses in the scale of the UK television market is testimony to the importance of the BBC, a corporation paid for by this means, which is heavily influenced by government policy as a quasi-autonomous, public service broadcaster.

The television market has been significantly influenced by technological changes throughout its history. Arguably the most significant change has been the competition between terrestrial, satellite and cable TV channels, which has resulted in an explosion in choice for the consumer. This growth has been accelerated in the UK by Freeview and Freesat, which, after the purchase of appropriate receiving equipment, provide free access to multiple digital channels. It is estimated that at the end of 2008, 86 per cent of UK households had digital reception on their main TV set. This is the highest rate among seven more economically developed countries examined by Ofcom (2008) (see Table 12.3). However, it is the compulsory switch to digital TV broadcasting in the UK through government legislation which has accelerated the purchase of digital televisions and digital set-top boxes.

The greater choice offered by digital channels is being formalised by the change to digital TV broadcasting. The consequences of these changes for TV employment and financing are significant. Employment in television, particularly in production and presenting, is expanding. Finance, however, is getting tighter as more and more channels compete for limited (and, in a recession, falling) advertising revenue. Television advertising in the UK yielded around £3 billion in 2008, but this figure is falling in the recession at the time of writing. Furthermore, it faces increasing competition for advertising revenue from the internet – UK internet advertising is now about the same value, £3 billion.

Many fear the possible knock-on consequences of greater competition and reduced advertising revenues on the quality of TV productions, i.e. the effects of limited budgets outweighing any high quality programme aspirations. On the other hand there is an argument that greater competition among TV channels and production companies should drive standards higher, not lower. This 'cost versus quality' dilemma, i.e. seeking high quality and

Table 12.3 Television statistics for seven countries, 2007

	UK	France	Germany	Italy	USA	Canada	Japan
Total income (£ billion)	10.4	7.0	9.3	6.3	66.6	4.4	17.7
£ revenue per head of population, of which	172	109	113	109	221	135	139
advertising	58	38	36	55	110	34	67
subscription	71	52	37	35	111	86	48
public funding	43	20	39	19	1	14	25
Annual license fee (£)	140	79	140	73	n/a	n/a	108
Viewing per head (mins/day)	218	207	208	230	272	223	n/a
Share of three largest channels (%)	50	63	38	54	22	18	53
Digital TV penetration (% of households)	86	66	32	56	70	53	65
% of households with any concerns about what is on TV	39	54	53	46	47	43	25

Source: Ofcom (2008).

lower cost at the same time, or attempting an appropriate compromise between the two, is quite common in leisure markets (e.g. hotels, holidays) and is an important consideration for leisure managers.

> ### Discussion question
>
> Does increased competition and choice in television supply mean that quality of programmes is falling?

In a comparison of seven developed countries by Ofcom (2008), as Table 12.3 shows, the USA had the highest television revenue per head in 2007, including by far the highest from advertising and subscriptions but by far the lowest from public funding. Compared with these other developed economies, UK television is quite well funded, with the second highest revenue per head and the highest from public funding. Furthermore, whilst in the USA the three largest channels attracted only 22 per cent of viewing in 2007, in the UK the three largest channels attracted half the viewing, despite facing increasing competition.

In the face of increasing choice and competition, what do customers feel? Ofcom (2008) investigated customer satisfaction with television – see the last row of Table 12.3. There does not appear to be a correlation between the level of customer concern and the degree of competition (low competition is indicated by a higher viewing share of the three largest channels, as shown by the eighth row in Table 12.3). On the one hand Japan has the lowest level of customer concern (25 per cent) and low competition (one of the highest shares of viewing for the three largest channels, 53 per cent). On the other hand France had the highest level of customer concern (54 per cent) but the lowest competition in Table 12.3 (i.e. the largest share of viewing for the three largest channels, 63 per cent). The two countries with the most competition, USA and Canada, are in the middle of the customer concern percentages.

One of the ways in which television companies can compensate for falling advertising revenue is to increase subscriptions for pay-TV. In the USA, 96 per cent of households buy pay-TV, while, at the other extreme, in Italy the figure is 22 per cent. The UK figure is 47 per cent. The growth in subscription revenue in recent years has been faster than the growth in advertising revenue. Sports and films have been the traditional drivers of pay-TV subscriptions' growth, particularly for the channels which buy the licenses for the top leagues' football in different countries. A successful example in the UK is Sky and Case Study 12.2 provides details of how important the synergistic relationship between football and television is for Sky. HD (high definition) television is a related technological innovation, since sport is one of the types of programme which benefit most from HD.

One of the major technological developments in television in recent years has been on-demand TV. This allows people to use computers, logging on to appropriate websites, to watch programmes from the recent past, typically for free. BBC's iPlayer service attracted over 700,000 showings every day in 2008. In the USA a similar service, Hulu, is supported by NBC Universal and News Corporation – it attracted 2,632,000 viewers in August 2008 (Ofcom, 2008). The most recent development of this 'catch-up' opportunity in television is the opportunity to pay for downloads of full-length feature programmes – including classic programmes from the past. The BBC and Apple have agreed for such downloading to be available from Apple's iTunes online media store. Another related technological development is internet-connected TVs, so that the on-demand services for television programmes or films can be viewed without having to switch to the computer.

CASE STUDY 12.2

Football and television

Broadcasting and sport have had a close relationship for a long time. As ownership of first radios and then televisions became universal in more developed countries, so sport became an important feature of broadcasting. In the UK the BBC dominated sports broadcasting for a long time and consequently sport received little financial reward for being broadcast. The arrival of ITV in 1955 ended the BBC's monopoly in the purchasing of broadcasting rights, and competition and fees increased gradually until the 1990s.

In 1992, BSkyB entered the competition for the broadcasting rights for Premier League football in England and brought a much more competitive ethos. Whilst ITV, a free to air terrestrial channel, had paid £44 million in rights fees in 1988 for four years of live first division football coverage, BSkyB paid £191.5 million in rights fees in 1992 for five years of live Premier League football coverage. Fifteen years later BskyB and Setanta together paid £1,700 million for three years' rights (Gratton and Solberg, 2007). They paid such historically high sums because they calculated there would be sufficient increases in subscriptions, and therefore subsequent advertising revenues. However, this was not the case for Setanta, which later went out of business.

Sport, and particularly Premier League football, has become the barometer for profitability at BSkyB. Football is a key driver for subscriptions. BSkyB's total subscriber numbers in the UK and Ireland rose from 3.9 million in 1994 to 6.9 million in 1998. Out of the latter, 2.7 million (nearly 40 per cent) were subscribers to one of more of Sky Sports' channels. Of these, 82 per cent regularly watched football, and for 47 per cent football was their favourite sport to watch (Gratton and Taylor, 2000). When asked in research what the main reason was for subscribing to Sky Sports channels, 40 per cent answered sport; 10 per cent answered football, whilst 5 per cent identified live Premier League football. Other sports were each identified by less than 1 per cent of subscribers (Monopolies and Mergers Commission, 1999).

It is not only BSkyB that has benefited from broadcasting live Premier League football. The distribution of the higher television revenues to Premier League clubs meant that it became a very significant proportion of most clubs' income. In 1996–7, for example, income from BSkyB's television coverage represented 20 per cent or more of total revenue for 11 out of the 20 Premier League clubs (Gratton and Taylor, 2000). Ironically it was only at Manchester United that the television income represented less than 10 per cent of the total – even though they received the second highest payment from BSkyB. This is because Manchester United receives so much income from other sources.

12.4.2 Radio

Listening to the radio is a very popular form of home entertainment in many countries, as shown in Table 12.4, which provides comparative statistics for seven developed countries. Typically between 70 and 80 per cent of adults listen regularly (at least once a week). Japan is the notable exception, with only 38 per cent of adults listening regularly, possibly because of a much clearer switch to television, even at breakfast time. Ofcom (2008) reports a parity

Table 12.4 Radio statistics for seven countries, 2007

	UK	France	Germany	Italy	USA	Canada	Japan
Total income (£ billion)	1.3	1.1	2.3	0.9	10.6	0.8	1.7
£ revenue per head of population	21	17	28	15	35	26	13
Percentage of public funding	56	57	79	54	0.7	19	58
Percentage of adults regularly listening	73	75	83	72	79	79	38
Listening per head (mins/day)	177	171	186	180	159	157	128
Public radio listening share (%)	55	26	49	24	n/a	12	15
Percentage of adults owning and using a digital radio	34	15	21	32	12	14	7

Source: Ofcom (2008).

in the UK between the percentage of revenue for radio which is by public funding (56 per cent) and the percentage share of public radio listening (55 per cent) (see Table 12.4). This differs from other countries in the comparison, which typically have a much higher percentage of public funding than the public radio listening share.

Radio is influenced by technological change and recently significant growth in Europe has been achieved by the sales of digital (DAB) radios, particularly in the UK. In North America and Japan, however, the percentage of adults owning and using a digital radio is low, as shown in Table 12.4. Another significant trend caused by technological change is that more people are listening to radio via the internet or through their mobile phones or MP3 players. The international comparisons provided by Ofcom (2008) show a similar pattern as for digital radios – the lowest figures in 2007 were for North America and Japan; with higher figures in Europe. The section on convergence below illustrates such multiple entertainment use of devices.

12.4.3 Format wars

Home entertainment is a commercial battleground between different formats – again showing the power of technological change. In recorded and recordable media these battles have included Betamax and VHS in video tapes in the 1980s (won by VHS), records, tapes and CDs in the 1980s and 1990s (won by CDs), videos and DVDs in the late 1990s (won by DVDs), and Blu-ray and HD in the first decade of the twenty-first century (won by Blu-ray). HD has emerged as a format with major growth prospects in TV reception, however.

The format wars in films seem to be giving way to the growing use of the internet for viewing films, with many predicting the continued decline of DVDs and pointing out the cost disadvantages of Blu-ray compared with streaming films (i.e. direct and specific broadcast to a computer) via the internet. In electronic games, the battle between Sony's PlayStation, Microsoft's Xbox and Nintendo's Wii continues without a clear winner as yet. The lessons are clear for anyone involved in the home entertainment businesses – always look for the next format and retain competitiveness in technology.

The entertainment rental market has seen increasing competition between high street DVD rental stores, internet rental stores, such as Lovefilm in the UK, which operate via the post, and more recently services from companies such as Apple and Amazon which allow customers to view streamed films on a rental basis – termed 'videos on demand' (VOD). The potential of VOD is considerable because it does not require a subscription cost for the consumer, compared with movie channels on TV, and it has higher profit margins because of lower costs compared with companies dealing with the transport and storage of DVDs. Ofcom (2008) report VOD to be more developed in the USA, France and Germany but a relatively small market in the UK.

> ### Discussion question
>
> Is there such a thing as too much choice for consumers? Discuss in relation to electronic devices for leisure in the home.

12.4.4 Listening to music

Listening to music has undergone considerable shifts in spending in recent years, which have meant that it is no longer just a part of leisure in the home but is portable to anywhere out of the home too. Traditional home audio equipment has faced increasing competition from television music channels, DVD players, PCs and laptops, and also more portable devices such as MP3 players and mobile phones with equivalent software and storage space. Another recent technological change is wireless technology, with music systems accessing internet supply and supporting a network of wireless speakers. Consumers are faced with an almost confusing choice of devices to play music on and in such circumstances there is a tendency to support market leaders to reduce the uncertainty. Apple's iPod is a clear market leader – in the last quarter of 2007 over 22 million iPods were sold worldwide.

The move away from traditional audio equipment has also been accompanied by a move away from records and CDs to internet downloads. In 2006, for example, CD sales in the UK fell by 11 per cent (Leisure Industries Research Centre, 2008). As well as the increasing popularity of iPods and MP3 players, the rise in internet downloads has been fuelled by the industry's inability to effectively police illegal downloads, which according to one estimate outnumber legal downloads by twenty to one (Leisure Industries Research Centre, 2008). The future of the market is said to depend on how much of the growth in downloading music can be translated into commercial gain. Nevertheless, legal downloads in the UK rose from 5.8 million in 2004 to over 50 million in 2006, so there is still growth in revenue, even though there is also lost revenue from illegal downloading. Supermarkets have profited from CD sales despite the growth of downloads, increasing their share of the CD market in the UK from 9 per cent in 2002 to 25 per cent in 2007 (Leisure Industries Research Centre, 2007). This success is very similar to their success in selling books and is based on both convenience and discounted prices.

12.4.5 Computers and electronic games

Computers are very important for home entertainment. For example, in 2007 the most popular uses of Google searches in various countries were for games (France), videos (Italy and Japan), lyrics (USA, Canada and Sweden) and the BBC (UK), according to Ofcom (2008). The strongest growth in Google searches in 2007 in Canada, Sweden and the UK was Facebook. Growth in computer systems is largely driven by lower prices and growing demand for laptops rather than PCs.

Broadband connection is a major recent technological change which is vital for the high speed of downloading important to many of the internet services referred to above. It is an important government objective in the UK, where 93 per cent of adults using the internet use a broadband connection (Ofcom, 2008). This is higher than the figure in many other countries – in Japan, for example, the equivalent figure is 67 per cent. However, an important innovation yet to come for home entertainment is for the broadband infrastructure to achieve more consistent, universal high speed capability.

Consumer spending in the UK on home computers is matched in scale by that for video games. A major difference between these two markets, however, is the relative importance of systems, add-ons (extra equipment) and software. Because over 80 per cent of households in the UK have a home computer, growth is constrained by market saturation and add-ons and software do not compensate for slowing sales of computer hardware. In video games, by contrast, the intensive competition between PlayStation, Xbox and Wii continues to feed growth, but more importantly the value of sales of add-ons and software exceeds the value of sales of games consoles.

Computers and video games are commonly blamed for the reduction in physical activity among 'Generation Y', particularly boys. However, it is too simplistic to blame one element of the competition for young people's time for any lack of physical activity. Television, parents, schools, eating behaviour, peer group pressures and many other factors contribute to physical activity behaviour. And there are now examples where electronic games directly promote physical activity, including Wii, DDR (Dance Dance Revolution) and XavixPORT.

12.4.6 Convergence in home entertainment

Ofcom (2008) provides evidence on convergence, the extent to which people are using the same devices to access different types of content – audio, video, text and other data. The convergence takes place in different types of device. Mobile phones and computers – laptops with dongles, or PCs – are the most obvious but it is also possible to access the internet from televisions for the streaming of services such as catch-up TV and video on demand; and to use electronic games consoles to download films or play DVDs. Some of this convergence is instrumental in taking previously at-home leisure out of the home, e.g. mobile phones, laptops and portable electronic games consoles.

Table 12.5 provides some comparisons across seven more developed countries for the two main vehicles for multiple home entertainment – the internet and mobile phones. It demonstrates how significant minorities of adults are using both the internet and mobile phones for multiple entertainment purposes. And the patterns are very similar across the different countries compared by Ofcom (2008). Furthermore, in most cases these percentages are increasing over time. Convergence feeds an important attribute in modern leisure consumption – convenience. And convenience is as much about where to enjoy entertainment as what to enjoy, i.e. much of it is no longer confined to the home.

In 2008, UK internet users spent on average just under 14 hours a week online, higher than other European countries covered by Ofcom (2008) but still short of the USA figure (over 15 hours a week). In all countries researched by Ofcom, the average time spent online by internet users increased in 2008 compared with 2007, and in the UK it increased by 21 per cent per annum in the four years up to 2008. However, internet use is not exclusive. Ofcom (2008) reports that significant minorities of internet users frequently watched TV at the same time, e.g. 39 per cent in Japan, 36 per cent in France and 28 per cent in the UK.

> ### Discussion question
> **Which is more important to leisure, the mobile phone or the internet?**

12.5 House and garden

This sector consists of two main parts – DIY and gardening. In terms of consumer spending in the UK, DIY is about twice the scale of gardening but both are among the largest expenditure elements of leisure in the home (see Table 12.1). They have also both demonstrated growth over the period 2002–8, as shown in Table 12.2.

12.5.1 DIY

Since much of DIY is maintenance of the home, cars, domestic equipment, etc. to either solve or prevent problems, there is an issue about whether or not such expenditure is truly leisure expenditure, or more akin to housework. Nevertheless, it is usually included in categories of leisure in the home.

Table 12.5 Entertainment use of home internet connections and mobile phones in seven countries, 2007

	UK	France	Germany	Italy	USA	Canada	Japan
Percentage of adults using home internet connection to:							
watch or download films, TV programmes	23	21	14	27	23	22	18
listen to the radio	33	37	34	31	26	27	17
listen to downloaded music or podcasts	35	27	18	39	36	40	31
access social networking sites	50	27	34	32	40	55	33
upload photographs	43	31	36	38	42	44	20
upload video content	11	15	5	16	11	10	9
Percentage of adults using mobile phones:							
to listen to music	25	21	26	28	14	12	20
to listen to FM radio	16	13	13	22	3	4	8
as a still camera	59	51	51	58	42	35	52
to record video clips	16	6	5	15	9	7	9
to upload pictures/video content to the internet	11	3	7	10	9	5	17

Source: Ofcom (2008).

In the long term, DIY benefits from the positive influence of rising home ownership, which was 70 per cent of UK households in 2008. In the shorter term, the DIY market tends to fluctuate in line with the housing market generally, such that the housing boom in the UK in 2001–4 was accompanied by annual growth rates in DIY spending of between 7 and 11 per cent in real terms. In contrast, a stalling house market in 2005 was accompanied by a decline in the value of the DIY market. In 2008, as the housing market and consumer confidence fell, together with bad summer weather, so DIY spending fell again.

There is a paradox to the tendency for DIY spending to follow the housing market. If the housing market went into decline it would be logical to expect DIY spending to increase, because this would protect the value of the house owner's major asset. However, this does not normally happen. The largest element of DIY consumer spending in the UK is household maintenance, i.e. fixing or preventing problems. Other significant elements of DIY spending are paint, wallpaper, timber and equipment hire. Supply of DIY products is dominated by large retailers in the UK, including B&Q, Wickes and Homebase, and also Halfords for cars and bikes. DIY is another example of the oligopoly structure identified as typical of commercial leisure in Chapter 4.

12.5.2 Gardening

Consumer spending on gardening follows a similar trend over time to DIY, also following the housing market. Gardening expenditure is negatively affected by the long-term shrinking of average garden size, which itself is the product of the increase in single occupancy flats. Garden plants and flowers are by far the most significant element of this market, accounting for over three-quarters of its value in the UK. Garden tools are another important element. Unlike DIY, supply of gardening products is highly fragmented, with many small, independent operators, although the major DIY stores have made major inroads into the gardening market sales – by 2003 they attracted one-third of garden-related expenditure in the UK.

Gardening is becoming one of the most successful sectors in internet retailing. The core of this growth is the so-called 'silver surfers', aged 50+ years, who are increasingly shopping online. Another trend in the gardening sector which is beneficial to growth in the value of the market is for greater convenience gardening – leading to growth in sales of ready-made plants and plug plants at the expense of seeds. Other growth areas with higher value in gardening are unusual plants, promoted by gardening programmes on television, and garden furniture, lighting and water features, which help to develop gardens into social spaces as well as places for gardening. It is estimated that 80 per cent of households with gardens have garden furniture (Leisure Industries Research Centre, 2003).

The house and garden sector has benefited from considerable exposure on television programmes, which has helped to transform the sector from one of functionality to one of aspirational lifestyles. However, this turns spending in the sector into less of an essential, functional expenditure and more luxury expenditure. Whilst this feeds growth in consumer spending in times of economic growth, when a recession hits, as at the time of writing, the 'luxury' image of the sector is more likely to lead to a downturn.

Discussion question

Is time spent on DIY and gardening leisure or housework?

12.6 Hobbies and pastimes

The main components of this sector for which data are available from *Leisure Forecasts* are photography, toys and games, and pets. Of these, consumer spending on pets is approximately twice the scale of spending on each of the other elements, as shown in Table 12.1. Table 12.2 shows that all three elements are healthy growth sectors, and photography in particular has achieved rapid growth in volume terms, thanks mainly to reducing prices of photographic equipment in the early 2000s.

12.6.1 Photography

Photography, like home entertainment, is an activity that is clearly not confined to the home, but it is conventionally treated as an in the home leisure activity. In the photography market, the biggest change in recent years has been stimulated by the change to digital technology. *Leisure Forecasts* (Leisure Industries Research Centre, 2008) estimates that ownership of digital cameras grew from 11 per cent of UK households in 2002 to 59 per cent of households in 2008. The year 2005 seems to have been a watershed, when at least one major retailer in the UK stopped selling film cameras and another reported digital cameras to be 97 per cent of sales (Leisure Industries Research Centre, 2005). The rise of digital cameras has boosted the relative importance of photographic equipment sales – now about half of the total photography market value – and has also led to a steep decline in consumer spending on photographic film.

Interestingly, however, spending on film processing has been maintained, as customers still demand professional prints from their digital cameras. However, it is estimated that 30 per cent of digital camera owners in the UK never print their pictures (Leisure Industries Research Centre, 2005). Furthermore, it is likely that an increasing proportion of camera owners print their photographs at home as home printing technology improves in both quality and convenience (e.g. editing and printing straight from camera memory cards).

As identified above, photography is just one of the multiple functions of mobile phones and it has been suggested that this popularisation of everyday photography has led to an increased demand for higher quality digital cameras – for both still photographs and videos. However, a threat to this effect is the technical quality of mobile phone cameras, which has improved to match the technical specifications of ordinary digital cameras. Mobile phone cameras have also led to a steep decline in the demand for throwaway film cameras. Another important driver for the photography market is the rising popularity of social networking and photo editing sites on the internet. Such sites as Flickr and Snapfish have facilitated the sharing of digital photographs.

12.6.2 Toys and games

The market for toys and games is difficult to predict because it is very socially driven, via contact between children. A substantial minority of toys are made under licence from film and television brands. However, each licence typically has a limited life-cycle – for example, sales of Lord of the Rings figurines grew while the films were in the cinemas in 2001–3, but have since fallen significantly – and series of the length of the *Harry Potter* films are few and far between. Nevertheless there are some enduring examples in toys and games, including the Disney brand. However, arguably the most durable and iconic toy is the Barbie doll (see Case Study 12.3).

CASE STUDY 12.3

Barbie dolls

The year 2009 was the fiftieth anniversary of the Barbie doll and, as the saying goes, 'there's life in the old girl yet'! The original inspiration for Barbie was to get away from the traditional baby dolls of the time and appeal to young girls' budding sense of fashion, so change was very much at the heart of the concept from the beginning. Since its introduction, Barbie has succeeded by continual transformation into new versions which capture the fashion of the moment, long before Kylie and Madonna adopted the same strategy. The doll has been reproduced in over 100 different forms, including astronaut, Olympic swimmer, rock star and even presidential candidate. There have been Afro-American and Hispanic Barbies.

The company which sells Barbie, Mattel, claims that 90 per cent of girls in the USA between three and ten years old own at least one Barbie doll and that every second two Barbies are sold somewhere in the world. There are two websites on which girls can design clothes, network and play games. The Barbie brand stretches to DVDs, MP3 players, bicycles and jewellery.

All this success has been achieved despite the fact that Barbie's figure, 36–18–38, is totally unrealistic. Barbie has been criticised for its figure (too idealised) and its materialism. But on the other hand it has been praised from the outset for representing a young lady in more than simply a domestic, gender-stereotyped role, but rather in a variety of professions, many of which women at the time were finding it difficult to succeed in. Mattel has always conducted careful research among young girls to establish what role models they admire, and this research informs the next transformation of Barbie.

In the final quarter of 2008 Barbie sales fell by one-fifth. Although the company blamed the global economic crisis, it may be that a longer term threat lies in the 'kids growing older younger' syndrome. Whilst Mattel see Barbie's main market as 3–10-year-olds, industry experts suspect that this may be shrinking to 3–6-year-olds. Barbie's main competitor, Bratz, was designed to have a harder edge and a more contemporary look and the dolls have been successful with both youngsters and 'tweens' (aged between 9 and 12).

Barbie is a truly global product, selling in 150 countries. Barbie's relaunch in 2009 featured an experimental flagship store in Shanghai, 'House of Barbie'. The store is attempting to broaden the doll's appeal to older girls and also to mothers – because there is a generation of women in China who did not have access to Barbie when they were children. Nevertheless, the core market remains young girls, and Mattel's strategy to continue to appeal to them is by keeping Barbie current. Arguably, there is no better indicator of Mattel's success in doing so than the fact that there are over 500 Facebook groups and about 1,000 YouTube channels featuring Barbie.

The toys and games market has changed character over recent decades. One feature is that traditional toys have faced intense competition from PC- and console-based video games. The main challengers to these products are hand-held video games such as Nintendo's DS and Sony's PlayStation Portable. However, the ubiquitous mobile phone offers competition in this market too, as some phones are heavily games oriented. Nintendo's latest DSi has attempted to match the flexibility of other media by including a camera and music playing capability – another element of convergence in entertainment media, as discussed above.

Although there has been something of a retro revival in the form of traditional childhood pastimes, many children's preferences are for electronic devices. This switch in preferences from traditional to electronic has caused problems for traditional toy manufacturers and retailers alike. The nature of toy retailing is shifting rapidly away from toy specialists and towards supermarkets and the internet.

Furthermore, the move from traditional to electronic devices is shifting to younger children – the 'kids getting older younger' syndrome. In 2004, for example, 28 per cent of Nintendo Game Boy players were estimated to be 11 years old or younger. Hand-held electronic games consoles are not always conspicuously expensive – some Nintendo DS consoles retail at less than £100 (at the time of writing). Profitability for Nintendo lies not so much in the selling of the DS consoles as in sales of games from its catalogue of over 600 titles, with prices per title varying from around £10 to £25 in the UK.

12.6.3 Pets

The pets market is one of the most consistently expanding leisure in the home markets in the UK. The poor years are few and far between and any declines in sales have been marginal. This consistency of growth is being tested by the recession at the time of writing. Reports on both sides of the Atlantic point to increasing rates of abandonment of pets, with the suspicion being that owners can simply no longer afford to keep them. However, in previous recessions such an effect has not been significant – a large majority of households will not abandon pets if their household income has declined.

Pet ownership and expenditure is influenced by changes in demographics and the housing market but sometimes these effects are uncertain. The greater number of single person households caused by higher divorce and separation rates, for example, might be a positive influence on pet ownership because pets are good company for single people. Alternatively it might be a negative influence because families are the traditional mainstay of pet ownership. The tendency for couples to have children later in their lives typically means lower numbers of children, which has a negative effect on pet ownership. However, many childless couples might see pets as almost surrogates for children, in which case the lack of children has less of a negative effect. Finally, increased life expectancy could have a positive influence on pet ownership because pets are good companions for older people, or a negative influence because of other expenditure priorities for older people and also restrictions on their housing tenancy agreements.

Higher levels of house ownership promote pet ownership, even the rise in urban apartments, which is more conducive to cat ownership than to dog ownership. In 1990 7.4 million dogs and 6.8 million cats were owned by UK households (Leisure Consultants, 1996), whilst in 2008, although the population of dogs had remained more or less static, the number of cats had expanded to 9.9 million. This possibly reflects the increasing time pressures perceived by modern households (see Chapter 3) in that cats are more independent than dogs and do not need taking for walks.

The nature of spending on pets has changed over time, as highlighted in Chapter 3. In 1990, consumer expenditure on pet food in the UK was nearly twice that on non-food pet items. Now expenditure on non-food items is greater than that on pet food (Leisure Industries Research Centre, 2008), boosted particularly by pet health care spending and pet insurance. In 1986, 70 per cent of animal medicines were bought for farm animals; now the largest share is for household pets (Leisure Industries Research Centre, 2005). However, non-food pet items may be easier to cut expenditure on than pet food, which may make the pet market as a whole more susceptible to decline at times of recession.

12.7 Gambling

Gambling is a leisure activity that is switching location from out of the home to in the home in the UK, largely because of the internet and particularly with the spread of broadband connections. However, several countries have taken action to either outlaw or severely restrict online gambling, including the USA, Germany, Scandinavian countries, Russia and China (Leisure Industries Research Centre, 2009). Internationally, therefore, the greatest uncertainty for online gambling lies in legislative and taxation action – either continued restriction or possibly liberalisation.

The reasons for some countries being more restrictive in allowing online gambling are partly fiscal, to protect tax revenues from land-based gambling enterprises, and partly moral, in fear of an explosion of uncontrollable gambling through people's homes. For example, in 2006 the USA brought in regulations which outlawed the processing of bets taken online by banks and credit card companies, which came into law in early 2009 and effectively block internet gambling.

In the UK a more pragmatic and liberal line was taken and in 2007 a 15 per cent remote gaming tax was introduced. This was clearly designed to protect tax revenues whilst not hitting the gambling industry too hard – many major gambling companies have diversified into online gambling. As a result, online gambling has been the fastest growing element of the UK gambling market, growing 650 per cent in the period 2002–7. However, this was growth from a very small base and in 2008 online gambling was still only 7 per cent of the total gambling market (Leisure Industries Research Centre, 2008). Several other European countries are also adopting a fairly liberal line and it is likely that in due course the most typical approach will involve taxation and regulation, rather than blocking and banning.

> ### Discussion questions
>
> How much regulation should there be for online gambling? And for what reasons?

12.8 Conclusions

Leisure at home includes some of the most dynamic sectors of the leisure industry. The speed of change in consumer behaviour is significant and this change is led in the main by technological developments. Arguably the leading markets in this respect concern home entertainment. Changes in television, mobile phones and the internet in particular represent a telling reminder to all leisure services, for in the home or away from home consumption, of the power of modern media. Whilst these media are important in their own right for consumers, they are also increasingly important in the promotion of leisure out of the home. Increasing numbers of holidays, for example, are researched and booked online.

It is important for all leisure businesses to react quickly to the speed of technological change. This is particularly the case in several leisure in the home markets – TV, radio, listening to music, electronic games and photography are conspicuous examples. Market leaders in these sectors have embraced and led technological changes which have enhanced their products in their consumers' eyes. Other markets are also influenced by technological change – reading, toys and gambling, for example.

An important feature of many technological changes is that they increase cost efficiency and profitability for leisure industries. For example, streaming music and films over the internet is much cheaper than producing, storing and transporting CDs and DVDs. However, profitability in both these markets is threatened by illegal downloading and the relevant industries still have to deal with this threat effectively.

A feature of electronic goods and services for leisure in the home in the last decade is that growth in sales has been helped by falling prices. The price reductions are partly because of intense competition in supply but mainly because of cost reductions in production. Cost reductions are the product of technological changes and cheaper labour, and whilst there is no reason to expect limitations in the former, the latter is very much in debate. Production bases have continually shifted to cheaper labour countries but this process is inevitably accompanied by rising standards of living and higher wage aspirations in these countries.

Another interesting feature of technological change is the danger of increasing confusion for consumers, who are faced with an array of technological choices and wonder if they will provide low value for money in the long term as they are superseded by new developments. An interesting concept which home entertainment industries in particular have embraced is that of convergence, whereby a particular medium can be used for a variety of leisure purposes, and not only in the home but also away from home. The mobile phone is the most conspicuous example, able to provide not just telephone services, but also music, games, still photographs, video camera, films and access to the internet, to name but a few. The internet is equally versatile and this convergence makes it so much more convenient for consumers wishing to access an array of leisure services both in the home and away from home. Even televisions and electronic games consoles are being adapted to provide internet access in order to capture the convergence factor.

Perhaps the next challenge for these industries is to demystify, even deskill, their products, so that they do not replicate the clichéd example of the washing machine – with a facility for multiple programmes but with the average consumer only using two. Many older consumers in particular are deterred by the technological demands of modern media. Deskilling leisure in the home products will increase their accessibility. A lesson here is arguably from another leisure in the home market, and one less explicitly dependent on technology – gardening. Part of the reason for gardening's success is that it has become less the province of the 'expert' and more accessible to ordinary consumers, who do not need to know the Latin names for plants or the scientific properties of their soil. They do not even have to plant seeds – plug plants have made it so much easier to participate and succeed in gardening.

Another key agent of change and growth in leisure markets is the transformation of the nature of spending by consumers. Good examples of this are DIY, gardening and pets. In the cases of DIY and gardening, the transformation was from functional expenditure to lifestyle choices, from necessity to image. In the case of pets the transformation was from the dominance of expenditure on pet food to the growth of non-food expenditure. In all three cases the development was from a concept of what is essential to a more mature and rounded concept of what is important and of value. The role of the media is very important in such transformations – obvious examples being the proliferation of home improvement and gardening programmes on television.

The increasing importance of technological changes in leisure in the home has also raised the critical issue of government or industry regulation. Such regulation is essential in organising the structure of television and radio broadcasting. It is vital for relevant industries in the battle to reduce illegal downloading of music and films. It is also an important feature of the future of internet gambling. Internationally, there is a great deal of difference between the regulatory stances taken by different countries. Some are more liberal and inclined to let market forces resolve issues, whilst others are more interventionist in attempting to mould the future of the markets.

Whether or not governments succeed in the regulation of key leisure in the home markets, these markets will continue to play a major part in the leisure lifestyles of consumers. No activities out of the home can match the ubiquitous nature of television, or the growth rates of the use of computers and the internet for leisure purposes. Yet it is important to remember that in overall terms it is leisure out of the home which dominates consumer spending and that it is growing at a faster rate than leisure in the home. Nevertheless, an increasing degree of crossover is evident between leisure in the home and leisure out of the home. Examples include the relationship between major books, the cinema, DVDs and toys; the convergence of different leisure contents within one form of technology; and the growth of research and purchase functions on the internet at home, for a variety of out of home leisure activities, particularly holidays.

Practical tasks

1   Conduct an audit in one house or flat of:
    (a) the percentage of space in the home that is used for leisure;
    (b) the percentage of each member of the household's time spent on leisure at home;
    (c) the value of the leisure equipment in the home (you will need to estimate this).
    What conclusions do you reach about the importance of leisure to this household?
2   Design and conduct a pilot survey of young people (16–24 years) and older people (50+ years) who you know, in order to find out:
    (a) how dependent they are on technology for consuming leisure in the home (i.e. television, computer, audio equipment, etc.);
    (b) how competent they feel in using such leisure technology.
    What are the implications of your results for the prospective marketing of a new piece of leisure technology such as HD television or digital radio?

Structured guide to further reading

For reporting and forecasting leisure in the home (and leisure away from home) in the UK:

Leisure Forecasts, an annual publication produced by the Leisure Industries Research Centre, at Sheffield Hallam University in England.

Government agencies produce reports of relevance to leisure in the home. A particularly relevant recent one is:

Ofcom (2008) *The International Communications Market*, Ofcom, London, available at http://www2.ofcom.org.uk/research/cm/icmr08/.

Part 4

Skills and techniques for successful sport and leisure management

Contents

This final part of the book concentrates in the main on a set of management disciplines considered to be important to sport and leisure. The study of these promotes an appreciation of the skills and techniques which help to improve management in this sector.

What is conceived of as management today is an amalgam of different theories, which were summarised in Chapter 1. The chapters in Part 4 reflect the thinking in all these theories, rather than just the most recent, because they have all contributed to a comprehensive understanding of best practice in management. Some of the chapters in this part (Chapters 13, 15, 18 and 19) review traditional functional disciplines important to management. Other chapters (Chapters 14, 17 and 21) examine more contemporary and interdisciplinary subjects which are considered important to good management. A couple of the chapters (Chapters 16 and 20) deal with decisions and contexts that are sufficiently important to sport and leisure management to be given explicit consideration.

Several themes run through all these chapters, e.g. rational thinking, logical processes, engagement with both staff and customers. A pattern develops of general management principles which entail:

- understanding the business environment, particularly the market;
- setting appropriate organisational objectives;
- designing a structure and strategy for operations;
- implementing plans to realise the strategic objectives;
- organising operations and adapting to internal or external circumstances;
- monitoring and evaluation;
- feedback, review and change.

Managing people in sport and leisure

Chris Wolsey and Jeff Abrams

In this chapter

- What are the relationships between changing customer needs, organisational behaviour, human resource processes, people management and business objectives?
- Why is it important to develop an empowered, skilled and motivated workforce?
- How important are effective leadership, management and communication?
- How are formal and informal organisational structures linked to organisational context and strategies?
- How can an understanding of organisational behaviour and human resource strategy be developed and implemented?

Michelangelo Gratton/Getty Images

Summary

It is often said that 'people' form a critical component of virtually all organisations worldwide. This truism is particularly appropriate to the sport and leisure sector of the economy. This sector often relies upon the lowest paid staff to provide the 'front of house' customer service that is pivotal to successful customer interactions and retention, which itself is essential in an increasingly competitive business environment. However, there can be no 'one size fits all' prescription relating to how this is achieved in practice. What does exist, though, is a number of principles and conceptual models that seek to frame some of the key issues. Broadly, these can be better understood and developed within the theoretical frameworks provided by the organisational behaviour literature.

Although it is important to have a feel for the external environment and the issues that could impact on organisational behaviour and people management decisions, it is critical that such decisions are made at a local level with a clear sensitivity to the needs of both staff and customers. This chapter looks at these issues from the point of view of developing appropriate structural and leadership models based upon an understanding of customer needs. Increasingly, this is seen to require staff engagement in order to elicit a better understanding of the local context, in all its various guises.

The extra ingredient is to frame such decisions in the context of organisational priorities, strategies and objectives. In this way, the people management role fulfilled by 'personnel' departments becomes a more fundamental corporate function, designed to extract maximum value from its 'human resources'. However, this leads to a number of tensions that have to be recognised and managed in a process of continual improvement. This is a dynamic process that is constantly evolving at individual, group and organisational levels.

The chapter interrogates such issues and concludes that there is a need to move away from traditional models of management based on 'command and control' in favour of a more flexible approach, designed to deliver an evolving customer experience based upon staff engagement, empowerment and innovation.

13.1 Introduction

Leading and managing 'people' is fundamental to the successful operation of virtually all organisations and businesses. This is particularly true of sport and leisure organisations, whose market 'product' often contains a substantial 'service' element which relies heavily on the real-time interaction of customers and employees. Often, it is this relationship that yields real competitive advantage and is pivotal to customer perceptions of both value and quality. An understanding of organisational behaviour seeks to provide a conceptual framework in which the interactions and motivations of individuals and groups can be better understood and subsequently managed; particularly with respect to the positive and negative performance consequences. Related to this, human resource management provides a more functional representation of management. This is, perhaps, best understood as a corporate attempt to squeeze as much value as possible from an organisation's employees. However, organisational and individual performance is often difficult to measure accurately (see Chapter 17). It should be considered relative to customer requirements, the goals of the organisation, the actions of competitors and the ever-changing external environment.

In an ideal world, once there is clarity around such issues, decisions can then be made about how employees, at all levels, can make a significant contribution to a competitive and profitable customer experience. Assuming one has a clear understanding of current and developing customer requirements, it is then important to design organisational structures that facilitate a flexible and appropriate fit between customer requirements, organisational constraints, individual/group needs and future business opportunities.

Human resource structures, systems and processes should be designed to both deliver and develop all levels of staff in relation to organisational objectives and customer value. An understanding of organisational behaviour helps consider the potential consequences of management decisions in this regard. As a consequence, this chapter seeks to provide a better understanding of the strategic fit between the deployment of staff and the needs of customers, organisations, markets and industries within the sport and leisure environment.

Excellent staff are as important as excellent facilities in meeting customer requirements. Therefore, senior professionals and managers must have knowledge, experience and understanding of staff matters: staff motivation, organisational structures and the impact of these important areas on both organisation and staff performance.

Staff – full-time, part-time, casual or voluntary – are the most important resource in any leisure organisation and their cost should be regarded as a highly valued investment rather than an expensive item of expenditure. The right staff need to be employed, trained, nurtured and enabled to perform well for their organisations and for themselves.

13.1.1 Sport and leisure employment

It is difficult to estimate the precise numbers of people employed in leisure-related jobs, not least because of the definitional difficulties of this very broad industrial sector. However, as the UK struggles with an unemployment rate that is set to approach three million people during 2010, leisure employment is likely to become a growth sector of national significance, both in social and economic terms.

If we look at the sport industry in particular, Skills Active (2005) reveals a higher than average proportion of young people (16–24 years) working in this area. The Office for National Statistics (2009c) reveals that the 18–24 age band recorded its highest unemployment rate on record (18 per cent) when compared against a national unemployment rate of around 8 per cent for the period July–September 2009. In a time of change and potential future growth, sport and leisure managers need to attract, motivate and retain high quality staff. Given the burgeoning pool of applicants, it is important that such managers do not become complacent but instead work even harder to identify and nurture staff, in an effort to not merely sustain but where possible grow the business.

13.2 The importance of staff training and development

Education and training are of vital importance at all levels of leisure and sport management. Without men and women of vision and standing, and without qualified and trained staff, no leisure service can hope to be efficient, let alone effective in meeting the needs and aspirations of its various stakeholders, most notably its staff and customers. Staff are an investment; training helps to get the best out of them, for their own job satisfaction and for the organisations of which they are an integral part. However, there exists some confusion over the use of the two terms 'training' and 'development'. At times these terms appear to be interchangeable, and sometimes one term may be all embracing, encompassing both meanings at once.

Overall, training is about learning specific, often vocationally oriented skills and knowledge that can be applied directly to work-based practice, typically in the short term. Broadly, it deals with relatively narrow questions with respect to 'what' and 'which' things should be done. In other words it perpetuates current practice. Development, however, is a wider educational concept that promotes personal growth. This encourages an approach to learning which is much broader and deeper, allowing a greater understanding of related issues and opportunities for the transfer of knowledge into a variety of problem solving situations. This promotes questions such as 'Why are things done in this way?' and gives the necessary insight and confidence to challenge prevailing orthodoxies by suggesting improvements to the way things are done. This, in turn, allows more flexible and progressive approaches to daily performance-related issues that affect customer value.

13.2.1 The need for a coherent training structure

> Unlike many professions, leisure does not have obvious educational or professional pathways, with clear entry qualifications leading onward to training and advancement. The profession covers a wide variety of specialisms including sport, the arts, tourism, heritage and countryside management. It is closely related to many other careers, such as planning, business management, marketing and teaching. Skills from these professions are often relevant and create opportunities to cross over into the leisure profession.
>
> (Griffiths and Randall, 2004)

Any coherent system of training must be structured around the management and staffing needs of sport and leisure organisations. If training is to be effective we need to ask, 'Why is it needed?' and 'Who is it for?' before we ask, 'What should it be?' Commercial organisations are likely to make training judgements based upon evidence-based systems that deliver proven and increasingly prioritised performance outcomes. As the UK Commission for Employment and Skills (2009) argues, this means '[c]reating a modular and flexible qualification system in which only employer recognised and accredited learning and qualifications that meet industry requirements are eligible to receive significant public funding'.

13.3 Leadership and decision-making

A successful manager must have both the management skills to ensure that customer needs are catered for and the people skills to inspire and lead a group of staff. Effective leadership requires an understanding of the goals of the organisation, the services, facilities, programmes, resources and the people involved. Leadership is an important aspect of management – the ability to lead effectively is one of the factors that produces an effective manager. Leadership has been described as a mixture of art, craft and humanity. It is an essential part of a manager's job.

Adair and Reed point to the need for leadership:

> Management has the overtone of carrying out objectives laid down by someone else. Moreover, there is nothing in the concept of management which implies inspiration, creating teamwork when it isn't there, or setting an example. When it is the case that inspiration and teamwork exist, you may well have managers who are in effect leaders, especially if they are the source of the inspiration. But it is, I believe, unfortunately more often the case that management does not ring bells when it comes to people.
>
> (Adair and Reed, 2003)

Discussion questions

Is it possible to be a good manager without being a good leader? Conversely, is it possible to be a good leader without being a good manager?

What is also critically important is a firm understanding of the political and power context in which the organisation is operating. This has consequences for leadership and management. Often leisure and sport organisations are dependent on other organisations, such as central government, for funding and survival. This context will influence the managerial and leadership behaviours. Therefore leadership and management cannot be fully understood unless there is a clear appreciation of the context faced by the organisation.

A good leader is concerned both with people and results. Leadership is a word with positive connotations. We look to leaders to inspire, direct and pave the way. In leisure and sport management, there is a need for excellent leaders at all levels – policy-makers, executives, middle managers and operational personnel. Sometimes, managerial leadership skills come from within the team or are exercised so subtly that they are not always evident. We can see evidence of this with some conductors of an orchestra, directors of a theatre production or with some coaches and captains in sport, who quietly get the best out of their players without shouting from the rooftops.

Much of the literature on leadership includes a range of interrelated concepts, variables and theories. These include concepts and theories of leadership attributes such as personal qualities, trait theories, power theories and behavioural theories. There can also be an element of teaching and coaching within the leadership model, as well as the need to understand 'following' in order to be an effective leader. Clearly there is much to consider, learn and apply in the complex world of the leader. It is useful therefore to reflect on the leadership styles of those sport and leisure practitioners who have been considered successful in their leadership roles. One such person is John Wooden (see Case Study 13.1).

In distinguishing leadership from other management functions, it has been suggested that most management functions can be taught, whereas leadership skills must be learned through doing. Leadership stems largely from a manager's personal dealings and personal

CASE STUDY 13.1

John Wooden

John Wooden is one of the most successful basketball coaches in American NCAA basketball history, with his team, UCLA, winning ten national basketball titles in 12 years. What is unique about John Wooden is the reserved and professional approach that he adopted on the sideline during games. Occasionally, he would become animated but for the most part he was reserved and in control, with his team more often than not coming out on top. This was very much in contrast to his contemporaries, who would often be seen shouting instructions to players from the sideline throughout the matches. It would appear to the uninitiated observer that Wooden was somehow different in his approach. His players without doubt had great respect for him and it seems clear that he had equally great respect for them. There is certainly something about John Wooden that all leisure and sport managers can learn from.

What was it about his leadership, coaching, teaching and management style that led to his success? John Wooden developed what he called the pyramid of success. This was based on years paying great attention to detail. Wooden would keep meticulous records of every training session. He would have detailed notes on every player and would regularly discuss each player's performance with them, with suggestions for adjustment and improvement. This not only included player performance but genuinely caring for the player as an important member of the team. Successful

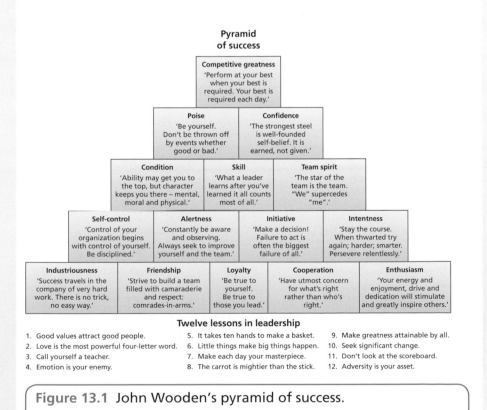

Figure 13.1 John Wooden's pyramid of success.

Source: Wooden (2005).

leadership, according to Wooden, included such attributes as industriousness, friendship, loyalty, cooperation, enthusiasm, self-control, alertness, initiative, intentness, condition, skill, team spirit, poise, confidence, patience and faith – all working together to create the structure for successful leadership and competitive greatness (Wooden, 2005). These attributes are combined to create Wooden's pyramid of success (see Figure 13.1).

Source: taken from Wooden (2005). For further information, visit Wooden's website: www.coachwooden.com

influence over others. Leaders need to inspire, communicate, support and direct. However, it is important to recognise that 'virtually every employee in the 21st century will be called upon to display leadership behaviours at some point in time' (Landy and Conte, 2009). As a consequence of this, leadership will become as much about 'followership' as it is about leadership. Leadership will need to become an important enabling behaviour rather than what has been traditionally accepted as a controlling function. One way of addressing this is through the use of 360 degree feedback and upward appraisal, where subordinates give feedback to superiors on their managerial behaviours and performance.

13.3.1 Leadership styles

There are several appropriate leadership styles (see Figure 13.2). It is not always possible to define precisely what good leadership is but, unlike good leadership, a person with poor leadership exhibits a wide range of easily recognisable traits: aloofness, insensitivity to others, intimidating manner, abrasiveness, overbearing, over-supervising, failing to delegate, seeking praise first instead of giving praise to colleagues, blaming, finding scapegoats, indecision and so on.

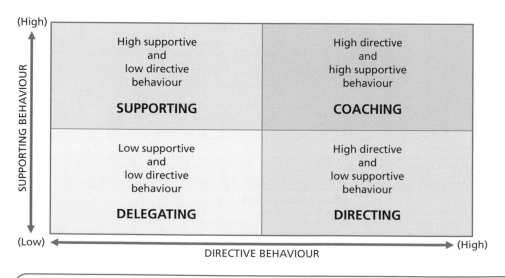

Figure 13.2 Leadership styles.

A leader's style should be flexible enough to change to suit the situation. Leaders have to balance the big picture – the vision – with the details. What they find is that little things matter – sensitivity, care, attention to detail. A false assumption is often made that a leader is one of autocratic, democratic or 'free rein'. However, most leaders tend to use many styles but with a leaning towards one, depending on the prevailing circumstances. In emergencies and critical situations – e.g. swimming pool safety or problems in opening a major event on time – autocratic and directive leadership is eminently suitable. The authoritarian/directive style can also be very effective when toughness is needed under certain conditions, even at some personal emotional cost to the leader. Leadership is not an easy option. It requires commitment, sensitivity and skill.

The 'art' of leadership involves the juxtaposition of both hearts and minds, where a blended balance is needed between the characteristics of the manager, the characteristics of the team, the type of organisation and the nature of the problem. It is in the strategy and the tactics of handling the problem that the manager's leadership skills are put to the test. Can they raise the level of employee motivation? Can staff and key user groups be persuaded to accept change readily? Can the quality and effectiveness of managerial decisions be improved? Can teamwork, morale and staff development be enhanced along with increased levels of satisfaction for the clients and customers?

Discussion questions

For a named sport of your choice, what tensions exist between the needs of the individual, the group and the organisation? For example, in professional sport there always seem to be perpetual battles between club and country. Who is best placed to resolve such issues and how?

13.3.2 Team building

A distinction needs to be made between the manager as the leader and leaders of discrete teams within the organisation, e.g. specific 'offensive' and 'defensive' teams within many sports, particularly in North America. Heller offers the advice:

> A leader must always be aware of the ultimate goals of the organisation, and know how their own objectives fit in with them. Once these goals have been established, you must ensure that your team understands the direction in which they are heading and why, and the purpose of their own activities within the overall plan. The ultimate objective should be broken down into attainable, yet challenging goals that ideally will be inspiring and motivating for the whole team. Aims should also relate directly to the specific skills of each individual within the team. Working together towards a shared goal gives people a sense of ownership and responsibility, and builds an atmosphere of team spirit.
>
> (Heller, 1998)

Heller (1998) suggests that for a team to function most effectively, there are key roles that should be filled, including: coordinator; ideas person; critic; external contact; implementer; team leader; and inspector. It is vital that all members of a team work together to maximise

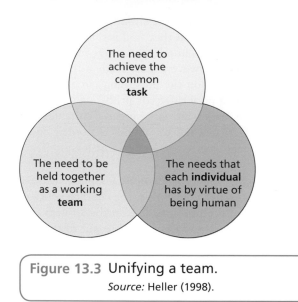

Figure 13.3 Unifying a team.
Source: Heller (1998).

team performance. Each member should be able to cover the role of at least one other member; members should be given responsibility to act on their own initiative within a team, but a large task will be better handled by the whole team being responsible for the entire project. Heller suggests that most teams place too much focus on the task and not enough on the individual. His model, shown in Figure 13.3, illustrates an 'ideal situation in which the needs of the individual, the dynamics of the group, and the requirements of the task coincide {…} to produce a unified, effective working team' (Heller, 1998).

The modes of behaviour within groups have been termed task oriented; maintenance oriented; and self-oriented. Both 'task' and 'maintenance of the team' are important in varying situations, depending on the objectives of management, whereas the behaviour within self-interested groups hinders the achievement of common goals. This behaviour can arise, for example, because individuals may be faced with problems of identity, and personal goals and needs dominate rather than the group goals and needs. For example, many health clubs operate a sales system based on individual numbers and associated commissions. This can create competitive tensions and conflict within the group, which could, in part, be resolved by introducing a commission system based more around team rather than individual targets.

Argyris (1966, 1976) suggested ten criteria, based on empirical research, that are necessary for group competence and effectiveness:

1 Contributions made within the group are additive.
2 The group moves forwards as a unit, is team spirited and there is high involvement.
3 Decisions are mainly made by consensus.
4 Commitment to a decision is strong.
5 The group continually evaluates itself.
6 The group is clear about goals.
7 It generates alternative ways of thinking about things.
8 It brings conflict into the open and deals with it.
9 It deals openly with feelings.
10 Leadership tends to go (or move) to the person most qualified.

Leaders have to deal with conflict and cooperation within and between groups. Conflict is not in itself undesirable; only through expression of differences can good problem solving take place. For everyone to agree is as unrealistic as expecting that no agreement is possible. But conflict so severe as to disable the participants and prevent the continuation of problem solving is unacceptable. One answer is to find an overriding goal – one which both (or all) groups accept as essential to reach and which all can reach. For example, the success of professional team sports is predicated upon maintaining a competitive balance between the teams and ensuring the uncertainty of outcome and thus excitement for the customers or fans. Even though competition between teams is intense, there is a collective recognition that equalising the power of teams is in the best interests of all major stakeholders. This applies to a range of different contexts from Formula One motor racing to the draft pick system in American sports, where the weakest teams are able to recruit the best college players with the most potential.

Bennis (1989) suggests that ingredients for good leadership today include: a guiding vision; passion; integrity; trust; and curiosity and daring. A great deal depends on what we want to accomplish. As Covey (1992) says, 'Begin with the end in mind'. Adair and Reed (2003) have a chapter entitled 'Humility' – leadership as a form of service. Adair and Reed use the strapline: 'the task of leadership is not to put greatness into humanity, but to elicit it, for the greatness is already there.'

In summary, the manager must be a successful leader in order to be effective. The manager must seek to better understand themselves, their staff and their customers. The manager recognises that a high degree of subordinate-centred behaviour in helping to run an organisation raises employee teamwork and morale. But this does not mean that a manager leaves all decisions to the staff. Situations vary and staff vary. Staff readiness and ability are important. The successful leader will behave appropriately in the light of their perceptions of the people and the situations. In addition to leading personally, the manager must recognise that many subordinates fulfil important leadership roles themselves. They too need training in the 'art' of effective leadership. Leadership may result in the successful completion of a task, but effective leadership occurs when the team of staff not only completes the task, but does so willingly and, typically, is involved in the decision-making process that produces positive results.

13.3.3 Management communication

Rather than persuading, communication should ideally be two-way. The argument for two-way communication is not only a moral one; it is also a practical one because the manager will become more effective by encouraging the group members to make full use of their abilities. Drucker put the argument against the purely persuasive approach to communication in the following way:

> In many cases human relations has been used to manipulate, to adjust people to what the boss thinks is reality; to make them conform to a pattern that seems logical from

the top down, to make them accept unquestionably what we tell them. Frankly, sometimes, I think it is better not to tell employees anything rather than to say 'We tell
them everything, but they must accept it, and it is our job to make them accept it.'

(Drucker, 1955)

Forcing one-way communication on to people without their understanding and without
understanding them makes for poor management. Such decisions could be classed as mis-
judgements, particularly where 'the boss' may not have the legitimate authority to make
such decisions. Commenting on the reaction of county cricket executives to the early
involvement of Giles Clarke, the Chairman of the England and Wales Cricket Board (ECB),
with the ill-fated American investment banker Alan Stanford, Wilde writes:

> By far their most damaging allegation, though, is that Clarke {...} and David Collier,
> his chief executive, did not inform other members of the 12 man ECB Board that
> Stanford had been granted options to sponsor the English Premier League starting in
> 2010 {...} 'It is a disgrace that board members were not informed of the details con-
> cerning Stanford's involvement with the EPL' one said, 'it is a very serious breach. At
> the end of the day they (board members) are held to account for what is done in their
> name.'

(Wilde, 2008)

In many ways this is no different from a manager of a sport or leisure organisation making
decisions without consulting staff that directly affect customers, which staff members are
then held to account for as part of their daily duties.

13.3.4 Coaching, mentoring and motivational leadership

Like sports players and teams, leisure management staff and teams can benefit from coaching and mentoring. Coaching and mentoring can inspire learning through practical experience and help promote real personal performance gains. Moreover, they may both facilitate
and enhance personal learning by an associated development in self-awareness. Through
both approaches staff can be encouraged to undertake new tasks, improve performance,
develop new skills, learn how to solve problems and become even more valuable members
of the team.

Good business coaching will work with staff to help release their latent potential, by
encouraging them to become more aware of their individual motivations and decision-
making processes. Good business coaches need to be very good listeners and work closely
with staff, usually over the relatively short term, to help them solve their own business or
sometimes personal challenges. They will encourage and facilitate self-reflection through
asking open questions such as: 'What would you say is the real issue here?', 'What's the
most important priority?', 'What barriers exist?', 'What options do you have?', 'What are
the first steps in moving this forward?', 'How will you know when you have achieved this?'
As such, business coaches do not offer specific advice, but skilfully encourage learners to
solve their own problems.

A mentor, on the other hand, is an experienced guide – a believer, an understander, promoting the cause and showing the way – who can make a lasting impression on an individual's life over the longer term by offering advice and guidance based upon direct personal
experience. An effective mentor–mentee relationship provides a helping hand, inspires
mutual trust, loyalty and friendship and, unlike businesses coaching, can be directive in

nature by offering advice such as 'I don't think that's the best way forward' and 'I think, based on my experience and knowledge, what you need to do is this'.

The bond between mentor and mentee is an emotional one, based upon mutual respect, and requires time to mature. In this process, the mentee absorbs an approach, a style, a life-view which can shape their future. The mentor can open doors for their mentee for which, without them, it's unlikely there would be a key. In contrast, the business coach works with employees over a relatively short period of time and offers no direct advice, instead helping the participants to develop their own, bespoke, problem solving skills in response to specific performance-related objectives.

We have considered the different interpretations of management versus leadership and shown how important the human side can be to the effective management of sport and leisure. Leadership, decision-making, communications and an understanding of group behaviour are key components. Management must be appropriate to different situations, and the manager must adapt his or her style of management to changing situations. It is clear that a manager armed with only one style of management may be ill equipped for the variety of different tasks and people to be handled – just like a golfer with only one club.

The business of sport and leisure requires staff to be flexible and work unsocial hours, and it calls for styles of leadership in keeping with providing good customer service and care of staff. In these circumstances, the 'democratic' manager with a professional 'executive style' is more likely to succeed. Such a manager will see the job as effectively maximising the efforts of others. The manager's commitment to both tasks and relationships will be evident to all. These managers often work with a team; ideas can come from any quarter; and the greater number of possibilities explored, the better the understanding of the problem. As Hammer (1996) argues, 'Managers will coach and design rather than supervise and control.' However, they still have to lead – they cannot hide behind the team – and they still have to make the ultimate decision; but both manager and staff feel involved in the successes and failures. Setanta, the sports broadcasting media organisation, provides a good example of this. After the collapse of its funding, caused by the worldwide financial crisis, employees are reported to have stood up and applauded when the owners told their staff that the company was to go into administration (Robinson, 2009). Staff appeared genuinely appreciative of the hard work and openness with which they had all attempted to push through the crisis and were aware that the deciding factors were largely outside the business's short-term control.

Of course, whilst issues of leadership are critical to the involvement, motivation and development of staff, they will always exist within the structural context of the organisation.

13.4 The impact and importance of organisational structure

An organisation's structure represents the way in which the work is organised and shared out and the manner in which an enterprise is managed. Every sport or leisure organisation, from the smallest to the largest, has an organisation and staffing structure of some kind. Used effectively, the structure provides the framework through which the work processes are operationalised in order to achieve organisational objectives.

Of course, whilst there are many 'structural' models that help us to understand such fundamental organisational building blocks, their 'effective' operation is always subject to a range of tensions. These include the developing needs of the customer in relation to constantly changing levels of competition. Such issues act collectively and cumulatively to create either a positive organisational culture or one that subverts the original intention of the initial structural arrangements. In other words, it is rarely as simple as merely delegating the roles and responsibilities needed for the organisation to fulfil its overall mission and underlying business objectives. In the real world, the ability to understand and respond positively to such challenges is critical to the role of the manager.

13.4.1 The need for appropriate structures

There is a considerable variance in the staffing structures, the types of staff and the levels of staffing needed within sport and leisure organisations. For example in public leisure, subsidised by the public purse and subject to local government administrative systems and standardised procedures, one might expect to find a considerable level of uniformity. However, different localities have different facilities and different circumstances and wide variations can and do exist in the structures employed by local authorities. Moreover, there are also likely to be differences in the backgrounds, interests and aspirations of staff at all levels of the organisational hierarchy, as well as differences in their employment status, e.g. full time, part time, temporary, casual and voluntary.

> ### Discussion question
>
> Identify the likely similarities and differences between full-time, part-time, casual, temporary and voluntary workers in terms of knowledge, experience, commitment and motivation. For a major sporting event such as the New York Marathon, what possible differences will the employment status of workers make to customer experiences?

Many leisure facilities, particularly in the voluntary sector, are managed by a leader and volunteers. They take responsibility for facilities, machinery, programme and personnel. However, as is often the case with voluntary sport organisations in particular, there is a lack of formal human resource systems and processes. Reporting on non-profit organisations in New South Wales, Australia, Taylor and McGraw (2006) found that 'despite pressures to become more strategic in their people management, only a minority of these sport organisations have formal HRM systems'.

This is also often the case in professional sports organisations, which typically have a relatively small number of employees and struggle to justify the expense of a functional human resources department or even human resources specialists. This leads to a particular culture within an organisation which can be difficult to change, as Case Study 13.2 demonstrates.

For most sport and leisure organisations, staffing takes the largest share of operating costs. This is particularly the case in professional sports, where player wages and transfer fees can have a significant effect upon the operational bottom line of the organisation. If the business model is not set up to deal with market variations, then companies can find themselves in financial difficulty. In times of economic stringency staffing reductions are a common method of reducing deficits and/or increasing net returns. It is therefore important to provide a clear justification for the most appropriate levels and methods of organising staff for the prevailing organisational objectives and market environment. Otherwise there is a risk of indiscriminate staff cuts, which may harm organisational performance.

Manchester City FC

Manchester City Football Club has seen huge changes during the period 2005–10, particularly during the latter part of the decade, with £200 million of new football talent brought into the club during 2009. This followed the takeover of the club, in September 2008, by the Abu Dhabi United group and a newly appointed club chairman, Khaldoon al-Mubarak, making them one of the richest football clubs in the world.

On the pitch changes have also been matched by off-field changes in the long-term strategic management and organisation of the club, including the decision by Garry Cook, the club's new Chief Executive, to initiate quarterly staff meetings at the new Eastlands Stadium. However, whilst this may seem great news for the club, it is not without its problems. Conn, commenting on his observation of the meetings, reveals:

> His shtick is not, it has to be said, going down noticeably well with the people who receive it mostly in silence, arms folded. Cook introduces Mark Allen, head of the newly established human resources department and part of an executive team recruited after Khaldoon expressed his shock at the 'amateurish' structure of the club on his arrival. Allen unveils an impending culture of appraisals, formal feedback and pay reviews, sweetened by a significant new benefit.
>
> 'We will be announcing,' he says proudly, 'private medical cover for all staff.' Even this is not greeted with quite the whooping and hollering that Cook might have expected in his previous job, at Nike's US headquarters. Manchester City have always been more of a National Health Service, not private medical cover, kind of a football club.
>
> (Conn, 2009a)

It will clearly take some staff some time to make the appropriate adjustments to the attention to detail and newly instigated human resources processes, focused around the needs of the key stakeholders (customers, players, etc.). This process needs to be handled sensitively as it would appear to involve a fundamental change in the prevailing organisational culture of the club. As such it is likely that there will be tensions between the old working practices and the new professional approach adopted by the new owners. Clearly, Cook appears to be adopting a 'carrot and stick' approach that identifies and rewards appropriate behaviours as a prelude to a more substantive shift in organisational values and performance. As Khaldoon explains, 'We like to take a long-term view {...} As long as the foundations are there, you have to allow the business to run. It is no different in football' (quoted in Conn, 2009a).

Cook's professional, business-oriented and customer-focused approach is, according to Conn (2009a), reported to have gone down well with another key set of the club's stakeholders, i.e. the Manchester City fans. These are reported to be eager to embrace the new era for the club and the newfound sensitivity to their needs. This is nothing overtly radical in management terms, but merely represents a willingness to listen to the needs of consumers in the new, professional culture of service provision and management. It is inevitable, therefore, that this will be reflected in the way that staff are organised and managed.

The way in which such organisational change is implemented will be key to ongoing performance enhancements. Conversely, at least over the short term, this may result in negative consequences as individuals struggle to adapt. This is equally applicable to the players. As Johnson *et al.* (2005) suggest, '[p]oor performance might be the result of an inappropriate configuration for the situation or inconsistency between structure, process and relationships'. In other words, the structure of Manchester City might seem right in managerial terms, but this may not reflect the uniqueness of the football club culture established over many years prior to the Abu Dhabi takeover. In real terms, this is likely to take some time to become embedded in the foundations and habitual practices of existing employees.

Portsmouth Football Club became the first Premier League club in England to go into administration during March 2010. According to Kelso (2010), 'drastic cuts saw 20 full-time and 65 part-time staff made redundant across all departments of the club, reducing the staff from 320 to 235 with the possibility of more redundancies to come'. Paradoxically the most expensive staff, the players, are not for sale as the administrator's objective is to sell on the club as a going concern. In order to accomplish this it is deemed necessary to retain the club's prize assets in order to attract potential buyers. Such short-term decisions may lead to longer-term negative revenue consequences, as both the staff and the customer experience are likely to be diminished.

Staff flexibility is required in sport and leisure, because of the multiplicity of tasks and the typically long opening hours. This should be mirrored by organisation and employer flexibility. It needs mutual dependency and interest to work together in the spirit of teamwork. This is difficult to achieve but when it is achieved the impact can be dramatic. Arguably, one of the greatest team sporting achievements of recent times is by the Great Britain track cycling team, which won nine out of a possible 18 gold medals at the 2008 Beijing Olympics. Although the performance director, Dave Brailsford, is formally the leader, in reality:

> For a sports team at the highest level, it is a highly unusual structure. This is no one-man operation headed by a forceful individual; while Brailsford is where the buck stops, the four senior managers seem to enjoy an equal say in decision-making at a strategic level.
>
> (Fotheringham, 2008)

One of GB track cycling's senior managers is the ex-Olympic gold medallist Chris Boardman, who is responsible for equipment and coach development. For Boardman, the critical ingredient is that they all have the same strategic goals of being the best in the world. These override any other personal agendas and produce a true team performance, designed to produce the very best track performances by blending management, coaches, athletes and equipment in perfect harmony. If only such ingredients could be easily replicated across all sport and leisure organisations!

13.4.2 The principles of management that affect staffing

Some top-level managers and senior personnel are called upon to formulate policies and organisational structures. Most managers, however, are appointed to positions in existing organisations, to which they have to adapt. It is important that managers at all levels understand the organisational structure, the principles on which it is based and the components which go to make it up.

According to the International City Management Association (1965), three basic principles of management must be considered in establishing an organisational structure, namely: unity of command; logical assignment; and span of control. In this context, it is also important to consider two further variables, namely employee engagement, and authority and power.

13.4.2.1 Unity of command

This principle states that each individual in an organisation should be responsible to only one superior. Adherence to this principle establishes a precise chain of command within the organisation. However, situations exist in sport and leisure organisations which do not follow such a principle. For example, the head groundsman can play a pivotal role in the outcome of any number of sporting encounters. However, always assuming the availability of appropriate staff at critical moments, does the groundsman answer to the chief executive, the stadium operations manager, the coaches, the sporting captain, the 'star' players or the referee/umpire? All represent important stakeholders in the process. Just with this relatively simple example, one can easily detect the potential for miscommunication, misunderstandings and structural problems to emerge.

As a consequence, sport and leisure managers need to be careful when considering unity of command as it is grounded in very traditional approaches to structure and management, based on the principle of control and command. This has benefits in terms of clarity of role and lines of responsibility and may function better in organisations where there are many habitual and non-contestable tasks to perform. However, in an increasingly dynamic and competitive environment, requiring more not less flexibility, sport and leisure organisations need staff who can take the initiative and welcome autonomy.

Discussion questions

Traditionally, it would be the decision-makers, towards the top of the organisational hierarchy, who would dictate structural arrangements within sport and/or leisure organisations, e.g. in a sports centre or a theatre. To what extent do you think staff would be comfortable in engaging in the process of deciding organisational structures? What would be the advantages and disadvantages of involving staff in this process?

13.4.2.2 Employee engagement

MacLeod and Clarke (2009) wrote a seminal government report looking at the issue of employee engagement. This has many different facets but central to it is the following supposition:

> If employee engagement and the principles that lie behind it were more widely understood, if good practice was more widely shared, if the potential that resides in the country's workforce was more fully unleashed, we could see a step change in workplace performance and in employee well-being, for the considerable benefit of the UK.
>
> (MacLeod and Clarke, 2009)

Despite this, there is recognition that there are a significant number of employees in the UK and elsewhere who do not feel engaged in their working life. This has much in common with the central concept of 'empowerment' developed throughout this chapter. MacLeod and Clarke (2009) identify several barriers to this within the workplace in both public and private sector organisations. There are many managers who cannot see the potential use of the idea and/or do not understand the concept or how to introduce it. Those managers who do recognise the potential relevance of employee engagement may not be well supported by others. Unsurprisingly, the report identified that leadership and management were seen to be pivotal to employee engagement. Leadership is fundamental in order to offer an appropriate organisational culture, based on mutual trust and integrity. Management should then enable a greater staff voice by supporting and encouraging staff participation, requiring regular feedback and appropriate coaching for staff, working towards common operational and strategic goals.

13.4.2.3 Logical assignment

This principle states that staff doing the same work should be grouped together and that work is planned and scheduled in a logical order. Without logical assignment, there can be duplication or overlap, confusion and power struggles. Effective structural arrangements can help to reduce the negative consequences of such micro-politics. Managers need to give much more consideration to wider issues of organisational health through actively promoting behaviours designed to deliver openness and trust within the organisation. This is as much to do with a consistent leadership style and organisational culture as it is to do with structural arrangements.

In September 2008 Kevin Keegan walked away from his job as manager of Newcastle United Football Club over a dispute with the owner concerning player recruitment. Keegan alleges that he was assured he would have the final word over player recruitment, while the club's owner, Mike Ashley, had recruited several 'inexperienced people to key positions because, it is said, they were his friends and he trusted them' (Conn, 2009b). These included an executive director of football, a vice president in charge of player recruitment and a technical coordinator. When it became clear to Keegan that his authority had been usurped by these structural arrangements, he decided that his position was untenable. Keegan's position was vindicated by the Premier League's arbitration panel when, in October 2009, he received £2 million in compensation for 'constructive dismissal'.

This was arguably the most high profile case of its kind at the time, but it was also reflective of a trend amongst Premier League clubs to move to a more 'continental system' of structuring football clubs. Under this system, managers are appointed to run the non-playing side of the game, with various titles such as 'Director of Football', whilst 'Head Coaches' are appointed to take care of first team football. This represents standard operating practice for a number of successful European clubs such as Bayern Munich, AC Milan, Barcelona and Real Madrid.

Professional sport often represents a multi-million pound business and so it is logical to argue that it makes little sense to make one person responsible for all aspects of the organisation, particularly when their only qualifications might be sports coaching related. Historically, football managers in the UK are appointed because of their football knowledge not because of their business qualifications and experience. The lesson here is that what might appear logical on paper may prove unworkable in practice.

13.4.2.4 Span of control

Span of control is a rather limited concept, as the need to 'control' staff has to be balanced with the need to also empower and engage them. A better term might be 'span of management'. It is not possible to state the exact number of people a manager should 'control'.

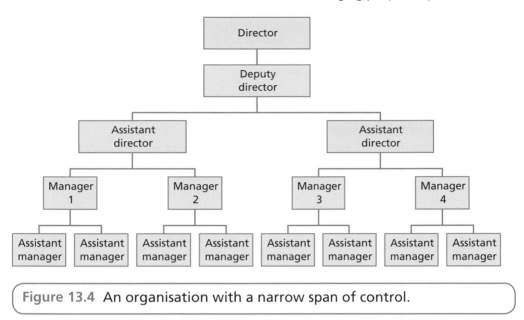

Figure 13.4 An organisation with a narrow span of control.

Much depends upon the organisational context, i.e. customer requirements, organisational culture, organisational systems, competence of subordinates and the manager's own knowledge, ability, time, energy, personality and leadership.

Organisations with narrow spans of control, i.e. a relatively small number of employees to supervise (see Figure 13.4) enhance the manager's ability to balance the need to both control and engage staff. This can improve horizontal communication within levels, but is likely to work against vertical communication up and down an increased number of hierarchical levels. Hence, narrow spans of control tend to require more tiers of management, more managers and therefore more expense, as in the Newcastle United example above. Alternatively, wider spans of control may result in more limited direct control, but should give managers greater 'reach' across the organisation's functions (see Figure 13.5).

As a rule of thumb, organisations should only have as much structure as is needed. Structural layers can always be added later but they are notoriously difficult to remove once they are in place. There is a correlation between the number of managerial layers and the degree of managerial control. The more layers, the more control. The more control, the less potential there is for autonomy and therefore innovation. This is a tricky balancing act to achieve

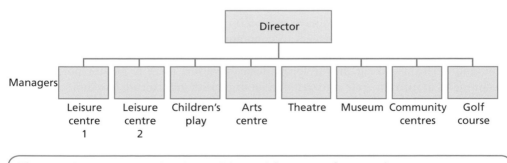

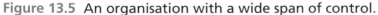

Figure 13.5 An organisation with a wide span of control.

because where the span of control is too wide both managers and their staff can become overloaded and performance can dip. Conversely, a narrow span of 'control' makes it possible to supervise work tightly but may not give staff the opportunity to make decisions or feel a sense of commitment and achievement.

> ## Discussion questions
>
> What are the main differences between span of control and span of management? How do these differences affect your view on whether a manager working closely with a small number of staff (i.e. a narrow span of control) is a good idea?

13.4.2.5 Authority and power

Too often these words are mistakenly treated as being synonymous. Authority is based upon a person's position within the organisational structure, incorporates the person's responsibilities, tasks, etc. and is, in theory, accepted by his/her subordinates as 'legitimate'. Power on the other hand is a much broader concept and relates to the person's ability to influence or persuade others to take a particular course of action. Power can come from being a leader, even without positional authority, and power can also come from being an expert – the power of knowledge.

Ideally, power will be exercised both explicitly (through direct decisions) and implicitly (through the prevailing organisational culture) for the common good of all stakeholders. As a consequence, employees will be both extrinsically and intrinsically motivated to perform well against their given role. However, in reality what may be claimed to be good for the fulfilment of wider organisational objectives may be to the detriment of staff, who are asked to do more with less.

Increasingly the role of a manager should be more about enabling and empowerment than it is about the use of managerial power as a form of command and control. Empowerment, in a human resource context, implies a genuine caring for colleagues and their development, in line with the prevailing organisational objectives and customer requirements. This is seen as a more effective way of achieving objectives than a model that is based on subordination and control. Unfortunately, many sport and leisure organisations are still dominated by more traditional roles, based on hierarchy, power and subordination of the many to the position and power of the few. This problem is illustrated by Case Study 13.3.

The traditional approach does have short-term benefits, as it is often perceived to be both quicker and easier for managers to communicate 'one-way' instructions than it is for them to engage in the trickier and more time-consuming process of 'two-way' dialogue and decision-making. In the longer term however, there is greater potential for commitment, motivation and innovation in an organisational culture based on empowerment and mutual development. This is particularly important for sports organisations, many of which are reliant upon governing bodies to both control and develop their sport.

Clearly, the environment (internal and external) is rarely fixed but instead is in a state of flux around changing perceptions of who holds the most power. For example, in October 2009 Jack Warner, a highly influential member of FIFA's Executive Committee, comment-

CASE STUDY 13.3

Formula One motor racing

Max Mosley was the President of the Fédération Internationale de l'Automobile (FIA) from 1993 until he agreed to relinquish the reins in October 2009 following a power struggle with key stakeholders in Formula One. The FIA is a non-profit-making organisation that controls worldwide motor sport. However, despite overseeing many positive developments, Mosley's reign was controversial during his final years and nearly led to the demise of Formula One motor racing, with many of the major teams threatening to start their own race series, complaining of the autocratic style of Mosley and his unwillingness to listen to their views. This demonstrates that sports governing bodies must seek to tread a fine line between exercising appropriate levels of control and balancing this with a willingness to listen to the views of stakeholders in an effort to develop the sport.

Importantly, it also demonstrates the key role that personalities and leadership style can play in fashioning the future of sport. Jean Todt, Mosley's successor, was elected FIA President on the promise of more collaboration, not conflict, and the prospect of a new commissioner for all of the FIA world championships. This represents another tier in the structure but does provide a means by which one person can work with the differing stakeholders involved in each of the FIAs worldwide race portfolios. Arguably, this provides a more appropriate span of management by providing a better unity of command and logical assignment of roles. The new structure provides the opportunity for much more constructive dialogue to develop between all the stakeholders who are fundamental to the future development of the sport.

What this example shows is that sport and leisure organisations do not exist in a vacuum and must look at both external and internal factors when considering changes to the way in which staff are managed. This, in turn, is influenced by the way that both formal and informal relationships are cultivated between key stakeholders.

ing on England's bid for the 2018 football World Cup warned 'My [FIFA] colleagues are saying very quietly that the guys who are coming to them are lightweight. This is the type of thing that loses you a bid' (quoted in Watt, 2009). Arguably, such comments precipitated difficulties within the England bid team, leading to resignations, recriminations and a restructuring of the team. It also led to a more high profile involvement from world sports stars such as David Beckham and to a subsequent meeting between Jack Warner and the UK's Prime Minister.

Discussion questions

To what extent are authority and power barriers to effective employee engagement? Are there any circumstances when it is not sensible to engage/empower staff?

13.5 Formal and informal organisations

There is a need to distinguish between informal and formal organisations. A formal organisation has a clearly defined structure that establishes relationships and differences in status, role, rank and levels of authority, in a controlled environment where rules exist with regard to channels of communication, accepted forms of behaviour and the manner in which key tasks have to be undertaken. Additionally, such organisations have defined outcomes and in order to achieve these the overall work is divided amongst the workforce in a coordinated way so that they function as a unit or a department. In contrast an informal organisation has a much less defined structure. It is also likely to be much smaller in size and more likely to have a shorter lifespan. In certain circumstances an informal organisation will be converted into a formal one, e.g. an interest group forming a club or society with rules and a constitution.

Handy's work on organisational culture is worth considering in relation to formal and informal organisational types. Handy (1985) usefully categorises organisations into four cultural types:

- **role culture** – based on rules and procedures;
- **people culture** – based on the needs of individuals;
- **power culture** – based on the dominance of powerful individuals and groups over others;
- **task culture** – based on the need to carry out and achieve tasks.

This last cultural type is considered to be the most effective as it focuses on activities and jobs of work. In practice each of the above cultural types exists side by side in most organisations, often with one dominant culture being evident.

Informal relationships facilitate lateral communication, rather than 'going through the channels', even in formal organisations. Informal, two-way communication leads to improved understanding with both internal and external stakeholders. Much of the important 'human' work which makes an organisation 'tick' is undertaken through informal communication. While formal structures are required, managers should also encourage effective informal structures to enable the essential human dimension and improve decision-making. For example, at Disney the park designers regularly consult cleaning supervisors, as they are best placed to receive market intelligence from around the parks concerning what works and what doesn't for customers. This process, which is both formal and informal in nature, cuts across organisational boundaries and space and time allocations for staff.

Discussion question

Do you think the balance of formal and informal processes differs between the three main sectors of provision: commercial, public and third sector? Think of sport or leisure examples to illustrate your discussion.

13.5.1 Designing formal structures

Forming an organisational structure is like creating a structure from building blocks – the work unit or the job of an individual worker is the smallest building block in the structure as a whole. Organising is the process of dividing up the work in a structured framework. Managers have distinct tasks in setting up the staffing structure:

- dividing the work tasks into jobs that are considered important to the customer experience;
- grouping similar tasks, usually by forming sections, units or departments;
- specifying and controlling the relationships between the groups;
- delegating authority for carrying out the jobs or group of jobs – this is normally done via 'chains of command';
- specifying the authority or control over the groups, which can be centralised or decentralised to varying levels.

In designing the above structural arrangements, managers need to be aware of the extent to which employees have control of the nature, flow and type of work that is allocated to them through the formal structural arrangements. Butler (1991) defines structure 'as providing a relatively enduring set of rules for decision making'. This is important, as the nature of decision-making will have an impact on employee engagement and the crucial relationship between managers and staff. Professional sport provides a good illustration of this. Sports coaches and managers are heavily involved in the preparation and training stages before matches. However, once the contest begins there is only limited support that can be given. Ultimately, it is the responsibility of the sportsmen and women to make the correct choices during the sporting contest. It is incumbent upon the support staff to prepare front of house staff to produce the results demanded by the customers.

Chandler (2005) suggests that structure should follow strategy. However, the creation of strategy is in itself a challenging task and does not always account for the political realities that managers face in their daily work situations. Sport and leisure managers often have to react to changes in the external environment that dictate the flow, pattern and types of decisions that are eventually taken. Structures need to be suited to strategy but also flexible enough to service change and innovation.

13.5.2 Departmental structures

To be effective, managers must divide the workload into manageable parts. The main purpose of dividing the work is to establish methods of determining section responsibilities, the distribution of authority to individuals and the processes of delegation. The most widely used method of dividing work is departmentalisation – dividing the workforce into units and departments. In constructing work patterns it is important as far as possible to match the needs of individuals to the needs of the work to be done, with the essential requirement for staff engagement and innovation.

Sport and leisure managers need to be careful when dividing workloads up that the process does not become overly mechanistic. This may stifle innovation and restrict the possibilities created by dynamic change and staff empowerment. Clearly a balance is needed between dividing work up and creating enough space for innovation, creativity and the ability to respond to dynamic change.

13.5.3 Different organisation structures

The various organisational structures used by sport and leisure organisations fall on a continuum between a mechanistic model which is rigidly structured, at one extreme, and an organic model which is flexibly structured, at the other (see Figure 13.6). The different

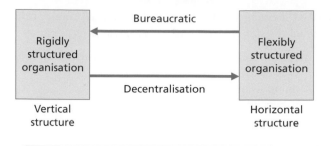

Figure 13.6 The mechanistic–organic continuum.

models are outlined below, together with their characteristics: either more 'vertical' or more 'horizontal', and more or less 'bureaucratic'. Within the compass of these various parameters are some specific 'models', and four are considered briefly: bureaucracy; the 'pyramid'; the matrix structure; and hybrid structures.

The mechanistic extreme is comprised of formal structures, hierarchical communications and standardised tasks, and power resides at the highest level. The organic extreme is more likely to have informal structures, with more lateral communication and shared ownership of tasks for those with the appropriate knowledge and experience. Control, authority and communications at the organic extreme move through a wide horizontal network.

13.5.3.1 Bureaucracy

The bureaucratic model is the most widely implemented form of organisational structure. It is a vertical structure. Authority is located at the top of the hierarchy and flows downwards through the organisation. The division of labour emphasises the hierarchical structure and establishes a superior/subordinate relationship. This allows the various activities to be subdivided into a specific set of tasks, with the roles of individuals clearly defined. There is great benefit in such an approach in terms of clarity of role and lines of communication and authority.

However, in Handy's terms the role cultures in this model are based on rules and procedures. In such organisational cultures there is the potential for what has been termed 'goal displacement'. This is where the means and ends get confused. In other words, the rules become more important than the outcomes. So, for example, it would be more important to follow rules and procedures even if objectives, customer needs and performance were negatively affected by this type of behaviour and action.

13.5.3.2 The pyramid

Peter (1986) demonstrates the ways in which proliferating bureaucracies sap human resources. He perceives that the problem with major organisations is that they are constructed upside down, with the point of the operation almost invisible underneath the baggage of top-heavy administration. Instead the pyramid should be turned upside down so that all senior staff are supporting more junior staff at the point of customer delivery – the primary purpose of most organisations in this area. Paradoxically, a sport/leisure organisation, looking to prune expenditure, often cuts jobs at the lower, delivery levels – the customer service elements such as receptionists, grounds staff, coaching staff, cleaners, attendants – often the solution least likely to affect a cure and one more likely to impact negatively on customer satisfaction (see the Portsmouth example on p. 352).

13.5.3.3 The matrix structure

The matrix structure (Figure 13.7) is normally a combination of a functional, departmental structure with an overlay of project managers, who are responsible for completing specific topics, e.g. a feasibility study for a new sport/leisure facility. In this example the project manager can call upon the expertise in the different departments to assist in the production of the feasibility study: personnel services on staffing aspects; technical services on producing the designs and projections of capital costs, etc. The advantage of this structure is that it concentrates on the task in hand; technical experts are used as and when required.

For example, part of the project brief for many new sports stadia involves a consideration of environmental impact and sustainability. Recent examples include the new Olympic stadium for the London 2012 Olympics and the proposed new stadium and training ground for Tottenham Hotspur Football Club. This requires specialist expertise to be integrated into an eco-friendly design brief, both for altruistic reasons and to promote a more acceptable image to future stakeholders, particularly sponsors.

Unfortunately, problems can also be encountered when using this form of organisation such as role conflict and role ambiguity – is he or she working for the department or for the project? This situation can produce tensions, work overload, or provide inadequate or too much authority to the project manager. Inadequate resources and authority can delay the project and result in time-consuming negotiation and meetings. In order to make a matrix organisation effective, there is a need for a multi-disciplinary team and effective teamwork. Objectives need to be clearly defined and known by all and delegated authority given at a senior level.

13.5.3.4 Hybrid structures

The delivery of leisure products and services calls for flexibility and adaptability – different forms of organisational structure will suit different situations. Commercial sports management, charitable trust management, partnership management and volunteer management have different psychological, structural and resource needs. As such, they may require a variety of 'hybrid' structural arrangements. Sports, arts and outdoor leisure often call for specially created forms of 'looser' organisational structures. In such leisure environments,

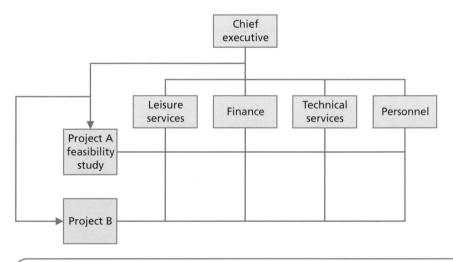

Figure 13.7 Matrix organisation.

with outreach workers, wardens, coaches, teachers and voluntary support groups, there will be a need to cultivate a flexible management regime. The roles and responsibilities may be fluid and subject to an iterative process of negotiation. As Wolsey and Whitrod-Brown argue:

> the management of people in sport represents a number of unique challenges for the industry. Whilst traditional industrial relationships are governed by employment contracts and the exchange of personal time and effort for monetary gain, this does not apply to many volunteers working across the industry. As a consequence, it is the psychological contract that is fundamental to understanding the perceptions, behaviours and success of many volunteers in this area.
>
> (Wolsey and Whitrod-Brown, 2003)

As a consequence, the motivations of a variety of full-time, part-time, casual and volunteer workers must be taken into account when considering the correct combination of organisational structures. For example, the ongoing training and development needs of an Olympic athlete are very different from those of a short-term volunteer at a one-off sporting event. Both need guidance and inspiration to give their best performance. However, whilst athletes may be willing to run through brick walls in the pursuit of personal excellence, this is not the primary goal for most sports volunteers. The organisational structure must reflect such differences and must serve to enhance personal motivations, not stifle them.

If used wisely, organisational structures provide a framework in which individual and group ambitions can flourish. For most volunteers, for example, the requirement to adopt a more professional approach is often viewed as a bureaucratic imposition from full-time governing body staff. Because most structures emphasise hierarchies, they confer status and 'pecking orders'. Some managers therefore become over-concerned with preserving and enhancing the organisational structure itself and their own position within it, rather than using it to serve the aims and objectives of the organisation.

All organisations, particularly those involved in sport and leisure, represent a social network of relationships and ongoing transactions, leading to the fulfilment, or otherwise, of customer requirements, individual needs and organisational objectives. The trick is to ensure that all these factors are catered for simultaneously and in a way that offers something valuable and unique to the market, particularly with reference to the people who work hard to deliver such products and services.

13.6 Conclusions

This chapter has demonstrated that sport and leisure management requires high quality leaders, managers and staff. Managers in the industry will need continuing professional development in order to respond positively to the dynamics of the external government and business environments. Managers need to be aware of more flexible ways of working, in order to deliver a committed, dynamic and highly motivated workforce. This workforce needs to be well placed to respond to both current and future competitive challenges in this important and expanding area of the economy. To accomplish this, there is an increased need to consider more progressive models of management, which are more about employee empowerment and development than about the traditional and arguably outdated models of management based only upon notions of command and control. This requires sensitivity, skill and, above all, effective leadership.

Practical tasks

1 Consider the structural arrangements of the sport/leisure organisation that you work(ed) for or that you are familiar with. Describe them in relation to the structural types outlined in the chapter (i.e. bureaucratic, pyramid, matrix and hybrid). Is this structure fit for purpose – does it service the organisation's objectives? What are its advantages and disadvantages for individual, group and organisational performance? How could it be improved?

2 Using generic and leisure-specific literature, identify the characteristics that are considered to differentiate sport and/or leisure provision from other areas of the economy. For example, what are the differences between providing products and services? Are there differences between sport and other parts of the leisure industry? What implications exist for people management and human resource practices in such areas?

3 Consider a sport governing body that you are aware of. Identify how it is structured by using its website or other documents. Who are the key stakeholders? Who are the key power brokers (individuals and organisations), and why? How does this relate to Handy's typology of organisational culture? What evidence can you find regarding how effectively the various stakeholders work together?

Structured guide to further reading

For generic textbooks on human resources management:

Bratton, J. and Gold, J. (2007) *Human Resource Management: theory & practice*, 4th edition, Palgrave Macmillan, Basingstoke.

Collings, D.G. and Wood, G. (ed.) (2009) *Human Resource Management: a critical approach*, Routledge, London.

Legge, K. (2005) *Human Resource Management: rhetoric & realities*, anniversary edition (Management, Work and Organisations), Macmillan Business, London.

Stewart, J., Rigg, C. and Trehan, K. (eds) (2007) *Critical Human Resource Development: beyond orthodoxy*, Prentice Hall, Harlow.

For sport and leisure human resources management:

Chellandurai, P. (2006) *Human Resource Management in Sport and Recreation*, 2nd edition, Human Kinetics, Champaign, IL.

Chellandurai, P. and Madella, A. (2006) *Human Resource Management in Olympic Sport Organizations*, Human Kinetics, Leeds.

Cuskelly, G., Hoye, R. and Auld, C. (2006) *Working with Volunteers in Sport: theory and practice*, Routledge, London.

Flannery, T. and Swank, M. (1999) *Personnel Management for Sport Directors*, Human Kinetics, Leeds.

Lashley, C. and Lee-Ross, D. (2003) *Organisational Behaviour for Leisure Services*, Butterworth-Heinemann, Oxford.

Taylor, T., Doherty, A. and McGraw, P. (2008) *Managing People in Sport Organizations; a strategic human resource management perspective*, Butterworth-Heinemann, London.

Wolsey, C., Abrams, J. and Minten, S. (forthcoming) *Human Resource Management in the Sport and Leisure Industry*, Routledge, London.

Useful websites

For general human resources management:
Chartered Management Institute, www.managers.org.uk
Chartered Institute of Personnel & Development, www.cipd.co.uk

For sport and leisure human resource management:
Skills Active, www.skillsactive.com
Institute for Sport, Parks and Leisure, www.ispal.org.uk
Institute of Sport and Recreation Management, www.isrm.co.uk/
UK Sport, www.uksport.gov.uk
Sports Business Publications, www.sportsbusiness.com
Sport Industry Group, www.sportindustry.biz
Street & Smith's, www.sportsbusinessjournal.com
Press Association, www.pressassociation/sport.html
http://pressassociation/entertainment.html
http://pressassociation/business-information.html

Chapter 14

Planning for sport and leisure

In this chapter

- What are the main purposes of planning for sport and leisure?
- What are the main processes and principles in planning?
- What is the government function in planning?
- How does government guide planning for sport and leisure?
- What practical leisure planning techniques are there?
- How is demand assessed?
- What is the role of public consultation in planning?

Summary

In this chapter, leisure managers are encouraged to understand key elements of the planning process and their potential involvement in it. The role of the government, the tiers in the planning system and planning processes are considered, with a focus on the UK to give the review of processes coherence. Practical techniques for sport and leisure planning are also examined, with a focus on understanding leisure demands.

The accurate assessment of leisure demand is at the heart of good leisure planning. This mirrors the importance of knowledge of the market in marketing (Chapter 15) and the importance of customers to quality management (Chapter 17). Several methods of assessing and forecasting demand are reviewed, with strengths and weaknesses identified. Many of these are quantitative estimation techniques, although an understanding of why people demand leisure is also important.

The chapter finishes with a suggested ten-point planning process for leisure managers to consider. Thereby, leisure managers can identify what roles they might play in this process. It is important for leisure managers to get involved in leisure planning at all levels of provision: local, regional and national. Their specialist knowledge of the nature of leisure demands is a vital ingredient in ensuring that supply matches demand.

14.1 Introduction

This chapter deals with local planning for sport and leisure, i.e. the considerations that government in particular lays down for the effective and appropriate planning of sport and leisure provision and development. Business planning, by individual organisations for a new sport or leisure development, is included in Chapter 21. Local planning is not irrelevant to commercial and third sector businesses, however, because any commercial sport and leisure development will be influenced by local plans. Local plans will also affect local communities more generally, because a key element in their construction is how accessible sport and leisure facilities and amenities are, and whether they fit local needs.

Government planning has always been concerned, albeit often peripherally, with the provision of facilities for leisure. The evolution of the planning movement was closely associated with the nineteenth-century fight for the retention of open spaces and commons, which were threatened by unplanned urban development. The movement has evolved from a concern for public health, education and moral standards to problems of inner cities and countryside recreation and conservation. Leisure planning as a discipline in its own right is not a new phenomenon. Indeed, leisure planning was at the forefront of the planning of the Garden Cities in the UK by Ebenezer Howard in the early twentieth century.

This chapter is not a text for planners but instead it provides information about planning processes and systems, and also reviews practical techniques for sport and leisure planning.

The context for planning involves legislation, government regulation, direction and guidance, public debate and consultation, the geography of an area, land use, and the need for sport and leisure facilities and amenities to fit within community plans and cultural strategies.

The planner's objective is to provide the right facilities, in the best location, at the right time and at an acceptable cost, for the people who need them. Planning is not a static process, but a dynamic and changing one. Planners themselves are only part of the planning process. They do not directly acquire and manage land and amenities. They identify locations for facilities according to acceptable planning principles. They seek to minimise conflicts of interest, traffic, noise, pollution and congestion. Planners help to make towns functional, attractive and healthy places; they also have to safeguard the public interest and help to conserve (and foster good use of) the environment.

One of the fundamental drivers of leisure planning is equitable distribution of opportunities. This is open to a variety of interpretations of the concept of 'equity', and equity is not necessarily synonymous with equality. Equal distribution of leisure facilities does not necessarily provide either equal opportunity or equal participation. Often, the more affluent people are the predominant users of public sector facilities, despite attempts to provide amenities in disadvantaged areas.

The leisure manager should be involved in the planning process at the earliest stage, to assist in assessing need and demand, identifying gaps in provision and proposing appropriate services and facilities. Unfortunately, however, there are too many examples of poor planning. The most common failure is that leisure facilities are often placed on land which is available because it is owned by the local authority, but which is not in an appropriate location for their market. In such circumstances, they are unlikely to achieve optimum levels of usage and hence they require increased levels of subsidy. Community built facilities located on the periphery of centres of population or away from main transportation routes, or alongside physical barriers such as rivers or difficult road systems, suffer from poor access and inevitably result in a restricted catchment.

14.2 The role of government in planning

Planning systems regulate development and land use and contribute to government strategy for sustainable development in towns, cities and the countryside. The systems help to plan for homes, schools, factories, transport, etc. and in doing so protect the natural and manmade environments. They differ in different countries so the UK is used as an example. In England there are over 400 planning authorities, including regional planning bodies, district councils, unitary authorities and National Park authorities. There are three main tiers in the planning system: national, regional and local. National policy is set out in a series of Planning Policy Statements. Regional planning bodies prepare Regional Spatial Strategies, whilst local authorities prepare Local Development Frameworks.

Planning issues in Wales are covered in *Planning Policy Wales* (2002), from the Welsh Assembly, and implemented by 25 local planning authorities. In Scotland there is a National Planning Framework, with 33 planning authorities to help implement it. In Northern Ireland a Regional Development Strategy has been written for the period up to the year 2025. National planning policies are supported by similar guidance notes to those in England, called Technical Advice Notes in Wales, Planning Policy Statements in Northern Ireland and Scottish Planning Policy in Scotland (see 'Useful websites', p. 393). These typically include separate guidance notes for nature conservation and planning; historic environment; tourism; coastal planning; and sport, recreation and open space.

The planning system aims to ensure that development occurs in the right place and that inappropriate development is prevented. However, no matter what planning systems are in place, planning and development decisions are taken by politicians, and therefore the political influence is important. For example, at the local level in the past it was not unusual for sport and leisure developments to favour the constituencies of specific politicians in power at the time.

The case of playing fields in the UK demonstrates how the government has felt the need to take action over a national concern – the development of playing fields for other purposes, e.g. housing, retail, and the consequent loss of sport and recreational opportunity. Legislation brought in the late 1990s requires any proposed development plans involving playing fields to be referred to the national sport agency, Sport England. This demonstrates how specific, reactive legislation is sometimes needed to support sport and leisure planning, in this case responding to a perceived threat to sport and leisure provision. Enforcement of the legislation is not through the courts but rather through a sport agency.

14.3 Key planning processes

This section reviews a selection of planning processes in England, to illustrate the complexity of planning but also to show how planning procedures are constructed. The processes are different in different countries – they are even slightly different in the four countries that make up the UK. It is therefore not possible to review the processes in detail for different countries.

14.3.1 Planning Policy Statements/guidance

In England, national planning policy is set out in Planning Policy Statements, which are gradually replacing Planning Policy Guidance Notes (PPGs). These form the basis for policies contained in regional and local plans. In 2004 there were 25 Policy Planning Guidance Notes, but at the time of writing some have been cancelled (including one on the Countryside and another on Tourism) and will be subsumed within new Planning Policy Statements. Most of the PPGs and Planning Policy Statements have implications for leisure and some are significant to leisure planning, including PPG 17 on Planning for Open Space, Sport and Recreation, PPG 20 on Coastal Planning, PPG 15 on Planning and the Historic Environment, and PPG 2 on Green Belts. PPG 17 features in Case Study 14.1 to illustrate best practice guidelines for planning in this sector.

14.3.2 Statutory plans

Planners have a legal duty to conform to statutory planning regulations. In parallel, they have to try to meet local needs. As noted above, two tiers of statutory plan in the UK are regional and local. Regional Spatial Strategies set out, for each region, a broad spatial planning strategy for how the region will look in fifteen to twenty years time, with the objective of ensuring sustainable development. They inform the preparation of Local Development Frameworks and Local Transport Plans. Important processes in producing Regional Spatial Strategies include the need to work in partnership with community organisations and conduct community consultation; an implementation plan, with targets and indicators relating to each policy objective; and also the statutory requirement to produce an annual monitoring report, reporting progress against its objectives and identifying any problems.

PPG 17 Planning for Open Space, Sport and Recreation

PPG 17 (Department of Communities and Local Government, 2002) is the guidance which has been of greatest interest to sport and leisure professionals in England. Even though sport and leisure is not a statutory service in English local authorities, PPG 17 contains one of the clearest statements of its importance to government policy, although this justification concerns sport's contribution to other government objectives, rather than valuing sport for sport's sake:

> Well designed and implemented planning policies for open space, sport and recreation are {…} fundamental to delivering broader Government objectives.
>
> (Department of Communities and Local Government, 2002)

The statement then goes on to detail the benefits of 'supporting an urban renaissance', 'supporting a rural renewal', promotion of social inclusion and community cohesion', 'health and well being', and 'promoting more sustainable development'.

Local authorities are expected to adopt a strategic approach to the provision of new facilities and to plan positively for their effective maintenance. Several key features of good planning identified in PPG 17 are now summarised.

Assessment of needs and opportunities

The government expects all local authorities to carry out 'robust assessments of the existing and future needs of their communities for open space, sports and recreational facilities'. In addition, audits of existing facilities are required, along with the use that is made of them, access to them in terms of location and entrance charges, and opportunities for new provision. Furthermore, PPG 17 suggests that '[a]udits of quality will be particularly important as they will allow local authorities to identify potential for increased use through better design, management and maintenance'. (For more on quality frameworks, see Chapter 17.) One key reason for effective needs assessment and audits of provision is that they will help plans to resolve potential conflicts that arise between different uses and users.

Setting local standards for provision

The government believes that open space standards are best set locally and that local standards should include:

- **quantitative elements** – how much new provision is needed;
- **a qualitative component** – to identify the need for enhancement of existing facilities;
- **accessibility** – including distance thresholds and assessment of entrance charges.

The point of standards is that they set a minimum level of required provision, and therefore enable the identification of quantitative and qualitative deficiencies. Later in the chapter, however, some criticisms of the use of standards are made, so, despite their inclusion in PPG 17, whether or not they represent best practice is debatable.

Maintaining an adequate supply

This element concerns defending existing provision. It states:

Existing open space, sports and recreational buildings and land should not be built on unless an assessment has been undertaken which has clearly shown the open space or the buildings and land to be surplus to requirements.

(Department of Communities and Local Government, 2002)

If a local authority has not undertaken such an assessment, then it is up to any potential developer of such assets to prove 'through an independent assessment' that the land or buildings are surplus to requirement. Furthermore, '[d]evelopers will need to consult the local community and demonstrate that their proposals are widely supported by them'. A particular concern explicit in PPG 17 is playing fields (see p. 369). The guidance suggests that 'local authorities should give very careful consideration to any planning applications involving development on playing fields', with detailed specification of circumstances under which such an application is approved.

Planning obligations

PPG 17 acknowledges that in some cases the development and loss of open space or sports facilities may provide an opportunity to improve provision, through the use of planning conditions or 'obligations' (see p. 372). Through these, in exchange for planning permission for another development, e.g. housing, the developers must develop new open space or sport and recreation facilities at an agreed location on the site or nearby.

Planning for new open space and sports and recreational facilities

PPG 17 sets out the general principles for such planning, including:

- to promote accessibility by walking, cycling and public transport, and for people with disabilities;
- to contribute to town centre vitality and viability;
- to avoid any significant loss of amenity to residents, neighbouring uses or biodiversity;
- to improve the public realm through good design;
- to add to and enhance the range and quality of existing facilities;
- to consider security and personal safety, especially for children;
- to assess the impact of new facilities on social inclusion;
- to consider the recreational needs of visitors and tourists.

PPG 17 then provides more detailed guidance on a number of types of leisure development, such as stadia, natural amenities and rights of way, as well as different types of area, such as urban fringes and rural areas.

However, planning policy statements and guidance are not legally enforceable and it is not known to what extent local authorities abide strictly by their criteria. As ever, providing best practice guidance is one thing, adhering to it is entirely different.

A Local Development Framework consists of a set of documents explaining how planning is managed in the local area, including:

- a core strategy;
- a map which identifies all site-specific policies;
- a statement of how the local community was involved in each document;
- an annual monitoring report.

A Local Development Framework sets broad targets for development of housing, industry and transport in relation to predicted changes in the population and the economy of the area. For leisure, the plans identify strategic land use policies for major initiatives, such as community forests, and projects affecting large areas or populations.

14.3.3 Planning obligations

Currently, local authorities in England may enter into planning obligations to secure the provision of public open space and sporting, recreational, social, educational or other community facilities as part of larger mixed developments. Planning obligation is the process whereby planning permission may be granted provided certain obligations are fulfilled. Councils can use this powerful tool (recently termed 'planning contributions' and formerly referred to as 'planning gain' and 'Section 106 agreements') to improve the provision of sport and recreation facilities by agreements with developers, planning applicants and land-owners. Sport England encourages local authorities to use planning obligations to benefit sport and recreation (see 'Useful websites', p. 393).

Government policy requires that planning obligations be sought only where they meet the following tests:

- They are necessary.
- They are relevant to planning.
- They are directly related to the proposed development.
- They are fairly and reasonably related in scale and kind to the proposed development.
- They are reasonable in all other respects.

The Planning Act 2008 gives local authorities in England and Wales the option of charging a Community Infrastructure Levy on new developments in their area. This levy would be related to the size and character of the development and the proceeds would be spent on local and sub-regional infrastructure, which may include open spaces and sport and recreation facilities. Detailed proposals for the introduction of the Community Infrastructure Levy are under consultation at the time of writing, but if they are accepted and if many local authorities implement this levy, it may replace planning obligations. This would mean a shift from a selective tax to a more general tax on development, which would remove discrimination but would also remove any direct responsibility for developers to provide community assets.

Discussion question

Should local commercial developers be penalised by planning obligations and/or a Community Infrastructure Levy for helping to redevelop local areas?

14.3.4 Local Cultural Strategies

In the UK the Department for Culture, Media and Sport (DCMS, 2000) provides guidance for local authorities on the production of Local Cultural Strategies. Local authorities are encouraged to provide opportunity to all people in their community to engage in cultural activities and for the strategy to support social and economic regeneration, lifelong learning, environmental sustainability and the development of healthy communities.

The guidance sets out underpinning principles. Local Cultural Strategies should:

- be guided by a vision;
- promote the cultural well-being of the area;
- meet needs, demands and aspirations;
- ensure fair access for all;
- develop a cross-departmental and inter-agency approach;
- take a holistic rather than a service viewpoint;
- have clear links with other national, regional and local strategies and plans;
- ensure meaningful, active consultation;
- take account of the wider central and regional government context;
- contribute to the government's key objectives.

The Local Cultural Strategy should be viewed as overarching, focussing on strategic choices, priorities and forward planning and ensuring that the strategy document contains an Action Plan. Developing a Local Cultural Strategy is complex and takes time. The guidance document illustrates a seven-stage strategy development process (Figure 14.1) which takes one or two years to complete. It suggests that the preparation before a strategy is actually written

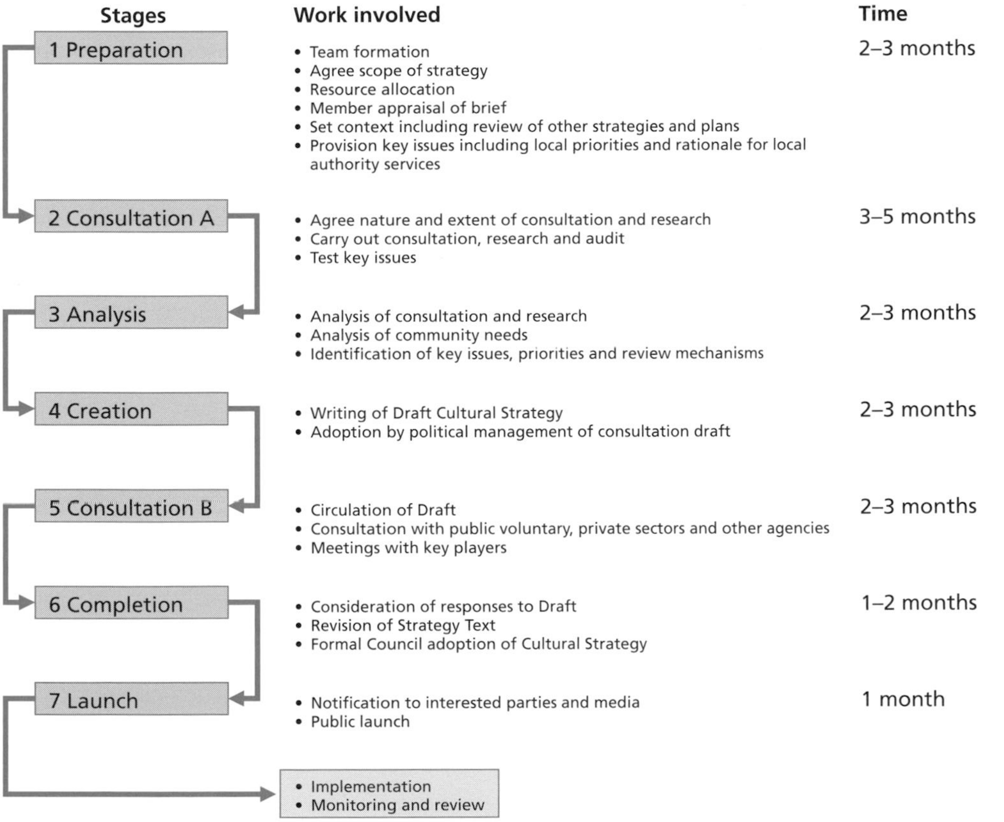

Stages	Work involved	Time
1 Preparation	• Team formation • Agree scope of strategy • Resource allocation • Member appraisal of brief • Set context including review of other strategies and plans • Provision key issues including local priorities and rationale for local authority services	2–3 months
2 Consultation A	• Agree nature and extent of consultation and research • Carry out consultation, research and audit • Test key issues	3–5 months
3 Analysis	• Analysis of consultation and research • Analysis of community needs • Identification of key issues, priorities and review mechanisms	2–3 months
4 Creation	• Writing of Draft Cultural Strategy • Adoption by political management of consultation draft	2–3 months
5 Consultation B	• Circulation of Draft • Consultation with public voluntary, private sectors and other agencies • Meetings with key players	2–3 months
6 Completion	• Consideration of responses to Draft • Revision of Strategy Text • Formal Council adoption of Cultural Strategy	1–2 months
7 Launch	• Notification to interested parties and media • Public launch	1 month
	• Implementation • Monitoring and review	

Figure 14.1 Seven-stage strategy development process.
Source: DCMS (2000).

may take up to a year. Importantly there are two stages of consultation with key stakeholders and citizens in this recommended process: first, to help design the strategy and, second, to generate feedback on the draft strategy. The model in Figure 14.1, however, is not prescriptive – different local authorities have designed different models, much depending on whether the strategy is for a local district, a city or a region.

> ### Discussion question
>
> What would happen if there were no government plans at the local level, i.e. land use and building use were left entirely to the market?

14.4 Planning techniques

The most authoritative source of information on planning techniques for sport, leisure and tourism is Veal (2002), who also has lots of information on his website (see 'Useful websites', p. 393). Much of the review that follows is informed by Veal's work.

Underpinning many of these techniques is both an understanding of demand for different sport and leisure activities and knowledge of the quantity and quality of existing sport and leisure opportunities. The fundamentals of sport and leisure planning are to compare demand with supply and then plan to remedy any likely unmet demand with changes in supply. In reviewing the planning techniques, it is important to identify the means by which both supply and demand can be measured. In the case of demand, this is more difficult because for planning purposes it is not just present demand that needs to be measured but also future demand. This needs to be forecasted for the period ahead appropriate to the plan – the so-called 'planning horizon'.

The techniques examined are:

- those focused more on supply:
  - standards of provision;
  - hierarchy of provision;
  - spatial analysis;
- those focused more on demand:
  - expressed demand and demand forecasting;
  - public consultation;
- those focused on both supply and demand:
  - matrix analysis;
  - social area/need index;
  - facilities planning model;
  - U-Plan system.

14.4.1 Standards of provision

One of the most developed and widely used approaches to the 'equitable' distribution of recreational services is the use of standards of provision, whereby the standards identify what type of provision should be made, typically for a specific size of population. Examples cited in Veal (2002, 2009a) include:

- for local sports centres:
  - 23 square metres of indoor sports centre floor space per 1,000 population, from the Sports Council in the UK, 1977;
- for open space planning standards (including children's play, playing fields and informal space):
  - 6 acres (2.4 hectares) per 1,000 population, from the National Playing Fields Association in the UK, since 1938 (the subject of an additional case study on the website accompanying this book);
  - 2.4–4.25 hectares per 1,000 population, from the National Recreation and Parks Association in the USA, 1983;
  - 4–7 hectares per 1,000 population, from the South Australian Urban Land Trust, 1988.

Many standards are not based on empirical research, but on long-accepted assumptions of what is 'needed'. Standards appeal to politicians and planners. Someone 'in authority' has done the thinking for you. Standards are simple and efficient; they invite the same level of provision area to area; they act as an external authoritative source; and they can be measured, monitored and assessed. Standards are important and useful when they have been based on sound methodology and are used with flexibility and local knowledge. They give yardsticks against which to measure existing provision, they are easy to understand and communicate and they cover many of the facilities provided by local authorities.

However, while standards have advantages, they also have disadvantages:

- Standards can become institutionalised, unmovable and be given greater strength and importance than they merit.
- Standards vary (as in the open space standards above). Most major pursuits have standards – pitches, pools, indoor sports centres, libraries and so on, but sometimes the same activity has different standards, which prompts the question: which one to choose?
- The validity of some standards is open to question. Playing space standards, for example, are based on participation rates, but participation is largely dependent on the level of supply. Changes in provision will lead to changes in participation, but the implications for possible changes in standards are unclear. As both supply and demand change over time, so standards can become out of date. The growth of fitness centres, driven by increased demand, may mean that the standards for provision for these facilities are too weak; whilst the decline in squash may make standards of provision too generous. Hence, some standards of just a decade ago are no longer valid or appropriate.
- Standards should always be tempered by local knowledge and circumstances. If they are unrealistic, they will be ignored. For example, national open space standards cannot be achieved in inner-city areas.
- While standards are easy to understand, they can be misinterpreted and used as a justification for taking no further action. Some authorities have been known to interpret standards to suit their own purposes. For example, they may say that they have more than adequate indoor playing space but analysis might reveal that most of the total space is made up of small units unsuitable for activities in demand, or that access by the general public is restricted.
- Standards are inanimate, inhuman. They are concerned with quantitative and not qualitative aspects of provision. They take no account of the leisure potential of the specific areas, i.e. local needs, local priorities, local differences and local environments.
- Many leisure pursuits are amenable to standards of provision, but many are not. Water

recreation, tourism, heritage, entertainment and arts have no comprehensive basis for evaluation.

In summary, standards of provision can involve a crude assessment of demand. As they are based on national information, they can often bear little relationship to local circumstances; they deal in quantities, thereby ignoring the quality of provision as well as key aspects of distribution, use and management. At best, standards of provision can be used as a starting point by providing a benchmark for measuring the adequacy of facilities and for identifying under- or over-provision, while recognising that most standards indicate minimum levels of provision. But more typically, standards have been replaced by more sophisticated techniques which attempt to measure supply and demand.

14.4.2 Hierarchy of provision

A modified version of the standards approach is the hierarchy of provision approach, normally applied to a range of facilities for a given population size. It has been used in the development of new towns, where the planning of leisure facilities and services is seen as a prerequisite for attracting people to the towns. For example, a town might have a three-tier hierarchy for sport:

- at a school level using facilities and services for school and community – a grassroots tier;
- specific club facilities and services, e.g. hockey or tennis at a second tier;
- flagship central facilities and services at the third tier.

A hierarchies approach helps to settle the debate over whether to provide a large centrally located facility or numerous smaller facilities strategically placed throughout the district. With scarce resources, often a choice has to be made. There will probably be savings in the capital costs if only one large centre is provided, as economies of scale would apply in both the construction and operation of the facility, e.g. the construction costs per cubic metre of internal space are lower for large buildings than for smaller buildings. However, the closer a person resides to a leisure facility, the more likely they are to use the facility, and the more frequently, compared with a person who resides some distance away. This is the principle of 'distance decay'.

An example of a hierarchy of provision is given in Table 14.1, which was developed specifically for use in the small communities along the Lambourn Valley in Berkshire, UK (Torkildsen and Griffiths, 1987). Such an approach is arguably more beneficial when used for small scale communities – when used for large scale projects, the limitations associated with the use of standards are likely to apply to this approach too. The hierarchies approach also requires an implicit understanding of facilities' catchment areas, which is more central to spatial analysis (discussed on p. 380).

Two further examples of the hierarchy approach are the Recreation Opportunity Spectrum (Clark and Stankey, 1979), for resource-based outdoor recreations, and the Tourism Opportunity Spectrum (Butler and Waldbrook, 1991), for nature-based tourist provision. Both of these identify standards for facilities and services, determined by environmental, social and managerial factors. They are an advance on a purely standards approach, however, because they consider the nature of demands, as well as the capacity of different resources to meet them.

Table 14.1 Suggested hierarchy of leisure provision for rural communities based on a specific location in Berkshire, UK

Community size	Recommended facilities that could be offered	Examples of activities relating to location	Additional comments
1 Hamlet/small village, 100–500 population	Village hall suitable for social functions. Kitchen, snooker table, depending on demand and local tradition	Meetings, dances/discos, concerts, table tennis, youth club, voluntary organisations, e.g. scouts, adult education classes	Centrally located – preferably linked to community open space
	Community open space, 2–3 acres, including children's play area with equipment	Children's play, football and cricket, informal recreation, village festivals, carnival, etc.	Location – central, avoiding the necessity for children to cross main roads. Possibly linked to a primary school
	Mobile library service – van	Books, DVDs, etc.	Preferably linked to the focal point of the village
2 Medium-sized village, 500–1,500 population	Community hall (15×10×6.7 metres) with kitchen, toilets, temporary stage, changing facilities, storage areas. Bar facilities depending on demand, car parking	Recreation, badminton, keep-fit, yoga, aerobics, meetings, drama, concerts, dances/discos, youth clubs	
	Community open space, 3–7 acres, including football pitch with pavilion (or linked to community hall), children's play area with equipment, seats, floral beds. Space for tennis and/or bowls, depending on local demand	Children's play, football club, informal cricket, informal recreation, village festivals, carnival, pony club	
	Mobile library service – trailer library	Books, DVDs, etc.	
	Community minibus – available for hire – provision dependent on public transport service and facilities available within village	Organised visits in connection with sports, arts, entertainment and social events	Hire costs and maintenance schedules important

continued

Table 14.1 continued

Community size	Recommended facilities that could be offered	Examples of activities relating to location	Additional comments
	Mobile recreation service	Offering sports and arts activities, particularly for the young, females, unemployed, the elderly, etc.	Depending on the range of opportunities available and the degree of initiative and leadership within the village. One half-day visit per week
3 Large village, 1,500–2,500 population	Community hall (20×10×6.7 metres), including bar facilities	A range of sports (including gymnastics, martial arts, badminton, possibly five-a-side soccer, etc.), arts and social recreation	Location – central, focal point of public transport
	Community open space, 9–14 acres, two or more football pitches, one cricket square, bowling green, two hard/synthetic surfaced tennis courts/netball courts. Pavilions for changing, plus bar refreshment facilities. Children's play area with kickabout and equipment	Activities to include club football/rugby, cricket, bowls, tennis, netball	Depending on the availability of open space, it might be necessary to have the facilities at more than one location. Each site should have a pavilion with changing facilities
	Library – fixed accommodation. Opening times staggered throughout the week to meet different people's needs	Books, DVDs, etc.	
	Mobile recreation service – depending on the facilities within the village and whether they are professionally managed	Sport and recreation activities	Visit restricted to half-day a week

Settlement	Facility	Activities	Notes
4 Small country town, 2,500–6,000 population	Sports hall (26×16.5×7.6 metres), depending on the size of the community. Consideration to be given to ancillary facilities such as a weight training area	Increased range of sporting activities, including five-a-side football, cricket, indoor bowls, basketball, volleyball, weight training, squash, archery, tennis	For economic reasons, dual use with a secondary school or a large sports club/voluntary organisation should be explored
	Swimming pool (20–25 metres)	Swimming, life-saving	As above; provision only if a dual-use arrangement can be achieved
	Community hall/arts centre – to include stage and projection facilities, plus meeting rooms, kitchens, bar, toilets, craft workshop	Meetings, drama, concerts, cinema, whist drives, bingo, table tennis, adult education classes, displays	Linked to other community provision – improve spin-off and awareness
	Community open space (15–40 acres), including park area, children's play areas with equipment, four football/rugby/hockey pitches, two to four tennis courts, bowling green and pavilions with refreshments, one cricket square, multi-purpose floodlit hard all-weather area	Children's play, town show, carnival, soccer, rugby, cricket, bowls, tennis, netball, five-a-side football, training purposes	Children's play areas, easy access to housing estates. Playing pitches best located near sports hall – economies of scale and spin-off
	Library facilities – branch library	Books, DVDs, pictures	Permanent accommodation – spread opening hours
	Mobile recreation service	Sports/recreation activities	Programmed to meet specific market segments, e.g. unemployed – off-peak times/one day per week

> ### Discussion question
>
> When they are accused of being a nuisance on the streets, it is often claimed by young teenagers that there is 'nothing to do' and 'nowhere to go'. How would you construct a hierarchy of sport and leisure facilities and services for young teenagers in your area?

14.4.3 Spatial analysis

When asked what were the three most important factors in the development of hotels, Conrad Hilton cited 'location, location, location'. This equally applies to most leisure facilities. Ideally, a public leisure facility should be located near a main road that is well served by a public transport system, in close proximity to other facilities. In recent years in the UK, extensive user surveys have been taken of many leisure facilities, and from these an indication of the size of a leisure facility's catchment area can be made. Using this approach, the geographical area covered by the facility's perceived catchment area can be identified, with areas beyond that, theoretically, not being served.

This is a useful planning tool, because by putting together the calculated catchment areas of all the facilities in an area for a specific purpose, e.g. multi-use leisure centres, it is possible to identify geographical gaps in provision. It also enables identification of the degree of overlap of catchment areas, which may have implications for the programming of 'competing' facilities.

However, there are a number of important issues which need to be considered when conducting such a spatial analysis, including:

- the quality of existing facilities, whether they have spare capacity or whether their demand exceeds supply;
- the density of population in the relevant areas;
- the shape of the catchment areas of leisure facilities, which are not circular but are distorted due to many factors, e.g. physical barriers such as rivers, railway lines and busy roads can restrict a catchment area, while access to a facility along a major road can extend the catchment area along its route;
- the respective catchment populations of different leisure facilities, which may differ in size, affluence, mobility and social composition.

14.4.4 Expressed demand and demand forecasting

Information on expressed demand is often provided by large scale, national participation surveys – such as the *Active People* surveys for sports participation in England and the *Taking Part* surveys for leisure participation in the UK. National surveys identify the way in which participation in a variety of leisure activities varies by gender, age, socio-economic group, ethnicity, etc. National surveys are often conducted by public agencies and the results are in the public domain. However, some are conducted commercially, such as the *Target Group Index* (TGI) in the UK, a national consumption survey by the British Market Research Bureau. One advantage of using the TGI is that it is linked with ACORN (the acronym for A Classification of Residential Neighbourhoods), which is a demographic and socio-economic categorisation of neighbourhoods.

A problem with most large-scale national surveys, however, is that the samples for local areas are insufficient for very much analysis. This leads to national demand evidence being assumed to be relevant to a local area, which is not necessarily the case. However, the *Active People* survey of sports participation in England (2005/6) was designed to produce 1,000 respondents in every local authority, which enables detailed analysis, and is therefore useful for planning purposes, at the local level.

As well as national surveys, it is often the case that information on expressed demand is collected locally. The analysis of sports facilities' booking sheets, for example, can reveal the amount of spare capacity available, and may indicate whether the demand for specific facilities at certain times exceeds the supply available – this would depend on records being kept of failed attempts to book because capacity was fully booked. The level of demand for existing facilities can therefore provide a useful guide to whether additional facilities are required in an area.

Discussion questions

How would you measure excess demand for a particular activity in your area? Could this be done on a continuous basis, rather than by occasional measurement?

It is not just knowledge of current or recent demand that is important to planning. Through the use of survey information, it is possible to forecast what would happen to participation if population levels or structures changed: for instance a growing population, an ageing population, or a population with higher numbers of immigrants from certain countries. Such forecasts can be achieved by quantitative techniques such as time series, regression analysis or the simpler cohort analysis.

14.4.4.1 Time series

If there is sufficient data over time on demand, from repeated surveys which are consistent, time series is a statistical method by which trend data over time can be extrapolated into the future to provide a forecast of demand. This is done by calculating a 'moving average' which exposes the underlying trend in the data over time as well as identifying normal seasonal fluctuations in demand (here is not the place for a detailed statistical explanation – you need to refer to a statistics textbook). The technique can be used for particular leisure activities and for specific population sub-groups, as long as there is sufficient reliable data for these. There are two main problems with this technique, however. First, it assumes that the future will exactly replicate demand patterns from the past, which often isn't the case. Second, the technique offers no explanation for changes over time – a problem which regression and cohort analyses attempt to remedy.

14.4.4.2 Regression analysis

In this technique, it is necessary to have data for whatever is being explained, called the 'dependent variable' – in this case a measure of sport or leisure demand – and also data for the so-called 'independent variables' which have an influence on demand, such as age, gender, ethnicity, education, socio-economic group, income, car ownership, etc. All these data are inputted into multiple regression software, which then estimates the separate effects of each of the independent variables on the dependent variable. This regression analysis will also disclose the statistical significance of each effect and the explanatory power of the whole model.

With such a model calculated using recent data it is then possible to input forecasted values for important independent variables in the future, e.g. an older population, to estimate the effect this has on demand. However, such analyses are rarely conducted by local authorities or even regional authorities, because of either the lack of sufficient data or the lack of expertise to run regressions. They are mostly conducted by academic analysts and national agencies. As such, regression analysis is not really feasible for local leisure plans.

14.4.4.3 Cohort analysis

This is a simpler technique than regression analysis. A cohort is simply a sub-group of the population, e.g. by age, gender, income, etc. Two pieces of information are needed to forecast demand for any cohort in the population: first, a forecast of the population changes for the planning area over the planning period; and, second, an estimate of the participation rate of that cohort in the leisure activity being planned – usually drawn from survey data. Multiplying the forecasted population by the estimated participation rate will provide the number of people it is anticipated will be interested in an activity.

With survey data also providing likely frequencies of participation, this technique will help to identify likely demand in the future, for any specific cohorts, as long as specific and reliable data exist on population forecasts and expected participation rates. The 'explanation' for these forecasts lies in the different cohorts selected for analysis – acknowledging the major structural variables which affect likely participation, such as age, gender, etc.

14.4.4.4 Latent demand

The level of expressed demand identified by surveys and used in techniques to forecast demand is to an extent dependent upon the level of provision. It does not take into consideration latent demand. This is demand that is real but is not yet realised because of major constraints, such as lack of supply. Occasionally, however, surveys include questions on latent demand. Examples include the *General Household Survey* in Britain in 2002 and the *Active People* survey in England in 2007–8. With the help of survey evidence, forecasts of demand can integrate not just expressed demand but also estimates of latent demand. In the case of swimming in England, for example, if latent demand were converted into actual swimmers another 4.3 million swimmers would be added to the 5.55 million swimmers already active (Bullough *et al.*, 2010).

14.4.5 Public consultation

Public consultation, along with intelligence on expressed demand, is an important indicator of public demand. The weakness is that people may demand facilities but never use them. In addition, the more articulate and organised leisure groups are often the most vocal. Nevertheless, public consultation remains invaluable in gauging local feeling and opinion. Not only is it politically desirable to consult with people, but the planning process itself is incomplete unless people are consulted about their leisure needs and demands, their perception of existing facilities and services and their expectations of future provision. Without such consultation, the planning process is paternalistic – dictating provision for people as opposed to planning with the people.

As with other methods, public consultations are not without their shortcomings. These are normally associated with the expressions of demand not being representative of the community as a whole, and with the subjective nature of many of the responses.

The major methods of consulting with the public include:

- community surveys;
- leisure facility user surveys;
- surveys of clubs, societies and organisations;
- public meetings;
- working parties;
- stakeholder interviews;
- focus groups.

14.4.5.1 Community surveys

Four surveys which have been used regularly are: household interviews; street surveys; postal surveys; and telephone surveys. More recently online surveys are becoming popular, as much for their economy in implementation as their effectiveness in generating results. The face-to-face household interview is a sound approach, but can be both time-consuming and expensive to administer. In order to avoid unnecessarily alarming residents, particularly the elderly, household interviews are best undertaken following an introduction, e.g. by telephone or post, which requires even more time. A face-to-face alternative is the street survey. This requires achieving randomised quota sampling, e.g. a reasonable cross-section of males and females, different age groups, etc. It also calls for trained, sensitive interviewers. The postal survey is much easier and cheaper to administer, although it has limitations. The response rate can be very low unless some interest has been created in the local media or an incentive is associated with the return of the questionnaire. A low response rate then raises the issue of sample bias – were the people who responded of a particular type? A telephone survey using skilful, sensitive researchers is comparatively easy to undertake, provided the questionnaire is short and simple. The problems are those of contacting the selected people and getting accepted. Many sales personnel use the telephone in an attempt to sell products such as financial products and double glazing. Hence, there is resentment towards this form of consultation.

14.4.5.2 Leisure facility user surveys

User surveys conducted in a face-to-face approach or by self-completion questionnaires can be informative, providing information on the user profile, the facility's catchment area (and also the areas not being served), participation data (e.g. activities, frequency), perceptions of provision, how it is managed and expectations for the future. When the questionnaires are self-administered, user surveys tend to be less representative and the response rate is reduced, although this method is easier and cheaper. Identifying users also provides a broad picture of the non-users, when comparisons are made with local population characteristics.

14.4.5.3 Surveys of clubs, societies and organisations

The voluntary organisations for sports and arts are often the backbone of leisure groupings. Hence, in any leisure planning process their contribution is essential. A survey of local clubs and societies can provide valuable information regarding membership levels, resources and current and future requirements. The drawbacks are that often databases of key contacts are out of date because of changes in club officials; and there is often a delay in the responses because of the seasonal nature of some clubs. Furthermore, many clubs are independent in outlook and are not prepared to look at aspects beyond those that directly affect their members. Levels of response from such organisations are often low.

14.4.5.4 Public meetings

Although opinions given at public meetings are not necessarily those representing all the community, they do give an indication of the strength of the support or opposition to particular proposals. Good promotion is necessary to ensure that reasonable and hopefully representative attendances are achieved at the meetings and that those who 'shout loudest' or have vested interests do not hold sway. Working with the press to give balanced reports of such meetings is also important and it requires good public relations.

14.4.5.5 Working parties

A much under-used approach is that of a working party, whereby relevant stakeholders get together with officers and members from the local council in a working party that has delegated authority to propose recommendations. A formal example of this approach in planning for sport in England is Community Sport Networks, which are working parties of local leaders in sport, set up to help plan the development of sport in their communities. It is important that such working parties have the authority to influence decisions, or they simply become talking shops and soon lose enthusiasm.

The advantages associated with this approach are considerable. It is democracy at work and, hopefully, the realistic expectations of the local community can be fulfilled. Unfortunately, in such a situation decision-making can be slow and the commitment of members will wane if progress is not seen to be made. But the greatest problem may be associated with working party members making unrealistic demands that it requires excessive amounts of space and finance to fulfil.

14.4.5.6 Stakeholder interviews

Interviews with community leaders, including politicians, teachers, leisure leaders, play-workers, youth leaders, social workers, police, ethnic minority representatives, disadvantaged and disabled groups and the business community, can be an invaluable source of information. Likewise, informal interviews with shopkeepers, publicans, postal workers – all those who come into contact with a wide range of residents – help to build a picture of how different people perceive the current provision and how it is managed and what deficiencies they think exist.

The main advantages of interviews – either semi-structured, with the main issues for discussion identified, or unstructured, with only the main topic identified – are that the interviewee drives the decision about which issues are covered and the responses. This contrasts with structured questionnaires, where the respondent is only required to address the specific questions asked, and these may not consider other issues important to the respondent.

14.4.5.7 Focus groups

The focus group differs from other methods of consultation in three ways:

1 All those interviewed have been involved in a real situation relevant to the subject.
2 The 'content' for the discussion has been previously identified, so participants have had time to think about it.
3 The discussion facilitates conflict and consensus between interested parties – it is not just a matter of adding up different responses, but also a matter of the strength of opinion and the judgement reached by the discussion.

The focus group interview generally involves eight to twelve individuals who discuss a particular topic under the direction of a moderator. The moderator promotes interaction, makes sure that everyone has a say and ensures that the discussion remains on the topic of interest. Smaller groups may be dominated by one or two members, while larger groups are difficult to manage. A typical focus group session will last for up to two hours. Depending on the intention of the research, the moderator may be more or less directive with respect to the discussion, but is more often non-directive. The moderator might begin with a series of general questions but then directs the discussion to more specific issues as the group proceeds.

14.4.5.8 Other consultations

There is a range of other methods, including: consultation clinics for individuals or small groups; stakeholder panels; local press and media; website interactions.

It is clear that, at present, there is no one way of determining the level of potential leisure demand for a particular activity. All the approaches reviewed have different advantages and limitations, and in order to be able to make a fairly accurate projection of the likely demand for a facility or service, it is desirable to use a range of different methods. Planning for people means putting people into the planning process. To make future leisure provision appropriate and meaningful, a greater understanding is required of people's needs and demands, what leisure means to people and the role it plays in their lives.

> ### Discussion question
>
> A town council is planning a new swimming pool but has little evidence of the likely demand for it and asks you to help. With limited resources, so that you cannot conduct all the methods of consultation reviewed above, what two methods would you select and why? (See the list on p. 383.)

14.4.6 Matrix analysis

This approach is more of a management technique than a planning approach, but it has an important function in specific situations, for example where planning criteria have been established for a range of possible developments on a particular site, or where the facilities within a park or geographical zone have to meet the demands of all sections of the community. If the community is divided into different cohorts, e.g. pre-school, young children, teenagers, adults, etc., listing their needs and matching these against the facilities available, each cell in the matrix will identify the degree of match between a particular population cohort and a particular type of provision. This will lead to the identification of deficiencies. Further applications can be used to place a list of facility/service deficiencies into a priority ranking order, or to select the most appropriate site from a range of possibilities.

14.4.7 Social Area/Need Index

The Social Area or Need Index approach determines whether a deficiency in provision exists in relation to need; and places different local areas into a priority ranking. At present, most of the methods of assessing demand concentrate upon the relationship between the resources available and potential users but little emphasis is attached to the concept of need. It is logical to assume that those areas with a low resource level as well as a high level of need should have a higher priority than areas with a high level of resources and a low level of need.

This approach is well illustrated when applied to the provision of children's play spaces. Case Study 14.2 describes the Need Index Approach to planning children's play provision as used in Basingstoke and Deane in the UK. It illustrates a logical process of measuring the needs of different areas and comparing them with a measure of existing resources in the same areas, in order to arrive at a priority order for investment in new provision.

CASE STUDY 14.2

The Need Index approach to children's play provision in Basingstoke and Deane, UK

Basingstoke and Deane Borough Council commissioned a study to design an equitable system for awarding funding for children's play areas, by local electoral ward areas. The result was a 'needs' minus 'resources' model which provided an index to establish gaps in existing provision; and also priorities for new provision.

Need index
In 1994, the Department of the Environment produced a set of indicators to measure the relative degree of deprivation to be found in the local authority areas of England. There were 13 indicators, 7 of which applied at the electoral ward level (each local authority is divided into several electoral wards):

- unemployment;
- overcrowded housing;
- lacking or sharing basic amenities;
- children in low income households;
- no car within a household;
- children living in 'unsuitable accommodation', e.g. flats;
- 17-year-olds not in full-time education.

Three indicators specifically refer to children and a fourth, overcrowding, rarely occurs without children. The other factors – unemployment, lacking basic amenities and no car – provide a picture of lack of affluence and mobility, which restricts access to play areas beyond a child's walking distance. The variables were combined with the total number of children in each ward, to provide a statistical index of need for play opportunities. The number of children in each ward is of critical importance as it is logical to assume that the areas with the greatest numbers of children will have the greatest demand for the use of playgrounds provided, all other variables being the same.

The indicators above were combined into a Need Index, such that each ward area had a score for its need for play areas, to compare with the other wards. This placed the electoral wards in order of priority need. The council initially allocated funding to the top 12 wards on the basis of the areas in greatest need. Wards lower down the priority scale moved up as their needs became greater in relation to those areas already refurbished. The process of taking into account not just need but also provision was formalised by the use of a resource index.

Resource index

The resource index measured 180 play areas by ward. Giving a score to the range and quality of playgrounds is a difficult exercise, as there is a wide range of factors to consider, many requiring subjective judgements, e.g. factors 2, 6, 7 and 8 below. Key factors taken into consideration when developing the resource index were:

1   the scale of play provision within each ward;
2   the quality of provision, facilities and equipment;
3   the distribution of playgrounds within each ward;
4   the size of the playgrounds – small, medium, large and extra-large;
5   the range of equipment, capacity and attraction of the playgrounds;
6   the maintenance and condition of the playgrounds and their equipment;
7   the safety factors, taking into consideration whether the playgrounds have impact absorbing surfaces, are enclosed by a fence and are safe from passing traffic;
8   the play value of the play area – an assessment of the overall physical, social, creative, educational and motivating features to be found.

Scores per play area were allocated for each of these factors, then the scores were combined into an index to represent the range and quality of play provision in each ward.

Priority ranking

The formula of 'Need – Resource = Deficiency = Priority' is possible with a need ranking by ward and resource ranking by ward. By using this formula, wards with a high level of need and a low level of resources were given a higher priority than areas with a high level of need and a high level of resources. In determining ward priority, the relative ranking in the two indices is important. For example, a ward with low ranking in both indices could achieve higher priority than a ward with higher need if the latter had higher resources too.

In summary, the formula resulted in a Play Area Index, giving a ranking by ward. This ranking changes as ward demographic data change or resources change, for better or worse. Information needs to be updated regularly and the formula needs to be reviewed on at least an annual basis.

Source: The index for Basingstoke and Deane was devised by George Torkildsen, Gwynne Griffiths and Pat Kendall; the play area inspection was carried out by Tony Chilton, consultant to the National Playing Fields Association.

More recently, needs in the UK are often represented by a government-produced Index of Multiple Deprivation (see 'Useful websites', p. 393). This combines a lot of indicators representing economic, social and housing issues into a single deprivation score for every local authority, and for smaller areas within the local authority – termed 'super output areas'. There is also now a Local Index of Child Wellbeing in the UK, which has been devised to assess need specific to children's issues.

14.4.8 Facilities planning model

The Facilities Planning Model is used by **sport**scotland and Sport England as a method of assessing the demand for sports facilities (sports halls, swimming pools, synthetic turf pitches and indoor bowls centres) at the community level of provision. The basic structure of the model is to compare demand for facilities with supply, taking into account how far people are willing to travel to a facility. Because demand and supply are compared, the same unit of measurement is used: number of visits per week at peak times. The approach has three components:

1 Demand is measured by the rate and frequency of participation using national data, i.e. from surveys.
2 Supply is measured by working out the number of attendances a facility can accommodate in a specified peak period.
3 Catchment area calculations are based on identifying, from national leisure surveys, the distance the regular participants (70–80 per cent of users) travel from and the travel modes they use.

The model identifies:

● where demand is located;
● whether, and to what extent, demand exceeds supply;
● whether, and where, spare capacity exists in existing facilities.

Local demand is measured on the basis of the number of visits per week in the peak period for any particular sports facility, determined by:

● the total number of people resident within the study area;
● their participation rate – the proportion of residents who want to use the facility type for particular sports;
● the desired frequency of visits – how often they want to visit;
● the proportion of visits which arise in the normal peak periods per week.

The benefits of the Facilities Planning Model include:

● assessing requirements for different types of sports facilities on a local, regional or national scale;
● helping local authorities to determine adequate levels of sports provision in their areas;
● testing 'what if {...} ?' scenarios, e.g. the effects of opening a new facility, relocating a facility, closing a facility, a change in the participation by local people, a change in the local population size or structure – all such changes can be factored into the model to see what impact they have on the existence of excess demand or spare capacity, and the precise locations of these.

The Facilities Planning Model can be used in urban and rural settings. It is a substantial improvement on a standards approach to planning facilities. However, it deals only with known demand and not with latent demand, or demand generated by new marketing efforts or innovative management. It calculates likely demand for facilities on the basis of an appropriate level of provision, but this is driven by a national model – it is not driven by local data on demand. The model relies on consistent information about existing facilities, which in the UK is provided by *Active Places*, a facilities database. It is also important to realise that it is only a planning tool which helps providers make decisions – it is not a policy-making instrument which makes the decisions for them.

Sport England takes a holistic approach to sports facility planning, known as the Facilities Improvement Service (see 'Useful websites', p. 393), designed to promote a set of planning tools for evidence-based needs assessment, to inform decision-making on what sports facilities are needed and where. The planning tools comprise:

- the Facilities Planning Model;
- Active Places Power, an interactive database of facilities' supply;
- Active People Diagnostic, an interactive database of demand for sport;
- Market Segmentation, a sports-specific analysis of market segments in England (see Case Study 15.2);
- Sports Facility Calculator, a tool to estimate the level of demand for a sports facility that is created by a given population;
- Improving Community Sports Facilities, a toolkit for the strategic planning of community sports facilities (Sport England, 2009c).

14.4.9 U-Plan system

Veal (2009b; and see 'Useful websites', p. 393) has devised a system for leisure planning which is called U-Plan. Although it is a participation-based approach, it entails three core components:

1 **objectives and outcomes** – establishing broad targets for the planning exercise, related to the organisation's mission and the key criterion of participation;
2 **participation** – measuring existing participation and evaluating likely future patterns;
3 **supply** – identifying the facility/service implications of the targets and projections from the participation analysis.

These components are broken down into 18 planning tasks, including a number of tasks reviewed earlier, i.e. surveying residents' leisure participation, surveying users of facilities/services, forecasting participation changes and auditing the existing supply of facilities/services. However, these tasks are prefaced by the refinement of organisation objectives, the clarification of decision-making responsibilities and the setting of budget constraints, which echo important features of other chapters in this book (see Chapters 17, 13, 18 and 21). Veal's U-Plan system is therefore more than a planning technique – it is a coherent and holistic approach to planning for leisure provision. And it is driven by participation, which echoes the importance of customers to both marketing (Chapter 15) and service quality (Chapter 17).

14.5 A ten-stage leisure planning process

The leisure planning process, in conceptual terms, is a simple model based on identifying leisure needs and demands and providing services and facilities to meet those demands. In reality, however, the process is far more complex. Figure 14.2 identifies a ten-stage leisure planning approach, representing best practice based on leisure theory and current practical application from a leisure management perspective, which summarises much of what has been reviewed in this chapter. This planning process runs parallel to, and in collaboration with, the formal planning process and local plans.

To explain this process a little more:

- **Stage 1: review policies, goals and objectives** – this concerns the philosophical basis of providing for the community and the roles of the key stakeholders (e.g. as providers, enablers, partners, etc.).
- **Stage 2: evaluate provision** – this stage identifies the type, range and ownership of facilities, whether public, voluntary or commercial. It also evaluates effectiveness and efficiency,

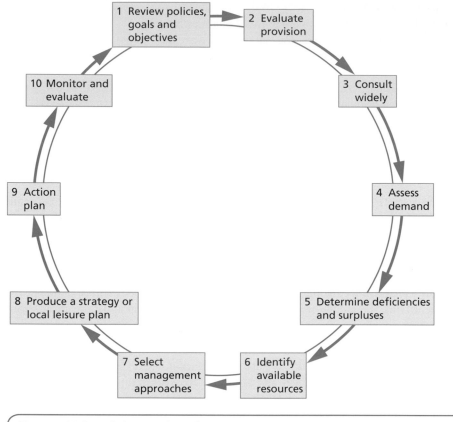

Figure 14.2 A leisure planning process.

usage and management. It determines levels of demand and spare capacity. A population study will identify resident concentrations and specific sections of the community that require special consideration, while a transport analysis will highlight the accessibility of existing and potential leisure sites.

- **Stage 3: consult widely** – this creates the opportunity to find out what needs to be provided for those the plan is intended to serve. Consultation is needed with local residents, workers and organisations. A range of techniques should be used. Consultation is also needed with agencies such as arts and sports governing bodies, with education authorities and schools, and with neighbouring authorities to avoid overlap and duplication.

- **Stage 4: assess demand** – although there is no single leisure planning technique that can accurately indicate what the potential demand may be for a particular activity or facility, a good indication can be obtained by using different leisure planning techniques, including demand modelling. These include national and, more specifically, local data; population profiling; the results of consultation; and identifying known and latent demands.

- **Stage 5: determine deficiencies and surpluses** – this stage analyses the supply–demand relationship. Comparing the level of potential demand with the actual provision should, theoretically, produce a list of deficiencies. It would be unrealistic for any authority to contemplate redressing all the perceived deficiencies; rather, the deficiencies should be ranked in order of priority.

- **Stage 6: identify available resources** – it will be necessary to examine all potential sites for leisure development and these should be assessed in terms of their suitability (e.g. size, terrain, accessibility, environmental considerations). A feasibility study should be undertaken, which should lead to a business plan encompassing capital and revenue costs, management and use. Grants and planning obligation opportunities will need to be considered.

- **Stage 7: select management approaches** – there now exists a range of management options and it is incumbent on local authorities to provide value for money. Options include: commercial contractors; trust management; buy-outs by existing managers; business concessions; partnerships; or a mix of these for different operations. Different facilities and services may well require different management approaches.

- **Stage 8: produce a strategy or local leisure plan** – leisure managers will also need to prepare a local leisure plan or series of specific plans (e.g. Arts; Sport and Recreation), incorporating short and medium term development plans for the area, with the council's role in these developments being clearly defined. A local leisure strategy will set out the roles of the council, the policies, the development and management objectives, and a plan of actions.

- **Stage 9: action plan** – to implement the strategies, it will be necessary to produce an action plan with clear objectives, targets and methods of measurement. Areas of responsibility will need to be assigned to key committees and officers with delegated areas of responsibility. In order to ensure that the tasks are completed on time, it is advisable that a detailed critical path analysis network be drawn up.

- **Stage 10: monitor and evaluate** – the progress made will need to be monitored and results measured. This should include the effect of the actions upon the community. The strategies will need periodic review in the light of economic, social and environmental changes.

14.6 Conclusions

The nature and scale of leisure provision are often the result of inheritance and possibly this may be the reason why local authorities often had no philosophy for the allocation of leisure resources – no stated purpose for their expenditure on leisure services or their planning for other providers. With greater recognition of leisure as a meaningful part of local, regional and national infrastructure, this ad hoc approach to leisure planning has changed, in the UK and in other countries.

As with marketing, a knowledge of customers is important to sport and leisure planning. However, there is no one method of accurately determining the demand for leisure activities or amenities. Each of the methods of assessing demand reviewed in this chapter has its strengths and its limitations; and used appropriately they can provide a good indication of the extent to which demand is unsatisfied. It would be wise, if resources allow, to use more than one method, as a form of triangulation – examining the same problem with different methods is a test of the validity of the results.

Leisure planning is an important discipline. Approached logically, it should result in eliminating previous examples of poor leisure planning, where provision is inappropriate to the market it is meant to serve. Leisure planning differs from general planning, as leisure outside the home is made up of an extremely wide variety of activities and choices; and leisure behaviour is not always predictable. Nevertheless it is important for the leisure manager to understand and participate in appropriate planning processes.

This will ensure an appropriate fit between supply and demand, moderated by the resources available.

Resources are also important to the scope and scale of leisure planning undertaken at the local level. It requires a lot of time and expertise to use the techniques reviewed in this chapter and, whilst external consultants can help, all such planning efforts will be constrained by the local authority's resources.

Practical tasks

1 Local plans:
   (a) Select an area. Find a local development plan/framework (they are usually publicly available through the local authority's website) and identify what elements of leisure are acknowledged in this plan.
   (b) For the same area, find a local leisure/cultural plan and identify what processes of consultation were undertaken to inform this plan.
   Is it possible to identify from these plans the importance of leisure to policies and people in the local area investigated?
2 Cohort analysis:
   (a) Find current population figures and population forecasts for a specific area. Identify specific population cohorts and their likely populations now and in ten years time.
   (b) Identify participation rates for a specific activity for the cohorts, using appropriate survey data. Assuming likely scenarios (e.g. policy initiatives, industry changes), estimate how these participation rates are likely to change in the next ten years.
   (c) Multiply the current populations for the cohorts by their current participation rates, to identify the number of people participating. Multiply by average frequency of participation to calculate average number of visits in a given time period. Repeat the process to calculate the number of people and visits in ten years time.
   (d) What are the implications of your results for planning provision?

Structured guide to further reading

For guidance on planning principles:

Department of Communities and Local Government (2002) *Planning Policy Guidance 17: planning for open space, sport and recreation*, HMSO, London (a new Planning Policy Statement is being prepared at the time of writing).

Sport England (2009) *Improving Community Sports Facilities: a toolkit for the strategic planning of community sports facilities*, Sport England, London.

For a review and discussion of planning techniques:

Veal, A.J. (2002) *Leisure and Tourism Policy and Planning*, 2nd edition, CABI Publishing, Wallingford.

Useful websites

For planning policy in England and Wales and a guide to Local Development Frameworks:
www.planningportal.gov.uk/
www.planningportal.gov.uk/uploads/ldf/text_ldfguide.html

For planning policy in Wales:
http://wales.gov.uk/topics/planning/policy/?lang=en

For planning policy in Northern Ireland:
www.planningni.gov.uk/index/policy/policy_publications/planning_statements.htm

For planning policy in Scotland:
www.scotland.gov.uk/Topics/Built-Environment/planning/National-Planning-Policy/newSPP

For planning obligations in England:
www.sportengland.org/facilities_planning/planning_contributions/what_are_they.aspx

For the Index of Multiple Deprivation in the UK:
www.communities.gov.uk/communities/neighbourhoodrenewal/deprivation/deprivation07/

For Sport England's *Facilities Improvement Service*:
www.sportengland.org/facilities__planning/planning_tools_and_guidance/facilities_improvement_service.aspx

For A.J. Veal's U-Plan resources:
www.leisuresource.net/service2.aspx

Marketing of sport and leisure

In this chapter

- What is marketing and who are the customers it is aimed at?
- How can information on customers be organised to help marketing?
- What is relationship marketing?
- How does assessing the internal and external environments contribute to marketing?
- What is the 'marketing mix'?
- How important is sponsorship to marketing in sport and leisure?

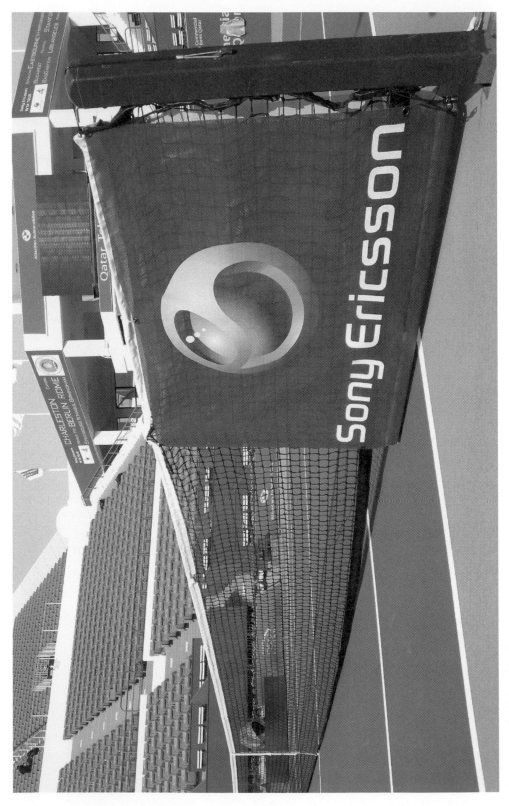

Summary

Much of the modern emphasis in sport and leisure businesses is on the customer. Satisfying customers is at the centre of notions of service quality. This chapter follows a marketing planning process which begins with identifying the organisation's objectives and understanding customers, particularly the market segments of interest to the organisation; proceeds through analysis of the organisation's internal and external environments and its market positioning; then involves a range of decisions about the 'marketing mix'; before implementing an action plan; and monitoring whether or not marketing objectives have been achieved.

Eight marketing mix decisions are considered in this chapter, because sport and leisure are largely service industries. This marketing mix consists of product, price, place, promotion, people, physical evidence, process and sponsorship. These are not separate considerations, however, but are interrelated and interdependent parts of an integrated plan. The one element of this mix which is different from many other industries is sponsorship, which is particularly important to some parts of the sport and leisure industry.

15.1 Introduction

Marketing is an essential part of good management practice. It is a process of identifying customer needs, wants and wishes, and satisfying them. Sport and leisure services and facilities depend on satisfied customers or they go out of business. Marketing involves creating appropriate goods and services and matching them to market requirements. Therefore, far from being just about selling, marketing is from the beginning an integral part of the business process. Marketing does the following:

- assesses the needs and wants of potential customers;
- analyses the internal organisational and external market environments;
- segments the market appropriately;
- positions the product in the market;
- implements a number of decisions, termed the 'marketing mix';
- secures appropriate relationships with customers;
- analyses, evaluates and adjusts.

However, marketing is as relevant to not-for-profit organisations, in the private and public sectors, as it is to the commercial profit-making sector. Any providers should be motivated to supply their customers with what these customers want. In the commercial world, marketing has proved to be an effective means of staying in business and making greater profits. For leisure services in the public and voluntary sectors, it can help to achieve a more complex set of objectives. The common link is the customer, because it is through satisfying customers that any organisational objectives are achieved. As Chapter 17 makes clear, the essence of quality management is satisfying customers.

Marketing is not a single function in a business or service organisation. It is a business philosophy, a business way of life. Traditionally, many companies used to be process led and product oriented; having a predetermined product or service, they found customers and convinced them to want their product. The approach is 'This is what we've got – now sell it'. Local government services in particular have often worked in this way. For example, facilities are built, equipment is installed, markings are put on to the floors, programmes are devised, times are decided, charges are determined, systems are established, and the council will proudly announce that the facility is open. Councillors might then say of the facility, 'It is there for them to use; if they don't use it that is their lookout. We provide plenty of opportunity in our town.' This approach is concerned with providing predetermined products.

The marketing approach reverses the process and starts with the customer. It is market led. It requires the manager to find out what the customer wants and then design, produce and deliver what is required to satisfy customers, and achieve the organisation's objectives. Blake (1985) said: 'Sports centres, pools, theatres, art galleries, libraries, museums, gymnasia, are merely warehouses holding tangible and intangible products that have no value except that brought to them by customers.'

15.1.1 The concept of social marketing

Marketing can be interpreted as much broader than just economic exchange and can also include exchanges dealing with social issues. Kotler and Zaltman (1971) define social marketing as '[t]he design, implementation and control of programmes calculated to influence the acceptability of social ideas and involving consideration of product planning, pricing, communication, distribution and market research'. Marketing can encompass political campaigns, community programmes and social causes, such as environmental issues, healthy living, child protection, disability issues, anti-smoking campaigns and equal opportunities. Social marketing, however, is less concerned with finding out what consumers want, and more concerned with convincing consumers that certain decisions are in their own interests and worth acting on for social reasons.

Of particular relevance to sport and leisure is healthy living social marketing, such as participACTION in Canada, where sport and physical activity has been stimulated by a national campaign (see Case Study 15.1). In the UK and other countries, health is currently a primary motivation for public policy to increase participation in sport and physical activity. ParticipACTION provides an important precedent in successful social marketing for this purpose.

A recent initiative on similar lines to participACTION in England is Change4Life (see 'Useful websites', p. 424). This is a three-year healthy living campaign run by a coalition of government, industry partners and other non-governmental organisations. Social marketing is at the heart of the campaign, which is designed to reverse the country's growing obesity problem by encouraging people to be more active and make healthier food choices. A similar campaign in Scotland is called Take Life On.

15.2 The marketing planning process

In order to market successfully, there needs to be a marketing plan. Sometimes this is used to mean the selection of the marketing mix (see p. 410) but it is a more holistic process than this. Figure 15.1 illustrates a ten-stage marketing planning process. This process establishes

ParticipACTION

ParticipAction (see 'Useful websites', p. 424) is one of the most successful social marketing campaigns to have aimed at increasing physical activity. It was established in 1971, ran until 2000, but then was revived in 2007 as the national voice of physical activity and sport participation in Canada.

The first participACTION programme was founded to create awareness of how inactive and unfit Canadians were, and educate Canadians on how to get more physically active. At its core was a very effective communications campaign, utilising commercial marketing methods, funded by government. One of the most effective messages claimed that, on the basis of international evidence, the average 30-year-old Canadian was in about the same shape as the average 60-year-old Swede. Edwards reports that one of the key principles in the communications strategy was to respect the audience:

> Communications campaigns that condescend or tell people what they *should* do inevitably fail. An effective campaign *shows* rather than *claims* that an idea is good, and how and why it is worth acting on.
>
> (Edwards, 2004: S9)

Throughout the campaign, surveys suggested that the prompted awareness level for participACTION was consistently in excess of 80 per cent of those questioned – much higher than equivalent campaigns elsewhere (Edwards, 2004). It has become a model for social marketing.

However, although the impact of participACTION in terms of awareness levels is undeniable, it is more difficult to report reliably on the effects of the social marketing on physical activity levels in Canada. Other factors affect physical activity, such as government 'community mobilisation programmes', of which several occurred simultaneously with participACTION. There is evidence that physical activity in Canada rose during the period of participACTION, including time-use evidence (Zuzanek, 2005) which shows that the average time given to physically active leisure by Canadians rose by 79 per cent between 1981 and 1998 – from 19 minutes to 34 minutes a day. How much of this increase was due to participACTION is difficult to quantify, although it undoubtedly had a role to play.

The major problem that the second phase of participACTION is designed to combat is unacceptably high levels of obesity and overweight in children and adults, with associated health problems. Participation in sport for both children and adults declined in the period of reduced funding and eventual closure of the original participACTION programme in 2000. ParticipACTION adopted a ten-point agenda for increasing population physical activity (Shilton, 2006), which demonstrates the integrated marketing approach required for such an ambitious social objective – effective communication is necessary but not enough by itself. The agenda was as follows:

1 Establish a multidisciplinary task force, from across government departments and the community, including health, education, transport, planning, sport and local government.
2 Develop and implement a comprehensive physical activity strategy.
3 Ensure appropriate investment in new resources.
4 Support population monitoring of physical activity.
5 Fund and implement communication and mass media campaigns.
6 Support mass participation through proven programmes.
7 Fund active transport initiatives, such as walking and cycling.
8 Partner with those who plan the built environment, so that design facilitates physical activity.
9 Take a life-stage approach, to meet the needs of market segments at greater risk from physical inactivity.
10 Require compulsory physical education.

These ten points include some of the basic principles of marketing, i.e. clear objectives as part of point 2, understanding customers in point 9, evaluating effects in point 4 and implementing appropriate elements of the marketing mix in points 5 (promotion), 3, 6 and 7 (product), and 10 (place).

Figure 15.1 The process of marketing planning.

the structure for the rest of this chapter. Whilst each element is reviewed separately, it is important to remember that this is an integrated set of issues and decisions which are dependent on each other.

15.3 Organisational vision, mission and objectives

Concise organisational statements of vision and mission are very important, not only to steer marketing planning but also for all stakeholders in an organisation, whether they are customers, staff, shareholders or partner organisations. An organisation's vision statement is a clear statement of where it wants to go. Its mission statement identifies the organisation's main reason for existing and indicates the values guiding its policies and strategies. The vision and mission statement are equivalent to aims, but they do not contain sufficient detail to enable them to be confidently translated into operational details and targets. For this objectives are necessary.

To be operationally useful, objectives need to have certain attributes – often summarised in the term 'SMART', but this is modified and has an extra letter added to form the term MASTER (**M**easurable, **A**chievable, **S**pecific, **T**ime-specified, **E**nds not means, **R**anked) (see Chapter 17). The essential point is that it must be possible to identify if and when objectives have been achieved.

> **Discussion question**
>
> Arts Council England's mission statement reads: 'Our mission for the next three years, ten years and beyond is clear and unequivocal. It is about great art for everyone' (www.artscouncil.org.uk). How useful is this as a steer for marketing the arts?

15.4 Understanding customers

An essential part of analysing external and internal environments for an organisation is understanding customers. Customers include:

- individuals;
- organisations (who buy for others);
- supporters;
- spectators;
- schools;
- clubs;
- parents of young users;
- the community.

Even non-users might be seen as potential customers and are therefore worthy of consideration from a marketing perspective. Different customers have different needs, a principle which is at the heart of market segmentation (see Section 15.4.2).

Chapter 2 identifies some dimensions to the concepts of customer need and market demand. Understanding customer needs and demands is a foundation stone for marketing. Market research and demand forecasting are tools to help with this (see Chapter 14). There are a number of other techniques to help, including customer profiling, market segmentation and analysis of customer relationships. Before reviewing these techniques, it is important to understand consumer behaviour.

15.4.1 Consumer behaviour

This is a branch of marketing analysis which examines the reasons for customer purchases. It centres on needs and motivations, which have already been reviewed in Chapter 2. Many theories of consumer behaviour are based on logical processes. For example, the theory of reasoned action suggests that consumer behaviour is driven by intentions, which are themselves driven by a variety of internal and external factors. Consumers have attitudes towards prospective purchases which will be driven partly by their perceptions of value, partly by their personal circumstances and partly by the social environment they live and work in (Pope and Turco, 2001).

With a particular focus on sport marketing, Mullin *et al.* (2007) identify a range of environmental and individual factors which influence consumer behaviour, either positively or negatively. Such factors include:

- Environmental:
  - significant others, such as parents, teachers and peer group leaders;
  - cultural norms and values, which may be inherited but may also be influenced by the media;

- class, race and gender relations;
- climatic and geographic conditions;
- market behaviour of sport organisations;
- Individual:
  - self-concept, including self-image, and self-confidence;
  - life-cycle stage;
  - physical characteristics;
  - income and employment;
  - education and learned skills;
  - perceptions;
  - motivations, including physiological, psychological and social;
  - attitudes.

In short, sport and leisure marketers have a significant task in understanding why consumers behave the way they do. But this understanding is an important foundation for the rest of marketing activity.

15.4.2 Market segmentation

Knowledge of consumer behaviour leads to the conclusion that customers are not one set of people with the same characteristics and preferences. Instead, customers comprise numerous groups of individuals within each of which there are similarities in needs, characteristics, motivations, etc. It is no longer appropriate to believe that an organisation is providing a service for all people. Even local authorities, with arguably the broadest remit in terms of a potential customer base, now recognise that if they indiscriminately market their services to all, it will probably result in particular types of people being over-represented among their customers and some groups, particularly the disadvantaged, being under-represented. Remedying this requires market segmentation and target marketing.

A market segment, then, is any relatively homogeneous subdivision of a market that is likely to be attracted to particular products or services. Several forms of market segmentation are available:

- **by demographics** – e.g. age groups, gender groups, ethnic groups, tourists;
- **by socio-economics** – e.g. by income, occupation, housing type, car ownership;
- **by geography** – i.e. different areas, from countries to communities, the latter often coinciding with socio-economic variables in formal classification systems such as ACORN in the UK (see Chapter 14);
- **by behaviour and benefits** – i.e. how customers respond to and what they get from the service, e.g. off-peak visitors, fitness motivated customers, visitors motivated by education/skill improvement;
- **by psychographics** – typically different attitudes, lifestyles and values.

Many practical segmentation exercises involve a mix of these different methods. It is possible to conduct clear and simple segmentation by using descriptive statistics such as age, gender and socio-economic profiles of populations, to identify major market segments suitable for marketing actions. It is unlikely that many sport and leisure organisations will have the resources to undertake a complex statistical analysis, such as that illustrated in Case Study 15.2 – particularly small and medium-sized enterprises and organisations in the voluntary sector. Sport England's segmentation analysis enables relevant organisations to utilise a ready-made system for identifying market segments and what motivates them, and designing appropriate marketing communications.

CASE STUDY 15.2

Sport consumers segmentation in England

Consultants Experian have produced for Sport England a 19-segment classification of people in respect of sport (see 'Useful websites', p. 424) – using national survey data to identify their activity levels, their socio-demographic characteristics, their motivations and their attitudes. This segmentation was conducted to provide those working in community sport with both an insight into the sporting behaviour, barriers and motivations of existing participants; and a practical marketing tool. The 19 market segments are identified in Figure 15.2 and comprise:

1 competitive male urbanites;
2 sports team drinkers;
3 fitness class friends;
4 supportive singles;
5 career-focused females;
6 settling down males;
7 stay at home mums;
8 Middle England mums;
9 pub league team mates;
10 stretched single mums;
11 comfortable mid-life males;
12 empty nest career ladies;
13 early retirement couples;

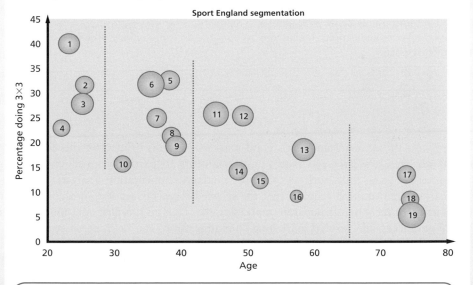

Figure 15.2 Sport England market segments.

Notes: The size of the circles relates to each segment's total percentage in the English adult population. The percentages refer to those doing three × 30 minutes moderate intensity sport per week.

Source: Sport England (2007b).

14 older working women;
15 local old boys;
16 later life ladies;
17 comfortable retired couples;
18 twilight year gents;
19 retirement home singles.

Figure 15.2 demonstrates that even though these segments are identified by multivariate analysis, age plays a significant role in discriminating between them. Within each age band, however, are several different segments, with different characteristics that are summarised by their titles but described in much more detail (see 'Useful websites', p. 424).

Detailed information on the size and composition of these segments has been produced at different geographical levels – street, community, local authority and region. It is also available for individual sports and broader sport groups (e.g. by type, such as racquet sports or martial arts, by facilities used, by individual/team). The information extends to how sport and active recreation fit into each segment's lives, the type of marketing communications messages they respond to, the communications media they respond to, the brands they identify and associate with, and how they make decisions. This is all very important for the detailed marketing planning for each segment.

Sport England also provides advice on how its market segmentation can be used for a variety of purposes, including catchment area analysis, funding decisions, planning new facilities, project evaluation, attracting new members and identifying appropriate partner organisations. In addition there are case studies demonstrating how County Sports Partnerships (sub-regional organisational networks) have used the segments for a variety of purposes. Humber County Sports Partnership in the North East of the country, for example, has used it to develop new marketing strategies for its constituent local authorities, matching programmes to motivations for key segments and modifying marketing communications, taking into account the decision-making processes of these market segments.

The process of segmentation needs good market research, to identify the different segments. It requires strategies and matching of segments to particular products within the overall service – using tools such as the Sport England segmentation analysis. In practical terms, market segmentation requires that the selected segments are measurable, substantial (of sufficient size to be worth separate marketing planning and implementation) and easily identified and accessible, so that marketing communications can be directed at them effectively and efficiently.

15.4.3 Customer relationships

Relationship marketing is an approach to marketing which is designed to improve the relationship between the customer and the service provider. Being led by considerations of what matters for customers, it contrasts with product-led and process-led marketing. Relationship marketing is increasingly important in sport and leisure marketing, as the many examples in Ferrand and McCarthy (2009) demonstrate. Through this approach, the understanding of customers is structured by their relationship with the product, the brand

and the organisation. Sport is an excellent example of this. At one extreme are fans of sports teams – the most loyal of customers, who turn out to support their teams no matter what, often home and away, who purchase associated merchandise in larger quantities than other supporters and who provide the most vocal sounding board for any matters the organisation wants to test, e.g. through fanzines. At the other extreme are commercial fitness clubs, whose greatest problem is often poor retention of members, because their customers tend to shop around to find the service most appropriate to their needs and at the best price.

The rationale for relationship marketing is undeniable, especially in sport and leisure. More loyal customers spend more and cost less than new or less loyal customers. Customers with a good relationship with the product, brand and organisation will act as ambassadors or agents for attracting further customers – their word of mouth is a powerful medium. Relationship marketing translates market segments into individuals, because a key objective is to establish a relationship with each individual customer.

The main marketing implications of relationship marketing are that it is important to:

- **build new and stronger relationships** – e.g. through personalised marketing communications to selected market segments;
- **retain and develop existing relationships** – e.g. through loyalty offers and rewards and added value services;
- **recover from problems with existing relationships** – e.g. through fast identification of problems and effective action to resolve them (see Case Study 17.1).

These are principles which any marketing strategy should adopt. However, Ferrand and McCarthy (2009) promote relationship marketing as an alternative strategic approach to more traditional marketing approaches such as that identified in Figure 15.1, which is the structure for this chapter. Their model consists of three key stages:

1 Change the internal marketing structure of the organisation to focus on developing relationships.
2 Create and develop relationships with targeted customers, i.e. with the market.
3 Create and develop relationships with key stakeholders, i.e. with the network or organisations relevant to supply.

> **Discussion question**
>
> Discuss the difficulties of professional sports clubs simultaneously developing good relationships with corporate clients, 'fair weather supporters' and relatively low income, long-term fans.

15.5 Analysing internal and external environments

Understanding customers is really part of a first stage of marketing planning, which involves auditing and analysing the internal (organisational) and external (market) environments of the organisation. This involves assembling appropriate data and then analysing it. The types of data which are relevant include:

- Internal:
  - mission, vision and objectives;
  - customers, e.g. satisfactions, dissatisfactions, expectations, relationships;

- resources, e.g. management structure, staff, finance, technology;
- stakeholders, e.g. staff, partners, funders, relationships.
● External:
    - PEST – **P**olitical, **E**conomic, **S**ocial and **T**echnological considerations which impact on the organisation's activities (also called STEP; see Chapter 7 for an overview in relation to tourism markets);
    - potential customers – needs, motivations, profiles, behaviour and locations;
    - competitors, both direct (same products) and indirect (appealing to similar customer needs) – profiles, market shares, critical success factors, limitations, strategies, trajectories over time;
    - markets – size, growth, product developments, prices, distribution characteristics, promotion norms and development.

15.5.1 SWOT

A traditional means of summarising the internal and external environmental analysis which is still in common use is SWOT: **S**trengths and **W**eaknesses summarise the internal analysis of the organisation; **O**pportunities and **T**hreats summarise the external environment for the organisation. SWOT analysis is typically concise, attempting to select the key issues important to marketing decisions. It is also often descriptive, but the word 'analysis' is important – it needs to both justify the importance of the selected SWOT features and make clear the marketing implications for the organisation.

> **Discussion question**
>
> Consider the main strengths, weaknesses, opportunities and threats of a sport or leisure organisation in your locality. What are the marketing implications of your conclusions?

15.6 Marketing objectives and strategies

Marketing objectives should aspire to the same attributes as organisational objectives (see p. 400) and they should be shared by the whole organisation, not just the marketing manager/department (see Chapter 13). They should specify marketing targets in relation to appropriate performance indicators (see Chapter 17 for a review of performance indicators and performance management). Marketing objectives are also likely to be specific to selected market segments. Examples include reaching a certain number of members from a particular demographic section of the catchment area, such as older people; and reaching a target for secondary income per attendance, from merchandise and catering.

> **Discussion question**
>
> For a sport or leisure organisation of your choice, discuss possible organisational objectives and marketing objectives to illustrate the differences between them.

A marketing strategy is a calculated approach to achieving objectives and targets. The strategy sets a direction for the specific marketing instruments – the marketing mix. One important element of the strategy is market segmentation (see pp. 402–4). Another is market positioning.

15.6.1 Strategic positioning

'Positions' are people's perception of where products fit in the market. A product's position can be easily recognised and favourable positions encourage continued sales. Products and services have long-term 'personalities', just like people. For example, the Bank of England – normally safe and dependable; Wimbledon – the pinnacle of tennis and its traditional values; Richard Branson's Virgin products – innovative and creative. Disney, McDonald's, Nike and hundreds of other brands have a position in our minds and in the marketplace. Positions, however, can be favourable or unfavourable. Local authority leisure services for years have had to battle with the public perception of their facilities as basic and cheap, in comparison with higher quality commercial sector facilities.

Positions are established through well-targeted marketing communications. For example, activity holiday resorts like Center Parcs established a strong market position in a relatively short time, principally through television advertising. Sponsorship enables companies to establish a strong position within their industries, e.g. insurance companies like Cornhill and Axa Equity and Law improved their market positions and market shares through sponsorship of cricket.

Repositioning is possible. The drink Lucozade used to be sold in chemist's shops for people who were ill. However, TV promotions using Olympic gold medal winners, like Daley Thompson, repositioned Lucozade as a refreshing energy drink for athletes – from a position of a drink for the sick to a drink for the fit. Crompton (2009) views repositioning as vitally important for the future of public leisure services. It is his claim that leisure services are still not central to public service provision, because they are not sufficiently positioned alongside major social concerns. Their future, therefore, depends on repositioning public sport and leisure so that the public and politicians associate them with solutions to such concerns, e.g. poor health, obesity, crime and vandalism, children's safety, etc.

Two other commonly cited tools can help in positioning products within the market place and within the organisation's portfolio of products. These are the Boston Matrix and the Ansoff Matrix.

15.6.2 The Boston Matrix

This matrix, shown in Figure 15.3, was designed for the Boston Consulting Group as a device to help analyse sources of cash flow within an organisation. Its two axes, market share and market growth rate, are associated respectively with cash generation and cash usage. The organisation's business units, or alternatively brands or products, can be positioned in this matrix by the use of data and judgement. The matrix helps to identify the balance of the portfolio of business units, brands or products, although not all the quadrants of the matrix are of equal merit with respect to cash flow:

● **Cash cows** – with high market share but low market growth, these are often described derogatively as mature and boring, but in fact because they are highly likely to be net cash generators, they are very valuable assets, with a market position which should be

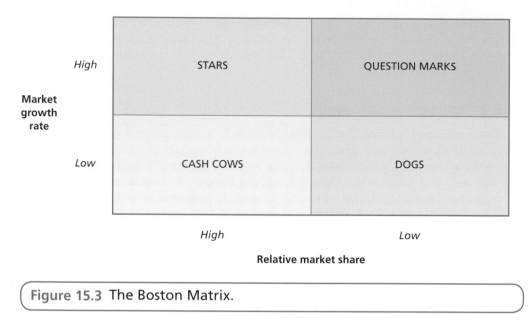

Figure 15.3 The Boston Matrix.

defended by rejuvenation tactics. In the UK, at indoor sports centres, five-a-side football leagues might be seen as cash cows.

- **Stars** – with high market share and high market growth, these typically attract all the attention as the best performers, although the high growth rate requires high cash usage. Gyms in indoor sport and leisure centres in the UK are a current example of 'stars'.
- **Question marks** – with low market share and high market growth, these are net cash users and although they may increase market share as a result of high market growth, there is a risk that their growth rate falls and they become 'dogs'. Specific forms of exercise class are possible 'question marks' because there is always uncertainty about whether they will become established or be replaced by a new form of exercise.
- **Dogs** – with low market share and low market growth, these are not worth continuing. In recent years in the UK, squash has been of this nature, and has been disposed of by a number of indoor sports centres.

The Boston Matrix gives a clear positioning of an organisation's products, but it requires a detailed knowledge of the market to be accurate. It does not reveal the profitability or social impact of the organisation's products. It is therefore useful for analysis of cash flow and its potential, but it should not be interpreted as more than this. Nevertheless, cash flow is important to organisations in all three sectors, not just commercial companies. And it is from this perspective that the Boston Matrix gives implications for marketing priorities and activities, e.g. defensive marketing for cash cows against threats to market share, and demarketing or disposing of 'dogs'.

15.6.3 The Ansoff Matrix

This matrix, shown in Figure 15.4, was devised in order to help organisations and their marketers identify the strategic choices for growth in their business. Each quadrant represents different potential for growth and risk:

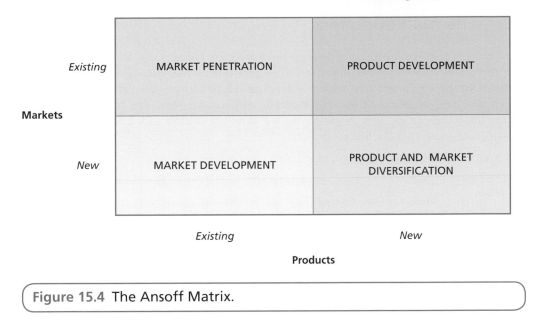

Figure 15.4 The Ansoff Matrix.

- **Market penetration** offers probably the lowest growth potential but also the lowest risk, i.e. more of the same product to the same market. Growth can be achieved by capturing customers from other suppliers, attracting non-users or encouraging existing users to buy/visit more frequently. The free swimming initiative in the UK could be viewed as largely market penetration, because it is likely to stimulate more swimming from the same markets that provide current swimmers.
- **Market development** requires marketing activity in new markets. These may be new geographical areas or new market segments that were previously not targeted. Outreach services are a typical form of market development in sport and leisure, i.e. taking the services into geographical areas where usage is low. The growth prospects are higher than market penetration, but so are the risks – the new market may not be as suitable as the existing market.
- **Product development** requires identification, supply and promotion of new products to existing customers. The growth prospects and risk depend critically on designing the right new product for the market – customer research is essential to reduce the risk. Commercial fitness centres are very good at developing new fitness products for their existing customers.
- **Diversification** is the most risky strategy and the one requiring most research because both the products and markets are new. Several sports, for example, have developed new variants of their activities for very young participants.

The Ansoff Matrix, like the Boston Matrix, is a descriptive device to categorise products. These devices are not prescriptive and need careful interpretation with respect to marketing strategies for brands, products and markets.

15.7 The marketing mix

Marketing is concerned with providing the right products and services, and then forging the best relationships between customers and those products and services. The 'marketing mix' is the means by which that relationship is developed. It has a number of ingredients, each of which will have a greater or lesser influence in different settings. The first four are commonly referred to as 'the four Ps', while the last three are usually added in consideration of services marketing to make 'the seven Ps':

1 product (including service);
2 pricing;
3 place;
4 promotion;
5 people;
6 physical evidence;
7 process.

An eighth element of the marketing mix which is particularly relevant to sport and leisure is sponsorship. The sections which follow review these components.

15.7.1 The sport and leisure product

The product (including the service) is the basis of all marketing. It is the unit of exchange with the client or customer. If it offers customers satisfaction, they may continue to buy it. Sport and leisure products are opportunities for customers and they can be of different types, including tangible and intangible elements. They include one or more of the following:

● goods, e.g. photographic equipment, sports clothing and footwear;
● facilities, e.g. tennis courts, museums;
● services, e.g. a lesson, a guided walk, outreach opportunities;
● events, e.g. a sports competition, a music festival;
● programmes (see Chapter 16), e.g. a Shakespeare production, a mother and child swimming session, an aerobics class.

These are the vehicles for realising demands. When these products successfully match customer demands, it leads to the realisation of service outcomes, in particular the benefits sought by customers. People want to enjoy, to be with friends, to learn, to look better, to feel better, to be skilful, to win. If customers do experience such benefits, they will want to 'buy' them again. Customers help to create the final product, which is the participation experience – this is the inseparability of leisure service products and consumption. Another key characteristic of many sport and leisure experiences is that they differ on each occasion. Every sports game is different, every drama production is different, every concert is different, even when there are some standard infrastructure elements supporting the delivery of the final product. It is this difference, or novelty, that is said to be a key driver of leisure demands (see Chapter 2).

The provision of services, facilities and programmes is important in providing opportunities but the purpose of the product is not realised until it is utilised. In this sense the sport and leisure product is highly perishable; for example, an unsold seat at a theatre production represents the permanent loss of an experience. Matching products to likely demand is a very difficult task, not just in terms of the timing of opportunities (around peak and off-peak fluctuations in demand, seasonal changes) but also in terms of the quantity and quality of the product offer. A sports centre which is too big for its catchment area, for example, will give rise to continual capacity utilisation problems, which represent a waste of product.

Products exhibit life-cycles. With most commercial products, that life-cycle consists of:

- product start;
- growth;
- development;
- decline and replacement by better products.

In sport and leisure services, many products have been with us for a long time but a number are relatively new (e.g. various forms of aerobic exercise classes) and some have declined (e.g. squash). Product development provides a continuous stream of new or changing products which fit customers' needs. Cinemas have changed from single to multi-screen. Tenpin bowling and bingo have changed to social venues with a wider range of products. In public sector sport, it is apparent that needs and motivations have changed over the years, with less demand for competitive team sports and growing demand for non-competitive, individual, fitness activities (see Chapter 10). This is not supply led, but rather is determined by changing motivations towards health- and fitness-related outcomes, such as losing weight for health reasons or looking good for social reasons.

Leisure products, like any other products, need testing and changing to suit customer needs. Hence market research and product testing need to be undertaken to have the best chance of matching products with markets. Capturing interest with the product is essential, and novelty is a desirable attribute. Good marketers should encourage levels of originality and be prepared to take risks. This is particularly the case in the arts, where new products are an important element of attracting repeat business. Originals and 'firsts' capture interest and can also create a lasting impression.

Packaging different products can generate customer benefits at all levels of participation, e.g. a daytime public leisure centre package might include sports activity, dietary clinic, sauna and a crèche for the children. Marketers have identified three levels of product and the packaging of products is clearly aimed at embracing all three:

1 The **core** product is the main motivation for the customer, e.g. a visit to an exhibition, or a fitness class.
2 The **actual** product wraps certain elements around the core product, such as changing facilities in the case of sport.
3 The **augmented** product includes a variety of optional extras, such as merchandising, drinks, food or transport arrangements.

Most sport and leisure programmes, even those designed with a specific activity in mind, tend to market more than one product. A combination of facilities can attract greater use, be more economical and also provide the spin-off to other activities, expanding the market.

Discussion question

Think of a core product, e.g. enjoying a theatre production, a game of sport, an art exhibition. Now think of additional product items that can be offered to create added value for the customer. Are all these typically on offer and if not why not?

15.7.1.1 Brands

Another form of product augmentation which has become important in its own right is brands. A product is the basic functional item for sale, whether it is a physical good or an intangible service. Often it can be easily copied. However, a brand is fundamentally an identifier, such as a logo, which helps to distinguish one seller from its competitors – it cannot be copied. Aaker (2002) suggests that brands add a number of intangible associations which augment the product, such as customer relationships, emotional benefits and user imagery.

The brand helps position the product in the market. A product takes on added value from a brand, because of the intangible associations and benefits which consumers relate to the brand. This added value is termed 'brand equity', which can be financial, such as increased sales and profits, and consumer based, such as perceived higher quality, brand associations and brand loyalty. The marketer uses brands because they help to enhance the relationship with the customer, generating greater customer loyalty and more repeat purchasing of the product.

> **Discussion question**
>
> Many customers buy only branded sports clothing and footwear, typically at considerably higher cost than unbranded equivalents. What are the main 'added value' reasons for this behaviour?

15.7.2 Pricing

It is important not only to match people's needs with appropriate products but also to do so at prices they are willing to pay. Otherwise demand remains latent, not revealed. Price is an important signal to both consumers and producers in the market system. Economists begin an explanation of the market system with a demand and supply diagram, with price as the controlling variable for both. Often the importance of price is overstated. In some art forms, where demand is dominated by customers without socio-economic disadvantage, evidence suggests that price is not very important compared with the product – the performance, e.g. theatre and music concerts. Nevertheless, for many products demand is more price sensitive, particularly in markets where there is strong competition between alternative providers, or for market segments which suffer from socio-economic disadvantage, such as older people without private pensions, the disabled and the unemployed.

Prices perform valuable functions for providers – they raise revenue, they ration demand and they can help discriminate in favour of certain types of customers. They are also important signals for customers, who may perceive prices as indicators of quality, e.g. low pricing may suggest low product quality, whilst high prices reinforce perceptions of high quality and exclusivity, e.g. exclusive holidays and yachts.

Pricing policy is an important factor in financial planning and a vital part of marketing. Important pricing decisions for any product include:

● **The level of price which is appropriate to the organisation's objectives and its market demand** – too low and there could be considerable excess demand, with queues for services and waiting time for goods; too high and there will be underutilised capacity in services, and unsold stocks of goods. Even a free product should involve an explicit decision by the provider, because it should match the organisation's objectives and a way needs to be found to recoup the costs of provision.

- **The structure of prices,** including whether or not to have different prices for different customers – in arts or sports events this is normal, with higher prices for better audience positions. In tourism, higher prices are charged in peak seasons. Many other leisure organisations charge discounts for various reasons such as socio-economic disadvantage, promotion at slack times of the day or week, to attract new customers, to build relationships or to reward loyalty and repeat purchasing.

In principle, pricing decisions should be made with respect to a number of criteria:

- **The financial and marketing objectives of the organisation,** which can vary from maximising profits, through maximising utilisation, to maximising social benefits such as health improvement and reduction in crime and vandalism.
- **The costs of provision to the organisation** – not just the operating costs but also capital costs.
- **Strength of demand,** particularly in response to changes in prices. In economics this is termed 'price elasticity of demand', i.e. the relative strength of response of demand to a change in price. For many sport and leisure services demand is typically price inelastic – examples include attendances at professional team sports events, sport and leisure centres, and arts venues such as theatres and concerts – meaning that the percentage change in demand is less than the percentage change in price.
- **Strength of competition,** not only from within the sector, e.g. between commercial firms, but also across sectors, e.g. between commercial firms and local authority providers. The greater the competition, the more responsive or 'elastic' demand is to changes in price, because it is easier for customers to find substitutes.

In practice, evidence suggests that not all these criteria are typically employed when pricing decisions are made. In the commercial sector the most common pricing determinant is costs, e.g. cost-plus pricing, where prices are decided by calculating average cost per unit of supply and adding a profit margin. There is sometimes fierce competition in the commercial sector which has to be considered (see Chapter 4), and which in an oligopoly situation (a few major competitors) sometimes leads to stable prices, for fear of a price war between competitors.

In the voluntary sector, the most likely pricing level is one which will result in a break-even on operational costs for the organisation, so again costs are the major criterion for setting membership fees. This is because most clubs in the voluntary sector are non-profit, e.g. Chapter 6 shows that the average financial surplus in UK sports clubs is very small. Aiming to break even, however, requires an appreciation of both the costs of supplying opportunities for members and how sensitive members are to different prices. One way of linking prices to costs more directly is to charge prices for different elements of costs, e.g. membership fees (for club overheads), NGB affiliation fees and match fees (for match day costs).

In the public sector, pricing has largely been based on tradition, e.g. previous prices plus an increment, with some consideration of what is an 'acceptable' level in other authorities (so-called 'copycat pricing'). Subsidies are common in the public sector, so the pricing decision needs to consider what subsidies are reasonable and can be afforded from the public purse and how big the subsidies should be. Figure 15.5 illustrates a common charging continuum for public sector leisure services. The bulk of public sector leisure activities are priced at a subsidised level, with the primary objective of making activities accessible to disadvantaged segments of the community.

		SUBSIDY	PROFIT	
Type of charge	**No charge**	**Some charge**	**Economic charge**	**Commercial charge**
Basis of policy	Social service – all residents have a recreational need – facilities available to all	Many people and groups have needs for specialist activities for health and recreation	Participants are main benefactors – hence have to pay full costs	Benefits participants exclusively. Charges include full costs and profit charges based on what market can bear. Profit used to subsidise other facilities
Types of facilities	Parks Libraries	Swimming pools Public tennis courts Arts centres Community centres	Entertainments Golf courses	Indoor tennis Health and fitness Squash Sauna Sunbeds
Profile of users	Representative of neighbourhood	High proportion of local people Youths/young people	Middle income groups Young adults	Middle to high income groups

Figure 15.5 The pricing policy continuum for public sector sport and leisure.

Discussion question

In attempting to attract a wide cross-section of the community to a public leisure attraction, what are the relative merits of (1) generally low prices for all customers and (2) specifically targeted price discounts for disadvantaged people?

15.7.3 Place

Products – facilities, programmes, activities – need to be accessible to the people they have been developed for. Place, or distribution, is the final contact with the customer, after other marketing decisions such as product, price and promotion have been taken. Once customers attend a facility or a service opportunity, or purchase a sport or leisure product, it is a sign of effectiveness in distribution. In sport and leisure services the product is often centred on particular types of facility, which means that instead of the distribution of goods to customers, as in manufactured goods, the customer very often has to attend a facility, e.g. a sports centre, a theatre, a country park. In these circumstances, one key product decision, facility location, is simultaneously a place decision.

Distribution decisions should be based on the market research about customers, their home and work locations, transportation and other accessibility factors. A critically important decision for facilities is where to locate them in relation to their anticipated markets.

This is arguably the most important marketing decision (see Chapter 14), because whilst programmes, activities, prices and promotion can all be changed in the short run, within weeks if necessary, facility location is typically only changed in the long run, every thirty years or more.

It is therefore very important for services and facilities to be placed in locations that customers can get to easily. Accessibility can also be influenced with directional signs, maps, an attractive welcoming entrance, and by lighting the parking areas and walkways. The general awareness of the leisure facility can be reinforced by attractive displays and exhibitions in public places and by leaflet distribution. Place is also important within facilities, i.e. locating key elements within facilities with customer convenience in mind, e.g. changing rooms near playing areas, crèche adjacent to outdoor play space, good viewing for spectators.

Time and information are also key aspects of accessibility. Activities need to be in the right place at the right time, so programming is essential to distribution. Different market segments have potential for visiting at different times, so conventional programming – such as evenings for the theatre and concerts, weekday evenings and weekends for sport and physical activity – may be restricting accessibility unnecessarily. Less conventional programming times can work, with the right products and promotion, such as theatre matinees on weekday afternoons (attracting older customers) and early morning fitness opportunities (attracting people in nine-to-five jobs). Similarly, information centres for sport and leisure opportunities often close in the evenings and weekends, when they may be most needed, although the internet has facilitated round the clock information.

Distribution of sport and leisure is often direct, from producer to consumer, e.g. participating in local public sports facilities, visiting a local library, museum or art gallery. Other forms of sport and leisure are increasingly distributed indirectly, i.e. by agents or intermediaries. A major example is music and sport events, with internet agencies such as Ticketmaster in the UK taking increasing shares of ticket purchasing, rather than the venues themselves. Other examples such as books, recorded music and sports equipment and clothing are increasingly showing a switch of agents, from normal retail outlets to online purchasing (see Chapter 12). Whether distribution is direct or indirect has an effect on accessibility and price – typically indirect distribution increases both accessibility, by promotion to a wider set of potential customers, and price – either to the customer through a booking fee or to the supplier through a commission on sales.

Many leisure facilities will be inaccessible to segments of the population, for example people living in rural areas. In these cases, needs can be met by organising mobile services, e.g. mobile library, play bus, travelling theatre, and by appointing artists in residence, 'animateurs' and sports development officers. Community facilities such as village halls can be utilised to widen the distribution of sport and leisure services. In the arts, many drama and music companies have devised innovative alternative locations to traditional indoor venues, for summer productions, using parks and the gardens of historic houses. Some of these are designed to be more attractive places for existing customers, rather than places which appeal to new market segments, but they demonstrate the effectiveness of imaginative place decisions.

15.7.4 Promotion

Many people mistakenly use the word 'marketing' when they really mean promotion. Promotion's purpose is twofold: creating awareness of the opportunities provided by the supplier; and seeking to attract and persuade customers to purchase the particular service or product. It is a process of familiarising, and creating and reinforcing favourable images, attitudes and a willingness to buy. Through this process it is also a means by which customer relationships can be enhanced.

Promotional activity can be defined as an exercise in communications. There are many factors affecting demand, some of which consumers may be not be conscious of. Restricted impressions or preconceptions, for example, can determine consumer responses, e.g. 'sports facilities are only for young, fit people', 'theatres are only for educated, well-off people', 'classical music is only for older people'. It is the job of promotion to correct such misimpressions and motivate anyone with a potential interest in an opportunity into actually moving towards the purchase stage.

Discussion questions

Is it asking too much of promotion to change the image of theatres from being only for educated, well-off people? What other parts of the mix have a complementary role to play in achieving this image change?

Promotional communications can provide information about such things as the existence of the opportunity, opening times, etc.; or they can simply create and reinforce a favourable image, through symbolic association. The general functions of promotion are summarised by the acronym AIDA, i.e.:

- Attention – drawing the customer's attention to the product;
- Interest – creating interest in the product, through promotion of its benefits;
- Desire – stimulating a desire to purchase the product;
- Action – purchase and consumption of the product.

Promotion can set off an important additional round of communication about the product through word of mouth and recommendation – a large proportion of sport and leisure customers come with friends and like-minded groups of people. Masterman and Wood (2006) demonstrate the complexity of the communications process, which involves:

- the organisation encoding the messages it wants the market to notice with the required images and information;
- the potential customer decoding the message with the required interpretation;
- 'noise' – external distractions in the communications process, which need to be minimised.

A promotional strategy should be built around a proper brief, taking account of the following:

- the benefits of the products to consumers;
- target markets;
- the information and messages to be conveyed to potential customers;
- the media and promotional methods to be used;
- offers and inducements.

Promotion consists of one or more of the following key components:

- **personal selling** – a direct 'presentation' to one or more potential customers with the objective of selling a service or a product;
- **advertising** – a paid form of non-personal presentation about the organisation and/or the opportunities it offers;

- **incentives/promotions** – a financial offer or 'gift' that is made to potential customers with the objective of encouraging them to purchase a particular service or product;
- **publicity/public relations** – favourable communication in the media (e.g. print or broadcast) which may be achieved at no direct cost to the organisation concerned.

These four methods are not necessarily independent of each other and different methods can be used to enhance both the message and the customer relationship, e.g. an incentive to introduce a friend to an organisation, promoted by direct mail, will provide added value for existing customers. Sponsorship is sometimes identified as a fifth promotional vehicle, but in this chapter it is covered later as another element of the marketing mix (see pp. 420–2).

15.7.4.1 Personal selling

Personal selling is important to sport and leisure and does not typically take place through such means as telesales, but rather through face-to-face contact with frontline staff, such as bookings or reception staff. To be effective in personal selling, it is necessary that the person concerned does it with enthusiasm, so that he or she is perceived as being able, efficient and caring. The function of personal selling involves a two-way communication process and can provide valuable feedback about existing and potential programmes and activities.

15.7.4.2 Advertising

Advertising encompasses many forms of communication and includes:

- posters – in prominent, eye-catching locations;
- brochures and leaflets that describe the facilities, services and programmes on offer;
- advertisements placed in the local media, i.e. newspapers and radio;
- newsletters and fully paid supplements in the local newspapers;
- direct mailing enclosing new information, e.g. offers of new benefits in new programmes;
- internet advertising, social network sites, texts.

Advertising is not just aimed at potential new customers but is also important for existing customers, i.e. to expand sales to people already buying the product, either by increased frequency of purchase, or by purchase of different products from the same supplier. For example, a customer who has used a travel agent for a certain type of holiday may, through targeted advertising, be attracted to other types of holiday arranged by the same travel agent.

Advertising does not provide immediate feedback and can be an expensive form of promotion. Television advertisements are extremely expensive, as are paid advertisements in the press. In contrast, the local cinema can be a relatively cheap form of advertising – as cinema-going audiences are largely young people, products, activities and services that appeal to young people could be effectively advertised in local cinemas. A 'mail shot' using an agency address list or compiling a database can be an effective way of getting directly to a target audience.

The message to leisure managers appears to be to look at the whole variety of ways of communicating, to try out various forms and 'shop around' and then act positively, measure results and make appropriate adjustments. Self-testing criteria for an advertising communication are that it should produce positive answers to the following questions:

- Is it eye-catching?
- Is the layout attractive?
- Do the headline and text stimulate the reader to proceed further?

- Does it provide adequate information?
- But at the same time, is the message clear and simple?
- Is the text persuasive and credible?
- Does the advertisement create a favourable public image of the organisation?

However, no matter how well designed an advertising communication is, it needs to be effectively targeted at appropriate market segments to achieve success in promoting sales.

Discussion questions

What advertising do you particularly remember and why? Did you purchase any of the associated products?

15.7.4.3 Incentives

Incentives in the form of an 'offer' have become a prime means of persuading people to buy. In contrast to the other forms of promotional activity, incentives should not be used on a regular basis but when offered should be restricted to a limited period of time. The main objective of using incentives is to stimulate participation from identified target markets, particularly from new customers. The incentives can take the form of an introductory offer such as no joining fee at a fitness centre for a specified period, discounts, two-for-one purchases, and gifts of CDs and t-shirts.

Financial incentives can be persuasive. We all like to think we are getting something for nothing. The offer of discounts such as reduced off-peak pricing without adequate promotion and publicity, however, is unlikely to have a great impact. One of the cardinal principles of attracting a positive and warm response is to give freely and generously. Professional sports clubs, for example, knowing that the capacity of their home venue is unlikely to be sold out for certain matches, often give free tickets to local schools – this attracts new customers and also creates a better atmosphere at the match.

15.7.4.4 Publicity

Publicity normally takes the form of press releases or feature articles, and in some instances a theatre or leisure centre may write its own weekly column in the local newspaper. Since most local authority leisure services departments have a minimal promotional budget, this has often resulted in many concentrating more on publicity than other forms of promotion. Local presses are often in need of appropriate features and they are unlikely to be critical in editing these features. Publicity is a useful method of informing the community of the results of programmes, fixtures and forthcoming events. To keep a facility continually in the public's mind, it is necessary periodically to have general interest stories relating to the facility in the local newspaper, since not all readers read the arts and sports pages.

Although publicity does not directly involve financial expenditure, the true cost of preparing the publicity material may be considerable, particularly if many senior personnel are involved. Publicity carries the risk that the press editorial staff may reject the 'press release' or prepared copy on the grounds that it is not adequately newsworthy. The press can sometimes give a negative image very forcefully and they can be seen as challenging and questioning towards a local authority. Therefore, the only effective approach is to influence the press coverage by well-organised public relations. This includes informing and involving the press, keeping them up to date with news. Good press coverage will help the public to say that taxpayers' money spent on leisure services is well spent.

Rather than treat the four elements of promotion as separate decisions, Masterman and Wood (2006) promote an integrated marketing communications approach. This requires one integrated communications strategy embracing all relevant mechanisms, a focus on building relationships with customers, and specific targeting of particular customer groups.

15.7.5 People

Because sport and leisure are often services, people are an essential part of the marketing mix. One of the defining characteristics of services is the inseparability of production and consumption. Face-to-face interaction between the supplying organisation and the customer is inevitable and the success of a service is very dependent on this people relationship. Avoiding this relationship is not a solution – a commercial fitness centre once tried to dispense with its line staff to reduce costs, by making everything card swipe controlled, including entry and use of all facilities. It failed as a business.

In Sport England's National Benchmarking Service for sport and leisure centres (see Chapter 17) staff attributes are typically ranked among the highest for customer satisfaction, particularly the helpfulness of staff and the standard of instruction. These 'people' attributes are also ranked by customers in the top half of the attributes for importance. Personal service, with genuine good intentions for the customer, is a core attribute for sport and leisure services. This needs careful recruitment of staff with appropriate interpersonal skills, and training in customer care. It also needs a customer orientation for all staff, not just the line staff working at the 'customer face'.

Bad news travels fast. It is passed on more readily than good news. Sport and leisure marketers must therefore be concerned not only with what motivates people to take part in sport and leisure, but also what demotivates them. Nothing demotivates customers more than being poorly handled: rudeness; a 'take it or leave it' attitude; double bookings; ruined expectations; dissatisfactions and broken promises. At the heart of these risks to service success is the quality of the people delivering the services.

Discussion questions

When did you last encounter a 'bad' people experience in consuming a leisure service? What might the organisation have done to prevent this experience from happening?

15.7.6 Physical evidence

Another defining characteristic of services is that they are intangible, yet ironically it is often the physical circumstances or 'tangibles' of a service that are most important to customers. In Sport England's National Benchmarking Service for sport and leisure centres, out of twenty service attributes certain tangibles are among the most important to customers, i.e. water quality for swimmers, and cleanliness of changing areas and activity spaces. These tangibles relate to the core or actual product. Other tangibles which are part of the augmented product are less important to customers, e.g. quality of food and drink, quality of car parking.

The setting of a sport and leisure experience and the design of a facility are further important ingredients of the physical evidence. They can reinforce the image of a service when they excite, when they give a sense of occasion. Alternatively there may be a danger of deterring the customer if these 'atmospherics' are missing and the setting/facility is dull and uninspiring.

15.7.7 Process

Because of the inseparability of consumption and production in services, the process of service delivery is under the spotlight throughout. This process runs from finding out about opportunities, through booking an activity, finding the facility, parking, entering the facility, finding the way round the facility, engaging in the activity, possibly buying food and drink, to leaving the facility. The whole process of service delivery determines the relationships between the organisation and its customers.

An obvious way to demonstrate an active and dynamic relationship with customers is through publicising customer suggestions and organisational responses in order to demonstrate and promote a process of continuous improvement. For example, on the website of Ponds Forge International Sports Centre in Sheffield, UK, there is a section on 'You said, we did' in which there is a monthly update of customer suggestions and the centre's responses. Typically these are about minor matters, such as the difficulty of opening doors, the range of food and drink, and the telephone response times for queries. But as the adage goes, it's the small things that matter.

15.8 Sponsorship

For sport and the arts in particular, sponsorship is another significant element of the marketing mix. Sport and leisure organisations are attractive vehicles for sponsorship because their products, services and events are associated with positive feelings, strong brand images and clear target markets. Sponsorship is different from other elements of the marketing mix, however, because rather than the marketing *of* sport's products, it is the marketing of the sponsor's brand *through* sport (Hoye *et al.*, 2009).

Meenaghan provides one of the clearest definitions of sponsorship:

> Commercial sponsorship is an investment, in cash or in kind, in an activity, in return for access to the exploitable, commercial potential associated with that activity.
>
> (Meenaghan, 1991: 36)

Sponsorship differs from patronage, where the finance or professional expertise is given by a commercial company for philanthropic reasons, without it looking for any material reward or benefit and often with it remaining anonymous. It differs from advertising in that the promotional messages are much less direct and the sponsor has much less control over the marketing communications.

The exact amount of sports sponsorship expenditure is difficult to ascertain. Many companies are reluctant to reveal exact information; and in addition to the payment for sponsorship rights, sponsoring companies spend two or three times this amount on 'leverage expenditure', i.e. complementary marketing activities to fully exploit the commercial value of the sponsorship. Nevertheless, IEG (2009a) report worldwide sponsorship expenditure as just over $41 billion in 2008. Mintel (2006) report that sponsorship expenditure in the UK rose from less than £200 million in 1986 to £800 million in 2005. Nevertheless, sponsorship expenditure is small compared with advertising – Masterman (2007) reports sponsorship as probably about 10 per cent of sponsors' overall market and communications budgets, compared with about 35 per cent spent on media advertising. However, sponsorship is rising partly because advertising is a very congested medium, and it is increasingly fragmented as the print, broadcast and internet media multiply. Sponsorship of a major event ensures consistent exposure across different media.

The scale of sponsorship can vary enormously, from contributions of millions of pounds from a multinational company for national sports to the donation of a cup or prize by a small sports shop to a locally run competition. Indeed, most local teams in sport have a sponsor. It is the major companies investing heavily in sponsorship that dominate the market financially. Sponsorship growth, worldwide, can be attributed in large measure to increased television coverage of major events in both sport and the arts. Mega events are extremely costly to the sponsor and potentially extremely beneficial – the Olympics and the football World Cup reach audiences of billions. Technology advances such as cable and satellite television and internet coverage will increase sponsorship further still.

Sport typically takes the lion's share of sponsorship expenditure – more than two-thirds of the total in the USA according to IEG (2009b) and 51 per cent in the UK according to Mintel (2006c). Other major areas of leisure to benefit from sponsorship are entertainment tours and attractions, the arts, festivals, fairs and events, broadcasting and membership clubs. According to Fenton (2005c), the top five industries globally for sponsorship expenditure are telecommunications, banking, cars, sports clothing and beer. In the UK, Mintel (2006) report that finance/insurance companies are the largest sponsors of sport.

Sponsorship is conventionally seen as a transaction, an exchange. On the one side it benefits sport and leisure organisations. Most obviously it brings in revenue, services or resources from the sponsor – without sponsorship, many events would be uneconomic even with large audiences and ticket sales. Sponsorship can also create interest, stimulate media coverage and consequently increase attendance numbers. It can help to attract major 'players' in sport or the arts; and it can assist in bidding for events or other projects. Sponsorship can also support good causes, e.g. social and environmental.

On the other side of the exchange, sponsorship benefits the sponsoring company in a number of ways:

- by helping to reinforce or change its corporate image, by association with the sponsored organisation's product and brand;
- by increasing publicity and improving public relations;
- by improving trade and employee relations (e.g. through corporate hospitality);
- by increasing awareness of the sponsor's brands;
- by possibly increasing sales, market share and gaining competitive advantage;
- as a complement to other marketing activities.

There are also costs to both parties. In particular the sponsor pays 'leverage expenditure' to realise the full marketing value of the sponsorship, whilst the sponsored organisation can devote considerable resources to servicing sponsors' needs, e.g. ensuring that corporate hospitality arrangements are suitable, and that star players or performers are available for corporate occasions and publicity.

Sponsorship is of local as well as national significance, and sponsors can raise their 'respectability profile' with the public and with government when sponsoring good causes, particularly those advocated by the government. Governments can get actively involved in promoting sponsorship. For example, Sport England has Sportsmatch, a grassroots sports sponsorship incentive scheme. It is funded by the Department for Culture, Media and Sport and for successful applicants matches new sponsorship money with a government grant. Since it started in 1992, Sportsmatch has awarded over £48 million to almost 6,000 projects which realised over £58 million in sponsorship from the commercial sector. It has proved highly effective in persuading sponsors to sponsor sport. Similar schemes exist in Scotland and Wales.

15.8.1 Key issues in sponsorship management

For sport and leisure managers, the key issues in sponsorship management depend on understanding the sponsor, just as the key issue in marketing management is understanding the customer. The key issues are as follows:

- **Objectives** – identifying not only what the sport or leisure organisation wants from sponsorship but what a potential sponsor is likely to want and how the sport can satisfy these business objectives. They may be similar to the benefits to sponsors listed on the previous page, but are likely to be specific to the sponsorships being considered.
- **Sponsors' selection of organisations** – a key factor is synergy of target markets for the sponsor and the sport or leisure organisation. This synergy provides opportunities to realise benefits by both partners, but in particular it enables the sponsor to benefit from increasing awareness of its brand by appropriate market segments that are attracted to the sport or leisure activity.
- **Costs and likely returns for both partners** – it is important for both partners to budget for the costs of servicing or leveraging the sponsorship and to have as clear an idea as possible of the evaluation criteria through which the returns can be assessed.
- **Implementation** – exclusivity is an important attribute of most sponsorship deals for the sponsor and defences need to be made clear against 'ambush marketing', where a commercial company associates itself with the sport or leisure product without actually sponsoring it. Other operational requirements include the need for clear lines of communication and for the sport to help service the marketing objectives of the sponsor, e.g. awareness, media exposure, content of communications, corporate hospitality, merchandising.
- **Evaluation** – historically the weakest part of the package. It is likely to include awareness and attitude surveys, and sales of the sponsor's products before, during and after the sponsorship deal. A commonly used measure is media coverage and equivalent cost, but this is problematic because the main purpose of the media coverage is to raise awareness of the activity, not the sponsor; therefore the quality of the marketing message for the sponsor is variable and the effectiveness of the marketing message received by the audience is difficult to measure. Evaluation is not a task that should necessarily be left to the sponsor – the sponsored organisation can usefully help in the task as part of its support services for the sponsor.

Discussion question

Select a sponsorship partnership in sport and leisure (e.g. in the UK Cornhill and cricket, RBS and rugby union) and discuss the synergies between the sponsor's products and brands and the customers of the sport or leisure organisation which is receiving the sponsorship.

15.9 Conclusions

This chapter has considered the marketing approach to sport and leisure services and facilities and the benefits that can accrue to organisations from systematised and detailed marketing planning. The marketing approach ensures that when a product or service is made available to the consumer, it has been planned, designed, packaged, priced, promoted and delivered in such a manner that the customer is not only persuaded to buy, but also to repeat the experience. While impulse buying, like attending an event or 'having a go', is important, repeat visits and repeat purchasing are even more so. Marketing affects people's awareness, attitudes and behaviour. Managers of sport and leisure should encourage people to look more favourably on their organisations and their products, services and brands.

Although this is not covered explicitly in this chapter, an appropriate and approved budget is needed for effective marketing. Very often, particularly in the public and private non-profit sectors, marketing budgets are inadequate for the task in hand. This is sometimes because marketing is seen as a cost, rather than as an investment. Yet the returns from investment in marketing are more interest in the products of the organisation, more purchases and more customer satisfaction.

Practical tasks

1 For a sport or leisure organisation that you are familiar with, use what data you can obtain on customers and/or members and suggest and justify a simple market segmentation appropriate to the organisation's objectives. Identify what other data would help with this task.

2 Visit a local leisure facility which you have not visited before, critically assess whether it is in a good location for its market; and whether accessibility is good both externally and internally. What place marketing recommendations can you make?

Structured guide to further reading

For lots of examples of relationship marketing:
Ferrand, A. and McCarthy, S. (2009) *Marketing the Sports Organisation: building networks and relationships*, Routledge, London.

For lots of examples of sports marketing:
Mullin, B.J., Hardy, S. and Sutton, W.A. (2007) *Sport Marketing*, 3rd edition, Human Kinetics, Champaign, IL.

Useful websites

For participACTION:
www.participaction.com

For Change4Life:
www.change4life.co.uk

For Sport England's market segmentation:
www.sportengland.org/research/market_segmentation.aspx

For worldwide data on sponsorship expenditure:
http.//www.sponsorship.com/Resources/Sponsorship-Spending.aspx

Chapter 16

Programming sport and leisure

Summary

Programming provides the services and products that sport and leisure managers are in business to deliver. It is the mechanism for meeting the needs of customers and organisational objectives. Programming is a continuous process characterised by repeated cycles of planning, implementation, evaluation and review.

Programmes can be classified by function; by geographical areas and facilities; by types of customers; and by the expected outcomes. The classification into functional activities such as education, fitness, etc. is the most common in public sports facilities. There are different approaches to and methods of programming. Two major strategic directions are 'social planning', where the locus of control is with the authority and professionals, and 'community development', which is a more people-oriented direction. It is possible to combine the best of both approaches.

Within the broad strategic alternatives, there exist a variety of specific methods of delivery. Good programming requires strategy, structure and coordination. The chapter finishes with a clear specification of programming stages, which clarifies the practical functions of the sport and leisure programmer. It consists of a logical sequence of actions through which leisure programmes may succeed.

16.1 Introduction

Programming is one of the most important functions of leisure managers. Everything that a service or department is concerned with – facilities, equipment, supplies, personnel, budgets, marketing, public relations, activities, timetabling and administration – is solely to ensure that opportunities exist for people to enjoy or experience leisure in ways satisfying to them. Studies of various leisure activities, particularly the arts, have indicated that the most important element in people's decision on whether or not to visit is the programme. It is not the only means by which opportunities are provided for people to enjoy their leisure time – natural amenities, for example, are typically provided without a set programme to adhere to – but for many types of leisure provision it is the mechanism by which the objectives of an organisation are realised.

Programming is equally important to sport and leisure managers in the public, commercial and voluntary sectors – all have to attract the public or they fail. A commercial fitness club manager has to programme the right activities at the right times to generate and retain a maximum number of members willing to pay the required fees. A voluntary sector club administrator has to programme sufficient playing and social opportunities to keep members satisfied. A public sector manager has to set a 'balanced' programme of opportunities, to reflect an array of policy objectives, from the quasi-commercial to those explicitly for community benefits.

Balance is important to all providers, i.e. an appropriate balance between the competing demands for the opportunities which a supplier is capable of providing. A balanced activity programme at a public sector leisure complex, for example, is likely to have some of the following features:

- opportunities to participate in a range of leisure activities on a structured or an informal basis;
- opportunities to take part actively (as a participant) or passively (as a spectator);
- opportunities to be involved as an individual or with a club or group;
- time set aside for a regular core programme of activities as well as time set aside for a variable programme of one-off opportunities, e.g. events.

Programming is equally important for a leisure facility with fixed spatial accommodation, such as a cinema or theatre with fixed seats, as it is in a more flexible space such as a sports hall which can be configured in a variety of ways. Major programming decisions in a theatre are about the appropriate artistic mix of performances and their timing and the duration of their run. In a relatively flexible space such as a sports hall, programming choices include choosing between many different activities that are possible, with some being continuous and others one-offs. Programming decisions in the public sector extend to outreach services too, where delivery is taken to local communities, rather than expecting customers to always travel to purpose built facilities.

An example of a programme for a leisure facility – in this case a swimming pool – is provided in Table 16.1. This programme demonstrates programming by types of user (e.g. schools, adults, adult and baby, over 60s, club) and different purposes (e.g. SwimRight lessons, Aqua Fit, Public Fun, birthday parties).

A programme provides order and structure; people know where they stand – they know when to come, what they can expect. This chapter concentrates on the programming process and the manager's role in that process. The rationale for excellent programming is basically to make the best use of resources – time, space, staff, money. This has the following requirements:

- the need to resolve conflicting claims of time and space for available facilities and alternative use of resources to provide opportunities;
- the need to utilise capacity as much as is feasible – sport and leisure experiences are among the most 'perishable' of services in the sense that an unsold space at a particular time is a permanently lost revenue opportunity;
- the need for balance in the programme, to accommodate a wide range of clients and potential customers – particularly in the public sector, where social inclusion is an important objective.

Table 16.1 An example of a swimming pool programme: Creswell Leisure Centre, England

Monday

07.45	09.15	Early Morning Swim Adults Only
11.00	12.00	Adult Lessons
12.00	13.15	Lunchtime Swim
13.30	15.00	School Swimming
16.00	17.30	SwimRight Lessons
17.30	18.45	Public Fun Session
18.30	19.45	Public Swimming Session
20.00	21.45	Adults Only Swimming Session

Tuesday

07.45	09.00	Early Morning Swim Adults Only
09.00	10.00	'Adult & Baby' Swim Sessions
10.00	11.00	Aqua Fit
11.00	12.00	Aqua Fit
12.00	13.15	Lunchtime Swim
13.30	15.00	School Swimming
15.00	16.00	Bolsover Wellness & Over 60s
16.00	17.30	SwimRight Lessons
17.30	18.45	Public Fun Session
19.00	20.00	SwimRight Lessons
20.00	21.45	Adults Only Swim

Wednesday

07.45	09.00	Early Morning Swim Adults Only
09.00	12.00	Parents, Baby, Disabled & OAPs
12.00	13.15	Lunchtime Swim
13.30	16.00	School Swimming
16.00	17.30	SwimRight Lessons
17.30	18.45	Public Fun Session
18.30	19.45	Bolsover Wellness & Over 60s
20.00	21.00	Adults Only Swimming Session
21.00	22.00	Adults Swimming Lesson

Thursday

07.45	09.00	Early Morning Swim Adults Only
09.00	10.00	Aqua Fit
10.00	12.00	School Swimming
12.00	13.15	Lunchtime Swim
13.30	15.00	School Swimming
15.00	16.00	Bolsover Wellness & Over 60s
16.00	17.30	SwimRight Lessons
17.30	18.45	Public Fun Sessions
18.30	19.45	Public Swimming Sessions
20.00	21.45	Adults Only Swimming Session

Friday

07.45	09.00	Early Morning Swim Adults Only
09.00	12.00	School Swimming
12.00	13.15	Lunchtime Swim
13.30	15.00	School Swimming
16.00	17.30	SwimRight Lessons
17.30	18.45	Public Fun Sessions
19.00	20.00	Aqua Fit

Saturday

09.00	12.00	SwimRight Lessons
12.00	15.15	Public Swimming 'A Pound All Round'
15.30	18.30	Pool Birthday Parties

Sunday

09.00	16.30	Public Swimming 'A Pound All Round'
17.00	19.00	Club Use

Source: Creswell Leisure Centre, www.bolsover.gov.uk.

> ### Discussion question
>
> Consider what would be likely to happen if a community sports centre was opened without a programme being specified, i.e. activity on demand, meaning that people just turn up and play what they want, when they want, for as long as they want. What would be the implications for choice and variety of activities, for the setting up and breaking down of activities' equipment, and for customer satisfaction?

16.2 What constitutes a programme?

What makes a programme? Does it have to be a schedule of activities, a timetable of bookings or a list of events? Or can it be the planned availability of a supervised playground, mobile attractions or a community event? Or can it exist through the organised distribution of services such as a sport and leisure information service which collates all that is going on? A programme is all these things and a good deal more. Rossman and Elwood Schlatter (2008) define a programme as 'a designed opportunity for leisure experience to occur', the critical word being 'designed' – it is a management responsibility to ensure relevant and diverse opportunities, subject to the resources available. A practical interpretation is that programmes revolve around activities, amenities and facilities, services, staff, money and time:

- **Activities** can range from the completely spontaneous to the highly structured and all stages in between. Informal activities can be anticipated within a community programme by creating opportunities, encouraging spontaneity, having resources available such as space, time and equipment, e.g. a ball to kick about, a wall to scribble on or deckchairs to sunbathe on. Structured activities, for programming purposes, fall into several major categories, such as: arts, crafts, dance, drama, entertainment, games, sport, health and fitness, hobbies, music, nature, social recreation, travel and tourism.
- **Amenities and facilities** cover open spaces, buildings, supplies and equipment. These can be designed and constructed for special purposes, for example public arts centres or swimming pools. Alternatively they can be designed for self-directed or spontaneous activity, for example an urban park, the natural resources available to the public such as riverside walks, forests and beaches. Or they can be mobile resources to facilitate outreach services in local communities, such as a mobile library or a sports bus with sports development staff.
- **Services** cover all methods and means through which people are enabled to enjoy sport and leisure. Primary services include the leadership of or guidance for activities provided by key people such as coaches, tutors and animateurs (see p. 432). Support services include information services, promotion and publicity, transport, discount card schemes in local authorities, member direct debit schemes in private clubs, and crèches.
- **Staff** are the enablers, connectors and controllers, including: duty managers, supervisors, coaches, countryside rangers, teachers, technicians, cleaners, stage hands, librarians, museum curators, sports development officers, youth and community workers and receptionists. They are all responsible for the programme provided for customers.
- **Money** is needed for the resources to set up and run services, facilities and programmes. All programmes are subject to the reality check of what resources can deliver.

● **Time** is a key element in programmes, in respect of both the specific times that opportunities for customers are available and the duration of opportunities, both for a single visit and over the weeks, months or seasons covered by the programme.

The sport and leisure manager/programmer must use the available resources efficiently to deliver programmes. The programme, however, is not a series of individual activities strung together. It is a carefully integrated and planned combination of many opportunities selected on the basis of individual and group interests and motivations. These opportunities are organised to achieve the objectives of the organisation and simultaneously meet the needs and demands of individuals and groups.

16.3 Programme classification

The type of programme needs to be known in order to communicate with the potential market. Programme classification should describe and communicate the different activities in the programme. It also helps in providing programme balance through analysis of each category. The commercial sector is particularly adept at 'segmenting' market sectors for profitable outcomes.

Simple classifications can aid communication and administration and make it easier for clients and customers to understand. 'Fun sessions' at a swimming pool will give a warning signal to adults that these sessions may best be avoided. Programmes can be classified in a number of ways and four are commonly used:

1 **by function** – the most usual classification, normally by listing a number of activities or groups of activities, such as sports, arts, crafts, social; often the functional classification is linked to the motivations of the customers: casual, classes, fitness, education, club training, etc.;
2 **by facilities and areas** – e.g. pitches, swimming pools, rooms and halls to be let; and by local communities in the case of outreach programmes;
3 **by groups of people** – who the programme is intended for, such as casual users, members, family days, over 50s, parents and toddlers;
4 **by outcomes** – e.g. 'Learn to swim' and other beginner sessions, skill development, keep fit, weight loss.

Sociologists and psychologists tend to group people for classification into life-cycle stages, i.e. determined by such factors as age, dependency on others, marriage, having children, etc., which are relevant to customers' motivations, their appropriate market segments and their desired outcomes. Farrell and Lundegren (1991), for example, identify a range of activities through several life-cycle changes. However, these can be merged for many programmes (e.g. youth, teenager and young adults can be grouped together), or the groups can be further broken down (e.g. pre-school into toddlers, infants and pre-school). Further classification can be made regarding the activities themselves: passive/active, structured/unstructured, planned/self-directed, high risk/low risk, etc. Marketers often identify market segments for the purposes of key decision-making, including programming. Market segmentation is covered in Chapter 15.

16.4 Planning strategies for sport and leisure programming

Two extremes of strategic directions for public-related sport and leisure programmes are:

1 **social planning** (Edginton *et al.*, 2004), i.e. programmes planned by professionals such as local authority officers, sport and leisure managers, or club officials – often termed 'top down';
2 **community development programmes**, i.e. which emanate from the community itself via community engagement in the decision-making processes – often termed 'bottom up'.

The social planning approach is the most common. The basic assumption underlying this process is that use of professional expertise and knowledge is the most effective way of meeting community needs and demands, balancing programmes and meeting organisational objectives. In programmes for theatres or art exhibitions, for example, there are experts in the art forms on whom reliance is frequently placed for programming decisions. In practice many strategies for programmes are developed by professionals, often in consultation with key stakeholders and possibly with customers, but with little decision-making engagement by customers. This is increasingly seen as paternalistic, even when community consultation occurs.

Community development, on the other hand, is a programming strategy in which the role of the leisure manager is to enable individuals and organisations to get involved in the programming process (see Case Study 16.1 for a Canadian example led by ideas from the community). The locus of control is the important factor. The social planning strategy is professional and authority controlled. Community development relinquishes at least some of the control of programme development to representatives of the community.

The community development strategy is ambitious. It typically needs capable, trained people 'out in the field'. Community developers have become known by many names: 'encourager', 'enabler', 'catalyst', 'friend', 'adviser', 'activator' and 'animateur'. Animateurs are well-trained, capable and sensitive professionals who work towards stimulating individuals to think about their own development and also the development of other people in the community, through community programming. They work to develop the leadership capabilities of others – typically volunteers. They assist by supplying information about methods and procedures; they enable others to act for themselves.

Experience in the UK has shown that on the whole outreach programmes are only successful as long as the support is available over a sustained period of time. When the

Kitchener's Festival of Neighbourhoods: an example of the community development strategy

The Festival of Neighbourhoods is an initiative of the City of Kitchener in Canada. Since 1994 the city authority held a draw for an annual $10,000 neighbourhood improvement grant, which local communities can apply for. It is designed to encourage individuals and families to build stronger relationships with their neighbours and celebrate their community. Applications for the draw need to be activities, projects or events hosted in neighbourhoods with the object of bringing people together and open to everyone.

The ideas suggested on the festival's website are largely leisure oriented and include evening walks, a music festival, a street party, a baseball game, a bike rodeo, a barbeque and a funfair. The winners of the draw since its inception include six park improvement projects, half of which incorporated playground improvement, a nature trail improvement and extension, and a skateboard park. They might more accurately be called projects rather than programmes, but the essence of community development is at the heart of the Festival of Neighbourhoods, not just for the winners of the draw, but for all the community groups that complete applications.

Essentially, the programme for Festival of Neighbourhoods is planned by communities, although they get support in their applications and planning from city officers, and, of course, the winners get funding support from the draw. Research by Johnson *et al.* (2009) focused on the role of the community representatives who act as voluntary liaisons between public officials and neighbourhood residents. They identified very positive responses in the main from these community representatives, with regard to, first, their relationship with public officials and, second, their relationship with neighbourhood residents.

Key to these successful relationships were the flexible and trusting nature of the public officials, who were willing to let community groups lead in the planning of their projects, and also the help the public officials gave the neighbourhood groups in seeking additional funding from alternative sources. Regarding the relationships between the community representatives and neighbourhood residents, the main issues that arose were the importance of the representatives soliciting views and support from their neighbourhoods on key issues regarding their proposals, and resolving fears and conflicts regarding the nature and effects of the proposed developments.

It seems that community representatives rose to their responsibilities commendably, in having to cope with the two types of relationships important to their communities' development. A couple of the community representatives who were interviewed in the research lamented a disappointing number of 'new people' in their neighbourhoods willing to get involved in the collective action. But in the main their responses were very positive. The Festival of Neighbourhoods provides a successful example of publicly funded urban regeneration, using leisure, aimed at marginalised neighbourhoods and led by the communities themselves.

Source: derived from Johnson *et al.* (2009)

programmes cease, through lack of funding, for example, the majority of the newly formed groups flounder after a period of time, due partly to the lack of physical, psychological or organisational support. Systems are needed which provide pathways and networks to maintain and sustain new programme developments. Or at the very least, exit routes should be clear and facilitated for people who want to continue participating in the activity elsewhere.

Traditionally, local authorities have often undertaken the social planning strategy, with much of the work being administered centrally, even remote from facilities. Such an approach, on its own, has the following disadvantages:

- The decision-makers are distant from the potential users of the facilities and even the immediate service providers.
- There is generally a lack of consultation and sensitivity concerning the needs and demands of the community.
- The facility staff are less likely to be involved in the decision-making process and this can lead to a lack of accountability and commitment at facility level – this can manifest itself in poor staff motivation and low job satisfaction.
- Decision-making tends to involve committees, may be slow, and can result in repetitive and unimaginative programmes.

Looking across the broad spectrum of leisure programming, it seems clear that to adopt one direction – social planning or community development – to the exclusion of the other would be inappropriate. The community development approach fosters participant independence but can nevertheless lead to inefficiencies, and frustrations for the professionals. Both strategies have merit. A blend of the two is not only possible, but also desirable. Bolton *et al.* promote such a compromise: 'Rather than accepting the rather hackneyed and sterile debate of "bottom-up" or "top-down", we argue that there is a need for practitioners to develop a more central position in relation to community development' (2008: 100). They propose a partnership between community, citizens and providers, each with clear roles in the development and delivery of programmes.

Discussion question

As a member of a community, would you prefer to be helped to create leisure programmes for yourself, or would you rather a professional organised the programmes and gave you options to choose from?

16.5 Specific approaches to programming

Within the broad framework of the two main programming strategies lies a range of specific approaches to programming. Providing leisure opportunity is so diverse and complex a task that there is no one approach, system or method which is suitable for all organisations, all situations or all types of customer. The different approaches are known by a variety of names; most of them have no agreed formal titles in practice.

The programming methods employed depend on the organisation, the aims, the community to be served, the strategy, staff skills, money, facilities and a wide variety of other factors. Most sport and leisure programmers do not use a single method. Most use a number of methods, but if they are poorly planned they can be an untidy mix, lacking coordination. This section groups together around 30 approaches which have been identified, including those of Farrell and Lundegren (1991), Edginton *et al.* (2004), Kraus and Curtis (1977), and Rossman and Elwood Schlatter (2008), into 13 approaches or methods. They each have benefits if used along with other methods. They are:

1 **The lettings 'policy' or laissez-faire approach** – commonly found in the management of smaller community centres. The facility is provided and promoted to the local community; the programme is decided by bookings and usage, rather than a designed programme. Optimal usage and balance are seldom achieved because the programming is entirely reactive to demand.

2 **The traditional approach** – whereby what has gone on in the past and is generally successful is likely to be repeated. It relies on the same format as the past and therefore assumes that this is sufficient. It is not necessarily based on needs, but on what has worked before. It does not take into account new ideas and changes in demand. Its main merit is continuity and stability. As a single approach, however, it is ineffective. It can be far more useful as part of a process which learns from the past and makes modifications for the future.

3 **The current trends approach** – this relies on reacting to recent trends or activities in vogue. This has benefits in meeting some new demands. However, the approach is totally experimental. It is likely to serve only a segment of the market, and what may work in one area may be a total failure in others. It is also likely to be unpopular with those seeking a continuous, predictable set of opportunities, e.g. many sports participants want to play their activities regularly. It is important to provide for fads, but they must be seen in context. It is a useful method to include in order to test the market.

4 **The expressed desires approach** – by asking people through surveys, focus groups, etc., and then programming for their wishes, the intention is to provide what they want. But will this result in actual participation? And which activities will meet which desires? Such an approach is difficult to administer but it is a valuable tool for the programme planner; it gives information about people's desires. This approach has its limitations, however, as many respondents may not really know what they want until they try it; and they cannot predict with any degree of accuracy what their future leisure behaviour is likely to be.

5 **The authoritarian approach** (also the 'prescriptive' approach) – clearly a method derived from the social planning strategy. Reliance is placed on the judgement of the leisure manager. The assumption is that he or she understands what the needs are and what the community wants. This is a quick and tidy approach at its design and planning stage but participants are denied any involvement in the programme process. Such an approach makes it difficult to adapt to more of a community development strategy. Programming by the manager's perception of what a community wants is a tempting approach to adopt because it appears to be based on needs, as interpreted by the professional. However, without community involvement there is a risk that the professional's diagnosis is not accurate for the particular population in the potential market.

6 **The socio-political approach** – where pressure from groups, often linked to social causes, is used as a basis for a community programme. Such causes often provide political advantage and carry local authority support. For example, crime, poverty, deprivation, discrimination and social disorder may call for particular kinds of programming, concentrating on specific target groups and areas. Leisure managers in the public sector do not operate in a political vacuum but have to respond to political and social pressure

and to changing conditions. This approach, however, needs careful handling by an experienced leisure manager who can add practicality to the political ideal while programming for the overall goals of the organisation.

7   **The action–investigation–creation plan approach** – a three-phase plan to programming (Tillman, 1974). The action element is a reaction to demands generated by the community. The investigation element is concerned with fact-finding about the nature of demands and service requirements. The creation element is the interactive relationship between participants and professionals. The professionals use their own expertise and actively seek the views and involvement of participants. This approach is a compromise between the social planning and community development strategies.

8   **The external requirements approach** – means that the programme is basically dictated by a key stakeholder, e.g. the local authority, a school or college, or a governing body. It tends to have uniform standards, leadership and resources across local organisations, and external assessment is conducted for the stakeholder's requirements. A Scout or Girl Guide troop, for example, will satisfy the association's requirements. Such organisations normally have vertical management structures, a hierarchical leadership pattern, similar resources, administration and an external reward system. This approach may also be relevant for some commercial organisations, such as fitness centres, where a centralised approach is demanded of local clubs.

9   **A cafeteria-style approach** – with a variety of choices available for customers to sample. This is useful in that people may not know what they want and can try things out. Additionally, such an approach can help to meet the diverse needs of clients, such as family groups where individuals can choose different activities. It is a safe approach but tends to be expensive. While it appears to be the answer to the leisure manager's dilemma, it is inefficient in the use of resources because it can plan and provide services which then go unused because they have not been chosen. In addition, it is very difficult to set objectives and measure success – some activities will be winners and others losers, but the reasons may not be known. For example, poor marketing rather than a lack of demand may be the cause of poor utilisation. Nevertheless, any comprehensive sport and leisure programme will need to indulge in a cafeteria approach for some of its programmes, if only as an initial tactic to establish demand patterns.

10 **The demand approach** – offers what people want. It is a common form of programming. Clubs, associations and interest groups make known their demands and managers devise a programme to match these. Managers are faced with scores of applications requesting specific facilities. However, the most vocal, the most aware and the socially articulate will make their demands known most readily. The approach is not concerned with equitable distribution and may result in a narrowly focused programme. Many people and groups will not even be aware of the options and benefits. Because there is lack of understanding of the complexity and importance of programming, community leisure services and facility programmes are often a mix of the traditional and demand approaches. A broader mix of programming methods would be more suited to the task.

11 **The community orientation approach** – a process where individuals are involved in the planning process. This approach is clearly derived from the community development strategic direction. It is typically facilitated by using skilled professionals, or community volunteers, to meet people on their own patch, for example through outreach programmes, associations and community counsellors. The discovery approach is an extension and continuation of community orientation. It assumes that people can work together, there being no superior or subordinate relationships. One person's knowledge, skills, abilities and interests are used to meet another's needs, without necessarily

imposing value systems or external expectations. The approach is a people-to-people approach of interactive discovery, which probably requires skilled community leadership to make it effective.

12 **The community leadership approach** – consisting of community and consumer inputs channelled through advisory boards, user committees, tenants' groups or other action groups. The concerns of the community are represented in a more structured way than in the previously described approach. Community leadership assumes that individual interests are represented by their group. This, of course, is not wholly possible, but it does indicate community interaction and a level of democracy. At least it opens channels of communication between providers and consumers, and as such it can be a valuable tool for the sport and leisure programmer. Few community leisure service programmes emanate from the community itself without an externally imposed structure and leadership. This kind of programming is difficult, time-consuming and expensive in terms of paid personnel, usually requiring subsidy or being managed by volunteers.

13 **The outcomes approach** (or benefits approach) – designed to secure the outcomes, particularly for individual participants, that the objectives for the programme identify. This approach was originally devised for at-risk youth, with specific personal outcomes from the programme in which young people engage, such as self-confidence, self-efficacy, social skills, etc., being identified and the programme being designed to achieve them. A similar approach can be taken for a variety of specific target groups with different needs and motivations, e.g. ethnic minorities, older people, young mothers, overweight people. In fact every participant has needs and motivations, so in principle the outcomes approach can be taken for all programmes.

> **Discussion question**
>
> Is the cafeteria approach the most democratic of those reviewed above, because it relies on people 'voting with their feet' and all votes are equal?

16.6 Programme planning

Whatever approach is taken to sport and leisure programming, it is vital, as in many other aspects of leisure management, to set out a programme plan before implementing it. A programme plan gives structure and logical process to programmes. It should minimise the 'nasty surprises' that require hasty decisions. And it is a clear specification of the reasons for the programming decisions and the detailed programming decisions themselves, which others can pick up and run with, or adapt for any new circumstances.

Table 16.2 identifies the key elements of a programme plan (adapted from Rossman and Elwood Schlatter, 2008). Many of these are either self-explanatory or covered elsewhere in this chapter or book (e.g. Chapter 13 for staffing, Chapter 15 for promotion, Chapter 18 for budgets, Chapter 19 for risk assessment). Some of the elements need further explanation. A flowchart identifies the critical stages and responsibilities in a programme. A Gantt chart identifies specific timings and responsibilities for the stages; it provides a specific schedule for the preparation and implementation of the programme. The cancellation contingency defines the circumstances in which a programme would not be offered, or would be stopped – e.g. severe weather, a health scare – and plans for the procedure to implement

Table 16.2 Elements of a programme plan

1 Programme name

2 Organisational mission and objectives = rationale for the programme

3 Objectives of the programme

4 Programme elements
- activities
- places and facilities
- legal requirements
- equipment and supplies
- staffing and animation
- flow chart and/or Gantt chart
- promotion
- pricing
- budget
- management/control/monitoring plan
- cancellation contingency
- set-up and breakdown
- risk assessment and risk management

5 Evaluation of programme

6 Sustainability or exit routes for participants

7 Criteria for continuation and change

Source: adapted from Rossman and Elwood Schlatter (2008).

cancellation. Risk assessment (see Chapter 19) considers what in the programme might cause harm to people – either customers or staff – and the organisation, and how such risks can be minimised.

Sustainability in the context of a programme plan means whether or not the programme will be sustainable after the planned programme period. Sustainability is a particularly important element for community development programmes, because it is likely that any public sector support, financial or from officers, will have a finite duration. Will the community be in a position to take over the management and operation of the programme? In the event that a programme is likely to stop at the end of the planned duration, it is important to plan exit routes for participants, i.e. where can they continue to participate in such activities when the programme stops and how can the transition to other opportunities be facilitated?

16.6.1 Co-ordinating the approaches to programming

In terms of leisure programming, organisations are therefore faced with two levels of decision-making. First, which strategic programming direction should be taken? Second, which methods should be adopted to meet the strategic objectives? This is where leisure managers should come into their own, because of their contextual knowledge and their training and experience. One of the guiding principles will be that programming must be situationally and culturally specific. There are different communities, facilities and areas, providing different contexts, demands and challenges. A good manager must be a realist and use whatever approaches and options are open to meet needs and demands effectively and to be resource efficient in planning and operating the programme.

Needs assessment is complex (see Chapter 2). Part of the solution is gradually to make it possible for people to interpret and express their own needs and which types of programme best suit them. Managers must, therefore, involve people in programme planning, if only in consultation. The leisure manager must:

- understand the lessons to be learned from the various strategies and approaches;
- understand the problems and opportunities within current leisure programming;
- understand the requirements of customers, actual and potential;
- devise a logical and objective approach to the situation, bearing in mind the goals of the organisation and the resources available.

16.6.2 Targeting specific groups

Leisure facilities in all sectors are used more by those who are more affluent and mobile than those who have social, economic and other forms of disadvantage. In the commercial sector this is not an issue – attracting paying customers and making profits are important objectives. A commercial leisure service will target groups which will serve its objectives and this means people with money and education – the latter being an important driver for demand in many forms of leisure, including the arts, heritage, countryside and sport (see Chapter 2). There are national data which will help commercial organisations target particular geographical areas, such as ACORN in the UK, a system which classifies neighbourhoods using multiple forms of socio-economic and demographic data from the National Census. National survey data also identify the activities and programmes most likely to attract paying customers from higher socio-economic areas, not only across different leisure forms, but also within specific leisure activities, such as sport. *Active People* surveys in England, for example, provide details for each sport and activity of how participation varies with income, employment status, socio-economic group, car ownership, house ownership and other variables. Such information can help a commercial provider set programmes which are likely to attract paying customers.

Public sector organisations have a wider brief, however, and will be interested in providing opportunities for all, with a possible focus on people suffering disadvantages – the socially excluded. Socio-economic disadvantage in relation to leisure participation is well documented by the same data sources referred to above, particularly national survey data (see Chapter 2). Effective public sector leisure management can be measured in part by the degree to which a reasonable balance of the various population market segments within a community has been attracted across the range of services. However, evidence typically shows that those least likely to use leisure facilities are characterised by having low socio-economic status, low income, low educational achievement and poor mobility. Out of home leisure in the form of sport, arts and heritage does not appear to be of much relevance to many disadvantaged people, due to constraints such as the unrelenting pressure of parenthood, lack of money, no use of a car, etc.; and also due to preferences which lead many of them to other uses of their leisure time. This is a major challenge for public sector leisure programmers.

Yet the options for achieving greater representation in the use of public sector leisure opportunities are many and varied. Table 16.3 summarises some of them, and demonstrates that the programming of existing facilities is not enough. It needs to be accompanied by appropriate outreach programmes, and by financial and marketing decisions to complement the programmes.

> ### Table 16.3 Positive programming to encourage wider community use

Financial
- Cost subsidies
- Reduced/free memberships
- Discount cards or free passes (not just for children)
- Avoidance of lump sum payments
- Bus passes

Programmes
- Play schemes and family holidays
- Young mothers' programmes
- Transport, e.g. minibus shuttle
- Crèches at minimal or no cost
- Leisure skill learning – arts, crafts, sports
- Taster courses
- Family events
- Open days
- Social and community programmes

Outreach
- Assistance to self-help groups
- Babysitting services
- Neighbourhood contacts
- Neighbourhood facilities
- Mobile facilities

Marketing
- Leisure counselling
- Advertising benefits
- Helpline services
- Leisure information service
- Links with other community services and voluntary groups

The single most limiting factor for many disadvantaged groups is often perceived to be the cost of taking part. Yet, even when providing facilities free of charge, the manager will still need to promote and provide support and backup services, such as more crèche facilities, taster sessions, and mother and child activities. Attracting people through promotion and incentives, however, is not enough. The style of management and operational services is also important. Those people lacking in confidence are the most vulnerable to 'take-it-or-leave-it' services and will be easily put off. First impressions count. The approach of sport and leisure staff to some users is easily interpreted as 'intimidating', particularly at receptions. Procedures, regulations, membership cards and having to ask for information about concessions, for example, are offputting for some potential customers. The benefits of leisure are most successfully promoted by face-to-face communication. Therefore, staff training in customer service is of vital importance

16.7 Programming leisure centres

Multi-purpose leisure centres provide some of the greatest challenges for leisure programmers. These typically comprise of a sports hall, swimming pool, gym, activities rooms and possibly outdoor pitches. Such leisure centres require programmes which use the same space in a variety of ways. Swimming pools, for example, can be programmed for 'lane swimming', 'water fun', 'water aerobics', 'water therapy', galas and canoeing. Sports halls are used for concerts, antique fairs, dances, fashion shows and Christmas parties, in addition to a large range of sports and other physical activities. Even gyms have flexible spaces for classes such as 'spinning', pilates, circuit training, tai chi and boxing-related exercise.

An example of programming for a large leisure centre is provided in Case Study 16.2. It demonstrates a mixture of programming approaches, as well as key issues relating to excess

CASE STUDY 16.2

Ponds Forge International Sports Centre

This centre in Sheffield, England, is one of the most technically advanced centres in Europe. Its facilities include three pools – an international competition pool, an international diving pool and a leisure pool – as well as a sports hall large enough for ten badminton courts and international volleyball, which has seating for up to 1,000 when set for a sports event. This case study concentrates on the 50 metre competition pool, which can be configured as one large pool, or two or three smaller pools, for programming purposes – an important element of flexibility. A consideration of the programming for the range of water activities highlights the need to have firm general policies, which include a balance between local and international, community and club, casual and group, training and recreation. Programming problems for the management to overcome include: competition demands versus participation; club squad and structured activity versus casual use; and income earning activities versus development of excellence and social needs criteria from the owner, Sheffield City Trust.

The problem of interrupted continuity is all too evident from the programme alterations signalled on the website for this facility (see 'Useful websites', p. 449). In the month from 21 November 2009, for example, 32 hours of lane swimming were unavailable on two successive weekends, because of national and local events; 15 hours of swimming or diving lessons were cancelled; and nine days of normal programmes were unavailable in the sports hall because of events. The dilemma is that Ponds Forge is a major events venue as well as one which has a regular sports activities programme for the usual array of customers, from casual participants to elite members of clubs. Events are held on all but four weekends in the year, and they raise a lot of income, so inevitably the regular participants have to establish routines which incorporate the centre's weekend events programme.

Ponds Forge was built as a nationally important events centre, and this is fully accepted by Sheffield City Trust. Events bring a lot of media attention and economic benefits to the city. Up until 2002 there were complaints about the lack of public recreational swimming opportunities. Then a major review of the swimming programme resulted in more public swimming opportunities being available. Furthermore, Ponds Forge have been very proactive in keeping regular swimmers informed of cancelled times because of events – not only through their website but also through press releases, Facebook and Twitter. The emphasis in these marketing communications is not just on informing customers about the cancellations due to events, but also on promoting revised and new opportunities for regular swimmers to maintain their swimming during events, e.g. by switching to evenings, when competition swimming is over, by using the leisure pool or even by using other swimming pools in the city at weekends.

The programme has to accommodate a variety of demands apart from events and casual recreational swimming, including elite and development squads, lane swimming for fitness, swimming lessons, and a variety of water-based activities such as water polo and canoeing. There is a general state of excess demand in a successful facility such as Ponds Forge – clubs would like more training time, the public would like more lane swimming, there are waiting lists for swimming lessons and there are more events than can be accommodated. Therefore, compromise and balance in programming are important, as is creative thinking about making more space/time available. Since the review in 2002, there have been no major problems with the programme, so any changes have been minor, e.g. holding four swimming lessons at the same time in one third of the main pool, in order to free up space for other activities. Many of the changes and experiments with new elements in the programme are in reaction to customer feedback.

(The author is grateful to Helen Broadbent, General Manager of Ponds Forge ISC, for providing information for this case study.)

> ### Discussion question
>
> What can Ponds Forge do to placate regular users who express dissatisfaction when their regular programmes are interrupted by events?

demand. However, it is not just the large centres that need good programming. Small centres with limited space and resources need even greater skill at times. For example, in a one-court sports hall (four badminton courts) programming may include a variety of sports (for schools, clubs, coaching and casual use), concerts, dances, exhibitions and antique fairs. The typical problem with such a multi-purpose space is a huge array of options for the programme, but with limited capacity to accommodate them, particularly at peak times of the day, week and year. The programming decision is the designed solution to this problem.

> ### Discussion questions
>
> Faced with a number of competing demands (including various clubs, classes, casual users and local firms) for a limited capacity sports hall on a Monday evening, which of the approaches reviewed earlier will cause the least trouble? Does that make it the best approach?

16.8 Programming stages

The basic assumption was made at the start of this chapter that programming is a process. It is logical therefore to make programming a systematic process, which takes a wide and open view of the variety of possibilities. First, the approach must be capable of incorporating either, or a mix, of the major strategies – social planning and community development. Second, the approach must be capable of handling any of the detailed options, from the authoritarian approach at one extreme to the community orientation approach at the other.

Different approaches will suit different situations at different times. But all programming is undertaken in stages, which are repeated to form cycles of preparation, delivery and review. Torkildsen (2005) referred to his specification of programming stages as 'Programming by Objectives' but in practice any programming approach should be driven by clear and measurable objectives. And most programming involves similar functions of clarifying objectives, setting targets, planning, implementing, monitoring, evaluating and reflecting. It is a practical approach which breaks the tasks down into sequential stages. It echoes similar processes in planning (Chapter 14) and marketing (Chapter 15).

Essentially, programming results in people taking part in leisure activities and benefiting from leisure experiences. One thing we know about leisure behaviour is that if the experience is satisfying it can become habitual. Programmes therefore need to offer levels of continuity. Once established, programmes are difficult to change in a hurry. Moreover, time is needed to set up programmes and resources and finances are needed to promote and organise them. Hence, participation programmes need to run for at least a few months, unless, for example, they are short-term holiday or one-off weekend programmes, or tasters.

Leisure programming, therefore, in most cases is an ongoing cyclical process. Once a programme has been set in motion, it can go on in repeated cycles like a long-running saga.

While it may be easier to just let matters take their cyclical course with the same content, good programmers will constantly review the programme, introduce new initiatives or refine them, re-plan, implement afresh, run the programme, evaluate and then review again, and so the cycle goes on. Demands change, markets change and leisure managers have to match their programmes to the market.

The process outlined below is concerned largely with setting up the programme in the first place. But most programming is concerned with dealing with ongoing programmes with regular cycles of review, forward planning, implementation and evaluation.

16.8.1 Interpret policy, establish aims and objectives

Understand the purpose of your organisation, its philosophy and its fundamental beliefs. To do this you need to:

- produce a 'mission statement' or 'statement of purpose', i.e. the aims and goals of the organisation;
- produce programme policy guidelines and directional strategies.

Where no written philosophy/policy exists, top managers should interpret the organisation's purpose, communicate with others, produce a written policy statement and obtain endorsement.

16.8.2 Assess current and potential needs and demand

Produce a profile of the current and prospective consumers and the type of services and activities required to meet their needs and demands. You should:

- evaluate the current performance of facilities and services, and determine the level of spare capacity and excess demand;
- collate all marketing information, including user surveys, complaints and suggestions, customer panels, resident surveys, and information from community councils and other relevant organisations;
- establish a profile of relevant populations – i.e. the individuals and groups likely to participate – and their likely needs and motivations;
- assess forthcoming opportunities, e.g. historic celebrations, national and international events;
- identify market gaps and determine areas of deficiency in terms of services and programmes.

16.8.3 Assess organisational resources

Specify the existing and potential capacity of the organisation for delivering programmes. To do this:

- identify current resources, facilities, organisations, services, programmes and opportunities;
- evaluate existing staff for delivering programmes, their skills and potential development;
- evaluate the actual contributions made by other agencies, e.g. voluntary sector, commercial enterprises, education and industrial clubs;
- evaluate the potential for enhanced resources, e.g. partnerships, sponsorship;
- evaluate potential community contributions to programme planning.

16.8.4 Set objectives

Translate policies, market demands and available resources into practical objectives; prioritise and make each objective measurable and within a timespan (see Chapter 17). As part of this:

- involve key stakeholders in the setting of objectives;
- set short-range targets in each area of the facility, or each geographical area, within a precise time period: weeks (e.g. holiday programmes); months (e.g. beginner courses); and years (e.g. financial targets, social objectives, etc.);
- set an appropriate balance between different programming approaches;
- set an appropriate balance between passive and active leisure, between different activities for different purposes, e.g. self-improvement, fitness, social, entertainment, to meet objectives;
- agree performance indicators, including participation and financial ratios, and targets (see Chapter 17).

16.8.5 Plan the programme

Adopt the programmer's motto: proper prior planning prevents poor performance. To plan:

- consider how the programme fits into the marketing strategy, e.g. corporate approach to marketing, specific promotions;
- as time is the basis on which most programmes operate, identify hourly, daily, weekly and seasonal patterns of use;
- consider both fixed and flexible timetables;
- determine programme areas, i.e. types of activities;
- determine programme forms, i.e. casual, clubs, courses, events, etc.;
- recognise the different needs of different people: relaxation, competition, beginners, high standard, for different age groups, genders, ethnic groups, etc.;
- choose and analyse activities which collectively are most likely, within resources, to meet objectives;
- establish priorities between conflicting claims on the programme from different types of user and different activities;
- consider not only the programme's implications for utilisation and revenue, but also its requirements for resources and costs;
- plan for added value elements to the programme, e.g. in fitness clubs the development of new classes led by a skilled animateur;
- build flexibility into the programme – it will lead to variety, wider use and greater balance;
- account fully for the resources and time necessary to set up and break down for programme changes, especially new events;
- consider the staffing implications and management style, division of labour, responsibilities, training, etc.;
- try to ensure that any community development programmes have fully considered sustainability, or exit routes to similar opportunities;
- avoid administration problems by establishing easily handled and easily understood systems and methods, i.e. which are easy for the user and easy for the organisation;
- make full use of information technology and modern computerised systems.

16.8.6 Implement and manage the programme

The stages in this are as follows:

- Activate the agreed marketing strategy, using aspects of the marketing 'mix' to complement the programme, e.g. promotion, pricing and place (see Chapter 15).
- Attend to staffing requirements – where community development is relevant, staff/helpers are needed to support newly formed groups until they become self-supporting; consider outreach skill development.
- Try new technologies for programming, e.g. video, computers, giant screen for information, visuals to show availability in spaces and programmes, self-service, do-it-yourself bookings, etc.; use information technology to advantage.
- Ensure flexibility to meet changing situations – the flexible approach needs skilful management to enable individuals to participate in the way they want to.
- Control the programme through appropriate staffing and delegation of authority, financial and operational systems.
- Design monitoring systems to provide management with information relating to the current level of usage, the profile of users, changing trends.
- Anticipate the likely problems and be ready with alternatives.
- Avoid incompatible activities in terms of health and safety, noise, age, level of play, etc.
- Expand the programme with new activities, new methods and new people.
- Programme 'packages', not just single items.
- Try some experiments; try out regionally or nationally fashionable activities; yet always enhance local success.
- Extend product life-cycles through changes, variety and new forms of delivery.
- Keep all stakeholders and particularly potential and actual users informed of what is going on – use a variety of communication systems.

Programme control is a management function; it helps if one manager has overall responsibility. It is important that the way the programme is delivered meets or exceeds customer expectations and that staff are fully committed to the success of the programme. Programming success is often hampered by seemingly small items, such as double bookings, which cause problems far in excess of the relatively minor mistake.

16.8.7 Evaluate the programme

How else will you know whether you are doing a good job? To what extent have the programme's objectives been met? You should:

- Evaluate inputs – what has gone into planning the programme: resources, staff, time, costs?
- Evaluate the process – what has occurred in carrying out the programme from start to finish?
- Evaluate the outcome, the results – how did they compare with objectives and targets? Were clients and customers generally satisfied with the opportunities provided by the programme?
- Measure the efficiency of the operation – how well has the job been carried out? How adequate has the staffing been? How well have staff performed?
- Use several criteria, not just financial, to measure the performance of each element of the programme.

- Use both quantitative and qualitative measures, i.e. not only throughput, socio-economic profile of users, income generation, cost-effectiveness, levels of sponsorship achieved, etc., but also attitudes by users to such attributes as ease of booking, helpfulness of staff, range of activity choices, the timing of activities, etc.
- Identify any changes in user profiles, catchment areas, etc. compared with previous programmes.
- Obtain feedback from users and possibly non-users, e.g. through community groups and representatives.
- Assess the effectiveness of the marketing strategy, e.g. awareness levels, attractiveness of opportunities, clarity of information, distribution of outreach services.
- Determine the effectiveness of the changes in the programme.

16.8.8 Modify the programme appropriately

- Reinforce and possibly expand the successful elements of the programme.
- If the programme or elements of it have been unsuccessful, first determine the reasons from the monitoring and evaluation; second, act to counteract the reasons, e.g. by changes to the components of the programme, staff training or retraining, staff areas of responsibility or complementary elements of the marketing mix such as pricing or promotion.
- Modify targets according to levels of performance – targets should be challenging but realistic (see Chapter 17).

16.9 Monitoring and evaluation

The vital function in ensuring that programming is a cyclical process is monitoring and evaluation. It is this which leads to comprehensive and systematic review, from which the programme stages above start again, even possibly starting with reconsideration of the organisation's aims.

16.9.1 Monitoring

Monitoring involves continuous and regular collection of relevant information, as part of the normal management information systems for the programme. Because this information is collected systematically, it can be checked regularly and appropriate short run actions can be taken to remedy any emerging problems, or to benefit from any unexpected opportunities. The information collected might include:

- the identities and registration details (if collected) of participants, their attendance records;
- the total number of visits to each session, compared with the plan;
- total revenue collected, compared with the budget;
- the costs of operating each session, compared with the budget;
- comments and suggestions from customers (and staff, if they are collected systematically).

16.9.2 Evaluation

Evaluation is more of a one-off, extra effort to collect information with which to judge a programme's successes and weaknesses. It may take place at selected points in time during the programme but more typically it is conducted at an appropriate time towards the end of the programme's season. Evaluation will employ the monitoring information already collected, to which it will add information from any number of other methods, such as surveys, focus groups and interviews with key individuals. Evaluation should seek the views of customers, key stakeholders, staff and managers. It should produce an action document – i.e. what to do next – because it feeds into the re-planning of the programme.

Resources are typically constrained in operating a programme, no more so than in evaluation. Indeed, many programmes take place without any evaluation, which is a serious mistake. The key resource decision is who will do the evaluation. Evaluation can be undertaken by one or both of two main sets of people:

1 **Internal evaluation by staff** can be more sensitive to staff feelings, but is more likely to be biased and less objective, and more likely to justify failures or to exonerate from blame. Furthermore, internal staff typically have enough to do running the programmes and see evaluation as an unnecessary extra if they are not sufficiently briefed about its importance.
2 **External evaluation, e.g. by educational establishments or management consultants,** is likely to be more objective, but can be hampered by staff suspicion or worry about the outcome and lack of detailed knowledge of programme implementation. And it is typically more expensive than utilising internal staff.

Whichever resource is utilised for evaluation, the important decision is to include an explicit component in the programme's budget for evaluation. Then it is more likely to be done.

16.10 Learning from past mistakes

One of the hallmarks of good programming, whatever the organisation, is the extent to which objectives have been met and client satisfaction has been paramount. Managers should learn from the successes and the problems of many of the programmes currently practised. Outlined below are a number of problem areas which have been found at community leisure centres. They are in no particular order of significance:

- Demands and needs are not being assessed (see Chapter 14).
- Objectives, so called, are not measurable (see Chapter 17).
- Programmes tend to be too traditional, static and much 'the same old thing' – the same activities, the same delivery.
- Programmes lack variety and novelty.
- Often a 'take it or leave it' approach is adopted, regardless of whether the programme is appropriate to the target groups in the community.
- The advantages and disadvantages of different user systems (e.g. casual user, member, discount cards) are not evaluated fully.
- The balance of casual use with club use and events is not based on policy, but expediency.
- The need to analyse the benefits of different activities is rarely considered.
- Regular, habit-forming activities (e.g. weekly sessions) are interrupted by insensitive one-off programming, which breaks into the pattern without consultation.

- Programme patterns, such as seasonality, are not given due consideration.
- Incompatible activities are sometimes programmed together.
- Insufficient flexibility is built into programming to adapt to new demands.
- Ways of expanding an already busy programme are insufficiently explored (e.g. early/late bookings).
- IT and computer systems are not being put to best advantage to aid efficiency (e.g. self-service); bureaucracy and cumbersome administration systems still abound.
- Programme worth is increasingly judged on numbers allied to financial viability; qualitative programming gives way under such strain.
- Risk avoidance leads to a lacklustre approach, with a lack of creativity, stifled programmes, lack of adventure and non-appeal for young people.
- Some community facilities are used for few purposes, which occupy only a proportion of time and attract a narrow market segment.
- Programmes do not take into account outreach possibilities; many potential satellite resources remain unused for the community: schools; church buildings; and clubs, business and industrial sport and leisure facilities.
- Programme monitoring and systematic evaluation are not often carried out to change and improve programme content and presentation.

Not all poor programmes can be changed overnight. It may well take several cycles of the programme, for example, due to established patterns and 'sitting tenants'. However, most problems can be ironed out by making changes in easy stages.

> **Discussion question**
>
> In a leisure facility or service that you are familiar with, do you recognise any of the failings above?

16.11 Conclusions

Good programming can offer choice, provide balance, attract the markets being aimed at and be responsive to the needs and wants of stakeholders and customers. Conversely, poor programming results in the organisation's objectives not being met, limited choice and too many dissatisfied customers. The centrality of the product in marketing, which in leisure services is the programme, is the rationale for this chapter. However, the programme needs support from other parts of the marketing mix, such as pricing and promotion (see Chapter 15), and from other aspects of management, including finance and human resources.

One of the key tensions in programming is that between continuity and innovation. On the one hand, existing customers like stability and predictability, particularly in sports programmes. On the other hand, innovation and new opportunities attract existing and new customers alike, particularly in the arts. The virtues of continuity can lull a leisure manager into thinking conservatively about their programme – play safe, play the odds. However, creativity is an important attribute and although it is accompanied by risks, particularly the risk of a weak response by customers, it is a gamble that must be taken.

Innovation and creativity in programming require boldness in forecasting future demands. Chapter 14 includes a review of demand forecasting techniques, but one of the main problems is that many forecasting techniques are based on previous patterns of demand – back to continuity again. Innovation in programming, particularly in the arts, means making bold decisions, taking risks and accepting some programme failures. But if failures occur it is important to learn from them, through incisive evaluation. Even successful programmes need to be analysed, in order to identify the key drivers of success within the programmes. Perceptive analysis of failures and successes can yield valuable lessons for future programming.

Practical tasks

1 For the same leisure facility or space, one person design a week's programme using the authoritarian approach and a second person design a week's programme using the cafeteria-style approach. Compare both the resulting programmes with the current programme and debate the merits of the different approaches.
2 For a leisure facility or service of your choice, obtain a typical week's programme and identify what the weakest elements of the programme are in terms of numbers of customers. Consider why such elements are on the programme and the costs of these elements.

Structured guide to further reading

For an overview of programming issues and a summary of programming theories:
Edginton, C.R., Hudson, S., Dieser, R. and Edginton, S. (2004) *Leisure Programming: a service-centred and benefits approach*, 4th edition, McGraw Hill, New York.

For a workbook of how to undertake programming effectively, and a review of key decisions relevant to programming:
Rossman, J.R. and Elwood Schlatter, B. (2008) *Recreation Programming: designing leisure experiences*, 5th edition, Sagamore Publishing, Champaign, IL.

For evaluation of programmes:
Henderson, K.A. (2008) 'Evaluating and documenting programmes', in G. Carpenter and D. Blandy, *Arts and Cultural Programming: a leisure perspective*, Human Kinetics, Champaign, IL.

Useful websites

For Ponds Forge International Sports Centre:
www.ponds-forge.co.uk

For Creswell Leisure Centre:
www.bolsover.gov.uk

Chapter 17

Quality and performance management in sport and leisure

Summary

Quality management and performance management are important contemporary redefinitions of what good management of organisations is about. Their popularity has grown in recent years and there are now a number of systems which are available with which to promote and recognise good management. Many systems are generic to all organisations, or to public sector services. However, there are a few systems which are sport and leisure specific.

Quality management concerns processes which are designed to achieve continuous improvement in an organisation and which are aimed at meeting and hopefully exceeding customers' expectations. Generic frameworks to promote self-assessment of quality management within organisations include the European Foundation for Quality Management, whilst the Culture and Sport Improvement Toolkit is an example of a framework specifically designed for sport and leisure services. Such frameworks translate the principles of quality management into practical evaluation criteria which organisations can use.

Performance management covers very similar principles to quality management, with more of a focus on specifying measurable objectives, selecting appropriate performance indicators, setting targets, measuring performance, and using the evidence to review objectives and actions. Performance management is facilitated by generic systems such as the Balanced Scorecard. There is also an array of performance measurement systems which promote performance management in sport and leisure organisations.

Finally, it is desirable to put an organisation's performance into perspective and benchmarking is a technique which does this. The performance measurement systems include comparison of an organisation's performance with other similar organisations in the sport and leisure industry.

17.1 Introduction

Quality is a key determinant in satisfying customers in the sport and leisure industries, as in other industries. Whether managing in the commercial, public or voluntary sectors, people have to be attracted to the services and facilities and these should be managed with excellence – that is, with quality. But quality does not just happen. It has to be worked for. It has to be managed.

Deming is renowned as the first guru of total quality management (TQM). TQM concerns a shared vision among all in an organisation and a continuing process of organisational improvement. Deming's quality improvement work revolutionised Japan's industrial productivity after the Second World War. He is noted for the Deming cycle, or PDSA cycle, a continuous quality improvement model consisting of a logical sequence of four repetitive steps – Plan, Do, Study and Act – through which continuous improvement is achieved (Deming, 1986). Another important figure in the development of quality principles is Juran, who did much to consolidate a holistic, integrated concept of quality management (Juran, 1988), with an emphasis on communication and people management, and 'fitness for purpose' or 'quality' of a product or service defined by a focus on customers.

In the 1990s the popularity of quality programmes in the public sector in developed countries, including public leisure services, accelerated. This was stimulated by a number of considerations (Robinson, 2001; Williams and Buswell, 2003), including:

- an increasing strategic focus on customers;
- promotion of quality management by key professional agencies;
- rising customer expectations, driven by higher service standards in commercial services;
- greater government pressure and legislation for accountability in public services.

The Chartered Quality Institute in the UK defines quality management as 'an organisation-wide approach to understanding precisely what customers need and consistently delivering accurate solutions within budget, on time and with the minimum loss to society' (see 'Useful websites', pp. 482–3). This institute describes quality in terms of innovation and care, as indicated in Figure 17.1, which demonstrates how all-embracing the concept of quality is.

Robinson (2004) reproduces definitions for a number of other terms important in quality management:

- **quality** – how consistently the product or service delivered meets or exceeds the customer's expectations and needs (from Clarke, 1992);

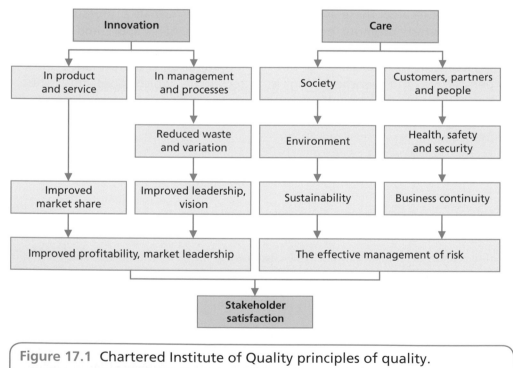

Figure 17.1 Chartered Institute of Quality principles of quality.
Source: Chartered Quality Institute, http://www.thecqi.org/.

- **quality control** – the operational techniques and activities that are used to fulfil requirements for quality (from BSI, 1987);
- **quality assurance** – all the planned and systematic actions necessary to provide confidence that a product or service will satisfy given requirements for quality (from BSI, 1987).

The term 'performance management' covers very similar principles to 'quality management', with a focus on performance measurement and consequent actions. It informs management decisions with appropriate planning, objectives, targets, performance measurement and review.

There is a wide range of quality management systems. Many require evidence of an organisation having gone through a formal process of applying quality management procedures and techniques, to then be awarded certification by an external body. These procedures are likely to involve consultation with customers, critical appraisal of the organisation and continuous quality management improvement. Certification can also provide a competitive edge. However, quality management systems can be costly, particularly for small organisations and those in the voluntary sector. Quality management certification is particularly useful in local government; it can help in meeting government's standards designed to assess how well a council delivers its services.

Discussion question

What is quality certification most useful for, improving management or reporting to stakeholders?

17.2 Total quality management

Total quality management (TQM) is an approach to improving the effectiveness of a business as a whole – i.e. a process which involves every person in an organisation – to ensure customer satisfaction. TQM thus focuses on customer needs and builds a logical linkage between these needs and the business objectives.

The principles behind such total quality management are identified by Mosscrop and Stores (1990):

- excellence as the objective and getting it right first time;
- everyone is a customer or a supplier in every transaction – every transaction in the business, every link in the chain, has a supplier and a customer;
- absolute clarity about customers' needs; the perceptions of customers are paramount;
- commitment from the top;
- measurement of all key outputs;
- prevention not blame; sharing responsibility;
- training and education;
- integration of total quality into the business – a core business activity which permeates every aspect of leisure operations.

In other words, excellence is called for and is worked for by every person in all aspects of the operation. All activity throughout all operations is continuously directed at satisfying client and customer requirements. Clearly this is an ideal and will never be completely achieved. Challenges in achieving TQM include the following:

● Organisations do not often act in unison and harmony but are often characterised by separate departmental interests.
● Identifying all customers' changing needs is very difficult and identifying customers' expectations is even more difficult.
● Organisational objectives are often not specified in a way that promotes TQM because they are too general and non-measurable.
● Measuring all outputs consistently is difficult and can be very resource intensive.

Some of these issues are explored in more detail in the sections below. Case Study 17.1, meanwhile, addresses an important consideration in quality management which is often overlooked in the quest for perfection – how to deal with mistakes.

Discussion question

In the light of its considerable requirements and challenges, is total quality management achievable?

17.3 Quality frameworks

Quality frameworks have been designed to help managers assess and promote total quality management in the workplace. They do not involve awards but rather establish a set of practical processes through which total quality management can be achieved. Two frameworks are summarised below: (1) one of the most commonly referred to generic models, the European Foundation for Quality Management's Excellence Model; (2) a recent government initiative in the UK specifically for sport and cultural services, the Culture and Sport Improvement Toolkit.

17.3.1 The European Foundation for Quality Management Excellence Model

The European Foundation for Quality Management (EFQM) was founded in 1988 to enhance the competitive position of European organisations and their effectiveness and efficiency. The EFQM Excellence Model (see 'Useful websites', pp. 482–3), also known as the Business Excellence Model, is a management framework that can be used to facilitate continuous improvement in an organisation. It is non-prescriptive and works on the basis of self-assessment against relevant criteria which go to make up quality performance.

By comparing the organisation against the model's criteria, it is possible to identify strengths and weaknesses, providing a clear indication of those activities which distinguish the organisation from World-Class or Best-in-Class organisations.

The EFQM Model is based on nine criteria (see Figure 17.2). Five of these, on the left side of the figure, are 'Enablers', i.e. actions and processes which the organisation undertakes. Four, on the right, are 'Results', covering the organisation's achievements. The interrelationships between them are logical: Enablers determine Results, whilst feedback from and review of Results helps to modify the Enablers.

CASE STUDY 17.1

Service failures and recovery in the restaurant industry: examples from the USA

Much of the quality literature concentrates on positives – what to do right to improve quality – whilst principles such as 'right first time' suggest there is no room for mistakes. However, mistakes do occur and in service industries the mistakes are all too quickly apparent. Furthermore, the received wisdom is that negative word of mouth resulting from dissatisfied customers is passed on to more people than positive word of mouth from satisfied customers. According to Mack *et al.* (2000), 'In order to balance the need for defect-free service and the inevitability of failure, organisations must be proactive in anticipating likely areas of failures/complaints as well as anticipating the appropriate needs for recovery'. To inform this process, Mack *et al.* examined service failures in restaurants in a south-eastern city in the USA by interviewing 20 respondents and asking them about critical incidents of service failure that they had experienced in restaurants.

The 20 respondents identified 14 service failures, most of which were failures attributable directly to staff (cook or waiter/waitress) such as unreasonably slow service, wrong orders or cooking errors. Most of these failures were perceived as major mistakes. Even so, almost half of the respondents indicated that they would dine again at the restaurant where the failure occurred, with only about one-quarter saying that they would not (the remainder were uncertain). So these customers experiencing service failure were remarkably forgiving of the mistakes. Nevertheless, the potential for negative word of mouth is considerable, even by those who are forgiving.

In over one-fifth of the service failures identified, the restaurant response was 'nothing'. However, in other cases there was a variety of recovery tactics, including correction and replacement of food (17 per cent), free replacement of food (17 per cent), apology (15 per cent), free drinks or appetisers (14 per cent) and what the researchers term 'free food overkill', i.e. replacement food plus free food or drinks (7 per cent). Importantly, 58 per cent of the respondents who had experienced a major mistake judged the recovery effort by the restaurants concerned as 'poor'.

As Mack *et al.* suggest, '[t]he importance of a good recovery cannot be overstated, demonstrated by the fact that 88.5 per cent of those indicating a good recovery in this study said they would dine again at the property'. When asked what else the restaurants could have done to recover from their mistakes, the interviewees' most frequent response was 'just admit that a mistake was made', although this was followed by a number of responses which required major actions to compensate for the failures, not just a correction or replacement.

Interestingly, Mack *et al.*'s study found no significant differences in failure perceptions or recovery judgements by the type of restaurant – experiences at McDonalds were similar to experiences in more expensive restaurants. The implications of the study are clear, however:

1 Try to anticipate causes of service failure and prevent them.
2 When mistakes are made, acknowledge them to the customer.
3 Plan and implement effective recovery tactics to minimise negative word of mouth.

Source: derived from Mack *et al.* (2000)

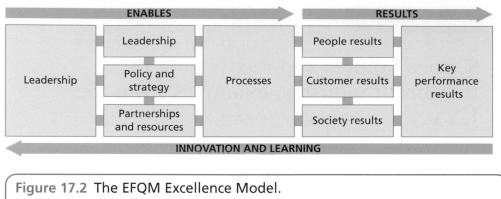

Figure 17.2 The EFQM Excellence Model.

Note: The EFQM Excellence Model is a registered trademark of EFQM.

Source: EFQM, http://ww1.efqm.org/en/Home/tabid/36/Default.aspx.

The EFQM is the most widely used organisational framework in Europe and has become the basis for the majority of national and regional Quality Awards, for example the UK Business Excellence Award, Investors in Excellence and Quest (the last two are summarised on pp. 461–3).

17.3.2 Culture and Sport Improvement Toolkit (CSIT)

CSIT is a national framework for performance management in cultural services in the UK (see 'Useful websites', pp. 482–3). It has been developed by IDeA, a UK government sponsored Improvement and Development Agency, in consultation with a number of other agencies, including professional bodies, the Department for Culture, Media and Sport (the central government department) and the Audit Commission (a public sector watchdog). In 2009 CSIT replaced and amalgamated three other systems, including Towards and Excellent Service.

CSIT is a self-assessment toolkit for improvement planning, designed to complement other quality systems such as EFMQ, Quest and Investors in People. It is described by IDeA (2008) as an 'improvement journey', because it is a continuous process of improvement. Continuous improvement is necessary because of ongoing changes in both community needs and customer expectations. CSIT incorporates not only self-assessment but also '360 degree feedback', a process of engagement with internal staff and clients and external stakeholders, through which alternative views of the service are generated.

CSIT identifies eight key 'themes' that influence the quality of cultural and sport services, listed below. Many of these echo the structural features of the EFQM model in Figure 17.2. Embedded in each of these themes are two principles – 'equality' and 'service access':

1 Leadership and corporate governance.
2 Policy and strategy.
3 Community engagement.
4 Partnership working.
5 Resource management.
6 People management.
7 Customer service.
8 Performance, achievement and learning.

(IDeA, 2008)

A ninth theme, efficiency, is being piloted at the time of writing. Within each theme, criteria have been developed which identify an excellent service. A number of key features further define each criterion and it is these which are the focus of self-assessment, each rated on a four-point scale: excellent, good, fair or poor. The results of the 360 degree feedback can be used to adjust the self-assessment scores.

Another important feature of CSIT is validation, accomplished largely by independent review and challenge, which includes interviews with staff and review of the documentary evidence used in the self-assessment. Peer review is another option. Once assessment and validation are completed, an improvement plan is written to convert the results into actions. IDeA (2008) states that improvement planning is the most important part of the CSIT process: it is the main reason for conducting the self-assessment and 360 degree feedback.

17.4 Quality awards schemes

Quality award schemes encourage and promote good practice in quality management. Awards, however, not only give recognition and status to an organisation; many come as a result of training, considerable collective effort, application of quality management systems and improvement. As such, they are significantly more than certificates and trophies.

Quality awards are based on assessment of an applicant organisation against criteria specified by the awarding body. Some are competitive, recognising the best; but others have no limit on the 'winners' because they are simply judged against the award criteria. There are international, national, regional awards and industry-specific awards. Examples of international awards include:

- European Quality Award, established in 1992 and offered by the European Foundation for Quality Management;
- Asia-Pacific Area Golden Quality Award;
- Deming Prize, established in 1951 (becoming international in 1984) and offered by the Japanese Union of Scientists and Engineers.

An example of a national award is The Malcolm Baldrige Award, established in 1987 by the US Congress and named after a former Secretary of Commerce. It aims to provide quality awareness and is based on a weighted score of seven categories of performance criteria: leadership; strategic planning; customer and market focus; measurement, analysis, knowledge management; human resource focus; process management; and business results. Another national award is the UK Excellence Award, which is run by the British Quality Foundation (see 'Useful websites', pp. 482–3), a National Partner Organisation of the European Foundation for Quality Management.

There are also industry-specific awards. The White Flag Award, in Ireland, is a quality award endorsed by Failte Ireland and the Irish Hotels Federation (see 'Useful websites', pp. 482–3). It is aimed at swimming pools, sports halls, gymnasiums and other indoor leisure facilities. The Green Flag Award, in England and Wales, is designed to recognise and encourage good quality public parks (see 'Useful websites', pp. 482–3). The Green Flag Award is managed by a consortium of Keep Britain Tidy, BTCV (the British Trust for Conservation Volunteers) and GreenSpace.

Many leisure, sport and recreation institutions have award schemes. Examples in the UK include the Institute for Sport, Parks and Leisure (ISPAL) Leadership Award, Innovation Award, and Health and Physical Activity Recognition Programme. In Australia, awards include the Parks and Leisure Australia Awards of Excellence. In the USA, the

Gold Medal Awards from the National Parks and Recreation Association are given to communities which demonstrate excellence in long-range planning, resource management and agency recognition.

17.4.1 British and International Standards

In the late 1970s, the British Standards Institute (BSI) developed the BS 5750 system to improve quality throughout the management process, by using a structured system of standards and procedures. During the 1980s, the Department of Trade and Industry (DTI) encouraged British industry to compete internationally using quality initiatives. In 1994, three existing standards – British, European and International – were merged and called ISO 9000 (Williams and Buswell, 2003). The relevant standard is now BN EN ISO 9001:2000 (see 'Useful websites', pp. 482–3).

This standard comprises a system which covers eight principles: customer focus, leadership, involvement of people, process approach, systems approach to management, continual improvement, factual approach to decision-making and mutually beneficial supplier relationships. It is a system of quality assurance rather than total quality management, however, because it concentrates on identifying whether stated operational procedures are followed, rather than on ensuring outcomes are achieved.

17.4.2 Customer Service Excellence

This is the UK government's standard for excellence in customer services in the public sector. It replaced another accredited standard, Charter Mark, in 2009. Customer Service Excellence (see 'Useful websites', pp. 482–3) is designed to act as a driver of continuous improvement, via an online self-assessment tool; it is a skills development tool; and it is an independently validated accreditation. It has five criteria for excellence:

1 **customer insight** – i.e. an in-depth understanding of customers, through identification, engagement and consultation, and through measurement of customer satisfaction;
2 **organisation culture** – i.e. a customer-focused culture via appropriate leadership and policy, and the professionalism and attitude of staff;
3 **information and access** – i.e. with an appropriate range and quality of information for customers, accessible services, and cooperative working with other providers;
4 **delivery** – i.e. excellent standards of service delivery, meeting customer expectations and dealing effectively with problems;
5 **timeliness and quality of services** – i.e. via measurable standards, timely outcomes and timely delivery.

Because the standard is designed for public services, three of these principal criteria are centred on the customer's experience, whilst the other two concern the extent to which the organisation is customer facing and informed of customers' needs and satisfactions. This is a narrower focus than frameworks such as the Culture and Sport Improvement Toolkit (see pp. 458–9), which includes more consideration of the service organisation itself (e.g. partnership, resource management, people management, performance and learning).

17.4.3 Investors in People

Investors in People UK (see 'Useful websites', pp. 482–3) is a UK non-departmental public body, established in 1991 by the government as a business support and advice service. The

Investors in People (IIP) Standard provides a framework for improving business performance and competitiveness through good practice in human resource development. According to the IIP, in 2009 there were over 35,000 IIP recognised organisations in the UK employing over 7 million employees – about 31 per cent of the workforce.

IIP is an award based on external assessment of ten indicators, organised in three stages:

- Plan: developing strategies to improve the performance of the organisation:
  1. business strategy
  2. learning and development strategy
  3. people management strategy
  4. leadership and management strategy
- Do: taking action:
  5. management effectiveness
  6. recognition and reward
  7. involvement and empowerment
  8. learning and development
- Review: evaluating the impact
  9. performance measurement
  10. continuous improvement

The ten indicators together contain 39 evidence requirements. In addition to these, an IIP assessor confidentially interviews a random selection of employees.

As leisure is often called a 'people industry', it is appropriate that IIP concentrates on performance in human resource management (HRM). A firm principle underlying IIP is that success in HRM will impact on wider organisational performance. Two studies in 2008 tested this relationship. Cowling (2008) investigated its effect on gross profit per employee, using a dataset of 2,500 UK private sector organisations. The results suggest that companies with IIP had gross profits per employee of £128.38, compared with a figure of £34.40 for companies without IIP. Furthermore, the research suggests that this higher performance is not just the result of better performing organisations choosing to undertake IIP.

Bourne et al. (2008) further endorsed the effectiveness of IIP. Their study used ten in-depth case studies of private commercial organisations, together with 196 responses to a survey from commercial organisations. The research concluded that IIP, through improvements in human resources policies, improved the organisations' social climates (trust, cooperation and engagement) and improved their employees' flexibility. This led to improvements in non-financial performance (including quality of products and services, customer satisfaction, and attraction and retention of employees), which in turn led to improvements in financial performance. However, it should be emphasised that both the Bourne and Cowling studies used commercial company data and covered a wide range of industries – they were not leisure specific.

17.4.4 Investors in Excellence

Investors in Excellence (IiE), was developed in the UK by Midlands Excellence in 2003. It is a not-for-profit and non-membership body with a range of quality improvement activities. Its IiE Standard is described as a framework for coordinating improvement activity, increasing performance and achieving recognition. The criteria against which achievement is assessed are those of the EFQM Excellence Model (see Figure 17.2).

17.4.5 Quest

Quest (see 'Useful websites', pp. 482–3) is also based on the EFQM Excellence Model but it is distinctive because it is the UK's quality award scheme for sport and leisure. It has been operating since 1996 and is managed by PMP, a sport and leisure consultancy. It has two awards:

1   **Quest Facility Management,** aimed at sport and leisure facilities in the commercial, voluntary and public sectors;
2   **Quest Sports Development,** aimed at Sports Development Units in local authorities, national governing bodies and voluntary organisations.

Quest is recommended by the British Quality Foundation for UK sport and leisure operations and is endorsed and supported by the four Sports Councils in the UK, plus a range of industry-representative organisations which have played an important role in developing the scheme. There are three main stages to achieving Quest:

1   **Self-Assessment,** in comparison to industry standards and best practice – this stimulates the right organisational culture for improvement and it facilitates the identification of strengths and weaknesses and the development of action plans;
2   **External Validation** – undertaken by independent assessors and, for facilities, including a mystery customer visit;
3   **Ongoing Maintenance** to maintain registration for two years – this involves an assessor visit, and includes a further mystery customer visit in the case of facilities.

Table 17.1 Quest assessment areas and issues

Facilities operation	Standards, systems and monitoring
	Cleanliness
	Housekeeping and presentation
	Maintenance
	Equipment
	Environmental management
	Changing rooms
	Health and safety management
Customer relations	Customer care
	Customer feedback
	Research
	Marketing
	Bookings and reception
Staffing	Staff supervision and planning
	People management
	Management style
Service development and review	Business management
	Programme development
	Partnerships
	Performance management
	Information and communication technology
	Continuous improvement

Source: Quest, www.questnbs.info/.

Quest assessment focuses on four key areas of management, with 22 management issues between them (see Table 17.1). The list of issues demonstrates how the general principles of such a system percolate down to very specific considerations of service delivery.

17.5 Quality awards and the performance of leisure facilities

An important 'bottom line' in most quality programmes is better performance by the organisation which succeeds in attaining the quality management award. Investors in People, for example, describes itself as 'a business improvement tool designed to advance an organisation's performance'. Robinson (2003) found that the two most commonly cited reasons for using quality programmes given by leisure facility managers were to improve services and to improve efficiency. Is there any evidence, then, that quality awards lead to better performance?

Two studies of IIP have been noted above, but they were not leisure specific. Ramchandani and Taylor (2011) investigated the effect of four different quality awards on the performance of sport and leisure centres, using a sample of 98 centres which had been processed through Sport England's National Benchmarking Service. Between them these centres had a number of awards, including Quest, Charter Mark, Investors in People and ISO 9002. Ramchandani and Taylor analysed 37 performance indicators, covering access to the centres by disadvantaged groups, finance, utilisation, satisfaction and importance-satisfaction gaps. They concluded that there was a statistically significant difference between centres with and without any quality awards for only one indicator out of the 37 – the percentage of visits which were first visits at the centre – and for this indicator it was centres without any awards that had the higher performance.

Ramchandani and Taylor also investigated the effects of individual awards and concluded that:

- Charter Mark was associated with higher access performance;
- Quest was associated with better finance, utilisation and customer satisfaction performance;
- Investors in People was associated with better utilisation and customer satisfaction performance;
- for all awards, some dimensions of performance are stronger in centres without the awards than in those with the awards.

Ramchandani and Taylor concluded that choosing to achieve a quality award does not necessarily improve all aspects of performance, and the selection of which award to go for depends on what aspects of performance are priorities for an organisation.

Discussion question

If you had to choose a quality management award for a leisure organisation to work towards achieving, which would you recommend and why?

Another study which investigates the impact of a quality system on the operations of organisations in sport is featured in Case Study 17.2. It demonstrates the design and effectiveness of sport-specific quality systems.

CASE STUDY 17.2

Quality management in Flemish sports organisations, Belgium

In 1997 the Flemish government published a Strategic Plan for Sporting Flanders (Flanders is the northern, Dutch speaking part of Belgium) which emphasised a shift to quality and performance management in all sports systems and structures. This, it was intended, would lead to all providers of sporting services – including federations, clubs and public services – monitoring the quality and effectiveness of their systems. It would also facilitate 'more professional quality and competence {…} in exchange for subsidies and other forms of support'. Federations and clubs are typically supported by government and local authorities.

The systematic promotion of total quality management in Flemish sport was related to other changes, particularly demands from some club members for a more contemporary approach to management, and a decrease in experienced volunteers. It was hoped that quality and performance management would help organisations to better deal with their internal and external challenges.

Van Hoecke *et al.* (2009) examine gymnastics clubs which have used IKGym, which began as an initiative to produce a guide to gymnastics clubs, including their service quality, but also set out to implement principles of quality and performance management; inform stakeholders about critical success factors; provide volunteer board members with professional advice and support; and improve the management of gymnastics clubs in order to enhance output and performance.

The IKGym system consists of an external audit to measure a club's performance over seven strategic dimensions (organisational management and strategic planning; internal communications procedures; external communication and image building; organisational culture; organisational structure; human resources management; and organisational effectiveness) and four operational dimensions (coaching; training group size, composition and intensity of training; quality of facilities and equipment; and performance and outcome). Each of these dimensions has an array of measures. A total score is calculated and certification of performance is provided, which lasts for three years, along with quantitative and qualitative reports which identify strengths and weaknesses.

Seventy-two gymnastics clubs which had participated in IKGym agreed that it provided a very good picture of their organisational performance (Van Hoecke *et al.*, 2009). In half of these clubs, the process of conducting the audit stimulated improvements in their organisation before the result was known. Nine out of ten clubs undertook targeted actions to correct weaknesses identified by the audit. IKGym was therefore an important influence on the change process in these organisations.

IKGym has been adapted in other more general quality systems for sports organisations in Belgium – including IKSport for sports clubs and PASS for youth academies in sports clubs. Research by Van Hoecke *et al.* (2009) suggests that these systems have been welcomed by their participating clubs for the accuracy of their audits and their usefulness in informing quality improvements.

Source: derived from Van Hoecke *et al.* (2009)

17.6 Performance management principles

Performance management is a cyclical, continuous process which relies on:

- specifying suitable objectives for the organisation;
- employing appropriate performance indicators to represent these objectives;
- setting challenging but realistic management targets for the performance of the organisation;
- taking the required actions to realise these targets;
- measuring performance;
- reviewing achievements and reconsidering objectives, indicators, targets and actions.

This process is compatible with the quality management systems reviewed above, but with a narrower focus on performance measurement and consequent action. This has not always been undertaken by leisure managers, particularly in the public and voluntary sectors. The Audit Commission in Britain, for example, exposed weaknesses in public leisure management in a series of seminal reports on sport (1989), entertainments and the arts (1991a) and museums and art galleries (1991b). However, since these reports, a range of performance management systems have been devised in the UK to help public sector managers achieve continuous improvement.

The Audit Commission (2000a) has made clear why performance measurement is central to performance management (see Table 17.2). Without the right evidence, it is not easy to see where you are, let alone what is right or wrong with an organisation, or where to go next.

Table 17.2 Why measure performance?

Performance measurement can contribute to effective services:
- What gets measured gets done.
- If you don't measure results, you can't tell success from failure.
- If you can't see success, you can't reward it.
- If you can't reward success, you're probably rewarding failure.
- If you can't see success you can't learn from it.
- If you can't recognise failure, you can't correct it.
- If you can demonstrate results, you can win public support.

Source: Audit Commission (2000a).

Discussion question

Many sport and leisure organisations do not measure performance very well. Discuss the possible reasons for this. If possible, use examples of organisations you are familiar with.

17.6.1 Objectives

An essential first stage in performance management is setting specific organisational objectives. An objective is a desired future position. Taylor (1996) identifies a number of desirable attributes for organisational objectives:

- Objectives should be specified so that, at the end of an appropriate period, it is clear whether or not they have been achieved. This means that objectives need to be measurable. Each objective requires appropriate performance indicators, by which measurement of performance is possible.
- Objectives are concerned with ends not means. For example, it is not an objective to 'set low prices for disadvantaged groups in the community'. Rather, the objective here is 'to increase visits to the service by people from disadvantaged groups'.
- The prioritisation of objectives is important, because sometimes objectives may conflict with each other. For example, 'increase revenue' might conflict with 'increase usage of a sport facility by disadvantaged groups'. Where trade-offs between conflicting objectives are apparent, priorities need to be identified. Otherwise, managers are put in a situation where some kind of failure is inevitable.

Such attributes for objectives can be summarised with the acronym MASTER:

- Measurable;
- Achievable;
- Specific;
- Time-specified;
- Ends not means;
- Ranked.

Often, particularly in the public sector, organisational objectives are expressed vaguely or generally, so that it is difficult if not impossible to identify whether or not they have been achieved. Examples of such mis-specified objectives include 'achieving sport for all' and 'serving the community's needs'. These are 'aims' rather than objectives – they are broadly based and non-measurable. They require more specific, measurable objectives to be monitored through performance indicators and used for management decision-making.

Public sector sport organisations have a more complicated task in framing appropriate objectives than commercial organisations, because social objectives are important to public sector organisations, such as usage by disadvantaged groups, the satisfaction of local communities with services and even impacts such as diversion of 'at-risk' youth from crime, as well as the more conventional financial and customer satisfaction objectives. Social impacts such as reduced crime and vandalism and improved health and citizenship are typically less easily expressed in a measurable form than more operational objectives such as usage and finance.

17.6.2 Performance

Performance for leisure organisations can mean any number of things, depending on what objectives are specified. This section identifies different aspects of performance that leisure managers will be most likely to be interested in:

- **Finance** – this is the most conventional dimension of performance found in the private sector. It is often specified simply as profits, but in fact financial performance covers much wider ground (see Section 17.6.3.1).
- **Economy** – this is concerned only with costs, i.e. inputs to the production process. Economy improves if inputs are acquired at lower cost. Overemphasis on economy, of course, carries some risk – for example if the inputs are of lower quality. For example, a major input in leisure services is typically labour and to reduce the costs of labour risks a 'false economy', with such problems as higher labour turnover or lower skilled labour.

- **Effectiveness** – this is concerned with outputs and reaching targets. A basic measure of effectiveness is throughput, such as the number of visits in a week. However, this is a rather basic indicator because it contains no indication of the types of visitors that have been attracted, or the extent to which the service has met the needs of the visitors – both of which can easily be measured by market research of customers. Assessing the effectiveness of such services may well extend to impacts in the local community, i.e. beyond the immediate use and satisfaction of customers.

- **Efficiency** – this is concerned with achieving objectives and targets at minimum cost, so it simultaneously takes into consideration both outputs and inputs. It is sometimes given the terms 'cost-effectiveness' or 'cost efficiency', and is also what is meant by the terms 'productivity' and 'value for money'. A contemporary term in much use in recent years, particularly in public sector services, is 'efficiency savings'; but this requires maintaining service outputs whilst cutting costs – a very difficult thing to achieve.

- **Equity** – this is particularly relevant to public sector services and means measuring fairness in the distribution of services to different types of customers, e.g. by age, gender, ethnicity and ability. It can be interpreted in a number of ways, for example fairness in the accessibility of services for all local citizens (i.e. equal opportunity) or fairness in the service received by different types of customers.

- **Customer satisfaction** – this is at the heart of quality management. It can be measured directly by such methods as questionnaire surveys, comments slips or complaints. Sometimes satisfaction with service attributes is compared with customer expectations of these attributes and sometimes it is compared with the importance of the attributes to customers. In the public sector, it is also important to measure the satisfaction with services by local citizens, regardless of whether or not they have actually used the service. This may seem contradictory – if a person has not actually used a service, how can they possibly comment? However, it is often the case that the community has a collective interest in the performance of a service, not least because they have collectively paid for it. An example is sport and leisure services for 'at-risk' young people. A wide range of people in local communities will have a view on whether or not such services are satisfactory, from parents and neighbours to anyone with a fear of nuisance or worse from bored young people.

> ### Discussion question
>
> Are social impacts too difficult to measure as performance dimensions for public sport and leisure facilities? Discuss in relation to such commonly cited impacts as improvements in health, reductions in crime and vandalism, and improvements in educational achievements.

17.6.3 Performance indicators

A performance indicator is a piece of empirical data which can be used to measure the performance of an organisation and which can be compared over time or between organisations. The UK Audit Commission (2000b) has identified criteria for good performance indicators (see Table 17.3). Although designed for the public sector, these criteria are transferable to other sectors.

Devising a set of performance indicators that fulfils all of the criteria in this table is challenging. For national indicators, the Audit Commission advises that a performance indicator should be clearly defined, comparable, verifiable, unambiguous and statistically valid. Indicators that are published for the benefit of the local community should first and foremost be relevant and easy to understand. It is also important that performance indicators should be capable of being measured for separate parts of a leisure service, since it is likely that different objectives and different targets are applicable to different parts of the service, even within one facility.

> ## Discussion question
>
> A very common performance indicator in use in sport and leisure facilities is annual visits per square metre of floor space. Discuss the extent to which this indicator fulfils the Audit Commission criteria in Table 17.3.

Good quality data is the essential ingredient for reliable performance information, so it is vital that the data used for the construction of performance indicators are up to the task. The Audit Commission (2007) defined six key characteristics that can be used to assess the quality of data used to construct performance indicator scores: accuracy; validity; reliability; timeliness; relevance; and completeness. Most of these directly echo those stipulated for performance indicators in Table 17.3. The additional consideration for performance data of completeness is an important reminder that validity and reliability are as much dependent on what is missing as on what is collected. However, it should be emphasised that in practice any set of indicators is unlikely to fulfil all of these properties. These data qualities are difficult to achieve and managers should, whilst striving to achieve them, accept and be open about the limitations of the data they use.

17.6.3.1 Private, commercial sector

For a private, commercial organisation, performance is largely specified in financial terms, although there are other important considerations. Business accounting ratios are designed principally for planning purposes (strategic appraisal) and control purposes (operational appraisal). The largely financial ratios are concerned not just with profit, but also with growth, liquidity, asset utilisation, defensive position and investment performance. A sample of such ratios is given in Table 17.4.

These ratios, and many more, are detailed for individual companies and industry sectors by commercial sources such as ICC British Company Financial Datasets, a part of Dialog's company and industry intelligence, which covers nearly half a million companies worldwide.

Ratios have to be interpreted very carefully. Many are more appropriate for comparing a single firm's performance over time than for comparing different firms, particularly if the firms are from different industries or sectors. Some ratios involve estimates which can be made in various ways, so comparing like with like can be problematic – for example valuing inventories and intangible assets. Some ratio values are annual averages, so getting the information from balance sheets is unreliable, merely averaging the beginning and end of the year situations, when more observations during the year are really required, e.g. liquidity ratios.

Private firms are also interested in other aspects of performance apart from financial ratios. Market share is an important objective that is normally measurable, even at the local or regional level. Market share is one of a number of possible indicators for the demand for the product. It is vital for any organisation to be informed about the nature of, and changes

Table 17.3 Criteria for a good performance indicator

Criteria	Explanation
Relevant	An indicator should be relevant to the organisation's strategic goals and objectives and cover all relevant performance dimensions.
Clear definition	A performance indicator should have a clear and intelligible definition in order to ensure consistent collection and fair comparison.
Easy to understand and use	A performance indicator should be described in terms that the user of the information will understand.
Comparable	Indicators should be comparable on a consistent basis between organisations and this relies on there being agreement about definitions. They should also be comparable on a consistent basis over time.
Verifiable	The indicator also needs to be collected and calculated in a way that enables the information and data to be verified. It should therefore be based on robust data collection systems, and it should be possible for managers to verify the accuracy of the information and the consistency of the methods used.
Cost effective	There is a need to balance the cost of collecting information with its usefulness. Where possible, an indicator should be based on information already available and linked to existing data collection activities.
Unambiguous	A change in an indicator should be capable of unambiguous interpretation so that it is clear whether an increase in an indicator value represents an improvement or deterioration in service.
Attributable	Service managers should be able to influence the performance measured by the indicator.
Responsive	A performance indicator should be responsive to change. An indicator where changes in performance are likely to be too small to register will be of limited use.
Avoids perverse incentives	A performance indicator should not be easily manipulated because this might encourage counterproductive activity.
Allows innovation	An indicator that focuses on outcome and user satisfaction is more likely to encourage such innovation to take place than one that is tied into existing processes.
Statistically valid	Indicators should be statistically valid and this will in large part depend on the sample size.
Timely	Data for the performance indicator should be available within a reasonable timescale.

Source: adapted from Audit Commission (2000b).

Table 17.4 Performance ratios for commercial organisations[1]

	Explanations
Growth	
$\dfrac{\text{(This year} - \text{last year)}}{\text{Last year}} \times 100$	Year on year percentage changes in key variables, e.g. income, expenditure, profit, assets, liabilities.
Profitability	
Either $\dfrac{\text{Gross or Net Profit}}{\text{Sales}}$	Gross profit ratio or net profit ratio. No rules of thumb. It varies widely between industries and firms.
$\dfrac{\text{Net Profit After Tax}}{\text{Total Assets}}$	'Return on Capital Employed'. No standard definitions, so care is needed in making comparisons between firms and industries.
Liquidity	
$\dfrac{\text{Current Assets}}{\text{Current Liabilities}}$	'Current Ratio'. Rule of thumb = at least 1:1 and preferably higher.
$\dfrac{\text{Current Assets} - \text{Inventories}}{\text{Current Liabilities}}$	'Acid Test', 'Quick' or 'Liquidity' Ratio. A more discriminating test of ability to pay debts.
$\dfrac{\text{Cash}}{\text{Current Liabilities}}$	'Cash ratio'. A more conservative measure which ignores less liquid assets such as stock.
$\dfrac{\text{Balance Sheet Trade Debtors} \times 365}{\text{Total Credit Sales}}$	Average collection period of trade debts, i.e. average number of days before accounts are paid.

Asset Utilisation

$$\frac{\text{Sales}}{\text{Fixed Assets}}$$

Indicates the effectiveness in using fixed plant to generate sales.

$$\frac{\text{Cost of Goods Sold}}{\text{Inventories}}$$

'Stock Turnover'. Varies a lot between industries.

$$\frac{\text{Sales}}{\text{Number of Employees}}$$

Indicates revenue productivity of labour.

Defensive position

$$\frac{\text{Net Worth}}{\text{Total Assets}}$$

Indicates shareholders' interest in the business. (Net Worth is ordinary shares + preference shares + reserves).

$$\frac{\text{Borrowing}}{\text{Net Worth}} \times 100$$

'Gearing ratio'. An indication of the riskiness of the capital structure.

$$\frac{\text{Total debt}}{\text{Total assets}} \times 100$$

'Debt ratio'. An indication of the powers of creditors over an organisation.

Investment

$$\frac{\text{Dividend per Share}}{\text{Market Price per Share}}$$

'Dividend Yield'. Indicates rate of return on investment in shares.

$$\frac{\text{Net profit} - \text{Preference Share Dividend}}{\text{Number of Ordinary Shares}}$$

Earnings per ordinary share.

$$\frac{\text{Market Price per Share}}{\text{Earnings per Share}}$$

'Price/Earnings Ratio'. Indicates the market's evaluation of a share.

Note:

1 Details of the use of these ratios can be found in any good accounting text.

Sources: Gratton and Taylor (1988); Wilson and Joyce (2010).

in, demand for the service they are providing. Market research is a typical means of generating this evidence.

Most large private leisure organisations have marketing departments with market research functions. As well as continually monitoring demand for their goods and services by this means, they regularly employ outside market research agencies or consultancies to conduct specialist market research. In addition, some consultancies produce regular reports with market research information alongside financial data for different industries. The 2009 reports from Mintel, for example, include UK reports on golf (March) and bingo (April); Ireland reports on food tourism (May) and the short breaks market (July); USA reports on recorded entertainment (February) and theme parks (April); and international reports on airlines (June 2009) and the future of the European package holiday (May). Key Note's 2009 market reports for the UK include ones on the film market (April), football clubs and finance (July), holiday purchasing patterns (June) and sports equipment (June).

17.6.3.2 Public sector

Public sector services have been subject to increasing pressure for accountability in recent decades. Accountability does not just mean spending the money as they should; it also refers to achieving value for money from public spending. This requires appropriate performance indicators. In the UK the process of reporting to standard performance indicators has been driven in recent years by Best Value legislation, and particularly by Comprehensive Performance Assessment (CPA) and more recently Comprehensive Area Analysis (CAA). These government requirements have obliged local authorities to publish performance information for a set of national performance indicators. Table 17.5 shows the indicators relevant to public sector cultural services. They were very restrictive under CPA but under CAA the list covers more activities, although now local authorities can choose which indicators to report. The final column in Table 17.5 shows that the adoption by local authorities of cultural indicators is variable, with two indicators quite commonly adopted (sport and active recreation participation, young people's participation in positive activities) but others being selected by fewer authorities and two being selected by very few (visits to museums and galleries, use of public libraries).

At the individual service level, much more comprehensive lists of performance indicators can be found. For example, Sport England's National Benchmarking Service for public sport and leisure centres (NBS) calculates 47 performance indicators across four dimensions of performance, shown in Table 17.6.

This NBS list is comprehensive but even so it doesn't cover all the aspects of public facilities' performance that managers and politicians would like it to. The NBS does not measure most of the wider social impacts of such facilities, such as improvements in health, improved quality of life, reduced crime and vandalism, or education benefits – these are considered too difficult to measure regularly in the specific context of these facilities. The NBS does not measure non-users' attitudes and barriers – this would require research in local communities, which is expensive. The NBS also does not record the views, behaviour, etc. of young people under 11 years old, who are not considered suitable for the questionnaire survey employed. These exclusions demonstrate the compromise that is often necessary in practical performance measurement systems between what indicators are desirable and what indicators can be measured reliably and at reasonable cost.

It is the responsibility of each organisation to choose a manageable array of indicators to reflect its objectives. For a public sector provider, this may include throughput indicators for particular groups of clients, such as women, the elderly, lower socio-economic groups

Table 17.5 Public sector national indicators relevant to cultural services in the UK

---

a) CPA 2007–8

Visits to/usage of museums and galleries (including research enquiries and website hits) per 1000 population

Visits to museums and galleries in person per 1000 population

Visits to museums & galleries by pupils in organised groups

Compliance with Public Library Service Standards

Source: Audit Commission, www.audit-commission.gov.uk/localgov/audit/bvpis/pages/guidance.aspx.

b) CAA 2009+

National Indicators	Number of local area agreements including each indicator	Rank in popularity, out of 152 indicators[1]
Adult participation in sport and active recreation	82	16
Young people's participation in positive activities	75	22
Participation in regular volunteering	42	43
Engagement in the arts	24	65=
Children and young people's participation in high quality PE and sport	24	65=
Use of public libraries	10	95=
Visits to museums and galleries	2	142=
Children and young people's satisfaction with parks and play areas	0 – definition still to be agreed	n/a

Note: 1 The ranks are according to how many local area agreements include each indicator. For example, adult participation in sport and recreation is in 82 agreements, which makes it the 16th most popular indicator in such agreements.

Source: IDeA, www.idea.gov.uk/idk/core/page.do?pageId=8399555.

> **Table 17.6** Performance indicators for Sport England's National Bench-marking Service

a) Access

Key
% visits 11–19 years ÷ % catchment population 11–19 years
% visits from NS-SEC classes 6 and 7 ÷ % catchment population in NS-SEC classes 6 and 7[1]
% visits 60+ years ÷ % catchment population 60+ years
% visits from black, Asian and other ethnic groups ÷ % catchment population in same groups
% visits disabled <60 years ÷ % catchment population disabled <60 years

Other
% visits 20–59 years ÷ % catchment population in same group
% of visits which were first visits
% visits with discount card
% visits with discount cards for 'disadvantage'[2]
% visits female
% visits disabled 60+ years ÷ % catchment population disabled 60+ years
% visits unemployed

Notes:

1 NS-SEC classes 6 and 7 are the two lowest socio-economic classes in the official classification used in the UK.

2 Disadvantage eligibility for discount cards includes over 50s, students, unemployed, disabled, single parents, government support, government-funded trainees, widows, exercise referrals and elite performers.

b) Utilisation

Key
annual visits per sq. m (of usable space, i.e. excluding offices and corridor space)

Other
annual visits per sq. m (of total indoor space, including offices and corridor space)
% of visits casual, instead of organised weekly number of people visiting the centre
as % of catchment population

c) Financial

Key
subsidy per visit

Other
% cost recovery
subsidy per resident
subsidy per sq. m
total operating cost per visit
total operating cost per sq. m
maintenance and repair costs per sq. m
energy costs per sq. m
total income per visit
total income per sq. m
direct income per visit
secondary income per visit

Table 17.6 *continued*

d) Service attributes for customer satisfaction and importance scoring

Accessibility	Activity available at convenient times
	Ease of booking
	The activity charge/fee
	The range of activities available
Quality of facilities/services	Quality of flooring in the sports hall
	Quality of lighting in the sports hall
	Quality of equipment
	Water quality in the swimming pool
	Water temperature of swimming pool
	Number of people in the pool
	Quality of car parking on site
	Quality of food and drink
Cleanliness	Cleanliness of changing areas
	Cleanliness of activity spaces
Staff	Helpfulness of reception staff
	Helpfulness of other staff
	Standard of coaching/instruction
Value for money	Value for money of activities
	Value for money of food/drink
Overall – satisfaction only	Overall satisfaction with visit

and the disabled, since this would monitor the effectiveness of the organisation in dealing with such target groups. It may also include very conventional indicators of financial performance, such as some of those relevant to the commercial provider given in Table 17.4, particularly for parts of the service which have no particular 'social service' function, such as the bar, cafe, vending machines and other merchandise sales.

How often should performance indicators evidence be produced? It is very common for performance indicators to be calculated on an annual average basis. However, there are good reasons for wanting operational performance indicators to be available on a far more regular basis. Decisions about promotion, programming and staffing arrangements may be modified at any time, so a regular flow of up-to-date information assists such decisions. Such a consideration reminds us that the primary purpose of performance measurement is to help management decisions. A secondary purpose, albeit important, is to report performance to the organisation's stakeholders.

17.6.4 Targets

Targets are precise statements of what is to be achieved, by when. They support the process of performance management because they are tangible manifestations of the aim of continuous improvement and they are important reference points against which improvement can be monitored. A target is typically quantitative, e.g. to increase the number of visits by ethnic minorities by 5 per cent.

How is a target decided? The most appropriate basis is evidence of previous performance by the organisation and evidence of the performance of similar organisations elsewhere. Such evidence enables the target setter to reach the difficult but necessary balance between ambition and realism. Targets need to be challenging but they also need to be achievable. If they are too easily reached, or if they are impossible to reach, they quickly fall into disrepute. Targets can and do change in the course of time. They need to remain under continuing scrutiny for their relevance to the operating circumstances of the organisation.

> ## Discussion question
>
> How easy is it to set targets for the following objectives: (1) improve customer satisfaction; (2) increase the diversity of visitors; (3) increase off-peak utilisation of a facility?

17.7 The Balanced Scorecard

The Balanced Scorecard was devised by Kaplan and Norton (1996). It is a system of performance measurement which is generic and used by a wide variety of organisations in all sectors and across the globe. A primary motivation for the Balanced Scorecard was to add strategic non-financial performance measures to the traditional financial measures to give a more 'balanced' view of organisational performance. The structure of the Balanced Scorecard is represented in Figure 17.3.

The figure demonstrates not just the development of performance measurement beyond the financial, but also a consistent process of specifying objectives, devising measures for these, setting targets and devising initiatives to achieve the targets. It is the last of these processes that turns the Balanced Scorecard into a performance management system, not just a performance measurement tool.

17.8 Benchmarking

So far we have been discussing the performance measurement that it is appropriate for an organisation to conduct, so that its managers can identify how the organisation is performing and whether or not changes are occurring as a result of their decisions. However, it is also likely that the organisation will want comparisons to be made with other similar organisations, to put their own performance into perspective. Benchmarking is a process which facilitates this and there are two main types:

1 Data benchmarking involves comparison with numerical standards (e.g. averages) calculated for performance indicators in a particular service. The benchmarks are typically organised into relevant 'families' of similar organisations.
2 Process benchmarking involves comparison of different procedures adopted in different organisations. Used in conjunction with performance data, process benchmarking helps a manager understand how to improve performance. It is often facilitated by 'benchmarking clubs' of similar organisations.

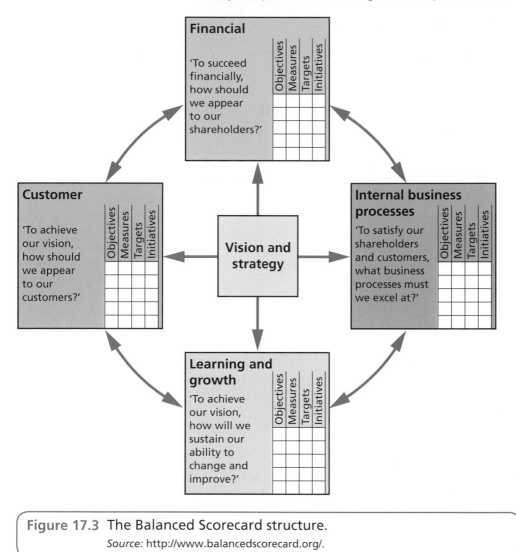

Figure 17.3 The Balanced Scorecard structure.
Source: http://www.balancedscorecard.org/.

External benchmarks for performance are important because they identify the performance of an organisation relative to other similar organisations. They also enable other agencies to assess the relative performance of all organisations participating in the benchmarking exercise. This is particularly important in the public sector, where central government is typically interested in monitoring the relative performance of individual local government services. In many countries this job is done by independent auditors.

Comparative performance information is available in both the private sector and the public sector. In the private sector, for example, ICC British Company Financial Datasheets provide detailed evidence for individual companies, including industry comparisons for a number of key business ratios. Similarly, Key Note provides Business Ratio Reports for each UK industry sector.

In the public sector in the UK, benchmarks are provided for sport and leisure in two annual publications by the Chartered Institute of Public Finance and Accountancy (CIPFA). These are *Culture, Sport and Recreation Statistics* and *Charges for Leisure Services*. The former in the main contains financial statistics, which are estimates for the year, rather than outturns. Three other explicit benchmarking services can be identified for sport and leisure – one in Australia and New Zealand (CERM), the other two in the UK (APSE Performance Networks and NBS).

17.8.1 CERM performance indicators

Operating in Australia and New Zealand, the CERM PIs Project is run by the Centre for Environmental and Recreational Management at the University of South Australia. It has clients from public sector, voluntary and commercial facilities. Originally designed for public aquatic centres and leisure centres, it now extends to a range of sport and leisure services, including golf courses, caravan and tourist parks, campgrounds, skate parks and outdoor centres.

CERM PIs provides benchmarks for 26 operational performance indicators, including services (e.g. programme opportunities per week), marketing (e.g. promotion cost as a proportion of total cost), organisation (e.g. cleaning and maintenance cost per visit) and finance (e.g. surplus/subsidy per visit). It also provides customer service quality benchmarks, covering gaps between customers' expectations and satisfaction in relation to a number of service attributes.

17.8.2 APSE Performance Networks

APSE Performance Networks covers 15 UK local authority service areas, including civic, cultural and community venues; culture, leisure and sport; sports and leisure facility management; and parks, and open spaces and horticultural services. APSE collects data and reports on the following dimensions of performance:

- customer satisfaction;
- cost of services;
- staff absence;
- human resources and people management processes;
- quality assurance and community consultation processes.

APSE compares an individual local authority's performance with other local authorities of a similar type, determined by similar overall scores for a series of drivers, which comprise facility type and size, location characteristics, competition, transport, car parking, pricing policy, programming and investment.

17.8.3 Sport England's National Benchmarking Service

The NBS measures performance standards for indoor sports and leisure centres. The performance indicators measured in this service are identified in Table 17.6. The NBS results for access, finance and utilisation performance are compared with benchmarks for four families which have been empirically tested and proven to have structural effects on performance:

1 **type of centre** – wet, dry (with/without outdoor facilities) and mixed (with/without outdoor facilities);
2 **the socio-economics of a centre's location** – high deprivation, medium deprivation, low deprivation – measured by the percentage of the catchment population in the bottom two socio-economic classes;
3 **size of the centre** – large, medium and small;
4 **management type at the centre** – in-house local authority, trust, commercial contractor.

Three benchmarks are employed. The 25 per cent, 50 per cent and 75 per cent benchmarks are the quarter, half and three-quarters points in the distribution of scores for a performance indicator, if all the centres' scores were organised from the lowest score at the bottom end of the distribution to the highest score at the top end.

> ### Discussion question
>
> If you managed a sport and leisure organisation which, according to benchmarking data, performed in the bottom quartile for an important performance indicator such as visits by young people, discuss the steps you would then take. (This should not include resigning!)

For the importance and satisfaction attributes (see Table 17.6), the NBS reports in three ways:

1 the satisfaction scores in comparison with industry averages for different facility types;
2 the gaps between importance and satisfaction mean scores from customers – the largest gaps being the strongest indication of problems;
3 the percentage of customers dissatisfied with each attribute.

17.8.4 Benefits of benchmarking

APSE (2009) suggests that '[t]he real benefit of benchmarking is the ability to learn from those authorities that have performed particularly well in order to improve service delivery'. APSE organises advisory groups, benchmarking meetings and seminars in order to promote this shared learning.

NBS clients have demonstrated a number of general learning responses to the processes of performance management, such as:

● generating the right information;
● interpreting the results meaningfully;
● utilising the results in performance planning, i.e. immediate action plans, and longer term contract specification and strategy development.

Case Study 17.3 discusses the benefits to facility managers in one English local authority which has been utilising the NBS for a number of years.

> ### CASE STUDY 17.3
>
> # The benefits of NBS to Milton Keynes leisure centre managers
>
> Milton Keynes has put five of its centres through the National Benchmarking Service (NBS) periodically since 2003. For Milton Keynes Council, a key benefit of the NBS is that it enables them to monitor the performance of the different centres in a consistent and comparable manner and compare them with national standards. It also provides performance data for inclusion in annual reports and cabinet/committee reports, and it helps to lever in funding for improvements and for further research.

Milton Keynes Council takes a collective approach to the discussion of performance and the NBS facilitates this. When the reports are completed, the council convenes a workshop for all the centres' managers, plus the key officers from the council, led by the national lead for the NBS technical service. As a result of these workshop discussions, the following benefits from NBS participation have been discussed:

1 Awareness of performance – facility managers are provided by NBS with an objective, externally validated set of performance measures. Local managers can explain and discuss this information with their knowledge of local circumstances. As one pointed out, though, it is only a 'snapshot' of performance in respect of customers, because the user survey is only over nine days.

2 Education of stakeholders – the NBS data help to educate politicians in particular about the realities of performance at the leisure centres. Indeed, one local politician has attended all the NBS workshops at Milton Keynes. Two of the centre managers feel that there are limits to the extent to which NBS information can be used for this purpose. They have not used it to inform customers, for example, because they feel the data need appropriate background knowledge for them to be properly understood.

3 Challenges to preconceived ideas held by managers and politicians – in fact the NBS data often confirm preconceived ideas but they occasionally throw up some unexpected surprises, both negative and positive, for managers. This has led to some detailed discussions at Milton Keynes, not just about revised expectations in the light of the NBS evidence, but also about the accuracy of the NBS evidence. For example, local knowledge can challenge the catchment area for a facility, which the NBS derives from a national model.

4 Expectations and targets – NBS data help managers and other stakeholders to form realistic expectations about what performance is possible, given not only the performance of their own centres but also comparisons with national benchmarks. At Milton Keynes the NBS data inform a process of pragmatic discussion between officers from Milton Keynes Council and the centres' managers, from which there are shared expectations for the year to come. The council then 'incentivises' the centres' improvement plans by making 10 per cent of their funding conditional on improvement in certain performance indicators' scores. One centre manager feels that the NBS data help Milton Keynes Council to identify different expectations for each centre, according to their strengths and their local circumstances.

5 Evidence-based management culture – experience of collecting data and receiving benchmarking reports helps to develop an awareness of further information needs. An example is qualitative research needed to identify exactly why customers have given a relatively weak satisfaction score to a particular service attribute. Although one centre manager feels that the current research is sufficient, others acknowledged that NBS performance data can lead to further research questions. However, there is then the matter of finding resources to address such questions.

6 Process benchmarking – benchmarking data facilitate the selection of partners with whom to discuss how to generate better performance for specific performance indicators. The Milton Keynes managers' NBS workshops are good examples of this process at a local level, with a refreshing openness to the discussions of both strengths and weaknesses in performance. One manager uses other NBS clients outside Milton Keynes to make comparisons and identify best practice.

7 Provide data for quality management systems – this benefit was endorsed strongly by most of the Milton Keynes managers. Their centres also participated in Quest and they emphasised how complementary the two systems are: NBS providing data, particularly from customers, to inform key requirements of Quest.

In addition, one Milton Keynes manager suggested that the NBS data give Milton Keynes Council the opportunity to examine how authority-wide systems are working – for example their leisure (discount) card system.

17.9 Conclusions

Quality and performance management are in effect restatements of what good management is all about. Many of the principles in the examples reviewed in this chapter are similar and they are all underpinned by the ethos expounded by Deming – plan, do, study, act. They service the aspiration for continuous improvement and this improvement is designed to better meet the needs of customers. They promote good systems for the collection and use of appropriate evidence.

It is idealistic to think that the culture of total quality management can be achieved, i.e. that every single person in an organisation is united by an excellence culture. Rather, it is an aspiration, a culture to be aimed for, and part of continuous improvement is to take the organisation closer to the TQM ideal.

Good performance evidence enables weaknesses to be identified, plans to be made, actions to be taken and outcomes to be improved – these are the essentials of performance management. However, acquiring appropriate evidence is not an easy matter. Some objectives, particularly in the public sector, are difficult to represent in performance indicators at reasonable cost. Generating accurate and consistent measurement data can also be a problem, e.g. financial data which can vary despite accounting regulations, and market research data which can all too easily fall prey to errors such as biased samples or misleading questions.

Another essential element of good performance management is to compare performance with other organisations. This is where benchmarking helps. However, rather than making comparisons within informal professional networks, a key advantage of the benchmarking systems reviewed in this chapter is that they offer objective, like-for-like comparisons. However, particularly for public leisure services, benchmarking systems do not cover everything – in particular they do not cover very well the ever-important impacts of public services on their local communities. This weakness exposes a limit to performance management which it is important to acknowledge – if measuring certain types of performance is too difficult, then managing them will be that much more difficult.

Practical tasks

1 Begin the process of taking a sport or leisure organisation that you are familiar with through the CSIT system (see pp. 458–9). To what extent does it help you to identify the strengths and weaknesses of the organisation? What other advantages do you perceive in adopting this framework?

2 Specify three objectives for a sport or leisure organisation that you are familiar with, e.g. a local club, a local facility. Design a set of performance indicators by which performance of these objectives can be measured. Identify what data would be needed to measure performance for your selected indicators. Evaluate the major problems the organisation would have in collecting such data.

Structured guide to further reading

For detailed discussion of quality issues:
Williams, C. and Buswell, J. (2003) *Service Quality in Leisure and Tourism*, CABI Publishing, Wallingford.

For rounded discussions of both quality and performance management in the public sector:
Robinson, L. (2004) *Managing Public Sport and Leisure Services*, Chapters 7 and 8, Routledge, London.

For the principles of performance measurement:
Audit Commission (2000a) *Aiming to Improve: The Principles of Performance Measurement*, Audit Commission, London.

For details of performance management systems:
Kaplan, R.S. and Norton, D.P. (1996) *The Balanced Scorecard*, Harvard Business Press, Boston, MA.
IDeA (2010) *Culture and Sport Improvement Toolkit*, IDeA, London.

Useful websites

For quality frameworks:
Chartered Quality Institute, www.thecqi.org/
Culture and Sport Improvement Toolkit, www.idea.gov.uk/idk/core/page.do?pageId=8722761
EFQM, http://ww1.efqm.org/en/Home/tabid/36/Default.aspx

For IDeA, the UK agency for improvement and development of local government services (work on culture, tourism and sport):
www.idea.gov.uk/idk/core/page.do?pageId=11216202

For quality awards:
UK Excellence Award, www.bqf.org.uk
British and International Standards, www.bsi-global.com
Customer Service Excellence, www.cse.cabinetoffice.gov.uk/homeCSE.do, and
www.cse.cabinetoffice.gov.uk/UserFiles/Customer_Service_Excellence_standard.pdf
Green Flag Award, www.greenflagaward.org.uk/
Investors in People, www.investorsinpeople.co.uk
Quest, www.questnbs.info/
White Flag Award, http://81.17.252.145/~whiteflag/

For performance measurement systems:
APSE Performance Networks, www.apse.org.uk/performance-network.html
Balanced Scorecard, www.balancedscorecard.org/
CERM Performance Indicators, http://unisa.edu.au/cermpi/
National Benchmarking Service, www.questnbs.info/

For performance measures:

CIPFA statistics, www.cipfastats.net/

ICC British Company Financial Datasheets, http://library.dialog.com/bluesheets/html/bl0562.html

Keynote, www.keynote.co.uk

Mintel, http://reports.mintel.com/

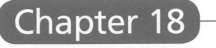

Financial management in sport and leisure

Rob Wilson

In this chapter

- What is the purpose of financial management in a sport and leisure context?
- What is the key terminology in finance?
- What are the key regulations for financial accounts?
- How is financial position reported and financial performance measured?
- How is financial planning and control exercised?
- What does financial management and evaluation mean for sport and leisure organisations?

Caspar Benson/Getty Images

Summary

Today's sport and leisure management students and employees are required to understand the financial side of the industry in order to offer the most cost-effective solutions to complex problems and an increasingly volatile market. Consequently, this chapter introduces the key financial regulations and procedures that need to be applied to begin to plan, make effective decisions and control a sport and leisure organisation. It acknowledges that sport and leisure organisations are often not financially driven or even based in the private sector, but stresses the importance of financial management and responsibility and the mandatory requirements placed upon all organisations. Finally, within the chapter, a framework is provided to fully appraise the financial health of an organisation in order to move an organisation forward financially.

18.1 Introduction

It is important before we start that we establish some ground rules; put simply, finance is *not* just about numbers and you *do not* have to be a skilled mathematician to understand a set of financial statements. Instead you need to understand the guiding rules and principles that help compile and structure a set of accounts. As students or managers who work within the sport and leisure industry it is important that you appreciate the importance of financial management and responsibility and that you can communicate key financial information to both internal and external stakeholders. Sport and leisure is now big business. Indeed the Sport Industry Research Centre (SIRC) (2008) indicates that the sport and leisure sector is worth around £20 billion, which roughly equates to 2.5 per cent of consumer expenditure. By 2011 this is expected to rise to an estimated £24 billion (SIRC, 2008). This proves that sport and leisure is far more serious and less frivolous than people believe.

The commodification and professionalisation of sport and leisure has led to vast sums of money being invested at all levels, for example Tom Walkinshaws' investment in Gloucester Rugby Football Club in 1997, shortly after the sport turned professional; and Malcolm Glazer's £700 million purchase of Manchester United in 2005. Stewart (2007) also identifies that sport and leisure has established itself as a mechanism for creating personal meaning, cultural identity (the purchase of a replica football shirt, for example) and a lucrative career path for many people all over the world. Deloitte's *Annual Review of Football Finance* (Deloitte and Touche, 2008) identifies that ten clubs earned in excess of €200 million a year. In the US, many professional sportsmen earn more than $1 million and in the UK the Leisure Company Blacks Leisure recorded a £14.5 million net profit for the year ended 2006.

Unfortunately sport and leisure has lagged behind other business sectors from a financial management point of view. For the most part sport marketing, planning and strategy have dominated sport business management education and led to a growing maturity in such areas. Financial management has often been overlooked, anecdotally because individuals claim to have some sort of fear with numbers. There are still many sport managers and graduates with sport management degrees who struggle to even understand the basics of an income statement or balance sheet, let alone have the confidence to make informed judgements on the financial health of an organisation. However, as Wilson and Joyce (2008) point out, every organisation, ranging from multi-million-pound operations through to small, local, voluntary sport clubs, needs to produce a set of financial statements every year. Therefore, if organisations have to do it, the chances are that should managers wish to be successful in employment, they will have to understand, communicate and use financial information too.

18.2 Key terminology

Essentially there are two types of accounts: financial and management. Depending on the nature of a user's information needs, the style of the accounts may be quite different. From the section above, you should have noticed that financial information can look two ways. When looking backwards, i.e. into the past, it is normal to examine financial accounts, as they are prepared for external use and are based on historical information; they are also required by law. A set of financial accounts will, for example, illustrate the past financial position and financial performance of an organisation.

> ### Key term
>
> **Financial accounting** – the term used to describe the system for recording historical financial transactions and presenting this information in summary form.

However, should managers wish to be more proactive and examine future trends and issues they will need to examine more forward-looking (future) accounting information. Such information will not be found in financial accounts, hence there are management accounts, i.e. accounts that look forward and are based on providing information for managers to help with the planning, decision-making and control of organisations. Unlike financial accounts, management accounts are not a statutory requirement. It is important that managers understand the distinction between the two types of accounts, as they dictate where they should look for information. These two types also structure the remainder of this chapter. First we examine financial accounting information, before moving on to management accounts towards the end of the chapter (see pp. 500–8).

> ### Key term
>
> **Management accounting** – the term used to describe more forward-looking financial data for planning, decision-making and control purposes.

In reality, managers should appreciate that financial and management accounts work together hand in hand. Even though the law stipulates that financial accounts should be constructed within the parameters set out by the International Accounting Standards (IAS), no manager in their right mind would record financial transactions and hope for the best. Instead they will plan their operations, consider the implications of their decisions and control their organisation in such a way that they reach (in most cases) their organisation's objectives. In order to plan and make effective decisions, a manager will have to adopt the principles of good management accounting, for example budgeting, break-even analysis and costing – some of which will be explored toward the end of this chapter (see pp. 501–8). Consequently, a rounded understanding of how the two types of accounting practice are applied is essential for a successful manager.

Before we continue, it is worth outlining more key terminology that you may encounter when moving through the financial accounting sections.

Key terms

Income statement or profit and loss account – a summary of financial performance and therefore actual income and expenditure over a period of time.

Balance sheet – a snapshot of a company's financial position at a specific point in time.

Cash flow – a forecast of funds coming in and out presented over a period of time.

Assets – those things of value that a company owns, e.g. buildings, equipment, vehicles.

Debtor – an individual or organisation who owes the company money or service, e.g. someone that you have lent money to.

Liabilities – think of liabilities as the opposite of assets, e.g. for a credit card company.

Creditor – an individual or organisation who you owe money or service.

Depreciation – the loss in value of assets over time, e.g. a computer will be worth less after it has been used.

18.3 The importance of financial management

The concept behind financial management is not the simplistic idea that you need to manage profit, but more importantly how to monitor, evaluate and control the income and expenditure of an organisation. It is vital for sport and leisure managers to understand the changing values of the three sector provision model (as covered in Part 2) and recognise that a large number of sport services are provided to achieve social objectives, which operate at a loss, and which it will normally require a government subsidy to operate. This does not mean, however, that proper financial controls are not important. It is vital that sport and leisure managers have an understanding of the costs of the products and services that they offer, in order to operate as effective business entities to generate profits, or ensure that taxpayers' money is not being wasted on frivolous plans or ideas.

Many organisations will borrow to fund their expansion plans; in fact borrowing is part and parcel of everyday life if organisations wish to remain competitive. However, borrowing is normally based on the simple assumption that the organisation's future returns will be sufficient to cover the borrowing and any associated business. Problems, however, often occur when organisations fail to meet their financial obligations. Consequently, an organisation's

Finance, football and Southampton Leisure Holdings

In 2003 Southampton Football Club narrowly lost to Arsenal in the FA Cup Final. By May 2005, after 27 years in the top flight of English football, Southampton FC was relegated to the football Championship. Following this relegation Southampton had a series of new managers, new playing staff and also new chairmen. By the time Rupert Lowe resigned in 2006 there was £3.4 million cash on deposit at Barclays Bank. In addition there were payments outstanding for players such as Theo Walcott. However, by the time Lowe returned in 2008 the cash deposit had been replaced by an overdraft of £6.3 million, and an overall operating loss of £4.9 million, this despite receiving £12.7 million profit on the sale of playing staff! Furthermore, and more importantly when we consider financial management, the club was running a player/coach wage bill of 81 per cent of turnover. Ostensibly, this meant that for every £1 of revenue that the club generated, 81 pence was being spent on players and coaches alone; leaving 19 pence to pay for everything else, including the upkeep of a 32,000 seater stadium.

What is central to effective financial management is the ability of the organisation to pay its debts as they fall due. Southampton was clearly not in a position to do so. Some further analysis of the organisation's income statement and balance sheet reveals more issues. Broadcasting revenue (often the Achilles heel of a football club) fell from £8.1 million to £3 million, match day revenue from £10.5 million to £7.9 million, commercial revenue from £4.6 million to £3.3 million, while operating expenses saw increases in the cost of players and coaches from £10.5 million to £12.2 million).

Football clubs often gamble finance with on-pitch performance, much in the same way as Leeds United did before they ran into financial difficulty due to the failure to qualify for the UEFA Champions League (see Wilson and Joyce, 2008). For Southampton, promotion back to the Premier League was not realistic in the 2007/8 season – their revenues fell while their costs rose. Disaster was on the horizon financially and strategically.

Although the loss for the year 2007/8 amounted to £5 million, the value of the company also fell (from £7.3 million to £2.3 million). This compounded an already precarious financial position (a net debt of £19.2 million for the football club) to an overall group net debt of £27.5 million. Most small organisations will go under when they reach a net debt of about £1 million!

On 25 April 2009, Southampton was officially relegated to League One. Going into administration ensured that Southampton started the next season, but in League One with a ten-point deduction. This is within six years of being FA Cup runners-up, UEFA Cup competitors and finishing eighth in the English Premier League. By the end of May 2009, the club was unable to meet its financial commitments to its staff, i.e. it could not afford to pay people's wages and had to ask employees to work unpaid. The club administrator warned that the club faced imminent bankruptcy unless a buyer was found, and while club legend Matt LeTissier fronted a consortium, they were unable to reach agreement to purchase the club. However, by 8 July 2009 a new buyer had been found in the form of Swiss businessman Mark Liebherr. Since then the club's fortunes have improved and by October 2009 Southampton had managed to erase the ten-point deduction and accrue 11 additional points, thanks in part to new signing Richard Lambert. While its future appears stable financially, at the time of writing it remains to be seen if the club can climb out of the relegation zone and reach safety.

(Figures extracted from Southampton Leisure Holdings PLC, Annual Report and Accounts 2008.)

There are two principal issues here to do with financial management. The first is that a manager needs to make an assessment of the market that he or she is operating within, as this will offer some direction as to how do deal with cost. In Southampton's case spending 81 per cent of turnover on players' and coaches' wages was not a financially acceptable thing to do. The second issue is to do with debt. Clearly Southampton has operated with a fairly high level of debt, compared to the value of the company. However, it was not the concept of debt, nor the concept of borrowing, that led to the company's downfall. The issue was that it could not service the debt and that wealthy owners do not lie around every corner.

ability to pay its debts as they fall due is usually the difference between financial success and eventual bankruptcy. If managers are to make effective plans and decisions, they need to control their organisation's finances. Borrowing is not necessarily a bad thing, nor for that matter is debt – the main issue is being able to service the debt. This is a problem that Southampton Leisure Holdings (the parent company of Southampton Football Club) found out the hard way (see Case Study 18.1).

Discussion questions

What were the most significant issues that caused the financial decline of Southampton FC? What other football clubs have faced similar issues?

18.4 The users of financial information

Financial information will be useful to a wide variety of stakeholders. These will often span several sectors and each will have slightly different needs for the information. For example, Malcolm Glazer (the owner of Manchester United FC) will want to know how much profit his company has made, to ensure that he can make the necessary interest payments on the loans that he took out to finance his takeover in 2005. Sheffield City Council will want to know how much subsidy they have to provide in order to keep all of their leisure services running across the city, so that their council taxpayers get value for money. The chairperson of the Cheltenham Swimming and Water Polo Club will want to ensure that enough money is being received through subscriptions and funding to cover their running costs.

Generally, information relating to the finance of an organisation is of interest to its owners, managers, trade contacts (for example suppliers), providers of finance (for example banks), employees and customers. All of these groups of people need to be sure that the organisation is strong, can pay its bills, make a profit if it is commercial, and remain in business. An indicative list of users and their areas of interest is illustrated in Table 18.1.

> ## Discussion question
>
> Who are the most important audiences for financial information (1) in a private commercial sport and leisure organisation; (2) in a local authority sport and leisure service; and (3) in a voluntary sport and leisure club?

Table 18.1 Users of financial information and their information needs

User groups	Areas of interest
Owners of a company	Owners will want to know how well the management of the organisation is doing on a day-to-day basis and how much profit they can take from the organisation for their own use.
Managers	Managers require financial information so that they can make future plans for the organisation and see how effective their decisions have been.
Trade contacts (i.e. suppliers)	Suppliers and other trade contacts need to know if they are going to be paid on time by the organisation.
Providers of finance (i.e. banks, etc)	Banks and other lenders of finance need to ensure that any loans and interest payments are going to be made on time, before they lend money and during the repayment period.
Her Majesty's Revenue and Customs (UK), Internal Revenue Service (USA) or the Australian Taxation Office, etc.	The tax authorities needs information about the profits of the organisation so that they can work out how much tax the organisation owes. They also need details for VAT and employees' income tax.
Employees	Organisations' employees often wish to know whether their jobs are safe and that they are going to be paid on time.
Customers	It is normal for customers to know whether goods/services purchased are going to be delivered/provided. They may also be interested in investing in the company and therefore will want to know whether it is a good prospect.

18.5 Statutory requirements for sport and leisure

Effective management of an organisation, whether it is in the sport and leisure industry or not, requires more than just an understanding of financial management, as it requires individuals to put financial tools to use. As Knott (2004) confirms, the understanding and application of the financial recording and reporting system enables quick and easy understanding of an organisation's financial health. This is essential for any manager, regardless of the size, style or type of the organisation, as they have to produce a set of financial statements which include a balance sheet and income statement (previously termed a profit and loss account). In a nutshell, the balance sheet is simply a list of all of the assets owned by an organisation and all of the liabilities owed by an organisation at a specific point in time. It will often be referred to as a 'snapshot' of the financial position of an organisation at a specific point in time (usually the end of the financial year). The income statement, on the other hand, illustrates financial performance by outlining the profits (or losses) recognised during a period in time. The profit is calculated by deducting expenditure from income.

Any limited company will produce an income statement for the period of one year; however, it is not uncommon for managers to construct interim income statements that are linked to budgets on a quarterly or even monthly basis – further illustrating the link between financial and management accounting, which will be explored in detail later (see pp. 500–8). Organisations that are 'not-for-profit', such as charities and many clubs or societies, will produce a similar statement called an income and expenditure account, which details any surplus as opposed to profit. Examples of these statements are presented in this chapter.

While financial statements might never satisfy all of the needs of the user groups, it is worth confirming that financial statements are a statutory requirement and that every organisation, be it in the public, private or voluntary sector, has to produce them. Companies listed on any international stock exchange, e.g. FTSE (UK), NASDAQ (USA) or the ASX (Australia), must go one step further and are obligated to publish their statements and send copies to shareholders.

18.6 The financial statements

The objective of financial accounts is to provide useful information for users regardless of who those users are. Consequently the information contained within the set of accounts is concerned with the resources employed and how they are used. This means that the accounts help to communicate how financially successful an organisation has been against its corporate objectives. However, it is often taken for granted that a professional accountant or accounts department will produce the following three principal reports:

1. **the statement of financial performance, or income statement,** which reports on the revenues earned and the expenses incurred;
2. **the statement of financial position, or balance sheet,** which illustrates the current levels of assets, liabilities and capital;
3. **the cash flow statement,** which provides details of more day-to-day activities such as the purchase and sale of assets and the securing and borrowing of funds.

Each of these three statements needs to be clearly understood by sport and leisure managers to ensure that they have the opportunity to effectively manage an organisation. Consequently, it is worth having a detailed look at the main statements so that you can see the

Arena Leisure Plc: an introduction

Arena Leisure Plc is a leisure group that manages seven racecourses in the UK, including Doncaster, Wolverhampton and Worcester. Overall the group hosts 25 per cent of all racing fixtures each year, making it the UK's largest operator of horse racing. Their race portfolio includes classic races such as the St Leger alongside more contemporary events such as the Monday Night Racing season at Royal Windsor.

Each of the seven racecourses within the organisation provides conferencing and banqueting facilities to ensure that they can provide services to consumers 365 days of the year. Two of the racecourses include an 18-hole golf course, one a leisure club and a third a branded hotel. Their future plans include the development of two further hotels, a casino, new spectator viewing areas and extensive conference and exhibition facilities.

Source: adapted from Arena Leisure Plc (2008)

general layout of the accounts and understand the key figures and their implications for the future prospects of the organisation. In order to make this information more consistent and accessible we shall use Arena Leisure Plc's annual accounts (see Case Study 18.2).

18.6.1 The income statement: a measurement of financial performance

One of the first things to note about the income statement is that it is referred to by a variety of terms. Although its new name is the income statement, it was previously known as the profit and loss account or, in the not-for-profit sector, the income and expenditure account.

The income statement indicates the historical financial performance, or in other words profitability, of an organisation over a period of time. Having already established that most organisations exist to make a profit, or at worst break even, the income statement provides us with some of the most important financial information. Put simply, the measurement of profit first requires the organisation to calculate the revenue generated. Subsequently, the organisation's expenses are added together before this expenditure is deducted from the revenue to establish whether a profit or a loss has been made (Wilson and Joyce, 2008).

Revenue, or income, or turnover as it is alternatively known, will typically be divided into both operating and non-operating items, i.e. what revenue has the organisation generated from all of the day-to-day activities (operating revenues) and what revenue has been generated by exceptional items, funds or grants, etc. (non-operating revenues). In general, as Stewart (2007) confirms, revenues in the sport and leisure sector have expanded dramatically over the last few years, but for the average not-for-profit sports club the reliance for revenue lies squarely on membership fees, gate receipts, fundraising activities, sponsors and hospitality.

While revenues are relatively simple to break down, expenses should be treated more prudently. Unfortunately, the IAS allows two methods for the presentation of expenses: by function or by nature. Essentially this means that organisations can choose the method which most appropriately represents the elements of the organisation's performance. However, in order to ensure that one organisation can be confidently compared to another, the standard explicitly states that information on the nature of the expense, including depreciation and staff costs, should be disclosed. To illustrate these points it is worth examining the income statement for Arena Leisure plc in Figure 18.1.

Figure 18.1 illustrates the usual 'by function' format as outlined by the IAS. The key components of revenue (i.e. income from trading), gross profit (i.e. profit before any expenses have been calculated), the profit from operations and the profit for the year are emboldened for ease of reading. The statement itself details that the profit before interest and tax was a little under £5.8 million (first column, halfway down) and that the overall profit for the year was about £3.8 million (first column, towards the bottom). Further information will be available in the notes to the accounts should we wish to see what items were recorded in a key component such as revenue. The notes for Arena Leisure plc can be seen in Figure 18.2.

Consolidated Income Statement

for the year ended 31 December 2008

	Note	Trading £'000	Separately disclosed items £'000	2008 Total £'000	Trading £'000	Separately disclosed items £'000	2007 Total £'000
Revenue	5	64,825	–	64,825	57,920	–	57,920
Cost of sales		(47,270)	–	(47,270)	(42,024)	–	(42,024)
Gross profit		17,555	–	17,555	15,896	–	15,896
Other operating income	7	760	1,667	2,427	1,352	–	1,352
Administrative costs excluding impairment losses		(12,848)	–	(12,848)	(11,351)	–	(11,351)
Impairment losses	16	–	–	–	–	(1,050)	(1,050)
Profit from operations	6	5,467	1,667	7,134	5,897	(1,050)	4,847
Non-operating income and expense	8	–	–	–	–	1,370	1,370
Share of post-tax results of joint venture	19	310	–	310	(215)	–	(215)
Profit before interest and taxation		5,777	1,667	7,444	5,682	320	6,002
Finance expense	12	(3,064)	(1,455)	(4,519)	(2,053)	–	(2,053)
Finance income	12	1,091	–	1,091	1,895	–	1,895
Net finance expense	12	(1,973)	(1,455)	(3,428)	(158)	–	(158)
Profit before taxation		3,804	212	4,016	5,524	320	5,844
Income tax expense	13	–	–	–	–	–	–
Profit for the year		3,804	212	4,016	5,524	320	5,844
Attributable to:							
– Equity shareholders of the parent company	14	3,871	212	4,083	5,615	320	5,935
– Minority interest		(67)	–	(67)	(91)	–	(91)
Profit for the year		3,804	212	4,016	5,524	320	5,844
				Pence			Pence
Earnings per share:	14						
Basic earnings per share				1.12			1.63
Diluted earnings per share				1.12			1.63

Figure 18.1 Arena Leisure Plc income statement.
Source: Arena Leisure Plc (2008).

5 Revenue

	2008 £'000	2007 £'000
Sale of services	64,825	57,920

The Group only has one segment: racecourse operations. Within this segment, turnover is analysed as follows:

	2008 £'000	2007* £'000
HBLB	18,993	18,918
BAGS (media rights income in relation to licensed betting offices)	10,399	9,883
Other racecourse-related revenue	35,433	29,119
	64,825	57,920

*The allocation in respect of 2007 has been changed for consistent presentation.

> **Figure 18.2** Arena Leisure Plc notes to the accounts.
> *Source:* Arena Leisure Plc (2008).

18.6.1.1 Interpreting the income statement

When users examine a set of financial reports, they will often only examine some of the 'key information'. In Figure 18.1 the key figure is 'Profit for the year' so it would stand to reason that a user would only really examine that figure and leave with the message that the company is performing well as it made a £3.8 million profit. Although this presents a useful yardstick to establish financial performance, effective managers should recognise it is only one measure of performance. While a thorough financial health appraisal is beyond the scope of this chapter, it is worth considering the other useful parts of the income statement before moving on to examine the balance sheet.

In order to fully appreciate financial performance it is necessary to establish how the 'profit for the year' was derived. In other words, what has the organisation done to make its profit and how does that compare to last year? The revenue figure for 2008 (£64.8 million) can be compared to the figure for 2007 (£57.9 million). This indicates that the company has been able to generate additional revenue of £6.9 million, an increase of about 11 per cent. Additionally, 'Gross profit' has risen by around £1.6 million (from £15.9 million in 2007 to £17.5 million in 2008).

However, although the expenses have seen a moderate increase, which you may expect from the increase in revenue, the overall profit for the year has fallen by around £2 million from 2007 to 2008. Principally this is due to 'Other income' being received in 2007. This straightforward analysis demonstrates how managers can become more rounded in their understanding and appreciation of finance. It also provides much more detailed information on which to base future decisions.

Discussion questions

The income statement measures an organisation's financial performance. What are the main limitations of this function? What do you think the main benefits are?

18.6.2 The balance sheet: a measurement of financial position

Unlike the income statement, the balance sheet cannot be used to determine a full view of financial performance, although you can see how much profit or loss an organisation has made in most cases. Instead the balance sheet provides details of an organisation's financial position by highlighting the value of assets owned by the organisation, the value of its liabilities (i.e. money owed to others) and the value of the organisation by virtue of its capital. To underpin the idea of financial position it is always worth remembering that Assets – Liabilities = Capital.

By definition, the balance sheet should balance, hence the equation outlined above. Consequently it is only ever accurate on the day on which it is produced, as the value of assets and liabilities will constantly change. This is why the balance sheet is often referred to as being a snapshot or static picture of an organisation. Although this picture will always be accurate on the day on which it was taken, it will quickly become dated and this presents a weakness in its worth to managers.

Normally the balance sheet will split its assets and liabilities up into Fixed and Current Assets and Current and Non-Current Liabilities. Before we examine a balance sheet, you need to familiarise yourself with the meaning of these key terms.

Key terms

Assets – items or resources that have a value to the organisation and things that are used by the organisation and for the organisation. Normally assets are classified as fixed or current. The basic difference is that a fixed asset is something that the organisation intends to keep and use for some time, whereas a current asset is held for the organisation to convert into cash during trading. Some good examples here are the organisation's premises and motor vehicles, which are fixed assets, and stock and cash, which are current assets.

Liabilities – amounts owed by the organisation to people other than the owner. Normally liabilities are classified as either payable within one year (current liabilities) or payable after one year (non-current liabilities). Some good examples here are bank overdrafts and supplier accounts, which are current liabilities, and bank loans, which tend to be non-current liabilities.

It is usual for a balance sheet to include a number of notes to the accounts, much like those on the income statement. The key issues that need to be considered are the values of the organisation's total assets, total liabilities and total capital. To illustrate these points Figure 18.3 presents the balance sheet for Arena Leisure Plc.

18.6.2.1 Interpreting the balance sheet

While the balance sheet has its limitations due to it being a snapshot of an organisation's financial position, it does provide some useful information that coupled with information from the income statement can be very powerful. The balance sheet for Arena Leisure, for example, indicates that the organisation is worth £72.6 million. Additionally, we can establish how in control of itself the organisation is or whether creditors really control things. Figure 18.3 shows that Arena is using a bank overdraft (the first item in Current liabilities) to ease any cash concerns and has total liabilities of £62 million.

It is also possible to examine the types of assets owned by the organisation. This is important should any creditors ask for their money back, as too many fixed assets (which are normally difficult to turn into cash) would mean that the organisation will struggle to pay things immediately. In the case of Arena, fixed (or non-current) assets equate to £128.5 million (about

Consolidated Balance Sheet

at 31 December 2008

	Note	2008 £'000	2007 £'000
Non-current assets			
Property, plant and equipment	16	119,734	108,283
Intangible assets	17	5,596	5,596
Investment in joint venture – Share of gross assets		2,699	2,624
– Share of gross liabilities		(6,073)	(6,437)
	19	(3,374)	(3,813)
Goodwill in respect of joint venture	19	1,580	1,580
Loans to joint venture	19	4,965	4,979
		3,171	2,746
Investment in associate	19	–	–
Total non-current assets		128,501	116,625
Current assets			
Inventories	20	544	415
Trade and other receivables	21	5,415	6,191
Assets classified as held for sale	22	100	–
Cash and cash equivalents	24	179	3,735
Total current assets		6,238	10,341
Total assets		134,739	126,966
Current liabilities			
Bank overdraft	24	(1,003)	–
Trade and other payables	23	(7,850)	(6,475)
Loans and borrowings	26	(2,940)	(2,796)
Accruals and deferred income	25	(6,691)	(6,585)
Total current liabilities		(18,484)	(15,856)
Non-current liabilities			
Loans and borrowings	26	(40,448)	(37,145)
Accruals and deferred income	25	(3,163)	(3,554)
Total non-current liabilities		(43,611)	(40,699)
Total liabilities		(62,095)	(56,555)
Total net assets		72,644	70,411
Equity			
Share capital	29	18,210	18,210
Share premium	30	223	223
Merger reserve	30	5,417	5,417
Retained earnings	30	46,985	44,685
Equity attributable to shareholders of the parent company		70,835	68,535
Minority interest	30	1,809	1,876
Total equity		72,644	70,411

Figure 18.3 Arena Leisure Plc balance sheet.

Source: Arena Leisure Plc (2008).

one-quarter of the way down Figure 18.3), whereas current assets make up £6 million in comparison (one-third of the way down). Although there is no golden rule for the split between fixed and current assets you could argue that Arena needs more liquid (easy to turn into cash) assets.

A final point to note about financial position is whether or not an organisation can cover its liabilities with its assets. Typically, professional sport and leisure organisations will run things very tight so that they can just about cover any liabilities that are outstanding – this is how clubs such as Manchester United FC can continue to operate. Even though the Glazer family borrowed heavily, the club's assets are sufficient to cover the debt should they need to redeem it in the future. In the case of Arena, there is £134 million worth of total assets compared to £62 million worth of total liabilities, so the future appears positive.

18.6.3 The cash flow statement

One of the simplest ways to monitor financial performance is to ensure that an organisation remains solvent. If for any reason the demands of creditors could not be met, the assets of an organisation would be sold with the aim of meeting those outstanding debts. Monitoring the cash position of a company is traditionally done through budgets (which will be examined on pp. 501–8) and cash flow statements. Without cash an organisation cannot continue to trade, regardless of its profit. Although the income statement helps us to establish an organisation's financial performance, it does not give us any idea about any problems that it may have with the flow of cash. This can be important for creditors to an organisation, as they will want to see that the organisation has sufficient cash to pay its bills on time. It is also important to managers, so that they know what cash they have available to purchase materials or to provide their services.

Cash flow statements, therefore, aim to illustrate all movements of cash under three main headings: operating activities, investing activities and financing activities. The purpose of this is to obtain a picture of the flow of cash in and out of an organisation. The cash flow statement for Arena Leisure Plc is illustrated in Figure 18.4. Such transactions listed in the cash flow statement are there to represent the following: day-to-day spending (operating activities), including things like wages and salaries (cash out) or membership income (cash in); the purchase (cash out) and sale (cash in) of assets (investing activity); and the procurement of capital and borrowing of funds (financing activities), including activities such as loans (cash in) and repayment of loans (cash out).

At first glance one could argue that the cash flow statement could be used to determine the profit or loss of an organisation rather than net cash flow. However, it must be noted here that there will be many items of expenditure that are not cash transactions and therefore only appear in the income statement. The cash flow for Arena Leisure in 2007 was very positive considering that it provided a net cash flow of over £3.7 million (bottom row in Figure 18.4, 2007 figure). However, that cash has been used up, predominantly through the repayment of financing activities in 2008 (see four rows from the bottom), so that the organisation needs to find £824,000 cash to complete its trading activities (bottom row, 2008 figure). Essentially the cash flow statement presents very clear details of what cash has been used for and the ease with which cash payments are supported by cash reserves. The Arena example proves that cash reserves (mainly net cash from financing activities) were essential in 2007.

Consolidated Cash Flow Statement
for the year ended 31 December 2008

	Note	2008 £'000	2007 £'000
Cash flows from operating activities			
Profit for the year		4,016	5,844
Adjustment for:			
Depreciation	16	3,370	2,616
Insurance surplus in respect of Southwell Racecourse flood damaged assets	8	–	(1,370)
Dilution gain	19	(129)	–
Impairment provision	16	–	1,050
Share-based payment expense	33	220	153
Net finance expense	12	3,428	158
Share of (profit)/loss of joint venture	19	(310)	215
Profit on sale of property, plant and equipment		(1,615)	(4)
Grant amortisation		(71)	(53)
Cash flows from operating activities before changes in working capital and provisions		8,909	8,609
Decrease in trade and other receivables		776	263
Increase in inventories		(129)	(398)
Decrease in trade and other payables		(1,003)	(125)
Net cash from operating activities		8,553	8,349
Cash flows from investing activities			
Purchases of property, plant and equipment		(13,905)	(27,250)
Proceeds from sale of property, plant and equipment		1,760	66
Insurance proceeds in respect of flood damaged assets	8	–	4,586
Sale of investment in associate	19	–	100
Decrease/(increase) in loans to joint venture	19	14	(1,003)
Interest received	12	1,091	962
Net cash used in investing activities		(11,040)	(22,539)
Cash flows from financing activities			
Minority interest equity contribution	30	–	2,000
Proceeds from bank and other borrowings		6,243	21,687
Capital grants received		–	882
Repayment of loans		(3,243)	(143)
Repayment of finance lease liabilities		14	(2)
Interest paid	12	(3,083)	(1,771)
Dividends paid	15	(2,003)	(1,858)
Net cash from financing activities		(2,072)	20,795
(Decrease)/increase in cash and cash equivalents	24	(4,559)	6,605
Net cash and cash equivalents at beginning of year	24	3,735	(2,870)
Net cash and cash equivalents at end of year	24	(824)	3,735

Figure 18.4 Arena Leisure Plc cash flow statement.
Source: Arena Leisure Plc (2008).

18.7 The value of management accounts

At the very beginning of this chapter you were introduced to the two main types of account-ing information: historical (financial) accounts, which include the three financial statements; and management accounts, which provide more forward-looking information. It is, however, important that the two types are recognised as two sides of the same coin and effective managers will be able to use both types in harmony, so as to be effective in their decision-making.

Management accounting will involve managers being much more proactive, as the information that is generated can be used for planning, decision-making and control purposes. The information will also be generated and presented in a way that suits the needs of the organisation that it is prepared for, rather than as financial accounts, where the use of information has to satisfy the needs of numerous users. Finally, it is important to understand that management accounting information is principally concerned with the efficient and effective use of resources. So it is vital that in order to make meaningful decisions, based on effective plans, as a manager you will need to use management accounting information.

While the breadth of management accounting information is beyond the scope of this chapter, we will consider one of its principal functions – budgeting – which will provide managers with the information required to plan, make effective decisions and control the future of the organisation. Other functions include capital investment appraisal, i.e. establishing whether investing money in alternative projects is a good idea or not, which is reviewed in Chapter 21.

18.8 Planning and budgeting

To support the planning, decision-making and control process, it is essential for managers to estimate the costs and expenses involved in implementing plans. They also need to ensure that a range of additional resources are available to support both strategic and operational planning. Understanding and applying conventional budgeting techniques can be the first step in managing finance effectively in an organisation. The purpose of introducing planning and budgeting is quite simple. Every organisation that has designs on being successful, whatever its organisational goals are, will form some sort of plan so that managers and employees work towards the same outcome.

In sport and leisure these outcomes can be quite different. In the private sector, Greens Health and Fitness Centre will want to make as much profit from its members as it can, while providing a high quality service. In the public sector, local authorities will want to provide sport and leisure services that meet the needs of their communities in a cost-effective way. In the voluntary sector, small sports clubs will want to generate sufficient revenue from their members, in many cases just to survive. Once these plans have been agreed, managers have to monitor and control activities by comparing what actually occurs with what was planned for. This is the first link between financial and management accounts. If managers can control the annual costs of their organisation, then they can manage the organisation's cash flow and ultimately help control activities to generate profits, or at least to cover costs. Providing that plans are controlled, any significant deviation can be compensated for, as managers can take action to get the organisation back on course to achieve its objectives.

So, back to budgets. A budget is essentially a plan of action that is expressed in financial terms. Often budgets will be prepared in summary form but they could quite easily be expressed with plenty of detail. Unlike the income statement, for example, the type of budget and the level of detail contained within it can vary a great deal between organisations, and as such they are not a statutory requirement. Ideally a budget should cover all of the activities of an organisation and should involve all of its personnel in its preparation. A common misconception with the preparation of a budget is that it should be done by an accountant and not the full team. If this occurs, an organisation will not be seen as inclusive by its staff and budgets will often not be met. Ultimately a budget should be realistic and ensure that goals and aspirations are met; it will facilitate other management functions such as planning, coordination, motivation, communication and control.

Management budgets can take a number of iterations to develop as an organisation moves through a growth curve. At the most basic of levels, however, they will list the expected income and expenditure for a project, planned activity or general business. If expenditure exceeds income the budget will need to be re-examined and consideration given to a cheaper alternative, to reduce costs. Budgets are often imperfect in their construction and will require constant monitoring and refinement.

18.8.1 The budgeting process

Budgeting will play a central role in keeping an organisation's finances on track and should ensure that debts are paid as they fall due. The budgeting process will include costing, estimating income and the allocation of financial resources so that the budget is realistic. Normally a budget will be based on the following information:

- the financial history of the organisation;
- the general economic climate;
- income and expenditure that is reasonably expected to be generated with the resources available;
- data from competitors.

In advance of the trading year, a good manager will spend time developing his or her budget, using all of the information outlined above and comparing it to the general organisational objectives. Budgeting effectively forces managers to think ahead and implement any corrective action required or explain any variance from the original projected costs. The budget should cover a defined period of time and a significant part of the actual budget can be used to provide information for the construction of the income statement. The two primary types of budgeting that will be explored during the remainder of this chapter are continuation budgeting and zero-based budgeting. An illustration of the budgeting process can be seen in Figure 18.5.

Organisational objectives are commonly monitored using performance measurement tools that are principally focused on financial budgeting and financial measurement (see Chapter 17). All three sectors of the sport and leisure industry can apply these measurement tools in order to enhance their operational effectiveness and ultimately their financial health.

18.8.2 Budgetary control

In business the meaning of control is quite straightforward: is what happens to an organisation supposed to happen? Providing that you agree and understand that a budget is simply an organisation's objectives expressed in financial terms, we can take this simple definition forward and you can begin to exercise more control over day-to-day operations. For any plan to be achieved, it has to be both monitored and controlled to ensure that the organisation is on target to achieve its goals. In the event that it is not on the right course, corrective action can be taken. If the implementation of the budget is not controlled, it is likely that the organisation will not meet its objectives. By providing a mechanism for translating an organisation's strategic plan into realistic financial objectives, staff in the organisation can see where they and the organisation are going. However, to control the budgets, managers must allocate responsibility for monitoring actual costs and revenues, to ensure that any problems are identified in a timely manner.

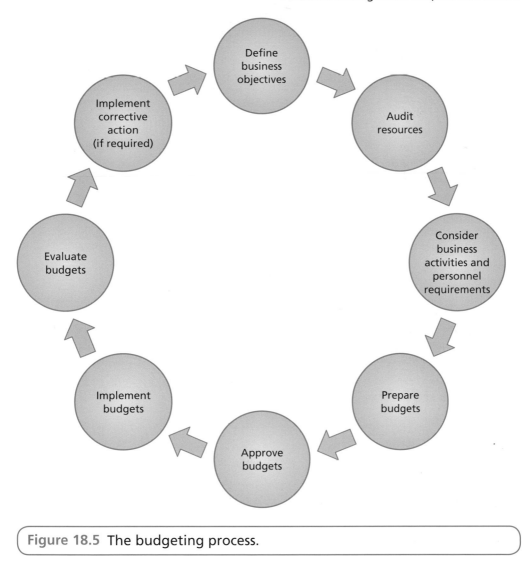

Figure 18.5 The budgeting process.

18.8.3 Continuation budgets

In the sport and leisure industry the most frequently used method of budgeting is continuation budgeting, especially for voluntary sector clubs and public sector leisure services. Essentially, this type of budgeting refers to the notion that an organisation will not change its objectives significantly from one trading period to the next. Such an assumption does not encourage an organisation to grow, as it will not challenge organisational goals and aspirations. It is, however, a very easy method of budgeting to apply and is used frequently in sport and leisure. On the positive side, if the organisation is already working efficiently and making a profit or achieving other objectives, one could argue that continuation budgeting is a sensible and cost-effective way of controlling the financial side of an organisation.

Within the continuation budgeting framework there are two types of budget: incremental and decremental. Incremental budgets will assume that the organisation will grow in line with inflation. Consequently, all a manager will have to do is obtain the budget from the

Table 18.2 Income and expenditure budget for a residential sports camp

Expenditure

Description	Units	Costs	Original budget, 2008	Projected budget, 2009
Facility hire	1	£6,000	£6,000	£6,180
ACCOMMODATION AND CATERING				
Residential campers B&B	130	£60	£7,800	£8,034
Residential staff	10	£60	£600	£618
STAFFING				
Coaches' salaries	12	£250	£3,000	£3,090
Assistant coaches' salaries	8	£100	£800	£824
Physio	1	£500	£500	£515
CRB checks	25	£36	£900	£927
EQUIPMENT				
Physio equipment			£200	£206
Radio hire			£300	£309
Van hire			£500	£515
MEDIA EQUIPMENT				
Media equipment			£150	£155
MARKETING & PROMOTION/ PRINTING				
Merchandise	100	£7	£700	£721
Promotional material	1	£1,058	£1,058	£1,090
Certificates design and printing	1	£1,000	£1,000	£1,030
Trophies			£–	£–
Prizes	1	£400	£400	£412
Staff uniforms	25	£30	£750	£773
Contingency 5%	1	£4,000	£4,000	£4,119
Total expenditure			**£28,658**	**£29,518**

Income

Description	Units	Fees	Total income	
Residential campers	130	£295	£38,350	£39,501
Merchandise	100	£20	£2,000	£2,060
Total income			**£40,350**	**£41,561**
Surplus/deficit			**£11,692**	**£12,043**

Source: adapted from Phoenix and Wilson (2009).

previous year and multiply everything by the rate of inflation to generate the new period's figures. Decremental budgeting, on the other hand, assumes that there will be a standstill within the organisation or a reduction in funding, so the budget will either roll over as it is or will provide reductions in specific areas. An example of an incremental, continuation budget is illustrated in Table 18.2.

> **Discussion question**
>
> What are the benefits and drawbacks of continuation budgets?

18.8.4 Zero-based budgets

Zero-based budgeting (ZBB) was developed initially to address some of the criticisms levelled at traditional budgeting techniques such as continuation budgeting (explained on p. 503). Continuation budgets do not present a manager with a challenge and do not encourage growth. ZBB takes an altogether different stance by applying a cost/benefit approach to creating a budget for an organisation. Ostensibly, ZBB requires a manager to challenge every single item of expenditure based upon the benefits that it is likely to generate.

The typical way of applying this technique is to begin with a blank sheet of paper and start at zero! For example, the expenditure for an entire department commences at zero and the activities that form part of that department's function are clearly evaluated to determine whether they bring an appropriate level of benefit and therefore whether they are really necessary. Given that resources are finite for all organisations, this method of budgeting allows managers to prioritise expenditure according to those inputs which bring about the greatest benefit. In sport and leisure, such budgeting techniques are becoming more popular in the not-for-profit sector, as output is often intangible. ZBB can be applied easily when using these simple questions:

1   What is the purpose of this expenditure?
2   On what exactly will this expenditure be made?
3   What are the quantifiable benefits of this expenditure?
4   What are the alternatives to this proposed expenditure?
5   What would be the outcome of cutting this expenditure completely?

ZBB enables managers to identify and remove operations that are inefficient and can encourage the avoidance of wasteful expenditure by asking crucial questions. However, it can mean that the emphasis is on short-term returns instead of long-term benefits because the former are more easily measured. Furthermore, it presupposes that commitments for expenditure are made at the time of preparing the budget so, for example, expenditures that are not supported by the ZBB can be stopped. Moreover, cost/benefit analysis is often problematic, takes time and requires the manager to have a detailed understanding of the organisation.

> **Discussion question**
>
> What are the benefits and drawbacks of zero-based budgeting?

18.8.5 Analysing budgets

This chapter is about financial management, so having appraised the financial statements and outlined the key components of planning and budgeting, it is important that you understand how to analyse budgets. The ultimate purpose of budgeting (and management accounting more generally) is to assist managers in the planning, decision-making and control of an organisation. In order to achieve this aim, it is necessary to have a framework which can provide periodic comparisons of actual performance with planned (or budgeted) performance. Table 18.3 illustrates in simple terms how this can be achieved. Essentially, here we are concerned with the variance between actual and planned performance and, providing you have produced your budget on a spreadsheet, this variance is easy to measure by deducting planned from actual performance. Once this is completed, it is possible to note the outcome – i.e. either Favourable or Unfavourable – and explain the reason behind the variance. Table 18.3 uses the income and expenditure budget from Table 18.2 and applies these concepts.

In the example there are five columns. The 'budget' column refers to the approved budget for the financial period. The 'actual' column provides details of the entries that have been made to the organisation's accounting system, which will be used to construct the financial statements and are often different from the budgeted figures. 'Variance' refers to the difference between the actual and budgeted performance as outlined above, while the 'direction' column provides details as to whether the variance has a positive (Favourable) or negative (Unfavourable) effect on the financial performance. Finally, 'note' is a cross-reference to a written explanation of a variance (see an example in Figure 18.6). The numbers in isolation do not have the ability to tell the full story, so it is always worth providing a qualitative version of events.

Any member of staff reading the management accountant's report should be able to clearly establish why reported variances have occurred and should be able to cross-reference them against any other relevant information. In the example in Table 18.3, action may be required as the increase in expenditure is not covered by the increase in income, leaving £400 less surplus at the end of the camp, which may or may not be acceptable. Before you move on to the chapter conclusions, take note of the key management accounting terminology.

To: Camp Director

From: Management Accountant

Re: Actual v. Budgeted Notes for Residential

Note 1:   Facility Hire

Facility hire was budgeted as £6,000. However, due to the increase in camp numbers an additional space was needed at the facility to store the equipment required. This was initially priced at £500 but was later discounted, due to next year's booking, to £200. The increase in facility hire has been covered by the increase in camp numbers (see note 8).

Figure 18.6 A qualitative explanation of variance.

Table 18.3 Variance analysis on income and expenditure budget for a residential sports camp

Description	Budget	Actual	Variance	Direction	Note
Facility Hire	£6,000	£6,200	£200	U	1
ACCOMMODATION AND CATERING					
Residential campers B&B	£7,800	£8,000	£200	U	2
Residential staff	£600	£600	£–	F	
STAFFING					
Coaches' salaries	£3,000	£3,000	£–	F	3
Assistant coaches' salaries	£800	£1,050	£250	U	
Physio	£500	£500	£–	F	
CRB checks	£900	£900	£–	F	
EQUIPMENT					
Physio equipment	£200	£200	£–	F	4
Radio hire	£300	£300	£–	F	
Van hire	£500	£500	£–	F	
MEDIA EQUIPMENT					
Media equipment	£150	£150	£–	F	5
MARKETING & PROMOTION/PRINTING					
Merchandise	£700	£800	£100	U	6
Promotional material	£1,058	£1,058	£–	F	
Certificates design and printing	£1,000	£1,000	£–	F	
Trophies	£–			F	
Prizes	£400	£400	£–	F	
Staff uniforms	£750	£750	£–	F	
	£–				
Contingency 5%	£4,000	£4,000	£–	F	
TOTAL EXPENDITURE	£28,658	£29,408	£750	U	7
INCOME					
Description	Total Income				
Residential campers	£38,350	£38,700	£350	F	8
Merchandise	£2,000	£2,000	£–	F	
TOTAL INCOME	£40,350	£40,700	£350	F	
SURPLUS	£11,692	£11,292	£400	U	9

Note: F = favourable; U = unfavourable.

Source: adapted from Phoenix and Wilson (2009).

> ### Key terms
>
> **Budget** – the business or overall plan of an organisation expressed in financial terms.
>
> **Cash budget** – an analysis of how the cash available to an organisation is expected to change over a given period of time.
>
> **Continuation budget** – budgets compiled on the basis of no change in policies or priorities.
>
> **Variance** – the difference between actual performance and planned performance.
>
> **Zero-based budgeting** – a method of budgeting which starts with the priorities of an organisation and allocates resources to the priorities according to their rank order of importance.

> ### Discussion question
>
> Why is it important to compare budgets with actual performance and how frequently should a manager do this?

18.9 Performance analysis

The budgeting process enables managers to set targets, while the control process allows for performance to be monitored and any necessary corrective action to be taken. The final step, however, within the management accounting framework for this chapter is a performance analysis. This will assist managers in making a successful transition into the next financial period, by enhancing their skills and moving the organisation forward.

In any management function it is essential that some sort of evaluation is considered (see Chapter 17). Without it, an organisation cannot review its performance and set budgets for the following year, while the users of financial information, as identified on p. 492, are not provided with sufficient detail to answer their information needs. Sport and leisure organisations in the private commercial sector will want to see that more profit has been made from one period to the next; public sector organisations will want to see active communities; and voluntary and not-for-profit organisations will want to provide services to their members in a solvent manner.

Providing an analysis of the main financial statements and an organisation's budget will help a manager prove his or her worth to an employer, as demonstration of financial management skills will help an organisation move forward. Arguably it might be more important to demonstrate these skills if an organisation is performing badly, as it will need to steer its way out of trouble. Although this chapter has only provided a framework for appraising the financial health of an organisation, it assumes a series of skills that the average sport or leisure manager does not yet possess, especially in the public and not-for-profit sectors.

18.10 Conclusions

The purpose of this chapter is to demonstrate the importance of financial management within a sport and leisure context. While any detailed analysis is beyond the scope of the chapter, provision is made to equip managers with the necessary skills to communicate, in basic terms, the financial health of an organisation. The cyclical process of planning, decision-making and control, coupled with the analytical techniques that can be applied to both financial and management accounting information, should enhance the toolbox of skills that any sport or leisure manager possesses. The importance of this process should not be underestimated in both for-profit and not-for-profit organisations, regardless of their size or stature.

The main objective of all organisations should be to operate within their own resources so that they can continue trading. The tools identified in this chapter, including budgeting, should help this process. Furthermore, using financial and management accounting information as two sides of the same coin – which is rarely acknowledged – will help provide managers with the discipline and confidence to plan, make effective decisions and exercise financial control.

The income statement, balance sheet and cash flow statement equip managers with information that can determine the financial performance and position of an organisation and demonstrate the difference between profit and the typically scarce resource of cash. The statements also illustrate how an organisation is structured in terms of its assets and liabilities, so that effective investment, borrowing and service decisions can be made. In addition, it can be determined whether or not business should be conducted with certain organisations and whether you or your competitors can pay debts as they fall due.

It is not possible within one single chapter to cover all of the financial health ratios and budgetary techniques. However, you should have grasped the idea that financial management is important enough to be considered an integral part of any organisation. Other skills are required to come up with a marketing campaign or a training and development plan, but only those who understand finance can establish whether or not they are financially viable, worthwhile or even necessary in the first place. The best way to ensure that you develop the full range of financial management skills is to achieve a thorough understanding of the theoretical concepts involved and some tangible experience of finance in practice.

Practical tasks

1 Identify the key figures that are discussed for Arena Leisure in the income statement, balance sheet and cash flow statement. Once you are happy that you can understand where these figures can be found, use the income statement, balance sheet and cash flow statement for a sport and leisure organisation of your choice to answer the following questions:
   (a) What is the organisation's financial performance?
   (b) What is the organisation's financial position?

> ### Practical tasks
>
> **2** Construct a budget for yourself for a typical calendar month. You could use an existing bank statement to provide you with the necessary information. Provide details of income and expenditure and calculate your financial performance during the month. Once you have produced this budget, try and reconstruct it using the principles of zero-based budgeting (see p. 505). Consider all streams of income and expenditure and establish whether or not you are financially viable. Remember to ask yourself all of the questions associated with this method of budgeting. For example, is a gym membership required? What is the cost of not paying for car insurance?

Structured guide to further reading

For guidance on recording and reporting financial information and for more detail on performing a financial health analysis:

Wilson, R. and Joyce, J. (2008) *Finance for Sport and Leisure Managers: an introduction*, Routledge, London.

For more information on general sport funding especially for not-for-profit organisations:

Stewart, B. (2007) *Sport Funding and Finance*, Butterworth Heinemann, London.

For a general view of accounting in leisure:

Owen, G. (1994) *Accounting for Hospitality, Tourism and Leisure*, Pitman Publishing, London.

Useful websites

For free annual reports from organisations in the sport and leisure industry:
www.precisionir.com/investors/ars.aspx

For a critical insight into academic papers concerning sport finance:
www.fitinfotech.com/IJSF/IJSF.tpl

For discussions of sport and leisure finance in the business and sport sections of daily publications:
http://news.bbc.co.uk/sport/default.stm
www.ft.com/arts-leisure
www.timesonline.co.uk/tol/sport/

Chapter 19

Law and sport and leisure management

Peter Charlish

In this chapter

- Why does a sport and leisure manager need to know about the law?
- What elements of the law are particularly relevant to sport and leisure managers?
- What is negligence and how can a manager avoid it?
- How is a sport and leisure manager subject to legal liability?
- How is working with children affected by the law?
- What employment law should a sport and leisure manager be aware of?
- What does good risk management entail?

Matt Cardy/Getty Images

Summary

This chapter concentrates on key legal areas of responsibility for sport and leisure managers. One of the most important is the avoidance of negligence, which means recognising a duty of care to all customers, volunteers, etc. who visit an organisation and ensuring that there is no breach of duty. Other key legal issues are occupiers liability and vicarious liability, the first of which involves a common duty of care to all visitors, whilst the second concerns liability for employees' actions.

Working with children is an area of law in which there has been considerable change in recent years, culminating in new legislation for anyone working with children and vulnerable adults in the UK – requiring registration with an Independent Safeguarding Authority. There are also specific precedents for the way in which liability in school sport is identified.

A brief overview of some important legal considerations for potential employers of staff is presented. Finally, the chapter closes with consideration of risk management, i.e. ensuring that negligence is prevented and liability is acknowledged in an organisation's systems, particularly in the recruitment and training of staff. A key element of risk management is risk assessment, which involves straightforward procedures to identify risks and take measures to minimise them.

19.1 Introduction

This chapter serves as an introduction to key legal issues that may affect or impact upon people working in the sport and leisure industries. Inevitably for such a broad discipline, the chapter only provides an insight into selected areas and if readers want further information there are references provided to signpost where that additional information may be found. Many of these references are to cases – case law is very important for setting precedents.

By its very nature, the law is different in different countries, so this chapter concentrates on the way the law operates in England and Wales, for consistency (Fafinski and Finch, 2007; Elliott and Quinn, 2007). However, many of the principles demonstrated will be valid in other countries' legal systems – but they will be enacted by different legislation, different processes and the legal details will be different.

In order to locate the case law and legislation cited in this chapter, it is necessary to become familiar with searching the major legal databases. There is a vast quantity of legal material (case reports, journal articles, statutes, etc.) available online. However, most of these are only available to organisations and libraries that pay the appropriate subscription fee. It is highly likely that most universities will have access to at least some of these databases and you should contact librarians for more details and instructions on how to use these databases. There are three main commercial databases – these are *Westlaw*, *Lexis-Nexis* and *Lawtel*. For ease of use, *Westlaw* is probably the most user-friendly. It has a clear, stripped down Google-like interface, with a whole battery of features available beyond the initial search. It also enables the user to search using a variety of terminology and in a variety of different ways.

19.2 Negligence

It is a fact of life that when people participate in sports and leisure activities they will sometimes suffer injuries. Sometimes these injuries may be viewed as 'just one of those things'. However, there will be other times when an organisation or an individual may be at least partially responsible for the injuries received and the injured party may therefore wish to pursue an action to claim compensation from those responsible. It is through negligence that such an action is most likely to be pursued.

There appears to be a perception amongst many that the threat of negligence liability is removing much of the risk in society, and that a compensation culture has grown up (Williams, 2005). This perception has developed to such an extent that legislation was recently enacted in the UK (The Compensation Act, 2006) aimed specifically at protecting those such as sport organisations that provide socially useful activities. In particular the legislation now asks the courts to specifically look at whether the steps that an organisation may have to take to protect itself from liability may in fact discourage it from providing a particular activity. The provision of school trips and outdoor pursuits courses are particularly relevant, where teachers or recreation providers may be under threat of being sued for accidents which happen whilst participants are taking part in activities such as hiking, canoeing, caving, orienteering, rock-climbing, etc.

With the new legislation, arguably there is now a reduced threat of being successfully sued, which will be a welcome boon for all involved in the sport and leisure industry. When considering negligence, however, a manager must remember that the basic requirement is for providers and customers to act reasonably. The requirement is not to make an activity 100 per cent safe by eliminating all risk; but rather to do what is reasonable to enable people to remain safe. Part of this equation is that the greater the risk of something going wrong, or the graver the consequences for someone should an identifiable risk occur, the greater the precautions that must be taken to prevent this risk from happening.

Negligence has a wide range of applications and these include helping to regulate the behaviour and actions of both individuals and organisations in a sport and recreational context. For an injured party to succeed in gaining compensation through a claim in negligence, they must satisfy the court that their injury was caused, at least in part, by the actions of another. They must demonstrate that this party failed to take reasonable care of their safety and that this lack of reasonable care caused or contributed to the injury suffered. The injury suffered may be physical (to person or property), psychological or financial. In order to win an action in negligence, the claimant (the person who has suffered the injury) must prove the following:

- that the defendant (the other party) owed the claimant a duty of care;
- that this duty of care was breached;
- that this breach of duty caused or contributed to the injury or loss suffered.

It is important to note that the claimant does not have to demonstrate this beyond reasonable doubt, as the prosecution would have to in a criminal trial. In a legal action in negligence, the requirement is merely to show *on the balance of probabilities* (i.e. 51 per cent), which is a far easier standard to reach. The following sections break a claim in negligence down into its constituent parts in order to explain the operation of this area of law in a sport and leisure context.

19.2.1 Duty of care

In order to establish a claim in negligence the claimant must first show that the defendant owed them a duty of care. Providers of sport and leisure facilities will almost certainly always owe their customers a duty of care. They will have a responsibility at all times to make sure that they consider their customers when going about their business.

There are many different relationships in sport and leisure where a duty of care is clearly owed by one party to another, for example (Hartley, 2009):

- participant to participant;
- teacher to pupil;
- event organiser to spectator;
- private club member to club member;
- sports governing body to participant;
- team doctor to sports participant;
- official to participant;
- adventure tour operator to tourist;
- manufacturer of a sport product to a consumer;
- employer to police on duty at an event;
- adult to adult on a skiing holiday;
- occupiers of a sports centre to lawful visitors (even trespassers);
- hypnotist/theatre/club to audience volunteers;
- teenagers to other teenagers in informal leisure/recreation.

In almost all relationships in a sports and leisure context, a duty of care will be owed – one party will need to have the other party in consideration when going about their business. So, for example, a tourism operator will have to make sure it does all that is reasonable to maintain the safety of its operations for the tourist. The owner and/or manager of a leisure centre will need to ensure that the centre is reasonably safe for those coming to use the centre, for whatever purpose (not just the sports facilities but even the cafeteria would need to be reasonably safe for its customers). It must also be the case that such premises are reasonably safe for employees of the centre to do their jobs.

It is in the area of breach of duty that the courts will assess whether a party has behaved reasonably or taken reasonable steps to maintain safety.

19.2.2 Breach of duty

Once a duty of care has been established, it must then be proved whether this duty has been breached or not (Deakin *et al.*, 2007). In a sport and leisure context the obligation is to do all that is reasonable to maintain the safety of the participant or spectator. However, the circumstances as to what amounts to 'reasonable conduct' are of fundamental importance. As has been said in an Australian case, the circumstances involved in chariot racing are far different from those involved in water-skiing. In other words, the nature of chariot racing means that it may take 'more careless' behaviour to breach duty.

To put this in a modern context, the nature of and inherent danger in an activity such as rugby union mean that mere careless behaviour may not breach duty – something more akin to reckless behaviour may be necessary before breach of duty is established. Alternatively, the circumstances in an activity such as bowls or badminton may be that if one party is careless and this carelessness injures another party, then this is sufficient to breach duty. The crucial factor here is the circumstances – a vital issue. What are the circumstances of the event, what are the inherent dangers of the event, what might the weather conditions be, the abilities of the participants, what about the presence or otherwise of protective equipment, etc.? These issues and many others will play a role in assessing whether behaviour has been reasonable and therefore there has been no breach of duty, or whether it has been unreasonable and therefore there has been a breach of duty.

Case Study 19.1 below contains a recent explanation of how to assess whether there has been a breach of duty of care in a sports and recreation context.

Discussion question

What kinds of circumstances may be important in assessing whether there has been a breach of the duty of care in a situation where a player is injured by a tackle in a game of football?

CASE STUDY 19.1

Caldwell v. MaGuire & Fitzgerald (2001) EWCA Civ 1054

This case is probably the most significant sports participant negligence case in the UK. It was heard in the Court of Appeal and its significance lies in the time the Court took to examine the standard of care owed by one participant to another. Previous to *Caldwell*, the examination of the standard owed had been rather vague and uncertain. The case involved an injury inflicted on a jockey when he was thrown from his mount when it was squeezed for position by two other horses. In the event, both defendants were held not to be liable for the injuries received by the claimant Peter Caldwell. In explaining its reasoning, the Court of Appeal tried to clarify the whole position of negligence in sport. The Court approved five major points, which are:

1   Each contestant in a lawful sporting contest (and in particular a race) owes a duty of care to each and all other contestants.
2   That duty is to exercise in the course of the contest all care that is objectively reasonable in the prevailing circumstances for the avoidance of infliction of injury to such fellow contestants.
3   The prevailing circumstances are all such properly attendant upon the contest and include its object, the demands inevitably made upon its contestants, its inherent dangers (if any), its rules, conventions and customs, and the standards, skills and judgement reasonably to be expected of a contestant. Thus in the particular case of a horse race the prevailing circumstances will include the contestant's obligation to ride a horse over a given course competing with the remaining contestants for the best possible placing, if not for a win. Such must further include the Rules of Racing and the standards, skills and judgement of a professional jockey, all as expected by fellow contestants.
4   Given the nature of such prevailing circumstances the threshold for liability is in practice inevitably high; the proof of a breach of duty will not flow from proof of no more than an error of judgement or from mere proof of a momentary lapse in skill (and thus care) respectively when subject to the stresses of a race. Such are no more than incidents inherent in the nature of the sport.

5   In practice it may therefore be difficult to prove any such breach of duty absent proof of conduct that in point of fact amounts to reckless disregard for the fellow contestant's safety. I emphasise the distinction between the expression of legal principle and the practicalities of the evidential burden.

(*Caldwell v. MaGuire & Fitzgerald*, 2001, para 11)

The first two propositions make it clear that sports participants owe one another a duty of care and that this duty is to behave in a reasonable manner taking account of the circumstances which you are in. In other words, the level of behaviour expected may be different in, for example, a competitive game of rugby than in a different activity. It is the circumstances which dictate the level of care required. The third proposition tries to introduce some of the kinds of circumstances which may be important in assessing whether a breach of duty has occurred. It raises issues such as the inherent dangers of the particular sporting activity and the level of skill of the participants. This is not by any means an exhaustive list; there is room for consideration of many different variables or circumstances. The fourth proposition then goes on to attempt to reassure those who worry that the threat of legal liability is dissuading some people from taking part in sport. It states very clearly that a finding of liability does not come easily and that it may only be quite serious behaviour that would lead to a finding of negligence. The final proposition attempts to reconcile an academic debate that has endured since another case in 1963, by stressing that the approach taken by the courts in sports negligence remains harmonious with that in other walks of life, in that breach of duty will occur where there is *unreasonable* behaviour. However, depending on the circumstances, *careless* behaviour might not be *unreasonable* and in fact it may not be until behaviour becomes *reckless* that the behaviour is deemed to be *unreasonable* and therefore negligent.

(Also see 'Useful websites', p. 533.)

It is perhaps pertinent for those involved in sport and leisure activities that the Court of Appeal in a 2004 case equated children's horseplay (i.e. boisterous fooling around) with organised sport, stressing that the only real difference between horseplay and organised sport is that in the former there are no formal rules. The implications of the decision of the Court of Appeal to equate horseplay by and large with organised sport is that sports negligence principles should be applied across a whole range of activities, wherever there is consensual recreational activity. This means that depending on the circumstances of the activity, *reckless* behaviour rather than ordinary *careless* behaviour may be required to breach that duty of care.

A sports governing body must have adequate safety measures in place to make sure that participants are protected from reasonably foreseeable risks. In *Watson v. BBBC* (2001), the boxer Michael Watson successfully sued the British Boxing Board of Control (BBBC) for injuries he received whilst fighting Chris Eubank for the world title. He was able to establish that the safety measures they had in place were insufficient to protect him from his foreseeable injuries. He suffered a brain haemorrhage after he was knocked out late in the fight.

It was the inadequacy of the immediate aftercare of Michael Watson which was the subject of the negligence action, rather than the events leading up to the knockout. Watson accepted the risks of boxing. What he did not accept, however, was that the safety procedures the BBBC had in place to deal with injuries such as those that Watson suffered (which were clearly foreseeable) would not be fit for purpose.

CASE STUDY 19.2

Wattleworth v. Goodwood (2004)

The interest in this case lies in the fact that an action was brought by the widow of the victim against three different parties – against the circuit itself (Goodwood), against the national governing body (the MSA) and against the international governing body for motorsport (the FIA). The claimant alleged that her husband's death had been caused by the negligent construction of the safety barrier. Goodwood Circuit agreed that as occupiers they owed a duty of care under the 1957 Occupiers Liability Act (see pp. 519–20), but claimed that they had discharged that duty by taking all reasonable steps to ensure that the track was reasonably safe by following all advice given to them by both the MSA and FIA.

It was quite clear from the judgement that there had been detailed analysis and several inspections of the safety provisions of the track by both Goodwood and the MSA, and to a lesser extent the FIA. For these reasons, Goodwood had indeed discharged its duty of care and so no liability was held against them. The MSA denied that it owed a duty of care, due to the fact that the event in which Mr Wattleworth was killed was not an official MSA event for which they would have issued a licence. However, the Court held that they clearly had assumed a responsibility and that their role as national governing body went far beyond merely issuing licences to circuits. They provided detailed safety advice and worked closely with the circuits to make sure all appropriate safety features were in place, providing guidance and expertise. It was thus fair, just and reasonable to impose a duty of care upon them. However, the construction of the safety feature was reasonable and they had taken reasonable care in inspecting it and approving it. Therefore there was no breach of duty. The Court made particular note of the experience and expertise of the MSA inspector and that at all times his priority was to keep risks to a minimum. The action against the FIA also failed. It was held that because of the remote nature of the organisation and the fact that the FIA took no direct responsibility for safety at national events (this they delegated to national sporting authorities), they owed no duty of care towards Mr Wattleworth. The conclusion of the Court was that the accident was caused by a momentary lapse in judgement by Mr Wattleworth. His car had gone a few feet off line at the fateful moment, causing him to collide with the safety barrier, which unfortunately caused his death. There was no negligence on the part of any of those involved in the organisation of the event. They had done all that was reasonable to look after his safety.

Parties only need do what is reasonable to guard against injury. However, it is also the case that the graver the consequences of any injury that may be suffered, the more that must be done to eliminate the risk. It is not necessary that every single risk must be eliminated. In *Bolton v. Stone* (1951) a pedestrian was struck by a cricket ball which had been hit out of the ground during a local match. The injured party sued for the injuries she suffered. In the case the Court was told that a ball had only been hit out of the ground in this manner six times in the last thirty years and due to the infrequency of this happening it would be unreasonable to ask the defendants to guard against this very small risk. Therefore it was held that there was no breach of duty as the injury suffered was not due to a reasonably foreseeable risk which the defendants would be expected to guard against.

If event providers and facility owners/managers are to ensure that they remain on the right side of liability it is important that they conform to appropriate recognised safety standards. Such considerations were important in two significant cases heard some thirty years apart. In the first, *Simms v. Leigh Rugby Football Club* (1969), a player was injured in a tackle and alleged that his injury was caused by a collision with a perimeter wall that was constructed around the rugby pitch. The Rugby Football League bylaws stated that any perimeter wall must be at least seven feet away from the touchline. This particular wall was seven foot three inches away and so exceeded the standard expected by the governing body. The Court dismissed the claim.

In the second case, *Wattleworth v. Goodwood* (2004), detailed in Case Study 19.2, a racing driver died during a race, following a collision with a safety wall constructed of tyres and an earth bank.

However, it is important to recognise that just because a particular practice or standard is approved by a governing body it does not necessarily mean that it will stand up to legal scrutiny. Ultimately, as seen in *Watson v. BBBC*, it may well be the case that liability will be held against the governing body and/or the event organiser, even though that party may be adhering to the governing body guidelines.

The responsibilities and duties of stadium owners and occupiers in the UK have been further defined by legislation concerning occupiers liability. The following section will look briefly at this legislation and its impact.

19.3 Occupiers liability

An issue of real importance for those organising sport and leisure events or providing facilities for such events is that of their potential liability. The Occupiers Liability Acts of 1957 and 1984 are of particular pertinence in this area. The Act of 1984 refers to unlawful visitors (typically trespassers) to the premises, whilst the 1957 Act refers to lawful visitors and, as such, encompasses all participants, officials, coaches/instructors and also obviously any spectators who may be present.

An occupier owes a common duty of care to any lawful visitor to their premises. Typically the occupier will be the owners of the premises or the managers of the premises. Usually the occupier will be defined as the person or business 'in control' of the premises. The duty owed by the occupier is to ensure that the premises are reasonably safe for the purposes for which the visitor has been invited. For any visitor to a premises there of course remains the possibility of an action in negligence in the event of them suffering an injury. However, where it is the state of the premises that has caused the accident, the statutory duty laid down by the Occupiers Liability Act 1957 means that an action against an occupier has far more chance of success and is therefore far more likely than under ordinary negligence principles reviewed earlier (see pp. 514–19).

If the premises are unsafe for the purposes for which someone is invited, then it is incumbent upon the occupier either to make the premises safe or to ensure that the visitor can remain safe whilst on the premises. In *Cunningham & Others v. Reading Football Club Ltd* (1991), police officers were injured when football hooligans broke pieces of concrete from the ground and used them as missiles, causing injury to the police officers attending the game. Despite the fact that the deliberate actions of the hooligans directly caused the injuries suffered, the club had failed to ensure that the ground was reasonably safe and they had exacerbated that by allowing hooligans access to the defective area. A solution may have been for the club to restrict access to the particular area of the ground which had the defective concrete.

It is not the premises themselves that necessarily need to be made safe. The focus is on making sure that the visitor is safe for the purpose for which they are/were invited. So, for example, a warning notice may enable someone to remain safe. However, it is very important to note that a warning notice must make it clear what the danger is and how to avoid it, rather than merely be an attempt to evade liability.

Furthermore, any warning must take into account individual characteristics of visitors, so more care will be needed where the visitor is a child or someone who is visually impaired (Harpwood, 2009). Occupiers may also be able to discharge their duty if all appropriate safety checks and recommendations have been undertaken and these are sufficient to ensure that the visitor is safe. In the *Wattleworth* and *Simms* cases referred to earlier, the Courts dismissed claims because the governing bodies' relevant technical recommendations had been followed.

Many people are also surprised to learn that trespassers are owed a duty of care (albeit a more limited one) by occupiers (persistent trespassers can sometimes attain the status of lawful 'visitors'). The duty, though, only covers personal injury and not damage to property. The duty owed is to take such care as is reasonable in the circumstances, to see that the trespasser does not suffer injury due to any danger identified. Warnings again may suffice to prevent a finding of liability. A case that illustrates these issues very well is *Ratcliff v. McConnell* (1999) (see Case Study 19.3).

19.4 Vicarious liability

If an employee commits a tort (a civil wrong, e.g. a negligent act) whilst acting during the course of their employment the employer is said to be vicariously liable for the tort committed. The practical implications of this are that it will be the employer (or their insurer) who will actually be responsible for paying the compensation to the claimant, if it can be demonstrated that:

- the defendant is an employee (who may, for example, be a lifeguard at a leisure centre or a fitness trainer at a gymnasium);
- the tort (such as negligence) was committed during the course of their employment.

If an employee has a contract of employment the first question is relatively simple to answer, but if the 'worker' is, for example, an independent contractor, this question becomes more problematic. The test as to whether someone is an employee for the purposes of vicarious liability is a difficult one to assess and seems to hinge on the facts of each case. It may well be that where a degree of 'control' is exercised by the employer over the activities of the defendant, this will be critical in assessing vicarious liability. For example, in *Hawley v. Luminar Leisure plc*, it was held that despite a group of doormen actually being employees of a security services company, the nightclub owner where they operated was vicariously liable for their acts as he exercised clear control over how they did their job.

Once it has been established that the defendant is an employee, the second hurdle to clear is to establish that the act which caused the injury was caused during the course of employment. It is difficult to find clear principles which are applicable in all cases. However, if the employee is providing some benefit to the employer, or the position of the employee enabled them to perform the action complained of, then it is likely to be interpreted as acting in the course of their employment.

Even if the employee is doing an act which is forbidden by the employer, if that act is bringing some benefit to the employer, or if the status of their employment has enabled them to carry out that task, then it is likely that they will have been acting in the course of their employment. For example, in *Limpus v. London General Omnibus Co.* (1862), the company was held

Ratcliff v. McConnell (1999)

This case involved an action brought by a student who broke into the college swimming pool with two friends after they had been drinking (although the student was not drunk). They climbed over a locked gate; there were two notices saying that the pool was closed and warning against taking glasses and bottles into the pool area at the pool entrance, another 'substantial' warning at the shallow end and another at the deep end stating, 'Deep end shallow dive'. There was also a motion activated security light (albeit one which did not throw out a great deal of light). The student dived in and hit his head, causing him permanent tetraplegia.

The High Court found for the claimant (subject to 40 per cent contributory negligence on his part), holding that the college was aware the pool was used regularly by its students during prohibited hours, that new students were not specifically warned against use, that no information was made available about specific opening hours, that there was no general prohibition against diving and that the college did not take such care as is reasonable in the circumstances to, for example, warn of the dangers or to discourage people from encountering the risk.

On appeal, the High Court judgement was quite strongly criticised by the Court of Appeal. It found that the student had actually dived deeper than he had intended and that alcohol may have played a part in this misjudgement. Moreover, it found (contrary to the High Court) that there was no evidence of persistent misuse of the pool by students at the college. Further, again contrary to the High Court, it was found that the student had been told that out of hours use of the pool was prohibited and that warnings were posted. In analysing the case in relation to the Occupiers Liability Act 1984, it was held that the college (the occupier) had done all that was reasonable in the circumstances in relation to this trespasser. The dangers in a swimming pool were twofold – that of drowning or having an accident, as the student had done. Both were obvious dangers to someone of his age and maturity. Furthermore, both dangers were common to all swimming pools and the defendants had done all that could reasonably be asked of them to guard against this risk. The Court of Appeal summed up the position thus:

> The question is whether the defendants should have offered other protection to the plaintiff from a risk which he should have been fully aware of, and indeed was aware of.

The Court of Appeal answered this question in the negative, leaving the plaintiff (i.e. the claimant, in this case the student) without any compensation at all. It is clear from this case that each case will be decided on its own facts. Issues which may be important in deciding if a duty is owed and has been breached may be things such as the age of the claimants, their mental capacity or indeed the nature of the danger and the resources of the occupier.

vicariously liable following a race between two drivers which injured the claimant, who was the driver of the other bus. Although drivers racing their buses was expressly forbidden by the company, the drivers were employed to drive and racing was merely an unauthorised method of doing what they were employed to do. In contrast, in *Beard v. London General Omnibus Co.* (1900) a bus conductor caused injury whilst moving his bus. The company was held not to be vicariously liable as the conductor was acting outside the course of his employment – he was employed to conduct, not to drive.

An employer may also be held liable for the deliberate acts (rather than negligent acts) of the employee, even if these acts are prohibited by the employer or against the law, if their employment placed them in a position which facilitated these acts or the employer derived some benefit from the act. This was established crucially in the case *Lister v. Hesley Hall* (2002), which involved children sexually abused by the warden at their boarding home. The House of Lords concluded that it was his employment status that had enabled the warden to commit his acts and that those acts were therefore closely connected with his employment status and thus it was fair, just and reasonable to hold his employers liable for the actions of the warden. This was later applied in *Gravil v. Carroll & Anor* (2008), where it was held that the part-time employers of a rugby union player were held vicariously liable and therefore had to pay the compensation for an off the ball punch that the player threw during a match, which caused his opponent a severe eye injury requiring substantial reconstructive surgery.

What these cases demonstrate is that employers/managers must at all times take care when employing staff, supervising staff and training staff, to ensure that they do not leave themselves open to compensation claims due to the principle of vicarious liability. The clearest way for an employer to protect themselves from potentially being held to be vicariously liable for the negligent acts of their employees is to ensure that their employees do not commit such acts in the first place. An employer may guard against an employee committing such acts by closer monitoring and training, or by regular staff assessments and appraisals. Such precautions may take place prior to staff taking up employment by closer checks and safeguards during recruitment. An employer must also, of course, always make sure that their systems of working are safe and, furthermore, that they always encourage and promote safe and best practice. It is important to remember that the fundamental requirement is once again that of reasonableness. There is no guarantee of safety and safe practice, and as long as an employer is doing all that is reasonable to ensure that their staff behave reasonably they should not find themselves on the wrong side of a legal claim in this area.

19.5 Working with children

A large part of work within the sport and leisure industry involves children, and this necessarily involves its own challenges. To this end, a guide to the UK legal framework has been produced by the Department for Education and Skills (HM Government, 2006) (see 'Useful websites', p. 533). The document is seemingly addressed to all organisations and individuals that may have a role in promoting the welfare and looking after the safety of children, which includes many sport and leisure organisations.

Under the Children's Act 1989, a person with care of a child in the UK must do all that is reasonable in the circumstances for the purpose of safeguarding or promoting the welfare of the child. All organisations which have a responsibility towards children must have in place proper procedures and measures to ensure the protection of the children under their care. The Protection of Children Act (PoCA) 1999 introduced the PoCA List, whereby the Secretary of State had to record a list of the names of individuals considered unsuitable to work with children – this placed an obligation upon all qualifying organisations working with children to refer the names of individuals who may be unsuitable for possible inclusion on that list. The consequence of this was that Criminal Records Bureau checks had to be made for all potential employees who might have contact with children. If any potential employee or current employee appeared on the list they could not be employed in that position by the provider. It was an offence under the Act to employ someone in a childcare capacity (or any other 'regulated' capacity) whose name appeared on the list.

This list worked in tandem with *list 99* (Information held under the Education Act 2002), which dealt with individuals barred from working in schools and education settings in England and Wales. These have now been replaced by the new Vetting and Barring Scheme, which was a recommendation of the inquiry into the Soham murders (a particularly harrowing crime in 2002 in which a school caretaker murdered two 10-year-old girls who had attended the school where he worked). This brought the POCA list, *list 99* and a Protection of Vulnerable Adults list under administration by the new Independent Safeguarding Authority (ISA). The rationalisation of the lists and bringing them under the supervision of one umbrella organisation was seen as a key constituent of the Safeguarding Vulnerable Groups Act 2006, which was passed as a consequence of the Soham murders.

The Vetting and Barring Scheme (see 'Useful websites', p. 533) has introduced new safeguards and it is now a criminal offence for individuals on the list 'to work or apply for work with children or vulnerable adults in a wide range of posts'. It will also be a criminal offence for anyone on the ISA list to engage in any regulated activity (which is essentially any activity which involves contact with children or vulnerable adults 'frequently, intensively and/or overnight' – see 'Useful websites', p. 533). Such an offence is punishable by up to five years in prison. Further:

> Employers, local authorities, professional regulators and other bodies have a duty to refer to the ISA, information about individuals working with children or vulnerable adults where they consider them to have caused harm or pose a risk of harm.

For anyone wishing to take up a paid position in one of the regulated activities, there is a charge to join the scheme, although it is free for volunteers. It is a criminal offence for an employer to allow a barred person to work in any regulated activity. The new UK Coalition Government at the time of writing has halted development of the Vetting and Barring Scheme and is aiming to review the scheme and 'scale it back to common sense levels' (see ISA in 'Useful websites', p. 533).

Discussion question

Discuss what your legal responsibilities would be if you were on the interview panel seeking to appoint a candidate for the position of a childrens', athletics coach at the local leisure centre. What might the consequences be of failing to comply with these responsibilities?

19.6 Negligence liability in school sports

There have been several cases when school pupils have sued their teachers for injuries that they have received whilst taking part in recreational activities in school. The implications of these cases for the schools are of course that, as the employers of the teachers, they are likely to be held to be vicariously liable, and these cases may also have important considerations for sports and recreation centre managers, who may employ coaches to work with children (or adults) and who will have the same kind of legal relationship with their charges that schoolteachers have. It is therefore in the best interests of the schools (and leisure centres) to recruit, train and supervise their staff appropriately to try and minimise the chances of injury in the first place.

A recent significant case involved an injury to a boy who had been playing rugby union (*Mountford v. Newlands School*, 2007). The 14-year-old boy sued the referee/selector and school for injuries inflicted by an overage player participating in an age group rugby match. The school was held liable despite the fact that the English Schools Rugby Football Union rules did not prohibit boys playing outside their age group. Furthermore, the tackle that caused the injury was not a foul tackle and nor did the older boy's additional size contribute to the injury.

It seems that if the selector/referee had given the rules and the older boy's suitability to play due consideration and concluded that he was suitable to play, or if he had conducted an appropriate risk assessment, there may have been no finding of liability. The fact that the selector/referee failed to consider the possible consequences of allowing an older boy to play was vital to the case (Heywood and Charlish, 2007).

The implications of this case for junior sport in particular are potentially far-reaching. Whilst it is impossible to say just how many students play 'down' in lower age groups in school sports, it is undoubtedly the case that it happens, and often for very good reasons. It may be the case that without an overage student playing, an institution may not be able to raise a team, making the over-age player a necessity. Therefore, an unfortunate consequence of this case may be a reduction in participation rates in junior level sports.

Other problems may arise with staff or coaches taking part in activities with children. Liability may arise, for example, if a tackle is performed which causes injury to a child. A teacher or coach must take reasonable care when performing or demonstrating tackles and, crucially, must be particularly mindful of the disparity in age, size and physical maturity between them as adults and the pupils/children.

Sometimes, young people need protecting from themselves, particularly if staff are aware of any issues which may make a particular activity unsuitable for any particular child. This was illustrated in *Moore v. Hampshire* CC (1982), where a 12-year-old girl who had congenital hip problems was allowed to do PE by her teacher, despite being forbidden from taking part in such physical activities. The teacher knew this but still allowed the girl to take part. The result was that the girl broke her ankle and the school was held liable for the teacher's negligence in allowing her to participate. Again, the implications of this for coaches and teachers are that they must know their pupils or students and if there are any known reasons that may place restrictions on participation in certain activities, then the employers of the teachers or coaches must ensure that their staff comply with these restrictions or face the consequences.

Liability is not just relevant to recognised sports. For example, in *A (a minor) v. Leeds* CC (1999) two girls collided with one another whilst taking part in a warm-up activity organised by the teacher during a PE lesson. Again the school was held vicariously liable for the failure of the teacher to properly organise the warm-up activity. However, it should be stressed once again that schools and others in a supervisory position only need take reasonable precautions when dealing with children and young people.

The Courts do not wish to minutely scrutinise all aspects of different activities which may be enjoyed. For example, in *Babbings v. Kirklees* MC (2004), a Year 4 schoolgirl was injured whilst in a mixed PE class with Year 3 children. The injury was caused when she was attempting a routine manoeuvre which involved jumping from a springboard to a high bar and holding onto the bar, then dropping from it and landing on her feet. Unfortunately she suffered a fracture of her right arm and sued the school, alleging negligence on the part of the experienced teacher. The Court found in favour of the school, making it clear that it would be unreasonable to expect classes to be absolutely free from any risk and, further, that any move towards complete risk aversion would do PE no favours at all.

This is obviously refreshing news for educators and providers of sport and leisure services, reiterating that the legal duty is to take reasonable care for the safety of your 'neighbour'. Such measures will ensure that those involved in the sports and leisure industries do not find themselves being held liable for all injuries suffered by participants in activities which they have organised.

Discussion question

You are the manager of a sports centre which runs several children's rugby teams. One weekend one of the teams is short of players so, without consulting you, the coach makes up the team with three players from the younger age group. In the event of a serious injury to one of the younger children, discuss the possible legal consequences.

19.7 Employment law issues

It is likely that any person involved in sport and leisure management will at some stage be involved either in hiring staff or in having to part company with staff. Therefore this section will deal briefly with some of the legal issues which may result from this.

It is important to remember that any contract of employment contains both express terms (terms written clearly into the contract) and implied terms. The latter are terms that are not written down but nevertheless are considered to be part of the contract and may include, for example, the duty to safeguard the health and safety of employees and the duty that, if provided, a reference will be written with reasonable care and skill. An employee has an implied contractual duty, for example, to adapt to new working conditions and to always exercise reasonable care and skill whilst carrying out their job. These terms are binding on both employer and employee.

19.7.1 The employment process

In the UK, within two months of the commencement of employment an employer must provide written particulars of that employment to the employee (Employment Rights Act 1996). Failure to do so will lead to an award of between two and four weeks wages in any case of unfair dismissal, redundancy or discrimination (Employment Act 2002).

19.7.2 Discrimination

It is unlawful for an employer in the UK to discriminate on the grounds of sex, race, disability, age, sexual orientation, religious belief or on the basis of whether the worker is full time, part time or on a fixed term contract. Such discrimination laws typically apply from the job advert stage before employment is commenced and any employer found guilty of discrimination on one of those grounds would be liable to pay a hefty sum in compensation.

Discrimination may be direct (for example not employing someone simply because of their gender) or indirect (for example setting a condition of employment that means that more men than women or vice versa are likely to qualify) – both forms are unlawful.

Discrimination laws, however, do not prohibit an employer from specifying gender or race requirements needed for a job due to the particular nature or genuine occupational requirements of that job. Similarly, an act of indirect discrimination may be lawful if the condition that is imposed is proportionate to a legitimate aim. So, for example, in the case *Panesar v. Nestle Ltd* (1980) it was lawful to prohibit workers from having beards and long hair for health and safety and hygiene reasons even though this was discriminatory against members of the Sikh religion, who could not comply with this rule. It is important that any indirectly discriminating measure must amount to the minimum possible restriction necessary to achieve the aim, and no more. An employer also has a duty not to discriminate on the grounds of disability and must make reasonable adjustments to their workplace to ensure that individuals with a disability are not discriminated against. This duty extends to organisations that provide access to the public, such as shops, leisure centres, etc., and means that reasonable adjustments to premises must be made to ensure equality of access for those with disabilities.

> ### Discussion question
>
> Discuss what changes you may have to make to a municipal sports facility (or your place of work) and its services in order to comply with the Disability Discrimination Act 1995.

19.7.3 Termination of contract

Two types of employment termination are subject to legal proceedings and therefore to be avoided by managers – wrongful dismissal and unfair dismissal. Wrongful dismissal occurs where employment is terminated contrary to the terms of the contract. It typically occurs where an employee has suffered unjustified, quick dismissal. If an employer follows the relevant notice period they will defeat a claim for wrongful dismissal. Also, if an employer can show that the employee was guilty of a fundamental breach of the contract of employment (such as gross misconduct) they will be able to dismiss an employee without providing a notice period.

In order to pursue a claim for unfair dismissal in the UK, an employee must typically have been employed in the job for at least one year. The legislation (Employment Rights Act 1996) provides for potentially fair reasons for dismissing an employee, such as their qualifications, their conduct, redundancy or reaching the default retirement age. It also provides details of reasons for dismissal that would automatically be judged as unfair. These include dismissal due to pregnancy or illness, dismissal due to trade union membership, to unfair selection for redundancy and also where an employee makes a protected public interest disclosure, i.e. a whistleblower. This list is not exhaustive and is considered so serious that the usual one-year employment qualification period to bring a claim for unfair dismissal is not applied.

In the event of a disciplinary process in the UK, it is important that the parties follow guidelines produced by the Advisory, Conciliation and Arbitration Service (ACAS) (see 'Useful websites', p. 533), which although not law are nevertheless recommended, and in the event that these are not followed it may lead to a higher award of compensation. The guidelines include the following principles:

- Raise issues quickly and promptly and ensure no unreasonable delays.
- The employer must carry out a reasonable investigation to ascertain the facts.
- The employer should afford the employee the opportunity to respond to concerns before any decision is taken.
- The employee should be allowed to be accompanied to any hearing by a trade union representative or work colleague.
- The right of appeal should be offered.

The onus is always on the employer to demonstrate that they have acted fairly and reasonably in dismissing the employee so, for instance, if others have committed the same offence, have they been dismissed? If an employer breaches a fundamental of the contract that causes the employee to resign, then that employee may also bring a claim for unfair constructive dismissal. This is designed to prevent the employer from seeking a way around the legislation by not dismissing the employee. Such reasons may include unilaterally reducing pay, failing to investigate allegations of sexual harassment, engaging in harassment or applying a disciplinary sanction out of all proportion to the offence. Where an employee has been unfairly dismissed or unfairly constructively dismissed there are three possible remedies:

1 reinstatement in the same job;
2 re-engagement in a comparable position in terms of salary, seniority, etc.;
3 compensation – factors looked at to calculate the compensation will include the age of the employee, length of service and salary; additional factors which may be included in any award might be possible overtime losses, pension losses or losses accrued by the employee seeking alternative employment.

19.8 Risk management: health and safety

Anyone involved in providing trips away, particularly with young people, will be familiar with the need for a risk assessment. It is important that any risks are identified and then managed if necessary. The statutory framework relating to risk management and health and safety at work in the UK is for the most part covered by the Management of Health and Safety at Work Regulations (MHSW) 1999 and the Health and Safety at Work etc. Act 1974. The MHSW 1999 states:

(1) Every employer shall make a suitable and sufficient assessment of –

(a) the risks to the health and safety of his employees to which they are exposed whilst they are at work; and
(b) the risks to the health and safety of persons not in his employment arising out of or in connection with the conduct by him of his undertaking {...}

(2) Every self-employed person shall make a suitable and sufficient assessment of –

(a) the risks to his own health and safety to which he is exposed whilst he is at work; and
(b) the risks to the health and safety of persons not in his employment arising out of or in connection with the conduct by him of his undertaking.

(the Management of Health and Safety at Work Regulations 1999, section 3)

It is therefore necessary for all employers and self-employed individuals to carry out a formal risk assessment covering both their employees and others who may be affected by what they do. The regulations pay specific attention to the position of young people within the workplace – particularly relevant for those working in the sport and leisure industry. The regulations make it very clear that an employer must not employ a young person unless a review or assessment of relevant material has been made. Particular account should be taken of:

- the inexperience, lack of awareness of risks and immaturity of young persons;
- the fitting-out and layout of the workplace and the workstation;
- the nature, degree and duration of exposure to physical, biological and chemical agents;
- the form, range, and use of work equipment and the way in which it is handled;
- the organisation of processes and activities;
- the extent of the health and safety training provided or to be provided to young persons;
- risks from agents, processes and work listed in the Annex to Council Directive 94/33/EC[8] on the protection of young people at work.

19.8.1 Health and Safety at Work etc. Act 1974

The Health and Safety at Work etc. Act 1974 lays out broad principles rather than specific requirements for both employers and employees in the UK. The most relevant sections of the Act are detailed below:

- **Section 1: Preliminary** – this section stresses the duty of employers to ensure the broad provisions that the health and safety of all people are protected from risks connected with the activities of people at work and, further, that dangerous substances are kept and used in a controlled manner. Section 1(1) of the Act specifically states:

  (1) The provisions of this Part shall have effect with a view to –

    (a) securing the health, safety and welfare of persons at work;
    (b) protecting persons other than persons at work against risks to health or safety arising out of or in connection with the activities of persons at work;
    (c) controlling the keeping and use of explosive or highly flammable or otherwise dangerous substances, and generally preventing the unlawful acquisition, possession and use of such substances.

- **Section 2: General duties of employers to their employees** – this section looks at the general duties of the employer to ensure as far as is reasonably practicable the health, safety and welfare of all employees, paying particular reference to the provision and maintenance of systems of work, the provision of training and supervision, and that a reasonably safe work environment is maintained. The section then goes on to detail the necessity to maintain and revise procedures as appropriate, to bring these updates to the notice of the workforce, and to consult with trade unions or other employee representatives when making and maintaining arrangements to ensure health and safety at work.
- **Section 3: General duties of employers and self-employed to persons other than their employees** – again there is a generic duty, as far as is reasonably practicable for employers and the self-employed, to ensure that persons other than employees (such as visitors and/or customers) are not exposed to risks to their health and safety. Further, both employers and the self-employed should furnish persons (other than their employees) with the information about how the business is conducted which might affect their health or safety.

● **Section 4: General duties of persons concerned with premises to persons other than their employees** – this section places a duty upon employers to ensure that their premises and equipment within those premises are as safe as is reasonably practicable.

The Act also deals with the duty imposed upon employees whilst at their place of work. It includes:

● **Section 7: General duties of employees at work**

It shall be the duty of every employee while at work –

(a) to take reasonable care for the health and safety of himself and of other persons who may be affected by his acts or omissions at work; and

(b) as regards any duty or requirement imposed on his employer or any other person by or under any of the relevant statutory provisions, to cooperate with him so far as is necessary to enable that duty or requirement to be performed or complied with.

Whilst the broad provisions of the Act may appear quite daunting, it is worth reiterating that the starting point for any risk management policy is that organisations must do all that is 'reasonably practicable' to protect people from risk. It is a legal requirement that employers look at any risks that may arise in the workplace and then control them by installing 'sensible health and safety measures'. It is not necessary to eliminate all risks, and for those in the sport and leisure industry this is particularly important as many activities linked to the industry by their nature carry risk; and if all such risk was to be eliminated then the nature of the activity would be destroyed. For example, a walking trip may be perfectly safe to engage in during the summer months but may become dangerous, depending upon location and weather conditions, during the winter. Similarly, whilst a kayaking trip across a small lake may be perfectly safe, a proper risk assessment may not come to the same conclusion about a similar trip across a much bigger lake or on coastal waters.

It is not the purpose of this section of the chapter to produce a scaremongering catalogue of various disasters that have befallen sections of the sport and leisure industry in this area. Rather, it is to point the reader in the direction of sound sensible advice in interpretation of the Act. With a little effort, this can help produce reasonable policies which will fulfil the legal and moral requirements placed on organisations to maintain safety for all at work, whilst at the same time retaining the central character of their business and the activities their business provides. Whilst all leisure providers have a duty to provide an appropriate risk assessment, it is worth pointing out that a failure to provide such an assessment will not by itself indicate a breach of duty on the part of a provider. In *Poppleton v. Trustees of Portsmouth Youth Activities* (2008), the claimant failed to establish liability against an activity centre which provided indoor low level climbing facilities. The claimant (an inexperienced climber) leapt from one wall and attempted to grab a buttress on another wall. He failed and fell awkwardly onto the matting below, breaking his neck and suffering permanent tetraplegia. Despite the fact that the defendants had failed to carry out a risk assessment, had provided no supervision and had not given the claimant any explanation of the risks, it was held that there was no breach of duty. The risk of injury from such a fall was an obvious and inherent risk of the activity. The Court stated:

The risk of possibly severe injury from an awkward fall was obvious and did not sustain a duty in the appellants to warn Mr Poppleton (the claimant) of it.

This is a very reassuring decision (not least given the failure to carry out a risk assessment) for all activity providers worried about the threat of legal liability. What this case and two subsequent cases (*Parker v. Tui Ltd*, 2009, and *Uren v. Corporate Leisure (UK) Ltd & Ministry of Defence*, 2010) emphasise is that there is risk involved in many activities and that it would be unjust, where an obvious or inherent risk manifests itself, to impose an overly burdensome legal duty upon activity providers; individuals must take care of their own behaviour.

19.8.2 Risk assessment guidance

The UK Health and Safety Executive (HSE), produce numerous very helpful leaflets detailing advice to organisations carrying out risk assessments (see 'Useful websites' p. 533). A central part of good risk management is effective risk assessment, defined thus by the HSE:

> A risk assessment is simply a careful examination of what, in your work, could cause harm to people, so that you can weigh up whether you have taken enough precautions or should do more to prevent harm. Workers and others have a right to be protected from harm caused by a failure to take reasonable control measures.

Whilst there are many ways of conducting risk assessments, the HSE very helpfully has produced a guide to conducting such assessments. It would be sensible for anyone working in the sport and leisure industry in the UK to follow the guidance laid down. The HSE identifies five distinct steps in the process. These are:

1 **Identify the hazards** – simply by walking around the workplace it is possible to identify what may reasonably be expected to cause harm. Consultation with employees will further enhance this identification. Other practical methods may involve contacting the HSE and any relevant trade association.
2 **Decide who might be harmed and how** – it is important to recognise that particular groups of people (such as expectant mothers, members of the public, people with disabilities and new workers) may have particular needs with regard to some risks. Similarly, people in the workplace outside normal office hours, such as cleaners, contractors or shift workers, may have particular needs that need dealing with.
3 **Evaluate the risk and decide on precautions** – the legal requirement is to do all that is 'reasonably practicable' to deal with a risk. It is not to eliminate all possible risks. The most sensible action to take is to try and comply with standard industry practice, paying particular attention to procedures followed, equipment used, warnings provided and welfare facilities provided. Again it is important to discuss issues with staff and involve them in any proposals or procedures you intend putting in place.
4 **Record your findings and implement them** – if an organisation has fewer than five employees there is no legal obligation to record findings. However, if any employer is serious about following good practice this is really something they should do. The HSE has examples of good practice that can be downloaded, but essentially an employer must be able to demonstrate five things:
   – that a proper check was made;
   – that the employer enquired about who might be affected;
   – that obvious hazards were dealt with and the number of people who might be affected by such hazards was taken into account (the more people who may be affected and the greater the consequences of the hazard, the greater the obligation to deal with it;

- that reasonable precautions were taken and any risk remaining is low;
- that staff (or their representatives) were properly involved in the process.

5 **Review your assessment and update if necessary** – it is recommended that a formal review takes place annually but that informally there is constant monitoring so as to ensure that any new staff, procedures or practices are fully embedded into the risk assessment procedure. The HSE concludes on this matter as follows:

> During the year, if there is a significant change, don't wait: check your risk assessment and where necessary amend it. If possible, it is best to think about the risk assessment when you're planning your change – that way you leave yourself more flexibility.

There should be a proper system of monitoring and updating – it is far preferable to set a date in the calendar for a formal update rather than wait until an incident requires attention. Whilst formal updates are important, remaining watchful and listening to employees plays a vital role in the process.

The HSE provides a clear summary of the overall responsibilities of both the employer and the employee when dealing with these matters (see 'Useful websites', p. 533); and also information on who to contact if problems arise in this area. If the guidelines produced by the HSE are followed there should be no need at all for sport and leisure providers to have any fear of legal liability stemming from an accident in their business. Sound risk assessments and coherent risk management policies play a vital part in the industry. Through such means good practice is encouraged, which in turn ensures that findings of liability in the event of accidents are unlikely. More importantly, they enable people to enjoy the benefits of all that the industry has to offer whilst being able to experience the ordinary risks of an activity but not being vulnerable to unreasonable risk.

19.9 Conclusions

How the law relates to sport and leisure is a vast area and this chapter has really just touched the tip of the iceberg. It has concentrated on some of the most significant issues. The recurring theme through much of the detail covered in this chapter is that if providers behave reasonably they are unlikely to find themselves on the wrong side of the law. The emphasis for anyone involved in these industries should not be merely to ensure that their behaviour, policies and practices are designed so that they do not find themselves being held liable for injuries suffered by another. Rather, they should ensure that safety is designed into all that they do, so that unnecessary danger is prevented or alleviated. This will, of course, have the effect of ensuring that they are not legally liable, but the emphasis remains on safety for the user rather than merely preventing liability.

If such an approach remains the focus for all involved in the area of sport, leisure and recreation, this will enable people to remain safe while at the same time providers will not be inhibited. The appropriate level of risk will be managed and, crucially, maintained if the nature of the activity demands it. The courts are not in the grip of a 'compensation culture' or 'health and safety mania'. The issues raised in relation to such concerns are necessarily one part of a much wider picture the courts must take into account in any case that comes before them. This can perhaps best be summed up by Lord Hoffman, who as long ago as 2003 commented:

> It is of course understandable that organisations like the Royal Society for the Prevention of Accidents should favour policies which require people to be prevented

from taking risks. Their function is to prevent accidents and that is one way of doing so. But they do not have to consider the cost, not only in money but also in deprivation of liberty, which such restrictions entail. The courts will naturally respect the technical expertise of such organisations in drawing attention to what can be done to prevent accidents. But the balance between risk on the one hand and individual autonomy on the other is not a matter of expert opinion. It is a judgment which the courts must make and which in England reflects the individualist values of the common law.

(*Tomlinson v. Congleton Borough Council* 2003, para. 47)

Practical tasks

1 Read the Australian case found at www.lexisnexis.com.au/aus/academic/text_updater/luntz_hambly/186_alr_145.pdf. What safety measures would need to be taken in England in a similar situation to prevent legal liability in the event of an injury to a spectator, a participant and a trespasser?

2 For a single trip for a club that you know (e.g. to an away match, to an event, to a concert) conduct a risk assessment, with reference to the HSE guidelines (see pp. 530–1). When it is completed, think of an accident that may happen to one of the club's members during this trip, and evaluate the legal implications of this accident.

Structured guide to further reading

For the structure of courts and judicial precedent:
Fafinski, S. and Finch, E. (2007) *Legal Skills*, Oxford University Press, Oxford.

For general principles of negligence:
Deakin, S., Johnston, A. and Markesinis, B. (2007) *Markesinis and Deakin's Tort Law*, 6th edition, Oxford University Press, Oxford.

For general principles of torts:
Harpwood, V. (2009) *Modern Tort Law*, 7th edition, Routledge Cavendish, London.

For legal guidance on working with children:
HM Government (2006) *Working Together to Safeguard Children: a guide to inter-agency working to safeguard and promote the welfare of children*, The Stationery Office, London.

For employment law issues:
Taylor, S. and Emir, A. (2009) *Employment Law: an introduction*, 2nd edition, Oxford University Press, Oxford.

For a pocket guide on health and safety law:
HSE (2009) *Health and Safety Law: what you need to know*, HSE, London.

Useful websites

For guidance on legal abbreviations:
http://learnmore.lawbore.net/index.php/Understand_Legal_Abbreviations

For case comment on *Caldwell v. MaGuire & Fitzgerald*:
http://digitalcommons.shu.ac.uk/cgi/viewcontent.cgi?article=1007&context=lrg_papers

For guidance on the legal framework for working with children in the UK:
www.dcsf.gov.uk/everychildmatters/resources-and-practice/IG00060/

For the Independent Safeguarding Authority (ISA) and the Vetting and Barring Scheme:
www.isa-gov.org.uk

For Advisory, Conciliation and Arbitration Service (ACAS) guidelines on disciplinary process:
www.acas.org.uk/

For Health and Safety Executive guidance on risk assessment:
www.hse.gov.uk/risk/fivesteps.htm

Cases

Vicarious liability:
Beard v. London General Omnibus Co. (1900) 2 QB 530
Gravil v. Carroll & Anor (2008) EWCA CIV 689
Limpus v. London General Omnibus Co (1862) 1 H & C 526
Lister v. Hesley Hall (2002) AC 215
Hawley v. Luminar Leisure plc (2005] EWHC 5 (QB)

Sports/recreation specific negligence:
Caldwell v. MaGuire & Fitzgerald (2001) EWCA Civ 1054
Parker v. Tui Ltd [2009] EWCA Civ 1261
Poppleton v. Trustees of Portsmouth Youth Activities [2008] EWCA Civ 646
Uren v. Corporate Leisure (UK) Ltd & Ministry of Defence [2010] EWHC 46 (QB)
Watson v. BBBC (2001) Q.B. 1134

School sport negligence:
Mountford v. Newlands School (2007) EWCA Civ 21
A (a minor) v. Leeds CC (1999) CLY 3977
Moore v. Hampshire CC (1982) 80 LGR 481
Babbings v. Kirklees Metropolitan Council (2004) EWCA Civ 1431

Occupiers liability:
Bolton v. Stone (1951) A.C. 850 HL
Cunningham & Others v. Reading Football Club Ltd, *The Times*, 22 March 1991 (HC)
Ratcliff v. McConnell (1999) 1 WLR 670
Simms v. Leigh Rugby Football Club Ltd (1969) 2 All ER 923
Tomlinson v. Congleton Borough Council (2003) UKHL 47
Wattleworth v. Goodwood Road Racing Company Ltd (2004) EWHC 140

Discrimination:
Panesar v. Nestle Ltd (1980) ICR 144

Legislation

Children's Act 1989
Compensation Act 2006
Employment Act 2002
Employment Rights Act 1996
Health and Safety at Work etc. Act 1974
Management of Health and Safety at Work Regulations 1999
Occupiers Liability Act 1957
Occupiers Liability Act 1984
Protection of Children Act 1999
Safeguarding Vulnerable Groups Act 2006

The importance and management of events

Guy Masterman

In this chapter

- Why are events important?
- Who are the key stakeholders for events?
- What are the short-term and long-term objectives for events?
- What are the different stages of the event planning process?
- What are the requirements for the successful planning of an event?

C. Brandon/Getty Images

Summary

The extent to which events impact on and affect peoples' lives is something that is not easily measured; but it is clear that throughout history events have been readily recorded as marks in time and as catalysts for great changes in society. At the other end of the scale, it is difficult to imagine a week going by without an event that an individual relates to and takes note of. Events of all scales are important throughout societies. In analysis they can be seen to be tools for the achievement of socio-cultural, economic, environmental and political objectives. They are also used to develop participation and competition in sport, art, music, dance, business and politics. In other words they touch all aspects of society and an event can be an agenda for the achievement of as wide an influence as is imaginable. The world's top events are now so important they are much sought after and bid for.

A successful approach to planning an event is a logical, staged process that works from objectives at the outset, to evaluation of results followed by feedback at the end. However, it is continuous evaluation throughout the process via an iterative approach that will lead to success. If the objectives are used to devise a concept and strategies, there can be evaluation at every stage to ensure that planning can be aligned and realigned to what is intended and that opportunities can be exploited as they occur.

20.1 Introduction

An event can be a lot more than 'just a game' and, whatever its size, it can be of great importance to its community. This chapter will explain why and how this is the case. It is important to start with one key message and this is that events are fun. They are fun to watch, take part in and organise. Event management is not for everyone, but for those that aspire to it, the thrill of seeing a 'sold out' sign, the running-order working to time and planning that provides solutions to complex problems means more than being in the spotlight on the stage or pitch. Event management is a 'behind the scenes' role, and planning and then implementing an event that meets its objectives can be both a vocation and a one-off experience that can be thoroughly enjoyable.

This chapter will provide an overview of the job of organising events by considering how to plan and then implement them, whatever their size or location. First, though, it is important to set the scene and consider why events are important, what they are and what they can achieve.

20.2 What are events?

In the literature there are a number of differences in the definitions and terms used to identify events. A dictionary definition, for example, describes an event as a 'thing that takes place', a public or social occasion, or as a contest (*Oxford English Dictionary*, 2008). Event management literature uses a wider range of terms. An event is transient, has a fixed duration and is unique (Getz, 1997). It can also be planned or unplanned. One of the most famous examples of an unplanned event is an inter-trench football match between enemies who temporarily halted fighting in the First World War. There was very little preparation beforehand and yet in retrospect we can still analyse this happening as an event. When it comes to event management, though, we are clearly concerned with those events that are planned. Some refer to these as 'special events' (Allen *et al.*, 2005; Getz, 1997; Goldblatt, 1997).

Unfortunately, there is insufficient consistency when it comes to the use of terms such as 'major', 'mega' or 'hallmark' events. For some, the Olympic Games (see 'Useful websites', p. 559) is a 'hallmark' event (Goldblatt, 1997; Hall, 1992). For others it is a 'mega' event, while hallmark events are recurrent in a particular city, e.g. the Wimbledon tennis championships occur every year in London (Getz, 1997; Allen *et al.*, 2005). Some refer to hallmark events as sizeable, with wide-ranging target audiences, considerable media interest, including broadcasters, regional and perhaps national government stakeholders, commercial sector partners and superior technical competencies and human resources (Getz, 1997; Westerbeek *et al.*, 2006). On the other hand, mega events might be sizeable, with a 'dramatic character, mass appeal and international significance' (Roche, 2000).

The term 'sizeable' also offers some confusion. For an indoor concert an audience of 5,000 might seem small if it is a venue like Wembley Arena, where the capacity is 12,500, while 1,000 participants at a harvest festival in a local village might be deemed very welcome by that community. Less than 70,000 for a Manchester United home game would be a commercial concern as the Old Trafford 'Theatre of Dreams' holds over 76,000 and is regularly sold out. So, establishing some kind of audience and/or participant number as a threshold is not wholly adequate for definition purposes (Emery, 2002).

The model offered by Jago and Shaw (1998) does go some way to providing a relationship between major, hallmark and mega events. It at least includes all the terms mentioned above and in a structure that alludes to size and scale. See Figure 20.1 for a number of examples of major and minor events, mega and hallmark events.

Further classifications of events can identify that events cut across all aspects of society – culture, sport, politics and business – and of course may be indoor or outdoor, in purpose built or temporary venues, predominantly participatory or spectator led, and competitive or recreational. For example:

- **cultural events** – art exhibitions; stage plays; pop, rock, classical and operatic concerts; dance displays; food and drink shows; film festivals;
- **sports events** – single or multi-sport events in schools and clubs; regional, national and international competitions; local, regional and national programmes for sport participation development; frequent league and infrequent cup competition;
- **political events** – local and national party rallies, conferences and conventions; marches and demonstrations; inaugurations and ceremonies;
- **business events** – expos; networking symposiums; conferences; trade exhibitions; conventions; media and press launches; product launches, experiential marketing events and demonstrations; tourism expositions.

Local events have always been important. While there are those mega, hallmark and major events that many people are aware of, it is local events that arguably have most effect on peoples' lives. They have appeal because they are fun, entertaining, possibly adventurous and glamorous. They can involve and integrate diverse communities, increase

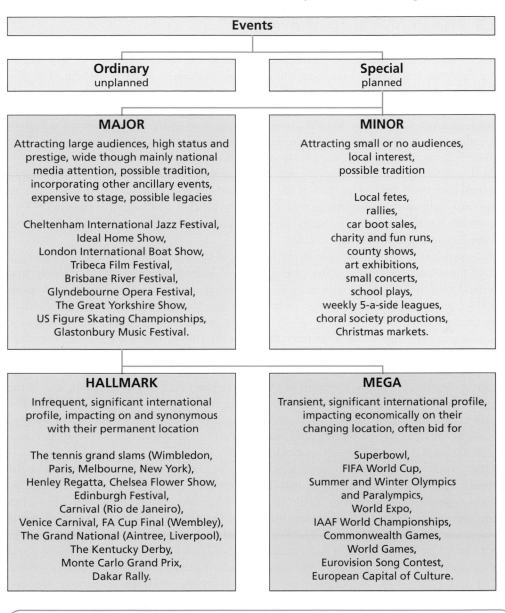

Figure 20.1 A definition for events.
Source: adapted from Jago and Shaw (1998).

awareness and promote all kinds of organisations and their objectives. Some attract 'A' list performers and others the more locally famous 'C' list, but they can also display the talents of beginners and local expertise. Consequently they are an important part of leisure and recreation programmes and as such an increasing importance is being placed on their organisation and the development of skills and competence in event management at this level.

20.3 The importance of events

Historically, events have played an important role in the development of society and in many cases key individuals have, sometimes against all odds, created something of significance from the smallest of beginnings. People have always celebrated or marked special occasions such as birthdays, deaths, anniversaries, moons, solstices and seasons; and through folklore some of the festivals, ceremonies, competitions and exhibitions we celebrate today were derived hundreds, even thousands, of years ago. In this way, events have been derivatives of society that have evolved into society-shaping agents.

In Ancient Greece events were of such importance that there were truces from war to accommodate them, and as recently as the First World War a game of football was able to temporarily halt warfare between enemies. It is reported that on Christmas Day in 1914 an inter-trench football match was contested and, while reports are varied, this feat has now become legend (Bancroft-Hinchley, 2000).

Religions have played a big role in the creation of the events that are now a traditional part of many societies and in some cases they have become so widely encompassing that they have become integrated with a wider culture that incorporates art, music and sport. The Olympics today are a celebration of sport but also dance, music and art. The Ancient Jews celebrated 82 sacred days, of which 59 were holidays from work, and to organise special events they appointed event managers with the title of director of the feast (Smith, 1831). More recently other church groups have played a role in developing sport. For example, basketball was originally a recreational game created at a New England School for Christian Workers by James Naismith in 1891 (Basketball Hall of Fame, 2003), and in the UK some of the earliest football clubs and teams were formed out of church groups. The Parish of St Domingo's Church in Liverpool founded a team that went on to become Everton FC in 1879 and, in Birmingham, Aston Villa FC was founded in 1874 by the Parish of Villa Cross Wesleyan Chapel (Masterman, 2009).

Other traditions have mixed derivations, some religious but also political, and what has evolved are events that are deeply rooted in culture: May Day and Hogmanay in the UK, Home Coming and Thanksgiving in the US and Independence Days throughout the world. Many individuals have risked all in their pursuit for their beliefs and some have used events as the catalyst for success. Tom Waddell is credited with having conceived the idea of the Gay Games first held in 1982 in San Francisco. The Glyndebourne Festival is now a world leading operatic event as a result of the efforts of John Christie and his wife Audrey following its opening in 1934. The Glastonbury Festival is an internationally famous rock music event dreamed up by Michael Eavis and started in 1970 on his own land (see 'Useful websites', p. 559). These varied examples demonstrate that society has been influenced by individuals and their creation and implementation of events. The previous edition of this book rightly refers to such events as landmarks of history.

Contemporary events touch all our lives. Events are both derivatives of as well as shapers of society. All scales of events are influenced politically, if only because there is a fundamental requirement to conform to laws and regulations for health and safety, employment, fiscal reporting and licensing. There are also political events such as rallies, congresses and, of course, marches. The opinion polls for prime ministers have been seen to increase at the time of successful events, such as in France in 1998 during the FIFA World Cup. Equally, if politicians get it wrong the reverse can happen, and the Millennium Dome in London and its construction delays, the mismanagement of the 2000 New Year celebrations and its initial lack of positive legacy were a negative for the UK government at the time.

The development of technology and events are interrelated. The development of materials for sports equipment such as rackets and balls, digital timing and sophisticated call centre operations for ticket selling are all intrinsically involved in the growth and development of sport events (Masterman, 2009). In 2008, technology was a contentious intervention for South African double-amputee sprinter Oscar Pistorius when he was not allowed to use his carbon fibre prosthetics in races as they were deemed to be technically giving him an illegal advantage by the International Association of Athletics Federations (Robinson, 2008). Pyrotechnics almost appear to be standard at many events, and fireworks, once used as enhancements for events, are now the focus of some. The Boston Harbor 4 July fireworks celebrations in the US are a spectacle that enthrals thousands of residents as well as visitors. Television, as an informer and broadcaster of events, also plays an ever-increasing role, as do the internet and now mobile and wireless communications. These media not only provide wide, sometimes global audiences, they are also available 24 hours a day as promotion tools and sales outlets, and as such enhance events while also providing important communications for society at large.

The development of the arts, music, dance and sport relies on the showcases that events supply. The more people who watch events, the greater is the opportunity for spectating and participation to increase. Events that invite participation, such as club open days, coaching workshops, summer schools and taster sessions, are direct approaches intent on widening participation. Events are therefore potentially significant development tools. However, it is important to recognise that for development to be sustainable there need to be strategies in place that follow up on initial participation. An 'open day' approach, for example, can lead to a number of people turning up to play a sport, try out theatre, appreciate art or play an instrument, but these events will need to be supported by strategies that ensure that these fresh recruits stay interested in the longer term. Nevertheless, events are important to society as developers of new ways to 'get involved'.

20.4 Event owners, promoters and managers

The requirement for excellence in events management is increasing, from audiences and participants as well as organisers. While larger events are organised by promoters, governing bodies and combinations of agencies that may be well trained and experienced, local events are controlled by leisure managers, facility and venue managers and often many volunteers, who may well be organising an event that lies outside their usual remit. Event owners are not always the organisers of their own events. Event management organisations, agencies and promoters can be brought in to run one-off events. Events can also be an integral part of a larger programme, where there may be any number of event organisations staging constituent events that may or may not require close collaboration. This happens a lot in sport, where there are local, regional and then national phases to competitions, particularly at school and club level. A typical format is to progress from local to regional to national rounds of competition. Stokesley FC's Under-13 football team, for example, progressed through district, county and regional competition to become national champions and then went on to beat their counterparts from Scotland, Northern Ireland and Wales to be UK Champions in the 2008–9 season. At international level the Association of Tennis Professionals (ATP Tour) and European PGA (golf) operate their tours in a similar way, whereby their year-long programmes consist of different events in cities throughout the world.

Generally each event has a different promoter, although there are some well-established and sizeable organisations such as International Management Group (IMG) that have bid for and won the right to promote several tennis and golf events on the respective tours (see 'Useful websites', p. 559). On the other hand, there are many independent promoters that prefer to keep their stable of events small, such as Ion Tiriac and partners, the organisers of the Madrid Masters. While a rock band can also take in a large number of cities, music tours generally consist of daily concerts over an intensive period of a month or two. Bruce Springsteen and his E Street Band toured in 2009, taking in dates in the US, UK, Italy, Spain, the Netherlands, Finland, Sweden, Norway, Switzerland, Germany, Ireland and Austria. Another difference here to the sports model is that music tours are generally organised by one promoter, but that does not prevent collaboration with others. During his six-week-long Working on a Dream tour, Springsteen also accepted dates at other promoted events, including Glastonbury in the UK, where he headlined. On the other hand, theatre tours are more usually organised by one promoter and involve longer stays at each venue. For example,the West End show *Joseph and His Amazing Technicolour Dreamcoat* and a recent UK TV phenomenon, *Britain's Got Talent*, both toured throughout 2008–9, performing in UK regional theatres and arenas respectively.

Event owners can also be promoters. Nova International owns and organises the Great North Run, the world famous half-marathon in the north-east of England; it has also rolled out a whole series of 'Great Runs' across the UK as well as abroad (see 'Useful websites', p. 559). Manchester and Sheffield City Councils in the UK both have event departments that own and manage events as well as spending considerable time actively attracting other owners and promoters to their cities. Nova International, for example, worked closely with Manchester City Council's Event Department in staging a 'Great Run' and in 2009 also laid a special 60 metre track on Deansgate, the main shopping street in the city, for a televised race that featured world 100 metres record holder Usain Bolt.

Governments, regional or local municipal authorities, educational institutions, clubs and commercial promoters can all independently own and/or stage events. If these are sports events, they will generally be required to run them according to prescribed rules, which might also require a more complex process of applying for official sanction from a governing body. Events can also involve more sophisticated management arrangements. Host cities, supported by collaborative organising groups made up of a number of partners and stakeholders, can bid to run an event by applying to event rights owners. Sheffield City Council's Event Unit has staged over 600 events since its inception in 1991 following its hosting of the World Student Games, for example, including many that it has had to bid for with a number of different partners.

Many major international events are bid for by organising groups that may consist of the city authority, regional development agencies, national governing bodies, commercial supporters and national government. These events can have significant impact and in the main are sports related. In Australia and the USA the model is based on State departments. Sport and Recreation Victoria, for example, is driven by a keen strategy that sees Melbourne regularly hosting the Australian F1 Grand Prix, International Air Show and the Australian Open (tennis), and has also bid for and hosted the 2006 Commonwealth Games and 2003 Rugby World Cup matches. The State of Utah, having hosted the 2002 Winter Olympics in Salt Lake City, also has a state-driven strategy and a focus on it becoming the USA 'state for sport' (Masterman, 2009). The growing importance of major events of all types is being increasingly recognised by municipal authorities and this is highlighted by the emergence of city and state departments such as these.

On a smaller scale, all schools, colleges and universities organise sports events for intramural as well as inter-institution competition, but they also organise exhibitions and conferences with a focus on showing off student and staff talent. Hence they are organisers of exhibitions for art, fashion and design, music concerts, plays and conferences for knowledge transfer. These events can be credit bearing in support of educational programmes but they can also be staged to attract research income, business and students. They can be to show parents what is being learned.

Other institutions and organisations have also recognised the importance of having event-led strategies. Fast moving consumer goods manufacturers have seen how events can increase product awareness and sales. For example, a number of drinks companies have associated themselves with or owned events, such as Coca-Cola and its Music Festival; Pepsi's lifestyle show Extravaganza; Red Bull's Air Race; and Guinness' Witnness music festival.

Whatever the size of the event, the volunteers can be critical. The use of 100,000 volunteers is becoming the norm for a Summer Olympics, with the organisers of the 2012 London Olympics seeking as many as Beijing did in 2008. However, the input from volunteers in the organisation of many local events is no less critical. Certainly in sport it is the volunteers who run the clubs, leagues and associations that ensure that players can take part. It is estimated that there are over six million volunteers in sport in the UK alone (Volunteering England, 2009). However, this is also true of other recreations and their provision of events. Local arts, music and drama societies provide entertainment for their communities with exhibitions, concerts, plays and pantomimes throughout the UK, with sometimes only a handful of members multi-tasking to ensure successful events.

20.5 The purpose of events

The key to minimising negative impacts and achieving potential positive impacts is in the effective planning of the event (Masterman, 2009). In order to plan an event, therefore, an event manager needs to work towards specified objectives. The following criteria form a broad set of purposes for staging events, many of which are interrelated.

20.5.1 Socio-cultural objectives

Events can be culturally and socially beneficial. First, they can be fun to attend, participate in and organise, and in this sense they will meet various individual personal needs. Because they are fun and can satisfactorily meet a number of values held by individuals, they can be readily undertaken and they are useful tools for society to use as conduits for social inclusion, cohesion and compliance. So events can bring those of different religion, race, age and sexual persuasion together. They can also be used to integrate these various sectors for a more harmonious society.

Equally, events are also perceived to provide opportunities for those members of society who might step outside the law and as such are seen to provide them with more acceptable activities. Harlem, in New York, is known for its efforts in this vein, with a number of boxing and other sports clubs founded. Events such as the Rucker Basketball Tournament, for example, founded by Holcombe Rucker, were created to inspire Harlem youths and provide them with 'discipline, dedication and teamwork' (Williams and Rivers, 2006). In 2009 the Aero Space Gym put on a Focus Mitt Boxing Championship featuring boxing champions and celebrities to aid East Harlem School to provide more opportunities for its pupils (NY 1, 2009).

The period leading up to an event as well as the event itself can be used to effectively widen the effect of such socio-cultural strategies. In general the International Olympic Committee

(IOC) recognises the importance of widening the Olympics and its sports focus so that it can impact right across society. For example, it regards a cultural programme as an 'essential element of the celebration of the Olympic Games', and therefore it is a requirement of a host city to provide one (Masterman, 2009). Salt Lake City, for example, provided an Arts Festival that included 60 performances, 10 major exhibitions and 50 community projects, again supported by Coca-Cola (Masterman, 2009; Salt Lake City, 2002).

20.5.2 Political objectives

Events of all sizes can be used politically. First, events can be used at a macro level, whereby party political objectives can be achieved. Also at a macro level there are examples of events that have been used to extol the benefits and values of certain political ideals. The gaining of worldwide recognition via 'mega event politics', and in particular via measurable economic gain via tourism and inward investment, is a fast emerging political strategy (Hall, 2001; Preuss, 2004). Barcelona is a much cited example of a city that used its 1992 Olympics to benefit over the long term (an example that we examine on p. 547 under economic objectives). It is claimed that the the city's main objective was to develop a profile for the city and the Catalan region that might compete with the Spanish capital, Madrid (Roche, 2000). Beijing also used its 2008 'Peoples Olympics' as a means of informing the world about Chinese culture and there are other controversial examples of nations attempting to develop national and cultural identity via political manipulation focused on the Olympics. In particular, Soviet and East German approaches in their use of sport as a political tool in the mid-twentieth century have been well documented.

Cultural events can also be used for diplomatic objectives. Orchestras, for example, have been the focus of 'soft diplomacy' for some time (Higgins, 2009) (see Case Study 20.1).

Discussion question

To what extent can or should events be apolitical? Discuss this in relation to one or more events you are familiar with.

20.5.3 Development objectives

An event is a showcase and can be used to widen awareness of the arts, music, sport, dance, a political idea or a commercial product, with the intention of widening participation and/ or increased support and interest. The latter may be to increase numbers of fans and followers generally, and numbers of paying spectators or members specifically. The 'come play an instrument' approach is a simple concept and the Peoples Music School, Chicago, founded in 1976 by Rita Sino, is a master of it. The school gives opportunities to young people of all financial backgrounds by providing free tuition and also puts on its own Street Festival. 'Come try art' is also a simple but effective idea and can involve adults and children alike. In Brisbane, Australia, drawing workshops are staged in the street by city agencies, with the objective of getting people to participate in art.

While all sports events can be used to promote the sports involved, newly created events can also be used for specific purposes. Following the lead of London and the founding of its Youth Games in the 1980s, there are now county Youth Games throughout the country

CASE STUDY 20.1

The diplomatic use of the arts

The use of music, artists and orchestras for political gain is not new; for example, it is more than fifty years since a Western orchestra, the New York Philharmonic, was taken to the former Soviet Union. While it might not be that clear, there is no doubt that a touring orchestra can be used in a 'soft' diplomatic approach where hardline international political relations are not as subtle or successful. The appeal is that orchestras and other artists are harmless and their art is their passport to a country even when relations are aggressive (Higgins, 2009). Art forms such as orchestras can be very good tools for diplomacy. An artistic tour can be seen as a sign that there is still room for a better relationship on a political front.

Recently there have been some quite sophisticated examples. The Royal Ballet has performed in Beijing's National Centre for the Performing Arts, adjacent to Tiananmen Square. The invitation to China, where dance culture is quite different, and to a particular area of the city that is perceived in the West to be steeped in controversial human rights issues, is meaningful. The tour is unlikely to have had an immediate effect on relations but as a part of a long-term strategy it might be an important step. On the other hand, the message is clearer from the West-Eastern Divan Orchestra, which features both Arab and Israeli musicians.

The beauty of this kind of implementation is that it can be mutually acceptable because both sides want it to happen. Cuba, for example, invited both the New York Philharmonic Orchestra and the Royal Ballet to perform in the capital Havana in 2009. This was a significant move, virtually unprecedented since Cuba became a communist state in 1959. It is perceived that in offering this invitation Cuba indicated its desire to develop positive relations with both the USA and the UK. The invitation might have been refused of course, but in this case President Obama lifted the forty-year-old embargo on Cuba to allow the visit of the orchestra. The visit of the Royal Ballet to Cuba is the first by such a company since the Bolshoi Ballet visited from the Eastern Bloc almost thirty years ago (Carroll, 2009).

The objective is not always to smooth the political waters; it might also be a more hostile threat that can be imposed. The Ossetian born conductor Valery Gergiev, a good friend of Russian President Vladimir Putin, was carefully selected to take a Russian orchestra to South Ossetia in 2008 at a time when the region was troublesome for the Russian government. While this was a selection that showed a willingness to work together, the choice of music was also significant – it included Shostakovich's 7th Symphony, a composition that relates the story of the siege of Leningrad (Higgins, 2009).

that are designed to get non-playing youngsters into sport as well as promote competition for those who are already participating (see Case Study 20.2).

20.5.4 Economic objectives

Commercial firms from the manufacturing and service sectors are not the only organisations that might derive revenue from an event. Cause-related events are designed to deliver funds for charities, and promoters of music, dance and sports events are typically intent on

The North Yorkshire Youth Games

The North Yorkshire Youth Games, run by North Yorkshire Sport (NYS), the County Sports Partnership, has been an annual event since 2000 and since 2005 has been staged at Ampleforth College. For its tenth anniversary in 2009, NYS managed to secure critical funding from a new sponsor, Leeds Trinity & All Saints College. While the culmination is one day in August for teams and young sportsmen and women of all school ages, the event as a whole is something that stretches over the entire year. Teams represent the eight local community sports networks in the county of North Yorkshire in boccia, kurling, rugby league and union, swimming, orienteering, cross-country, athletics, cheerleading, football, hockey, kwik cricket, netball, tennis and gymnastics. To reach the finals at the Games they compete in leagues and knock-out competitions throughout the year within their districts.

The aim of the Games is to develop and sustain participation and competition in sport. Many of the sports governing bodies are involved via their regional offices in the administration and coaching that is required to improve performance and also to enthuse young athletes into sport. The key, though, is for this enthusiasm to be sustainable and for these athletes to carry on in sport after the Games. Of course, there is the ongoing opportunity to compete for as long as the young people are at school and therefore in as many Games as that allows, but the critical factor is ensuring that they participate after they are eligible, in other words in out of school hours and once they have reached school leaving age. The dropout from sport at this latter stage of the life-cycle is of particular concern for Sport England.

NYS as a partnership consists of not only the local district councils but also the various school sports partnerships in the region and the national governing bodies with regional representation. This allows NYS to hold dialogue and build programmes with schools and sports clubs. It operates the Games to encompass both school and club teams in order to build the links so that the bridge for sport participation between schools and clubs can be created.

In addition to hosting 1,500 young people at the Games and the many more that compete throughout the year, NYS also supports this activity with a government-sponsored programme, Sport Unlimited, that provides investment which impacts on over 27,000 young sports people between the ages of 5 and 19.

Discussion question

How might the North Yorkshire Youth Games be commercially developed?

realising a profit. Event owners, whether they have development objectives or not, may also seek a profit so that funding may be raised to add to their overall development effort. Small as well as large events can be designed for economic objectives and while events can be used as loss leaders at the outset, the ultimate aim for all event managers is at least to break even. Most will seek a surplus, driven by a budget, whether the surplus is to be used for commercial or non-profit purposes.

While the event is a budget-driven project in itself, there is a further area of economic gain to be considered. For major, hallmark and mega events there is the critical importance of a wider economic impact. A negative impact on the economy can result in a lasting legacy that taxpayers have to bear. The cost of the 1976 Montreal Olympics and Sheffield's 1991 World Student Games, for example, have both been heavy and long-term financial burdens on those two cities. However, there can be a positive outcome via the attraction of inward investment prior to an event, event tourism during an event and then the 'image' gained from the event can be leveraged to attract business after the event is over (Preuss, 2004).

For example, Barcelona attracted sufficient inward investment to regenerate its water-front with infrastructure for its 1992 Olympics and has since further utilised the intial benefit in the long term for what is now a well-recognised positive legacy. The original Olympic zone is now a thriving resort area consisting of a marina, retail outlets and residential housing in what was once a rundown area. The city also claims to have increased its meetings, incentives, congresses and exhibitions (MICE) business as a result of its staging of the event. Prior to the Games, in 1990, there were 100,000 congress attendees, which grew to over 200,000 after the Games in 1996.

While sports events in particular are prominent media topics when it comes to reviewing economic legacies, there are other examples of cities gaining economic impacts from hosting cultural events. For example, the Eurovision Song Contest and the European Capital of Culture have been sought and used as economic catalysts. Helsinki's hosting of the Eurovision Song Contest in 2008 is claimed to have entertained 40,000 guests and generated €12.6 million, whereas Liverpool, as European Capital of Culture in 2008, used its event to help boost tourism numbers between 2002 and 2006 by 16 per cent and tourist expenditure by 24 per cent (Helsinki, 2008; Liverpool 2009a, 2009b). World Expo is a major event that has been sought for economic impact and Shanghai is intent on using its hosting of Expo 2010 not only to create new infrastructure and develop business but also to create links between its two key areas, which sit on opposite sides of the river: Puxi, the home of the famous skyscraper skyline, and Pudong, the more popular tourist area (Wasserstrom, 2009).

An issue with all economic impact studies of events is that they can only be perceived to deliver a positive legacy. While cities perceive there to be a possibility of developing their economies as a result of hosting major events, this is not universally accepted among academics. The scepticism derives from our lack of capacity to measure such benefits over the long term and then be assured that the impacts are undoubtedly as a result of staging an event (Jones, 2005).

20.5.5 Environmental objectives

Major events are recognised as having the potential to be catalysts for 'greening' regeneration and development projects. The Department of Environmental Affairs and Tourism in South Africa, for example, appointed the Environmental Evaluation Unit and Steadfast Greening to provide greening guidelines for large sporting events in 2009. In particular, the guidelines focused on the 2010 FIFA World Cup, but also considered the greening of other sporting events (EEU, 2009). Such initiatives are widely acknowledged as being initiated by the precedent set at the Sydney Olympic Games in 2000, where standards that addressed waste management and recycling as key contemporary issues for event managers were instigated (Allen *et al.*, 2005). Since then 'green' Games have been a controlled requirement for the IOC. For the Games in 2004, for example, Athens addressed waste management, water quality and air pollution and, for 2008, Beijing went to some effort with afforestation, air pollution prevention, recycling and water installation in particular (Masterman, 2009).

All events, whatever their size or location, have the potential and now responsibility to be greener. Even users of temporary venues for music concerts need to adopt good practice when it comes to waste disposal, sanitary utility provision and also the handing back of the site to owners in a state at least as good as before. Waste disposal is a constant activity for most events throughout their duration and in many cases it is a job that is outsourced.

An environmental issue that will prevail within the event industry is that of carbon footprint evaluation. Clearly many of the events used as examples in this chapter involve a lot of travel, worldwide tours and international events that attract the world's best performers, while tourists from around the globe require significant air travel. The dilemma here is that while technology such as television and internet broadcasting has allowed audiences to see events they cannot attend, all events are nevertheless successful because they are 'live' and the experience of attending an event is the main product on offer. There may therefore be continuing reluctance from event organisers to detract from that offer.

20.5.6 Regeneration objectives

There are benefits that can be gained by incorporating regeneration projects into event planning and the use of events as catalysts for the achievement of municipal objectives. An event that necessitates the development and utilisation of land that would have otherwise been redundant can then leave physical legacies for future social, cultural and economic benefit, and for some cities this can help justify the initial event staging costs. This capacity is generally limited to major events and mainly mega sports events: for example the 2000 Olympic Games and the regeneration of the Homebush area of Sydney; the 2002 Commonwealth Games and the regeneration of the Eastlands area of Manchester; and East London is being transformed in connection with the 2012 Olympics. The transformation of urban space via event-led strategies is a form of 'urban boosterism' whereby events are an attractive municipal proposition because they are perceived as stimulants to urban economic redevelopment (Andranovich *et al.*, 2001; Hiller, 2000).

20.5.7 Physical build or renewal objectives

This is a contentious area of objectives, not because events cannot be catalysts for new facilities, but because many facilities that have been built as a result of hosting events have turned out to have negative legacies or be 'white elephants' because of underutilisation. In particular these are sports and Olympics related. Stadium Australia, for example, remains a financial challenge to date and the main Olympic site created for the 2004 Games in Athens is now almost completely unused and derelict. The key issue is planning – it is entirely possible to plan for and achieve physical legacies out of the planning of major events and Manchester has shown this to be the case in relation to the facilities it built for its Commonwealth Games, which have been in continuous use since 2002 (Masterman, 2009).

Essex and Chalkley (2003) suggest that over time there have been three types of Olympic host city – those that have sought to keep the scale of transformation to a minimum (Los Angeles 1984, Salt Lake City 2002); those that have produced substantial sports facilities but little in the way of wider urban provision (Munich 1972, Moscow 1980, Calgary 1988); and those that have produced sports and/or major urban infrastructure (Grenoble 1968, Sapporo 1972, Seoul 1988, Atlanta 1996, Sydney 2000, Athens 2004). Noticeably these were not in three distinct periods through time; there are cities that were early developers of infrastructure, as well as later and very recent examples of more frugal approaches.

There is an important link to be made between the new facilities that are built for major events and the other physical infrastructures that are put in to support them, in particular structural 'hard factors' such as housing, telecommunications and transportation (Preuss, 2004). For example, in building facilities in disused and outer-city areas, there arises the need to provide adequate transportation, if only for the event itself. Clearly this requires further investment – for example AU\$80 million for Sydney's 2000 Olympics (Holloway, 2001) – and its future use becomes reliant upon the long-term success of the facility it serves.

In contrast, events do not in general provide a great stimulus for legacies in the form of accommodation, hotels and room increases, etc. There are few examples in the industry of new build, refurbishment and even renovation of hotels, simply because the increases in event tourism are not proven as sustainable (Essex and Chalkley, 2003; Hughes, 1993).

There are two types of post-event usage – sports, leisure and recreational use by the local community and/or the staging of other future events. The 1992 Barcelona Olympics were a part of a wider long-term city strategy for modernisation and provide an example of both types of after-use. The strategy, 'Barcelona 2000', was implemented in the mid-1980s, and included six new sports stadia, an Olympic village on the waterfront, a new airport and communication towers. Two distinct organisations were created to manage the legacies, one to attract and run major events and the other for public sports participation. This strategy helped to 'popularise the Olympic event, to develop public–private sector partnerships in the post-event management of facilities and also to promote the after-use of the facilities by the mass public' (Roche, 2000).

> ### Discussion question
>
> What objectives do you think are important in order to gain local political and commercial support for a new event in your community?

20.6 The event planning process

In order to achieve any combination of the objectives considered above, whatever the scale or nature of the event, an event manager needs to undergo an event planning process. The remainder of this chapter is devoted to explaining this process, which encompasses both short-term requirements for the implementation of the event and the long-term objectives regarding the legacies of the event (Masterman, 2009). Figure 20.2 contains a model of this planning process.

The event planning process model consists of up to ten different stages. As can be seen from Figure 20.2, each stage may be revisited iteratively so that realignment with objectives can be undertaken if required. A description of each stage in the process now follows (adapted from Masterman, 2009).

20.6.1 Objectives

The first stage in the planning of any event is to determine its purpose – the previous discussion provides a number of options. The Great North Run was originally designed to widen participation in running in the north-east of England. The Tribeca Film Festival was created by Robert De Niro with the City of New York to further promote the city as an international centre for filmmaking (see 'Useful websites', p. 559). Manchester aimed to use

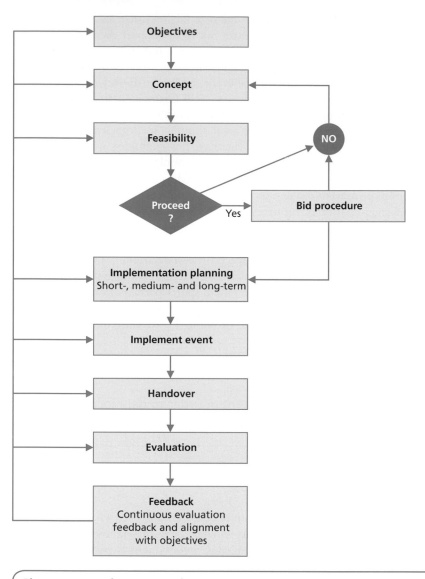

Figure 20.2 The event planning process.
Source: Masterman (2009).

its 2002 Commonwealth Games as a catalyst for the regeneration of derelict areas and to increase employment opportunities.

The setting of specific and measurable objectives provides direction for the planning, execution and evaluation of the event. In order to do this, all stakeholders should be identified and consulted so that their requirements can be considered and incorporated if necessary into the planning of the event. Stakeholders in events can be any of the following:

- **Customers** – individual and corporate ticket buyers, participants or competitors, advertisers, corporate package buyers (e.g. franchised spaces), sponsors, merchandise buyers.
- **Suppliers** – the organisations that are used to supply equipment, services or goods in

connection with the event, for example equipment, legal advice, food and beverages, transportation, security and emergency services.

- **Partners** – many sports events are not possible without the sanction of the relevant regional, national and international governing body. Other partners may well be local, regional or national governments or their agencies. Separate event management organisations may well combine forces to put on an event, as may clubs, societies and associations. Sponsors are often referred to as partners both in their title rights and because of the longevity and/or closeness of the relationship, as too are media organisations that purchase event rights.
- **Investors** – some of the above partners may also be investors in that they have a vested interest as a result of providing funding either financially or via in-kind services. Municipal or agency investment may require non-financial returns such as sporting, cultural or social development.
- **Staff** – permanent staff, short-term event hired personnel, sub-contracted staff and volunteers.
- **External influencers** – these include the event publics that are important for the success of the event and therefore influence any decision-making, even if they are not directly connected to the event in any of the above terms. For example, the local community in which the event is delivered, pressure groups, local and national governments, individual politicians and the media.

Following stakeholder analysis and any consultation, the key questions for those managing the event are:

- Why is the event to be held?
- What is to be achieved?
- Who is to benefit and how?

If the event is to be managed by an appointed agency, then it is important to consider any briefs that have been received for the event from the event owners as these will form the basis of the objectives. Often it is the brief that forms the invitation to pitch for the right to manage the event and so it forms the earliest of guidelines for the planning that follows.

Once the objectives have been formulated, they then become the basis for the design of the event which follows at the next stage. These objectives are essentially built in as mechanisms to align subsequent planning. At all stages of the process, there should be regular evaluation to see if planning is still on track. If planning has gone awry, or indeed new opportunities may be possible, then realignment is possible. Alignment can be achieved with the identification of performance indicators and targets that are tied to the objectives, both for the short and long term.

For all scales of event the planning process identifies its own integrated indicators, i.e. through the setting of deadlines for the achievement of budgeted levels of income, appropriate cashflows, prescribed levels of media coverage, or the signing of appropriate contracts with suppliers and partners. It is also important to incorporate mechanisms to allow for the exploitation of any new opportunities for improving the project during implementation.

20.6.2 Concept

Once the objectives have been determined the event can be designed. The design or event concept is guided by the clear and measurable objectives. The Beijing Olympics adopted an approach that utilised new and existing facilities all over the city, including on its outskirts and further afield by partnering with other cities such as Shanghai and Quingdao. London's

Millennium Dome year-long 'show' in 2000 set out to provide a snapshot of as wide a picture of the world as possible and did that by creating zones that showcased technology in particular but also fun elements like the circus.

Having undertaken a stakeholder analysis, it is possible to identify the decision-makers for the planning that follows. The key questions asked at this stage are:

- What is the event?
- What does it look like?
- Who are its target audiences and customers?

Using environmental analysis tools, including competition analysis (see Chapter 15) will ensure that the concept can be fully developed to achieve the objectives. Consideration of the following should also be undertaken:

- the scale of the event;
- how it will operate;
- when it will be staged;
- where it will be staged – locations and venues;
- what facilities and equipment will be required;
- who the key partners are – local or national government, governing bodies, event owners, and promoters and charities.

At this stage consideration should also be given to what kind of show will be put on. All events are entertainment and can be expensive to stage, so it is necessary to determine what will be the base requirement and what the possibilities are for enhanced provision. The location and venue may be supplied with some of the requirements already intact; while sponsors may supply other enhancements such as ancillary entertainments, decorations and special effects. The quality of the performance is critical and so the level of performer is also a consideration at this stage. The items that may be costly and which it may be tempting to ignore in order to keep costs under control may also be the factors that are essential if customer satisfaction is to be achieved. For example, waste disposal, clean toilets, accessible parking, pleasant and informative stewarding may all be costs, but they may also be factors that can affect competitive advantage.

After-use is also an important consideration at this stage. Whatever the scale of the event, facilities, equipment and venues may need to be handed on or back to their owners; alternatively divestment may be an option. There will be cost and effort involved and so it is critical that this be considered and planned so that handover can be executed effectively at the right time, even though at this stage this might appear to be a long way off.

Discussion question

What event concept would you develop for your local town to meet the following objectives?

- Integrate all sections and age groups in the community.
- Involve local groups, associations or societies.
- Encourage local retail and business interest.
- Utilise local outdoor facilities and spaces.
- Develop regional interest and awareness of the town and its assets.

20.6.3 Feasibility

This stage of the planning process is concerned with deciding if and how the concept can run. As long as this is approached with flexibility, the concept can be revisited until feasibility is ensured.

The concept needs to be tested. This might require a dress rehearsal, or a run-through of key aspects. For major events this may involve the delivery of one or more events that are used as learning curves. Beijing, for example, as was required by the IOC, put on a number of high profile events prior to 2008 and in the Olympic venues, including international taekwondo, swimming, diving and water polo championships (Beijing 2008, 2008).

There needs to be a thorough audit of how financially robust the concept is at this stage. Whatever the scale of event, a cost/benefit evaluation needs to be undertaken in order that the budget can be set. This will enable organisers to forecast cash flows, which, as indicated on p. 470, will help form appropriate performance indicators. By determining costs prior to any decisions to proceed, organisers can ensure that unnecessary costs can be kept to a minimum and that there will be no surprises. It may be a peculiarity of the UK, but both Manchester and London's Olympic bid books for 2000 and 2012 respectively contained unresolved tax issues. London, to date, still does not know if the government will require VAT payments to be made.

Further consideration at this stage should be given to the feasibility of long-term after-use, or the need for handover of legacies at the end of the event.

In order to identify costs and a firm budget, the following questions need to be answered:

- Who is responsible for the delivery of the objectives (short- or long-term) and the timings that are involved?
- What resources are required, from where and when – financial, personnel, facilities, equipment, marketing, services?
- If there is a bidding process, what criteria are to be met and at what cost – can this be written off or is a return on the investment required, even from a losing bid?
- What is required for event implementation, execution and evaluation, and when?
- Are there any intended legacies, how will they be handed over and to whom – are there any requirements for the long-term after-use of facilities that need to be addressed at this stage?

Whatever the scale of the event, a Master Plan is required. This might be a manually derived and maintained schedule, and for many small events this will be handwritten or produced at home on a word processor. However, the more complex the event, the greater the requirement for each individual aspect of planning to be planned so that they create the Master Plan, which comprises:

- facilities;
- staff and personnel;
- administration, documentation and finance;
- sales and marketing;
- equipment;
- presentation and media;
- support services;
- health and safety.

For large events the Master Plan is more complex; for example, for Beijing 2008 it consisted of the following departments, each of which provided a separate contributory plan, coordinated by a Project Management Department (Masterman, 2009; Beijing 2008, 2008):

- international relations – liaison with the IOC and national Olympic committees;
- sports – organisation of all competitions;
- media and communications;
- construction and environment;
- marketing – sponsorship and licensing;
- technology – office and event communications;
- legal affairs – contracts and legal counsel;
- Games services – housing, transportation, registration and spectator services;
- audit and supervision – overseeing of funding and staff performance;
- human resources – recruitment, training and management of staff;
- finance – budget management;
- cultural services – festival management;
- security;
- media relations – press centre operations;
- venue management;
- logistics – materials and services for the Games;
- Paralympic Games – liaison with the IPC;
- transportation;
- Torch relay;
- accreditation – for athletes, officials and dignatories;
- ceremonies;
- villages – accommodation operations;
- volunteering – recruitment, training and management;
- ticketing – ticket sales and distribution.

20.6.4 Proceed

If the event is feasible, the decision on whether to proceed or not can be made. If the event is deemed infeasible there is an opportunity to revisit the objectives and the concept to determine a way forward. If this can be achieved the decision to go ahead can be made, but if not, there is also the option to abort the event.

20.6.5 Bidding

For some larger-scale events there is a bidding process to undergo. For example, many major international sports events are bid for (for Olympics bids, see 'Useful websites', p. 559). This is also now an approach that rights owners from the arts are beginning to adopt, or at least consider, in strategies to take their events to cities around the world. The 2007 International Indian Film Festival Awards, for example, were hosted by Bradford in the UK. The city beat New York and Melbourne to be the host and its subsequent successful staging of this event led to it being declared by UNESCO the world's first City of Film in 2009. Clearly a bid can be expensive and as there can only be one winner there are a number of losers with sunk costs. Therefore the decision to proceed to bid and the costs that will be incurred should be a consideration at the feasibility stage of the planning process.

With bidding costs high, it is becoming more common for cities to look carefully at the objectives that might be achieved just by bidding – in other words, gaining a return on the bidding investment, even if the bid fails. For example, it is not unreasonable to say that Havana, Cuba, submitted its bid for the 2012 Olympics with a low probability of winning.

Even though its bid was rejected in the early rounds of the process, it might be assumed that there were diplomatic, possibly even trade, benefits to be realised from bidding.

20.6.6 Implementation planning

The next stage is the planning for the implementation of the event. This is when both short- and long-term strategies are developed to achieve the objectives set. For the delivery of the event itself, the short-term operational strategies need to cover a number of key areas, each of which may be organised into a unit and coordinated by a dedicated team. Every event is unique, but below is a general indication of what might be planned for.

The skills of those involved, whether they are full time or volunteers, are clearly varied, and for major events specialists in administration, finance, marketing and public relations, support services, catering, sponsorship, facility and media management may well be employed. Skilled event directors can adapt themselves to run all kinds of events and as such can also become much sought after. However, for those events with lower profiles there will be smaller management teams and in many cases the personnel involved will have to be multi-skilled.

If there are long-term objectives, such as those highlighted on pp. 543–9, it is important that long-term strategies are also implemented at this stage. For these events, expertise in economic generation, urban regeneration, town planning, city marketing, cultural and sport development and environmental sustainability may be required.

Both the short and long-term strategies that are required to deliver the event need to be included in the development of a critical path. Their alignment with event objectives is again an important element in an approach that requires continuous evaluation. Readdressing the budget requirements and assessing performance indicators throughout this stage will help to ensure event planning stays on course.

20.6.6.1 Critical path

An event is a complex project and as such requires project management skills. A successful event manager will adopt a process that looks to identify and then break down all the tasks that are involved in staging the event and then place them into a time plan that maximises effectiveness and efficiency. A critical path is such a time plan, with the sequencing and pre-requisites for each key task clearly identified. There are several areas and types of tasks that are critical for every event and these have to be identified in advance, together with the timelines required to complete them. This approach provides a backbone for event implementation planning and a calendar with deadlines for all tasks.

The chart can become overcrowded and extremely complex, and to identify any clashing schedules, tasks need to be prioritised. Network analysis can be used to determine a critical path, identifying deadlines by which tasks absolutely have to be achieved. This analysis shows how many tasks will impact upon others and limit effectiveness. An event manager can then identify the consequences of not achieving each task and also identify who will coordinate each one.

Complexity can limit use of a Gantt approach and so many international events use other software or adopt their own processes. The objective remains the same, however: an effective and efficient set of tasks performed in the right sequence. To initiate this process, the following general areas of work should be considered:

- **programme** – coordination of the schedules, the running order of each component, main stage and ancillary activities, liaison with acts, players and performers, choreography, rehearsal, show entertainment;

- **staff** – management and accreditation of full-time and volunteer personnel, human resource issues, training, welfare and payments;
- **administration and services** – financial and resource management, legal agreements and contracting, venue bookings and arrangements, facility and equipment coordination, recruitment and coordination of sub-contractors and suppliers, licenses, security, transportation, accommodation;
- **marketing** – product, prices, distribution and promotion management;
- **commercial** – sponsor recruitment and relationship management, franchised space, licensing and merchandising, advertising, retail sales, ticket sales;
- **technical** – coordination of the purchase, hire, supply and return of equipment, provision of effective and legal health and safety, creation and execution of audio-visual effects and communications, environmental sustainability, sanitation;
- **catering** – management of retail, hospitality and staff catering;
- **media** – press and broadcaster relationship management;
- **public relations** – government liaison, governing body liaison, stakeholder development and enhancement.

20.6.7 Event implementation

Once plans have been made they can be executed, so this stage of the process is a separate one. However, it is neither essential nor practical to assume that all planning can be done prior to all of the implementation that has to be undertaken. Some decisions can be made and implemented before others, provided that the impacts they have on each other have been fully considered. There is also a degree of flexibility required in all planning, especially the longer the time period, in order to allow for opportunities that were initially unforeseen. For example, the organisers of the 2012 London Olympics have had to address a global recession since they won their bid and the effect that has had on construction and purchasing costs as well as reduced interest in sponsorship.

If the planning for implementation has been in accordance with the objectives set, a successful event may be achieved. The reality, of course, is that events will always throw up opportunities and issues both during planning and during the event itself, and so these will need to be addressed. There is significantly more time and capacity to do this if the planning has been as comprehensive as possible. The unforeseen can be addressed if the foreseen is well planned for.

20.6.8 Handover

The event is not completed for another three stages yet. This stage begins with the shutdown of the event and concludes with the handing back of facilities and equipment to the owners. An example is parkland, seating and staging following a jazz concert at Kenwood in London. Other examples include forestation after the conclusion of an orienteering event on farmers' land, and the Intercontinental Hotel in Beijing following its use as a media centre for the 2008 Olympics. There is also the handover of any legacies that are to be managed in the long term, such as new facilities to new owners. This might be newly developed staging, seating and backstage facilities provided so that the arts might be staged in the long term at ancient venues such as the Acropolis in Athens (theatre), the ampitheatre at Verona (opera) or the new Globe in London (Shakespeare).

Shutdown involves returning the site to its original state or to a state that has been agreed with the incoming management. This might involve cleaning up as well as clearing out and a strategy has to be in place so that this is as efficient and effective as possible, not least because this is a costly time that has no income return. This is therefore a stage of the process that should already have been planned. For some events this might also be a long period and particularly costly. The Sydney Olympic Park was not handed over for a year following the closing of the 2000 Olympics and the City of Manchester Stadium also took a year to reconfigure before it was handed over to lessees Manchester City FC following the 2002 Commonwealth Games. The handing over of the responsibility for evaluating the legacy over the long term was also a consideration for both these events (Adby, 2002; Bernstein, 2002).

20.6.9 Evaluation

There is general agreement that evaluation is performed in the short term after an event, but there is less consideration of long-term evaluations. The subjective of evaluating an event after it has ended, in the short term, is common. However, measurement against the objectives set is a practice that is often seen as time-consuming and costly. Assessing the impact of an event in the long term is not a widespread practice for similar reasons. It may also be a case of the responsibility for this task being unassigned. This is prevalent at the highest levels with the IOC itself – only committing to a comprehensive approach to short-term evaluation in 2002 via its Transfer of Knowledge programme. Even now the IOC is less conclusive about how it should encourage long-term evaluation in its host cities.

As a minimum, a formal overall evaluation report is always required that at least covers the process up to the close of the event. It is this that will enable the managers of the next event to easily decide how the new event should be delivered (Felli, 2002). However, evaluation is not just necessary at the end of the process, as has already been discussed. Continuous alignment with objectives, whatever the scale of the event, is a requirement throughout the planning process.

20.6.10 Feedback

The final stage of the process is one that ensures that everything that can be learned from planning is fed into the next event. So the evaluation of whether it went well or not, achieved some or all of its objectives, the strategies, tactics and tools that were used, all need to be used to guide future decision-making. Processes are therefore required to ensure that evaluation reports and formal discussions are used and that any changes to planning and new developments for planning are made possible.

20.7 Conclusions

Given the increasingly recognised importance of events, there is a call for greater advances in the field of event management. Practitioners can now be trained and educated in many aspects of event management and there is burgeoning academic support in research and theory. However, there are few standards and professionalism varies. Event evaluation, for example, is not consistent either in application or in commonly accepted tools. Similarly, approaches to planning vary greatly.

It is, though, early days for a subject that did not have a university degree until the mid-1990s and there are successful events to be found throughout the world that continue to beat expectations. These successes, as well as failures, are gradually feeding into the field, informing us of better ways to use and manage events.

Practical tasks

1 Select an event of your choice from your neighbourhood that has only local interest. Analyse who the stakeholders are and determine what objectives this event seeks to achieve.

2 For a small, local event such as a sports tournament or a festival in a park, devise a first draft of a critical path which identifies the key tasks to deliver the event and the minimum timescale necessary to achieve them.

3 For past events that you know well, from personal experience or from media reports, identify key problems and discuss whether better continuous evaluation might have prevented these from happening.

Structured guide to further reading

For a text covering event management and planning:
Getz, D. (1997) *Event Management and Tourism*, Cognizant, New York.

For a text covering sports event management and planning, with a wide range of examples of all scales of event and specific reference to the Beijing 2008 Olympics:
Masterman, G. (2009) *Strategic Sports Event Management: Olympic edition*, Elsevier, Butterworth-Heinemann, Oxford.

For a text focusing on marketing communications planning for events:
Masterman, G. and Wood, E. (2006) *Innovative Marketing Communications: strategies for the events industry*, Butterworth-Heinemann, Oxford.

For a text covering project management and its application to the management of events:
O'Toole, W. and Mikolaitis, P. (2002) *Corporate Events Project Management*, John Wiley & Sons, New York.

For a text specifically covering the economics of major events and in particular the Olympic Games:
Preuss, H. (2004) *The Economics of Staging the Olympics: a comparison of the Games 1972–2008*, Edward Elgar, Cheltenham.

For an Olympic bid book of your choice, visit any Olympic Studies Centre (www.olympic. org) or download documents from bidding/successful host city internet sites, e.g. www. london2012.com, www.vancouver2010.com.

Useful websites

For information on the Olympic Movement and Games:
www.olympic.org

For the Tribeca Film Festival in New York:
www.tribecafilmfestival.org

For the Glastonbury Festival:
www.glastonburyfestivals.co.uk

For IMG, one of the largest sports, arts and events management organisations in the world:
www.imgworld.com

For Octagon, another international sports management organisation:
www.octagon.com

For Nova International's site for all its Great Run events:
www.greatrun.org

For Olympic bidding cities and up-to-date information on their progress towards the IOC decision on the next hosts for Olympic Games:
www.gamesbids.com

For daily updated information on the business of sport:
www.sportsbusinessdaily.com

For Ticketmaster, a leading international event ticket sales agency:
www.ticketmaster.com

For the official site of the National Outdoor Events Association:
www.noea.org.uk

Chapter 21

Enterprise and entrepreneurship in sport and leisure

In this chapter

- What are enterprise and entrepreneurship?
- How can enterprising individuals be identified?
- How can the current business position be identified?
- What strategies are needed to stimulate innovation and change?
- What are the key elements of a business plan?
- How can risk be reduced?

Summary

Enterprise involves creating new business development, whilst it is achieved by entrepreneurial skills. Enterprise and entrepreneurship involve much of what is termed 'best practice' in management. They are to be found in all sectors of the economy and are not confined to individual, new ventures in the commercial sector. Enterprise also occurs in existing organisations, and in the non-profit sectors too – termed social enterprise. Innovation and change are at the heart of enterprise.

To analyse enterprise and entrepreneurship requires many of the skills and techniques introduced in previous chapters, which is why this is the final chapter – in many ways it is a summary chapter. The principal new material in this chapter relates to what qualities an entrepreneur demonstrates; commercial and governmental sources of finance for enterprise; business and financial planning; and managing risk. But the chapter is also a synthesis of previously covered material and as such it makes repeated cross-references to previous chapters. The core of the chapter is organised according to three stages of business development: assessing the current position; deciding the strategies for change; and then planning how to achieve the desired change.

21.1 Introduction

Enterprise encapsulates the essence of good organisational leadership and decision-making. It is traditionally discussed in the context of new ventures and commercial businesses but it is more general than that, embracing innovations in existing sport and leisure organisations and in the public and voluntary sectors. It is not confined to the successes of a few self-made, inspirational individuals such as Richard Branson (Virgin) or Tim Smit (Eden Project), but is also achieved by countless managers who seek to innovate and improve their organisations' activities. Because of its general relevance, it is fitting that enterprise is the subject of the final chapter of this book – analysing the principal ingredients of successful entrepreneurship serves as a summary of best practices in management which are referred to elsewhere, particularly Part 4. In enterprise, the name of the game is innovation, so the best practices reviewed in this chapter necessarily service change in organisations.

The chapter begins by summarising the characteristics of entrepreneurs, the key individuals driving new developments. It then examines three stages of enterprise:

1   positioning of a business – i.e. where it is now;
2   strategies for the business – i.e. where you want it to go;
3   business planning – how it will get to where you want it to go.

(Barrow *et al.*, 2006)

The principles and techniques reviewed are relevant to new independent ventures, and strategies and business planning are essential elements in the start-up phase in the life-cycle of a business. However, the chapter adopts the more general and common concept of enterprise as innovation within existing organisations, as well as the more specific development of entirely new organisations.

Some definitions are necessary at the outset. Put at their simplest, **enterprise** is the development of a new initiative/venture/project; whilst **entrepreneurship** is a set of skills and techniques which facilitate enterprise. This chapter concentrates more on entrepreneurship. Two other concepts are important to introduce. First, **intrapreneurship** is a term used to describe corporate entrepreneurship, i.e. a new initiative within an existing organisation, rather than a new independent venture. Much enterprise in sport and leisure is created by intrapreneurship, the creation of a new service in an existing organisation, e.g. the introduction of personal trainers in fitness centres. **Social entrepreneurship** represents entrepreneurship in the voluntary and public sectors, as opposed to the traditional commercial sector entrepreneur. **Social enterprises** are businesses operating for a social purpose, often with charitable status – an example, the Trinity Sailing Trust, is featured in Case Study 21.2. The Office of the Third Sector in the UK estimates that there are 62,000 social enterprises in the UK, contributing £24 billion to UK output.

Entrepreneurs are risk-takers, because for new ventures they typically have to raise substantial funds to realise their dream. However, whereas many small firms are the realisation of enterprise by entrepreneurs, not all small firms demonstrate entrepreneurship. In hospitality, for example, there are many bed and breakfast establishments and cafes which are small, steady-state businesses which do not demonstrate innovation or change. These are not examples of entrepreneurship, although they might have been when they were first set up.

The innovations which are the subjects of entrepreneurship are of various types (Wickham, 2006), all of which exploit an opportunity to do something differently and better. They include:

- new products, services and brands;
- new production or service delivery techniques;
- new distribution methods;
- new ways of informing customers;
- new ways of managing relationships within an organisation.

One of the most significant demonstrations of new services in the travel and tourism market in recent decades is budget airlines. Southwest Airlines in Texas introduced the simple but devastatingly effective innovation of cutting costs in order to reduce prices for customers. Other companies worldwide have successfully followed this business model, including Ryan Air, Easy Jet and BMI Baby in Europe. Such airlines have reduced costs by such means as using smaller airports, and eliminating travel agents, tickets and free in-flight meals.

Another compelling example of enterprise is the case study of Brawn GP (Case Study 21.1), a combination of new product and brand, together with new finance, brought about by extreme circumstance. It demonstrates that entrepreneurship can be inspirational, especially when it emerges from such a negative stimulus.

21.2 Enterprising individuals

Enterprise is a function of entrepreneurship and individuals are at the heart of entrepreneurship. Hisrich *et al.* (2005) identify three sets of skills required in entrepreneurs – technical (including communication and technology), business management (including planning, marketing and

Brawn GP, 2009

With three weeks to go until the beginning of the 2009 Formula One season, Honda pulled out of the sport. In a classic twist on the old saying 'Necessity is the mother of invention', the team principal, Ross Brawn, organised a buy-out of the team and rebranded it as Brawn GP. Thus began one of the most successful examples of enterprise in recent sport history.

Whilst the financing of the deal was not disclosed, reports suggested that Honda and Bernie Ecclestone (the sport's commercial rights holder) contributed to it – the former substantially less than their budget for the 2008 season. In addition, Bridgestone and Ray-Ban remained as sponsors and they were joined in the spring of 2009 by sponsorship from Virgin, MIG Investments, and Henri Lloyd. Despite this essential funding from sponsorship, one of the innovations that Brawn had to make was to radically cut costs, including significant cuts to the pay of the two principal drivers, Jenson Button and Rubens Barrichello, as well as not running a spare car and reducing the support team at GP races to 55, compared with 100 the previous season.

Brawn also instigated two important technical changes, among others. First, he changed the engines to Mercedes-Benz and, second, his were two of the few cars utilising KERS, a system of providing a periodic boost to the engine's power through kinetic energy recovery. Although there is a perennial argument about how important the car and the driver are to winning, there is little argument that the car has to be right. Brawn GP's technical achievements in such a short time were outstanding.

The immediate and most publicised successes of this enterprising rejuvenation of a defunct racing team were that in 2009 Brawn GP won the World Constructors' Championship and Jenson Button won the World Drivers' Championship. Not so well publicised, but equally important for the business future of the company, was that at the end of 2009 Brawn GP was bought out by Daimler and an investment fund, Aabar, which together took a 75.1 per cent stake. The new name for the company is Mercedes Grand Prix – the first time Mercedes has had a team in the sport since 1955. Ross Brawn and his chief executive Nick Fry retained a 24.9 per cent stake in the company, so they have achieved significant financial rewards for the risks taken at the beginning of 2009 and they continue to lead the team in 2010.

Sources: articles in the *Financial Times*, 1 March 2009 and 17 November 2009; and in the *Independent*, 18 April 2009

finance) and personal (including risk-taking, innovation and leadership). Wickham (2006) and Kuratko and Hodgetts (2007) concentrate on the personal attributes of entrepreneurs (see Table 21.1). It's easy to get the impression from such a list that entrepreneurs are extraordinary individuals and in many ways they are. However, whilst many people work hard, seek information, are problem solving, receptive to change and committed to others, entrepreneurs add to these qualities some less common attributes, such as being risk-taking, self-starting and opportunistic, having vision and not being afraid to fail.

A powerful personal vision is one of the defining characteristics of entrepreneurs; it is a management skill which is particularly relevant to the identification of where the business needs to go and how to get there. A personal vision can be a driving force for an entrepreneur, just as a vision statement can be important as a signpost for an organisation (see Section 15.3). Vision helps to define project objectives and is important for both the leadership of a development and the motivation of the team involved. Creativity is an important element of vision, and entrepreneurs are often creative not only about their core idea but also about the ways to achieve it, including financing.

> ## Discussion question
>
> Are Wickham's attributes of entrepreneurs things that they are born with or can they be developed, e.g. through education and training?

There is a debate in the literature on entrepreneurship about whether entrepreneurial attributes are things entrepreneurs are born with or things that are the product of, or developed by, social processes, including education. This is the same 'nature v. nurture' or 'genetics v. environment' debate which occurs in a number of fields. However, it is very difficult to measure the extent of such attributes as those in Table 21.1, let alone identify the effect of possible causal factors on them; so the debate is likely to continue. As well as personal attributes, Morrison *et al.* (1999) summarise the environmental or social influences on entrepreneurship, reproduced as Table 21.2. Some of these are also difficult to measure and scientifically associate with entrepreneurial behaviour. Like many aspects of the 'nature v. nurture' debate, it is likely that both sets of major influences, genetic and environmental, are important in determining an individual entrepreneur's behaviour.

Entrepreneurship is more than having a good idea; it requires sound planning and risk-taking to see the idea through. Coming up with the idea is the essence of **creativity**; making the idea work is termed **innovation**. As Jennings (2009) suggests, creativity is a fundamental driving force for individual entrepreneurship, but in combination with logical analysis. He gives the McDonalds concept, developed by Ray Kroc, as a good example of this combination – a simple and flexible idea at the heart of a global franchising system.

Kuratko and Hodgetts (2007) and Jennings (2009) distinguish left brain activity, which promotes rational, linear, logical analysis, from right brain activity, which stimulates greater challenge to custom and routine, through intuition and imagination, and looks for better ways of doing things. Creative thinking is more the domain of right brain activity, but logical analysis is the product of left brain activity and is needed to develop creativity into a sustainable enterprise, i.e. innovation. A formal version of creative thinking, typically in a group setting, is 'brainstorming', whereby random ideas, not limited by any boundaries, are invited in relation to a particular problem or issue.

Entrepreneurs also have to cope with what Kuratko and Hodgetts (2007) call the 'dark side' of entrepreneurship. This entails coping not just with a variety of risks, to finances, family, career and their own confidence, but also with the negatives associated with stress. Stress can be summarised as the gap between expectations and outcomes and entrepreneurs are particularly exposed to stress because they can be prone to what is termed 'role overload', i.e. taking on too much, with multiple tasks and the excessive responsibility often associated with 'control freaks'.

Where do enterprising ideas come from? Bragg and Bragg (2005) suggest that nearly half of new business ideas are stimulated by the existing work environment; just over one-quarter of ideas come from secondary sources, such as trade journals or venture capital firms; 15 per cent of ideas come from the desire to improve an existing technology, product or service; whilst 10 per cent of ideas are stimulated by a vision of an opportunity. Hisrich *et al.* (2005)

Table 21.1 Attributes of entrepreneurs

Attributes	Notes
Hardworking	Entrepreneurs typically (but not always) work long hours.
Self-starting, proactive	They do not wait for instructions, but are leaders in identifying and progressing tasks, taking personal responsibility for progress.
Has vision and sets personal goals	They are visionary, with a strategic orientation – just as objectives are important for organisations, so clear and demanding goals are important to entrepreneurs, against which to measure progress.
Resilient, determined	Failures are part of the process of learning and a good entrepreneur is not afraid to fail and willing to learn from mistakes.
Efficacy	Entrepreneurs get things done – they have a strong desire to compete and succeed.
Confident, positive and risk-taking	Entrepreneurs are typically confident, not only of themselves but also of their proposed innovations. They are therefore used to risk-taking and managing risk.
Realistic	Entrepreneurs seek practical solutions and do not gamble but take calculated risks.
Receptive to new ideas	Confidence does not mean refusal to learn from others – entrepreneurs should recognise their limitations and seek appropriate advice.
Assertive and motivational	These are essentially communications attributes – being able to carry important others with the idea – which translate into leadership skills.
Information seeking	An enquiring mind is important to ensure that developments are as well informed as possible.
Eager to learn, problem solving	Entrepreneurs are aware of potential improvements, and a learning attitude helps to achieve them. Even business failures are experiences from which to learn and improve with the next venture.
Resourceful, versatile	Entrepreneurs adapt to different circumstances and respond positively and practically to change.
Attuned to opportunity	This means both seeking appropriate opportunities and seizing them.
Receptive to change	Change is the very nature of entrepreneurship and a willingness to embrace and promote change is essential
Committed to others	A recognition that you cannot do it all yourself, but will necessarily rely on good people around you.
Comfortable with power	Power can, of course, corrupt, but it is also a part of the outcomes for a successful entrepreneur. Power is one of the facilitators for continued development.

Sources: adapted from Wickham (2006); Kuratko and Hodgetts (2007).

> **Table 21.2** Social influences on entrepreneurial behaviour

Availability of appropriate role models
Career experience over the life-cycle
Deprived social upbringing
Family background
Family position
Inheritance of entrepreneurial tradition
Level of educational attainment
Negative or positive peer influence
Social marginality
Discomfort with large bureaucratic organisations

Source: Morrison *et al.* (1999).

emphasise the importance of existing or potential customers as sources for new ideas. They can be consulted formally, through such methods as focus groups and brainstorming, for example, or informally through listening to their complaints and needs.

So creativity, innovation and entrepreneurship are important to, but not just the province of, individuals starting up new enterprises. Individuals working in an existing organisation are not handicapped in their creativity, because their working environment and particularly existing customers can be a strong motivator for new ideas. What is needed, though, is that the individual can identify associated business opportunities and drive the idea through the start-up phase of business development. It is also important that the organisation where the intrapreneur works facilitates the creation of new ideas and is receptive to evaluating, testing and developing these ideas.

> **Discussion question**
>
> For a sport and leisure organisation that you know well (e.g. a club you belong to or a professional team that you support) think of an enterprising idea for changing what it does or how it does it. This could concern, for example, the service or product it provides, or the markets that it distributes to.

21.3 Evaluating the current business position

Unless the enterprise is a completely new venture, an essential first stage in promoting the development of an innovation is to understand the current business position of an organisation. This evaluation will necessarily stimulate ideas for improvement. It involves many issues covered in previous chapters, including:

● mission and core objectives (see Section 15.3 and Section 17.6.1);
● SWOT and PEST (see Section 15.5);

- finances (see Section 18.6);
- people, structures and systems (see Chapter 13).

A key concept in evaluating the current business position is organisational or strategic 'fit', i.e. the extent to which the organisation's activities fit the business environment. Morrison *et al.* (1999) suggest that the required 'fit' is three ways – between the individual entrepreneur or intrapreneur, the organisation and the environment. Strategic fit is particularly important because the business environment can change so rapidly – obvious examples being the growth of e-commerce, or legislation such as a smoking ban in public places. Case Study 4.1, of changes in the regulation of public houses in the UK, demonstrates the power of legislation to change the environment for enterprise in a market. After the Beer Orders legislation in 1989, the number of independently managed pubs rose by over 70 per cent in the subsequent ten years.

Benchmarking is also important to identify an organisation's position relative to best practice (see Section 17.8). Such benchmarking can involve comparative data, or comparisons of structures and processes. Barrow *et al.* (2006) identify seven best practice characteristics of organisations against which an organisation should compare itself:

1 **outward looking** – monitoring the organisation's understanding of customers, competitors, market, technology and relevant legislation;
2 **vision** – clarity of purpose which is shared by everyone in the organisation;
3 **culture** – pride and identification of employees with the organisation;
4 **empowerment** – sense of ownership of problems within the organisation; staff proactive in taking actions;
5 **flexible structures** – i.e. adapting to requirements; typically smaller and flatter structures, with possible outsourcing of certain tasks;
6 **teamwork** – creating a corporate identity by rotating job roles, cross-department meetings, etc. to enhance an understanding of the collective function;
7 **reward and recognition** – identifying what matters in performance and giving credit for it.

> ### Discussion question
>
> Is it always necessary to compare oneself with the best in order to come up with ideas for changes in an organisation, or are examples of failure just as inspiring of creativity?

21.4 Strategies for improving the business

Once it is clearly established what shape the current organisation is in and what the current business position is in relation to its external environment, there is a secure basis for plotting the future direction of the organisation and specific new enterprises within it. This requires a number of strategic decisions, particularly about marketing and financing. Similarly, for new enterprises, once a creative entrepreneurial idea starts to take shape, a strategy puts the idea into a business framework.

Two marketing tools which will help have already been introduced in Chapter 15 (Sections 15.6.2 and 15.6.3) – the Boston Matrix and the Ansoff Matrix. The former analyses the product portfolio of existing organisations and raises important implications for changing a business. To what extent is it possible, for example, to use the money generated by 'cash cows' (with high market share and low market growth) to invest in 'stars' (with high market growth as well as high market share)? How quickly is it possible to disinvest in 'dogs' (which have low market share and low market growth)? How much risk should be taken on by continued investment in 'question marks' (with low market share and high market growth)? These questions need active answers, otherwise inertia will hold back change and entrepreneurship because the resources devoted to 'cash cows' and 'dogs' will constrain the potential of 'stars' and 'question marks'.

The Ansoff Matrix is a useful tool for deciding in which forms growth and development is going to be attempted – again for an existing organisation. The options range from the low risk market penetration (existing products to existing markets) to the high risk diversification (new products to new markets). They are not alternatives but a decision is required about the appropriate combination of products in the growth portfolio of an organisation. Many public sector sport organisations, for example, are led by short-term funding into high growth activities, only to realise that when the funding finishes the enterprise is unsustainable. Key factors influencing the growth decision are rewards and risks. A high risk growth strategy has potentially high returns, but it is risky! Lower risk market penetration, on the other hand, typically offers lower prospects for growth, although it can provide reliable cash with which to invest in higher risk ventures.

Strategic options appraisal helps to identify the best prospects for change and new enterprise in an organisation. It requires consideration of a number of factors, in addition to those highlighted by both the Boston and Ansoff matrices. These factors include:

- organisational objectives;
- critical success factors (according to customers);
- growth potential;
- cash potential;
- risk;
- financing requirements.

Any options appraisal lends itself to quantitative analysis. For example, each option for development, such as expansion into a new market or development of a new service in existing markets, can be scored according to important factors such as those above. The factors might even be weighted to reflect their importance to the strategic direction of an organisation, according to key stakeholders. The result will be a quantitative ranking of different options, to help guide the strategic decisions of the organisation.

When considering the competitive strategy for entry into a market, consideration needs to be given to the key elements of business success. According to Porter (2004) there are five competitive forces which combine to determine the success of commercial organisations, and indeed the ability of an industry to sustain commercial success, particularly by new organisations. These are as follows:

1 **The entry of new competitors** – conditioned by barriers to entry into markets, which include the existence of economies of scale required to start efficient production (including initial capital funding requirements); absolute cost advantages; the degree of brand loyalty within the market, possibly created by significant advertising expenditure; access to distribution channels; and legal barriers imposed by patents, licenses or the government. In the restaurant business, for example, entry is relatively easy because there are low barriers to entry, including weak brand loyalty, and relatively small initial capital funding requirements.

2   **The threat of substitutes** – not just immediate substitutes. In sport and leisure generally there is a wide range of alternative ways for a consumer to spend their time and money. The relative prices of substitutes are important, as is the consumer's likelihood of buying substitutes (conditioned, for example, by the degree of brand loyalty). The fitness club industry is relatively competitive, for example, because of the range of alternative means of maintaining health and fitness, as well as low brand loyalty and considerable choice of clubs (in most urban areas in developed countries).

3   **The bargaining power of buyers** – retail or wholesale. Influences on this include brand loyalty; sensitivity to price changes; product differentiation (i.e. key differences in products); and buyer concentration (the fewer there are, the more power they have). In most sport and leisure industries, for example, the buyers are individual people or small groups, so their bargaining power is weak. Furthermore, they are typically but not always relatively insensitive to price changes. Such factors give greater scope for success in the business.

4   **The bargaining power of suppliers** – influences on this include important differences in inputs such as labour and materials, and the ability to substitute inputs; supplier concentration (the fewer suppliers there are, the more power they have); and the possibility of taking over suppliers (i.e. backward integration). An example of the bargaining power of suppliers is trade unions, particularly in the public sector. The success of commercial contract companies and trusts in the business of managing public sports and leisure facilities in the UK, for example, is partly because over time their labour contracts have not been so conditioned by national agreements with public sector trade unions.

5   **The intensity of competition between rival firms** – entering a highly competitive market will reduce profit margins and leave the enterprise open to the tactics of competitors, such as price discount wars, substantial competitive advertising or even a takeover. Tourism and hospitality companies, for example, have historically shown a high intensity of competition between rival firms, leading to not only price wars and considerable takeover activity, but also a high rate of business failure, even for the largest of firms.

Morrison *et al.* (1999) identify a number of strategic options in terms of the organisational form with which to take an enterprise forward. As well as the conventional forms of an independent organisation, or a new section in an existing organisation, these include the following forms:

1   **Franchising** – particularly important in service industries where the customer has to come to the product. With franchising the original concept is rolled out to a wider market by attracting the motivation and finance of other individual entrepreneurs, thereby achieving growth but spreading the risk. It is particularly prevalent in the fast food business and relates closely to three of Porter's principles above: it enables a company to reduce both barriers to entry and competition by attracting and assisting franchisees to enter the company rather than set up rival companies; and the scale of the operation increases the company's bargaining power with suppliers.

2   **Takeovers** – these provide opportunities for existing organisations to move into other businesses that are felt to be strategically compatible. This can reduce competition if the firm being taken over is in a similar business, or reduce the bargaining power of suppliers if the firm being taken over is a supplier. Also, being taken over is a means by which successful entrepreneurs can capitalise on their success and finance other ventures.

3   **Buy-outs** – where a particular operation within an existing organisation splinters off as a new, independent enterprise. A clear example of this is commercial contract management companies which run public sport and leisure facilities in the UK. Many originated

as discrete business units within local authorities, after compulsory competitive tendering was introduced in the late 1980s. The more entrepreneurial of these business units then bought the business out from the local authority, thus becoming commercial enterprises. This demonstrates weak barriers to entry because such organisations can develop a critical mass of expertise and experience before the buy-out.

4 **Strategic alliances and joint ventures** – a means of securing economies of scale and facilitating new developments while sharing the risks. Strategic alliances are quite common among airlines and hotel groups, because of obvious synergies in their operations and markets. The oneworld alliance, for example, is a global alliance between 11 airlines.

Whatever strategies for change are devised, Johnson *et al.* (2008) emphasise the need for evaluation of their appropriateness and timing. They identify three basic aspects of strategy evaluation:

1 **suitability** – i.e. the extent to which strategy addresses key issues regarding positioning of the organisation/development;
2 **feasibility** – i.e. whether or not the new development will work in practice and deliver the strategy; whether it has the right resources – human, financial and operational;
3 **acceptability** – i.e. whether the strategy will deliver the expected performance outcomes for key stakeholders, particularly funders, and possibly planners and relevant government agencies.

Discussion question

If a Premier League football club from England had a strategic intention to increase its fan base in the USA, how would you assess the suitability, feasibility and acceptability of this strategy?

21.4.1 Financing commercial enterprise

An essential factor in the development of enterprise is financing. For a commercial business, the two main options are internal and external financing. Internal financing, through profits and working capital in an existing organisation, or from savings for a new venture, is typically more limited but should nevertheless not be ignored. Increased profits, for example through greater cost control or the realisation of cash from 'cash cows', may contribute significantly to the financing of new enterprises. External financing takes two principal forms for commercial businesses: debt and equity. The ratio of debt to the net worth of the organisation (principally equity) is a key ratio – gearing – and a normal expectation of banks is that for small and medium-sized enterprises it should be 1:1 (Barrow *et al.*, 2006). A higher gearing, e.g. 2:1, gives a greater return on share capital for a given profit, but exposes the enterprise to a higher risk of not meeting interest payments on the debt if profits fall. Appropriate gearing depends on the nature of risk for the business – with high business risk (e.g. with diversification) a high gearing is not wise, because whatever happens the interest on debt has to be paid.

Banks are generally the usual source of debt financing, but there are also specialist lenders for people starting up new enterprises, such as, in the UK:

- Prime, for people aged over 50;
- the Prince's Trust, for young people;

- the Industrial Common Ownership Finance Fund, for cooperatives, employee-owned businesses and social enterprises;
- Community Development Finance Institutions, for businesses in disadvantaged communities.

(See Business Link in 'Useful websites', p. 583.)

Governments often supplement banks with other arrangements to facilitate debt financing. In the UK, for example, the Enterprise Finance Guarantee (previously known as the Small Firms Loan Guarantee Scheme) is a government-organised scheme to help the financing of business plans for small and medium-sized enterprises. It provides lenders with a government guarantee for 75 per cent of the lenders' exposure on individual loans; and it requires the borrower to pay the government department a 2 per cent premium on the outstanding balance of the loan. UK businesses with an annual turnover of up to £25 million are eligible to apply but the banks take a commercial decision on whether or not to lend. The European Investment Bank also has an arrangement with high street banks for low cost, longer term loans to small and medium-sized enterprises. The loans can be for a variety of purposes, including the purchase of physical assets, increasing working capital, or research and development.

Equity is finance raised from external investors, typically in return for a share in the business. Two major sources of equity are venture capital and business angels. Venture capitalists are companies which can organise a total funding package for a fast growing business, for a few years. They expect a high return and take an important stake in the business. Business angels are wealthy individuals, rather than companies, and they are typically entrepreneurs themselves. They use their own capital to finance new developments and, unlike in other forms of business finance, they like to get involved, using their experience and skills to provide business advice as well as finance. Their return is a share of the new business. The television programme *Dragons' Den* has a panel of business angels deciding which ideas to back with finance and advice. In addition, in the UK the government is active in facilitating equity finance (see Business Link in 'Useful websites', p. 583), particularly through its Capital for Enterprise Fund, which can provide businesses with longer term funding when traditional sources have been unsuccessful; and an Enterprise Investment Scheme, which helps smaller companies raise finance by providing tax relief to investors who buy shares in them.

Discussion question

In seeking funding for a new enterprise, consider the advantages and disadvantages of asking a bank manager rather than one of the *Dragons' Den* investors (i.e. a business angel).

21.4.2 Financing social enterprise

For non-profit organisations, debt and equity are not the normal means of financing new developments. Instead, fundraising can be vital in the voluntary sector, whilst a range of government grants are often available in the short term for specific initiatives in both the public and voluntary sectors. In sport in England, for example, *Sport Unlimited* project funding is cascaded through County Sports Partnerships to organisations which can fulfil the remit of encouraging semi-sporty young people to engage more in sport.

The Office for Civil Society (formerly the Office of the Third Sector) coordinates central government funding opportunities for the voluntary sector in the UK. In total in 2009–10 it provided over 4,000 grants, loans and contracts for third sector organisations, although this number is across the board, not specifically for sport and leisure. Many are available through generic programmes, however, and as such may be open to certain voluntary sector sport and leisure organisations. At the time of writing these programmes include:

- **Capacitybuilders** – aimed at support services to increase the effectiveness of voluntary organisations;
- **Futurebuilders** – to help frontline third sector organisations increase the scale and scope of their public service delivery;
- **grassroots grants** – to boost local community organisations, administered through a Community Development Foundation;
- **V** – an independent charity tasked with delivering improved quality, quantity and diversity of volunteering opportunities to young people in England.

A feature of such programmes is that they are designed to stimulate change and development in voluntary organisations – key features of social enterprise. Case Study 21.2 reviews one Futurebuilders funded project and demonstrates the importance of such funding to improving the capacity of a third sector organisation.

21.5 Business planning

For any new enterprise, especially in the commercial sector, it is important to have a detailed and persuasive business plan. This is not only the consolidation of all relevant considerations relating to the enterprise, but also an important tool for communicating with others, especially potential funders. Furthermore, the business plan is a tool for future and continuing operational business management, as the enterprise matures beyond the start-up phase. A business plan comprises of such elements as the following:

- **a clear and compelling mission, vision and objectives** (see Section 15.3 and Section 17.6.1);
- **an understanding of the business's environment and positioning** – exploiting organisational fit, using PEST and benchmarking (see Section 15.5 and Section 17.8);
- **a strategy** – developing the product portfolio, using methods such as the Boston Matrix and Ansoff Matrix (see Section 15.6);
- **an operations plan** – location, facilities, plant and equipment, suppliers;
- **a financial plan** – enhancing the financial position (see Sections 18.8 and 18.9), identifying a budget, appraising capital investment, securing appropriate finances;
- **a marketing plan** – exploiting critical success factors, seeking to improve the SWOT, utilising the marketing mix (see Sections 15.2 and 15.7), and forecasting sales with due regard to daily and weekly peak and off-peak fluctuations and longer term seasonal variations;
- **a people plan** – enhancing leadership, building around the personal capacity of the leader, recruiting and retaining key staff, developing an organisational culture, planning the numbers of staff and their required skills and development, designing effective structures, systems, communications and incentives (see Chapter 13);
- **risk assessment** – planning contingencies, managing risk.

Trinity Sailing Trust: an example of public funding of social enterprise

Trinity Sailing Trust, a charity established in 1999, is based in Devon in England and has two main objectives: to assist the personal development of disadvantaged and disabled young people through offshore sailing on traditional vessels; and to restore and preserve its vessels as important examples of maritime heritage. A team of administrators and ships' crews are backed by a network of other helpers, including volunteers, trustees and patrons. The result is that over 500 disadvantaged young people a year are given opportunities to develop through 'sail training', via contracts through which the Trinity Sailing Trust is paid to provide such training. As with many such programmes run through social enterprises, sport and physical activity are the catalyst to motivate young people, change their attitudes and expectations, and encourage them to take steps that may change the course of their lives.

The Trust has received the support and endorsement of many statutory, government and youth organisations, but has also engaged in extensive fundraising activities, including the Three Ships Appeal, through which approximately half its expenditure is covered. However, the considerable efforts required to pay for operating costs mean that there is little left for business development.

The government-sponsored programme Futurebuilders invested £20,000 in the Trust to undertake a feasibility study into acquiring and restoring a fourth sailing vessel, through which it can expand its business by fulfilling more public service contracts for the personal development of disadvantaged young people. Subsequently, a further £63,000 was invested for the refurbishment of the fourth vessel and to boost the Trust's capacity to undertake more business.

The Trinity Sailing Trust is an excellent example of capital funding for an extension of business for a social enterprise. The funding satisfied a one-off, capacity building requirement, which means that it is more likely to lead to a sustainable increase in business than a short-term revenue expenditure grant to cover operating costs – less than 10 per cent of the Futurebuilders funding was for operational expenditure.

Not untypically, it was necessary to fund a feasibility study and business plan before the capital funding was released. Social enterprises often do not have the resources to develop business plans independently, so an increasingly important direction for government advice and funding is to help create these plans and make sure that the development of social enterprise is on a sound footing.

Sources: www.futurebuilders-england.org.uk/ and www.trinitysailingtrust.org/

Discussion question

Discuss the conflict between needing to be concise in a business plan and needing to put such a lot of detail into it. Which parts do you think need more detail and which less detail?

Most of these elements have been covered in previous chapters (particularly Chapters 13, 15, 17 and 18) in relation to existing businesses. They are about first ensuring that the objectives, mission and vision are clear and persuasive; that the market environment and, for existing businesses, the nature of the current business are understood; and that a strategy for 'realising the dream' has been decided. Then the overall strategy has to be disaggregated into a series of separate functional strategies – marketing, finance, human resources and production. These strategies paint a broad picture of direction – e.g. key market segments, sources of finance, organisational structure, quality of product, etc. – and justify it with respect to the business environment and the chosen objectives.

The core of the business plan is specifying operational details, i.e. operational plans for each functional department. These require detailed operational objectives and outlines of the physical and human capital, systems and processes used to achieve the objectives. Techniques to help stitch the detailed plans together, in terms of the tasks to be completed, their sequencing and the times it takes to complete them, include the following:

- critical path analysis;
- programme evaluation and review technique (PERT);
- network diagrams;
- Gannt charts.

(For details of these techniques, please refer to project management texts.)

Business plans are about managing change in terms of introducing a new business venture in an existing organisation or starting up a new independent enterprise. They are proactive rather than reactive and they promote desired and well thought through change, rather than the crisis-motivated change that all too often strikes in organisations. Business plans for new developments are designed to improve outcomes, and often the change in outcomes takes time to achieve – months, even years. Barrow *et al.* (2006) refer to a U-shaped curve after change is implemented, with productivity immediately falling as staff adjust to major changes, then rising hopefully to a higher level than the pre-change situation, when staff are comfortable with the new development. The initial result of significant changes in the structures or processes of existing organisations is almost always negative, as people take time to adjust and resistance takes time to be broken down. Only after such adjustment is it likely that positive change is achieved.

In existing organisations, change has to be for a purpose, not change for change's sake. Arguably the sector with the greatest inclination for the latter is the public sector, because the identity of the politicians in charge alters so frequently. There is no clearer example of this than Sport England, which has had to endure endless structural changes over more than twenty years as new political masters have enforced new reviews. When change is for change's sake, the result is often to lose key staff rather than gain and motivate key staff, and the implications for outcomes are not good. Whereas change is a fact of business life, some stability also has its benefits. Barrow *et al.* (2006) suggest that both internal (push) and external (pull) factors are required to stimulate change in an organisation.

Discussion questions

Discuss likely internal and external reasons to change what is done in a specific sport or leisure organisation that you are familiar with, e.g. a local or sports club, leisure centre, theatre, or museum. Is the external market changing? Is the internal organisational structure suited to change? Is the physical infrastructure flexible enough to accommodate change?

21.5.1 Financial plans

The financial 'bottom line' is critically important to a business plan for a new venture, particularly for the funding organisation. Financial forecasts, or budgets, are assembled by six stages:

1 **Forecast sales revenue** – this derives from the marketing plan in particular, requiring forecasted sales volumes at planned prices (see Section 14.4.4 for demand forecasting).
2 **Identify the required capital spending** – and demonstrate through capital investment appraisal the return that will be achieved (see below).
3 **Identify operating costs** – i.e. especially labour, a vital resource and for sport and leisure services typically the principal operating cost (see Chapter 13), plus annual premises costs, materials, marketing, support services, etc.
4 **Derive an income statement** – identifying the main income and expenditure flows (see Section 18.6.1).
5 **Draw up a balance sheet** – showing assets and liabilities (see Section 18.6.2).
6 **Check cash flow requirements** – showing the movement of cash in the organisation (see Section 18.6.3).

(Stutely, 2002)

An important technique to employ in arriving at these budgets is sensitivity analysis. This involves varying the assumptions made on key factors, and reworking the forecasts. Sensitivity analysis demonstrates how sensitive the bottom line is to changes in key variables, such as the demand for the products at the anticipated prices, the extent of competition, the time for capital investments to become operational, the quantity and quality of required staff, or the interest payments due on debts. Sensitivity analysis is often simplified as a 'worst case scenario' and 'best case scenario' but, however it is conducted, it is important to recognise that any forecast is built on assumptions which may be wrong.

One specific set of techniques usually has an important function in financial planning – capital investment appraisal. Because physical capital assets have a relatively long lifetime, it is important to assess whether investment in such assets, as part of new enterprise, generates sufficient return over their lifetime. The best techniques for assessing new capital expenditure are discounting techniques, because they take account of the changing value of money over time (because of inflation and the alternative return that can be made over time). Two discounting techniques are Net Present Value and Internal Rate of Return – here is not the place to detail the mathematics of these techniques but accounting textbooks will provide details. Many organisations still use non-discounting techniques such as Pay-back. This basically requires calculation of the time it will take for an investment to pay back its initial capital costs. Three to five years is a typical period over which a commercial firm would expect capital costs to be paid back. For small-scale capital investment, such as a new piece of equipment, the expected pay-back period might be as short as a year. For very large-scale investments the expected pay-back may be ten years or more.

Whatever investment appraisal method is used, it relies critically on an accurate identification of both capital costs and the resulting increase in revenues from the new enterprise. Costs are perceived as the more accurate to estimate, but many projects suffer from cost escalation. A notorious example in the UK is the new Wembley Stadium in London, which was originally budgeted at £326 million but eventually cost £827 million to construct. Revenues can be even more unpredictable, because of unforeseen changes in the external business environment. Yet again, sensitivity analysis is a wise procedure in conducting investment appraisal, e.g. to identify how long pay-back will take to achieve during adverse trading conditions.

21.5.2 Planning for and managing risks

The consideration of sensitivity analysis above is an example of a process of identifying risks to the business plan and building scenarios and plans to deal with them. The following examples of sources of risk are adapted from Stutely (2002):

- increasing competition, especially from new market entrants;
- changing market/reduced sales, e.g. the recent recession;
- product/service quality problems, e.g. cleanliness in sports facilities;
- resource constraints, e.g. skill shortages and gaps, particularly in high labour cost locations such as London;
- unused service capacity at off-peak times, e.g. sports centres, museums;
- insufficient investment, e.g. lack of car parking at urban locations;
- IT system problems, e.g. inadequate real-time management information;
- internal politics and relationships, e.g. between key stakeholders;
- unproductive staff;
- cash flow problems;
- increasing interest rates;
- changes in currency exchange rates.

One way to reduce risks from competition is to seek to protect the intellectual property rights of the new development with legal protection, such as patents or copyright. From the initial idea to the creation of a new business venture, entrepreneurs invest a lot of their intellect into their enterprise, and legal protection is one way to ensure that this advantage can be exploited fully by the entrepreneur. There are different arrangements in different countries to protect intellectual property, and some global agreements. They ensure that for a specified time period entrepreneurs can exploit their idea without direct competition, unless, of course, the idea is licensed or franchised for others to exploit. The main forms of intellectual property rights include:

- **patents** – registered with the government and can cover product design or production processes;
- **trademarks** – also registered and typically apply to words or logos that represent a brand, e.g. Apple, Virgin and Microsoft;
- **copyright** – not registered but applies to the creation of a new and original work such as a book, a film, a work of art or a piece of music.

Apart from legal ways of reducing competitive risks to a business, Elliott (2004) identifies the steps necessary to manage risk more generally:

1 Identify hazards and threats.
2 Assess the likely impact of hazards on business activity.
3 Assess the probability of risks and decide priorities.
4 Consider alternative options, including prevention and control measures, insurance or modifying plans to avoid specific risks.

Acknowledging risks and planning for them is half the battle with new ventures – and much easier than ad hoc crisis management. If the risks can be quantified in terms of possible changes in sales, resources, costs, etc., then techniques such as those used in business planning can be replicated with different numbers to identify possible alternative outcomes. It is then necessary to plan remedial actions in the eventuality of risks becoming reality. If sales of gym memberships fall in a recession, for example, what impact are reduced membership fees going to have on the number of members, and on sales revenue? What cost reductions are possible in the short term in order to compensate for a fall in sales revenue? Planning exercises such as these are necessary to identify contingencies, i.e. rehearsing for the unexpected.

> ### Discussion question
>
> How might a sport and leisure organisation, which is reliant on member-ship subscriptions, reduce the risk of members deserting the organisation and going to competitors?

As important as planning for risk, though, is monitoring performance in order to identify emerging risks as soon as possible when they occur. Chapter 17 is relevant here. In the National Benchmarking Service in England, for example, the best financial performers are very sensitive and responsive to variations in their organisations' performance from their business plans, as shown in Case Study 21.3.

21.5.3 Practicalities

A business plan should be as short as possible, and is typically less than 50 pages long. This is primarily because of the communication function – those you want to win over are unlikely to have the time to plough through hundreds of pages of detail. However, a diffi-cult compromise to achieve is between necessary detail and being concise. A business plan needs to tell a coherent story and not be an endless collection of bullet point lists.

Stutely (2002) recommends that the principal features of the business plan should be relayed three times, for effective communication:

1 Tell them what you are going to tell them – i.e. the executive summary.
2 Tell it to them – the main body of the plan.
3 Tell them what you just told them – the conclusion.

The shorter messages, particularly at the beginning, are as important as the long one in the middle. Barrow *et al.* (2006) suggest that the executive summary is the single most important part of the plan. Many different types of people will need to be persuaded by the business plan and some will only be interested in the executive summary. Indeed, the concept of the 'elevator pitch' – where you have one minute to persuade an influential person of your busi-ness idea – has a sound logic. The essence of the business plan has to grab the intended target quickly – this is the concept behind the television programme *Dragons' Den*. If the executive summary fails to attract attention, then the detailed body of the plan is already handicapped.

The targets for a business plan are many and varied. If it concerns a new development for an existing organisation they will include senior managers in the organisation, internal compet-itors for development funds, and people who just like to ask awkward questions. If it concerns a development which needs external funding, then the business plan needs to convince either commercial financiers such as venture capitalists or business angels, or possibly government-sponsored sources of finance – either way the plan needs to shine in a very competitive environ-ment. Whoever the intended targets of the business plan are, they will all be looking for different things. Some will concentrate on the bottom line, and evaluate its feasibility. Others will concentrate on whether the leadership and management potential is there to carry the

CASE STUDY 21.3

Managing risk in commercial management of public facilities

About one-third of the sport and leisure centres using the National Benchmarking Service in the UK (NBS – see Chapter 17) are run by commercial contract companies. Many of these companies were 'born' after the legislation which introduced Compulsory Competitive Tendering in the late 1980s (see Chapter 5). About 10 percent of all UK public leisure facilities are managed by commercial contract companies, according to the Department for Communities and Local Government (2007).

Every year the NBS gives awards for the best performing centres in its dataset, including a category for finance. Commercial contract companies have featured heavily in these finance awards over the years and a fundamental reason is that the companies' ethos is strongly focused on the bottom line and mitigating risk. They typically have very frequent (weekly) and detailed monitoring of sales revenue and costs, in order to identify deviations from those planned. This signals actions to correct the situation as fast as possible. This is not just for the benefit of the companies' head offices – the centre managers value such reporting because it provides near-instant feedback on how they are performing and what their immediate priorities are, so that they can take fast corrective action if necessary.

The production of budgets is an integral part of the contract companies' business plans, and one enterprising element to the fulfilment of these budgets is to incentivise staff at all levels in the centres to increase revenue and cut expenditure. This includes commission for sales-related proactive action, such as suggesting that a customer might save money by subscribing to a membership by direct debit. A bonus from this sales culture is that satisfaction scores from customers have improved – customers are getting more attention, not simply to get them to spend more but rather to improve service provision, which might in turn lead to more revenue.

On the cost side, continual expressions of enterprise include rewarding staff for ideas to improve productivity, such as increasing their work flexibility, which of course requires staff development and training to cope with multi-tasking in a people service environment. Rewards are also provided for energy saving suggestions.

The feedback from the NBS award winners for finance suggests that there is no simple fix to achieve financial excellence, but that also it is not 'rocket science'. The 2009 finance workshop report suggests that:

> Success comes from culture, a focus on the business essentials, proper planning, ownership of budgets by all staff, attention to detail, the provision of timely feedback, an appropriate system of rewards, recognition of good work, and a good product which enables the delivery of excellence.

Source: National Benchmarking Service Improvement Conference workshops, 22 April 2009

development through. In an existing organisation another concern will be with the internal synergy of the proposed development. The business plan must anticipate a variety of questions and answer them all.

Kuratko and Hodgetts (2007), Hisrich *et al.* (2005) and Stutely (2002) identify several reasons why business plans fail. These include the following:

- Objectives are unrealistic or not measurable.
- The entrepreneur shows a lack of commitment to the enterprise.
- The entrepreneur has no experience in the planned business.
- The entrepreneur does not accurately anticipate potential threats to or weaknesses in the business case.
- There is poor evidence of customer need or what the market is.
- There are presentational weaknesses, e.g. too scruffy.
- The text is too long or too short.
- There is insufficient sensitivity analysis.
- The financial forecasts are unreasonably optimistic.

Stutely also suggests that a reason for failure is if the plan is produced by professional consultants, not the entrepreneur, because it should be the entrepreneur who drives the business plan. However, the use of consultants can be important to compensate for technical weaknesses in the entrepreneur's skill set. Also, in the third sector of voluntary and charitable organisations it is often necessary to seek professional help at the feasibility stage. The earlier case study of the Trinity Sailing Trust (Case Study 21.2) is a good example of initial funding for professional business planning followed by investment funds for the capital expenditure required.

On a more positive note, Barrow *et al.* (2006) suggest that business plans that succeed include the following:

- **evidence of market orientation** – i.e. an awareness of the market context for the development, the relevant market segments for the product;
- **evidence of customer acceptance** – i.e. the results of market research and market testing;
- **exclusive rights** – through patents, copyright, or trademark protection, etc., which reduces risk and competition;
- **believable forecasts** – based on appropriate precedents and using facts rather than hope;
- **due diligence** – i.e. demonstrating that the track record and competencies of key people are up to the task.

21.6 Enterprise failures

It might seem odd to include a section on business failure in a chapter on enterprise but the fact is that only half of new firms live as long as 18 months and only 20 per cent live for ten years (Morrison *et al.*, 1999). Failure rates are worse for specific parts of the sport and leisure industry; for example, UHY Hacker Young (2007) reported that hospitality and catering businesses were three times more likely to fail than the average business. Therefore it is important to identify the major reasons for new business failures and, as good entrepreneurs do, learn what might be done to avoid them. Whilst evidence relating to business failures typically applies to all businesses – not just new ones, and also not just sport and leisure – nevertheless there is no reason to believe that new sport and leisure business failures will be different.

According to Morrison *et al.* (1999), management deficiencies and financial shortcomings are common factors in business failures. Some of the research reviewed by Morrison *et al.* (1999) examines the concept of 'management deficiencies' more closely and suggests that it is attitudes and actions that are at fault, rather than technical managerial skills. In particular, the evidence points to two more detailed reasons for business failures: reliance on intuition and emotion in decision-making, rather than planning; and inflexibility when things start to go wrong. Another contributory factor appears to be managerial inexperience, but that is why failure is an important part of the learning process for many entrepreneurs – it is an unforgettable experience!

Morrison *et al.* (1999) point out one other factor in business failure that might be particularly appropriate in sport and leisure – when a hobby becomes a business. It has become a cliché over time that many professional football clubs run by successful businessmen from other industries are not successful businesses. Similarly, many restaurants and small gyms have been started as a result of taking a serious hobby (e.g. cooking, sport) into a business enterprise. Whilst these entrepreneurs will have tremendous enthusiasm, this might prejudice a sound business plan. However, this discussion is speculative – more research is needed into the reasons why sport and leisure businesses end up failing.

21.7 Conclusions

Given that enterprise represents the heart of good management, it is fitting to end the chapter and the book with reference to Barrow *et al.* (2006), who provide 12 golden rules for dynamic and successful businesses. These are:

1 **Invest in employees** – a critical resource, particularly in sport and leisure services.
2 **Have a business plan and follow it** – a plan is useless unless it is used as a blueprint.
3 **Demonstrate financial discipline** – finance is another critical resource, particularly the monitoring and controlling of cash flow.
4 **Keep passionate about the business** – i.e. commitment to the business by its leaders.
5 **Monitor performance** – i.e. accountability to the business plan by all employees.
6 **Communicate performance internally** – to generate continued commitment and unity of purpose.
7 **Know the competition** – to avoid nasty surprises.
8 **Work smarter, not longer** – i.e. it is the quality of decisions that counts, not the hours of work.
9 **Get online** – e-commerce is of increasing importance to most businesses.
10 **'Stick to the knitting'** – i.e. for existing organisations the core business is selling existing products to existing markets.
11 **Be financially flexible** – don't rely on one funding source but have a range.
12 **Think globally** – particularly for supply sources.

Although these 12 golden rules are clearly oriented to commercial businesses, many are also relevant to successful organisations in the public and voluntary sectors. And it is important to remember that such advice applies as much to existing operations as it does to new ventures. Change is inevitable, particularly in the dynamic environment that sport and leisure management is conducted in – standing still is not an option. All sport and leisure managers can benefit from being entrepreneurial, helping themselves and their organisations to thrive in an industry which is becoming increasingly important in people's lives.

Practical tasks

1 Think of a new idea for an existing sport or leisure organisation that you are familiar with. It could be a new product, a new service, taking a variant of a different service to a new type of client (e.g. young people, or older people) or delivering the service in a different way. Then think about the market for the new idea and what kind of marketing mix would attract this market; how much it would cost to set up and operate; where the money to achieve this would come from; and what skills are needed to implement the idea. Finally, design a one-minute 'elevator pitch' to sell your idea to an influential person, i.e. a relevant manager or a significant funder.

2 For a new piece of equipment, e.g. a pool table, research how much it would cost to buy, install and run at an appropriate site (e.g. club or pub); estimate how busy it is likely to be at whatever price you decide to charge for it; and calculate how long it would take to pay back its capital cost. Is it worth investing in?

Structured guide to further reading

For an overview of entrepreneurship:
Barrow, C., Brown, R. and Clarke, L. (2006) *The Successful Entrepreneur's Guidebook*, Kogan Page, London and Philadelphia.

For an overview of business planning:
Stutely, R. (2002) *The Definitive Business Plan*, 2nd edition, Pearson Education, Harlow.

For examples in hotels and restaurants:
Morrison, A., Rimmington, M. and Williams, C. (1999) *Entrepreneurship in the Hospitality, Tourism and Leisure Industries*, Elsevier Butterworth-Heinemann, Oxford.

Useful websites

For the Department of Business Innovation and Skills:
www.bis.gov.uk/policies/enterprise-and-business-support

For Business Link, an advisory service for enterprise:
www.businesslink.gov.uk

For the Prince's Trust:
www.princes-trust.org.uk

References

Aaker, D.A. (2002) *Building Strong Brands*, Simon and Schuster, Free Press, New York.

Adair, J. and Reed, P. (2003) *Not Bosses but Leaders*, 3rd edition, Kogan Page, London.

Adby, R. (2002) Interview with the Director General, Olympic Co-Ordination Authority, Sydney 2000 by email questionnaire on 9 July 2002.

Aguiar, M. and Hurst, E. (2007) 'Measuring trends in leisure: the allocation of time over five decades', *Quarterly Journal of Economics*, 122, 3, available at http://faculty.chicago-booth.edu/erik.hurst/research/aguiar_hurst_leisure_qje_resubmit2_final.pdf (accessed 25 February 2009).

Alexandris, K. and Kouthouris, C. (2005) 'Personal incentives for participation in summer children's camps: investigating their relationships with satisfaction and loyalty', *Managing Leisure*, 10, 1, pp. 39–53.

Allen, J., O'Toole, W., McDonnell, I. and Harris, R. (2005) *Festival and Special Event Management*, 3rd edition, John Wiley & Sons, Queensland.

Andranovich, G., Burbank, M. and Heying, C. (2001) 'Olympic cities: lessons learned from mega-event politics', *Journal of Urban Affairs*, 23, 2, pp. 113–31, Urban Affairs Association.

Annan, K. (2005) *Report on the International Year of Sport and Education*, United Nations, New York.

APSE (2009) *Performance Networks Prospectus: benchmarking for success*, APSE, Manchester.

Arai, S. (1997) 'Volunteers within a changing society: the use of empowerment theory in understanding serious leisure', *World Leisure and Recreation*, 39, 3, pp. 19–22.

Arena Leisure Plc (2008) *Annual Report and Accounts 2008*, Arena Leisure Plc, London.

Argyris, C. (1966) 'Interpersonal barriers to decision making', *Harvard Business Review*, 44, 2, pp. 84–97.

Argyris, C. (1976) *Increasing Leadership Effectiveness*, Wiley, New York.

Arts Council for England (1998) *International Data on Public Spending on the Arts in Eleven Countries*, Research Report Number 13, Policy, Research and Planning Department.

Arts Council of Great Britain (1993) *A Creative Future*, HMSO, London.

Ashley, C., Boyd, C. and Goodwin, H. (2000) 'Pro-poor tourism: putting poverty at the heart of the tourism agenda', *Natural Resource Perspectives*, 51 (March), pp. 1–12.

Athens 2004 (2002) www.athens.olympics.org/Home/Legacy (accessed 24 April 2002).

Attwood, C., Singh, G., Prime, D. and Creasey, R. (2003) *2001 Home Office Citizenship Survey: people, families and communities*, Home Office, London, available at www.homeoffice.gov.uk/rds/pdfs2/hors270.pdf.

References

Audit Commission (1989) *Sport for Whom? Clarifying the local authority role in sport and recreation*, HMSO, London.

Audit Commission (1991a) *Local Authority Entertainments and the Arts*, HMSO, London.

Audit Commission (1991b) *The Road to Wigan Pier? Managing local authority museums and art galleries*, HMSO, London.

Audit Commission (2000a) *Aiming to Improve: the principles of performance measurement*, Audit Commission, London.

Audit Commission (2000b) *On Target: the practice of performance indicators*, Audit Commission, London.

Audit Commission (2006) *Public Sport and Recreation Services*, Audit Commission, London, available at www.audit-commission.gov.uk/reports/NATIONAL-REPORT. asp?CategoryID=&ProdID=3CC48D79–9F95–40cf-80BA-1BD14E044A43.

Audit Commission (2007) *Improving Information to Support Decision Making: standards for better quality data*, Audit Commission, London.

Audit Commission (2009) *Tired of Hanging Around*, Audit Commission, London, available at www.audit-commission.gov.uk/hangingaround/.

Australian Bureau of Statistics (2010) *Australian National Accounts: tourism satellite account, 2007–08*, ABS, Canberra.

Babbidge, A. (2007) *Local Authorities and Independent Museums: a research study*, AIM & MLA, London.

Bancroft-Hinchley, T. (2000) 'Football match between First World War enemies on Christmas Day 1914 really took place', available at www.english.pravda.ru/sport/2001/01/01/ 1795 (accessed 22 May 2003).

Barrow, C., Brown, R. and Clarke, L. (2006) *The Successful Entrepreneur's Guidebook*, Kogan Page, London and Philadelphia.

Basketball Hall of Fame (2003) www.hoophall.com/halloffamers/Naismith (accessed 22 May 2003).

Battram, A. (1999) *Navigating Complexity*, Industrial Society, London.

Beech, J. and Chadwick, S. (2004) *The Business of Sports Management*, Pearson Education, Harlow.

Beijing 2008 (2008) www.beijing2008.cn (accessed 11 February 2008).

Bennis, W. (1989) *On Becoming a Leader*, Business Books, London.

Bernstein, Howard (2002) Interview with the Chief Executive of Manchester City Council, Chief Executive Office, Manchester Town Hall, 28 June 2002.

Big Lottery Fund Research Issue 7 (2004) *The People's Network: evaluation summary*, November.

Bird, W. (2007) 'Practical applications of green space and health', paper presented at the Natural Health Conference, 4 July, available at www.tiny.cc/gR6bt.

Blackmore, A. (2004) *Standing Apart, Working Together: a study of the myths and realities of voluntary and community sector independence*, National Council for Voluntary Organisations, London.

Blake, T. (1985) 'Image', *Leisure Management*, 5, 11 (November), pp. 14–15.

Bolton, N., Fleming, S. and Elias, B. (2008) 'The experience of community sport development: a case study of Blaenau Gwent', *Managing Leisure: an international journal*, 13, 2, pp. 92–103.

Boniface, B. and Cooper, C. (2009) *Worldwide Destinations: the geography of travel and tourism*, Elsevier, Butterworth-Heinemann, Oxford.

Bourne, M., Franco-Santos, M., Pavlov, A., Lucianetti, L., Martinez, V. and Mura, M. (2008) *The Impact of Investors in People on People Management Practices and Firm Performance*, Centre for Business Performance, Cranfield School of Management, Cranfield.

Bradley, P. (2007) 'The internet and libraries', in J.H. Bowman (ed.) *British Librarianship and Information Work 2001–2005*, Ashgate, Farnham, Surrey.

Bradshaw, J. (1972) 'The concept of social need', *New Society*, 30, 3, pp. 640–3.

Bragg, A. and Bragg, M. (2005) *Developing New Business Ideas*, FT Prentice Hall, Harlow.

Breuer, C. and Wicker, P. (2008) *Sports Clubs in Germany*, German Sports University, Cologne.

British Beer and Pub Association (2008) News release 05/2008, available at www.beerand-pub.com/documents/publications/news/NR%200508%20-%20pub%20numbers.pdf (accessed 26 February 2009).

Brown, F. and Taylor, C. (2008) *Foundations of Playwork*, Open University Press, Maidenhead.

BSI (1987) *Quality Vocabulary: Part 1, international terms: BS44778*, British Standards Institute, London.

Bull, A. (1995) *The Economics of Travel and Tourism*, Longman Australia, Melbourne.

Bullough, S., Moriarty, C., Wilson, J. and Panagouleas, T. (2010) *The Nature of Latent Demand Compared to Expressed Demand, Using Active People 2*, a Strategic Insights Paper, Sport England, London.

Butler, R. (1991) *Designing Organisations: a decision making perspective*, Routledge, London and New York.

Butler, R.W. (1980) 'The concept of a tourist area cycle of evolution', *Canadian Geographer*, 24, pp. 5–12.

Butler, R.W. and Waldbrook, L.A. (1991) 'A new planning tool: the tourism opportunity spectrum', *Journal of Tourism Studies*, 2, 1, pp. 1–14.

CABE (2009) *Public Space Lessons: designing and planning for play*, Commission for Architecture and the Built Environment, London, available at www.cabe.org.uk/publications.

CAF/NCVO (2008) *UK Giving 2008*, CAF/NCVO, London, available at www.cafonline.org/pdf/UK%20Giving%202008.pdf.

Campaign for National Parks (2009) www.cnp.org.uk (accessed October 2009).

Carpenter, G. and Blandy, D. (2008) *Arts and Cultural Programming: a leisure perspective*, Human Kinetics, Champaign, IL.

Carroll, R. (2009) 'Obama administration grants exemption from 40-year embargo', *Guardian*, 14 July.

Carter, P. (2005) *Review of National Sport Effort and Resources*, DCMS, London, available at www.culture.gov.uk/images/publications/Carter_report.pdf.

Casey, M.M., Payne, W.R. and Eime, R.M. (2009) 'Building the health promotion capacity of sport and recreation organisations: a case study of Regional Sports Assemblies', *Managing Leisure: an international journal*, 14, 2, pp. 112–24.

CCPR (2009) *Survey of Sports Clubs 2009*, CCPR, London.

Centre for Leisure and Tourism Studies (1996) *A Survey of Local Authority Service Budgets in England and Wales, 1995/6*, University of North London, London.

Centre for Leisure Research (1993) *Compulsory Competitive Tendering Sport and Leisure Management: national information survey report*, Sports Council, London.

Chalip, L. (2003) 'Tourism and the Olympic Games', in M. de Moragas, C. Kennett and N. Puig (eds) *The Legacy of the Olympic Games 1984–2000*, IOC, Lausanne.

Chandler, Alfred D., Jr (2005) *Shaping the Industrial Century*, Harvard University Press, Cambridge, MA.

Children's Workforce Network (2009) *The Integrated Qualifications Framework*, available at www.iqf.org.uk/.

References

Clark, R. and Stankey, G. (1979) *The Recreation Opportunity Spectrum: a framework for planning, management and research*, General Technical Report PNW{hy}98, US Department of Agriculture Forest Service, Washington, DC.

Clarke, F. (1992) 'Quality and service in the public sector', *Public Finance and Accountancy*, 23, 10, pp. 23–5.

Cnaan, R., Handy, F. and Wadsworth, M. (1996) 'Defining who is a volunteer: conceptual and empirical considerations', *Non-profit and Volunteer Sector Quarterly*, 25, pp. 364–83.

Coalter, F. (2007) *A Wider Social Role for Sport: who's keeping the score?*, Routledge, London and New York.

Coalter, F., Long, J. and Duffield, B. (1986) *Rationale for Public Sector Investment in Leisure*, Sports Council and Economic and Social Research Council, London.

Colbert, F. (2000) *Marketing Culture and the Arts*, 2nd edition, HEC, Montreal.

Cole-Hamilton, I. and Gill, T. (2002) *Making the Case for Play*, NCB, London.

Collins, M.F. and Kay, T. (2003) *Sport and Social Exclusion*, Routledge, London.

COMPASS (1999) *Sports Participation in Europe*, UK Sport, London.

Conn, D. (2009a) 'The deals are done, now for a place in the top four: inside Manchester City part three', *Observer*, Sport Section, 20 September, pp. 6–7.

Conn, D. (2009b) 'Kevin Keegan's case at Newcastle sheds light on the grubby deals we seldom see', available at www.guardian.co.uk/football/blog/2009/oct/02/kevin-keegan-newcastle-united-arbitration-panel (accessed 12 March 2010).

Conway, M. (2009) *Developing an Adventure Playground: the essential elements*, Play England, London, available at www.tiny.cc/sddFR.

Cooper, C., Fletcher J., Fyall, A., Gilbert, D. and Wanhill, S. (2008) *Tourism Principles and Practice*, Prentice Hall, Harlow.

Council of Europe (1992) *European Sports Charter*, Strasbourg.

Countryside Agency (2004) *GB Leisure Day Visits Survey 2002/03*, Countryside Agency, Wetherby.

Countryside Commission (1970) *Countryside Recreation Glossary*, Countryside Commission, Cheltenham.

Countryside Recreation Network (2007) *Volunteering in the Natural Outdoors*, CRN, Sheffield.

Covey, S. (1992) *The Seven Habits of Highly Effective People*, Simon and Shuster, London.

Cowell, B. (2007) 'Measuring the impact of free admission', *Cultural Trends*, 16, 3, pp. 203–24.

Cowling, M. (2008) *Does IIP Add Value to Businesses?*, Institute of Employment Studies, Brighton.

Crompton, J. (2009) 'Strategies for implementing repositioning of leisure services', *Managing Leisure: an international journal*, 14, 2, pp. 87–111.

Crowe, L. (2005) *Promoting Outdoor Recreation in the English National Parks: guide to good practice*, Countryside Agency CA214, Cheltenham.

CRRAG (1977) *Providing for Countryside Recreation: the role of marketing*, CRRAG, Cardiff.

Csikszentmihalyi, M. (1975) *Beyond Boredom and Anxiety*, Jossey Bass, San Francisco, CA.

Curry, N. (1994) *Countryside Recreation, Access and Land Use Planning*, E & F Spon, London.

Cushman, G., Veal, A.J. and Zuzanek, J. (eds) (2005) *Free Time and Leisure Participation: international perspectives*, CABI Publishing, Wallingford.

Cuskelly, G. (2004) 'Volunteer retention in community sport organisations', *European Sport Management Quarterly*, 4, pp. 59–76.

Cuskelly, G., Hoye, R. and Auld, C. (2006) *Working with Volunteers in Sport: theory and practice*, Routledge, London.

Davies, R. (2008) 'Europeana: an infrastructure for adding local content', *Ariadne*, 57, available at www.ariadne.ac.uk/issue57/.

Davis Smith, J. (1998) *The 1997 National Survey of Volunteering*, National Centre for Volunteering, London.

Davis Smith, J. (2003) 'Government and volunteering', *Voluntary Action*, 5, 3, pp. 23–32.

DCMS (2000) *Creating Opportunities: guidance for local authorities in England on local cultural strategies*, DCMS, London.

DCMS (2003) *Framework for the Future: libraries, learning and information in the next decade*, DCMS, London.

DCMS (2007a) *Taking Part: the national survey of culture, leisure and sport, annual report 2005/2006*, DCMS, London.

DCMS (2007b) *Taking Part: England's survey of culture, leisure and sport: headline findings from the child survey*, DCMS, London.

DCMS (2007c) *Winning: a tourism strategy for 2012 and beyond*, DCMS, London.

DCMS (2008) *Playing to Win: a new era for sport*, DCMS, London, available at www.culture.gov.uk/images/publications/DCMS_PlayingtoWin_singles.pdf.

DCMS/Cabinet Office (2002) *Game Plan: a strategy for delivering government's Sport and Physical Activity Objectives Report*, DCMS, London, available at www.sportengland.org/gameplan2002.pdf.

DCSF (2009) *The Play Strategy*, available at www.tiny.cc/cE6ly.

Deakin, S., Johnston, A. and Markesinis, B. (2007) *Markesinis and Deakin's Tort Law*, 6th edition, Oxford University Press, Oxford.

Debbage, K.G. and Ioannides, D. (1998) 'Conclusion: the commodification of tourism', in D. Ioannides and K.G. Debbage (eds) *The Economic Geography of the Tourist Industry: a supply side analysis*, Routledge, London.

Defra (2004) *Delivering the Essentials of Life*, available at www.defra.gov.uk/corporate/5year-strategy/5year-strategy.pdf (accessed March 2009).

Deloitte (2009) *Economic Impact of British Racing 2009*, British Horse Racing Authority, London, available at www.britishhorseracing.com/resources/media/publications_and_reports/Economic_Impact_of_British_Racing_2009.pdf.

Deloitte and Touche (2008) *Annual Review of Football Finance*, Deloitte and Touche, Manchester.

Deming, W.E. (1986) *Out of the Crisis*, The Press Syndicate, Cambridge.

Department for Communities and Local Government (2002) *Planning Policy Guidance 17: planning for open space, sport and recreation*, HMSO, London.

Department for Communities and Local Government (2007) *Developing the Local Government Services Market: working paper on the future for the leisure services market*, Communiities and Local Government Publications, London.

Department of Education and Science (1965) *Support for the Arts: the first steps*, Cmnd 2601, HMSO, London.

Department of Education and Science and Ministry of Housing and Local Government (1964) *Joint Circular 11/64 and 49/64: Provision of Facilities for Sport*, DES, London.

Department of the Environment (1975) *Sports and Recreation*, Cmnd 6200, HMSO, London.

Department of the Environment (1977) *Policy for the Inner Cities*, Cmnd 6845, HMSO, London.

Department of Health (1992) *White Paper, The Health of the Nation: a strategy for health in England*, Cmnd 1986, HMSO, London.

Department of Health (2004) *At Least Five a Week: evidence on the impact of physical activity and its relationship to health*, DoH, London, available at www.dh.gov.uk/en/Publicationsandstatistics/Publications/PublicationsPolicyAndGuidance/DH_4080994.

Department of National Heritage (1995) *Sport: raising the game*, Department of National Heritage, London.

DFES (2008) *2020 Children and Young People's Workforce Strategy*, available at www.tiny.cc/CkjYS.

Dodd, F., Graves, A. and Taws, K. (2008) *Our Creative Talent: the voluntary and amateur arts in England*, DCMS, London.

Doyal, L. and Gough, I. (1991) *A Theory of Human Needs*, Macmillan, London.

Drucker, P.F. (1955) *The Practice of Management*, Pan Books, London.

Dumazedier, J. (1967) *Toward a Society of Leisure*, W.W. Norton, New York.

Dunnell, K. (2008) *Ageing and Mortality in the UK*, Population Trends 134, London, ONS, available at www.statistics.gov.uk/downloads/theme_population/Population-Trends-134.pdf (accessed 26 February 2009).

Eden Project (2009) www.edenproject.com (accessed 4 August 2009).

Edginton, C., Coles, R. and McClelland, M. (2003) *Leisure Basic Concepts*, AALR, Reston, VA.

Edginton, C.R., Crompton, D.M. and Hanson, C.J. (1980) *Recreation and Leisure Programming*, Saunders College, Philadelphia, PA.

Edginton, C.R., Hudson, S., Dieser, R. and Edginton, S. (2004) *Leisure Programming: a service-centred and benefits approach*, 4th edition, McGraw Hill, New York.

Edwards, P. (2004) 'No country mouse: thirty years of effective marketing and health communications', in *The Mouse that Roared*, a special issue of the *Canadian Journal of Public Health*, 95, Supplement 2 (May/June), available at www.participaction.com.

EEU (2009) www.eeu.uct.ac.za (accessed 4 August 2009).

Elliott, C. and Quinn, F. (2007) *English Legal System*, 8th edition, Pearson, Harlow.

Elliott, D. (2004) 'Risk management in sport', in J. Beech and S. Chadwick (eds) *The Business of Sport Management*, Pearson Education Ltd., Harlow.

Else, P. (2005) 'The "3 Frees" Standard', in *Local Play Indicators*, Play England, London.

Else, P. (2009) *The Value of Play*, Continuum International Publishing Ltd, London and New York.

Elson, M. (1982) 'The poverty of leisure forecasting', in M. Collins (ed.) *Leisure Research*, SSRC/SC/LSA, London.

Elson, M., Heaney, D. and Reynolds, G. (1995) *Good Practice in the Planning and Management of Sport and Active Recreation in the Countryside*, Sports Council and Countryside Commission, London and Cheltenham.

Emery, P. (2002) 'Bidding to host a major sports event: the local organising perspective', *International Journal of Public Sector Management*, 15, 4, pp. 316–35.

Emery, R. and Weed, M. (2006) 'Fighting for survival? The financial management of football clubs outside the "top flight" in England', *Managing Leisure, an International Journal*, 11, 1, pp. 1–21.

English Nature (2003) *England's Best Wildlife and Geological Sites: the condition of SSSIs in England in 2003*, English Nature, Sheffield.

Ershova, T.V. and Hohlov, Y.E. (eds) (2002) *Libraries in the Information Society*, IFLA Publications, The Hague.

Essex, S. and Chalkley, B. (2003) 'Urban transformation from hosting the Olympic Games', university lecture on the Olympics, Centre d'Estudis Olimpics, Univesitat Autonoma de Barcelona, available at www.olympicstudies.uab.es/lectures (accessed 19 March 2005).

European Environment Agency (2009) www.eea.europa.eu (accessed March 2009).

European Union (2007) *White Paper on Sport*, European Union, Brussels, available at http://ec.europa.eu/sport/white-paper/whitepaper8_en.htm.

European Union (2009) *2009 Annual Work Programme on Grants and Contracts for the Preparatory Action in the Field of Sport and Special Annual Events*, available at http://ec.europa.eu/dgs/education_culture/calls/docs/sport09.pdf.

Fafinski, S. and Finch, E. (2007) *Legal Skills*, Oxford University Press, Oxford.

Farrell, P. and Lundegren, H.M. (1991) *The Process of Recreation Programming*, 3rd edition, Venture Publishing, State College, PA.

Felli, G. (2002) 'Transfer of Knowledge (TOK). Architecture and international sporting events: future planning and development', paper presented at the International Conference, Lausanne, June 2002. Lausanne, IOC, Documents of the Museum.

Fenton, W. (2005) 'Sports sponsorship in first place', *Brand Strategy*, 191 (April), pp. 37–9.

Ferrand, A. and McCarthy, S. (2009) *Marketing the Sports Organisation: building networks and relationships*, Routledge, London.

Fitness Industry Association (2009) *2009 FIA State of the UK Fitness Industry Audit*, FIA, London.

Fotheringham, W. (2008) 'Revolutionaries', *Observer*, Sport Supplement, 23 November, p. 53.

Fox, K. and Rickards, L. (2004) *Sport and Leisure: results from the sport and leisure module of the 2002 General Household Survey*, The Statistics Office, London.

Gambling Commission (2009) *Industry Statistics, 2008/2009*, Gambling Commission, London.

Garcia, B. (2003) 'Securing sustainable legacies through cultural programming in sporting events', in M. de Moragas, C. Kennett and N. Puig (eds) *The Legacy of the Olympic Games 1984–2000*, IOC, Lausanne.

Garvey, C. (1977) *Play*, Harvard University Press, Cambridge, MA.

Gershuny, J.I. (1997) 'Time for the family', *Prospect* (January), pp. 56–7.

Gershuny, J.I. (2000) *Changing Times: work and leisure in postindustrial society*, Oxford University Press, Oxford.

Gershuny, J.I. and Fisher, K. (1999) *Leisure in the UK across the 20th Century*, Social Policy Research Unit, Colchester, University of Essex.

Getz, D. (1997) *Event Management and Tourism*, Cognizant, New York.

GHK (2010) *Volunteering in the European Union*, Educational, Audiovisual and Culture Executive Agency, Directorate General Education and Culture, Brussels, available at http://ec.europa.eu/citizenship/news/news1015_en.htm.

Girlguiding UK (2009) www.girlguiding.org.uk/xq/asp/sID.1008/qx/whoweare/article.asp.

Glasgow Caledonian University (1998) *To Charge or Not to Charge?*, Museums and Galleries Commission, Glasgow.

Godbey, G. (1976) *Recreation and Park Planning: the exercise of values*, University of Waterloo, Ontario.

Goldblatt, J. (1997) *Special Events: best practices in modern event management*, John Wiley & Sons, New York.

Goodale, T. and Godbey, G. (1988) *The Evolution of Leisure*, Venture Publishing, State College, PA.

Goodall, B. (2003) 'Environmental auditing: a means of improving tourism environmental performance', in C. Cooper (ed.) *Classic Reviews in Tourism*, Channel View, Clevedon.

Government Office for Science/Foresight (2007) *Tackling Obesities: future choices – project report*, GOS, London, available at www.foresight.gov.uk/OurWork/ActiveProjects/Obesity/Obesity.asp.

References

Gratton, C. and Solberg, H.A. (2007) *The Economics of Sports Broadcasting*, Routledge, London and New York.

Gratton, C. and Taylor, P. (1991) *Government and the Economics of Sport*, Longman, Harlow.

Gratton, C. and Taylor, P. (1988) *Economics of Leisure Services Management*, Longman, Harlow.

Gratton, C. and Taylor, P. (2000) *Economics of Sport and Recreation*, E & FN Spon, London.

Gratton, C. and Taylor, P. (2005) 'The economics of work and leisure', in A. Veal and J. Howarth (eds) *The Future of Work and Leisure*, Routledge, London.

Gray, C. (2002) 'Local government and the arts', *Local Government Studies*, 28, 1 (Spring), pp. 77–90, Frank Cass.

Green, E., Hebron, S. and Woodward, D. (1987) *Leisure and Gender: a study of leisure constraints and opportunities for women*, Sports Council/Economic Social Research Council, London.

Griffiths, H. and Randall, M. (2004) *Careers in Leisure*, Institute of Leisure and Amenity Management, ILAM House, Lower Basildon, Reading.

Grindlay, D.C.J. and Morris, A. (2004) 'The decline in adult book lending in UK public libraries and its possible causes', *Journal of Documentation*, 60, 6, pp. 609–31, Emerald Group Publishing Limited.

Hall, C. (1992) *Hallmark Tourist Events: impacts, management and planning*, Bellhaven Press, London.

Hall, C. (2001) 'Imaging, tourism and sports event fever', in C. Gratton and I. Henry (eds) *Sport in the City: the role of sport in economic and social regeneration*, Routledge, London.

Hall, C.M. and Jenkins, J.M. (1995) *Tourism and Public Policy*, 4th edition, Routledge, London.

Hall, C.M. and Page, S.J. (2002) *The Geography of Tourism and Recreation: environment, place and space*, Routledge, London.

Hall, L. (2009) 'High culture and the Pitmen Painters', in *The Pitmen Painters Programme Notes*, National Theatre, London.

Hammer, M. (1996) *Beyond Reengineering*, HarperCollins Business, London.

Handy, C.B. (1985) *Understanding Organisations*, 3rd edition, Penguin Books, Harmondsworth.

Harpwood, V. (2009) *Modern Tort Law*, 7th edition, Routledge Cavendish, London.

Harrison, S. and Bland, N. (2009) *A Pause in Consolidation?*, Attractions Management online, available at http://attractionsmanagement.com/.

Hartley, H. (2009) *Sport, Physical Recreation and the Law*, Routledge, London.

Health and Safety Commission (2006) *'Get a Life', says HSC*, available at www.hse.gov.uk/press/2006/c06021.htm.

Heilbrun, J. and Gray, C.M. (2001) *The Economics of Art and Culture*, Cambridge University Press, Cambridge.

Heller, R. (1998) *Managing Teams*, Dorling Kindersley, London.

Helsinki (2008) www.hs.fi/english/article/Eurovision+Song+Contest+40000+guests+to+Helsinki+last+year (accessed 4 August 2009).

Henley Centre (2005) *Online Research Supporting the Outdoor Recreation Strategy*, available at www.naturalengland.org.uk/ourwork/enjoying/research/futuretrends (accessed March 2009).

Henry, I. (2001) *The Politics of Leisure Policy*, 2nd edition, Palgrave, Basingstoke.

Heywood, R. and Charlish, P. (2007) 'Schoolmaster tackled hard over rugby incident', *Tort Law Review*, 15.

Higgins, C. (2009) 'Striking a conciliatory note', *Guardian*, 14 July.

Hill, E., O'Sullivan, C. and O'Sullivan T. (2003) *Creative Arts Marketing*, 2nd edition, Butterworth-Heinemann, London.

Hiller, H. (2000) 'Mega-events, urban boosterism and growth strategies: an analysis of the objectives and legitimations of the Cape Town 2004 Olympic bid', *International Journal of Urban and Regional Research*, 24, 2, pp. 439–58.

Hinch, T. and Higham, J. (2004) *Sport Tourism Development*, Channel View, Clevedon.

Hisrich, R.D., Peters, M.P. and Shepherd, D.A. (2005) *Entrepreneurship*, 6th edition, McGraw-Hill Irwin, New York.

HM Government (2006) *Working Together to Safeguard Children: a guide to inter-agency working to safeguard and promote the welfare of children*, The Stationery Office, London.

HM Treasury (2002) *The Role of the Voluntary and Community Sector in Service Delivery: a cross-cutting review*, HM Treasury, London.

Holden, A. (2008) *Environment and Tourism*, Routledge, London.

Holden, J. (2005) *Capturing Cultural Value: how culture has become a tool of government policy*, DEMOS, London.

Holloway, G. (2001) 'After the party, Sydney's Olympic blues', www.europ.cnn.com.2001 (accessed 13 March 2002).

Holmes, K. (2007) 'Volunteers in the heritage sector', in R. Sandell and R.R. Janes (eds) *Museum Management and Marketing*, Routledge, London.

Home Office (1998) *Compact: getting it right together, Compact on relations between government and the voluntary and community sector in England*, CM 4100, Home Office, London.

Home Office (2003) *2001 Home Office Citizenship Survey: people, families and communities*, Home Office, London, available at www.homeoffice.gov.uk/rds/pdfs2/hors270.pdf.

Home Office (2007) *Positive Futures: review of the year*, Home Office, London, available at http://drugs.homeoffice.gov.uk/publication-search/183400/positivefuturesreview?view=Binary.

House of Commons (1995) *Environment Committee Report on the Environmental Impact of Leisure Activities*, HMSO, London.

House of Commons (2004) *Trade and Industry Second Report*, available at www.publications.parliament.uk/pa/cm200405/cmselect/cmtrdind/128/12802.htm.

House of Lords (1973) *Second Report from the Select Committee of the House of Lords on Sport and Leisure*, HMSO, London.

Hoye, R., Smith, A., Nicholson, M., Stewart, B. and Westerbeek, H. (2009) *Sport Management: principles and applications*, 2nd edition, Butterworth-Heinemann, Oxford.

Hudson, S. (2000) *Snow Business: a study of the international ski industry*, Cassell, London.

Hughes, B. (1996a) *Play Environments, a Question of Quality*, Playlink, London.

Hughes, B. (1996b) *Playworker's Taxonomy of Play Types*, Playlink, London.

Hughes, B. (2001a) *Evolutionary Playwork and Reflective Analytic Practice*, Routledge, London.

Hughes, B. (2001b) *The First Claim: a framework for playwork quality assessment*, Play Wales, Cardiff.

Hughes, B. (2003) *The First Claim: desirable processes*, Play Wales, Cardiff.

Hughes, B. (2006) *Play Types: speculations and possibilities*, London Centre for Playwork Education and Training, London.

Hughes, L. (1993) 'Olympic tourism and urban regeneration', *Festival Management & Event Tourism*, 1, pp. 157–62.

IDeA (2008) *Culture and Sport Improvement Toolkit*, IDeA, London.

IEG (2009a) 'Sponsorship spending', available at http.//www.sponsorship.com/Resources/Sponsorship-Spending.aspx.

IEG (2009b) *Stateside Report*, reported in Hollis Sponsorship Bulletin, available at http://news.hollis-sponsorship.com/tag/ieg-sponsorship-report/.

IFER/DART (Institute of Family and Environmental Research and Dartington Amenity Research Trust) (1976) *Leisure Provision and Human Need: Stage 1 Report (for DoE)*, IFER/DART, London.

Institute of Sport and Leisure Policy (ISLP) (2005) *Academic Review of the Role of Voluntary Sports Clubs*, ISLP, Loughborough University, England.

Institute for Volunteering Research (1998) *National Survey of Volunteering*, IVR, London.

Institute for Volunteering Research (2002) *UK-wide Evaluation of the Millennium Volunteers Programme*, research report 357, Department for Education and Skills, London.

International City Management Association (1965) *Basic Concepts of Organisation. Bulletin 3, Effective Supervisory Practices*, ICMA, Washington, DC.

Ioannides, D. and Debbage, K.G. (eds) (1998) *The Economic Geography of the Tourist Industry: a supply side analysis*, Routledge, London.

Irvine, D. and Taylor, P.D. (1996) 'Globalisation and leisure, theory and application', paper for Free Time and Quality of Life for the 21st Century, WLRA 4th International Conference, Cardiff.

Irvine, D. and Taylor, P.D. (1998) 'The value and structure of commercial leisure', in M.F. Collins and I.S. Cooper (eds) *Leisure Management: issues and applications*, CABI Publishing, New York.

Jago, L. and Shaw, R. (1998) 'Special events: a conceptual and differential framework', *Festival Management & Event Tourism*, 5, 1.2, pp. 21–32.

Jennings, P.L. (2009) *Identifying Business Opportunities*, course notes for Enterprise Development and Business Planning, School of Management, University of Sheffield.

Johnson, A.J., Glover, T.D. and Yuen, F.C. (2009) 'Supporting effective community representation: lessons from the Festival of Neighbourhoods', *Managing Leisure: an international journal*, 14, 1, pp. 1–16.

Johnson, G., Scholes, K. and Whittington, M. (2008) *Exploring Corporate Strategy*, 8th edition, Pearson Education, Harlow.

Jones, C. (2005) 'The potential economic return to stadia and major sporting events or a month on the lips, a lifetime on the hips?', paper presented at the Regional Studies Association, The Regeneration Games conference, 14 December, Goonerville.

Jung, B. (2005) 'Poland', in G. Cushman, A.J. Veal and J. Zuzanek (eds) *Free Time and Leisure Participation: international perspectives*, CABI Publishing, Wallingford.

Juran, J.M. (1988) *Juran on Planning for Quality*, Collier Macmillan, London.

Kane, P. (2004) *The Play Ethic*, Pan Macmillan, London.

Kaplan, R.S. and Norton, D.P. (1996) *The Balanced Scorecard*, Harvard Business Press, Boston, MA.

Keirle, I. (2002) *Countryside Recreation Site Management: a marketing approach*, Routledge, London.

Kelso, P. (2010) 'Portsmouth dismiss 85 staff as Peter Storrie takes 40 per cent pay cut', *Telegraph*, 10 March 2010, available at www.telegraph.co.uk/sport/football/leagues/premierleague/portsmouth/7415616/Portsmouth-dismiss-85-staff-as-Peter-Storrie-takes-40-per-cent-pay-cut.html (accessed 12 March 2010).

Kew, S. and Rapoport, R. (1975) 'Beyond palpable mass demand, leisure provision and human needs – the life cycle approach', paper presented to Planning and Transport Research and Computation (International) Company Ltd, summer annual meeting.

Knott, G. (2004) *Financial Management*, Palgrave Macmillan, London.

Knulst, W. and van der Poel, H. (2005) 'The Netherlands', in G. Cushman, A.J. Veal and J. Zuzanek (eds) *Free Time and Leisure Participation: international perspectives*, CABI Publishing, Wallingford.

Kotler, P. (2000) *Marketing Management*, the millennium edition, Prentice Hall, Upper Saddle River, NJ.

Kotler, P. (2003) *Principles of Marketing*, 2nd edition, Prentice Hall, Frenchs Forest, New South Wales.

Kotler, P. and Zaltman, G. (1971) 'Social marketing: an approach to planned social change', *Journal of Marketing* 35 (July), pp. 3–12.

Kotler, P., Bowen, J. and Makens, J. (2005) *Marketing for Hospitality and Tourism*, 4th edition, Prentice Hall, Upper Saddle River, NJ.

Kraus, R. (2001) *Recreation and Leisure in Modern Society*, 6th edition, Jones & Bartlett, Sudbury, MA.

Kraus, R.G. and Curtis, J.E. (1977) *Creative Administration in Recreation and Parks*, C.V. Mosby, Saint Louis, MO.

Kuenzel, S. and Yassim, M. (2007) 'The effect of joy on the behaviour of cricket spectators: the mediating role of satisfaction', *Managing Leisure*, 12, 1, pp. 43–57.

Kuo, F.E. (2001) 'Coping with poverty: impacts of environment and attention in the inner city', *Environment and Behaviour*, 33, pp. 5–34.

Kuratko, D.F. and Hodgetts, R.M. (2007) *Entrepreneurship: theory, process, practice*, Thomson South-Western, Mason, OH.

Lader, D., Short, S. and Gershuny, J. (2006) *The Time Use Survey 2005: how we spend our time*, HMSO, London.

Landy, F.J. and Conte, J.M. (2009) *Work in the 21st Century: an introduction to industrial and organisational psychology*, 3rd edition, Wiley-Blackwell, Malden, MA.

Leiper, N. (1990) *Tourism Systems*, Massey University Department of Management Systems Occasional Paper 2, Auckland.

Leisure Consultants (1996) *Leisure Forecasts, 1996–2000*, Leisure Consultants, Sudbury.

Leisure Industries Research Centre (2003) *Leisure Forecasts 2003–2007*, SIRC, Sheffield Hallam University.

Leisure Industries Research Centre (2005) *Leisure Forecasts 2005–2009*, SIRC, Sheffield Hallam University.

Leisure Industries Research Centre (2007) *Leisure Forecasts 2007–2011*, SIRC, Sheffield Hallam University.

Leisure Industries Research Centre (2008) *Leisure Forecasts 2008–2012*, Leisure Industries Research Centre, Sheffield.

Leisure Industries Research Centre (2009) *Leisure Forecasts 2009–2013*, Leisure Industries Research Centre, Sheffield.

Lester, S. and Russell, W. (2008) *Play for a Change*, Play England/National Children's Bureau, London.

Lew, A., Hall, C.M. and Williams, A.M. (eds) (2004) *A Companion to Tourism*, Blackwell, Oxford.

Liverpool 2008 (2009a) www.econstudy.net (accessed 4 August 2009).

Liverpool 2008 (2009b) www.liverpoolcapitalofculture2008.co.uk (accessed 4 August 2009).

Liverpoolculture.com (2004) www.liverpoolculture.com (accessed 31 March 2004).

Local Government Association and the Museums Association (2008) *Unlocking Local Treasure: collections management and the local authority museum*, LGA & MA, London.

Loomis, J.B. and Walsh, R.G. (1997) *Recreation Economic Decisions, Comparing Benefits and Costs*, Venture Publishing, State College, PA.

Lord Redcliffe-Maud (1969) *Report of the Royal Commission on Local Government in England 1966–1969*, HMSO, London.

Lord Redcliffe-Maud (1976) *Support for the Arts in England and Wales*, Calouste Gulbenkian Foundation, London.

Lord Redcliffe-Maud (1977) *Local Authority Support for the Arts*, Calouste Gulbenkian Foundation, London.

Lord Wolfenden (1960) *Report of the Wolfenden Committee on Sport, Sport and the Community*, Central Council for Physical Recreation, London.

Lord Wolfenden (1978) *The Future of Voluntary Organisations*, Croom Helm, London.

Louv, R. (2006) *Last Child in the Woods*, Alonquin Books, Chapel Hill, NC.

Low, N., Butt, S., Ellis Paine, A. and Davis Smith, J. (2007) *Helping Out: a national survey of volunteering and charitable giving*, Office of the Third Sector/Cabinet Office, London, available at www.cabinetoffice.gov.uk/media/cabinetoffice/third_sector/assets/helping_out_national_survey_2007.pdf.

Lynch, R. and Veal, A.J. (2006) *Australian Leisure*, 3rd edition, Pearson Education, Sydney.

Maas, J., Verheij, R.A., Groenewegen, P.P., de Vries, S. and Spreeuwenberg, P. (2006) 'Green Space, urbanity and health: how strong is the relation?', *Journal of Epidemiology and Community Health*, 60, pp. 587–92, BMJ Journals.

McGuigan, J. (1996) *Culture and the Public Sphere*, Routledge, London.

McIntosh, R.W., Goeldner, C.R. and Ritchie, J.R.B. (1995) *Tourism Principles, Practices, Philosophies*, Wiley, New York.

Mack, R., Mueller, R. and Crotts, J. (2000) 'Perceptions, corrections and defections: implications for service recovery in the restaurant industry', *Managing Service Quality*, 10, 6, pp. 339–46.

Mackett, R. (2004) *Making Children's Lives More Active*, Centre for Transport Studies, University College London, available at http://eprints.ucl.ac.uk/1346/.

MacLeod, D. and Clarke, N. (2009) *Engaging for Success: enhancing performance through employee engagement*, Department for Business, Innovation and Skills, London, available at www.berr.gov.uk/files/file52215.pdf.

McMaster, B. (2008) *Supporting Excellence in the Arts*, DCMS, London.

Maddern, D. (2002) 'Driving libraries toward a sustainable future', in T.V. Ershova and Y.E. Hohlov (eds) *Libraries in the Information Society*, IFLA Publications, The Hague.

Marcuse, H. (1964) *One Dimensional Man*, Sphere Books, London.

Martin, W.H. and Mason, S. (1998) *Transforming the Future Quality of Life: rethinking free time and work*, Leisure Consultants, Sudbury, Suffolk.

Maslow, A. (1954) *Motivation and Personality*, Harper, New York.

Maslow, A. (1968) *Towards a Psychology of Being*, Van Nostrand, New York.

Masterman, G. (2007) *Sponsorship: for a return on investment*, Butterworth-Heinemann, Oxford.

Masterman, G. (2009) *Strategic Sports Event Management: Olympic edition*, 2nd edition, Elsevier, Butterworth-Heinemann, Oxford.

Masterman, G. and Wood, E. (2006) *Innovative Marketing Communications: strategies for the events industry*, Butterworth-Heinemann, Oxford.

Masters, D., Scott, P. and Barrow, G. (2002) *Sustainable Visitor Management Systems: a discussion paper*, Scottish Natural Heritage, Inverness.

Matarasso, F. (1997) *Use or Ornament: the social impact of participation in the arts*, Comedia, London.

Mathieson, A. and Wall, G. (1982) *Tourism: economic, physical and social impacts*, Longman, Harlow.

MEA (2005) *Ecosystems and Human Well-being: a framework for assessment*, available at www.maweb.org/en/index.aspx (accessed March 2009).

Meenaghan, T. (1991) 'The role of sponsorship in the marketing communications mix', *International Journal of Advertising*, 10, 1, pp. 35–47.

Miao, Q. (20002) 'To be or not to be: public libraries and the global knowledge revolution', in T.V. Ershova and Y.E. Hohlov (eds) *Libraries in the Information Society*, IFLA Publications, The Hague.

Miller, G. and Twinning Ward, L. (2005) *Monitoring for a Sustainable Tourism Transition: the challenge of developing and using indicators*, CABI Publishing, Wallingford.

Minihan, J. (1977) *The Nationalization of Culture: the development of state subsidies to the arts in Great Britain*, Hamish Hamilton, London.

Ministry of Education (1960) *The Youth Service in England and Wales: Report of the Committee November 1958* (Albermarle Report), Cmnd 929, HMSO, London.

Mintel (2006a) *Skiing Holidays – International*, Mintel, London.

Mintel (2006b) *Children's Play Areas – UK*, Mintel, London.

Mintel (2006c) *Sponsorship Special Report*, Mintel International Group Ltd, London.

Mintel (2008a) *Snowsports – UK*, Mintel, London.

Mintel (2008b) *Theme Parks – UK*, Mintel, London.

Mintel (2008c) *Nightclubs – UK*, Mintel, London.

Mintel (2008d) *Multi-leisure Parks – UK*, Mintel, London.

Mintel (2009) *Eating Out Review – UK*, Mintel, London.

Monopolies and Mergers Commission (1999) *British Sky Broadcasting plc and Manchester United plc: a report on the proposed merger*, The Stationery Office, London.

MORI (2003) *Young People and Sport in England: trends in participation 1994–2002*, Sport England, London, available at www.sportengland.org/young-people-and-sport-2002-report.pdf.

Morrison, A., Rimmington, M. and Williams, C. (1999) *Entrepreneurship in the Hospitality, Tourism and Leisure Industries*, Elsevier, Butterworth-Heinemann, Oxford.

Moss, P. and Petrie, P. (2002) *From Children's Services to Children's Spaces: public policy, children and childhood*, Routledge Falmer, New York.

Mosscrop, P. and Stores, A. (1990) *Total Quality Management in Leisure: a guide for directors and managers*, Collinson Grant Consultants, Manchester.

Mullin, B.J., Hardy, S. and Sutton, W.A. (2007) *Sport Marketing*, 3rd edition, Human Kinetics, Champaign, IL.

Myerscough, J. (1988) *The Economic Importance of the Arts in Britain*, Policy Studies Institute, London.

National Playing Fields Association (2001) *The Six Acre Standard: minimum standards for outdoor playing space*, NPFA, London.

Natural England (2006) *England Leisure Visits: report of the 2005 survey*, NE13, Natural England, Wetherby.

Natural England (2008) *State of the Natural Environment*, NE85, Natural England, Sheffield.

Natural England (2009) *Childhood and Nature: a survey on changing relationships with Nature across generations*, a report for Natural England by England Marketing.

NCB (2006) *Play and Health*, National Children's Bureau, London, available at www.tiny.cc/PtR3b.

NCVO (2009) *The UK Civil Society Almanac 2009: executive summary*, NCVO, London.

Nebelong, H. (2002) *Keynote Speech to Designs on Play*, available at www.freeplaynetwork.org.uk/index.html.

Neulinger, J. (1974) *The Psychology of Leisure*, Charles C. Thomas, Springfield, IL.

Newsome, D., Moore, S.A. and Dowling, R.K. (2002) *Natural Area Tourism: ecology, impacts and management*, Channel View Publications, Bristol.

NHS Information Centre (2006) *Statistics on Obesity, Physical Activity and Diet: England 2006*, London, NHS, available at www.ic.nhs.uk/statistics-and-data-collections/health-and-lifestyles/obesity/statistics-on-obesity-physical-activity-and-diet-england-2006 (accessed 27 February 2009).

NHS Quality Improvement Scotland (2004) *Health Indicators Report – December 2004 A Focus on Children*, available at www.nhshealthquality.org/nhsqis/2231.html.

Nichols, G. (2005) 'Stalwarts in Sport', *World Leisure*, 2, pp. 31–7.

Nichols, G. (2007) *Sport and Crime Reduction*, Routledge, London and New York.

Nichols, G. and King, L. (1998) 'Volunteers in the Guide Association: problems and solutions', *Voluntary Action*, 1, 1, pp. 21–31.

NPFA, CPC and PLAYLINK (2000) *Best Play: what play provision should do for children*, NPFA, London, available at www.tiny.cc/AztUk.

NY 1 (2009) www.ny1.com/content/ny1_livinh/99171/boxing-benefit-helps-out-harlem-school (accessed 4 August 2009).

O'Sullivan, R. (2005) 'Raising children in an age of ritalin', *Journal of Andrology*, 26, 3 (May/June), American Society of Andrology.

Ockenden, N. and Moore, S. (2003) *The Community Networking Project*, GreenSpace, Reading.

Ofcom (2008) *The International Communications Market, 2008*, Ofcom, London, available at http://www2.ofcom.org.uk/research/cm/icmr08/ (accessed 14 April 2009).

Office for National Statistics (ONS) (1996) *General Household Survey, 1996*, ONS, London.

Office for National Statistics (ONS) (2001) *UK 2000 Time-use Survey*, ONS, London.

Office for National Statistics (ONS) (2002) *General Household Survey, 2002*, ONS, London.

Office for National Statistics (ONS) (2006) *Social Trends 36*, ONS, London. available at www.statistics.gov.uk/downloads/theme_social/Social_Trends36/Social_Trends_36.pdf (accessed 27 February 2009).

Office for National Statistics (ONS) (2008a) *UK Snapshot: income and wealth*, ONS, London, available at www.statistics.gov.uk/cci/nugget.asp?id=1928, (accessed 27 February 2009).

Office for National Statistics (ONS) (2008b) *UK Snapshot: income inequality*, ONS, London, available at www.statistics.gov.uk/cci/nugget.asp?id=332 (accessed 27 February 2009).

Office for National Statistics (ONS) (2008c) *Family Spending*, ONS, London, available at www.statistics.gov.uk/downloads/theme_social/Family_Spending_2007/FamilySpending2008_web.pdf (accessed 27 February 2009).

Office for National Statistics (ONS) (2008d) *Social Trends 2008*, ONS, London.

Office for National Statistics (ONS) (2009a) *General Household Survey 2007: overview report and data*, ONS, London, available at www.statistics.gov.uk/Statbase/Product.asp?vlnk=5756 (accessed 27 February 2009).

Office for National Statistics (ONS) (2009b) *UK Snapshot: internet access*, available at www.statistics.gov.uk/CCI/nugget.asp?ID=8 (accessed 25 February 2009).

Office for National Statistics (ONS) (2009c) *Statistical Bulletin: Labour Market Statistics*, 11 November, available at www.statistics.gov.uk/pdfdir/lmsuk1109.pdf (accessed 20 November 2009).

Office for National Statistics (ONS) (2009d) *Lifestyles and Social Participation*, Chapter 13, Social Trends 39, ONS, London, available at www.statistics.gov.uk/StatBase/Product.asp?vlnk=13675&Pos=&ColRank=1&Rank=96.

Office for National Statistics (ONS) (2010) National Statistics Online, time series data, available at www.statistics.gov.uk/ (accessed 29 March 2010).

Oxford English Dictionary (2008) 3rd edition, Oxford University Press, Oxford.

Palicki, M. (2009) *Projecting Growth*, Attractions Management Online, available at http://attractionsmanagement.com/.

Parker, S. (1997) 'Volunteering – altruism, markets, causes and leisure', *World Leisure and Recreation*, 39, 3, pp. 4–5.

Pearson, N. (1982) *The State and the Visual Arts*, Open University Press, Milton Keynes.

Peter, L. (1986) *The Peter Pyramid*, Allen & Unwin, London.

Petrie, P., Boddy, J., Cameron, C., Heptinstall, E., McQuail, S., Simon, A. and Wigfall, V. (2005) *Pedagogy: a holistic, personal approach to work with children and young people, across services*, Briefing Paper June 2005, Thomas Coram Research Unit, London.

Phoenix, F. and Wilson, R. (2009) 'Managing events', in K. Bill (ed.) *Sport Management*, Learning Matters, Exeter.

Pick, J. (1986) *Managing the Arts? The British experience*, Rhinegold, London.

Pieper, J. (1952) *Leisure: the basis of culture*, New American Library, New York.

Pine, J.B. and Gilmore, J.H. (1999) *The Experience Economy*, Harvard Business School Press, Boston, MA.

Play England (2008) *Design for Play: a guide to creating successful play spaces*, available at www.playengland.org.uk.

Play England (2009a) *How Children's Play Contributes to the National Indicator Set*, available at www.tiny.cc/LO5cI.

Play England (2009b) *Play Shaper Guidance*, available at www.tiny.cc/tjPfU.

Playwork Principles Scrutiny Group (2005) *Playwork Principles*, held in trust by Play Wales, available at www.playwales.org.uk/page.asp?id=50.

Pope, N. and Turco, D. (2001) *Sport and Event Marketing*, Irwin/McGraw-Hill, Roseville, NSW.

Porter, M.E. (2004) *Competitive Advantage*, The Free Press, New York.

Preuss, H. (2004) *The Economics of Staging the Olympics: a comparison of the Games 1972–2008*, Edward Elgar Publishing, Cheltenham.

Putnam, R.D. (2000) *Bowling Alone: the collapse and revival of American community*, Simon & Schuster, New York.

Ramchandani, G. and Taylor P. (2011) 'Quality management awards and sports facilities' performance', *Local Government Studies*, 37, 1 (in press).

Rapoport, R. and Rapoport, R.N. (1975) *Leisure and the Family Life Cycle*, Routledge & Kegan Paul, London.

Ritchie, B.W. and Adair, D. (2004) *Sport Tourism: interrelationships, impacts and issues*, Channel View, Clevedon.

Ritchie, J.R.B. and Crouch, G.I. (2003) *The Competitive Destination: a sustainable tourism perspective*, CABI Publishing, Wallingford.

Roberts, K. (2004) *The Leisure Industries*, Palgrave Macmillan, Basingstoke.

Robinson, J. (2008) 'Amputee ineligible for Olympic events', *New York Times*, 14 January, available at www.nytimes.com/2008 (accessed 29 January 2008).

Robinson, J. (2009) 'Setanta thought it had a sporting chance. It lost', *Observer*, Business and Media Section, 28 June, p. 4.

Robinson, J. and Godbey, G. (1999) *Time for Life: the surprising ways Americans use their time*, Pennsylvania State University Press, PA.

Robinson, L. (2001) 'Service quality and the public leisure industry', in C. Wolsey and J. Abrams, J. (eds) *Understanding the Leisure and Sport Industry*, Pearson Education, Harlow.

Robinson, L. (2003) 'Committed to quality: the use of quality schemes in UK public leisure services', *Managing Service Quality*, 13, 3, pp. 247–55.

Robinson, L. (2004) *Managing Public Sport and Leisure Services*, Routledge, London.

Robinson, T. (2008) 'We know we belong to the land: and the land we belong to is grand', *Countryside Recreation*, 16 (Autumn/winter).

Roche, M. (2000) *Mega-events and Modernity: Olympics and expos in the growth of global culture*, Routledge, London.

Rodgers, B. (1977) *Rationalizing Sports Policies, Sport in Its Social Context: international comparisons*, Council of Europe, Strasbourg.

Rojek, C. (2000) *Leisure and Culture*, Palgrave Macmillan, Basingstoke.

Rossman, J.R. and Elwood Schlatter, B. (2008) *Recreation Programming: designing leisure experiences*, 5th edition, Sagamore Publishing, Champaign, IL.

Royal Society for the Protection of Birds (2004) *Natural Fit: can green space and biodiversity increase levels of physical activity?*, RSPB, Nottingham.

Royal Yachting Association (2007) *Watersports and Leisure Participation Report*, available at www.bcu.org.uk/files/RYA%20Watersports%20Participation%20Survey%202007.pdf (accessed June 2009).

Ruskin, H. and Sivan, A. (2005) 'Israel', in G. Cushman, A.J. Veal and J. Zuzanek (eds) *Free Time and Leisure Participation: international perspectives*, CABI Publishing, Wallingford.

Russell, B. (1935) *In Praise of Idleness*, Allen & Unwin, London.

Salt Lake City (2002) www.saltlake2002.com (accessed 24 April 2002).

Scarman, L. (1981) for the Home Office, *The Brixton Disorders: first report of an inquiry*, 25 November, Cmnd 8427, HMSO, London.

Schor, J. (1992) *The Overworked American*, Basic Books, New York.

Schor, J. (1998) 'Beyond work and spend', *Vrijetijdstudies*, 16, pp. 7–20.

Schor, J. (2006) 'Overturning the modernist predictions: recent trends in work and leisure in the OECD', in Chris Rojek, Susan Shaw and A.J. Veal (eds) *A Handbook of Leisure Studies*, Palgrave, Basingstoke.

Scitovsky, T. (1976) *The Joyless Economy*, Oxford University Press, New York.

Scott, C. (2007) 'Measuring social value', in R. Sandell and R.R. Janes (eds) *Museum Management and Marketing*, Routledge, London.

Scottish Natural Heritage (2004) *Scottish Outdoor Access Code*, available at www.snh.org.uk/strategy/access/sr-afor01.asp (accessed May 2009).

Scouting Association (2009) http://scouts.org.uk/cms.php?pageid=6.

Secretary of State TLGR (Transport, Local Government and the Regions) (2001) *Strong Local Leadership – Quality Public Services*, The Stationery Office, London.

Sellick, J. (2002) *Leisure Education: models and curriculum development*, RLS 209, California State University, Sacramento.

Selwood, S. (ed.) (2001) *The UK Cultural Sector: profile and policy issues*, Policy Studies Institute, London.

Selwood, S. and Davies, M. (2005) 'Capital costs: Lottery funding in Britain and the consequences for museums', *Curator*, 48, pp. 439–65.

Senge, P.M., Kleiner, A., Roberts, C., Ross, R.B. and Smith, B.J. (1994) *The Fifth Discipline Field Book*, Doubleday, New York.

Shibli, S. (2009) 'The relationship between demand and supply for adult swimming in England', paper presented to the European Association of Sports Management 17th Annual European Sport Management Conference, Best Practices in Sports Facility and Event Management, Amsterdam, 16–19 September.

Shilton, T. (2006) 'Advocacy for physical activity: from evidence to influence', *IUHPE Promotion and Education*, 13, 2, pp. 118–26.

Shivers, J.A. (1967) *Principles and Practices of Recreational Services*, Macmillan, New York.

Sidaway, R. (1991) *Good Conservation Practice for Sport and Recreation*, Sports Council and Countryside Commission, London and Cheltenham.

Simmons, R. (2003) *New Leisure Trusts*, SPORTA and ILAM, London and Reading.

Sinclair, A. (1995) *Arts and Cultures: the history of the 50 years of the Arts Council of Great Britain*, Sinclair-Stevenson, London.

Skills Active (2005) *Skills Need Assessment for Sport and Recreation*, Skills Active, London, September.

Smiers, J. (2003) *Arts Under Pressure*, Zed Books, London.

Smith, H. (1831) *Festivals, Games and Amusements: ancient and modern*, Colborn and Bentley, London.

Social Exclusion Unit (2001) *Policy Action Team 10*, DCMS, London.

Society of London Theatre (SLT) (2009) *About Theatreland*, SLT, London, available at www.solt.co.uk/about/about.html.

Southampton Leisure Holdings Plc (2008) *Annual Report and Financial Statements 2008*, Southampton Leisure Holdings Plc, Southampton.

Sport England (1997) *A Sporting Future for the Playing Fields of England: policy on planning applications for development on playing fields*, Sport England, London.

Sport England (2002) *Participation in Sport: results from the General Household Survey 2002*, Research Briefing Note, Sport England, London.

Sport England (2003a) *Sports Volunteering in England, 2002*, Sport England, London, available at www.sportengland.org/volunteering-in-england.pdf.

Sport England (2003b) *Condition and Refurbishment of Public Sector Leisure Facilities*, Sport England, London.

Sport England (2007a) *Economic Importance of Sport, England, 2003*, Sport England, London available at www.sportengland.org/research/economic_importance_of_sport.aspx.

Sport England (2007b) 'Introductory guide to segmentation', available at www.sportengland.org/research/market_segmentation.aspx.

Sport England (2008a) *Sport England Strategy 2008–2011*, Sport England, London, available at www.sportengland.org/sport_england_strategy_2008 {hy}2011.pdf.

Sport England (2008b) *Shaping Places through Sport*, Sport England, London, available at www.sportengland.org/shapingplaces.

Sport England (2009a) *Active People Survey 2: key results for England*, Sport England, London.

Sport England (2009b) *Active People Survey 2: individual sports results*, Sport England, London.

Sport England (2009c) *Improving Community Sports Facilities: a toolkit for the strategic planning of community sports facilities*, Sport England, London.

References

Sport England (2010) *Active People Survey 1: headline results England*, Sport England, London, www.sportengland.org/research/active_people_survey/active_people_survey_1.aspx.

Sport Industry Research Centre (SIRC) (2008) *Sport Market Forecasts 2007–2011*, Sport Industry Research Centre, Sheffield.

Sport Industry Research Centre (SIRC) (2009) *Sport Market Forecasts 2009–2013*, SIRC/Sport England, Sheffield and London.

Sports Council (1972) *Provision for Sport*, Sports Council, London.

Sports Council (1982) *Sport in the Community: the next ten years*, Sports Council, London.

Sports Council (1998) *Facilities Planning Model: a planning tool for developing sports facilities*, Sports Council, London.

sportscotland (1999) *Sports Participation in Scotland*, sportscotland, Edinburgh.

sportscotland (2008) *Child Protection Legislation and Volunteering in Scottish Sport: summary report*, sportscotland, Edinburgh.

Standeven, J. and De Knop, P. (1999) *Sport Tourism*, Human Kinetics, Champagne, IL.

Stebbins, R.A. (2004) *Between Work and Leisure*, Transaction Publishers, New Brunswick, NJ.

Stewart, B. (2007) *Sport Funding and Finance*, Butterworth-Heinemann, London.

Stokowski, P.A. (1994) *Leisure in Society: a network structural perspective*, Mansell, London.

Sturrock, G. and Else, P. (1998) 'The playground as therapeutic space: playwork as healing', known as 'The Colorado Paper', in *Therapeutic Playwork Reader One* (2005), Common Threads, Southampton.

Stutely, R. (2002) *The Definitive Business Plan*, 2nd edition, Pearson Education, Harlow.

Taylor, C. (2008) 'An advocacy for playwork', in *Possible Futures for Playwork*, discussion papers, available at www.tiny.cc/LMFfn.

Taylor, P.D. (1996) 'The role of management information systems in sport', in G. Ashworth and A. Dietvorst (eds) *Policy and Planning for Sport and Tourism*, CAB International, Wallingford.

Taylor, P.D., Hart, G., Panagouleas, T. and Nichols, G. (2008) *Child Protection Legislation and Volunteering in Scottish Sport*, sportscotland Research Report 112, sportscotland, Edinburgh.

Taylor, S. and Emir, A. (2009) *Employment Law: an introduction*, 2nd edition, Oxford University Press, Oxford.

Taylor, T. and McGraw, P. (2006) 'Exploring human resource management practices in nonprofit sport organisations', *Sport Management Review*, 9, pp. 229–51.

Thompson, G. (1987) *Needs*, Routledge, London.

Tilden, F. (1977) *Interpreting Our Heritage*, 3rd edition, Chapel Hill, NC: University of North Carolina Press.

Tillman, A. (1974) *The Program Book for Recreation Professionals*, National Press Books, Palo Alto, CA.

Tokarski, W. and Michels, H. (2005) 'Germany', in G. Cushman, A.J. Veal and J. Zuzanek (eds) *Free Time and Leisure Participation: international perspectives*, CABI Publishing, Wallingford.

Tomas, S.R., Scott, D. and Crompton, J.L. (2002) 'An investigation of the relationships between quality of service performance, benefits sought, satisfaction and future intention to visit among visitors to a zoo', *Managing Leisure*, 7, 4, pp. 239–50.

Tomlinson, A. (1979) *Sports Council/Social Science Research Council Review: leisure and the role of clubs and voluntary groups*, Sports Council/SSRC, London.

Toohey, K. and Veal, A. (2000) *The Olympic Games: a social science perspective*, CABI Publishing, Wallingford.

Torkildsen, G. (2005) *Leisure and Recreation Management*, Routledge, London and New York.

Torkildsen, G. and Griffiths, G. (1987) *Lambourn Valley Recreation Study* (commissioned by Newbury District Council), LMGT, Harlow.

Travers, T. (1998) *The Wyndham Report*, Society of London Theatre, London.

Travers, T. and Glaister, S. (2004) *Valuing museums: impact and innovation amongst national museums*, National Museums Directors' Conference, London.

UHY Hacker Young (2007) 'Restaurants three times more likely to go bust than other businesses', press release, UHY Hacker Young, London.

UK Commission for Employment and Skills (2009) *Towards Ambition 2020: skills, jobs, growth*, London, October.

UK Sport (1999) *Compass 1999: sports participation in Europe*, UK Sport, London.

UNCRC (1989) *Convention on the Rights of the Child*, United Nations, available at http://www2.ohchr.org/english/law/crc.htm.

UNICEF (2007) *Report Card 7, Child Poverty in Perspective: an overview of child well-being in rich countries*, United Nations Children's Fund.

United Nations (2004) *World Population to 2300*, Department of Economic and Social Affairs, Population Division, United Nations, New York.

Uysal, M. (1998) 'The determinants of tourism demand: a theoretical perspective', in D. Ioannides and K.G. Debbage (eds) *The Economic Geography of the Tourist Industry: a supply side analysis*, Routledge, London.

Van Hoecke, J., De Knop, P. and Schoukens, H. (2009) 'A decade of quality and performance management in Flemish organised sport', *International Journal of Sports Management and Marketing*, 6, 3, pp. 308–29.

Vargo, S.L. and Lusch, R.F. (2004) 'Evolving to a new dominant logic for marketing', *Journal of Marketing*, 68 (January), pp. 1–17.

Veal, A.J. (2002) *Leisure and Tourism Policy and Planning*, 2nd edition, CABI Publishing, Wallingford.

Veal, A.J. (2009a) *Open Space Planning Standards in Australia: in search of origins*, U-Plan project paper 1, 3rd edition, School of Leisure, Sport and Tourism Working Paper series, University of Technology, Sydney.

Veal, A.J. (2009b) *U-Plan: a participation-based approach to planning for leisure*, U-Plan project paper 8, 4th edition, School of Leisure, Sport and Tourism Working Paper series, University of Technology, Sydney.

Visitor Safety in the Countryside Group (2005) *Managing Visitor Safety in the Countryside: principles and practice*, RSPB, Nottingham.

Vogel, H.L. (2007) *Entertainment Industry Economics: a guide for financial analysis*, 7th edition, Cambridge University Press, New York.

Volunteering England (2009) www.volunteering.org.uk (accessed 4 August 2009).

von Hinke Kessler Scholder, S. (2007) *Maternal Employment and Overweight Children: does timing matter?*, CMPO Working Paper series No. 07/180, Centre for Market and Public Organisation, University of Bristol.

Wall, G. and Mathieson, A. (2006) *Tourism: change, impacts and opportunities*, Pearson, Harlow.

Ward, R. (2007) 'Public libraries', in J.H. Bowman (ed.) *British Librarianship and Information Work 2001–2005*, Ashgate, Farnham, Surrey.

Wardle, H., Sproston, K., Orford, J., Erens, B., Griffiths, M., Constantine, R. and Pigott, S. (2007) *British Gambling Prevalence Survey 2007*, National Centre for Social Research,

London.

Wasserstrom, J. (2009) www.csmonitor.com (accessed 4 August 2009).

Watt, N. (2009) 'World Cup 2018: Gordon Brown meets FIFA's Jack Warner to back England's bid', *Guardian*, 27 November, available at www.guardian.co.uk/football/2009/nov/27/gordon-brown-jack-warner-meeting (accessed 15 January 2010).

Wearden, G. and Allen, K, (2009) 'Competition Commission opposes Ticketmaster and Live Nation merger', *Guardian*, 8 October, available at www.guardian.co.uk/business/2009/oct/08/competition-ticketmaster-live-nation-merger.

Weed, M. and Bull, C. (2004) *Sports Tourism: participants, policy and providers*, Elsevier Butterworth-Heinemann, Oxford.

Westerbeek, H., Smith, A., Turner, P., Green, C. and van Leeuwen, L. (2006) *Managing Sport Facilities and Major Events*, Routledge, London.

Wickham, P.A. (2006) *Strategic Entrepreneurship*, 4th edition, Pearson Education, Harlow.

Wilde, S. (2008) 'Clarke feeling the heat from county chiefs', *Sunday Times*, Sport Section, 2 November, p. 16.

Williams, C. and Buswell, J. (2003) *Service Quality in Leisure and Tourism*, CABI Publishing, Wallingford.

Williams, K. (2005) 'State of fear: Britain's "compensation culture" reviewed', *Legal Studies*, 25, 3, pp. 499–515.

Williams, L. and Rivers, V. (2006) *Forever Harlem*, Sports Publishing LLC, New York.

Williams, M. and Bowdin, G.A.J. (2007) 'Festival evaluation: an exploration of several UK arts festivals', *Managing Leisure*, 12, 2&3, pp. 186–203.

Wilson, B. and Smallwood, S. (2008) *The Proportions of Marriages Ending in Divorce*, Population Trends 131, ONS, London.

Wilson, R. and Joyce, J. (2008) *Finance for Sport and Leisure Managers: an introduction*, Routledge, London.

Wilson, R. and Joyce, J. (2010) *Finance for Sport and Leisure Managers: an introduction*, 2nd edition, Routledge, London.

Witcomb, A. (2003) *Re-Imaging the Museum: beyond the mausoleum*, Routledge, London.

Wolsey, C. and Whitrod-Brown, H. (2003) 'Human resource management and the business of sport', in L. Trenbirth (ed.) *Managing the Business of Sport*, Dunmore Press, Palmerston North, New Zealand.

Wooden, J. (2005) *Wooden on Leadership*, McGraw Hill, New York.

Woolf, F. (2004) *Partnerships for Learning: a guide to evaluating arts education projects*, Arts Council for England, London.

Work Foundation & NESTA (2007) *Staying Ahead: the economic performance of the UK's Creative industries*, DCMS, London.

WTO (2001) *Sport and Tourism Shaping Global Culture*, WTO, Madrid.

Yeoman, I., Robertson, M., Ali-Knight, J., Drummond, S. and McMahon-Beattie, U. (2004) *Festival and Events Management*, Elsevier, Butterworth-Heinemann, London.

Zuzanek, J. (2005) 'Canada', in G. Cushman, A.J. Veal and J. Zuzanek (eds) *Free Time and Leisure Participation: international perspectives*, CABI Publishing, Wallingford.

Name index

Subject index